Latina/os in the United States

2nd edition

To my wife, Janie Valadez, for her love, support, and encouragement, and to Remy Sáenz, our beautiful precious grandson who has brought so much joy to our lives.

Rogelio Sáenz

To Brian Roebuck, who provided immense support as I was writing this book, and my children Brianna and Joaquin, whose love makes me a better human.

Maria Cristina Morales

To my children Grace and Carlitos whom I love with all my heart. For my husband, Carlos, who has been by my side through it all. *Los amo.*

Coda Rayo-Garza

Latina/os in the United States

Diversity and Change

2nd edition

ROGELIO SÁENZ
MARIA CRISTINA MORALES
CODA RAYO-GARZA

polity

The right of Rogelio Sáenz, Maria Cristina Morales, & Coda Rayo-Garza to be identified as Authors of this Work has been asserted in accordance with the UK Copyright, Designs and Patents Act 1988.

First edition published in 2015 by Polity Press
This second edition first published in 2025 by Polity Press

Polity Press
65 Bridge Street
Cambridge CB2 1UR, UK

Polity Press
111 River Street
Hoboken, NJ 07030, USA

ISBN-13: 978-1-5095-3710-5 (hardback)
ISBN-13: 978-1-5095-3711-2 (paperback)

A catalogue record for this book is available from the British Library.

Library of Congress Control Number: 2024937086

Typeset in 9.5 on 13pt Utopia
by Cheshire Typesetting Ltd, Cuddington, Cheshire
Printed and bound in Great Britain by CPI Group (UK) Ltd, Croydon

The publisher has used its best endeavors to ensure that the URLs for external websites referred to in this book are correct and active at the time of going to press. However, the publisher has no responsibility for the websites and can make no guarantee that a site will remain live or that the content is or will remain appropriate.

For further information on Polity, visit our website:
politybooks.com

Contents

Tables and Figures   vi

Prefaces   x

1   Introduction   1

2   The Diverse Histories of Latina/os   16

3   Latina/o Social Thought   35

4   Historical and Contemporary Latina/o Immigration   53

5   The Demography of Latina/os   89

6   Gender and Sexuality   110

7   Political Engagement   121

8   The Latina/o Arts   146

9   Education   165

10   Work and Economic Life   185

11   Families   207

12   Religion   228

13   Health and Health Care   251

14   Crime and Victimization   280

15   Mass Media   301

16   Conclusions   328

Appendices

A.   List of Occupations Comprising "Latina/o Immigrant Jobs" by Sex   343

B.   Results of Multiple Regression Analysis Examining the Relationships between Selected Predictors and the Logged Wage and Salary Income by Place of Birth and Sex, 2022   345

References   347

Index   390

Tables and Figures

Tables

1.1 Percentage of Latina/os in Twelve Largest Latina/o Groups Choosing Selected Race Categories, 2019 and 2021 — 9

1.2 Percentage of Latina/os in Twelve Largest Latina/o Groups Choosing Selected Race Categories by Nativity, 2021 — 10

4.1 Persons Obtaining Legal Permanent Resident Status by Region and Period — 76

4.2 Spanish-Speaking Latin American Countries Ranked by Most Persons Obtaining Legal Permanent Resident Status by Period — 77

4.3 Number of Latina/o Immigrants and Related Statistics for Selected Groups, 2022 — 79

4.4 Annual Number of Immigrants to the US by Latina/o Group, 2012, 2017, and 2022 — 82

4.5 Number of Title 42 Expulsions and Non-Citizen Apprehensions by Country of Nationality, 2013 to 2022 — 84

5.1 US Population in 2022 and Projected Populations in 2040 and 2060 for Selected Groups — 101

5.2 Demographic Characteristics of Latina/o Groups — 104

7.1 Percentage Perceptions of Which Party is Most Concerned About Latina/os, 2018 — 129

7.2 Latina/o Lawmakers in Congress 2022 Making History — 138

7.3 Cities with the Largest Latina/o Population and Local Political Representation, 2023 — 139

7.4 States with Anti-Diversity, Equity, and Inclusion Legislation Introduced, Approved, or Failed, June 2023 — 141

9.1 Percentage of Persons 16 to 24 Years of Age who are Dropouts by Race/Ethnic Group, Sex, and Place of Birth, 2022 — 175

9.2 Percentage of Persons 25 Years of Age and Older who are High-School Graduates by Race/Ethnic Group, Sex, and Place of Birth, 2022 — 176

9.3 Percentage of Persons 25 Years of Age and Older with a Bachelor's Degree or Higher by Race/Ethnic Group, Sex, and Place of Birth, 2022   177

10.1 Percentage of Persons 25 to 54 Years of Age Employed by Race/Ethnic Group, Place of Birth, and Sex, 2022   192

10.2 Selected Characteristics Related to Job Quality by Race/Ethnic Group, Place of Birth, and Sex among Persons 25 to 54 Years of Age, 2022   194

10.3 Median Job Income by Race/Ethnic Group, Place of Birth, and Sex among Workers 25 to 54 Years of Age, 2022   197

10.4 Disparities in Wage and Salary Income of Workers 25 to 54 Years of Age Obtained from Multiple Regression Analysis for Selected Race/Ethnic Groups Relative to Whites by Place of Birth and Sex, 2022   199

11.1 Selected Marriage and Divorce Characteristics among Persons 25 to 44 Years of Age by Race/Ethnic Group, Sex, and Nativity, 2022   214

11.2a Race/Ethnic Identity of Latina Wives Married in Last Ten Years by Place of Birth and Husband Race/Ethnic Identity, 2022   216

11.2b Race/Ethnic Identity of Latino Husbands Married in Last Ten Years by Place of Birth and Wife Race/Ethnic Identity, 2022   217

11.3 Same-Sex Couple Rates by Race/Ethnic Group, Sex, and Nativity, 2022   219

11.4 Percentage of Children Living in Family Households with Female Householders No Husband Present by Race/Ethnic Group and Nativity, 2022   220

11.5 Selected Household Arrangement Characteristics by Race/Ethnic Group, Sex, and Nativity, 2022   221

12.1 Percentage Distribution of Selected Latina/o Groups by Religious Affiliation, 2014   243

13.1 Death Rates for Selected Race/Ethnic Groups by Age and Sex, 2022   259

13.2 Age-Adjusted Death Rates for Fifteen Leading Causes of Death by Race/Ethnic Groups and Sex, 2019   261

13.3 Causes of Death For Which Latina/os Have Higher Age-Adjusted Death Rates Compared to Whites, 2019   263

13.4 Percentage of Students in 9th to 12th Grade Engaging in Selected Health Risk Behaviors by Race/Ethnic Group and Sex, 2019   265

13.5 Percentage of Children and Adolescents Who are Obese by Race/Ethnic Group and Sex, 2015–2018   266

13.6 Percentage of Persons by Health Care Needs by Race/Ethnic Group and Age, 2015–2016   270

13.7 Selected Foreign-Born Latina/o Groups with the Highest Percentages of Persons Lacking Health Insurance by Age, 2022   271

14.1 Percentages of Concern Regarding Deportations of Self, Relatives, or Friends, 2008–2018   295

Figures

1.1 Percentage Racial Distribution of Latina/os by Year   8

3.1 Jovita Idár around 1905   37

4.1 Annual Number of Latina/o Immigrants to the US by Year, 2012–2022   81

4.2 Annual Immigration for Hondurans, Nicaraguans, and Venezuelans by Year, 2012–2022   83

4.3 Number of Asians and Latin American Immigrants Moving to the US in the Past Year by Period   85

4.4 Number of Immigrants Moving from China, India, and Mexico to the US in the Past Year by Period   85

5.1 Latina/o Population in the US, 1980–2020   90

5.2 Percentage Change in the Latina/o and US Populations by Period   91

5.3 Percentage of US Population Growth Due to Latina/o Population Growth by Period   92

5.4 Percentage Share of Latina/os in US Population, 1980–2020   92

5.5 Age-Sex Pyramid for Latina/os and Whites in the US, 2022   94

5.6 Percentage Share of Latina/os and Whites by Age Group in the (a) California and (b) Texas Populations, 2022   95

5.7 Latina/o and White Immigrants Arriving in the Past Year Per 1,000 Population, 2000–2022   96

5.8 Total Fertility Rates of Latina and White Women, 2003–2022   97

5.9 Life Expectancy at Birth for Latina/os and Whites by Sex, 2006–2021   99

5.10 Total number of Latina/o and White Births and Deaths, 2018–2021   100

5.11 Indices of Dissimilarity Representing the Difference between Latina/o Groups and the US Population in States of Residence, 2021   105

5.12 Two Categories of Latina/o New Destination States, 2020   107

7.1 Percentage of Latina/o Registered Voters by Political Party   130

7.2 Percentage of Latina/o Registered Voters by Level of Education   131

7.3 Percentage of Latina/o Registered Voters by Level of Education and Political Party   132

7.4 Percentage of Latina/o Registered Voters by Political Party and Sex   132

7.5 Percentage of Latina/os Who Approve of the 2017–2021 Trump Presidency   133

7.6 Photograph of the Immigrant Rights, March, 2006 134

7.7 Percentage of Latina/o Registered Voters by US-Born and Naturalized Citizens 135

9.1 Percentage of Parents with Access to Internet and Computer Device by Race/Ethnic Group and Nativity, 2020 173

10.1 Percentage of Latina/os among US Workers by Year, 1980–2021 202

10.2 Percentage of Latina/o Workers Foreign-Born, 1980–2021 203

12.1 Percentage of Latina/os by Religious Affiliation, 2010–2022 242

12.2 Latina/o Political Party Affiliation for Selected Religious Groups, 2014 244

13.1 The Social Determinants of Health 255

13.2 The National Institute on Minority Health and Health Disparities Research Framework 256

13.3 Life Expectancy at Birth for Selected Race/Ethnic Groups by Sex, 2021 260

13.4 Percentage of Persons with a Disability for Selected Race/Ethnic Groups by Age and Sex, 2022 267

13.5 Percentage of Persons with a Disability among Native-Born Latina/os, Foreign-Born Latina/os, and Whites by Age and Sex, 2022 269

13.6 Percentage of Persons Without Health Insurance by Race/Ethnic Group, Age, and Place of Birth/Citizenship Status, 2022 270

13.7 Infant Mortality Rates for Latina/os and Whites by Year 274

13.8 Percentage of Latina Women Giving Birth in Past Year Who Are Foreign-Born by Year 274

13.9 COVID-19 Age-Adjusted Death Rates by Race/Ethnic Group and Sex, 2020 and 2021 276

13.10 Life Expectancy at Birth by Race/Ethnic Group and Sex, 2019, 2020, and 2021 276

14.1 Percentage Perceptions of Racial and Ethnic Discrimination by Race/Ethnic Group, 2020 296

15.1 Number of Articles in the *New York Times* Containing "Hispanic" or "Latino" by Period 323

15.2 Percentage of Articles in the *New York Times* Containing "Hispanic" or "Latino" That Also Contain "Immigrant" or "Immigration" by Period 323

Prefaces

Ever since I discovered sociology back in the late 1970s when I was an undergraduate student at Pan American University (now University of Texas at Rio Grande Valley), I have used the sociological framework to make sense of the world and to seek ways to improve the lives of people on the margins of society. While I have written on a wide variety of topics, the major constancy of my work has been a focus on Latina/os. I have used my writing to call attention to major problems, including structural racism, that confront Latina/os and to try to find ways to improve the conditions of *nuestra raza*.

The dreams that I had as an undergraduate student involved writing about Latina/os, as I found very little written about us then. A book? That would be great! I was very fortunate that Polity Press reached out to me nearly two decades ago to write such a book. My dear friend and colleague and former student, Maria Cristina Morales, collaborated with me on the book, which came out in 2015. Like the first edition of the book, the second edition took too much time to complete – in large part due to my penchant for overextending myself with writing projects, doing public sociology/demography, and serving on the board of directors of countless non-profit justice organizations. Cristina and I reached out to a very talented doctoral student, whose dissertation I am directing, to join us as a co-author of the second edition. Coda Rayo-Garza delivered and helped us get to the finish line. *Muchísimas gracias* Cristina y Coda!

I am very thankful for the Polity folks, starting with Emma Longstaff, who first reached out to me to write the book, and to Jonathan Skerrett, whose patience and firm hand, made the writing of the two editions of this book possible and, more recently, to Karina Jákupsdóttir, who was a constant source of support. Thank you Polity Press! I have enjoyed the support of numerous colleagues locally and beyond who have contributed to my intellectual development, including Benigno Aguirre, Eduardo Bonilla-Silva, David Embrick, Roger Enriquez, Joe Feagin, Juan Flores, Mark Fossett, Mark Garcia, Felipe Gonzales, Willis Goudy (my mentor and dissertation advisor), Lourdes Gouveia, José Ángel Gutiérrez, Nancy López, Ramiro Martinez, David Montejano, Verónica Montes de Oca, Maria Cristina Morales, Ed Murguia, Michael Olivas, Marco Portales, Dudley Poston, Joseph Spielberg Benitez, Edward Telles, Marta Tienda, Norma Willimas, Jesse Zapata, and René Zenteno.

Finally, I provide the most special gratitude to the people closest to me, whom I love with all my heart and soul. I thank my wonderful sons – Daniel, Joseph, and Jesse – and stepdaughter, Jennifer, for their constant love, for being wonderful human beings, and for doing the great work that they do. I also thank my beautiful grandson, Remy, for the joy that he has brought to me, and my step-grandchildren, Sebi and Abbie, for their love and for making me part of the family. I also love and very much treasure my sister, Dalia, and brother, Balde, for their love, support, and humor throughout our whole lives. And, finally, I am so grateful and appreciative of my wife, Janie Valadez, for her endless love, support, and encouragement, and for her patience with my extremely overextended work schedule. *¡Te adoro con todo mi corazón y alma!* I have very much enjoyed the journey that we are on and very much look forward to our future years together.

Rogelio Sáenz
San Antonio, Texas

When I think of how I developed my interest in the sociology of Latina/o/x, I can trace it to my childhood in El Paso, Texas. I grew up along the US–Mexico border, in a place that looks ethnically homogeneous from the outside but where one is straddling between two cultures and not being fully incorporated into either. The complexity, structural violence and injustices, and the beauty of the border challenge me daily and are the source of my sociological imagination. This is the place that I have contin ued to call home, now as a professor of sociology at the University of Texas at El Paso (UTEP).

From my office at UTEP, I can see Cuidad Juárez, Chihuahua, Mexico, the sister city of El Paso, where I spent a significant portion of my childhood visiting family and various other social activities living the life of a *fronteriza* (a transborder person). I cannot simply go about my day and pretend that the violence and injustices at the border do not happen. This is a heaviness that most of us borderlanders carry with us. Yet, I also look to Juárez with a lot of gratitude and acknowledgment of the sacrifices my parents, Maria de Jesus and Oscar Morales, made as they migrated to the US and worked very hard to provide a better life for me and my siblings. I also would not be the person I am today without my *Abuelita* Aurora, who looked after us as my parents worked many, many hours. She truly was the kindest person that I've known. The saying "she never knew a stranger" truly applies to her as she loved and cared for many people and animals. She taught me to see the good in everyone and to love nature. Although she passed away while I was in graduate school, I continue to see her strength in my daughter Brianna. Life has presented many challenges for Brianna, and despite her young age, she handles things with more grace and wisdom than most adults. My son, Joaquin, is my safe place. Joaquin gives me peace and love and shields my wounds with his laughter and sense of humor. Brianna and Joaquin, I admire and love you both tremendously. My husband, Brian Roebuck, always puts me and the kids ahead of himself; without him, life as an academic would be nearly impossible. *Familismo* is not just a sociological concept; the support from my siblings Cindy and Oscar, my nephew Noah, nieces Alessandra, Andrea, and Bella, my brother-in-law Andres, and sister-in-law Debbie are invaluable.

Writing this book with my mentor and friend, Rogelio Sáenz, is a great privilege. Academia can be a very isolating place for a first-generation Latina like me, so his belief in me and mentorship for over two decades has been instrumental. Coda, I am in awe of how much you do for your family and community. I have enjoyed collaborating with you on this manuscript. I am also grateful for the emotional support that my academic friends gave me during this time, in particular, Leisy Abrego, Cynthia Bejarano, Selfa Chew, Angela Frederick, Amado Alarcon, Joe Heyman, Danielle Morales, Amelia Rau, Nadia Flores, and Nancy Plankey-Videla, during the writing of this manuscript.

Maria Cristina Morales
El Paso, Texas

I am deeply honored to have had the opportunity to contribute to the second edition of this book. When I first began my PhD journey, I never imagined I would have an opportunity like this. I am so grateful to have the mentorship and guidance of Rogelio Sáenz, or as we fondly refer to him as "el profe". To have contributed to a book like this is a dream come true, but to have done so alongside two incredible scholars that I admire and respect, Rogelio and Cristina, is a wonderful blessing. I have much to learn from you both. *Gracias por confiar en mí.*

As I think back on my childhood experiences, I am grateful that despite all the challenges my family faced, we made it through with the wisdom of a better understanding of life, justice, faith, and perseverance. I am grateful for the sacrifices of my mom and dad. Thank you for always encouraging me to keep my efforts focused on a better future. Finally, I am grateful for my husband Carlos. I appreciate everything you do for our family and everything you have done to support me through it all. We started this journey together many years ago, and now we have two beautiful children who we get to watch grow every day. Carlitos and Grace, you are everything to me. I hope to make you all so proud. I love you all so much.

Coda Rayo-Garza
San Antonio, Texas

We are deeply grateful to our editors, Jonathan Skerrett and Karina Jákupsdótti, and their team at Polity for their patience and insightful feedback that helped to shape the second edition of *Latina/os in the United States*. To our readers, thank you for your support, and we are honored to be part of your journey of learning about the contributions and structural challenges of Latina/os living in the US.

Rogelio Sáenz
Maria Cristina Morales
Coda Rayo-Garza

1 Introduction

> Hispanics set foot in this country long before the Pilgrims, one of many truths lost in the telling of American history. Now more Latinos are demanding answers from those who fail to acknowledge this continuing amnesia. Compared with white Americans, Latinos earn less, face more barriers to education and health care, and find themselves underrepresented in higher-paid areas of the workforce, as well as in popular culture. As long as our stories and voices continue to be written out of textbooks, omitted in film, TV, and print, and minimized in the halls of power, people will continue to see Latinos as something other than inherently American.
>
> (Stephania Taladrid)

Journalist Stephania Taladrid (2021), who is a contributing writer to *The New Yorker* on issues related to the Latina/o population, aptly illustrates the overall US ignorance and exclusion of Latina/os. Despite common perceptions that Latina/os are newcomers to the US, they have a long presence in the US extending back nearly two centuries. Over this long period of time, countless numbers of Latina/os have been born in the US, while others continue to make their journey to this country. Over their long history in the US, Latina/os have made important contributions to this nation. In particular, Mexicans were initially incorporated into this country more than one and a half centuries ago, with Puerto Ricans becoming associated with the US more than a century ago. The US, especially in the Southwest (especially Arizona, California, Colorado, New Mexico, and Texas), bears profound Latina/o – particularly Mexican – roots. Indeed, much of the land in the Southwest (including California, Nevada, Utah, New Mexico, most of Arizona and Colorado, and parts of Oklahoma, Kansas, and Wyoming) belonged to Mexico until 1848 with the signing of the Treaty of Guadalupe Hidalgo at the end of the Mexican–American War (National Archives 2024). As a result of this treaty, Mexico lost about 55 percent of its land to the US. Indeed, Latina/os living in the Southwest exist in land that once was part of Mexico.

Over the last several decades, Latina/os have played an important role in the changing demography of the US. The increasing prominence of Latina/os makes them the engine of the US population. The growing presence of Latina/os in the US is having an impact on the nation's culture and institutions. Population projections indicate that Latina/os will increasingly drive the nation's demography throughout the twenty-first century. It is estimated that the Latina/o electorate will nearly double between 2012 and 2030, largely due to the rapidly growing number of young Latina/os turning eighteen years of age (Taylor et al. 2012a). Latina/os also accounted for more than three-fifths (62%) of the growth in people eligible to vote between the 2018 presidential and the 2022 mid-term election, increasing at a rate of 16 percent, higher than the change among other racial or ethnic groups (Natarajan and Im 2022). The potential political power of Latina/os is immense. At the national level, 65 percent of the US Latina/o citizens of voting age population (CVAP) are concentrated in five of the six most populous states (California, Texas, Florida, New York, and Illinois) compared to 32 percent of US non-Latina/os. At the state level, the Latina/o population is larger than the white population in California, New Mexico, and Texas.

This book provides a sociological overview of Latina/os to help readers better understand the past, present, and future of the diverse groups that comprise the Latina/o population in the US. In the following section we will identify the extensive roots and some of the major influences of Latina/os in this country in the realms of history, culture, language, and cuisine.

The Deep Roots and Influences of Latina/os on the US

The influence of Latina/os on the US reaches far back in history. A testament of this historical presence are the many cities across the Southwest that bear Spanish names, including Casa Grande, Guadalupe, Mesa, Nogales, Sierra Vista in Arizona; Chula Vista, Fresno, Los Angeles, Merced, San Diego, San Francisco in California; Aguilar, Alma, Blanca, Dolores, Las Animas, and Pueblo in Colorado; Belen, Española, Las Cruces, Las Vegas, Raton, and Santa Fe in New Mexico; and Amarillo, Del Rio, El Paso, La Feria, San Antonio, and Zapata in Texas.

In addition, the influence of Latina/os on the US can be seen in the English language. In the Southwest, Spanish words that have become part of the English language stem from the ranching past of Mexicans. The list of Spanish words that are part of the English language includes arroyo (stream), avocado, barbeque, buckaroo (derived from vaquero, the Spanish word for cowboy), burro (donkey), chaparral (thicket), conquistador, corral (pen), desperado (bandit), dolly welter ("a term for wrapping a lasso around a saddle horn . . . comes from '*dale vuelta*' [Spanish for 'give it a turn'], see Ponce 2022), junta (meeting), lariat (derived from *la riata*, Spanish word for rope), lasso (same as with lariat), mesa (plateau), mesquite, patio, pimento (pepper), rodeo, salsa, savanna, sierra (mountain range), tango, ten-gallon hat, tomato, and vanilla (see Wikipedia 2024).

Furthermore, Spanish language instruction in the US has increased dramatically over the last several decades and Spanish became the most popular language studied by American students at the university level in the mid-1990s (Gearing 2010). For example, according to a study of college enrollment in foreign languages in 2009 by the Modern Language Association (Furman et al. 2010), approximately 865,000 students in the US were enrolled in a Spanish language course, with French, the second most popular foreign-language course, having an enrollment only one-fourth that of Spanish. Nonetheless, the most recent Modern Language Association report indicates a decline in non-English language instruction with the number of persons enrolled in Spanish courses dropping by 17 percent between 2009 and 2016, compared with a decline of 13 percent for all other non-English languages combined (Looney and Lusin 2019). Still, Spanish continues to be the most popular foreign language taught in higher education today, with half of all the students enrolled in a foreign-language course taking Spanish (Maria 2023).

Similarly, according to the 2021 American Community Survey (ACS) (Ruggles et al. 2024), Spanish was the most common language among persons five years of age and older who spoke a language other than English in the US, with 41.3 million persons speaking Spanish at home (Ruggles et al. 2024). Furthermore, approximately 2.7 million non-Latina/o individuals – 69 percent of these being whites – spoke Spanish at home at that time (Ruggles et al. 2024). Who are these whites who speak Spanish at home? There are three possibilities. First, they could be persons who have a Latina/o-related ancestry but they do not identify as Latina/o today. Second, they could be whites born in Latin America, the Caribbean, or Spain, places where Spanish is spoken. Third, they could be married to a Latina/o spouse. We examined these possibilities using data from the 2021 ACS for whites who speak Spanish at home. There is no support for the first two possibilities: only approximately 9 percent of white Spanish speakers who reported one or two ancestries in the ACS listed a Latina/o-related ancestry, and only 4 percent of white Spanish speakers were born in a country where Spanish is spoken. However, white Spanish speakers are disproportionately married to Latina/o spouse, who are likely to have been born outside of the US. Approximately 37 percent of married white Spanish speakers have a spouse who is Latina/o, two-thirds of these Latina/o spouses being born outside of the US. This represents an interesting illustration of how Spanish-language use is maintained even in cases involving intermarriage.

The influence of Latina/os – especially of Mexicans – can also be seen in the food that Americans consume. Indeed, the three most popular ethnic cuisines in the US are Chinese, Mexican, and Italian (Williams 2020). In addition, Mexican food accounts for the largest share of the overall food market and Mexican restaurants account for 11 percent of all restaurants in the country, behind only those designated as "American" food restaurants, which supposedly serve traditional "American" food (Danziger 2023). The dethroning of ketchup by salsa for the title of the most popular condiment in 1991 is emblematic of the rising popularity of Mexican food in the US (O'Neill 1992). More recently, in June 2023 Modelo beer supplanted Budweiser beer as the US top seller of beer, after the latter's nearly two-decade reign at the top (Moreno 2023; Tse 2023).

Furthermore, Mexican businesses have also made important inroads into the US and global markets. Cemex the second top cement supplier in the US (Leonard 2023) and Cinépolis (Kolmar 2023) and Grupo Bimbo (Bizvibe 2020) being the second largest movie theater chain and the fourth largest baker in the world, respectively. Moreover, Latina/o-owned small businesses have grown tremendously. For example, over the last decade, the number of Latina/o-owned small businesses rose by 34 percent compared to 1 percent for all other non-Latina/o-owned businesses (Cimini 2020; Mills et al. 2018).

In the world of music, *Rolling Stone* began a section on Latina/o music in late 2012 (Newman 2012). A significant number of Latina/o musicians have gained popularity as "crossover" artists who rank highly in Spanish and English language music charts. Historically, the list of leading Latina/o crossover performers has grown to include Marc Anthony, Raymond Ayala (aka Daddy Yankee), Celia Cruz, Gloria Estefan, Jose Feliciano, Luis Fonsi, Enrique Iglesias, Ricky Martin, Carlos Santana, Selena, Shakira, Richie Valens (see DeVitt 2011). Of course, there are other Latina/o performers who excel in English, including Jennifer Lopez and Sixto Rodriguez, among others.

Thus, it is clear that Latina/os have had major influences on diverse dimensions of the US, including its history, culture, language, architecture, and cuisine. This influence is likely to expand significantly throughout the twenty-first century with the disproportionate growth of Latina/os (see Chapter 5).

The Diversity of Latina/os

Before continuing, it is important to understand the population changes Latina/os have experienced over the last six decades. In the early 1960s, the Latina/o population was largely comprised of persons of Mexican origin alongside a relatively small Puerto Rican population and an even smaller Cuban population, with the great majority (approximately 85%) born in the US. More than a half century later the Latina/o population is much more diverse. While Mexicans still account for approximately three-fifths of the Latina/o population, Latina/os today originate from the Caribbean, Central and South America, as well as Spain, with close to one-third born outside of the US. In the last decade, we have seen a significant reduction of the Mexican-origin population and foreign-born persons, largely due to the decline in Mexican immigrants since the Great Recession beginning in 2008. Indeed, over the last decade and a half, the most significant shifts in the Latina/o population have been the reduction of Latina/os who are of Mexican-origin and who were born outside of the US. To be sure, the growth of the Latino population beyond Mexicans has been associated with significant levels of immigration from the Caribbean and Central and South America over the last few decades (see Chapter 4).

The combination of an established population that has been in this country for many generations alongside a newcomer group reflects the great diversity that exists within the Latina/o population in the US. Latina/os also differ significantly on the basis of language, physical attributes (e.g. skin color), family and household formation, socioeconomic status, among many other variations. Furthermore, as elaborated in Chapter 2, Latina/o subgroups differ significantly in their histories and particularly in the ways they were first incorporated into the US. Mexicans and Puerto Ricans were initially incorporated into the US through warfare directly involving the US in the nineteenth century. In contrast, Cubans were embraced as "golden exiles" and granted refugee status when they immigrated in significant numbers to the US in 1959 as they were fleeing communism and Fidel Castro with less favorable receptivity when immigrant flows became poorer and Black (Eckstein 2009). Dominicans were initially allowed to immigrate to the US in the form of a safety valve guarding against the rise of dissension in the Dominican Republic in the 1960s. Moreover, Salvadorans and Guatemalans came in large numbers, beginning in the late 1970s to escape the ravages of vicious civil wars in their countries, but their pleas for refugee status were largely rejected despite them fleeing brutal governments supported by the US. Finally, Colombians began immigrating to the US in the 1980s as they sought haven from the brutal cartel wars that devastated the country and its people. These varying histories of incorporation into the US led to diverse paths of inclusion with some groups enjoying easier routes than others, although the context of reception has grown increasingly hostile to all immigrants over much of the twenty-first century. This leads us to ask, how can groups with varying histories and migratory trajectories at different time periods and disparate conditions all be labeled as "Latina/os"?

The Making of Latina/os in the US

The US government and the US Census Bureau, have historically had difficulty in identifying and naming Latina/os. For example, in the 1930 census during the period surrounding the Great Depression and the Repatriation Program seeking to return persons of Mexican origin to Mexico, Mexicans were treated as a racial category – the only time ever in the history of the US census. As the Latina/o population grew during the 1940s and 1950s, the Census Bureau, in trying to identify this population, defined people as "persons of Spanish surname" and "persons of Spanish language," with terms used on the basis of the region of the country. Toward the end of the 1970s, the US government came up with the term "Hispanic" to identify the Latina/o population, although the 1980 census used the category "person of Spanish origin." The mass media celebrated and glorified the "Hispanic" term during the 1980s. For instance, *Time* featured a story on the Latina/o population and dubbed the 1980s the "decade of Hispanics" with Hispanic Heritage Month initiated in 1988 (Dávila 2001). Nonetheless, certain Latina/os were critical of the Hispanic term because they felt that it was imposed on the group by the national government and that the label highlighted and celebrated the Spanish roots of the group. By the 1990s, the Latino term began to be used increasingly in the mass media. Yet, some still expressed disapproval of the term because these individuals see it as neglecting their Hispanic and Spanish ancestry in favor of their Latin American ancestry.

We use the term Latina/o in this book. It should be understood that the terms Latina/o and Hispanic (and the Latinx and Latine designations that emerged in the last decade or so) represent the same people, though there are differences in their preference for labels. For example, a national survey of Latina/os/Hispanics found that half of the sample did not have a preference for one label over the other; however, of those that had a preference for one identity, the Hispanic term was favored over the Latina/o designation (Taylor et al. 2012b). More recent research has shown a greater preference for the Hispanic term, with 61 percent of respondents opting for this label compared to 29 percent preferring Latino, 4 percent Latinx, and 5 percent some other label (Noe-Bustamante et al. 2020). This Pew Research Center survey also observed that only one-third of Latina/os were aware of the Latinx term, but two-thirds of people who had heard this label opposed its use. Yet, US-born Latina/os in California have a more favorable connection to the Latinx term, with more than half familiar with the term (Mora et al. 2021) and approximately one-fourth identifying with the term (Mora et al. 2022). Younger Latina/os who are more politically progressive are the most likely to embrace the Latinx term.

While Latina/o and Hispanic represent "pan-ethnic" terms, in that they are umbrella designations that comprise the varying specific subgroups that make up the larger population, Latina/os tend to prefer labels that describe their national origin, i.e. Mexican, Puerto Rican, Cuban, etc. Indeed, slightly more than half of Latina/os picked a national-origin label over the pan-ethnic Latina/o or Hispanic term (Taylor et al. 2012b). This is particularly the case for migrants from Latin American and the Caribbean, who view themselves not as Latina/o or Hispanic, but as Mexican, Puerto Rican, Cuban, Guatemalan, Bolivian, or Spanish. Certainly, people in say, Colombia, regard themselves as *colombianos* or Colombians rather than Latina/o or Hispanic, as the latter two terms are not even appropriate pan-ethnic terms in their home countries – that is, they are labels constructed in the US. Nevertheless, regardless of their own preference, when immigrants come to the US they become recipients of the Latina/o or Hispanic pan-ethnic identities. While gradually they may come to adopt the "Latina/o" or "Hispanic" labels, the preference for the national-origin labels remains.

Similarly, social constructions of race vary tremendously between Latin American countries in the US. For example, Latin American and Caribbean countries use a variety of designations along the racial color line and there is a common saying in Latin America and the Caribbean that "money whitens," suggesting that persons with darker skin who are economically prosperous are treated as white. In contrast, the US has consistently featured a Black/white racial dichotomy in which a "single drop of Black blood" results in a person being considered and treated as Black (Hickman 1997). Thus, dark-skinned individuals, who may be viewed in their home country as white, are considered and treated as Black in the US. For example, considerable segments of people in the Dominican Republic, despite their historical ties to Africa, tend to deny their African ancestry in favor of their Spanish and indigenous roots (Candelario 2007; Torres-Saillant 2000). Many dark-skinned Dominican immigrants are surprised to learn that in the US they are Black.

Racial Matters

While social scientists view race as a social construction, it is real in its consequences. Thus, although there is greater variation in the genetic structure within racial categories than across racial categories, societies continue to place individuals into racial categories on the basis of physical features, namely skin color. Racial groups are then stratified along a variety of dimensions including social, economic, and political realms. Given the long history of white supremacy, persons who are white are at the top of the stratification system, while those who are the darkest are situated at the base of the stratification system. Latina/os vary widely on the skin color spectrum;

some Latina/os are dark while others are characterized by light skin. People who have populated Latin America and the Caribbean, as well as Spain, have a wide array of features associated with different racial categories. The mixture of racial features stems across African, Arab, Asian, European, and indigenous roots.

According to the Office of Management and Budget (OMB), which oversees the US Census Bureau, Latina/os represent an ethnic group rather than a racial category. Nonetheless, on census-related forms, Latina/os are asked to classify themselves racially. In the 2020 census there was a significant change in the question design, data processing, and coding procedures, with the consequences being greater options for people to identify their own race. The expanding race options included an expansion of the number of characters for the identification of multiple races along with an increase in the number of multiple races that people could choose (see Marks and Rios-Vargas 2021). For Latina/os, these changes brought about a major change in the way Latina/os identified themselves along the lines of race. Between the 2010 and 2020 censuses, the number of Latina/os identifying their race as white alone fell by 53 percent and those classifying themselves as Black alone declined by 6 percent, while the number of Latina/os identifying themselves as multiracial grew six-fold and those choosing the category of American Indian and Alaska Native alone more than doubled (Jones et al. 2021; for the concept of Latina/o displacement of indigenous people through settler colonialism, see also Pulido 2018). Of course, there is a need for caution in interpreting these changes, as they largely reflect the way in which the race question was designed and the way that the data were coded and processed rather than a massive change in racial identification.

This shift can be further identified in the comparison of the racial composition of Latina/os across four time periods: the first two (2010 and 2019) based on the procedures used in the 2010 census, and the latter two (2020 and 2021) based on those of the 2020 census. As Figure 1.1 shows, while the white racial designation was the most popular in the 2019 ACS, with about a little more than half (53.0%) and two-thirds (65.7%) opting for white, respectively, in 2010 and 2019, only one-fifth (20.3%) and one-sixth (16.4%) did so in 2020 and 2021, respectively. In the 2021 ACS, multiracial was the most popular racial designation, with 44.1 percent choosing this category, followed by "Some Other Race" at 35.3 percent and white at 16.4 percent. Again, we reiterate that these shifts reflect the change in the design of the race question and in the processing of the responses, rather than significant shifts of this magnitude in racial identification. Moreover, one of the major worrisome implications of these dramatic shifts in racial identification produced by these design and processing changes is the likely instability of statistics including poverty rates, death rates, median incomes, and so forth in making comparisons before and after 2020, when the procedural changes took place.

The racial identification changes occurred among all Latina/o subgroups (Table 1.1). Even groups that historically have identified almost exclusively as white changed their racial classification in 2020. For example, while 87 percent of Cubans identified themselves as white in 2019, only 20.5 percent did so in 2021. Spaniards, too, experienced a drop from 75.6 percent to 23.2 percent in the choice of white between

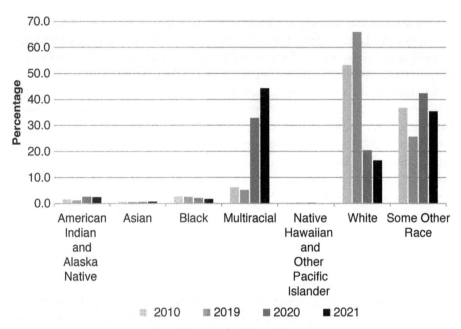

Figure 1.1 Percentage Racial Distribution of Latina/os by Year
Source: Data from 2010 and 2020 Census and 2019 and 2021 American Community Survey 1-Year Estimates Public-Use File (Ruggles et al. 2024).

2019 and 2021, respectively. In fact, in 2021, the selection of the white racial category was even much lower (below 20%) among all other Latina/o subgroups, aside from Cubans and Spaniards. Furthermore, in 2021, seven of the largest Latina/o subgroups selected multiracial as their most common racial designation: Cubans, 65.7 percent; Spaniards, 62.7 percent; Venezuelans, 55.8 percent; Columbians, 53.2 percent; Peruvians, 44.8 percent; Puerto Ricans, 44.7 percent; and Mexicans, 43.2 percent. The other five groups most commonly selected the Some Other Race category as their race: Salvadorans, 53.4 percent; Guatemalans, 52.0 percent; Dominicans, 49.9 percent; Ecuadorians, 48.9 percent; and Hondurans, 46.4 percent. As was the case with the white racial category, all groups selected Black less frequently in 2021 than in 2019, with only Dominicans (5.9%) and Puerto Ricans (5.7%) choosing it by more than 5 percent of their members. It is the case that the racial designation of Latina/os has undergone a major shift. Finally, despite most of the Latina/o subgroups having indigenous roots, relatively few identified racially as American Indian and Alaska Native with only three groups having more than 2 percent of their members choosing this racial category in 2021 (Guatemalan, 5.9%; Mexican, 2.8%; and Salvadoran, 2.3%; for the precarious nature of indigenous identity of Latina/os, see Pulido 2018). To reiterate, these changes are most likely to reflect the change in the design of the question and the processing of the responses rather than actual significant shifts in racial identity.

Yet, racial identification among Latina/os generally varies by nativity (i.e. place of birth) with the distinction being people born in the US and those born outside of the

Table 1.1 Percentage of Latina/os in Twelve Largest Latina/o Groups Choosing Selected Race Categories, 2019 and 2021

Latina/o Group	American Indian & Alaska Native 2019	American Indian & Alaska Native 2021	Black 2019	Black 2021	Multiracial 2019	Multiracial 2021	White 2019	White 2021	Some Other Race[a] 2019	Some Other Race[a] 2021
Mexican	1.2	2.8	0.7	0.6	4.0	43.2	68.3	16.9	25.5	36.0
Puerto Rican	0.6	0.8	8.0	5.7	9.0	44.7	60.5	18.4	21.3	29.5
Cuban	0.2	0.2	3.7	2.3	3.4	65.7	87.0	20.5	5.4	20.5
Salvadoran	0.7	2.3	0.9	0.5	4.0	33.8	53.6	9.7	40.6	53.4
Dominican	0.6	0.9	14.7	5.9	7.7	35.9	34.9	7.1	41.8	49.9
Guatemalan	2.4	5.9	0.6	0.5	3.5	32.7	51.2	8.6	42.0	52.0
Colombian	0.3	0.5	1.9	0.9	5.1	53.2	74.9	15.9	17.6	29.3
Honduran	0.8	1.8	4.1	1.1	5.2	41.8	56.5	8.6	33.4	46.4
Spaniard	1.5	1.8	1.0	0.7	12.4	62.7	75.6	23.2	7.3	10.3
Ecuadorian	0.4	1.2	1.3	0.6	4.9	36.4	56.0	12.5	37.0	48.9
Peruvian	1.1	1.8	0.8	0.5	6.5	44.8	59.9	13.9	31.2	38.1
Venezuelan	0.6	0.2	1.8	0.6	3.3	55.8	77.0	15.1	17.3	27.8

[a] The Some Other Race category does not include the Asian and Native Hawaiian and Other Pacific Islander race categories.

Source: Data from 2019 and 2021 American Community Survey 1-Year Estimates Public-Use Files (Ruggles et al. 2024).

US and immigrating here. For example, ACS data for 2021 show that across all twelve Latina/o subgroups, those born in the US were more likely to identify as white and as Black compared to those born outside of the nation (Table 1.2). In contrast, foreign-born individuals were more likely to choose the Some Other Race category, with the exception being Spaniards. This may suggest that Latina/os born outside of the US may be less likely than their US-born counterparts to find a racial category among the available list of options with which they can identify. There were fewer differences along the lines of nativity for the selection of the American Indian and Alaska Native and multiracial categories. Overall, in examining the most popular racial category for nativity groups across Latina/o subgroups, there are some general patterns. First, both foreign- and native-born persons preferred the multiracial category, particularly among Cubans, Colombians, Spaniards, and Venezuelans. Second, both nativity groups opted the most for the Some Other Race category among Salvadorans, Dominicans, Guatemalans, Hondurans, and Ecuadorians. Finally, foreign-born persons preferred the Some Other Race category, while Mexican, Puerto Rican, and Peruvian native-born individuals preferred the multiracial category.

It is important to note, however, that as the US Census Bureau prepares for the upcoming 2030 census, there is an initiative within the OMB to continue discussions that failed to materialize into changes in the racial designations leading to

Table 1.2 Percentage of Latina/os in Twelve Largest Latina/o Groups Choosing Selected Race Categories by Nativity, 2021

Latina/o Group	American Indian & Alaska Native		Black		Multiracial		White		Some Other Race[a]	
	FB[b]	NB[b]	FB[b]	NB[b]	FB[b]	NB[b]	FB[b]	NB[b]	FB[b]	NB[b]
Mexican	3.4	2.6	0.1	0.9	42.3	43.6	8.7	20.3	45.5	32.1
Puerto Rican	0.4	0.8	3.7	5.8	39.0	44.8	14.0	18.5	41.2	29.2
Cuban	0.0	0.4	1.2	3.6	73.2	57.0	14.2	27.7	11.0	10.3
Salvadoran	2.5	2.1	0.0	1.0	33.9	33.7	6.6	13.3	56.9	49.4
Dominican	0.9	0.8	3.7	8.1	33.8	38.1	4.4	9.8	56.9	42.6
Guatemalan	6.6	5.0	0.2	1.0	31.8	34.0	6.2	11.8	55.1	47.7
Colombian	0.3	0.7	0.4	1.6	54.9	51.0	10.9	22.5	33.4	23.8
Honduran	1.8	1.9	0.5	2.2	43.5	38.9	6.0	13.1	48.0	43.6
Spaniard	0.2	2.0	0.4	0.7	76.3	60.8	11.2	24.8	8.7	10.5
Ecuadorian	1.6	0.8	0.0	1.3	35.6	37.3	8.0	17.7	54.5	42.3
Peruvian	2.1	1.4	0.1	0.9	43.6	46.6	8.1	22.2	45.3	27.9
Venezuelan	0.1	0.5	0.3	1.6	57.0	52.0	12.7	22.7	29.5	22.5

[a] The Some Other Race category does not include the Asian and Native Hawaiian and Other Pacific Islander race categories.

[b] FB refers to foreign-born and NB to native-born.

Source: Data from 2021 American Community Survey 1-Year Estimates Public-Use File (Ruggles et al. 2024).

the 2020 census. One of these possible changes involves Latina/os. While Latina/os have been considered an ethnic group based on an ethnic identification of Latina/o and Hispanic alongside any racial category, there is now the discussion on Latina/os becoming a racial category. There is much debate with some proponents of the change arguing that it will clarify the confusion among many Latina/os concerning a racial identification, after they have already classified themselves as Latina/o or Hispanic in the census questionnaire, while opponents contend that mixed-race Latina/os, predominantly Afro-Latina/os, may opt for a single category, resulting in their elimination from the Latina/o or Black racial category (see López and Hogan 2021).

Thus, the varying groups that constitute the Latina/o population differ greatly on a wide variety of characteristics, including how they are viewed and how they perceive themselves racially in the US. Despite this great diversity within the Latina/o population, as noted earlier, many Americans continue to view members of this population as a homogeneous group with only shallow roots in the US. This book will examine the varying groups that constitute the Latina/o population as well as how they vary across different social, economic, political, and demographic dimensions. Finally, the book will engage readers through our highlighting of many of the major issues that Latina/os face and the trends they experience in the various aspects of their lives. Indeed, there are many critical concerns that affect the lives of Latina/os today that will ultimately impact the kind of future that they experience in this country.

The Larger Context: Historical and Contemporary Latina/o Boundaries

We started off this chapter with a quote from journalist Stephania Taladrid on the long history of Latina/os in the US and the continued inequality and neglect that they face as minoritized people. This is very much in line with the framing of the Latina/o people and their experience in this country. However, we call attention here to new frameworks that address difficult questions in the field regarding the concept of settler colonialism and the experience of Latina/os in subjugating indigenous people. We also provide a discussion on the boundaries that place some people firmly in the Latina/o category as well as contested boundaries that seek to include or exclude other people as Latina/o, and still other prescriptive boundaries that eliminate "neighboring" or "related" people, such as Brazilians, Filipinos, and Haitians, who are excluded because of not speaking Spanish or the color of their skin (see below).

Scholars have paid increasing attention to the concept of settler colonization, which involves settler states, such as Australia, Canada, Israel, and the US. Pulido (2018) notes that "[r]ather than seeking to control land, resources, and labor, settler colonization eliminated native peoples in order to appropriate their land" (p. 309). As Pulido (2018) has noted, while work on settler colonization has traditionally focused on white settlers, more recently there has been attention to the role of people of color in colonizing indigenous people. Pulido (2018), in particular, has called attention to the lack of engagement of scholars in Chicana/o Studies regarding the role that Chicana/os have played in subjugating indigenous people. She argues that part of this neglect has been due to their conceptualization of Chicana/os as a colonized and conquered people. Pulido (2018) suggests that "[r]ecognizing ethnic-Mexicans' role in settler colonization is threatening because it would force Chicana/o studies to recognize multiple subjectivities, which, in turn, would require rethinking the dominant narrative. She also reminds us that while Chicana/o activists in the Chicana/o Movement of the 1960s and 1970s celebrated Aztlán, the mythical homeland of Aztecs in today's US southwest, as a galvanizing force, at the same time they ignored the conquest of Aztecs over other indigenous people in Mexico. Pulido (2018) also suggests that another reason for the reluctance of Chicana/o Studies to engage in settler colonization is the "precarious nature of Chicana/o indigeneity" (p. 318). Despite the clear indigenous roots of many Chicana/os – and Latina/os, for that matter – in some respects the indigenous identity of many falls outside rules of tribal membership and ancestry, credentials that they do not possess.

This context of settler colonization involving Chicana/os and, more broadly, Latina/os is important for understanding the historical and contemporary context of the Latina/o people and their experiences. The ancestors of many of these individuals have been not only minoritized people, but also people who have played a role in the colonization and subjugation of indigenous people. This is important in also understanding variations in who is a Latina/o person in the US. One group of individuals are readily accepted as Latina/os: persons who identify as Latina/o and are generally seen by people in the ethnic community as being Latina/o. A second group consists of individuals who may not be truly accepted as Latina/os due to particular views that some Latina/o in-group members may hold regarding who is a Latina/o. For example, persons who were born in Spain and their descendants are not readily viewed as Hispanic or Latina/o by some in-group members because of the colonization of Spain over Latin American and Caribbean countries (Kang and Torres-Saillant 2010) and, in fact, some Spaniards and their descendants may not see themselves as Latina/o because they were not born in Latin America and the Caribbean (Benavides 2020; Soto-Márquez 2019). Despite this ambiguity, Spaniards and their descendants are defined as Hispanic or Latino by the OMB and the US Census Bureau (Kang and Torres-Saillant 2010). In addition, Afro-Latinos have for long not been embraced as Latina/o by certain segments of the Latina/o population (Dzidzienyo and Oboler 2005; Haywood 2017; T.K. Hernández 2022). Afro-Latina/os often report that they are commonly not fully accepted by African Americans, who do not accept them because they speak Spanish, and by Latina/os, who do not accept them because of the color of their skin (Gosin 2017; Howard 2018). Moreover, we can also think of other multiracial Latina/o persons who may experience a feeling of rejection because of their physical features (not looking Latina/o enough), non-Hispanic surnames, and the language that they speak (English, indigenous languages, and other non-Spanish languages). This is a growing population, with the number of Latina/os who are intermarried to non-Latina/os tripling between 1970 and 2000 (Rosenfeld and Kim 2005; Vasquez 2014). In 2015, the most common combination of intermarried spouses featured a Latina/o and a white spouse, accounted for 42 percent of all intermarried couples in the nation (Bialik 2017). There will be increasing numbers of children of intermarried parents that involve one Latina/o parent. Finally, there is another group of individuals who have a geographic or cultural affinity to Latina/os but certain rules exclude them from being Latina/o. In this regard, Black skin color and non-Spanish language generally keep out Belizeans, Brazilians, Filipinos, Haitians, and other groups tracing their ancestry to Latin American and the Caribbean from being part of the Latina/o population. Despite the important recognition that race and ethnicity are social constructions, they continue to play an important role in Latina/o membership boundaries today.

Changes from the First Edition of the Book

A lot has changed over the course of the completion of the first edition of this book and this updated version. Shortly after the first edition of the book, Donald Trump announced that he was running for US president, while verbally assailing Mexicans as criminals, rapists, and drug pushers. He would go on to win the presidential election with his disdain toward Mexicans and other people of color becoming more vicious and his policies hurtful to people of color overall. Trump's policies toward building a wall to keep Mexicans out of the country certainly played to the anti-immigrant and nationalist sentiments of his supporters. Never mind that the volume of immigration from Mexico fell tremendously from the time of the Great Recession onward (Sáenz 2019). The COVID-19 pandemic also disproportionately took the lives of Latina/os, American Indians and Alaska Natives, and Blacks, groups with pre-existing chronic diseases who were disproportionately on the frontlines toiling as essential workers. The continual killing of unarmed Blacks by police, most prominently the murder of George Floyd in Minneapolis in 2020, led to protests in the early midst of the pandemic. There have also been horrendous mass killings directed at Latina/o and Black people, with the killing of 23 Latina/os in El Paso in 2019 and ten Blacks in Buffalo in 2022.

Furthermore, throughout the 2010s there were rising numbers of people from Latin America and the Caribbean – most notably Cubans, Guatemalans, Haitians, Hondurans, Nicaraguans, Salvadorans, and Venezuelans – along with people from other continents coming to the US southern border seeking refugee status against the violence and persecution that they face in their countries. The Trump and Biden administrations used the pandemic to halt these individuals from gaining entrance into the US. Increasingly, the border region and immigrants have become political pawns, with politicians painting the border as a warzone that is out of control and many immigrants seeking asylum stranded in Mexican border communities to fend for themselves or entering the US and being shipped to large progressive cities. Texas Governor Greg Abbott has taken it upon himself with taxpayer money to continue to build the border wall and to strategically place concertina razor wire in parts of the Rio Grande River to keep undocumented immigrants out of Texas, along with shipping persons seeking asylum who arrive in Texas to New York, Chicago, and other large cities located far away from Texas.

Moreover, many states around the country, most prominently Texas and Florida, have established laws against the teaching of Critical Race Theory (CRT) in high schools (even though it is not taught in high schools) and colleges and universities and have ended DEI (diversity, equity, and inclusion) programs, and laws have been passed to make it more difficult for people to vote. Finally, there was the January 6, 2021 attack on the US Capitol Building by Trump supporters, who were trying to stop the count of electoral votes that would officially name Biden as the president. Many see the sum of these events, which have split the nation along political lines, as an attack on democracy, at a time, ironically, when the population of Latina/os and other people of color continues to grow, while that of whites has declined over the last several years.

We made four significant changes in this second edition of the book. First, we expanded our focus to additional Latina/o-origin groups, depending on the availability of data, with the most prominent new groups being Hondurans Afro-Latina/os, and Spaniards. In 2022, Hondurans, with a population of 1.2 million, were the eighth largest Latina/o subgroup, Afro-Latina/os (persons who identified as Latino or Hispanic and who identified racially as Black) with one million were the ninth largest, and Spaniards with 972,000 were the tenth largest subgroup. As we discussed above, we realize that some in the Latina/o community do not view Spaniards as part of the Latina/o population. We spent a considerable amount of time debating about whether or not to include Spaniards as one of the ten Latina/o subgroups that we highlight. In the end, we opted to include them in this capacity. This decision was, in large part, due to Spaniards already being part of the Latina/o category, as defined by the OMB and US Census Bureau (Kang and Torres-Saillant 2010). Our decision does not imply that we merely follow the lead of the OMB blindly, but rather the statistics that we use throughout the book are based on the Latina/o population, which does include Spaniards. In addition, Spanish-origin identity is considerable in some states, with 16.6 percent of Latina/os in New Mexico and 8.8 percent in Colorado, for example, identifying themselves as Spaniard, Spanish, or Spanish American in 2022. We will be able to assess the standing of these three subgroups alongside the other seven Latina/o subgroups that were featured in the first edition of our book. It continues to be the case that Afro-Latina/os have been neglected and overlooked in the study of the Latina/o population and that they tend to fare worse compared to other Latina/os on a variety of social and economic characteristics. Moreover, the inclusion of Spaniards will allow us to illustrate how some subgroups with whiter skin complexion and European features fare much better socioeconomically compared to subgroups that experience a greater degree of racialization. Second, we have added three chapters related to the development of intellectual thought in the Latina/o community, gender and sexuality, and the Latina/o arts. Third, as we did in this chapter, we begin each chapter with a vignette that highlights and illustrates with human voices the topics and issues we cover in the chapters. Finally, we have added questions at the end of each chapter that call attention to some of the issues that we cover and which will be particularly useful for students as they reflect on and organize their thoughts on the materials that they have read. These additions serve to expand our understanding of the Latina/o experience and facilitate engagement of the materials that we present and issues that we address.

Structure of the Book

This new edition of the book consists of a total of sixteen chapters. The book begins with an introduction (this chapter) to Latina/os, with the following chapter providing a historical overview of the largest Latina/o groups in the US (Chapter 2) and the development of Latina/o intellectual thought (Chapter 3). Subsequently, the next three chapters of the book provide an examination of the Latina/o population through the discussion of the group's immigration experience (Chapter 4), demography (Chapter 5), and gender and sexuality (Chapter 6). The book then proceeds to overview and understand the experience of Latina/os in societal institutions, including political engagement (Chapter 7), the Latina/o arts (Chapter 8), education (Chapter 9), work and economic life (Chapter 10), family (Chapter 11), religion (Chapter 12), health and health care (Chapter 13), crime and victimization (Chapter 14), and mass media (Chapter 15). This series of chapters examining Latina/os within particular institutions begins with a discussion of relevant theoretical perspectives to inform the contemporary patterns of Latina/os across selected characteristics associated with the institution. Subsequently, the chapters highlight important issues or questions that we will need to monitor in the future. The book ends with a concluding chapter (Chapter 16) that provides an overview of the major patterns associated with Latina/os, and offers a portrait of what the future is likely to hold for Latina/os in the future in the US.

To better understand the diversity of the Latina/o population and the various modes into which they initially arrived in the US, and the ways they have been incorporated into this country, it is useful to examine in the next chapter the historical origins of the variety of groups that form the Latina/o population.

Discussion Questions

1. What are some examples that illustrate the deep roots of Latina/os in the US and their impact on this country?

2. What are the two ways in which the composition of Latina/os in the US has changed over the last decade and a half?

3. What are the major changes in the racial identification of Latina/os between the period prior to 2020 and from 2020 to the present? Why did this shift in racial identification change? Do you believe that the racial differences are real or due to procedural changes?

4. What is meant by settler colonialism?

5. What is Aztlán and what is its significance?

6. What change is the Office of Management and Budget currently considering in the way Latina/os are identified?

7. What are the boundaries that are created that result in some people being readily accepted as Latina/os, others not easily considered Latina/os, and still others not allowed to be part of the Latina/o designation?

2 The Diverse Histories of Latina/os

The Fruit Company, Inc.
reserved for itself the most succulent,
the central coast of my own land,
the delicate waist of America.

(Excerpt from "The United Fruit Co," Neruda 1991, p. 179)

In this poem, penned in 1950, Chilean Nobel-Laureate poet Pablo Neruda (1991) imagines Jehovah parceling out the world's lands and resources to various multinational companies.

The lines above illustrate the vast riches that US corporations gained, along with the powerful intrusion of US imperialism into the political and economic affairs of many countries in Latin America and the Caribbean. The roots of Latina/os in the US today can be traced to these regions. These countries from which Latina/os originate share a common Spanish language, although indigenous languages are also spoken there. Aside from the common Spanish language, Latin American and Caribbean countries have additional commonalities. In particular, these countries share an experience of colonization from Spain, beginning in the late fifteenth century and, except for Puerto Rico, independence from Spain starting in the early nineteenth century. Moreover, Latin American and Caribbean countries also are linked to the US, extending back to the mid-nineteenth century through a variety of means, including warfare, political intervention, economic investment and exploitation, globalization, and free trade. The linkages between Latin American and Caribbean nations and the US represent the roots of the migration of millions of people from these regions to the US over nearly two centuries and continuing today with the large-scale movement of people fleeing violence in El Salvador, Guatemala, and Honduras.

Migration theory, as we will observe in Chapter 4, demonstrates that political, economic, and social linkages between developed countries and developing countries spur the movement of people from the latter to the former. In particular, the world system theory developed by Wallerstein (1974) and applied to the field of migration by Massey et al. (1993) helps us understand how developed countries in the core area of the world system enter developing countries on the semi-periphery or periphery of the world system and upset the traditional political, economic, and social patterns. International migration to developed countries represents one way in which people in affected developing countries respond to these disruptions. The US for long has been involved economically, politically, and socially in the affairs of countries throughout Latin America and the Caribbean as we will illustrate below. The encroachment of the US into these countries includes the exploitation of resources and labor, the protection of US economic interests, and intrusion into the political affairs of countries through the policies of manifest destiny, gunboat diplomacy, and the propping of right-wing dictatorships and dismantling of left-wing administrations. It is important to consider the role that the US played in the political, economic, and social activities of Latin American and Caribbean countries and how these conditions set the stage for international migration to the US. It is important also to consider how different Latin American and Caribbean groups of immigrants have been incorporated into the US and their subsequent experiences in this country.

Because space does not allow us to provide a historical overview of each country from where Latina/os originate, and how these countries are linked to the US, we will focus on doing this for the seven Latin American countries with the largest populations in the US. These countries are Mexico, Puerto Rico, Cuba, the Dominican Republic, El Salvador, Guatemala, and Colombia. This group of countries provides us great diversity with respect to types of linkages with the US, timing of initial immigration to the US, modes of incorporation into the US, and the subsequent experiences of immigrants in the US.

Historical Linkages between Latin American and Caribbean Countries and the US in the Making of Immigrants

Immigration does not happen in a vacuum. Rather a wide set of factors influences whether or not people contemplate uprooting themselves and their families and heading out to a foreign land. As we will see below, the US through its political actions and economic interests has played an important role in spurring Latin Americans and Caribbeans to move to the US over more than two centuries. González (2000) provides a fitting description of the process, involving the entrance of US interests, the exploitation of resources, the support for right-wing governments, the uprooting of the poor, and the eventual immigration of many to the US. González (2000) notes that:

> (A) series of military occupations in the century . . . allowed US banks and corporations to gain control over key industries in every country. Latin American ventures sprang up on Wall Street overnight, as sugar, fruit, railroad, mining, gas, and electric company executives raced south on the heels of the marines. Thanks to the aid of pliant local elites and of US diplomats or military commanders, who often ended up as partners or managers of the new firms, the newcomers quickly corralled lucrative concessions, while the host countries fell deeper into debt and dependence. Whenever conflict erupted with a recalcitrant nationalist leader, the foreign companies simply called on Washington to intervene. The pretext was usually saving US citizens or preventing anarchy near our borders. To justify those interventions, our diplomats told people back home the Latin Americans were incapable of responsible government . . . They fashioned and perpetuated the image of El Jefe, the swarthy, ruthless dictator with slick black hair, scarcely literate broken-English accent, dark

sunglasses and sadistic personality, who ruled by fiat over a corrupt banana republic. Yet, even as they propagated that image, our bankers and politicians kept peddling unsound loans at usurious rates to those very dictators. Critical details of how the dictators rose to power and terrorized their people with Washington's help, or how regimes provided a "friendly" business climate for North American firms, remained hidden deep in diplomatic correspondences. As US-owned plantations spread rapidly into Mexico, Cuba, Puerto Rico, the Dominican Republic, Honduras, and Guatemala, millions of peasants were forced from their lands . . . (B)eginning with World War II, which shut down the supply of European labor, North American industrialists initiated massive contracting of Latin Americans for the domestic labor front. Thus began a migration process whose long-term results would transform twentieth-century America. (59–60)

We highlight below the historical context involving the encroachment of the US into the political and economic affairs of the seven countries listed above and the subsequent movement of people to the US.

Mexico

The first direct link between the US and a Latin American country involves conflict between the US and Mexico. As soon as Mexico gained its independence from Spain in 1821, the US already had its Manifest-Destiny-colored glasses clearly focused on Mexico (Alvarez 1973). Trying to avert US plans to take Mexican land, the Mexican government opened up its northern frontier region (Texas) to foreign settlement from the US. Within a short period, white settlers from the US outnumbered Mexicans by a ratio of five to one (Alvarez 1973). Tensions mounted as settlers did not abide by two requirements – including pledging allegiance to Mexico and converting to Catholicism (Alvarez 1973). Hostilities heightened after Mexico abolished slavery – most of the settlers were from the South and owned slaves – and halted immigration. Finally, internal conflicts within the Mexican government between the centralists forces – which favored "administrative control over all Mexican territory by the governing elite" (Alvarez 1973, p. 923), and which Santa Ana, who presided over Mexico, supported – and the federalist forces – which favored the implementation of "noble political principles of the rights of man as enunciated by the US Constitution" (Alvarez 1973, p. 923), and which was the form of government favored by the Texas outpost including Mexicans living in the region.

With Texas a stronghold of federalism and stirrings of a revolt in the air, Santa Ana marched his troops to quell the rebellion forces in Texas, an event culminating on March 6, 1836, when the Mexican army defeated the Texans at the Alamo in San Antonio. Approximately six weeks later, Texas troops caught Santa Ana and his army off guard in the Battle of San Jacinto. Santa Ana surrendered Texas, at which time Texas became an independent nation.

Nonetheless, the nationhood of Texas was short-lived. In a decade, the US annexed Texas. Mexico considered this a slap on the face. Yet, there was still a major dispute between Mexico and the US regarding the boundary between Texas and Mexico.

Mexico considered the Nueces River as the boundary, while the US regarded the Rio Grande as the border (Alvarez 1973). The disputed territory between the two boundary lines represented a "no man's land." When General Zachary Taylor marched his troops into the area in 1846, Mexico considered this act an invasion marking the beginning of the Mexican–American War (Alvarez 1973). The war ended with the signing of the Treaty of Guadalupe Hidalgo on February 2, 1848. With the signing of the treaty, Mexico ceded approximately half of its land to Mexico. In addition, Mexicans who lived on their land and who were now on US soil were given a year to decide on whether to move south to Mexico or to remain on their land and become US citizens. Most of these Mexicans opted to become US citizens. Moreover, the Treaty stipulated that the culture, language, and religion of Mexicans who became US citizens would be respected.

Thus, the Treaty of Guadalupe Hidalgo marked the creation of the Mexican American population – what Rodolfo Alvarez (1973) described as "Mexican by birth" and "[US] citizens by the might of arms " (p. 924). The initial incorporation of Mexicans into the US was through warfare, portending barriers that Mexican Americans would experience in their new country. Indeed, when incorporation is not voluntary – that is, when people do not voluntarily choose to move to a new country – members of the host society do not readily accept the newcomers and may treat them as less than human, and members of the incorporated group may also express hostility toward members of the host society. Despite their US citizenship status and guarantees that their culture, language, and religion would be respected, Mexican Americans largely became a landless proletariat, as they lost their land through both legal and extralegal means (Acuña 1972; Alvarez 1973; Montejano 1987).

Over time, the links between the US and Mexico would intensify. As we will see in Chapter 3, US growers lobbied to ensure that they continued to have access to cheap Mexican immigrant labor, while Congress sought to drastically curb immigration from Southern and Eastern Europe. In addition, the US and Mexico governments established the Bracero Program, a guest-worker program that brought approximately 4.8 million Mexicans to work as contract laborers to assist the US during its labor shortage associated with World War II. US corporations also took advantage of Mexico's Border Industrialization Program (BIP), which began in 1965 and which gave the US access to cheap Mexican labor along the US–Mexico border. The establishment of the North American Free Trade Agreement (NAFTA), which went into effect in 1994, formalized the economic bonds between the US, Canada, and Mexico. These linkages between the US and Mexico have been associated not only with the movement of capital and goods, but also the flow of Mexicans to the US.

While Mexicans have been in the US for many generations, more than 175 years after the signing of the Treaty of Guadalupe Hidalgo, they continue to occupy the bottom structures of the US stratification system. As we will see in later chapters, even US-born Mexicans continue to lag behind whites and other Latina/o groups in such areas as educational attainment, occupational attainment, and income. Racial and ethnic groups that were initially incorporated into the US through non-voluntary modes, such as Mexican Americans, have been seen as colonized groups

(Barrera 1979; Blauner 1972), although here we remind readers of the role that persons of Mexican origin in the US have played in the subjugation of indigenous people through settler colonialism (see Pulido 2018).

Cuba

Toward the end of the nineteenth century, as Cuba sought to gain its independence from Spain, the US served the role of mediator between Spain and Cuba, an offer that Spain rejected. President McKinley sent the USS Maine to Havana in January 1898 to protect its interest and people in Cuba. About three weeks after its arrival, the Maine suffered an explosion in which 260 crew members lost their lives (Cavendish 1998). Although the cause of the explosion was not fully determined, rabid sentiments fomenting in the US press pushed for laying blame on Spain, resulting in the US going to war against Spain. The war was relatively short-lived, lasting less than four months. At the conclusion of the war, the Treaty of Paris was signed on December 10, 1898. With the signing of the treaty, Spain gave independence to Cuba, ceded Puerto Rico and Guam, which became US territories, and allowed the US to purchase the Philippines for $20 million (Cavendish 1998). The passage of the Teller Amendment earlier in 1898 ensured that the US would not have permanent control over Cuba, other than in a transitional stage.

Consistent with the stipulations of the Teller Act of 1898, the US exhibited control over Cuba for only a few years, as Cuba transitioned to a state of independence and US occupation of Cuba ended in 1902 (González 2000). Cuba's first Congress began governing the country on May 20, 1902, and Thomas Estrada Palma became the first president of the nation (González 2000). Nonetheless, the US did not disappear entirely, as it had significant economic and political interests in Cuba. Thus, following the provisions of the Teller Act, the US established a provisional government, following a revolutionary uprising within the country in 1906, and, eventually, pulled out in 1909 (González 2000).

A couple of decades later, Fulgencio Batista emerged as a powerful kingpin, who governed the country directly as president himself, and indirectly through his hand-picking of presidents (Argote-Freyre 2006). Batista led the Revolt of the Sergeants and took over the government on September 4, 1933 (Argote-Freyre 2006). Batista's rule was supported by the US, who saw him as a stabilizing force to counter liberal forces (González 2000). Batista ruled Cuba with a strong hand for approximately 25 years. Under Batista's rule, corruption flourished with drug and gambling interests making their way into Cuba (English 2009). Using government funds, Batista built luxurious hotels, which enriched himself and his cronies, who included US mafia kingpins (English 2009). Havana was dubbed the "Latin Las Vegas" (Sierra 2014). Batista quelled opposition with violence against his opponents. Nonetheless, oppositional forces led by a young lawyer, Fidel Castro, sought to overthrow Batista.

Fidel Castro assumed political power on January 1, 1959. Shortly after, many middle- and upper-class Cubans fled Cuba, as they stood to lose their property and wealth. Unlike their Mexican and Puerto Rican counterparts, who made their way to the US mainland with limited resources, the first wave of Cuban immigrants – commonly referred to as "golden exiles – were drawn from the elite of Cuban society. Because they were fleeing a US communist enemy, Cubans fleeing Castro were allowed to enter the US as political refugees, and were granted social and economic services to help them settle and adjust to life in the US. Given their own social, economic, and political capital, with which they immigrated to the US, along with the generous treatment that they received in that country as political refugees, in a relatively short period of time Cubans were able to become integrated into the US, specifically in the Miami area, where they formed successful ethnic enclaves in which their businesses thrived (Portes and Bach 1985).

A couple of decades later another wave of Cuban immigrants was allowed to enter the US. In April 1980, faced with a weakening economy, Castro encouraged Cubans whom he labeled "anti-social elements" to leave Cuba (Powell 2005: 185). Over a period from April to October in 1980, approximately 125,000 Cubans were transported to the US from Mariel Bay in Cuba, leading to these individuals being referred to as "Marielitos." The group included 24,000 with a criminal record (Powell 2005). While Marielitos were originally allowed to enter the US as refugees, their swelling numbers caused a change in policy in June 1980, when sanctions were leveled against persons transporting Cubans, and the classification of the asylum-seekers was changed from "refugees" to "entrants (status pending)," thus placing them in the same category as Haitian immigrants (Powell 2005, p. 185). Compared to the earier wave of Cuban immigrants, Marielitos included more individuals with limited resources as well as persons with darker skin, compared to the earlier wave of Cuban immigrants. While Marielitos faced greater problems adjusting than the earlier wave of Cuban immigrants (Aguirre et al. 1997), they were readily absorbed into the ethnic enclave economies of Miami, thus benefiting from the favorable economic position of the established Cuban community (Card 1990). Nonetheless, with the decreasing selectivity of Cuban immigrants, along with the increasing hostile environment to all immigrants over the last few decades, the welcoming of Cuban immigrants has become increasingly unfriendly (Eckstein 2009).

Puerto Rico

Puerto Ricans share a colonized group status with Mexican Americans. The initial incorporation of Puerto Ricans into the US also involved warfare, this time in the form of the Spanish–American War. As noted above, the terms of the Treaty of Paris meant that Spain gave independence to Cuba and ceded Puerto Rico and Guam, which became US territories.

In contrast, US control over Puerto Rico in one fashion or another has been more long standing. There have been three phases associated with the relationship between the US and Puerto Rico. Immediately after Puerto Rico became a commonwealth of the US, white Americans, who represented the dominant group bolstered by their large numbers, were faced with the question of what to do with a territory that was not white. The choice was to keep it as a commonwealth rather than to make it a US state. The Foraker Act of 1900 pretty much established Puerto Rico as a colony of the US (González 2000). The Act's provisions included the stipulation that Puerto Ricans would be citizens of Puerto Rico and not the US; the US president would appoint Puerto Rico's governor and Supreme Court; and the US Congress had veto power on any laws in Puerto Rico. It was obvious that the US was calling the shots, while Puerto Ricans had no say over their own affairs. In fact, under the Foraker Act, Puerto Rico enjoyed a weaker degree of self-governance compared to when it was under Spanish rule (González 2000). To make matters worse, a provision of the Foraker Act allowed for the devaluation of the Puerto Rican peso, which allowed US sugar companies to amass vast amounts of land, readily transforming coffee farmers into an agricultural proletariat (González 2000). It is estimated that approximately 5,000 Puerto Ricans left the island as contract workers to toil in the sugar plantations of the Hawaii Sugar Planters' Association (González 2000).

The second phase of US and Puerto Rican relations took effect with the signing of the Jones Act in 1917. The stipulations of the Acts included the provision that Puerto Ricans were granted US citizenship and were allowed to travel freely between the island and the mainland, thus opening a migration route to New York (Aranda 2007). However, the US president retained the power to appoint the governor, the Supreme Court, and other top officials. Thus, there were some gains among the Puerto Rican population, but the US government was still in charge (González 2000). The Jones Act was amended by the US Congress in 1947 through the passage of the Elective Governor Act. The act allowed Puerto Ricans to elect their own governor. In 1948, Luis Muñoz Marin became the first governor of Puerto Rico, elected by its own people.

A year earlier, Marin had instituted Operation Bootstrap, a program designed to industrialize Puerto Rico through foreign investment – mostly US corporations – by "offering them low wages, a tax-free environment to set up their factories, and duty-free export to the mainland" (González 2000, p. 63). The program resulted in a "massive displacement of agricultural workers and heavy urbanization" (Aranda 2007, p. 16). Puerto Rico's excess labor made its way from rural areas to urban areas of the island as well as to the US mainland (Aranda 2007; Duany 2004).

The inequity between Puerto Rico vis-à-vis states in the US mainland is readily apparent. For example, no other state – excluding Nevada – sent more soldiers on a per capita basis to Iraq or Afghanistan than Puerto Rico (Lakshmanan 2008). However, while Puerto Ricans can only participate in the presidential primaries (having a total of 78 delegates in 2024: 55 in the Democratic presidential primary and 23 in the Republican presidential primary) (Ballotpedia 2024), they are not allowed to cast their vote in the final presidential elections in November (Lakshmanan 2008).

Puerto Rico has held six plebiscites on the island's status – to remain a commonwealth of the US, become a US state, or gain independence from the US. These elections have occurred in 1967, 1993, 1998, 2012, 2017, and 2020. The vote has shifted, with the majority favoring commonwealth status in 1967 (60%) and a plurality in 1993 (49%), a plurality favoring "none of the above" (50%) followed by statehood status (46%) in 1998, and the majority (61%) preferring statehood in 2012 (61%), 2017 (97%), and 2020 (53%) (Puerto Rico Report 2022).

Like Mexican Americans – the other Latina/o group considered a colonized minority – Puerto Ricans in the US mainland occupy the lowest levels of the social and economic stratification system in the US. This, despite the fact that almost all Puerto Ricans are US citizens, and the group has been in the US mainland since first gaining US citizenship in 1917. Indeed, Puerto Rican newcomers to the mainland have tended to occupy the low social and economic status of their predecessors, who have been in the US for generations.

Dominican Republic

Another Caribbean country – the Dominican Republic – for long attracted the attention of the US. In particular, the US attraction to the Dominican Republic has centered on its protection of US economic interests as well as deterring communism in the Caribbean region. Great political instability characterized the country, beginning at the time of its independence in 1844 to the early 1930s, a period that witnessed 123 political rulers in the Dominican Republic (Crandall 2006). The US, nonetheless, viewed the Dominican Republic as a strategic location that could serve as a coaling station for war ships and, in 1869, the US sought to annex the country into the US (Crandall 2006). While Dominicans, under the strong-arm pressure of then-president Buenaventura Báez, overwhelmingly voted to become part of the US, the annexation treaty was not supported by the US senate (Crandall 2006).

For the next several decades the Dominican Republic continued to exist in a state of political and economic instability, much of this period under the despotic leadership of General Ulisés Heureaux, who ruled with great brutality between 1882 and 1899, when he was assassinated (Crandall 2006). His assassination was followed by heightened instability, as various rebel groups fought for control of the country. In order to bring some order, some groups called for US protectorate status, while still others sought a reconsideration of US annexation (Crandall 2006). Although the US hesitated to enter militarily at this time, it did take action to protect US financial interests in order to collect debt from the Dominican government (Crandall 2006).

The country established some political stability with the presidency of Ramón Cáceres in 1906, but this was short-lived, as his assassination in 1911 ushered in magnified political turmoil (Crandall 2006). Within five years, the country found itself in another civil war, resulting in President Wilson sending in US troops to occupy the Dominican Republic (Crandall 2006). The US occupation lasted eight years until November 1924, leaving behind "an elected government, a professional police force, a stronger financial position, and seeming internal stability" (Crandall 2006: 44). Nonetheless, the calm and stability proved deceiving as significant changes and turmoil were on the near horizon.

One of the soldiers, Rafael Trujillo, quickly ascended the scale of the military hierarchy during the period of US occupation. As the US ended its occupation of the country, Trujillo became president of the Dominican Republic in 1930 (Crandall 2006). Trujillo would go on to rule and terrorize the country as a brutal dictator for three decades. Still, because of his staunch opposition to fascism and communism, the US government supported his presidency (Crandall 2006). Trujillo bolstered US support by spending luxuriously on political lobbyists in Washington, DC, and entertaining congressional delegations who visited his country (Crandall 2006). Trujillo quashed an invasion by Cuban forces shortly after Castro gained political control of Cuba, thus demonstrating his importance to the US as a useful force for deterring communism in the region (Crandall 2006).

Nonetheless, President Kennedy began to distance the US government from Trujillo, as he feared an uprising by communist forces in the Dominican Republic. On May 30, 1960, with the support of the US Central Intelligence Agency (CIA), Trujillo was assassinated outside of Santo Domingo (Crandall 2006). Yet, the death of Trujillo did not end his dictatorship, as members of his family, especially his son Ramfis, continued to rule the country indirectly during Joaquín Balaguer's presidential administration (Crandall 2006). Political instability followed, with the overthrow of Balaguer by General Rafael Echevarría in 1962, who, with pressure from the US government, was promptly arrested and exiled, and replaced by Captain Elías Wessin y Wessin (Crandall 2006). The death of Trujillo and the political instability that ensued resulted in the start of a massive wave of immigration to the US, beginning in 1962, as migration had been virtually impossible under Trujillo's reign (Hernández 2002). The US government facilitated this immigration as a way of defusing political opposition (Grasmuck and Pessar 1991; Grasmuck and Grosfoguel 1997; Riosmena 2010).

The presidential elections in December 1962 resulted in the election of Juan Bosch, who had returned to the island after being in exile for 25 years (Crandall 2006). The US government was uneasy with Bosch's leadership, as he was viewed as an ineffective leader who was too lenient on local communist forces (Crandall 2006). With the US government refusing to provide defense to Bosch, as opposition forces nipped at his heels, the Dominican army overthrew Bosch in 1963 with a three-person civilian junta led by Donald Reid Cabral, who assumed leadership until elections took place in 1965 (Crandall 2006). Yet, several months after the 1963 coup, Cabral would become president of the junta, as two of the original members stepped down (Crandall 2006). Economic problems and austerity measures imposed by the International Monetary Fund (IMF) intensified political instability in the country. As Cabral sought to postpone the presidential election until September 1965, he was overthrown in a coup on April 24, 1965.

This overthrow led to complete bedlam, as the military and civilians openly revolted. The instability and violence resulted in President Johnson sending 1,700 marines in on April 27, 1965, to evacuate Americans from Santo Domingo (Crandall 2006). It was clear that Johnson feared a communist uprising through the return to power of Bosch and, shortly after, he dispatched an escalating number of troops in efforts to deter communism. The number of US troops nearly quadrupled – from 6,200 on May 1 to 23,000 ten days later (Crandall 2006).

As order was restored, the presidential election took place in June 1966. The US government directed funds to support the campaign of Balaguer, whose primary opposition was Bosch. Balaguer, the US-supported candidate, won the presidency with the majority of the vote (56%) (Crandall 2006). The Balaguer administration had two major goals, as Hernández (2002) points out: economic development and political stability. Economic development was promoted through the increase of investments from the US, alongside the expansion of industrial production, commercial trade, and finance (Hernández 2002). While these measures served to create significant economic development, unemployment rose due to industrial intensification (Grasmuck and Grosfoguel 1997; Hernández 2002). Political stability was pursued through iron-fist rule involving political repression, murder, and incarceration, with approximately 3,000 killed during Balaguer's first two presidential terms (Hernández 2002). In addition, political stability was also advanced through the emigration of political discontents. Indeed, through a tacit agreement with the US government, political dissidents of the government found easy passage to the US (Hernández 2002). As Hernández (2002) observes, in 1959, prior to Trujillo's assassination, 19,631 Dominicans requested a passport, with only 1,805 granted one; in contrast, a decade later, every one of the 63,595 petitioning for a passport received one.

Though Dominicans were not incorporated as colonized minorities into the US, in many respects their socioeconomic standing in the US has resembled the position of Mexicans and Puerto Ricans. The low socioeconomic status of Dominicans is likely to be related to their racial characteristics. Recall from Chapter 1 that Dominicans are the Latina/o group with the greatest share, viewing themselves racially as Black. Indeed, a significant amount of research has shown that people with darker skin tend to fare worse socioeconomically and experience discrimination, compared to persons with lighter skin (Allen et al. 2000; Espino and Franz 2002; Gómez 2000; Morales 2008; Murguia and Telles 1996; Santana 2018; Telles and Murguia 1990; Telles and Ortiz 2008; Visser 2019).

El Salvador

In some ways, historically, the US has not been as directly involved in the political, economic, and social affairs of El Salvador as has been the case with the four countries that we have examined thus far (White 2009). Certainly, much of the conflict that El Salvador has experienced throughout its history has involved hostility with the other countries forming Central America: Costa Rica, Guatemala, Honduras, and Nicaragua, with animosity being particularly acute with Guatemala. Yet, while the influence of the US over El Salvador has historically been more sporadic than those of the other countries, the US strongly supported the right-wing dictatorship during the country's civil war, which occurred between 1980 and 1992. The roots of the civil war, however, originate almost a century earlier.

After a tumultuous period of nation building during the half century from 1821 to 1871, El Salvador entered a new era in 1871, as it experienced a dramatic shift in its major crop from indigo to coffee (Menjívar 2000; White 2009). This transformation resulted in the rise of an oligarchy composed of the "Fourteen Families" that dominated the coffee industry (White 2009: 66). The emergence of the coffee oligarchy seriously reshaped political, economic, and social relations in the country. White

(2009) points out that during the 1871–1932 period associated with the establishment of the coffee oligarchy:

> El Salvador became more liberal economically, yet less democratic, more milita-
> rized, and thus more violent. At the same time, there were reformers, but they tended
> toward increasing the consolidation of power into the hands of the elite and away
> from the majority of the population. (65)

The sixty-year period between 1871 and 1932 saw the consolidation of lands from indigenous peasants to the coffee oligarchy. Indeed, in 1882 a law was established that outlawed communal land holdings (Menjívar 2000). Further, the military, as protectors of the interest of the coffee oligarchy, suppressed and lashed out with vio-lence against peasants. The US government had a hand in this violence. White (2009) observes that the Military History Museum located in San Salvador features 100 US-made weapons, with the earliest one originating in 1872. While indigenous peasants revolted against the military in protest against their loss of land and suppression, such insurgency was consistently quelled.

El Salvador's coffee product flourished on the world market during the second half of the nineteenth century. White (2009) illustrates the burgeoning sales of coffee by noting that "in 1855, a population of 394,000 exported a total of 765,324 pesos worth of goods, while in 1892, 703,000 people exported close to 7 million pesos worth of goods" (p. 67).

The beginning of the twentieth century saw the continuation of the oligarchy amassing lands, with coffee grown increasingly on large coffee plantations. The loss of land and the continued transformation of coffee production led to peasants work-ing on such large-scale operations. White (2009) describes the conditions under which peasants worked:

> A typical coffee plantation well into the twentieth century consisted of a poor work
> environment for the peasant, who labored all day for an owner who provided only
> two meals plus a meager wage. Unions were strictly prohibited through most of the
> country . . . well, which severely limited the peasantry's ability to improve their lot.
> This occurred due to the power of the elites within politics . . . [B]etween 1898 . . . and
> 1931 every president was a coffee grower. (72)

The coffee oligarchy continued to flourish economically throughout the first decades of the twentieth century, peaking in the 1920s (Menjívar 2000; White 2009). This prosperity was associated with a shift toward more favorable conditions for workers. Menjívar (2000) indicates that "at this time the government allowed a wide range of openness and reform, including relaxed labor policies, such as the creation of a ministerial-level workers advocate, the right to unionize and the eight-hour workday (39). Furthermore, a communist party emerged alongside other political parties and, in 1931, El Salvador carried out its first free presidential election, with Arturo Araujo winning the presidency (Menjívar 2000).

Yet, this political shift was short-lived, with the worsening economic conditions associated with the Great Depression. Araujo was overthrown, after serving only a few months as president, with his vice president, General Maximiliano Hernández Martínez, assuming the reins of power, thus signifying the return of the military presidency (Menjívar 2000).

As in earlier times, peasants prepared to revolt against their oppressors. The uprisings were not successful, as the military, as protectors of the coffee oligarchy, simply had too much power. The worst carnage occurred in 1932, with the massive crushing of a revolt against the government in western El Salvador. This event, known as *La Matanza* (the Massacre), resulted in the killing of an estimated 30,000 people, many Pipil, an indigenous group (González 2000; Menjívar 2000). For indigenous peasants, this event resulted in "a heightened culture of fear of the government forces that lasted until 1992" (White 2009: 75). In addition, La Matanza led to a crushing of these people's spirit and suppression of their ways of life. As White (2009) observes:

> Many of the surviving Indians resolved to eschew or hide their traditional culture in order to protect themselves from future persecution, indicating yet another level of destruction accomplished by the military. They knew that the government had targeted their fellow Pipils especially and therefore chose to blend in more as a result. (75)

The massacre served to provide calm and tranquility for the oligarchy "free of unions and organizations . . . to implement economic policies in their own interests" (Menjívar 2000: 40).

In response to this violence, along with the usurpation of land, many peasants left their areas of origin during this period. Many relocated to other parts of the country, while others immigrated to neighboring Honduras, which featured more favorable employment opportunities, especially in its banana industry (Menjívar 2000). Estimates suggest that Salvadorans accounted for approximately half of the residents of some communities located in the northern portion of Honduras (Anderson 1981; Menjívar 2000). Furthermore, the volume of Salvadorans immigrating to Honduras continued to rise, with the number quadrupling from roughly 25,000 in the 1930s to 100,000 in the 1940s (LaFeber 1984; Menjívar 2000). Such movement took a heavy toll on the rural communities from where these migrants originated.

Over the period between 1950 and 1980 the government generally promoted industrial development, specifically import-substitution industrialization (Menjívar 2000). These policies led to the development of a small middle class alongside a working class in urban areas. However, the large number of peasants who migrated to urban areas lived on the margins economically. Thus, there was great unrest among the poor, countered with immense repression on the part of the US-supported military (Menjívar 2000).

In the early 1960s, economic policies shifted toward the encouragement of export-based industry, which tended to further attract investments from the US (Menjívar 2000). El Salvador's economy thrived during this period with the country boasting the largest number of small manufacturing firms in Central America during the mid-1960s (Menjívar 2000). However, economic prosperity was not evenly distributed, as the poor continued to lag further behind economically. Menjívar (2000) relates that:

> Profits continued to leave the country, more land evictions occurred, and the mecha-
> nization of production contributed to an increase in unemployment among rural
> and urban workers. Commercial agriculture grew at the expense of subsistence
> agriculture. (43–44)

Economic pressures on the poor were exacerbated during the mid-1960s, when coffee prices dropped in the global market, disease took a toll on cotton, and private investments fell (Menjívar 2000; Montgomery 1982). Unemployment increased four-fold from 5 percent in 1961 to 20 percent in 1971 (Menjívar 2000; Montes 1987). The continued usurpation of land by the coffee oligarchy further drove peasants off their land, with the number of landless peasants quadrupling between 1961 and 1975 (González 2000). Governmental budget cuts, rising unemployment, and enhanced movement of peasants into urban areas further devastated the lot of the country's poor (Menjívar 2000). Nonetheless, military spending rose during this period. Unrest fomented in urban areas assisted by the growth of revolutionary guerrilla groups that had emerged in these places (Menjívar 2000). Many Catholic priests, who had long been supporters of the coffee oligarchy, turned their attention to the plight of the poor (González 2000). The military reacted with force and "paramilitary networks of informers such as ORDEN (Nationalist Democratic Organization)" were charged with conducting surveillance for the government (Menjívar 2000: 44). The network of informers had a devastating effect on people, as they could easily be accused of being a guerrilla sympathizer, which subjected them to harsh violence, including kidnapping and murder (Menjívar 2000).

Political and economic conditions in El Salvador plummeted by the late 1970s. As Menjívar (2000:48; see also Gorostiaga and Marchetti 1988) notes, "(b)y the end of that decade [1970s], the two main stabilizing forces that held the Salvadoran economy together – a solid demand for Salvadoran exports in the international market and easy access to foreign credit – had collapsed." In this context, wages were cut drastically for workers in urban and rural areas alike and, as the political situation declined alongside economic stability, multinational corporations left the country (Menjívar 2000). Rising levels of political repression against voices calling for social justice resulted in escalating levels of organization on the part of oppositional forces. In the 1977 elections, represented by large-scale fraud, General Carlos Humberto Romero gained power. As a stalwart defender of the oligarchy, Romero sought to control oppositional forces through increased levels of repression (Menjívar 2000). He ruled with an iron fist between 1977 and 1979, when he was overthrown by a military-civilian junta (Menjívar 2000). While the new government sought to make progressive changes, it met resistance from the extreme right and extreme left (Menjívar 2000). The extreme right opposed the progressive changes and viewed the new government as communist, while the extreme left criticized it for being merely a puppet for the military (Menjívar 2000).

Political changes in the US fomented further political discord in El Salvador. In light of overt political repression of the Romero administration, President Carter completely ended all military support for the government (Menjívar 2000). However,

President Reagan, fearing takeover from communists, strongly reversed this decision in a strong fashion. As Menjívar (2000: 50) observes "by 1982 Washington was sending approximately $1.5 million a day to keep the Salvadoran economy afloat." Indeed, approximately 70 percent of the $3.7 billion that the US gave to El Salvador between 1981 and 1989 went to fund weapons and related war assistance (González 2000). The rising US involvement escalated the war between the political establishment on the right and the oppositional left, with mounting armed warfare taking a dramatic toll on the Salvadoran people for a dozen years (Menjívar 2000). Menjívar (2000) aptly describes the horrendous violence that the Salvadoran people experienced, when caught between the government and the oppositional forces:

> The low-intensity warfare project in El Salvador involved direct armed confrontation and undercover paramilitary operations against all sectors of society that supported or were suspected of supporting or even sympathizing with the guerilla combatants . . . It also involved terror tactics such as death squad operations and attacks against civilian populations (mainly in rural areas), including massacres of entire villages believed to be sympathetic to the guerillas. Landless peasants and the unemployed were frequently suspected of involvement with oppositional organizations. But potentially anyone who was disliked or had an enemy who could point a finger could be branded a guerilla sympathizer. To demand justice in this environment would have meant an act of resistance, and consequently a threat to existence . . . But the use of intimation and violence to retain political and economic power in El Salvador was not novel. What was new . . . was the use of systematic terrorism based on the organized use of murder, kidnapping, and destructive violence by extremist groups as a means to obstruct the political process. The implacable opposition of the organized left and the extreme right unleashed a spiral of violence that affected . . . all sectors of Salvadoran society. The report by the United Nations Truth Commission . . . attributes culpability to both the government and guerilla forces for the violence that ravaged the country during the war years. (50–51)

In the end, the twelve-year war resulted in more than 75,000 deaths and the disappearance of an untold number of persons (United Nations 1993).

The bloodshed uprooted Salvadorans to other parts of the country, to other Central American countries, to Mexico and, even further, to the US (Menjívar 2000). The movement of Salvadorans to the US skyrocketed, doubling between the 1960–1969 and 1970–1979 period and rising nearly five-fold from 29,428 in 1970–1979 to 137,418 in 1980–1989. The numbers would double again between 1980–1989 and 1990–1999 (US Department of Homeland Security 2023). Furthermore, the population of Salvadorans living in the US rose eight-fold from 94,000 in 1980 to 701,000 in 1990 (González 2000). The increasing movement of Salvadorans to the US during the war was facilitated by "vital social, cultural, and historical linkages established over many years of US influence in [El Salvador]" (Menjívar 2000: 56).

However, unlike Cubans, who fled communism, Salvadorans were overwhelmingly turned down as political refugees. While it was clear that Salvadorans were fleeing vicious violence, this bloodshed was at the hands of the US-supported government. Indeed, the US Immigration and Naturalization Service (INS) only approved

2.6 percent of petitions for political asylum on the part of Salvadorans between 1983 and 1990; in contrast, during the same period INS authorized 25.2 percent of political refugee requests of Nicaraguans, a group that was fleeing a left-wing government that the US was seeking to overthrow (González 2000). Thus, Salvadorans have by and large lived a life in limbo and uncertainty in the US. This instability, along with the lack of US citizenship, resulted for many in difficult economic, social, and political conditions for Salvadorans in the US. Nonetheless, the US Department of Justice in the fall of 1990 granted temporary protected status (TPS) to Salvadorans who had entered the country on or prior to September 19, 1990 (Menjívar 2000). TPS allows persons in the US who cannot return to their countries due to violence, natural disasters, and related impediments to remain in the US under protected status. Despite the temporary protected status alongside the ruling in the *American Baptist Churches v. Thornburgh* case that INS policy is discriminatory against Salvadorans, and the 1997 Nicaraguan Adjustment and Central American Relief Act (NACARA), toward the end of the twentieth century the majority of Salvadorans remained undocumented in the US (Menjívar 2000). In the twenty-first century, Salvadorans with TPS have remained in limbo, with constant threats of their TPS status not being renewed, and a series of extensions allowing them to stay. The latest TPS extension allows approximately 239,000 Salvadorans to remain in the country between September 10, 2023 and March 9, 2025 (Telemundo 2023).

Guatemala

El Salvador's history has much in common with that of its neighboring country of Guatemala. As in the case of El Salvador, the interest of a particular industry dominated the economic and political affairs in Guatemala, which resulted in the appropriation of land and the making of a landless peasantry. In the case of Guatemala, the dominating industry is the banana. However, unlike El Salvador, where a coffee oligarchy consisting of fourteen Salvadoran families dominated the industry, in Guatemala it was the United Fruit Company (UFCO), a US corporation (recall words from Pablo Neruda's poem at the beginning of this chapter). Yet, another difference between El Salvador and Guatemala is that while the civil war of the former lasted twelve years (1979–1992), the Guatemalan civil war endured over a period of more than four decades (1954–1996).

As González (2000) points out, Guatemalan presidents over the first several decades of the twentieth century served to promote and support the interest of the United Fruit Company (UFCO). UFCO particularly benefited through the presidency of Jorge Ubico, who presided with an iron fist over Guatemala between 1931 and 1944. By the end of his administration, UFCO boasted over a million acres of banana plantations throughout Central America (González 2000). UFCO and one of its affiliates, International Railways of Central America (IRCA), were the two largest employers in Guatemala. The nation's poor, composed primarily of Mayan peasants, suffered greatly during the Ubico administration. For example, they were forced to work on government projects. In addition, vagrancy laws and the requirement that

Mayan peasants needed to carry passbooks tied them to UFCO and other large land-owners (González 2000). Ubico ruled the country with an iron fist.

Yet, in 1944 a voice for democracy emerged at the hands of a "coalition of middle-class professionals, teachers, and junior officers, many of them inspired by Franklin D. Roosevelt's New Deal liberalism" (González 2000: 136). The coalition gained momentous support, including from the nation's trade unions and eventually succeeded in forcing Ubico to resign (González 2000).

The following year, Guatemala had its first democratic election, resulting in the selection of Juan José Arévalo, an academician who had lived in exile, as president (González 2000). Arévalo instituted a variety of progressive changes. González (2000) notes that Arévalo "abolished Ubico's hated vagrancy laws, recognized labor rights, established the country's first social security and rural education programs, and offered government loans to small farmers" (136). Such policies upset UFCO and the country's upper class. Nonetheless, through the support of communist groups, alongside that of trade unions, Arévalo's policies gained public support.

In the next election in 1951, Arévalo's disciple, Jacobo Arbenz Guzmán, a military officer, became Guatemala's new president (González 2000). Arbenz sought to distribute land more equitably, as "only 2 percent of the landholders owned 72 percent of the arable land, and only a tiny part of their holdings was under cultivation" (González 2000: 136). In 1952, the Guatemalan congress enacted Decree 900, which expropriated lands of 600 acres or more not under use (González 2000). As part of the decree, landowners would be compensated for the assessed value of their property and peasants would be granted low-interest loans to allow them to pay for their land. While the law affected mostly large landowners, UFCO was particularly impacted. González (2000) notes that the expropriated land "covered the vast holdings of the United Fruit Company, which owned some 600,000 acres – most of it unused" (137). UFCO additionally complained about the sum of money – $1.2 million – that it would receive from the government, a figure derived from UFCO's own accountants' assessments of their property values prior to the decree being enacted (González 2000). UFCO and the US State Department requested a sum of $16 million, which the Guatemalan government did not accept (González 2000).

The powerful Dulles brothers – Secretary of State John Foster Dulles and CIA director Allen Dulles – convinced President Eisenhower to launch the CIA-directed "Operation Success" to overthrow Arbenz (González 2000). As an aside, the Dulles brothers were "former partners of United Fruit's main law firm in Washington" (González 2000: 137). After the successful coup, the leader of the operation, Colonel Carlos Castillo Armas, was appointed president of Guatemala, with his administration quickly receiving US recognition and financial support. Castillo promptly took the country to the pre-democracy era. As González (2000) observes "he quickly outlawed more than five hundred trade unions and returned more than 1.5 million acres to United Fruit and the country's other big landowners" (137).

González (2000) describes the violent bloodshed that Guatemalans endured: "over the next four decades, its people suffered from government terror without equal in the modern history of Latin America" (137). González (2000) notes that, with

US assistance, by the mid-1970s a total of 20,000 people had been killed, with the number murdered and disappeared reaching 75,000 a decade later.

Guatemalans, like their Salvadoran counterparts, began fleeing to the US by the late 1970s and early 1980s, seeking refuge against the massive violence. The number of Guatemalans immigrating to the US legally increased nearly five-fold from 29,428 in 1970–1979 to 137,418 in 1980–1989 (US Homeland Security 2023). Nonetheless, in the US, Guatemalans met the same fate noted above that Salvadorans experienced. Over the period of 1983–1990, of all Guatemalans seeking refugee status in the US only a mere 1.8 percent received approval (González 2000). As was the case with Salvadoran immigrants, Guatemalan immigrants were fleeing from a vicious government supported by the US. In the US, Guatemalans lived a life in limbo and uncertainty, aggravated by the undocumented status of many.

Colombia

South Americans have increasingly immigrated to the US, beginning in the 1980s and 1990s. The country of Colombia has led the pack in this movement to the US, and Colombians now represent the seventh largest Latina/o group in the US. In many ways, Colombians differ from other Latina/o groups that have immigrated recently to the US. For example, the major factor that propelled Colombians to move to the US was the drug cartel violence that claimed so many lives during the 1980s and 1990s, although its own bloody civil war had occurred decades earlier – a vicious civil war that lasted nearly a decade, beginning in 1948. In addition, in general, the earliest waves of Colombians tended to possess relatively high levels of education and light skin, traits that are useful in gaining a foothold in the US mainstream. Because of this, Colombians tend to resemble the earliest waves of Cuban immigrants, who relocated to the US after Fidel Castro took power in Cuba in 1959.

Stemming back to its formation as a nation, when it became independent from Spain under the name of Gran Colombia (name changed to New Granada in 1830 and finally to Colombia in 1863), for long there was tension between conservative and liberal forces. The former wanted a centralized government linked to the Church, while the latter called for a decentralized government separate from the Church. Relative ease was maintained through an agreement that the two parties would alternate power, with each holding the presidency for a given period of time. At the turn of the century (1899–1902), tension heightened between the Conservative and Liberal parties, which resulted in a bloody civil war that claimed the lives of approximately 100,000 people. A civil war reemerged in the period from 1948 to 1957 as a result of the assassination of Jorge Eliecer Gaitan, the leader of the Liberal Party (González 2000). His killing led to a massive riot in Bogotá, with approximately 2,000 persons killed. The riot brought about a decade-long vicious bloody civil war that took the lives of an estimated 180,000 to 200,000 lives (González 2000). Due to its vicious nature and the toll of lost lives, the civil war became known as *La Violencia* (the Violence). The war not only split families but also uprooted many persons from rural areas, who resettled in urban areas (González 2000). The civil war came to a close in

1957, when negotiators agreed to the two parties alternating power, as was the case earlier (González 2000).

Nonetheless, the conclusion of the war spurred the emergence of guerilla groups that dominated urban (M-19) and rural (Fuerzas Armadas Revolucionarias de Colombia, FARC – Armed Forces of the Colombian Revolution) areas (González 2000). The guerilla groups exerted much violence throughout the country. Yet, opportunities arose for many marginalized guerrilla-trained youth when warfare broke out in the cities of Cali and Medellín between drug cartels competing for control of the global cocaine market (González 2000). The youth were recruited as drug couriers and as assassins (González 2000). Murder and terrorism became rampant in the midst of the cartel wars. González (2000) observes that a Bogota newspaper in 1987 relayed that "43 people were killed on the streets of Bogotá, Cali, and Medellín, the three largest cities, assassinated by armed hoodlums who indiscriminately gunned down women, children, beggars, and garbage collectors for fun and target practice" (158). González (2000) points out that, in 1997, 31,000 persons were killed in the country. Meanwhile, violence continued in rural areas, as soldiers and right-wing paramilitary groups wreaked havoc and murdered people accused of supporting left-wing guerrillas (González 2000). Colombia became one of the deadliest countries in the world.

This violence prompted many Colombians, especially those from the educated segment of the population, to immigrate to the US. In fact, the flow of Colombians had actually started at the height of La Violencia, with the number of Colombians immigrating legally to the US increasing from 3,454 in 1940–1949 to 15,567 in 1950–1959 and to 68,371 in 1960–1969 (US Department of Homeland Security 2023). Still, the violence of the cartel wars was associated with increasing numbers of Colombian immigrants to the US: 71,265 in 1970–1979; 105,494 in 1980–1989; 137,985 in 1990–1999; and 236,570 in 2000–2009 (US Department of Homeland Security 2023). González (2000) points out that the earliest waves of Colombians became well established and integrated economically in New York City, where they are predominantly located. Nonetheless, González (2000) notes that the later waves have created schisms, as a certain share of Colombian immigrants have included people associated with drug cartels, thus creating tension between the earlier and more recent arrivals.

Summary

We examined in this chapter the histories of the seven largest Latina/o groups. These groups differ on their pasts, modes of incorporation into the US, and the time frame in which people began immigrating to the US in significant numbers. Yet, there are some similarities as well. For example, the groups are bound together by their conquest and eventual independence from Spain (except for Puerto Rico), as well as their common Spanish language. People originating from these seven countries as well as from throughout Latin America and Spain became Latina/o and/or Hispanic in the US, or took on newer identities such as Latinx and Latine. Furthermore, the seven

countries had a variety of ties to the US involving warfare, as well as the US intervening in the political affairs of countries, and providing military and financial support
to prop up right-wing governments that ruled with an iron fist, often protecting US
business and political interests. The establishment of such links between the US and
many Latin American countries, intensified more recently through free-trade agreements, has served to promote immigration of Latin Americans to the US. Finally, as
noted earlier, the initial mode of incorporation of Latina/os in the US has woven a
path toward integration with some groups, such as Mexicans and Puerto Ricans,
experiencing hardships, while others, such as Cubans and Colombians, have enjoyed
easier upward mobility and integration into the US.

The next chapter shifts the focus to the intellectual development of social thought
regarding the Latina/o population in the United States, extending back to early
pioneer thinkers who helped establish the field and more recent scholars who have
made important contributions over the last half century

Discussion Questions

1. How has US involvement in the affairs of countries in Latin America and the Caribbean contributed to the immigration of people to the US?

2. Which two Latina/o groups covered in this chapter are considered colonized groups? Why?

3. What is the significance of the Treaty of Guadalupe Hidalgo?

4. What is the significance of the Treaty of Spain?

5. What is Operation Bootstrap?

6. Who are *Marielitos*?

7. Can you draw linkages between the violence that Salvadorans and Guatemalans experienced in their home countries and the current migration of people from these countries to the US in search for refuge and better lives?

3 Latina/o Social Thought

Over the course of the history of Latina/os in the US, non-Latina/os, mostly white, have written the narrative of the Latina/o people, much of this writing not complimentary and not serving to defend the rights of Latina/o. In 1914, Jovita Idár, a teacher, writer, and activist from Laredo, who was located on the South Texas border, stood up to the Texas Rangers, the loosely organized military force that policed Texas, and particularly its borders, in the nineteenth and early twentieth centuries. The Texas Rangers, known for their violence toward Mexicans, turned up at the offices of the newspaper *El Progreso*, aiming to shut it down, following an editorial in the paper that criticized President Woodrow Wilson's order to send military troops to the Texas–Mexico border amid the Mexican Revolution. Idár defended the office, as well as the newspaper's right to freedom of the press.

Her activism and fight for civil rights is a hallmark of her legacy. Idár was a defender of Mexican American civil rights, fighting for equal rights for women and better education (Medina 2020). Her writings, which disseminated ideas about equality and justice, continue to be influential. In 2020, as part of the "Overlooked No More" obituary series, the *New York Times* finally gave her the recognition that was long neglected. Idár was an important voice that was a pioneer for journalists and social scientists and educators who seek to do public-intellectual work.

Unlike Blacks, who had Historically Black Colleges and Universities (HBCUs) that helped develop the Black intelligentsia, Latina/o academic institutions did not exist for Latina/os. It was not until the end of World War II when there was a trickle of Latina/os enrolling in Historically White Colleges and Universities (HWCUs). The work of early Latina/o scholars is often overlooked, like the work and legacy of Idár. Nonetheless, the heritage and contributions of Latina/o scholars did take place in academia, political history, and social movements. In academia, Latina/o scholars have made significant contributions to scholarship on the Latina/o population. While Latina/o representation within academia, and within the curricula that dominate US classrooms, are still in the margins, it is not for lack of their existence. The troubled history of the marginalization of the histories of communities of color, including Latina/os, has led to the perception that Latina/o contribution is thin. It is the case that Latina/os continue to be underrepresented across different disciplines, reflecting the historical and contemporary lack of access to academia tied to discrimination and oppression then and now. Latina/o consciousness and knowledge production have contributed greatly, and through a variety of modalities, to how we better understand the Latina/o experience in the US.

In this chapter, we will highlight some of the many important Latina/o thinkers who have made important intellectual, social, and political developments within academia and beyond. The scholars, activists, and leaders highlighted here represent only a few in the gamut of Latina/o leaders from a variety of fields. We begin the chapter by providing an important historical background that impacted the development of Latina/o social thought in the institutional settings. Early Latina/o academic and organic intellectuals, including Jovita Idár, highlighted above, fought for the fair treatment of Latina/os in education and civil rights, while advancing the Latina/o perspective in academia. Their actions, writings, and words challenged harmful stereotypes of Latina/os. Some of these Latina/o critical thinkers articulated ideas about the Latina/o experience that are now formalized in institutional settings. The contemporary Latina/o scholars highlighted in this chapter continue to educate us about Latina/os in the US and progressive theories across multiple academic fields.

Historical Roots

Jovita Idár and Her Post-Reconstruction Fight for Latina/o Education

In the era that followed the reconstruction years, the civil rights movement ignited mobilizations that eventually ended legal segregation. In Texas, Jovita Idár, a Mexican American activist, writer, and educator, born in the border town of Laredo, fought for fair treatment of Mexican Americans. In the generational framework of Chicana/o history, Idár would form part of the Mexicanist Generation, spanning the late nineteenth century up until the early 1920s. This cohort, according to some scholars, included Mexican people who considered themselves US outsiders but whose ancestors had lived in Mexico prior to the US annexation of the US Southwest (Blanton 2014), as noted in Chapter 2. Idár's life work contributed to a wider understanding of Latina/o civil rights, struggles for education equity, migration experiences, and life on the borderlands.

Idár was born in 1885 to a family that was civically engaged in the borderlands in the aftermath of the Mexican–American War (1846–1848) and the Mexican Revolution (1910–1920) that followed. As Masarik (2019: 284) wrote, "Jovita and the Idár family were what historian Benjamin Johnson terms 'Tejano Progressives,' who adhered to many of the economic and social proposals of the larger Progressivism of the US." For Tejana/o Progressives, the answer to white racism was the economic and educational success of Tejana/o and Mexican people living in the borderlands. Jovita's father became the publisher for a Spanish-language newspaper called *La Crónica*, which reported on lynchings, segregation, and violations of people's rights (Turner et al. 2015). The motto of the newspaper, according to the Texas State Historical Association, was: "We work for the progress and the industrial, moral, and intellectual development of the Mexican inhabitants of Texas" (Turner et al. 2015, pp. 229–230). After her father's death, in the first decade of the 1900s, Jovita, along with her siblings, Clemente and Eduardo, were the principal writers for *La Crónica*. The newspaper maintained its mission of uplifting the Mexican–Tejana/os and calling out injustices in South Texas.

Figure 3.1 Jovita Idár around 1905.
Source: General Photograph Collection/UTSA Libraries Special Collections.

Specifically, Jovita's articles about the educational injustice that Mexican American children were experiencing in South Texas represented a call to action (Turner et al. 2015). While Jovita's brother's articles uncovered the horrors of Jim Crow segregation in Texas public schools, Jovita directly experienced the injustices, having been a schoolteacher in Los Ojuelos, Texas (Turner et al. 2015). Her activism for educational equity stemmed from her belief that education was not only a way out of poverty, but also out of second-class citizenship and discrimination, despite citizenship or legal residency. In 1911, the Idár family organized the First Mexican Congress in Laredo. The political convention united Mexicans and Mexican Americans to discuss and formulate solutions to the social, political, and educational injustices they confronted daily. After the gathering of the First Mexican Congress, Idár went on to found and serve as the first president of the *Liga Femenil Mexicanista*, or the League of Mexican Women (Library of Congress 2022b).

The education of poor children was a primary concern of the League of Mexican Women (Turner et al. 2015). Idár highlighted the failures of the US school system to educate Mexican–Tejana/o children. She called for quality bilingual education and the establishment of *escuelitas* or an alternative school system, established in the late 1940s and 1950s, which taught Spanish literacy and Mexican history along the borderlands (Masarik 2019). Idár's advocacy for the escuelitas centered on the morality and need for bilingual education, given the understanding of the power of language and culture for nation–state building (Turner et al. 2015). In her time, Idár called out the educational system for purposefully excluding Mexican history and heroes, which unfortunately continues to be of concern today. For instance, Idár reflected that:

> If in the American school our children attend, they are taught the biography of Washington and not the one of Hidalgo, and if instead of the glorious deeds of Juárez they are referred to the exploits of Lincoln, as much as these are noble and just, that child will not know the glories of his nation, he will not love her, and he might even see his parents' countrymen with indifference. (Turner et al. 2015, p. 235)

Idár recognized the power of group identity through education in a country that, to this day, still struggles in this endeavor (see Chapter 9). Idár also went on to organize mutual-aid groups to offer free kindergarten to Mexican–Tejana/o families.

Idár's advocacy and social thought went beyond education. She worked to help create a volunteer nursing unit called *La Cruz Blanca* (The White Cross), to care for soldiers injured in the Mexican Revolution (Masarik 2019). Adding to the list of issues of concern, Idár also assisted undocumented people to understand and complete the paperwork necessary for naturalization. Her ideological origins were rooted both in her transnational advocacy for *la raza* (the people or community) and in modernity and liberalism (Turner et al. 2015). We can now see that Idár's advocacy provided a lens to understand the status of Latina/o children and immigrant families in South Texas at an early period in its history.

Jovita Idár leaves a legacy of advocacy and understanding of the Latina/o condition within a transnational space after the Mexican–American War, when Latina/o social identities were formulating on both sides of the border. During a time when violence against Mexican people was normalized, Idár's writings and activism uplifted the experiences of Mexican Americans and Tejana/os, long before a Chicana/o identity was an option. Idár's advocacy preceded the Chicana/o Movement, beginning in the 1960s, and even earlier efforts for Mexican American recognition in the political sphere and in academia. While her contribution to the fight for Mexican American civil rights, access to education, and recognition, are not often included in the path toward the development of Latina/o social thought, Idár's pivotal work on Latina/o racialization and dehumanization speaks to the complexities of nation-building and racial-identity formation at an early point in the history of the US Southwest. While Idar's work took place outside of academia and before any Latina/os became scholars, her legacy on public scholarship has lasted the test of time.

Latina/o Intellectuals of the Early to Middle Twentieth Century

In the early to middle of the 1900s, educational struggles made a path for Latina/o intellectuals in academia (Blanton 2014). Among these Mexican American pioneers were George I. Sánchez, Julian Samora, Octavio I. Romano, Deluvina Hernandez, Ernesto Galarza, and Americo Paredes. Below we discuss each of these Latina/o intellectuals.

In terms of early Latina/o scholars, Ernesto Galarza (1905-1984), George I. Sánchez (1906-1972), Américo Paredes (1915-1999), and Julian Samora (1920-1996) represented the W.E.B. Du Boises of Latina/os, each of them having particular qualities and accomplishments that contributed to the development of Latina/o scholarship. Galarza, Samora, and Sánchez's work in public policy led to the creation of important Chicana/o or Latina/o institutions, including the National Council of La Raza (NCLR) (now called UnidosUS), the largest Latina/o nonprofit advocacy organization that addresses the most important issues for Latina/os.

George I. Sánchez (1906-1972), a professor at the University of Texas at Austin, was also an activist and pioneer in the fight for Mexican American civil rights, who made important contributions to the development of Latina/o scholarship and to seeking solutions to issues that Latina/os faced. Like Idár, Sánchez called out the blatant racism against Mexican Americans in the educational system. In the 1940s, Sánchez relentlessly challenged school segregation and pushed his fellow Mexican Americans and liberal sympathizers to further understand the roots of educational injustices and to examine their unintentional contributions to inequalities in the school system through support for "special" education for Spanish-speaking Latina/os (Blanton 2014). In 1947, Sanchez spurred an investigation into segregated Mexican schools in Travis County's unincorporated areas. He was fully involved in the trial, supplying materials from a 1947 victorious case (*Mendez v. Westminster*) in California. In the Texas case, *Delgado v. Bastrop Independent School District,* Sánchez brought together an incredible group of expert witnesses from different parts of Texas to testify against educational segregation. Some of these experts included J. W. Nixon of the Laredo Independent School District and H. L. Barber of the Mission Independent School District (Blanton 2014). In 1948, Sánchez triumphed as Bastrop ISD was legally ordered to stop the segregation of Mexican American students. He did not stop there, as Sánchez continued his legal advocacy to end the segregation of Mexicans in the school system in *Hernández v. Driscoll* case. This case reaffirmed *Delgado v. Bastrop* and found that the school district had illegally segregated Mexican American students (Blanton 2014). Furthermore, from 1941 to 1942, Sánchez served as the president of the League of United Latin American Citizens (LULAC). It is evident that George I. Sánchez was among the most politically engaged Mexican American scholars of his generation.

Julian Samora is famously known as one of the pioneers of Latina/o scholarship. In 1953, Samora became the first Mexican American to have earned a doctorate in sociology and anthropology. Samora's work focused on highlighting the disparate and unequal experiences of Mexican Americans, from documenting differences in the hospital treatments of Latina/os to Latina/o poverty in the Midwest. After earning his Ph.D. in 1953, Samora received his first academic appointment at the University of Colorado School of Medicine where he broke ground by introducing studies of folk medicine and the role of ethnicity in health outcomes (López 2010). He is also credited for his role in pioneering the study of medical anthropology, which observes the different "cultural, linguistic, and historical similarities and differences among populations" (López 2010, p. 493).

In 1959, after an appointment at Michigan State University, Samora began his tenure at the University of Notre Dame, where he continued his research on inequality toward Mexican Americans and expanded his scope of work to include border studies, immigration, education, and more (Rios 2008). While at Notre Dame, Samora established the Mexican American Graduate Studies program where from 1972–1985 he mentored more than fifty students who went on to earn advanced degrees in many different fields (López 2010).

Samora's contribution to Latina/o social thought also came from his advocacy work. In 1968, he co-founded the Southwest Council of La Raza (later renamed to National Council of La Raza and in 2017 renamed again as UnidosUS). That same year, Samora also played a prominent role as a founding member of the Mexican American Legal Defense and Educational Fund (MALDEF), a non-profit organization providing litigation support for Latina/os, as well as advocacy and educational outreach that continues to be relevant today (López 2010). His work and advocacy were recognized through his appointment to various boards and commissions such as the US Commission on Civil Rights, the National Institute of Mental Health, and the President's Commission on Rural Poverty (University of Notre Dame 2024). Samora also published several impactful books that included *La Raza: Forgotten Americans* (1966), *Los Mojados: The Wetback Story* (1971), *A History of the Mexican American People* (1977), and *Gunpowder Justice: A Reassessment of the Texas Rangers* (1979).

Samora's contributions to Latina/o social thought was publicly cemented in 1989 when Michigan State University named a research institute in his honor: The Julian Samora Research Institute's mission entails "the generation, dissemination and application of knowledge to serve the needs of Latina/o communities in the Midwest and across the nation, with emphasis on health disparities, entrepreneurship, and service delivery system gaps" (Julian Samora Research Institute 2024). Samora's career is an important marker for Latina/os in academia and beyond, especially since he spearheaded some civil rights initiatives that are still with us today.

Another impactful Chicano scholar is Octavio I. Romano (1923–2005), whose work contributed to the Chicano Renaissance through the creation of Quinto Sol Publications in 1965. Romano, born in Mexico, earned his Ph.D. in anthropology from UC Berkeley, where he taught until his retirement in 1989 (Hendricks 2005). Romano is credited for publishing in 1967 the first journal on Chicano issues called *El Grito: A Journal of Contemporary Mexican–American Thought. El Grito* was among the first journals to print bilingually and included drawings, photography, short stories, poetry, and research papers (Martínez 2017). In fact, *El Grito* was the first to publish the works of Chicano scholars Rudolfo Añaya and Tomás Rivera (see Chapter 8). In an interview with a San Francisco news outlet, Anaya spoke of the significance of Romano's work in *El Quinto Sol* as a much-needed tool for Chicana/o writers and scholars. Specifically, Añaya recalled "It was a very difficult time to get our works known and to have a national public realize there was a Chicano literary movement going on . . . The press and Octavio were prime movers" (Hendricks 2005).

Many Latina/o scholars, including Maxine Baca Zinn, Alfredo Mirandé, Nick Vaca, and Deluvina Hernandez, among others, emphasized that Octavio Romano was pivotal in "exposing the social science stereotype of Mexican Americans" (Baca Zinn and Mirandé 2021, p. 306). Indeed, the first issue of *El Grito* opens with a message about the American ideological rhetoric developed to "neatly explain away both the oppressive and exploitative factors maintaining Mexican–Americans in their economically impoverished condition . . ." (Vaca 1967, p. 4). In the same issue of *El Grito*, Romero published "Minorities, History, and the Cultural Mystique," an article about the need to rethink the false rhetoric that has informed a faulty sociological framework. The cultural mystique referred to a rationale promoting a separatist idea about ethnic culture without contextualization. Specifically, Romano (1967) wrote, "This particular rationale has remained with us to this day, as witness the ubiquitous terminology of contemporary American social science that repeatedly describes people in the lower rungs of society as underachievers . . . fatalist, tradition bound" (p. 9). Romano pointed to the need for a new rhetoric that should begin with the premise that cultures do not evolve in isolation independent from the world around them. Felipe de Ortego y Gasca (2008) wrote about Romano's intent noting that the "Chicano achievement was not predicated on the approval of the mainstream" (p. 34). Indeed, Romano's argument in the editorial of the first issue of *El Grito* was that Chicana/o studies would provide the missing pieces of American history by accentuating Mexican Americans and the rich indigenous past (de Ortego y Gasca 2008).

Ernesto Galarza is another scholar/activist who made important contributions to the development of Latina/o scholarship and to seeking to end oppression against Chicana/os. Galarza, a graduate from Columbia University, was a scholar, activist, and organizer, who was recruited in the late 1940s by the National Farm Labor Union (later renamed as United Farm Workers) (Quinnell 2020). His community activism created a tremendous impact on the lives of many Latina/os in the US. Galarza advocated before congressional hearings against the oppressive Bracero program (see Chapter 4), and his research on the disparate treatment of Braceros including their living conditions and wages was influential (Valdés 2005). Indeed, Galarza's testimony led to the dismantling of the Bracero program. In the 1960s, Galarza campaigned on behalf of farm workers in California, taking on a significant leadership role in many important strikes, including those against DiGiorno and the cotton strikes (Valdés 2005). In fact, he transformed the social sciences through his social-action research, the combining of research and activism. Social-action research offered another major inspiration and model for early Chicana/o studies (Valdés 2005). During the 1960s and 1970s, like Samora and Sánchez, Galarza helped to form the Mexican American Legal Defense and Educational Fund (MALDEF) and the National Council of La Raza (NCLR).

With regard to Galarza's scholarship, he is famously known for his 1971 autobiography, *Barrio Boy*, based on approximately thirteen years of his life (Galarza 2011).

Barrio Boy told the story of his own struggles to acculturate beginning with his own migration experience and then with sharing the complexity of ethnic-identity formation. His work offered an early exploration into the subjective transnational experience. Galarza also published *Strangers in Our Fields* (1956), *Merchants of Labor: The Mexican Bracero Story* (1963), *Spiders in the House and Workers in the Fields* (1970), and *Farm Workers and Agri-Business in California* (1977). In 1993, the University of California, Riverside, became home to the Ernesto Galarza Applied Research Center.

Yet, another prominent Latina/o intellectual is Américo Paredes, born in Brownsville, Texas, who is recognized as the founder of Mexican American studies (see Chapter 8). Prior to earning his Ph.D. in English from the University of Texas at Austin in 1956, Paredes served as an army journalist during World War II (Humanities Texas 2022). Parades wrote largely about border issues along the Texas–Mexico region. In a 1994 interview with Miguel Medrano, Paredes recalled his childhood and growing up as a "Brownsville boy":

> I was born in Brownsville . . . on September 3, 1915, during the height of the border troubles when there was an ethnic cleansing, to use a current term, along the border when Rangers and others murdered a number of Mexicans and intimidated a lot of others to leave the country . . ." (Medrano 2010a, pp. 6–7)

Parades' literary studies of Mexican culture, such as the origin of ballads, or *corridos*, called attention to the cultural context of the Texas–Mexico border or South Texas (Limón 2012).

One of Paredes' best-known concepts was "Greater Mexico," which he used to refer to as *México de Adentro* (Mexico from inside) and *México de Afuera* (Mexico from outside) (Paredes 1995). By "México de Adentro," Paredes referred to the political borders of the Republic of Mexico and by "México de Afuera" he referenced "all those other parts of North America where people of Mexican descent have established a presence and have maintained their Mexicanness as a key part of their cultural identity" (Paredes 1995, p. xi). This distinction between two Méxicos is particularly important for distinguishing Mexicans who are away from their homeland due to migration, and those separated from Mexico through the establishment of the US–Mexico border. Paredes' literary publications (see Chapter 8) include *With His Pistol in His Hand: A Border Ballad and Its Hero* (1958), *George Washington Gómez: A Mexico–Texan Novel* (1990), *The Hammon and The Beans and Other Stories* (1994), *Between Two Worlds* (1991), *Folktales of Mexico* (1970), *The Shadow* (1998) and more. One of his well-known novels is *George Washington Gómez*, written in the 1930s and 1940s, but not published until the 1990s (Limón 2012). This is a semi-autobiographical novel recreating the Mexican people's struggle in South Texas against the backdrop of the Great Depression, the onset of World War II in Europe, and the over 100-year-old conflict of cultures in the Lower Rio Grande Valley of Texas (Medrano 2010a). Moreover, Paredes captured many historical events, including real-life figures, and covered the "effects of a North American capitalist economy and the tension it created among the traditional ranching communities along the Lower

Río Grande border" (Morín 2006, p. 49). The novel has been described as the greatest contribution to Chicano fiction literature (Medrano 2010a).

Paredes received many recognitions and awards for his contributions to Latina/o scholarship, including being one of five people to be awarded the Charles Frankel Prize of the National Endowment for the Humanities and, along with César Chávez and Julian Samora, the Orden del Aguila Azteca. Two years before his passing in 1997, Paredes received the University of Texas Presidential Citation for research, and contributions to the understanding of the Texas–Mexico border (Medrano 2010a). Paredes continues to inspire many Mexican American and Latina/o scholars and will be remembered as a significant Latina/o intellectual.

Deluvina Hernandez is another scholar who was part of the Chicana/o resistance against the stereotyping of Mexican Americans, and whose work contributed to the birth of Chicana/o studies. Hernendez is best known for her book *Mexican American Challenge to a Sacred Cow*, published in 1970. In this work, Hernandez provided a critical review of two published articles in which she highlighted "researcher bias, inadequacy and inappropriateness of theoretical framework, sophistry and irrationality, inappropriateness and subjectivity of survey techniques, and interpretation of findings" (Hernandez 1970, p. x).

Most of Hernandez's scholarship focused on stereotypes against Mexican Americans and how they impacted educational research (Limón 1973). She is also recognized for shifting the paradigm in Chicana/o scholarship, and is credited with "(r)esisting the racist epistemologies, ethics, logics, and metaphysics of gringo theorization [creating] new categories of knowledge grounded in a Chicano/a logics, where Chicano/as are the creators of reason, theory, history, and philosophy" (Soto 2020, p. 10). In an article titled "La Raza Satellite System," Hernandez utilized the philosophical viewpoints of Kant, Marx, Weber, and Mannheim to examine different facets of what she specified as the movement or *El Movimiento*. The movement, Hernandez claimed, is made up of different group activities, in particular:

> This study is intended to introduce for consideration the premise that Chicano (or Mexican American) activities in all social spheres are a practical set of directed behavior patterns in terms of a heterogeneous ethnic satellite system with thrust and objectives emerging from, revolving around, and converging at a collective focal point: LA RAZA. (Hernandez 1970, p. 13)

Fundamentally, Hernandez was exploring the phenomenology of the Chicana/o or Mexican American, during a time when Chicana/o leaders were resisting a system of oppression within and outside of academia, in many forms. Hernandez experimented with the philosophical frameworks of idealism, materialism, subjective understanding, and utopianism, and applied real-life examples or vignettes of the Chicana/o state of *being-in-the-world* from different perspectives of *El Movimiento*. She concluded that while Mexican American or Chicana/o works have some aspects of idealism, materialism, and utopianism, these interpretations do not sufficiently interpret the real social phenomenon of Chicana/os (Hernandez 1970).

Hernandez's epistemological contributions to the Latina/o experience examined in the "La Raza Satellite System" were unique, given their philosophical and phenomenological inflection. Moreover, Hernandez also attempted to unify the different facets of Chicana/o activism, thus referring collectively to all efforts as a satellite system, with La Raza as its nucleus (Hernandez 1970). Not much else is known about Deluvina Hernandez, but her existing writings have, no doubt, made a significant contribution to the establishment of Chicana/o studies and offered a unique contribution to the discipline of philosophy, where Latina/os continue to be particularly underrepresented.

Latina/os of all backgrounds have played an important role in building up theoretical frameworks and shifting narratives about Latina/os. Mauricio Miguel Gastón, born in Habana Cuba in 1947, has also left a significant mark in and out of academia as a scholar, architect, and community activist. Gastón immigrated to the US with his family, shortly after the Cuban Revolution, as a young boy (University of Massachusetts Boston, n.d.). He went on to earn a master's degree in City Planning from Massachusetts Institute of Technology in 1981. Gastón became a housing organizer and early advocate against injustices at the intersection of urban development, social equity, race, and class (University of Massachusetts Boston 2024). Gastón's scholarly endeavors were deeply rooted in his understanding of the symbiotic relationship between local activism and global solidarity, notably within the Puerto Rican Socialist Party and the Latina/o communities of Boston (University of Massachusetts Boston 2024). Transitioning to academia at U Mass Boston, his research spotlighted the nexus between decades-long disinvestment in urban areas and the subsequent wave of reinvestment, with a specific focus on empowering marginalized communities to shape the redevelopment process (University of Massachusetts Boston 2024). His academic contributions were distinguished by a blend of astute political insights, analytical rigor, and effective leadership, all of which significantly enriched the grassroots movements in Boston (University of Massachusetts Boston 2024). The Gastón Institute for Latino Community Development and Public Policy was established in 1989 at the University of Massachusetts Boston. The establishment of the institute was in response to the voices of the community urging the legislature for more research and understanding of Latinos' lived experiences in Boston (University of Massachusetts Boston 2024). Gastón's scholarship and activism are an important contribution to the manifold movement of Latina/o social thought in the United States.

Early Latina/o Sociologists in the Mainstream

The 1960s and 1970s represented a period when cohorts of Latina/os in the US were emerging in growing numbers from graduate programs with doctorate degrees. Some of the first Latina/os to gain entrance into prominent mainstream sociology programs, where their work received wide notoriety, included Alejandro Portes and Marta Tienda. Portes, from the Cuban exile generation, and Tienda, originating from Donna, Texas in South Texas and a daughter of immigrants, eventually became colleagues as full professors at Princeton University. Portes' career trajectory took him to the University of Texas at Austin, Duke University, before arriving at Princeton, and Tienda went through the University of Wisconsin at Madison and the University of Chicago, prior to arriving at Princeton. While their work was within the sociological mainstream, Portes and Tienda played a significant role in bringing notice of the study of Latina/os among mainstream academic circles. In the case of Tienda, her research transitioned to a focus on public policy, with one of her most prominent works in this area related to the Texas top-10-percent policy, following the *Hopwood* decision, which made it illegal to consider race directly in the admission of college and university students (Niu et al. 2008).

The Debate over Sociology of Chicanos and Chicano Sociology

In the 1970s, a debate evolved in the field of sociology over the need for a new paradigm through which to study the Chicano experience. In 1978, Alfredo Mirandé proposed a Chicano sociology that would liberate the Chicano experience from the traditional methodologies, a social science that perpetuates the misrepresentation of Chicanos. At the time, traditional or scientific methodologies would force the experiences of Chicanos into the Anglo/white framework (Lowry and Baker 1988). According to Mirandé, Chicano sociology offered a new paradigm based on decolonization (Baca Zinn and Mirandé 2021). For instance, Mirandé (1978) in his article titled "Chicano Sociology: A New Paradigm for Social Science" argued that "From a colonial perspective the family is not the tangle of pathology depicted by social scientists, but a stable and enduring institution that has helped Chicanos resist the onslaught of colonialism" (p. 301). Soon after the publication of Mirandé's article, Maxine Baca Zinn proposed an alternative perspective on the sociology of Chicanos. In her response to Mirandé, Baca Zinn (1981) acknowledged the need for a new paradigm to study the Chicano experience but argued that Mirandé ignored the contribution of other theories, especially structural (versus cultural) perspectives. Colonial theory, Baca Zinn (1981) stressed, is only one perspective and "no study of Chicanos and their social worlds can be complete if it is not informed by such a wide-ranging but finely disciplined imagination" (p. 269). Mirandé (1982) responded to Baca Zinn the very next year in his article titled "Chicano Sociology: A Critique and Evaluation of Prevailing Theoretical Perspectives," where he examined three models (assimilationist, colonial, and Marxist) and their contribution to the new Chicano sociological paradigms. Fundamentally, Mirandé argued that his "call for a Chicano/a paradigm was broader than Baca Zinn's examination of theories in that it could signal the onset of a social science revolution" (Baca Zinn and Mirandé 2021, p. 306).

Four decades after the onset of their debate, in 2021, Baca Zinn and Mirandé came together to propose a new paradigm for understanding the race and racialization of Latina/os in the twenty-first century. In their article titled "Latina/o Sociology: Toward a New Paradigm" both scholars are firmly rooted in the idea that a Latina/o sociology exists, but "lacks a definitive statement of what constitutes Latina/o sociology, including its basic frameworks, underlying assumptions, and relationship with the larger discipline" (Baca Zinn and Mirandé 2021, p. 305). Baca Zinn and Mirandé point to the continued underrepresentation of Latina/os in the field, while at the same time the broader acceptance and demand for Latina/o sociology in institutions of higher education signals an increasing acceptance of this area of study. The authors identified characteristics, from epistemological to theoretical to political, of what constitutes Latina/o sociology (Baca Zinn and Mirandé 2021). Importantly, Baca Zinn and Mirandé also proposed that Latina/o sociology build on the "principle of situated knowledge" (p. 309), which fundamentally emphasized the importance of centering the Latina/o voice in sociological work. In particular, Baca Zinn and Mirandé (2021) argued:

> This premise calls not for excluding researchers who are not Latino/a but for making the lived experiences of Latinos/as a focal starting point and for harnessing the tools of social science to examine Latinos/as in their own contexts. (p. 309)

Additionally, Baca Zinn and Mirandé's (2021) new theoretical lens is important for the understanding of race in the US more broadly, as it moves beyond the Black–White paradigm by uncovering the complexity of the racialization of Latina/os. Baca Zinn and Mirandé (2021) highlight the theoretical advancements in understanding the racialization of Latina/os in the work of Robert Blauner (1972), Eduardo Bonilla-Silva (2004), Joe R. Feagin (2013), Laura Gómez (2018), Rogelio Sáenz and Karen Manges Douglas (2015), to name a few.

The conversation that Baca Zinn and Mirandé initiated, and which has evolved over the four decades, marks an important contribution to Latina/o social thought. From questioning the traditional standards of sociological practice to incorporating existing approaches, and eventually to offering the academic community the fundamental infrastructure for a Latina/o sociology is a marker of how Latina/os have carried their own epistemological weight and uniqueness in a very white institutional and social space.

Contributions from Gloria Anzaldúa and the Borderlands

In advancing the study of Latina/os, Baca Zinn and Mirandé (2021) also stressed the importance of "narrative methodologies such as autoethnography, testimonios, and visual ethnography" (p. 309) as part of the movement toward incorporating marginalized voices. One of the prominent voices in this area is the work of Gloria E. Anzaldúa, an early Latina intellectual leader. Among the many Latina/os who have led movements and paved the theoretical pathways for Latina/o contributions to both academic and non-academic epistemology, the work of Anzaldúa is one of the most iconic and pivotal contributors to the understanding of the Latina/o experience. Often described as a Chicana-lesbian-feminist writer, Anzaldúa and Keating (2009) described herself as a "feminist, visionary, spiritual activist, poet-philosopher, fiction writer" (p. 3). Anzaldúa was born in the South Texas Rio Grande Valley to migrant farmers. At the young age of eleven, Anzaldúa herself worked the fields along the Texas–Mexico border. In the fall of 1963, she attended Texas Women's University in

Denton, but left after only two semesters because of financial difficulties (Anzaldúa and Keating 2009). After a year of working and saving to pay for college, she attended Pan American University (now University of Texas Rio Grande Valley) and graduated with a bachelor's degree in English (Anzaldúa and Keating 2009). Anzaldúa went on to teach from preschool to high school for four years in the Pharr-San Juan-Alamo (PSJA) Independent School District in South Texas. Anzaldúa earned her Master's in English from the University of Texas at Austin, but it was during her time enrolled in the doctorate program at the university where she was introduced to feminism, Chicana/o studies, and "gay life" (Anzaldúa and Keating 2009).

For the next decade, Anzaldúa dedicated herself to drafting essays titled "La Prieta" and "Speaking in Tongues." She also continued working on her anthology *This Bridge Called My Back: Writings by Radical Women of Color* (Moraga and Anzaldúa 1981), which she co-edited with Cherríe Moraga, and which continues to be very influential, with nearly 6,000 citations. During this time, Anzaldúa also held writing workshops and engaged in speaking engagements as a way to support herself financially. In 1985, Anzaldúa began working on her most influential book titled *Borderlands/La Frontera: The New Mestiza* (Anzaldúa 1987), which has nearly 26,000 citations! *Borderlands/La Frontera* had a deep impact in Latina/o social thought and was among the first to discuss intersectionality, although she did not use that term. Through her powerful poetics Anzaldúa metaphorically describes the hybridization of living in the borderlands. While commonly the concept of the border had only been described as a geographical region, i.e. where the US and Mexico meet, she extended this concept of being in-between to cultural, racial, sexual, and psychological borders. This status of being in-between is then used to describe the marginalization of Chicanas and Chicana-lesbians, which is rooted in the cultural-structural-historical characteristics of the region.

Anzaldúa also made a contribution to Chicana/o studies by using history to draw a connection between her Chicana identity and her indigenous ancestors, in particular the Indian woman's history of resistance. Yet, she also made the painful connection that she did not sell out her people, but it is her culture that betrayed her by not accepting her sexuality and seeking to make women subservient. Such experiences with marginalization led to Anzaldúa's development of a new mestiza consciousness that entailed the development of a counter-stance, where the key is to act and not react. Therefore, out of the social and internal struggles is the possibility for a new consciousness that provides an avenue to form connections with other marginalized groups and develop deeper insights into the culture, social, and psychological wounds of marginalized groups.

In *Borderlands/La Frontera: The New Mestiza*, Anzaldúa (1987) also makes contributions to transnationalism and border studies. She described an ontological experience of transnationalism in describing the borderlands. In particular, Anzaldúa (1987) wrote:

> The US–Mexican border *es una herida abierta* [an open wound] where the Third World grates against the first and bleeds. And before a scab forms it hemorrhages

again, the lifeblood of two worlds merging to form a third country – a border culture. Borders are set up to define the places that are safe and unsafe, to distinguish us from them. A border is a dividing line, a narrow strip along a steep edge. A borderland is a vague and undetermined place created by the emotional residue of an unnatural boundary. It is in a constant state of transition. (p. 3)

Here Anzaldúa described the duality of the border as a place where one is connected to both the homeland and the host-land, fundamentally exemplifying how the processes of migration and immigration can be consequential in psychological and physical ways. Transnational nation–state relationships are also complex and can be misrecognized. In this same book, Anzaldúa (1987) protests to white America when she stated, "Admit that Mexico is your double, that she exists in the shadow of this country, that we are irrevocably tied to her" (p. 86). The US–Mexico border has been a uniquely positioned transnational community and continues to be the nexus for border relations, where foreign policy comes to life, all the while serving as a medium for cultural passage and mixing.

In her post-Borderlands writings, the mestiza consciousness evolved into the concept of *nepantla* which is the Nahuatl word claimed by Anzaldúa to refer to an ontological state of being in-between. In an interview with Karin Ikas (2012), Anzaldúa intimates:

And I now call it Nepantla, which is a Nahuatl word for the space between two bodies of water, the space between two worlds. It is a limited space, a space where you are not this or that but where you are changing. You haven't got into the new identity yet and haven't left the old identity behind either – you are in a kind of transition. And that is what Nepantla stands for. It is very awkward, uncomfortable and frustrating to be in that Nepantla because you are in the midst of transformation. (Ikas 2012, p. 276)

Anzaldúa's writings provided both a physical and metaphysical understanding of the Latina/o experience in the world, but also within the geographic confines of the US. Anzaldúa's writings were at the forefront of Latina phenomenology and we see her work influencing philosophy today (Martinez 2014) and also having an impact on art, poetry, sex and sexuality, intersectionality, and sociology, especially in the Chicana feminism scholarship.

Gloria Anzaldúa went on to continue writing, lecturing, and leading workshops across the country, including a reading and writing workshop in San Antonio, Texas at the Esperanza Peace and Justice Center (Anzaldúa and Keating 2009) The life of Gloria Anzaldúa was riddled with experiences that shaped the development of her theoretical and philosophical perspectives, from her near-death experiences to her exposure to the world outside of the borderlands. She earned a National Endowment for the Arts in fiction in 1991 and a little over a decade later passed away in 2004 from diabetes-related complications. In her honor, Norma Elia Cantú founded the Society for the Study of Gloria Anzaldúa which has an annual conference at the University of Texas at San Antonio.

Latina/os Building Institutional Power

The road to building institutional power for Latina/os was preceded by the hard work and activism of thought leaders in the US, including those highlighted in this chapter who contributed to the development of the National Council for La Raza (NCLR), now UnidosUS, the Mexican American Legal Defense and Educational Fund (MALDEF), the Julian Samora Research Institute (JSRI), the Ernesto Galarza Applied Research Center, and the Society for the Study of Gloria Anzaldúa. Moreover, Latina/o scholars have also been instrumental in establishing their own academic organizations and in creating spaces within mainstream academic organizations. For example, the National Association of Chicana and Chicana/o studies (NACCS), which was started in 1972, brought a critical perspective based on the Chicana/o Movement. NACCS brought together scholars from the humanities and social sciences and championed gender and queer/lesbian perspectives as well. In addition, the Section on Latina/o Sociology, within the American Sociological Association (ASA), celebrated its thirtieth anniversary in 2021. The Section has not only expanded Latina/o scholarship through cutting-edge research but has supported and mentored hundreds of Latina/o sociologists. Another organization is the Latina/o Studies Association which has brought together the humanities and social sciences in the last seven years. Latina/os have also held leadership roles in a variety of professional associations including Marta Tienda as president of the Population Association of America (PAA) in 2002 and four Latina/os as presidents of the American Sociological Association (Alejandro Portes in 1999; Eduardo Bonilla-Silva in 2018; Mary Romero in 2019, and Cecilia Menjívar in 2022).

Contemporary Latina/o Thought Leaders

Latina/os' influence on academic and theoretical developments within various academic fields is stronger than ever. Contemporary scholars such as Eduardo Bonilla-Silva, Pierrette Hondagneu-Sotelo, Ramón Grosfoguel, Mary Romero, Cecilia Menjívar, and Michael Rodríguez-Muñiz have made important intellectual contributions toward the understanding of the Latina/o experience in the US using different methodologies and theoretical approaches. They are a few of the many Latina/o leaders evolving the understanding of Latina/os, their experiences, their perspectives and how this translates to an episteme that was early neglected. We highlight here a few of these scholars.

Pierrette Hondagneu-Sotelo is a Latina sociologist whose work "strives to understand people's lives and situations in relation to broader social and historical forces" (Hondagneu-Sotelo 2022). Hondagneu-Sotelo's research is centered around the following topics: gender and migration, informal sector work in the immigrant city, religion and immigrant integration and Latina/o community development. Her methodological approaches include interviews and participant observation ethnography. In her book *Gendered Transitions: Mexican Experiences of Immigration*, Hondagneu-Sotelo (1994) examined the intersection of gender and migration to show how one influences and interacts with the other, through the ethnography of settlement. Hondagneu-Sotelo explored the gendered process of migration and also addressed the impact of macro and micro forces. Hondagneu-Sotelo (1994) argues that "immigration is not the outcome of households strategizing or adapting to macrostructural economic pressures, but of the exercise of multiple interests and hierarchies of power that come to life within households" (p. 187). In their article, "I'm Here, but I'm There: The Meanings of Latina Transnational Motherhood," Hondagneu-Sotelo and Avila (1997), explore the concept of *transnational motherhood*. They capture a type of motherhood that is unique to immigrant women where women who work and reside in the US while their children remain in their countries of origin. In essence, transnational motherhood is a variation of motherhood that disrupts the normalized concepts of motherhood in a temporal and spatial sense. In her book titled *Domestica: Immigrant Workers Cleaning and Caring in the Shadows of Affluence* (2001), Hondagneu-Sotelo further explores mothering and the Latina immigrant experience through the informal labor activities of care workers. She highlights the voices of Mexican and Central American immigrant women in Los Angeles who care for other people's children, sometimes leaving their own children in their home country. In this book she is able to capture the experiences of a hidden population through a deeper understanding of domestic work. Hondagneu-Sotelo's (2017) research also adds to the understanding of gender and migration by examining the role of men and masculinity in an article titled "Place, Nature and Masculinity in Immigrant Integration: Latino Immigrant Men in Inner-City Parks and Community Gardens." In this work, she sets out to answer the question: How do Latino immigrant men create a sense of place, belonging and civic culture through their homosocial gatherings in parks and community gardens, and what is the role of these activities in processes of immigrant integration?

Latina/o scholars have historically examined connections and intersections between migration, economics, gender, and more. Today, Latina/o scholars continue to advance theories across different disciplines, such as sociology and philosophy. Ramón Grosfoguel's work, which focuses on the decolonization of knowledge and power and international migration and the political-economy of the world-system, is one example. Grosfoguel is a Puerto Rican sociologist, whose writings and work reach into topics such as racism through deep ontological and philosophical exploration. In his article titled "What is Racism?," Grosfoguel (2016) articulates a definition of racism influenced by the philosophical frameworks of Franz Fanon, Boaventura de Sousa Santos, and contemporary Caribbean Fanonian philosophers. Grosfoguel (2016) argued that a universalized understanding of racism can potentially hide the different forms of racism as they appear in different parts of the world. Racism, Grosfoguel (2016) argued, can be marked by color, language, religion, culture, and more. Grosfoguel, therefore, positioned an understanding of racism in the framework of Fanon's zones of being and non-being, essentially concluding that intersectionality of oppressions function differently for oppressed people in both zones. In the zone of non-being, intersectional oppression is aggravated by racial oppression, whereas in the zone of being, oppression may be mitigated by racial privilege (Grosfoguel 2016).

Eduardo Bonilla-Silva is a distinguished Puerto Rican sociologist making major contributions to the study of race today. He has essentially transformed how scholars study, conceptualize, analyze, and understand race. The reach of his work has been extraordinarily wide, in disciplines beyond sociology and academia. Bonilla-Silva's (2021) book titled *Racism without Racists: Color-Blind Racism and the Persistence of Racial Inequality in America* is now in its sixth edition. Rogelio Sáenz, one of the authors of the book you are now reading, in his blurb of *Racism without Racists* writes, "Eduardo Bonilla-Silva is one of the most influential, insightful, and engaging scholars writing on race. His pathbreaking book, now in its sixth edition, continues to be the gold standard for understanding the dynamics of racism and developing a blueprint for what whites and people of color must do to dismantle white supremacy and create a more 'humane, inclusive, and democratic' world." Bonilla-Silva's (2004) research has also argued that as the demography of the US changes with whites declining in numbers, the US will increasingly move from a bi-racial to a tri-racial framework (see Chapter 16) in which race becomes more fluid, with whites expanding boundaries to allow lighter-skinned successful persons of color into the white category, as well as designating other people of color as "honorary whites," allowed in the group under certain circumstances but not completely accepted. He also argues that there is a third category consisting of the "collective Black" where people of color are placed with limited opportunities for upward mobility. Finally, Bonilla-Silva's (2019) American Sociological Association presidential address titled "Feeling Race: Theorizing the Racial Economy of Emotions" provides a theoretical framework for understanding the role that emotions play in sustaining racism with this work opening up theoretical and conceptual paths for scholars of race.

There are many other Latina/o scholars beyond those whose work is highlighted here making major intellectual contributions on the understanding of Latina/os and their experiences in the US, not only in sociology but across many other disciplines. Unfortunately, the lack of space does not allow us to expand our discussion here.

Summary

In this chapter, we have provided a wide overview of the many contributions that Latina/o scholars, writers, and thinkers have made to the understanding of the experience of Latina/os in the US. Beginning with the important work of journalist and activist Jovita Idár to early generations of Latina/o scholars in the early to middle part of the twentieth century, and to contemporary scholars today, we have outlined the temporal course of the development of scholarship on Latina/os. It is important to realize that while some of these scholars have done traditional mainstream sociology and social science, many have also developed unique paths and careers combining research/scholarship, advocacy, and activism to put their research and scholarship to call attention to racism, discrimination, and inequality and to develop solutions through a variety of means to improve the lives of Latina/os and people of color.

Many have also crafted new theoretical approaches, methodological and analytical techniques, and stepped outside of the ivy walls of academia to improve the world and to get into what the influential and iconic John Lewis referred to as "good trouble," to challenge the systems of oppression.

We now turn to the next chapter which examines the historical and contemporary immigration to the US followed by the demography of Latina/os and gender and sexuality.

Discussion Questions

1. How did early Mexican American and Chicana/o scholars resist Anglo culture in their work?

2. How did transnationalism influence the work of early Latina/o thought leaders such as Gloria Anzaldúa and Américo Paredes? How does it vary from how transnationalism is captured in more contemporary scholarship?

3. Why did Alfredo Mirandé and Maxine Bacca Zinn propose an alternative perspective on Chicana/o sociology?

4. What is the meaning of borders in Gloria Anzaldúa's work? How does the *mestiza consciousness* connect to resistance?

5. How do the social barriers that Latina/os face influence the directions and focus of Latina/o social thought?

6. Analyze the contributions of contemporary Latina/o scholars such as Pierrette Hondagneu-Sotelo, Ramón Grosfoguel, and Eduardo Bonilla-Silva to the understanding of Latina/o experiences in the US. How do their methodologies and theoretical approaches differ, and what insights do they offer into issues of migration, race, and gender?

7. What was the significance of the debate over the sociology of Chicanos in the 1970s, particularly focusing on the arguments proposed by Alfredo Mirandé and Maxine Baca Zinn? How did their perspectives contribute to the development of Chicana/o sociology?

4 Historical and Contemporary Latina/o Immigration

A *New York Times* article in 2019 published an image of a drowned father and daughter, "[lying] face down in the muddy water along the banks of the Rio Grande, her tiny head tucked inside his T-shirt, an arm draped over his neck" (Ahmed and Sample 2019). Lamentably, this horrendous tragedy is not an isolated incident. Over the last three to four decades, US border operations have militarized the border and have fortified areas where undocumented immigrants have entered in the past. The result is that people seeking to enter the country have been diverted to perilous routes, where many lose their lives. A recent CBS news report called attention to the record-high 853 people who lost their lives trying to cross the US–Mexico border (Montoya-Galvez 2022). Many like Alberto Martínez Ramírez and his infant daughter from El Salvador seek political asylum in the US fleeing violence in countries in their countries of origin. For many, life is so perilous and dangerous that they risk all – even their lives – to survive.

Over the last three decades, there have been escalating efforts to militarize the border along with the building of the border wall and self-appointed armed vigilantes patrolling the border to keep immigrants out of the US (Correa and Simpson 2022). Throughout the 1990s and to the present there have been policies and practices to criminalize immigrants with the term "crimmigration" used to describe and call attention to these actions. During this period, there has been a growth of the big business of immigrant detention centers and the number of deportations has risen (Goodman 2020; Tapia 2022). Although animosity and hate against immigrants, particularly people of color, was getting worse, enter Donald Trump, who campaigned for the presidency in 2015 in which he referred to Mexicans as criminals and rapists – bad people who need to be kept out of the country. His hateful rhetoric toward Mexicans and immigrants galvanized his supporters. Over the last few years, the animosity and violence against undocumented immigrants has escalated even more, as people have come from many parts of the world to the Texas–Mexico border in search of asylum as they escape violence in their home countries. As Title 42 was used to keep undocumented migrants out of the US due to health reasons associated with the COVID-19 pandemic, many immigrants found themselves stranded in Mexico along the border. Republican governors have also battled with the Biden administration with efforts to make it even more difficult for undocumented immigrants to enter the country. Texas Governor Greg Abbott is at the forefront in calling the Texas border area a war zone, and using concertina wire to discourage immigrants from entering the US. He has also bussed countless numbers of immigrants to Democrat-led cities such as New York City, Chicago, and other communities.

The three of us, the authors of this book, grew up on the Texas border in El Paso (Maria Cristina Morales), Laredo (Coda Rayo-Garza), and the Rio Grande Valley (Rogelio Sáenz). We do not recognize our communities from an earlier time. As politicians have described the border as a warzone, the militarization and the presence of border-patrol agents, Homeland Security personnel, and the National Guard have multiplied. Many community leaders and business owners are very concerned that people will be scared to come to the border. The mass media and politicians regularly refer to the situation at the border as a major crisis. A recent Pew Research Center (2024) survey asked respondents their views regarding the immigrant situation at the border, the reasons why they believe that unauthorized immigrants come to the border, and their assessment of how the US government is performing, and whether or not they consider the situation a crisis. The results of the survey show that where one is on the political spectrum is important in whether people see the case at the border as a crisis or a problem – with Republicans and those who lean Republican more likely to view it as a crisis, and Democrats and those who lean Democrat to view it as a problem. There are also differences along political lines on the reason(s) why immigrants come to the border in search of gaining entrance into the United States. There are also significant differences along racial and ethnic lines and age on respondents' views regarding immigrants. One thing on which politicians and the general public across the political spectrum agree is that the immigration system is broken and needs to be fixed. Unfortunately, agreement and consensus stop there, as people have radically different solutions to deal with the broken immigration system. Trump continues to use hateful rhetoric against immigrants and has expressed concern that immigrants "are poisoning the blood of our country" (Gibson 2023). This is the context that we are in, one in which it is practically impossible to develop effective immigration policy.

This chapter provides an overview of the historical and contemporary Latina/o immigration. We begin with an examination of theoretical perspectives that have been developed to understand the international movement in order for readers to gain a framework for making sense of the sustained Latina/o immigration over the last century. These theoretical perspectives remind us that the movement of people across international borders does not occur in a vacuum; rather they are driven by economic, global, historical, and structural forces. Subsequently, we provide a discussion of policies that have shaped and affected Latina/o immigration and, concomitantly, describe the changing volume of immigration associated with such policies. Furthermore, we review the historical and contemporary shifts in immigration to the US with particular emphasis on the expanding immigration from Latin America and the Caribbean, beginning in the 1960s and peaking in the 1990s. We will then provide an analysis of the current levels of immigration among Latina/os in the context of the immigration situation described above. Finally, we outline the major and most pressing issues related to Latina/o immigration in the US.

Theoretical Perspectives

Over the last half century, demographers, economists, and sociologists have developed theoretical frameworks to understand the movement of people. In general, these perspectives have focused on the internal migration of people within countries, the push-and-pull factors that drive the movement, and the economic factors that propel people to move (Greenwood 1985; Lee 1966). In the last several decades, theoretical perspectives have been advanced to capture the broader context in which international migration occurs. In particular, these theoretical frameworks have called attention to the role that labor markets, households, globalization, historical forces, and social networks play in the movement of people across international boundaries. We draw below on the inventory and assessment of immigration theoretical perspectives undertaken by Massey and his colleagues (Massey et al. 1993; see also Massey et al. 2005; Massey and Espinosa 1997). We next provide a brief overview of these theoretical perspectives. We began with a discussion of the theories associated with the initiation of migration.

Initiation of International Migration

Neoclassical Economics
Economics push–pull perspectives have a long tradition in efforts to understand human migration. The neoclassical economics perspective draws on assumptions that humans are rational, seeking to increase their net economic benefits, and that they have complete information regarding conditions across labor markets. The neoclassical economics framework features two forms – macro and micro – based on the level of unit of analysis (e.g. labor markets, individual, etc.).

The macro variety of the neoclassical economics perspective focuses on the disequilibrium of the supply and demand for labor across labor markets. On the international stage, there are some countries, such as the US, which have favorable economic conditions characterized by low levels of unemployment and high wages, reflecting a high demand for labor. On the other hand, other countries, such as Mexico, are depicted by high levels of unemployment and low wages, evincing a high supply of labor. The labor saturation is especially evident in light of high fertility levels and large shares of young people entering the labor market. The neoclassical economics perspective suggests that flows of labor will be directed from countries with excess labor to those with labor needs, such as the movement of workers from many countries in Latin America and the Caribbean to the US. The theory proposes that the movement of workers across labor markets is a response to disequilibrium across those markets and that eventually equilibrium is restored when the supply and demand for labor is in balance. Certainly, the excess labor in many Latin American and Caribbean countries and labor needs in the US has been associated with the movement of people to the US. More recently, however, the flow of immigrants from Latin America, especially from Mexico, has slowed dramatically (Passel et al. 2012; Sáenz 2019). Among a variety of factors that have been associated with this decline has been a dramatic drop in the fertility rate in Mexico and Latin America, which has resulted in a smaller labor force (Cave 2013).

The micro form of the neoclassical economics perspective spotlights the decision making that potential migrants conduct as they evaluate costs and benefits associated with the potential place(s) of destination and site of origin. Benefits related to the place of destination include favorable labor market conditions, such as high wages, low unemployment, and the possibility of job advancement. Costs associated with the movement include the monetary cost of relocation, money foregone in the job search, as well as psychic expenditures related to cutting ties with family and friends in one's place of origin. The theory proposes that the likelihood of movement is enhanced when the benefits of the movement outweigh costs related to the relocation. As noted above, the theory suggests that people are rational and that they have complete information about varying labor markets. However, in the case of international migration, especially of people with limited resources, we will see below that people rely on social networks and social capital to navigate movement. For this reason, the individual form of the neoclassical economics perspectives is relevant to understanding Latin American and Caribbean immigration to the US, but as part of a larger framework that incorporates reliance on social networks and social capital (see below).

The New Economics of Migration

While the new economics of migration, similarly, highlights economic factors, it is broader than the neoclassical economics perspective in a few respects. For example, the center of attention is not individuals or labor markets, but households where members are mobilized to maximize household resources. In addition, the framework broadens the context to account for the numerous ways in which households survive economically in light of financial and environmental uncertainty. People in many developing countries have limited options at their disposal to protect themselves against a variety of risks that can devastate their economic well-being. For example, in Mexico small-scale farmers are vulnerable to unexpected downturns in the economy, the weather, and other related events. Thus, a significant drop in the value of the peso as well as the absence of rain can tremendously affect the livelihood of the country's poor. In addition, the poor do not have access to financial and insurance institutions that can protect them against such calamities.

As a strategy for protection against such distress, household members perform a diverse set of activities to minimize risks. Accordingly, households behave in a similar fashion as smart investors that diversify their investment portfolios. For instance, in the case of households engaged in small-scale farming, certain household members may tend to the raising of crops, others may take off-farm employment in the local or surrounding area, and still others may immigrate to the US from where they can send remittances to the household. Therefore, immigration represents a strategy that allows the household to minimize the risks of uncertainty while amassing resources from the business of migration. Historically, remittances have been a major part of the economy of Mexico and other Latin American and Caribbean countries (Khan and Merritt 2023; Massey and Parrado 1994). It is estimated that $142 billion in remittances flowed to Latin America and the Caribbean in 2022, with $60 billion directed to Mexico alone (Ratha et al. 2022).

Dual Labor Market Theory

The neoclassical and new economics of migration perspectives focus primarily on decisions that individuals and households make to maximize income or minimize risks. The dual labor market perspective shifts attention to the links between labor market demands in developed countries and the movement of labor from developing countries (Massey et al. 1993; Piore 1979).

As opposed to international migration driven by push factors in the country of origin and pull factors in the country of destination, the dual labor market perspective argues that the movement is due simply to the latter factors. This argument claims that the structure of labor markets makes international migrants an essential component of the economies of developed countries (Massey et al. 1993). Four attributes of the economies of developed countries, such as the US, are particularly important to understanding the inherent demand for migrant labor. First, developed countries face situations involving large demand alongside a small supply among their native populations for low-skill jobs. In order to make such jobs attractive to native-born workers, employers would need to raise wages. However, the boosting of wages for low-skill jobs would put pressures on employers to elevate the wages for jobs slightly higher in the hierarchy of occupational prestige, with the raising of such wages leading to further pressures to increase wages at still higher levels of the echelon of occupational prestige – a situation referred to as "structural inflation." Thus, developed countries have a need for immigrant labor that takes jobs at such low levels, thus ensuring the smooth operation of the economy without having to raise wages across the board.

Second, occupational hierarchies are essential for the motivation of workers, who can earn status for holding certain jobs as well as seeking to climb higher in the job echelon (Massey et al. 1993). Dead-end jobs at the bottom of the occupational structure are devoid of status and provide little upward mobility, thus not being attractive to native-born workers. The elimination of the bottommost jobs would simply result in the next tier of workers becoming the new basement level jobs. Hence, employers are attracted to low-wage immigrant labor that is primarily concerned with obtaining income rather than job status. Indeed, the low wages that immigrants receive for dead-end jobs are higher than those that they receive in their home country. In fact, as many immigrant newcomers continue to see themselves as part of their home country, they also derive status through remitting money to their family back home.

Third, due to the duality of capital which is fixed and labor which is flexible, labor markets are segmented into the primary sector and the secondary sector (Massey et al. 1993). The primary sector consists of capital-intensive labor in which employers invest heavily through training and education. Because employers invest in primary-sector workers, employers seek to retain them; primary-sector workers receive favorable wages and benefits, and have an opportunity for upward mobility within the organization. In contrast, the secondary sector is characterized by a labor-intensive workforce that is largely expendable, as employers let go of this segment of the labor force when they are not needed or the economy is not doing well. Thus, workers in this sector of the labor receive low wages, limited benefits, and, at best, have little opportunity for upward mobility. Again, native-born workers are not attracted to this segment of the labor force, with immigrant laborers filling this labor niche.

Fourth, the need for immigrant labor to fill low-wage, dead-end jobs has been exacerbated by the decline of two segments of the labor force whose supply has dwindled due to demographic forces. In particular, in the past, women and teenagers filled such jobs. However, over the last several decades, women have experienced increasing levels of labor force participation and divorce rates, both of which cemented their status as income earners, and they have experienced significant declines in their fertility, which has limited the labor supply of teenage workers. The decline of women and teenagers as occupants of low-wage, dead-end jobs has made immigrant labor even more attractive to employers.

In sum, the dual labor market perspective illustrates the forces that made low-wage immigrant labor a necessary part of the labor force of developed countries. Simply put, the economies of developed countries, such as the US, depend very heavily on immigrant labor stemming from developing countries, such as Mexico and other Latin American and Caribbean countries.

World System Theory

The world system perspective for understanding the initiation of international migration stems from the theoretical insights of Wallerstein (1974). This framework focuses on the development and expansion of the structure of the world market with roots in the sixteenth century (Massey et al. 1993). According to this perspective, the penetration of capitalists from developed countries and multinational corporations into the economic markets of developing countries sets the emergence of international migration from developing countries to developed countries. In particular, the entrance of capitalist interests into the economies of developing countries is associated with disruptions and dislocations to the traditional labor markets of developing countries. Furthermore, in order to protect the economic interests of their capitalist corporations, developed countries often intervene in the political affairs of developing countries, as illustrated in Chapter 2, thus setting off added forces stimulating immigration.

As capital interests enter developed countries, land becomes an increasingly valuable commodity. Capitalist farmers in developed countries usurp land from the hands of subsistence farmers and other small-scale operators and turn to high-yield seeds, expensive fertilizers, and mechanized production. Recall earlier the case of El Salvador's coffee oligarchy who wrested land from subsistence farmers. The lives of small-scale operators who cede their land are transformed dramatically, as they lose their livelihood. Some of these individuals work for the increasingly large planta-tions, others move to urban areas, and still others immigrate to developed countries.

The penetration of capital affects other industries aside from agriculture. For instance, capitalists from developed countries and multinational corporations enter developed countries to take advantage of their cheap labor through the forma-tion of assembly plants under the guise of helping the country industrialize. The US has a long history of such programs in Latin America and the Caribbean, most notably in the form of Operation Bootstrap in Puerto Rico in 1947 and the Border Industrialization Program (BIP) in Mexico in 1965, which was the precursor of the North American Free Trade Agreement (NAFTA) in 1994 and the new iteration of NAFTA, the United States–Mexico–Canada Agreement in 2018 under the Trump administration. Such industrialization efforts sever relations and transpose peasants into laborers making them increasingly mobile and subject to migration (Massey et al. 1993). As was the case in Puerto Rico and Mexico involving the industrialization programs noted above, many laborers working in assembly plants eventually sought to improve their fortunes in the mainland US.

Moreover, transportation routes are established between the developed country and the developing country to ship products. Such transportation paths serve to not only move capital and products but also people who immigrate to the developed country to pursue economic opportunities or join family members.

The set of theories just reviewed provides us an understanding of how interna-tional migration is initiated. The theoretical perspectives point to the importance of labor market forces involving the imbalance between labor supply and labor demand as well as the economic-related calculations that migrants undertake to decide whether or not migrate, the survival strategies that households use to maximize eco-nomic resources and minimize economic risks, the structural labor market forces involving developed countries needing low-wage labor from developed countries, and the dislocation of workers when capitalist enterprises enter developing coun-tries. We now turn to a discussion of the theoretical perspectives that provide insights into how immigration is sustained.

Perpetuation of International Migration

Network Theory

International migration is not a solitary act. Rather, people rely on their social net-works to facilitate movement across international borders. Massey et al. (1993) define migrant networks as "sets of interpersonal ties that connect migrants, former migrants, and nonmigrants in origin and destination areas through ties of kinship, friendship, and shared community origin" (p. 448). In particular, networks repre-sent a form of social capital that people can tap in order to facilitate international migration and secure employment in the place of destination (Massey et al. 1993). A valuable and instrumental feature of social networks is that information derived from one's social networks serves to reduce the costs and risks associated with immigration.

Potential migrants draw on the stock of knowledge accumulated by members of the community, including relatives and friends, to gain valuable information as they seek to immigrate and subsequently look for employment in the place of destination. Once the potential migrant, himself or herself, engages in migration and settles in the place of destination, he or she becomes another potential link to other potential migrants contemplating an international move. Thus, we can imagine a particular rural community in Mexico that initially did not have anyone who had immigrated to the US. Given the lack of a stock of knowledge of immigration in the community, the first person moving to the US would find it difficult and costly to set out abroad and would also face hardships in locating employment and assistance. The difficulties would be slightly less for the second person moving to the US because he/she could draw on the experience and information of the earliest immigrant. Hence, the difficulty, cost, and risk of migration decline as increasingly more people engage in immigration and attain vital information that can be shared with other potential immigrants. As Massey et al. (1993) point out: "Once the number of migrants reaches a critical threshold, the expansion of networks reduces the costs and risks of movement, which causes the probability of migration to rise, which causes additional movement, which further expands the networks, and so on" (pp. 448–449). Moreover, while originally the immigration flow consists of a selective population, such as young men, over time the immigration stream includes a broader segment of the population (Massey et al. 1993).

Institutional Theory
As the flow of immigration expands, private institutions and voluntary, non-profit organizations arise to meet the imbalance between the substantial number of people who seek to enter a developed country, such as the US, and the limited number of slots available to accommodate people's desire to immigrate (Massey et al. 1993). As the country of destination erects barriers and obstacles, including policies, to keep out persons from entering the country without proper authorization, entrepreneurs and institutions arise to provide goods and services to immigrants to increase their probabilities of entering the country. For the most part, these are underground activities that assist immigrants, such as human smugglers (e.g. *coyotes* in the case of human smugglers who provide their services to assist immigrants to enter the US from Mexico), businesses providing fraudulent documents (e.g. social security cards, passports, etc.) and arranged marriages between US citizens and immigrants, contract laborers who arrange for employment of unauthorized labor, as well as people and businesses who cater to the food and lodging needs of immigrants (Massey et al. 1993). Furthermore, voluntary, non-profit humanitarian organizations also emerge to assist immigrants. Such organizations assist immigrants through the provision of water and food during their journey, social services, counseling, as well as protecting them from human rights and related abuses (Massey et al. 1993).

As these individuals, businesses, institutions, and organizations providing goods and services to immigrants become firmly established and known to immigrants, they become part of the stock of knowledge and social capital on which immigrants draw to navigate immigration and facilitate settlement in the country of destination and these entities serve to ensure the continuation of immigration.

Cumulative Causation

Immigration is sustained in yet another way. In this case, immigration itself alters the social context into which other persons in the sending community make decisions regarding whether or not to engage in international migration (Massey et al. 1993). Thus, each episode of immigration makes subsequent immigration more likely because the act of immigration increasingly alters the environment of the community of origin, resulting in other individuals being more likely to immigrate as well. This is a process known as *cumulative causation*, which stems from the work of Gunnar Myrdal (1957).

There are numerous ways in which immigration alters the social context, which leads to ensuing immigration being more likely. These alterations involve the distribution of income, the distribution of land, the organization of agrarian production, the culture of migration, the regional distribution of human capital, and social labeling (Massey et al. 1993). For example, as people start moving from the sending community, immigration widens income inequality in the community. Immigrants attain more income from their jobs abroad, which they remit back home. Other individuals in the community experience relative deprivation as their own income lags behind those of migrants, leading to greater probabilities of others immigrating to earn higher income levels. In addition, with their remittances, immigrants purchase land, which they typically take out of production with the long-range plan for returning or retiring to live in a home built on the land. As more immigrants make similar purchases of land and take it out of production, there is a declining need for agricultural labor, which stimulates these individuals to immigrate in search of employment. Furthermore, in cases where immigrants purchase land to farm, due to their favorable economic position, they are able to engage in more capital-intensive forms of agriculture than is typical of the sending community, again leading to a decline in the need for agricultural laborers, who seek better economic opportunities abroad. Moreover, immigration alters immigrants themselves, along with their tastes, preferences, and lifestyles, so that, in order to satisfy the newly acquired lifestyles, immigrants are more likely to continue to engage in immigration, as well as to stimulate others to seek such pursuits through the vehicle of immigration. Hence, the culture of migration becomes deeply entrenched in people's behavior, leading increasingly to an expectation that people will immigrate. Additionally, as immigration becomes more widespread in the community of origin, the home community experiences a significant loss of its human capital, which negatively affects the need for labor locally, further stimulating people to immigrate in pursuit of better economic opportunities. Finally, as immigrants are drawn to certain low-paying jobs in the country of destination, those positions become known as "immigrant jobs," which reduces the likelihood that native workers will take such employment.

In sum, we have provided an overview of the different theoretical approaches that help us understand how immigration is initiated and how it is sustained over time. These perspectives can be used to comprehend the movement of people from Latin America and the Caribbean to the US over the course of more than a century. Below we discuss US policies and programs over the last century, which at times have facilitated the movement of people from Latin America and the Caribbean, especially from Mexico, and at other times made it increasingly difficult for individuals from this region to immigrate to the US.

US Immigration Policies and Programs

The US has established a variety of policies and programs, at times in conjunction with Mexico, over the last century, which has impacted the flows of immigrants from Mexico and the rest of Latin America and the Caribbean to the US. To a certain extent, these actions have at times welcomed Mexican and other Latin American and Caribbean immigrants and at other times have shunned these individuals.

Over the course of the nineteenth century and into the first couple of decades of the twentieth century, US immigration policy toward Mexico and Latin America and the Caribbean was mute (LoBreglio 2004). Indeed, during this period the movement of Mexicans across the US–Mexico border was fairly unregulated. This situation contrasted sharply from the major US immigration policies and programs that sought to limit immigration of certain groups including Chinese with the creation of the Chinese Exclusion Acts of 1882 and 1892, Japanese with the signing of the Gentlemen's Agreement in 1907, and Southern and Eastern Europeans with the passage of the Immigration Acts of 1917, 1921, and 1924. In fact, while many Americans rabidly called for policy to curtail or eliminate immigration from Southern and Eastern Europe, which led to the establishment of immigration policy between 1917 and 1924, US agriculturalists from the Southwest argued vociferously to exempt Mexicans from the literacy requirement and head tax imposed by the Immigration Act of 1917, and from the quota system that limited the number of people allowed to immigrate from specific countries, which was stipulated by the Immigration Acts of 1921 and 1924 (LoBreglio 2004). This incident more than a century ago illustrates the long and established dependence of US employers on cheap labor from Mexico and subsequently from other parts of Latin America and the Caribbean.

The Establishment of the Border Patrol

As a compromise for Mexico being exempted from immigration quotas constituted by the Immigration Act of 1924, the US established the US Border Patrol in 1924 as part of the US Department of Labor, with the passage of the Labor Appropriation Act of 1924. While the Border Patrol was created to curb the entrance of undocumented immigrants on US borders, its focus was on the prevention of Mexican immigrants on the US–Mexico border. The creation of the Border Patrol marked the criminalization of the Mexican immigrant in the US, although it was not illegal for an employer to hire undocumented laborers (Bustamante 1972). Border-patrol agents are referred to as *"la migra"* by Mexicans on both sides of the border.

The Repatriation Program

The Great Depression ushered in a new economic era, which displaced people from their jobs and placed them on breadlines. This meant that, despite efforts to curtail immigration legislatively at the beginning of the 1920s, by the end of the decade the flow of immigration to the US came to a close due to the Great Depression. In efforts to protect the handful of jobs available, the US sought to eliminate foreign job competition. Due to the proximity of Mexico along with the deep-seated racism against Mexicans in the US, Mexicans became a convenient scapegoat. Quickly President Hoover authorized the Mexican Repatriation Program in 1929 and his predecessor, President Franklin Delano Roosevelt, elongated the program until 1939. Balderrama and Rodríguez (2006) illustrate the context in which the US government fervently sent Mexicans back home:

> Americans, reeling from the economic disorientation of the depression, sought a convenient scapegoat. They found it in the Mexican community. In a frenzy of anti-Mexican hysteria, wholesale punitive measures were proposed and undertaken by government officials at the federal, state, and local levels. Immigration and deportation laws were enacted to restrict emigration and hasten the departure of those already here. Contributing to the brutalizing experience were the mass deportation roundups and repatriation drives. Violence and "scare-head" tactics were utilized to get rid of the burdensome and unwanted horde. An incessant cry of "get rid of the Mexicans" swept the country. (p. 1)

Countless numbers of Mexicans, along with persons born in the US, were deported or coerced into voluntarily returning to Mexico, with the estimates ranging from 400,000 to 2,000,000 individuals (Sáenz and Murga 2011). The most commonly cited figure of 500,000 (Hoffman 1974) suggests that approximately one-third of Mexicans counted in the 1930 US census were returned to Mexico. This repatriation program illustrates the way in which the US government has tended to view Mexican immigrants – as a workforce that is welcome when needed – but an easily disposable labor pool and convenient scapegoat during economic downturns.

Bracero Program

Within a few years from the termination of the Mexican Repatriation Program, the US took to the warfront in World War II. As young men went off to war, women picked up the job slack as they joined the labor force. However, there were still major labor shortages, particularly in agriculture. Mexicans, now, represented a much needed and welcome source of labor. The US in an accord with Mexico established the Bracero Program in 1942 with "bracero" referring to the Spanish term for manual labor or someone who works with his arms. The program allowed Mexico to send contract laborers to the US to work for a specific amount of time. US employers found the program extremely attractive, so much so that the Bracero Program was extended way beyond the end of World War II, with the initial extension occurring in 1951 with the signing of Public Law 78 and lasting until 1964.

Most academics simply think of the Bracero Program as an effort that mutually helped Mexico and the US. Mexico profited through a portion of its population working in the US; the US benefited from a cheap source of labor that the country desperately needed. However, we need to understand the context in Mexico in which the Bracero Program was developed. At the time, Mexico was undergoing an industrialization of its agricultural industry (Hernández 2006). As outlined above in the discussion of the cumulative causation theoretical perspective, Mexican workers were being uprooted at the time through the privatization of land, the mechanization of agriculture, and a focus on the exportation of agricultural production (Hernández 2006). Still, Mexico, especially in the case of large agricultural growers, had an eye on its own low-wage labor as being an essential part of the country's effort to industrialize its rural areas (Hernández 2006).

Consequently, there was a certain level of opposition in Mexico to the Bracero Program, with fears that Mexican laborers would seek better opportunities in the US through the Bracero Program or through undocumented immigration. Mexico could regulate the flow of those of its laborers who went to the US as braceros, a task that was much more difficult in the case of undocumented immigration (Hernández 2006). As an incentive for braceros to return to Mexico, the Mexican government withheld 10 percent of their wages and held those funds in Mexican banks, money they would supposedly receive upon their return migration. Years later, the Mexican government did not return the funds, which was the impetus for the Bracero Movement in 2004. As former braceros began to enter retirement, they began mobilizations to recover the 10 percent of the wages that had been held from their pay. Furthermore, to curtail the flow on undocumented immigration to the US during the Bracero era, Mexico negotiated initially and subsequently strengthened its demand that the US police its southern border to prevent undocumented immigration. Hernández (2006) points out that "beneath the [Bracero Program] agreement to import *braceros* were commitments to prevent Mexican laborers from surreptitiously crossing into the US and to aggressively detect and deport those who had successfully affected illegal entry" (p. 423). The US and Mexico governments worked bi-nationally to prevent Mexicans from entering the US without proper documentation.

Nonetheless, as soon as Mexican laborers found out about the initiation of the Bracero program, many ventured to Mexico City, where the Bracero Program recruitment center was headquartered. Upon arriving, however, many discovered that they were not eligible to participate in the Bracero Program. In particular, Hernández (2006) notes that "(o)nly healthy young men with agricultural experience, but without land, who had secured a written recommendation from local authorities verifying that their labor was not locally needed, were eligible for *bracero* contracts" (p. 425). Consequently, these prohibitive conditions stimulated a large number of individuals to go to the US as unauthorized persons in search of employment without the blessing of the Mexican and US government.

The outflow of Mexican laborers as undocumented immigrants resulted in an uproar among agribusiness employers who complained about the decimation of the local labor force. Indeed, Mexican President Manuel Ávila Camacho received significant grievances from landholders in such states as Baja California, Jalisco, and Tamaulipas who demanded a stop to the outpouring of Mexican laborers (Hernández 2006). Bracero workers, too, leveled complaints against the large flow of undocumented immigrants who they reasoned brought down wages and worsened labor conditions in general (Hernández 2006).

By 1943, the US dramatically increased the US Border Patrol's budget and border-patrol personnel along its southern border (Hernández 2006). When the enhanced border-patrol resources did not lead to a rise in deportations, the Mexican government pressed the US even more strongly to stop the Bracero Program, due to its own labor needs, which were aggravated by the outmigration of its workers (Hernández 2006). In response, Hernández (2006) observes that the chief supervisor of the US Border Patrol, W.F. Kelly, "launched an 'intensive drive on Mexican aliens' by deploying 'Special Mexican Deportation Parties' throughout the country" (p. 428). These efforts were successful in increasing the number of apprehensions of Mexican immigrants, with the sum more than doubling from 11,775 in 1943 to 28,173 in 1944 (Hernández 2006). Furthermore, the concentration of border-patrol efforts on the US southern border targeting Mexican immigrants resulted in Mexicans accounting for an annual average of 90 percent of all persons apprehended between 1943 and 1954 (Hernández 2006).

The US and Mexican governments made adjustments to make it more difficult for undocumented immigrants to return to the US after they were deported. Traditionally, unauthorized immigrants were deported at the US–Mexico border, making it easy for them to reenter. By April 1945, Mexican immigrants were routed to the interior and to places in Mexico that needed agricultural laborers, thus making it more difficult for them to return to the US (Hernández 2006). Mexico also placed its own border-patrol agents in its northern border, in such places as Tamaulipas, to make it more difficult for undocumented immigrants to enter the US, as well as to arrest those who tried to cross back into Mexico (Hernández 2006). Furthermore, as entry of undocumented immigrants shifted toward California, the US Border Patrol erected chain-link fences to deter immigration, thus sending immigrants toward more dangerous routes that placed them at risk of dehydration and hypothermia (Hernández 2006), hazards that we continue to see today.

Nonetheless, despite the concerted efforts by the US and Mexico governments to curtail undocumented immigration, the volume of apprehensions continued to climb in the early 1950s. For instance, the number of apprehensions of Mexican undocumented immigrants by US border-patrol agents along the Mexican border increased by 80 percent from 279,379 in 1949 to 501,713 in 1951 (Hernández 2006). Yet, one needs to keep in mind that the apprehensions represent episodes of apprehensions rather than individuals. Thus, a given individual could be apprehended, say, five times in a month, with the five apprehensions – instead of the one individual – tallied in the summation of apprehensions. It is estimated that by the end of the 1940s, one-third of apprehended individuals were "repeat offenders," i.e. they had been apprehended multiple times (US Immigration and Naturalization Service 1948; see also Hernández 2006).

Early in the 1950s, the US Border Patrol shifted its tactics toward an all-out attack on apprehending and deporting undocumented immigrants, a strategy that would serve as a model for Operation Wetback which would shortly come to fruition. Hernández (2006) describes this heightened approach:

> In February of 1950, US Border Patrol Inspector Albert Quillin of South Texas launched a new strategy that would soon form the core of US Border Patrol activities. "At 5 am, Tuesday, February 11, 1950, Quillin convened a detail of twelve border patrolmen with 'two buses, one plane, one truck, a carryall and . . . nine automobiles' at a 'point four miles east of Rio Hondo, Texas.'" There, the officers set up a miniature immigration station and split into two teams. Each team was given maps of the area and instructions to apprehend as many undocumented immigrants as possible, quickly process them through the temporary immigration station, and then place them on one of the waiting buses that would take deportees directly to the border. That day, about 100 undocumented Mexicans were deported from the Rio Hondo area. The next day, this same detail moved on to Crossroads Gin near Los Fresnos, Texas, and raided farms. By the end of the second day, an additional 561 undocumented Mexicans had been deported. On the third and fourth days, this detail moved into San Benito, Texas, from where they deported 398 Mexicans. Altogether, Quillin's detail apprehended over 1,000 undocumented laborers in four days of work. Word quickly spread regarding Quillin's accomplishments and within two weeks his model was being applied throughout South Texas. (pp. 440–441)

Quillin's model was dubbed "Operation Wetback." It was highly lauded and became a part of the operations of border-patrol agents across the Southwest. US border-patrol apprehensions nearly doubled from 459,289 in 1950 to 827,440 in 1953 (Hernández 2006). While the volume of apprehensions was inflated by repeat-offenders, the general public in the US and Mexico associated the rising numbers with a crisis (Hernández 2006).

Operation Wetback

In response to the increasing public concern, the US government officially launched Operation Wetback on May 1954. President Eisenhower picked retired Army general Joseph Swing as commissioner of the Immigration and Naturalization Service to lead the operation (Hernández 2006). Operation Wetback continued the practice established by Quillin along with the cooperation of the Mexican government which, as before, relocated deportees in areas within Mexico that had labor shortages. As Hernández (2006) notes, despite the lack of novelty with the official Operation Program compared to Quillin's model, Swing boasted about the success of the program which netted nearly 1.1 million apprehensions. This figure, however, truly overestimated the impact of the official Operation Wetback program as it reflects the number of apprehensions during Fiscal Year 1954, which terminated on June 30, 1954 (Hernández 2006). The existence of the official Operation Wetback program occupied only the last two weeks of Fiscal Year 1954 (Hernández 2006). The following fiscal year (1955), which contained the largest segment of Operation Wetback, resulted in only approximately 254,000 apprehensions (Hernández 2006). Operation Wetback officially was terminated in the late 1950s, coinciding with the end of the Eisenhower administration. The Immigration and Naturalization Service estimates that approximately 1.3 million apprehensions took place during the course of the program, although some suggest that this figure is inflated (Koestler 2013). Yet, Operation Wetback failed to stop the flow of Mexican undocumented immigrants, whose labor continued to be welcome by US growers (Ngai 2004). Still, in both its official and unofficial form Operation Wetback apprehended and deported countless Mexican undocumented immigrants through the collaborative efforts of the US and Mexico governments. It also reflects variations in the way the US government has viewed Mexican immigrants, in which the country welcomes them when they are needed and the economy is favorable and shuns them when they are unwanted and the economy is suffering.

The Bracero Program would go on to outlive Operation Wetback. Due to its popularity with US growers, the program survived significantly past the end of World War II. The Bracero Program finally ended in 1964. Approximately 4.8 million Mexicans came as contract workers as part of the Bracero Program (Cohen 2011; Gamboa 2000). It is important to understand that the Bracero experience was quite instrumental in the development of social capital and social networks on the part of braceros. Indeed, persons participating in the labor contract program gained a significant amount of information regarding distinct parts of the US and labor conditions, knowledge that helped people navigate the immigration route as well as wisdom that they could share with relatives and friends contemplating movement to the US. Such knowledge is essential for building and sustaining immigration ties between Mexico and the US, as illustrated by the network and cumulative causation theoretical perspectives described above.

There is a postscript story to the termination of the Bracero Program that needs to be told here, even though it does not involve US-based policy. The end of the Bracero Program brought a significant amount of concern to community leaders and public officials along Mexico's northern border. It was feared that once the program ended, braceros would remain in Mexican border communities rather than return to their homes in the interior of Mexico, thus exasperating the already high unemployment rates along the border. To avert such problems, the Mexican government established the Border Industrialization Program (BIP) in 1965 as a way of stimulating foreign investment and developing its northern border region. The program stipulated that foreign corporations establish "twin plants," one on the Mexican side and the other on the US side. The plants were referred to as *maquiladoras*, reflecting the Spanish term, signifying the portion of the product that the miller retains after grinding the stock. Videla (2008) notes the factors that BIP capitalized on in establishing the program: "proximity to the US; use of favorable articles of the US Tariff Code, which permits firms to import goods manufactured abroad with US components to reenter the US, paying duty only on the value-added, cheap labor; and a Mexican government friendly to investors" (p. 592). Videla (2008) intimates that BIP translated into "tax incentives for foreign firms, lax enforcement of environmental laws, and a blind eye to the breaking of labor laws" (p. 592).

From the beginning of BIP, US firms have taken advantage of the program incentives and Mexico's cheap labor force. Maquiladora operations soared after its implementation and were especially a bright economic spot in the Mexican economy during the 1980s, when the country experienced a major economic crisis that saw the peso plummet significantly (O'Neil 2013). In 2019, there were more than 3,000 maquiladoras, employing slightly more than 1.1 million workers along the northern Mexican border (Cross Border Freight 2019). The geographic and economic impact of maquiladoras expanded dramatically with the passage of the North American Free Trade Agreement (NAFTA) in 1994.

Again, the BIP and NAFTA and its newer iteration the United States–Mexico–Canada Agreement (see below) represent routes into which the US made inroads into the Mexican economy in search of labor and consumer markets. Furthermore, consistent with the world system theory, the movement of capital and products across international borders begets the immigration of people as well.

While the mid-1960s saw the termination of the movement of contract labor from Mexico to the US as part of the Bracero Program, it would result in a major shift in immigration policy that led to a notable change in the source of immigrants to the US.

Immigration and Nationality Act of 1965 (Hart–Celler Act)

The 1960s represented an era of social change in the US. In particular, groups that had been historically marginalized, most notably Blacks, called for their inclusion in all societal institutions. The Civil Rights Act of 1964 ushered in significant policies that sought to do just that in the areas of education, housing, employment, and voting. It was in this era that marked changes took place in immigration policy in the US. Recall that up to this point, immigration quotas favoring some groups, most notably northern and western Europeans, and limiting or completely excluding others (e.g. southern and eastern Europeans and Asians) were still in place. The Immigration and Nationality Act of 1965, also referred to as the Hart–Celler Act, ended the immigration quota system. In signing the bill, President Lyndon B. Johnson (1965) observed that the policy will ". . . repair a very deep and painful flaw in the fabric of American justice. It corrects a cruel and enduring wrong in the conduct of the American Nation . . . And this measure that we will sign today will really make us truer to ourselves both as a country and as a people" (p. 1).

The Immigration and Nationality Act of 1965 additionally included two major provisions. First, the act created two broad preference categories concerning family members and skilled workers. US citizens could petition to have three categories of immediate relatives gain entry into the US. The three immediate-relative categories included spouses of US citizens, children under 21 years of age of US citizens, and parents of US citizens (Liu et al. 1991). Individuals entering as immediate relatives were excluded from the hemisphere and country numerical limits of immigrants (see below). The preference system included six categories based on preferences: first preference: unmarried children (over 21 years of age) of US citizens (not more than 20% of total); second preference, spouses and children of permanent residents (26%, plus any slots not used for the first preference); third preference, professionals and scientists or artists of exceptional ability (not more than 10%); fourth preference, married children of US citizens (10%, plus any slots not allocated in the first three preferences); fifth preference, brothers and sisters of US citizens (24%, plus any slots not allocated in the first four preferences); and sixth preference, skilled and unskilled workers in occupations for which labor is in short supply in the US (not more than 10%) (Liu et al. 1991). Second, the act placed numerical limits on immigration, excluding exempted immediate family relative immigrants, based on hemisphere (170,000 for eastern hemisphere with a maximum of 20,000 for a given country in this hemisphere and 120,000 for western hemisphere with no limit imposed on any country in this hemisphere) (Reimers 1983).

There is a romanticized interpretation of the Immigration Act of 1965 as a policy that corrected a temporary lapse of the equitable and democratic American character (see, for example, Glazer 1987). However, as Luibheid (1997) argues, the Immigration and Nationality Act of 1965 was meant as rhetoric rather than to open the doors for non-white groups such as Asians, Africans, and Latin Americans. In fact, at the time that the bill was signed, President Johnson (1965) indicated that the policy was "not a revolutionary bill" and that it would "not affect the lives of millions" (p. 1). Many supporters of the bill argued that few Asians would immigrate to the US following the signing of the bill given that there were relatively few Asian immigrants in the country due to the Asia-Pacific Triangle which barred immigration from Asia. For example, Attorney General Robert Kennedy noted at most 5,000 Asians would enter the US the first year with the number virtually disappearing afterward (Center for Immigration Studies 1995). Similarly, Senator Edward Kennedy (D-MA) expressed assurance that immigrants, especially those from Africa and Asia, would not flood into the US and thus would not affect the current racial/ethnic composition of the country (Center for Immigration Studies 1995). Further, Senator Hiram Fong (R-HI) asserted that the bill would not change the culture of the US (Center for Immigration Studies 1995). Indeed, the bill was meant to erase the racist blemish associated with restrictive quotas and to alleviate the immigration of southern and eastern Europeans into the US (Reimers 1983). It was believed that because there were few Asians in the country, they would not benefit greatly from the new immigration policy. Similarly, Mexicans would now be subjected to immigration limits due to the ceiling of 120,000 for the western hemisphere.

In reality, the Immigration and Nationality Act of 1965 dramatically transformed the source of immigration from Europe to Latin America and Asia. The policy's focus on family benefitted Mexicans tremendously as US citizens were able to petition for close relatives to enter the US and undocumented immigration from Mexico rose with approximately one million undocumented immigrants apprehended along the US–Mexico border by the end of the 1970s (Reimers 1983). In addition, Cubans also benefited through provisions which allowed them to immigrate to the US as refugees (Reimers 1983). In addition, Asians were able to enter the US in large numbers through occupational and skill preferences with subsequent family sponsorship once the newcomers had obtained US citizenship alongside the admission of refugees from Indochina – from Vietnam, Cambodia, and Laos – into the US following the end of the Vietnam War (Liu et al. 1991; Reimers 1983). In the end, Reimers (1983) observes that "Clearly they [US policymakers] did not see how the new law would work, nor could they predict the fairly generous response to the US to the post 1965 refugee crisis, both of which have brought about a fundamental shift in historic immigration patterns to the US" (p. 25). Indeed, from the 1960s to the present, immigrants originating from Latin America have constituted at least two-fifths of all immigrants admitted to the US with Asians accounting for at least an additional one-third, with the percentage of immigrants from Europe ranging from 10 percent (1981–1990) to 18 percent (1971–1980) (Sáenz and Murga 2011).

Immigration Reform and Control Act of 1986 (Simpson-Mazzoli Act of 1986)

By the mid to late 1970s as undocumented immigration, particularly hailing from Mexico, rose significantly, many Americans were calling for major changes in immigration policy. After much debate, President Ronald Reagan in 1986 signed into law the Immigration Reform and Control Act (IRCA) in 1986 also known as the Simpson-Mazzoli Act of 1986. IRCA consisted of four major provisions: (1) amnesty for individuals who could document that they had been living in the US continuously since January 1, 1982, as well as for persons who could prove that they had worked at least 90 days in agriculture within the past year; (2) employer sanctions for persons who knowingly hired undocumented workers; (3) an assurance that there would be an adequate amount of seasonal and replacement agricultural workers for agricultural employees; and (4) an increase in funds to bolster enforcement at the US–Mexico border. Approximately three million persons received permanent residence status through IRCA with approximately three-fourths of these being Mexican (Massey et al. 2002).

IRCA had a significant impact on the structure of immigration in several ways. For example, immigrants gaining legal status through IRCA saw their wages increase (Aguilera 2004; Amuedo-Dorantes and Bansak 2011), though other research does not support this finding (Donato and Sisk 2012; Donato et al. 2008; Durand and Massey 2003). In addition, the attainment of legal status through IRCA freed immigrants to move in search of employment beyond traditional areas, resulting in the increasing movement of immigrants to new destination areas (see Chapter 5) primarily in the South and Midwest (Hernández León and Zúñiga 2000). Furthermore, US employers adapted to employer sanctions by using subcontractors to obtain workers, so not having to worry about whether or not their employees are documented (Phillips and Massey 1999; Taylor et al. 1997). Thus, employers are not liable given that they do not directly hire undocumented workers and the subcontractors benefit by retaining a portion of workers' wages for the provision of the legal buffer (Durand and Massey 2003).

North American Free Trade Agreement (NAFTA)

In the heels of the construction of the European Union (EU) signed on February 7, 1992, the US, Canada, and Mexico signed the North American Free Trade Agreement (NAFTA) in December 1992 with President Clinton signing NAFTA into law in the US in December 1993 and the program going into effect in 1994. In many ways, NAFTA formally marked the long economic association between, in particular, the US and Mexico. Indeed, Mexico opened its doors for business to the US extending back to the mid-nineteenth century under the Benito Juárez presidency and intensified under the 27-year Porfirio Díaz regime commonly known as the Porfiriato (O'Neil 2013). American economic moguls such as William Randolph Hurst along with the likes of the Guggenheims and Rockefellers invested heavily in Mexico and reaped massive wealth at that time (O'Neil 2013). More recently, as noted above, the BIP beginning in 1965, after the termination of the Bracero Program, opened up Mexico's northern border to foreign businesses, especially American ones. Unlike the EU agreement which saw stronger countries propping up weaker countries, such as Spain and Portugal, and opening up borders not only for capital and goods but for workers as well, NAFTA maintained the unequal relationship between Mexico and its northern neighbors and only allowed the movement of capital and products but not workers.

As the world system perspective (see above) suggests, the implementation of NAFTA led to major transformations in the Mexican economy including the uprooting of workers in some industrial sectors that could not compete with American producers. As NAFTA went into effect on January 1, 1994, the Zapatista Nationalist Liberation Army, under the direction of Subcomandante Marcos, rose to protest NAFTA and the anticipated negative economic impact on the population in Mexico's poorest regions, such as Chiapas. Corn producers were especially hurt economically by NAFTA as they were unable to compete with American corn producers who enjoyed government subsidies. As O'Neil (2013) notes, "some of the biggest aggregate losers from NAFTA were Mexico's small farmers, and rural poverty increased in the years following the passage of the free trade agreement" (p. 97). Not coincidentally, following the inception of NAFTA, Mexican emigration increased significantly in corn-producing states with large indigenous populations, notably Chiapas, which had traditionally not engaged in migration to the US (Batalova and Terrazas 2010). Thus, just as we saw global forces affecting the meat-packing industries in the late 1970s and 1980s with the ensuing development of Latina/o new-destination areas in the US Midwest and South regions (see Chapter 5), so too do we see international elements creating new-sending areas in Mexico (Batalova and Terrazas 2010).

NAFTA was eventually replaced by the United States–Mexico–Canada Agreement (USMCA) in 2018 and which went into effect in 2020. Many observers view that the NAFTA accord has been a win-win situation for Canada, Mexico, and the US. O'Neil

(2013) points out that while it is difficult to pinpoint success or failure associated directly with NAFTA due to major economic changes over the period since it has been in existence, she notes that the following are general patterns:

> In the years after NAFTA's signing, the economies of all three countries grew faster than the OECD average. Trade between the partners, too, increased much faster than overall world levels. Mexico's exports to the US grew fivefold and US exports to Mexico quadrupled, bringing the annual trade total to approximately US$460 billion in 2011. While the US was already Mexico's most important export market, it is now even more so, and Mexico has become the second most important destination for US exports in the world (following Canada). (95–96)

In addition, poverty has dropped significantly since the mid-1990s. For example, the percentage of people classified as poor under Mexico's governmental measures dropped from 70 percent to nearly 40 percent today (O'Neil 2013). Concurrently, there has been an expansion of Mexico's middle class. O'Neil (2013) observes that "In the last fifteen years, Mexico's middle [class] has blossomed. An open and diversifying economy, expanding home ownership and credit, new schools, new products, and new opportunities have all worked in its favor" (p. 106).

The Militarization of the Border

While the US opened its borders to the movement of capital and products into and out of Mexico with the establishment of NAFTA, the US sealed its southern border with the creation of a series of programs designed to make it more difficult for immigrants to enter the country at the most popular entry points. In September 1993, about three months before President Clinton signed NAFTA into law, the US Immigration and Naturalization Service (the precursor of the Department of Homeland Security) established Operation Blockade (later becoming Operation Hold the Line) in El Paso, Texas (Dunn 1996). Roughly a year later, in October 1994, INS launched Operation Gatekeeper in San Diego. Operation Safeguard was also mounted in Nogales, Arizona, in October 1994 and then again in 1999 as the flow of undocumented immigrants made their way into Arizona once the southern California entry point had been blockaded. Moreover, Operation Rio Grande was launched in August 1997 in the South Texas border (Brownsville and McAllen).

These operations have militarized the border and have made it difficult to enter the US through traditional entry routes (Dunn 2009). As conventional routes were sealed off, undocumented immigrants circumvented their way by taking dangerous and inhospitable routes through mountains and deserts, and the launching of operations to seal off the border at common entry points has resulted in significant increases in deaths among immigrants attempting to enter the US (Eschbach et al. 1999; Santos and Zemansky 2013). For example, the number of deaths associated with border crossing more than doubled between 1995 and 2006 in the Border Patrol's Tucson sector which includes much of the Arizona desert (US Government Accountability Office 2006). Over the last few years, as immigrant entry points have moved to South

Texas, there has been a significant increase in immigrant deaths in this region (Maccormack 2012). The irony, of course, is that while the NAFTA accord opened borders to the exchange of capital and products between countries, labor was not allowed to freely move across borders.

The Criminalization of Immigrants

These efforts to make it increasingly difficult for immigrants to enter the US through its southern border represented a harbinger of policies that criminalized immigrants. Two laws that President Clinton signed into law in 1996 set the stage for the criminalization of immigrants: Anti-Terrorism and Effective Death Penalty Act (AEDPA) and the Illegal Immigration Reform and Immigrant Responsibility Act (IIRIRA). Together, these policies further empowered the Immigration and Naturalization Service (the precursor of the Department of Homeland Security to apprehend, detain, and deport undocumented immigrants and minimized the rights of immigrants to appeal decisions affecting their deportation (Douglas and Sáenz 2013). AEDPA allowed for the deportation of unauthorized immigrants who committed any of a litany of crimes without any review (Douglas and Sáenz 2013; Verdeja 2002). The policy allowed immigrants to be deported for misdemeanors and considered offenses retroactively, e.g. they could be subject to deportation for committing crimes for which they had already served their time (Douglas and Sáenz 2013).

The IIRIRA policy further added a series of additional measures that criminalized unauthorized immigrants. In particular, IIRIRA "authorized the construction of a fourteen-mile fence along the US–Mexico border; doubled the force of border-patrol agents; allowed for summary exclusion of immigrants (for example, immigration officials were granted the authority to summarily deport individuals apprehended within one hundred miles of the border); expanded the grounds for deportation; reduced the allowable documents to satisfy I-9 requirements; and prohibited legal immigrants from federal welfare provisions for the first five years of their US residency" (Douglas and Sáenz 2013: 205; see also Fragomen 1997). Furthermore, IIRIRA "required the detention of all immigrants, including permanent residents, facing deportation for most criminal violations until the final resolution of the case" (Hines 2006, p. 17; see also Douglas and Sáenz 2013). In addition, IIRIRA's section 287(g) established authorized federal immigration officials to sign a memorandum of agreement (MOA) with state and local law enforcement officials which allowed the latter to execute federal immigration law enforcement activities (Douglas and Sáenz 2013).

Policy measures that criminalized immigrants were intensified immediately after the terrorist attacks of 9/11. A month after the strikes, President George W. Bush established the Department of Homeland Security to replace the Immigration and Naturalization Service (INS). Furthermore, in late October 2001 he signed into law the USA PATRIOT (Uniting and Strengthening America by Providing Appropriate Tools Required to Intercept and Obstruct Terrorism) Act of 2001. USA PATRIOT "significantly increased the budget for immigration enforcement; tripled the number of border-patrol agents on the northern border; expanded the government's ability to detain and deport terrorists, however defined; instituted a 'Special Registration' program [that] required men aged 16 to 45 from Arab and Muslim countries in residence in the US to register with the Department of Homeland Security and answer questions" [this program ended in May 2003] (Douglas and Sáenz 2013, p. 206).

The three programs outlined above (AEDPA, IIRIRA, and USA PATRIOT) led to a massive increase of immigrant detainees held in detention centers, many operated by the private sector (e.g. Corrections Corporation of America and the GEO group) (Douglas and Sáenz 2013). The average daily immigrant detainee population skyrocketed from 6,785 in 1994 to 33,330 in 2011 (Douglas and Sáenz 2013; Siskin 2007, 2012). The immigration detention business is quite lucrative and has been characterized as an immigration–industrial complex which benefits individuals with ties to the corporate, governmental, and criminal justice sectors (Douglas and Sáenz 2013; Dow 2004; Fernandez 2007; Golash-Boza 2009). Deportations have also increased noticeably over the last several years during the Obama administration. Indeed, the number of immigrant deportations reached an all-time high during the 2012 fiscal year (October 1, 2011 to September 30, 2012) at 409,849, 11 percent higher than the 369,221 immigrants deported during the 2008 fiscal year associated with the George W. Bush administration (Dinan 2012).

The election of Donald Trump as US president in 2016 led to greater animosity against immigrants seeking entrance into the US's southern border, many seeking political refugee status to protect them against violence and persecution not only in Central America, but more broadly from the Caribbean (Haitians and Cubans) and South America (Venezuela) and from other continents of the world. The Trump administration erected walls on the US–Mexico border to keep immigrants out of the country and used the COVID-19 pandemic to prevent immigrants from entering the US with immigrants largely stranded in Mexico's northern border.

As can be seen, over the last century there have been major changes in immigration policy. At certain periods, immigration policies and associated programs have been favorable toward Latin American immigration – particularly originating from Mexico – while at other times these have sought to deport immigrants or halt immigration to the US. One thing is certain – immigration policies have shifted the face of immigrants in the US.

Historical Latin American Immigration to the US

It is difficult to obtain the data necessary to directly enumerate the volume of immigration. This is particularly the case when we try to tally the flow of immigration over time. We draw here on historical immigration data from the US Department of Homeland Security (2023) on the volume of persons obtaining legal permanent resident status extending back to 1820. A few caveats are in order. First, the data represent a proxy for the level of immigration from a given region in the world for a certain time period given that the statistics enumerate the number of persons obtaining legal permanent resident status – as such, they could have lived in the US for any periods of time prior to being granted this status. Second, the immigration statistics do not account for all other immigrants who came during a given period through other routes including, for example, those who arrived as visitors or undocumented immigrants. Third, the data are based on the country of last residence rather than country of birth. Finally, the data presented here are aggregated across Latin America and, thus, includes some groups living in certain parts of Latin America such as the Caribbean (e.g. Haitians and Jamaicans), Central America (e.g. Belizeans), and South America (e.g. Brazilians, Guyanese, and Surinamese) that are not classified as Latina/o. In one part of the analysis (see Table 4.2 below), we are able to focus directly on Spanish-speaking countries in Latin America which is consistent with definitions on the Latina/o population.

Historically, nearly 88.5 million immigrants have obtained legal permanent resident status in the US between 1820 and 2022 (Table 4.1). Of these, the country of last residence is known for about 87.4 million individuals with approximately 47 percent originating from Europe. Latin Americans account for one-fourth of all immigrants who have secured legal permanent residence status. A considerable number of Latin American immigrants, largely originating from Mexico, have attained legal permanent residence status since the beginning of the twentieth century. For example, in the two decades (1910s and 1920s) surrounding the Mexican Revolution and its aftermath Latin Americans accounted for 9.4 percent of all immigrants who received legal permanent resident status in the US at that time.

Nonetheless, the passage of the Immigration Act of 1965 (Hart–Celler Act) represented a watershed event for Latin American immigrants. They constituted the largest segment of all immigrants who attained legal permanent residence status between the decades of the 1960s and that of the 2010s, with the peak taking place during the 1990s, when they comprised about 51 percent of this total. The percentage of Asians has also grown since the 1960s when they made up 11 percent of immigrants, who obtained legal permanent resident status at that time to a high of more than two-fifths in the 1980–1989 period. For Latin American and Asian immigrants, the decade of the 1990s represented each group's pinnacle with respect to the number of persons becoming legalized, with more than 4.9 million Latina/os and nearly 2.9 million Asians becoming legal permanent residents at that time. Thus far, between 2020 and 2022, Asians (922,546) who have obtained permanent resident status at that time outnumbered their counterparts from Latin America (908,892).

In contrast to the overall expansion of Latin Americans and Asians since the decade of the 1960s, the share of US immigrants obtaining legal permanent resident status who are European has dropped from 35 percent in the 1960s to a low of 9 percent in the 2020–2022 period. The peak level of Europeans receiving legalized status occurred more than a century ago, when close to 7.6 million Europeans obtained legalization in the 1900–1909 decade.

Overall, approximately eighteen million persons from Spanish-speaking Latin American countries have obtained legal permanent status over the last two centuries from 1820 to 2022 (Table 4.2). Persons from Mexico have accounted for more than half (52.6%) of these individuals. Mexicans along with Cubans, Dominicans,

Table 4.1 Persons Obtaining Legal Permanent Resident Status by Region and Period

Period	Latin America	Europe	Asia	Africa	Oceania	Other America	Not Specified	Total
1820–1829	7,358	99,618	34	19	2	2,298	19,173	128,502
1830–1839	20,030	422,853	55	66	1	11,881	83,495	538,381
1840–1849	16,231	1,369,423	121	67	3	34,296	7,196	1,427,337
1850–1859	19,974	2,622,617	36,080	104	110	64,227	71,442	2,814,554
1860–1869	12,372	1,880,389	54,408	458	107	118,055	15,472	2,081,261
1870–1879	21,036	2,252,050	134,071	441	9,094	324,853	592	2,742,137
1880–1889	32,318	4,638,684	71,152	768	7,341	497,527	778	5,248,568
1890–1899	34,682	3,576,411	61,304	432	3,279	4,074	14,112	3,694,294
1900–1909	154,742	7,572,569	300,441	6,326	11,677	123,140	33,493	8,202,388
1910–1919	361,824	4,985,411	269,736	8,867	12,339	708,715	488	6,347,380
1920–1929	641,963	2,560,340	126,740	6,362	9,860	949,315	930	4,295,510
1930–1939	67,591	444,404	19,292	2,120	3,240	162,728	0	699,375
1940–1949	142,240	472,524	34,532	6,720	14,262	186,195	135	856,608
1950–1959	508,335	1,404,973	135,844	13,016	11,319	413,309	12,472	2,499,268
1960–1969	1,218,990	1,133,443	358,563	23,780	23,659	455,204	119	3,213,758
1970–1979	1,723,766	826,327	1,406,526	71,405	39,983	179,870	326	4,248,203
1980–1989	2,538,108	669,694	2,391,356	141,987	41,432	156,396	305,406	6,244,379
1990–1999	4,942,317	1,349,219	2,859,899	346,410	56,800	194,825	25,928	9,775,398
2000–2009	4,205,161	1,349,609	3,470,835	759,734	65,793	236,368	211,930	10,299,430
2010–2019	4,249,599	906,816	4,062,777	1,037,674	59,663	183,495	133,422	10,633,446
2020–2022	908,892	200,173	922,546	223,889	14,445	37,270	158,498	2,465,713
Total	21,827,529	40,737,547	16,716,312	2,650,645	384,409	5,006,775	1,095,407	88,455,890

Source: US Department of Homeland Security (2023).

Table 4.2 Spanish-Speaking Latin American Countries Ranked by Most Persons Obtaining Legal Permanent Resident Status by Period

Country	1820–2022	1960–1969	1970–1979	1980–1989	1990–1999	2000–2009	2010–2019	2020–2002
Mexico	9,464,237	441,824	621,218	1,009,586	2,757,418	1,704,166	1,506,738	317,340
Cuba	1,749,333	202,030	256,497	132,552	159,037	271,742	479,818	69,122
Dominican Republic	1,705,789	83,552	139,249	221,552	359,818	291,492	503,978	89,962
El Salvador	971,984	14,405	29,428	137,418	273,017	251,237	198,974	56,804
Colombia	871,581	68,371	71,265	105,494	137,985	236,570	186,833	42,749
Guatemala	532,828	14,357	23,837	58,847	126,043	156,992	115,704	30,896
Peru	480,554	19,783	25,311	49,958	110,117	137,614	112,753	17,039
Ecuador	462,025	34,107	47,464	48,015	81,358	107,977	107,624	24,325
Honduras	344,532	15,087	15,653	39,071	72,880	63,513	98,276	32,030
Venezuela	330,989	20,758	11,007	22,405	35,180	82,087	103,671	41,488
Nicaragua	256,502	10,383	10,911	31,102	80,446	70,015	31,775	9,096
Argentina	249,592	49,384	30,303	23,442	30,065	47,955	37,981	9,446
Panama	157,223	22,177	21,395	32,957	28,149	18,120	12,290	2,478
Costa Rica	127,932	17,975	12,405	25,017	17,054	21,571	22,320	5,698
Chile	114,073	12,384	15,032	19,749	18,200	19,792	17,142	4,990
Bolivia	85,876	6,205	5,635	9,798	18,111	21,921	17,164	3,308
Uruguay	51,236	4,089	8,416	7,235	6,062	9,827	11,420	2,084
Paraguay	22,611	1,249	1,486	3,518	6,082	4,623	4,117	837
Total	17,979,608	1,038,120	1,346,512	1,977,716	4,317,022	3,517,214	3,568,578	759,692

Source: US Department of Homeland Security (2023).

Salvadorans, Colombians, and Guatemalans make up 85 percent of all persons from the Spanish-speaking countries of Latin American who have gained legal permanent resident status. In the post-1960 period, the share of Mexicans among people from Latin America receiving legal permanent resident status peaked in the 1990s (64%) but their share has fallen since then to 48.5% in 2000–2009 to 42.2% in 2010–2019 and to 41.8% in 2020–2022.

The peak period for the attainment of legalized status for the ten national-origin groups with the most immigrants has occurred in the last several decades. For example, the largest number of persons obtaining legal permanent resident status occurred in the 1990–1999 period, for people moving from Mexico and El Salvador, while the peak decade of legalization took place in the 2000–2009 period, for people migrating from Colombia, Guatemala, Peru, and Ecuador and the peak decade was 2010–2020 for those originating from Cuba, the Dominican Republic, Honduras, and Venezuela. The case of Venezuelans is quite unique. Over the last couple of decades Venezuelans have fled economic and political problems and violence in their home country to seek a better life in surrounding countries and the United States. Of the nearly 290,000 Venezuelans who have ever received legal permanent resident status, half of these have obtained this status since 2010.

The increasing diversity of Latin Americans and Caribbeans gaining legalized status is reflected in the rising prevalence of particular groups of immigrants. For instance, four Latin American and Caribbean countries (Cuba, the Dominican Republic, Honduras, and Venezuela) made up 28 percent of all Latin American and Caribbean immigrants legalized during the 2010–2019 period. While information on legal permanent residents in the country is useful to gain an understanding of historical trends on the volume of people who have obtained this status, it is important to remember that these individuals did not necessarily immigrate at the same time that they attained their legalized status.

We can obtain an estimate of the number of Latina/o immigrants who were in the US in 2022 through the examination of data from the 2022 American Community Survey (ACS) Public-Use File (Ruggles et al. 2024). While the data are not historical, they do have a few advantages over the US Department of Homeland Security (2023) used in the analysis described above. In particular, the data are based on foreign-born persons who identified themselves as Latina/o and who immigrated to the US regardless of their method of entry as well as their current legal status. Note that we include Afro-Latina/os in the analysis below, but they are not a mutually exclusive groups as their numbers are also part of the specific national-origin group of which they are members.

In 2022 there were 20.3 million Latina/os who immigrated at some time to the US (Table 4.3). Mexicans account for 52 percent of Latina/o immigrants in the US, down from 62 percent in 2010. Seven other groups (Salvadorans, Cubans, Dominicans, Guatemalans, Colombians, Hondurans, and Venezuelans), each with more than a half million immigrants, made up an additional 35 percent of Latina/o immigrants in the country. Altogether, then, these seven groups along with Mexicans account for 87 percent of all Latina/o immigrants in the nation.

Table 4.3 Number of Latina/o Immigrants and Related Statistics for Selected Groups, 2022

Latina/o Group	Number Immigrants	Pct. of Population Immigrants	Pct. of Immigrants Naturalized Citizens	Immigrant Median Years in US
Afro-Latina/o[a]	144,864	14.1	51.4	19
Argentinian	172,915	56.7	58.3	21
Bolivian	73,072	52.9	62.6	22
Colombian	869,639	60.7	58.4	20
Costa Rican	89,088	45.7	58.3	22
Cuban	1,311,359	53.5	64.2	19
Dominican	1,238,763	51.5	55.9	18
Ecuadorian	492,224	55.9	50.5	21
Guatemalan	1,062,463	56.8	27.4	16
Honduran	756,559	63.0	22.2	10
Mexican	10,578,153	28.3	35.2	24
Nicaraguan	286,787	57.6	54.5	23
Panamanian	103,735	51.0	53.5	23
Paraguayan	15,082	64.6	61.8	21
Peruvian	424,513	56.6	63.7	22
Puerto Rican	119,851	2.0	48.6	22
Salvadoran	1,334,354	53.7	35.9	21
Spaniard	144,401	14.7	49.8	19
Uruguayan	43,766	58.4	54.4	21
Venezuelan	600,553	76.3	30.2	6
All Other Latina/os	617,227	17.4	50.2	23
Total	20,334,504	32.0	40.8	22

[a] Afro-Latina/os are also included in their specific Latina/o national-origin group.

Source: Data from 2022 American Community Survey 1-Year Estimates (Ruggles et al. 2024).

The twenty million Latina/o immigrants account for approximately one of every three Latina/os. Yet, there is significant variation across Latina/o immigrant groups. Of the twenty-one Latina/o groups included in the analysis, fifteen have more than half of their members being immigrants with the highest level being among Venezuelans, with more than three-fourths (76.3%) being born outside of the US, which is consistent with the legal permanent resident status analysis presented above, showing that half of all Venezuelans who have received this status obtained it since 2010. Three other groups have upwards of 60 percent of their members being immigrants (Paraguayans, 64.6%; Hondurans, 63.0%; and Colombians, 60.7%. On the other hand, only 2 percent of Puerto Ricans are immigrants with Spaniards (14.7%), all other Latina/os (17.4%), and Afro-Latina/os (14.1) also having relatively low levels of immigrants. Despite the stereotypical image of Mexicans as immigrants, a little fewer than three of every ten Mexicans (28%) in the US are immigrants. The relative low percentage of immigrants among Mexicans is due to their long history in this country, spanning in some cases seven or more generations in the US.

Overall, a little more than two of every five Latina/o immigrants have become naturalized citizens. Yet, fourteen of the twenty-one groups have naturalization rates above 50 percent, with four groups having rates above 60 percent (Cubans, 64.2%; Peruvians, 63.7%; Bolivians, 62.6%; and Paraguayans, 61.8%). On the other hand, five groups have naturalization rates below 36 percent (Salvadorans, 35.9%; Mexicans, 35.2%; Venezuelans, 30.2%; Guatemalans, 27.4%; and Hondurans, 22.2%). In general, the low naturalization rates of Mexicans, Salvadorans, Guatemalans, and Hondurans reflect their relatively low socioeconomic levels, while the recency of immigration of Venezuelans to the US accounts for their low level of naturalization.

Finally, overall, Latina/o immigrants have resided in the US a median of twenty-two years. This signifies that, in general, immigrants have been in this country for a good amount of time. Mexican immigrants have the longest median stay in this country with a median of twenty-four years, which reflects their long immigration experience compared to other Latina/o immigrants. On the other side of the spectrum, Venezuelans, who are much more recent immigrants, have the lowest time spent in the US with a median of six years. Guatemalan and Honduran immigrants also have a relative short stay in this nation with a median of sixteen and ten years, respectively.

Latina/o Immigration in the Last Decade

The last couple of decades have seen a significant decline in immigration from Mexico and a slowdown from the rest of Latin American. Compared to fertility and mortality, immigration is less stable, as it is impacted by the state of the economy, immigration policies, political factors, and, as we recently observed, a pandemic, among other factors. Certainly, the Great Recession and the loss of construction jobs, alongside massive detention and deportations during the Bush, Obama, and Trump administrations, played a factor in the immigration decline from Mexico. But what has taken place more recently?

To answer this question, we examine the annual number of non-US-citizen Latina/os who migrated from abroad to the United States in each year between 2012 and 2022. We use data from the annual ACS public-use files to conduct the analysis. Because of response issues associated with the 2020 ACS during the first year of the pandemic, data are not available for that specific year.

Annual immigration data for the overall Latina/o population are presented in Figure 4.1. Before the pandemic, there was an increase in immigration from 2012 to 2016, followed by a decline in 2018 and another increase in 2019. The volume of Latina/o immigration fell by 25 percent between 2019 and 2021. However, immigration increased significantly between 2021 and 2022, with a rise of 72 percent. The 475,000 persons who immigrated to the US in 2022 represents the highest number of immigrants over the last decade.

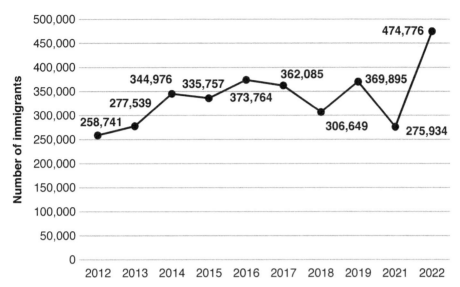

Figure 4.1 Annual Number of Latina/o Immigrants to the US by Year, 2012 to 2022

Source: Data from 2022 American Community Survey 1-Year Estimates (Ruggles et al. 2024).

In general, Latina/os groups experienced increases in their levels of immigration across three time periods (2012, 2017, and 2022) (Table 4.4). Of the twenty Latina/o groups that we examine, eighteen had immigration increases between 2012 and 2017, as did fourteen between 2017 and 2022. Six groups experienced an increase in immigration between 2012 and 2017 but a decline between 2017 and 2022 (Afro-Latina/os, Dominicans, Paraguayans, Puerto Ricans, Salvadorans, and Spaniards). Mexicans and Ecuadorians had a decline in immigrants between 2012 and 2017 but an increase between 2017 and 2022. Some additional trends emerge from the analysis. First, Mexicans had the largest number of immigrants in each of the three time periods. However, their percentage share of all Latina/o immigrants declined from 45.6 percent in 2012 to 30.6 percent in 2017 and to 27.4 percent in 2022. Second, Venezuelan immigration soared from 7,258 in 2012 to 51,955 in 2022, a seven-fold increase. Among the twenty Latina/o groups, the ranking of Venezuelans based on annual immigration climbed from 8th in 2012 to 2nd in 2017 and 2022. Third, Cubans and Colombians were generally among the top four groups in the ranking on immigration. Fourth, Honduras experienced significant increases in immigration nearly tripling between 2012 and 2022, as was the case with Nicaraguans, whose volume of immigration ascended eleven-fold between 2012 and 2022.

We highlight three Latina/o groups that stand out with their increasing levels of immigration. Figure 4.2 shows the annual number of immigrants for each of the years between 2012 and 2022. Venezuelans, Hondurans, and Nicaraguans have been prominent groups that have made their way to the Texas border in search of political asylum and better economic conditions. Between 2021 and 2022, the number of Nicaraguan immigrants to the US quintupled, while the number of Venezuelans

Table 4.4 Annual Number of Immigrants to the US by Latina/o Group, 2012, 2017, and 2022

Latina/o Group	2012	2017	2022
Afro-Latina/o[a]	3,999	7,732	6,573
Argentinian	2,209	2,358	8,773
Bolivian	423	599	1,158
Colombian	16,409	27,097	43,972
Costa Rican	622	2,034	3,775
Cuban	27,295	34,593	49,357
Dominican	17,584	27,123	21,992
Ecuadorian	7,028	6,059	15,268
Guatemalan	15,077	19,088	25,803
Honduran	10,232	21,234	38,677
Mexican	117,983	110,689	130,268
Nicaraguan	2,264	3,456	24,847
Panamanian	2,260	2,832	5,095
Paraguayan	1,120	1,233	319
Peruvian	6,382	8,439	11,550
Puerto Rican	42	1,763	1,015
Salvadoran	15,250	28,578	20,851
Spaniard	5,572	11,050	7,117
Uruguayan	423	525	711
Venezuelan	7,258	46,029	51,955

[a] Afro-Latina/os are also included in their specific Latina/o national-origin group.

Source: Data from 2012, 2017, and 2022 American Community Survey 1-Year Estimates (Ruggles et al. 2024).

increased 3.5 times. Honduran immigration peaked in 2019 with the level of immigration increasing between 2012 and 2022.

In sum, we have provided a historical and contemporary overview of immigration from Latin America and the Caribbean. There is one cautionary word. The data that we have just analyzed are based on people who have immigrated to the US and who were part of the American Community Survey. There is certainly an undercount of actual immigrants. In addition, there are undocumented individuals who are not counted because they are either in detention centers or have been deported.

Expulsion and Apprehensions of Latina/os

The rising immigration of Latina/os originating from Latin America and the Caribbean has been associated with growing deportations. Table 4.5 presents the number of persons from Spanish-speaking Latin American and Caribbean nations involving Title 42 expulsions and non-citizen apprehensions. Unfortunately, we are not able to disaggregate the numbers of Trade 42 expulsions and non-citizen apprehensions.

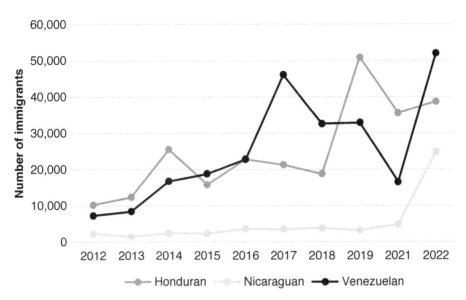

Figure 4.2 Annual Immigration for Hondurans, Nicaraguans, and Venezuelans by Year, 2012 to 2022

Source: Data from 2012 to 2022 American Community Survey 1-Year Estimates (Ruggles et al. 2024).

Between 2013 and 2022, 9.3 million people from Spanish-speaking Latin American and Caribbean countries have been removed from the country or apprehended. The number doubled from 1.1 million in 2019 to 2.3 million in 2022. Mexico, with 4.3 million people from this country removed or apprehended in the US, accounts for 46 percent of all persons expulsed or apprehended during this period, followed by Guatemala (1.5 million), Honduras (1.4 million), El Salvador (726,000), Cuba (336,000), Venezuela (283,000), and Nicaragua (263,000).

New Immigration Patterns from Mexico and Latin America

Despite the major increases in the volume of immigration from Latin America during the twentieth century, as shown in the analysis above, there has been a noticeable slowdown in Latin American immigration to this country. This can be shown by examining data from the ACS on the volume of persons who are not US citizens and who migrated within the last year to the United States from abroad over four time periods (2000–2004, 2005–2009, 2010–2014, and 2015–2019). Figure 4.3 shows that the volume of immigration from Asia surpassed that from Latin America in the 2010–2014 and 2015–2019 periods, the first time ever in the twentieth and twenty-first centuries. Overall, the number of persons migrating from Asia to the US between the 2000–2004 and 2015–2019 periods rose by 50 percent while the number moving from Latin America declined by 28 percent.

However, the decline in immigration from Latin America was particularly acute for the movement originating in Mexico (Figure 4.4). Despite the sliding number

Table 4.5 Number of Title 42 Expulsions and Non-Citizen Apprehensions by Country of Nationality, 2013 to 2022

Country	2013	2014	2015	2016	2017	2018	2019	2020	2021	2022	2013–2022
Mexico	472,720	405,844	330,921	325,348	264,716	307,535	312,130	362,105	695,582	836,844	4,313,745
Guatemala	75,041	101,695	73,111	97,967	93,519	153,814	292,022	62,848	293,954	243,913	1,487,884
Honduras	65,965	112,530	45,228	68,778	67,225	103,533	276,805	52,920	331,397	230,593	1,354,974
El Salvador	52,389	81,651	53,336	88,097	67,500	47,993	102,484	23,887	104,586	104,261	726,184
Cuba	15,432	3,724	3,014	3,739	5,076	10,065	36,082	15,048	40,549	233,602	366,331
Venezuela	679	640	683	1,333	2,383	4,210	10,465	4,265	52,590	206,075	283,323
Nicaragua	2,968	3,228	1,900	2,086	2,005	4,547	15,641	3,123	52,633	175,054	263,185
Ecuador	6,032	6,640	3,995	4,222	3,308	3,277	15,451	13,808	102,575	33,255	192,563
Colombia	3,007	2,568	2,807	3,256	3,491	4,066	4,705	2,970	10,381	140,059	177,310
Peru	2,054	1,952	1,256	1,424	1,415	1,631	1,822	1,120	4,053	55,677	72,404
Dominican Republic	5,201	4,634	3,788	3,708	3,496	3,581	3,836	3,056	3,934	8,628	43,862
Chile	217	302	420	522	689	698	1,171	1,345	7,933	10,047	23,344
Costa Rica	535	532	378	430	469	556	543	395	780	1,174	5,792
Argentina	373	348	280	246	367	338	469	423	724	1,179	4,747
Panama	311	189	190	167	170	174	193	131	615	1,694	3,834
Bolivia	292	265	166	192	225	231	227	135	306	1,442	3,481
Uruguay	164	122	70	72	117	100	133	60	208	417	1,463
Paraguay	55	41	37	37	43	55	61	66	107	88	590
Total	703,435	726,905	521,580	601,624	516,214	646,404	1,074,240	547,705	1,702,907	2,284,002	9,325,016

Source: US Department of Homeland Security (2023).

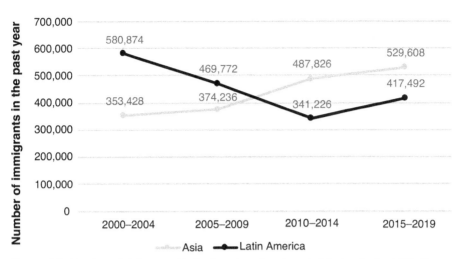

Figure 4.3 Number of Asians and Latin American Immigrants Moving to the US in the Past Year by Period
Source: Data from 2004, 2009, 2014, and 2019 American Community Survey 5-Year Estimates (Ruggles et al. 2024).

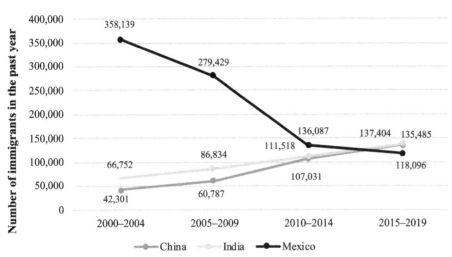

Figure 4.4 Number of Immigrants Moving from China, India, and Mexico to the US in the Past Year by Period
Source: Data from 2004, 2009, 2014, and 2019 American Community Survey 5-Year Estimates (Ruggles et al. 2024).

of immigrants originating from Mexico through the four periods in the twenty-first century, Mexico accounted for the most immigrants coming to the United for three of the four time periods. This changed in 2015–2019 when Mexico was ranked third behind India and China. Indeed, the volume of persons immigrating from Mexico to the US in the 2015–2019 period was only one-third of the volume that occurred in the

2000–2004 period. In contrast, the number of immigrants from China in 2015–2019 was 3.2 times larger than the number of immigrants in 2000–2004, with the respective ratio being 2.1 times larger for immigrants from India.

Latina/o Immigration in the Future

The movement of people from throughout Latin America and the Caribbean to the US has occurred over a sustained time period. This is particularly the case among Mexicans. Mexican immigration to the US has been unique in various ways, for no other group immigrating to the US from throughout the world has the experience of Mexican immigrants. For example, Mexican immigrants coming to the US are moving to land that once belonged to their country. Through the Treaty of Guadalupe Hidalgo in 1848 at the conclusion of the Mexican–American War, Mexico ceded more than half of its territory to the US, forming much of the southwestern portion of the US today. In addition, substantial immigration from Mexico to the US has occurred virtually unaltered for a century. Furthermore, the proximity of Mexico to the US has historically allowed Mexicans to move back and forth relatively easily, although the militarization of the border after 9/11 has made this more difficult.

Immigration has been important in other ways besides altering the demography of the Latina/o population. The constant flow of immigrants from Latin America has served to reinforce and enrich the Spanish language and cultures stemming from the countries of origin. Immigrants bring with them their Spanish language (and increasingly indigenous languages) and their cultural values and practices. This means that the perpetual arrival of newcomers strengthens the Spanish language and cultures of the Latina/o community in the US. In addition, as noted in Chapter 1, with the growth of the Latina/o population we have also seen the increase of Spanish-language instruction as well as the rising popularity of Latina/o foods and music.

Yet, as the Latina/o population has expanded in the US, there has been a backlash against the group, with immigrants becoming a primary target of those that want to halt immigration. Over the last several decades there has been continual debate over the economic and social impact of Latina/o immigrants – especially Mexican immigrants – on the US. One of the latest treatises warning against the detrimental impact of Latina/o immigrants on the country's cultural fabric is Samuel Huntington's (2004) book *Who Are We? The Challenges to America's National Identity*. He contended that the values of Mexicans clash with those of the puritanical and British values that form the foundation of the US. In addition, there has also been a rise of anti-immigrant sentiment against Latina/os, immigrants and native-born alike, through the formation of vigilante groups, hate speech, and local policies targeting Latina/o immigrants, particularly since the beginning of the Trump era. At the same time, however, there are opposing forces, most notably the business community, that recognize the value of Latina/o immigrants, particularly in the domain of the economy. Latina/o immigrants represent the bedrock of many industries that depend on them heavily as the primary labor force, including the agriculture, construction, homecare, hotel, landscape, and restaurant sectors. Severe cuts in the availability of Latina/o immigrant labor in these industries would have a tremendous effect on these sectors of the economy and would drive up consumer costs significantly.

However, as we opened this chapter, animosity and hate against undocumented immigrants has grown in this country, especially as countless numbers of immigrants not only from Latin America but from many other parts of the world have come to the US's southern border seeking asylum from violence and political persecution. The border region has been the center of controversy, with many calling this area a war zone. Princeton University sociologist and demographer Douglas Massey (2020) has reminded us that the situation at the border is not an immigration emergency but a humanitarian emergency. He asserts that there is a major need for humanitarian policies but is skeptical that it can happen within the current political divide.

Summary

In this chapter, we provided an overview of theoretical perspectives that have been used to explain international migration. We also overviewed policies and programs that have been associated with shifts in immigration to the US. In addition, we examined the changing source of immigration to the US from Europe to Latin America and Asia over the last half century. One major change over the last few years has been the decline in immigration from Mexico. Whether this is a short- or long-term situation remains to be seen. While people on the political left and right disagree on ways to deal with the immigration issue, both sides do agree that the immigration system is broken. The current situation at the border amply illustrates the major need for the establishment of humanitarian immigration policy. It has been nearly four decades since immigration policy was enacted in the form of IRCA. We now turn in the following chapter to provide an overview of the demography of the Latina/o population and the significant role that immigration has played. We will point out in the next chapter that as the US population ages, alongside declining birth rates, there will be major needs for workers. Many children who have risked their lives and everything they have to come to the US in search of a better life, many fleeing for their lives, represent a potential workforce for this country.

Discussion Questions

1. What are the immigration theories that help us understand how immigration begins? What about the theories that help us understand how immigration is sustained?

2. What is the significance of the Mexican Repatriation Program?

3. What was the Bracero Program?

4. Which immigration policy helped change the face of immigration to the United States becoming more Latin American and Asian?

5. What is one of the most significant historical events related to Mexican immigration in the twenty-first century?

6. Do you think that the volume of Mexican immigration will rebound to levels seen at the close of the twentieth century and beginning of the twenty-first century?

7. Do you think the current situation involving large numbers of immigrants arriving at the border is a crisis? Why, or why not?

5 The Demography of Latina/os

Leobardo Estrada (1945–2018), who spent most of his career at UCLA, had a long and distinguished career as a demographer. He made many important contributions to the conceptualization, definition, and understanding of the Latina/o population. Estrada had a deep passion for putting to use demographic research to make a difference in the real world. He dedicated his demographic skills and insights to numerous nonprofit organizations, most prominently the Mexican American Legal Defense and Education Fund (MALDEF) and the National Association of Latino Elected Officials (NALEO) (see Braswell 2019). Estrada had a front-row seat in the transformation of the Latina/o population from a small population concentrated in a few regions of the country to the nation's second largest group behind the white population. He was a mentor to many students and young scholars and inspired generations of students to do the good work – using demography to improve the conditions of Latina/os.

As Estrada observed during his career, the Latina/o population has changed tremendously over the last half century and has grown dramatically during this period. In 1965 the Latina/o population was largely composed of Mexicans with a small Puerto Rican population and an even smaller Cuban population. In addition, at that time only about 15 percent of Latina/os were born outside of the US. More than a half century later, the Latina/o population is much more diverse, encompassing groups from throughout Latin America and the Caribbean as well as Spain. Moreover, this change has occurred through the increasing immigration from throughout Latin America and the Caribbean, with nearly one-third of Latina/os today born outside of the US.

With the increasing demographic prominence of the Latina/o population over the last several decades, Latina/os have become the engine of the US population. Today, Latina/os account for approximately half of the overall population growth of the US. If it were not for Latina/os, the US would be a tremendously different country demographically. Indeed, it would resemble many European countries and selected Asian countries that are characterized by minute population growth or even declining populations brought about through a significant aging of the population alongside exceptionally low levels of fertility. Instead, the US has a higher percentage of persons less than 15 years of age and a lower percentage of persons 65 and older than all but a handful of European countries today (Population Reference Bureau 2022), largely due to the demographic influence of its Latina/o population.

This chapter describes the major population growth of the Latina/o population over the recent past. It highlights the various factors that have produced this growth, including the group's young age structure, high fertility, low mortality, and high immigration and the slowdown in population growth that Latina/os have experienced since the Great Recession. The chapter examines population projections which point to the increasing presence of Latina/os in the US population over the coming decades. Subsequently, the chapter ends with an overview of the significant variations across Latina/o subgroups.

Latina/o Population Trends

We can examine the population trends in the US over the last four decades to illustrate the increasing importance of Latina/os to the demographics of the US population. Over the last four decennial censuses the Latina/o population has increased rapidly from 14.6 million in 1980 to 22.4 million in 1990 to 35.3 million in 2000 to 50.5 million in 2010 and to 62.1 million in 2020 (Figure 5.1). Hence, the Latina/o population increased 4.25 times during the last forty years. In fact, if the US Latina/o population were a country in 2020, it would have been the twenty-second largest country in the world, outnumbering Italy, Tanzania, and South Africa (Population Reference Bureau 2020).

The Latina/o population has expanded at a rapid clip over the last four decades. The growth was especially fast during the 1990 to 2000 period when the Latina/o population increased by 58 percent, while the percentage change has been the slowest at 23 percent during the last decade (2010–2020) (Figure 5.2). The slower growth in the last decade reflects the significant decline in immigration from Mexico and in births among Latinas, beginning in 2008 during the Great Recession. Still, the Latina/o population has grown much more rapidly compared to the nation's overall population,

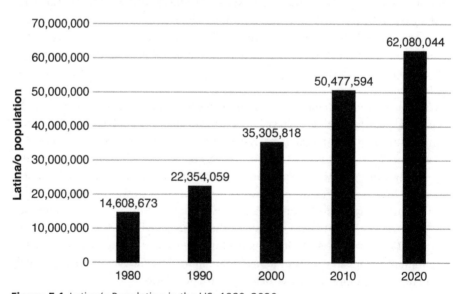

Figure 5.1 Latina/o Population in the US, 1980–2020

Sources: Hobbs and Stoops (2002) and US Census Bureau (2024).

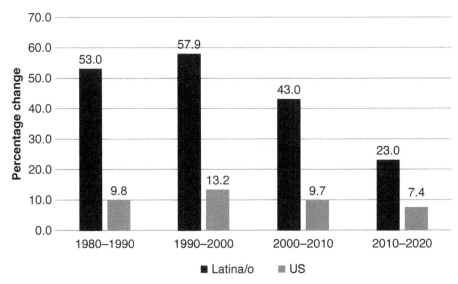

Figure 5.2 Percentage Change in the Latina/o and US Populations by Period
Sources: Hobbs and Stoops (2002) and US Census Bureau (2024).

increasing 5.4 times faster in 1980–1990, 4.4 times faster in 1990–2000 and 2000–2010, and 3.1 times more swiftly in 2010–2020.

Over the last three decades the Latina/o population has accounted for a disproportionate share of the US overall population growth each decade. For example, despite its relatively small percentage share of the US population in 1980 (6.4%), Latina/os accounted for more than one-third (34.9%) of the nation's total population growth in the 1980–1990 period, expanding to approximately two-fifths (39.6%) in the 1990–2000 period, and to more than half (55.5%) in the 2000–2010 and 2010–2020 (51.1%) periods (Figure 5.3). These trends support the notion that Latina/os represent the engine of the US population.

Illustratively, the Latina/o population has expanded its percentage share of the total US population over the last four decades. Latina/os comprised one of every sixteen (6.4%) persons in the US in 1980 with its share magnifying to one of every eleven persons in 1990, to one of every eight persons in 2000, to one of every six individuals in 2010, and to nearly one of every five in 2020 (Figure 5.4).

Why has the Latina/o population grown so rapidly compared to other segments of the US population? In fact, Latinos and whites represent polar opposites concerning the rate of population change. As noted above, Latina/os have accounted for a major part of the US population growth, while the percentage share due to whites has waned. There are four demographic factors that account for the rapid growth of the Latina/o population – a youthful age structure, relatively high levels of immigration, relatively high rates of fertility, and low levels of mortality. Each of these factors is illustrated below to understand the dynamics behind the swift growth of the Latina/o population relative to the white and other populations.

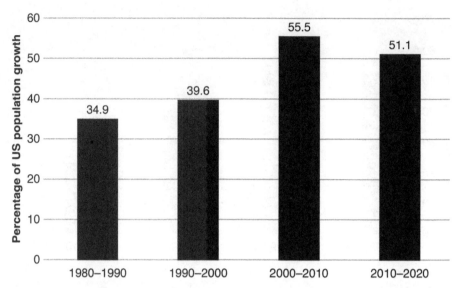

Figure 5.3 Percentage of US Population Growth Due to Latina/o Population Growth by Period

Sources: Hobbs and Stoops (2002) and US Census Bureau (2024).

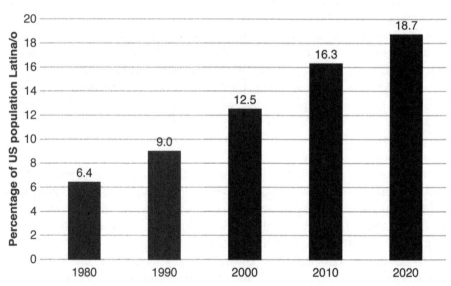

Figure 5.4 Percentage Share of Latina/os in US Population, 1980–2020

Sources: Hobbs and Stoops (2002) and US Census Bureau (2024).

Age Structure

The disparate growth of Latina/os and whites in the US is due principally to the distinctions in the age structures of these groups. In particular, Latina/os represent the youngest racial or ethnic group in the US with a median age of 30.7, while whites are much older, with a median age of 44.1 in 2021.

The differences in age structure can be viewed graphically by examining the age–sex pyramid of the two groups (Figure 5.5). Demographers use the age–sex pyramid to depict how youthful or old a given population is, as well as the relative presence of males and females across age groups. The age–sex pyramid consists of a vertical axis of five-year age groups, while the horizontal axis provides an indication of the percentage of males or females in each age group as a percentage of the entire population of interest. To illustrate an examination of the Latina/o age–sex pyramid in Figure 4.5 shows that boys from nought to four years of age constitute 3.9 percent of the entire US Latina/o population. A comparison of the Latina/o and white age–sex pyramids clearly displays the youthfulness of the Latina/o population as evidenced by a wider base at the younger ages, indicating a large presence of youngsters in the Latina/o population. In addition, the needle-like shape associated with the older ages signifies relatively few older people among Latina/os. In contrast, the age–sex pyramid of whites deviates quite a bit from that of Latina/os. In particular, the white age–sex pyramid is dominated by baby boomers – persons between the ages of 55 and 74. The base of the white pyramid is much narrower compared to that of Latina/os, indicating that youth comprise a relatively smaller share of the white population, while the top of the pyramid has wider bars than that of Latina/os, showing that older persons constitute a larger portion of the white population.

The distinction in the age structure between whites and Latina/os can be illustrated by examining the ratios of children (0 to 17) to older persons (65 and older) in each of these populations. In the Latina/o population, there are approximately 3.6 persons less than eighteen years of age per one individual 65 and older. In contrast, the ratio is 0.8 to one among whites with fewer persons less than eighteen years of age than persons 65 and older. The differences in the age structures of Latina/os and whites have major implications for future growth favoring Latina/os.

Furthermore, there is a significant age divide between Latina/os and whites. In the US, while whites still outnumber Latina/os across all age groups, the share of whites falls progressively from older to younger groups, while the opposite is the case for Latina/os.

However, the age divide is particularly acute in the two largest states in the country – California and Texas (Figure 5.6). Latina/os outnumber whites in age groups less than 55 years of age in California and less than 50 in Texas, with whites outnumbering Latina/os in older age categories. Again, these trends portend significant alterations to the nation's population in the near future. In fact, Latina/o births outnumber white births in 2021 not only in California and Texas, but also in Arizona, Nevada, and New Mexico (see Osterman et al. 2023).

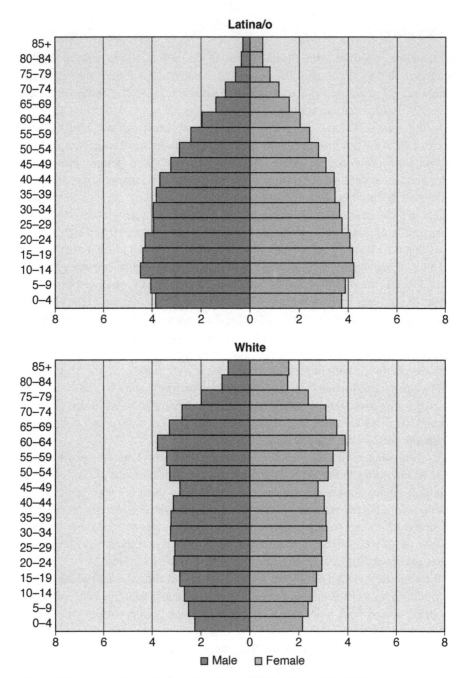

Figure 5.5 Age–Sex Pyramid for Latina/os and Whites in the US, 2022

Source: Data from 2022 American Community Survey 1-Year Estimates Public-Use File (Ruggles et al. 2024).

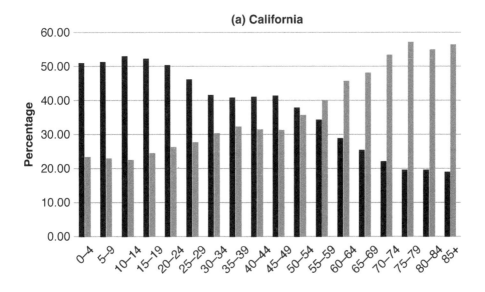

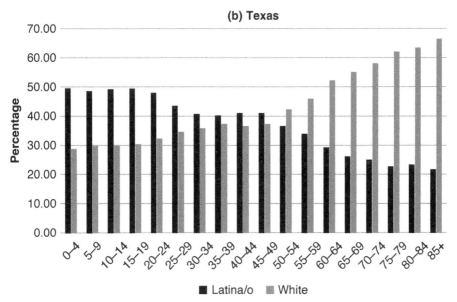

Figure 5.6 Percentage Share of Latina/os and Whites by Age Group in the (a) California and (b) Texas Populations, 2022

Source: Data from 2022 American Community Survey 1-Year Estimates Public-Use File (Ruggles et al. 2024).

Immigration

As illustrated in Chapter 4, Latin America and the Caribbean has long dominated the flow of immigrants coming to the United States since the mid-1960s. For the analysis presented here, we focus on the number of people who are not US citizens

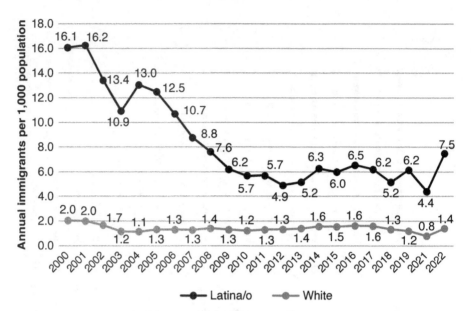

Figure 5.7 Latina/o and White Immigrants Arriving in the Past Year Per 1,000 Population, 2000–2022

Source: Data from 2000–2022 American Community Survey 1-Year Estimates Public-Use File (Ruggles et al. 2024).

and who immigrated to the US in the past year. Figure 5.7 shows the annual immigration rate (number of non-US citizens immigrating to the US per 1,000 persons in the population) for Latina/os and whites between 2000 and 2022. Despite the decline in Latina/o immigration observed in Chapter 4 since the mid-2000s, Latina/os have had a significantly higher immigration rate than whites. Over the 2000–2022 period, for every 1,000 persons in the population, Latina/os have had an average annual immigration rate that is six times higher than that of whites. Even in 2012, when the Latina/o immigration rate was at its nadir (4.9 immigrants per 1,000 population), Latina/os still had an immigration rate that was 3.7 times higher than that of whites. The fact that immigrants tend to be relatively young contributes to additional persons in their childbearing ages.

Fertility

For long, Latina women have had relatively high levels of fertility, much of this due to their low level of education. Figure 5.8 shows the total fertility rates (TFR) of Latina and white women between 2003 and 2022. The total fertility rate (TFR) is a measure of the average number of births that women would have if they went through their fertility-age years (15 to 44) conforming to the fertility levels as they age from one five-year age group to the next. The Latina fertility level is higher than that of white women over all the years, but especially between 2003 and 2010. The Latina TFR peaked at 2.85 in 2006. Nonetheless, Latina women have experienced a significant drop in their

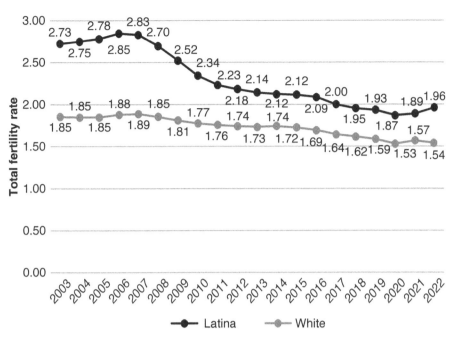

Figure 5.8 Total Fertility Rates of Latina and White Women, 2003–2022
Source: Centers for Disease Control and Prevention (2024c).

fertility levels and have been below the replacement level of 2.1 (the fertility level needed for a couple to reproduce itself) since 2016, while white women have been below the replacement level throughout the entirety of the 2003–2022 period. Indeed, on average, Latina women had almost one fewer births in 2020 compared to 2003, a percentage decline of 34 percent, while the fertility reduction for white women was much smaller (a 19 percent decline).

While the economic hardship of Latina/os due to the Great Recession played a key role in the significant decline of Latina fertility, the rising levels of educational attainment among Latina/os (see Chapter 9) and the major decline in immigration from Mexico (Chapter 4) have also contributed to the fall in fertility. The decline of immigrants among Latina women in their childbearing ages (15 to 44) has been massive over the last fifteen years. Latina immigrant women, who have higher fertility rates than their US-born counterparts, represented 47 percent of Latina women in their childbearing ages in 2007, but only 30 percent in 2022.

Despite the significant drop of Latina fertility, their higher rates of fertility, and the fact that Latina women aged fifteen and older are much more likely to be in their childbearing ages (15 to 44), have contributed to the much higher growth rate of the Latina/o population compared to the white population. In 2022, 60 percent of Latinas aged fifteen and older were in the childbearing ages of fifteen to 44 compared to only 41 percent of white women and to 51 percent of American Indian and Alaska Native, Asian, and Black women.

Mortality

Sociologists and demographers have for long observed that individuals with low socioeconomic standing tend to die at higher rates and live shorter lives compared to people of higher socioeconomic levels (Kitagawa and Hauser 1973). Latina/os possess a bundle of characteristics that place them at risk for elevated levels of mortality and truncated lives. These include low levels of education, high rates of poverty, high prevalence in dangerous jobs, low levels of health insurance coverage, and high rates of obesity and diabetes. However, in actuality, despite this configuration of risk factors, Latina/os have lower mortality rates and live longer than whites. This unexpected phenomenon has baffled demographers and epidemiologists and bears the name of the Latina/o epidemiological paradox (Markides and Coreil 1986; McDonald and Paulozzi 2019; Sáenz and Morales 2012). The Latina/o epidemiological paradox, along with the explanations that have been proposed to account for the paradox, will be covered in greater detail in Chapter 13.

Here, we provide an illustration of the mortality and life expectancy advantage that Latina/os enjoy over whites. We use the latest mortality data from the Center for Disease Control and Prevention (2023a). Statistics for 2019 (before the pandemic), 2020, and 2021 (the latter two years during the pandemic) show age–sex-specific mortality rates across eleven age categories (33 age categories for males and females across the three years). These data (not shown here) demonstrate that Latina females have lower mortality rates than white females in 28 of the 33 age groups for females across the three years (the exceptions being the less than 1 age category in 2019 and 2021, the 1–4 age category in 2021, and the 5–14 age category in 2020 and 2021) and Latino males have lower mortality rates than white males in 26 of the 33 age categories across the three years (the exceptions being the less than 1 age category in 2019, 2020, and 2021, the 15–24 age category in the same three years, and the 65–74 age group in 2020), the latter consistent with the research findings of Sáenz and Garcia (2021) that Latina/os aged 65–74 had higher all-cause death rates than whites, from the beginning of the pandemic to the end of August 2020, threatening at that time the loss of the Latina/o epidemiological paradox.

The disparities in age-specific death rates favoring Latina/os over whites contribute to greater longevity among Latinos. This can be shown through the examination of life tables on the Latina/o population available across sixteen years from 2006 to 2021. Life tables represent the most versatile tool of demographers and can be used for many applications. The life table, which can be broken down by race/ethnicity and sex, starts off with a cohort of 100,000 babies, who are subjected to probabilities of death (derived from current mortality rates) at each age until the entire cohort dies off (Poston and Bouvier 2017). One of the most-used functions of the life table is to determine the life expectancy of a population, given the existing mortality rates. Across the period from 2006 to 2021, Latina baby girls, on average, were expected to live 2.8 years longer than white baby girls, while Latino baby boys were expected to outlive white baby boys by 2.4 years (Figure 5.9). The life-expectancy advantage of Latina/os is consistent across the sixteen years, with the exception of one year for males – 2020, the first year of the

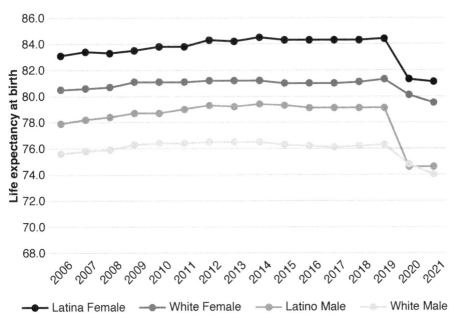

Figure 5.9 Life Expectancy at Birth for Latina/os and Whites by Sex, 2006–2021
Source: Centers for Disease Control (2024b).

pandemic. In fact, the COVID-19 pandemic narrowed the Latina/o–white gap in life expectancy. As can be seen in Figure 5.9, between 2019 (before the pandemic) and 2020 (the first year of the pandemic), the life expectancy of Latino males dropped by 4.5 years compared to a decline of 1.5 years among white males, with the respective life-expectancy declines of Latina females being 3.1 years and that of white females being 1.2 years. The larger drop in life expectancy at this time reflects the disproportionate impact of the pandemic on Latina/os (especially Latino males) compared to white, a topic that will be covered in Chapter 13.

Thus, as a whole, it is clear that the lower level of mortality among Latina/os relative to whites plays a significant role in the comparatively rapid pace at which the Latina/o population has grown. The impact of mortality is intensified when we consider the youthful age structure of Latina/os. Indeed, not only do relatively few Latina/os die because a substantial portion of the population is young, but the rate at which Latina/os die at each age is also relatively low.

Natural Increase

The age structure differences between Latina/os and whites strongly impact the relative volume of births and deaths within these groups. Demographers use the term *natural change* to represent the difference between births and deaths, with natural increase occurring when there are more births than deaths and natural decrease resulting when deaths outnumber births. Figure 5.10 shows the number of births and deaths for Latina/os and whites during the 2018–2021 period. The two

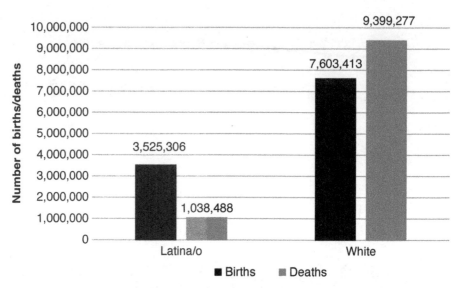

Figure 5.10 Total number of Latina/o and White Births and Deaths, 2018–2021
Source: Centers for Disease Control and Prevention (2024a, 2024c).

groups vary dramatically in the volume of births and deaths during the four-year period. In particular, over the 2018 to 2021 period, Latina/os experienced natural increase, i.e. more births (3.5 million) than deaths (1 million), while whites had natural decline, i.e. more deaths (9.4 million) than births (7.6 million). Thus, over the four-year period, the birth-to-death ratio (BDR) of Latina/os was 3.39 births for every one death compared to 0.81 births to every one death among whites. Again, the disproportionate number of deaths among Latina/os in the COVID-19 era impacted the birth-to-death ratio (BDR), as before the pandemic in 2019 the BDR of Latina/os was 4.17 births to every one death, compared to 0.88 births to every one death among whites.

The much higher BDR of Latina/os relative to whites reflects the younger age structure of Latina/os and the older age structure of whites. Put simply, a youthful population, such as that of Latina/os, produces a large number of births with relatively few people dying. In contrast, an older population such as that of whites generates a large quantity of deaths and a much smaller number of births. Given that older persons aged 65 and older outnumber children less than 18 years of age in the white population, whites will continue to have natural decline, i.e. more deaths than births, while Latina/os will continue to experience natural increase, i.e. more births than deaths. This leads to a situation where the major differences in the current and expected BDRs between Latina/os and whites will have major implications for the future of the US population.

The Latina/o Population Growth Slowdown

We have seen a slowdown in the Latina/o population growth, as noted by the much slower growth (23%) in the 2010–2020 period compared to earlier periods. This population growth slowdown has been due to the significant decline in Latina fertility and the significant decline in immigration from Mexico (see Chapter 4). The percentage of the Latina/o population who are foreign-born fell from 41 percent in 2012 to 30 percent in 2022. Nonetheless, despite the deceleration in the growth of the Latina/o population, it continues to be the engine of the US population growth. Indeed, the overall US population growth is at one of its lowest levels ever. The Latino population growth between 2010 and 2020 was still slightly more than three times as high as the nation's non-Latina/o population growth. In fact, Latina/os accounted for more than half (51%) of the overall nation's population growth between 2010 and 2020. Certainly, the Latina/o population will become older in the coming decades, but it will still have a younger population than other groups, thus contributing to the Latina/o continued strength in leading the US demographic change over the coming decades.

Latina/os and the Future US Population

The newest population projections conducted by the US Census Bureau are based on the 2020 decennial census (for a description of the methodology and assumptions used to generate the population projections, see US Census Bureau 2023). Overall, it is projected that the US population will increase from 333.3 million in 2022 to 364.3 million in 2060, a 9 percent increase. The Latina/o population is projected to increase from 63.7 million in 2022 to 81.7 million in 2040 and to 98.0 million in 2060 (Table 5.1), with the Latina/o population increasing by 54 percent between 2022 and 2060. In contrast, the white population is projected to decline from 196.2 million in 2022 to 185.6 million in 2040 and to decline further to 163.6 million in 2060, a decline of approximately 17 percent between 2022 and 2060. All other racial groups are

Table 5.1 US Population in 2022 and Projected Populations in 2040 and 2060 for Selected Groups

Group	Population in Millions			Pct. Share of US Population			Pct. Change
	2022	Projected 2040	Projected 2060	2022	2040	2060	2022–2060
Latina/o	63.664	81.650	97.994	19.1	23.0	26.9	53.9
White	196.226	185.644	163.630	58.9	52.2	44.9	−16.6
All Other	73.398	88.015	102.663	22.0	24.8	28.2	39.9
Total	333.288	355.309	364.287	100.0	100.0	100.0	' 9.3

Source: 2023 National Population Projections Tables: Main Series (US Census Bureau, 2023).

projected to increase by 40 percent between 2022 and 2060. Examination of the direct population projections shows that non-whites (all persons who are not non-Hispanic white) with a population of 179.7 million will outnumber non-Hispanic whites with a population of 179.2 million in 2046.

Growth in the US population will continue to be driven largely by the increase of the Latina/o population. The population projections indicate that the 34.3 million Latina/os that will be added to the US population between 2022 and 2060 will more than offset the decline of 32.6 million whites during this period. Thus, the percentage share of Latina/os in the US population is expected to ascend from 19.1 percent in 2022 to 26.9 percent in 2060. This is an amazing expansion of Latina/os in the US population especially given that in 1980 they only accounted for 6.4 percent of the nation's population. By way of contrast, the percentage share of whites in the country's population is expected to decline from 58.9 percent in 2022 to 44.9 percent in 2060. Again, the differing demographic future of Latina/os and whites is propelled largely by the major variations in their age structures today.

We have seen the major growth of the Latina/o population over the forty years, as well as its projected increase over the next half century. It is clear that Latina/os will continue to lead the US population in the coming decades into the end of the twenty-first century. We now turn to an examination of the demographic variation that exists across groups that comprise the Latina/o population.

Demographic Variations in Latina/o Groups

As noted in the earlier chapters, the diverse groups that comprise the Latina/o population differ on a variety of dimensions including their demographic characteristics. To a certain extent, these variations are due to the length of time that groups have been in the US, mode of incorporation, and the socioeconomic resources that immigrants bring with them to this country. Of particular interest is the Afro-Latina/o population which is part of the analysis below. One caveat is that the Afro-Latina/o population is not mutually exclusive, as members of this group are also part of the Latina/o national-origin group to which they belong.

Due to the largest percentage of the Latina/o population that is Mexican (59% in 2022), the characteristics of the other Latina/o groups tend to be lost if we only examine the overall Latina/o population. Table 5.2 provides a demographic overview of twenty Latina/o groups and the Afro-Latina/o population. As noted in Chapter 1, the ten most populous Latina/o groups, in order of population, are: (1) Mexicans, (2) Puerto Ricans, (3) Salvadorans, (4) Cubans, (5) Dominicans, (6) Guatemalans, (7) Columbians, (8) Hondurans, (9) Afro-Latina/os (although they are also counted in their specific national-origin group), and (10) Spaniards. For the most part there was general stability in the rankings in 2012 and 2022. Yet, there were four shifts in population-size hierarchy with Salvadorans rising from 4th to 3rd, Cubans dropping from 3rd to 4th, Hondurans ascending from 9th to 8th, and Afro-Latina/os declining from 8th to 9th. Undoubtedly, the drop in ranking of Afro-Latina/os involves the change in the processing of race data beginning in the 2020 census (see Chapter 1). They continue to be the only Latina/o group that experienced a decline in their population between 2012 and 2022 with a decline of one percent.

Overall, the fastest population growth between 2012 and 2022 occurred among Venezuelans, a group that has seen a significant increase in immigration to the US over more than a decade (see Chapter 4), with their population more than tripling from 258,000 in 2021 to 787,000 in 2022. Four other groups experienced percentage increases exceeding 45 percent between 2012 and 2022: Panamanians (57.7%), Hondurans (54.9%), Guatemalans (47.9%), and Dominicans (45.8%). On the other hand, Mexicans had the slowest growth at 10 percent during this period, undoubtedly due to their declining immigration and their large numerical base which mathematically makes it difficult to have high percentage increases.

There is significant variation in the age of Latina/o subgroups. Afro-Latina/s are the youngest group, with a median age of twenty-two in 2022, followed by Hondurans (26), Guatemalans (27), and Mexicans (29). In contrast, the four oldest groups include Uruguayans (41), Cubans (40), Argentinians (39), and Peruvians (38). Demographers use the sex ratio (the number of males per 100 females) to describe the sex composition of given populations. Males outnumber females in nine groups including Uruguayans (sex ratio of 120.5), Guatemalans (124.8), Costa Ricans (104.9), Mexicans (104.5), Panamanians (103.9), Cubans (103.1), Hondurans (102.6), Salvadorans (101.6), and All Others (101.2). The four groups with the greatest presence of females based on sex ratios below 90 include Paraguayans (71.7), Colombians (82.8), Dominicans (84.8), and Bolivians (89.2). Generally, such high sex ratios tend to be associated with male-selective immigration and low sex ratios with female-selective immigration.

There is much variation in the percentage of persons born outside of the US across the 21 Latina/o groups. Still, the majority (over 50%) of members of 14 Latina/o groups are foreign-born, led by Venezuelans with more than three-fourths (76.3%) born outside the US, Paraguayans (64.6%), Hondurans (63%), and Colombians (60.7). In contrast, four groups stand out with low percentages of persons who are foreign-born with only 2 percent of Puerto Ricans, due to those born on the island and the mainland being US citizens, followed by 14.1 percent of Afro-Latina/os, 14.7 percent of Spaniards, and 28.3 percent of Mexicans. Overall, due to the decline in immigration from Mexico (see Chapter 4), today only approximately 30 percent of all Latina/os are foreign-born with this figure influenced principally by the 28 percent figure of the large Mexican population.

The Geography of Latina/os

While Latina/os increasingly span across the US, they continue to be concentrated in particular states. Specifically, as is the case with other racial and ethnic groups, Latina/os tend to reside at a close proximity to those who are similar to them in national origin. This form of residence is helpful when people have limited resources and must rely on kin and friends and their social networks for various types of

Table 5.2 Demographic Characteristics of Latina/o Groups

Latina/o Groups	Population		Pct. Change	Median Age	Adult Sex Ratio	Pct. Foreign-Born
	2012	2022	2012–2022	2022	2022	2022
Afro-Latina/o[a]	1,041,071	1,030,894	−1.0	22	94.3	14.1
Argentinian	240,171	305,106	27.0	39	97.1	56.7
Bolivian	99,929	138,045	38.1	35	89.2	52.9
Colombian	1,080,843	1,433,285	32.6	37	82.8	60.7
Costa Rican	137,724	194,906	41.5	36	104.9	45.7
Cuban	1,973,108	2,449,775	24.2	40	103.1	53.5
Dominican	1,648,209	2,403,874	45.8	31	84.8	51.5
Ecuadorian	664,408	880,869	32.6	34	97.5	55.9
Guatemalan	1,265,400	1,870,908	47.9	27	124.8	56.8
Honduran	774,866	1,200,002	54.9	26	102.6	63.0
Mexican	33,972,251	37,368,050	10.0	29	104.5	28.3
Nicaraguan	408,261	497,784	21.9	35	97.5	57.6
Panamanian	129,074	203,587	57.7	34	103.9	51.0
Paraguayan	19,427	23,357	20.2	33	71.7	64.6
Peruvian	582,662	749,652	28.7	38	93.0	56.6
Puerto Rican	4,929,992	5,948,988	20.7	32	96.2	2.0
Salvadoran	1,969,495	2,484,592	26.2	30	101.6	53.7
Spaniard	723,519	980,003	35.5	35	98.4	14.7
Uruguayan	63,709	74,927	17.6	41	120.5	58.4
Venezuelan	257,807	787,084	205.3	36	91.8	76.3
All Others	1,991,628	3,554,424	78.5	30	101.2	17.4

[a] Afro-Latina/os are also included in their specific Latina/o national-origin group.

Source: Data from 2012 and 2022 American Community Survey 1-Year Estimates (Ruggles et al. 2024).

assistance including social support, financial assistance, housing accommodation, assistance locating employment, and so forth (Flores-Yeffal 2012).

Compared to the overall US population, Latina/os are gathered in a handful of states. For example, based on data from the 2020 census, 54 percent of the overall US population lived in ten states in 2020 (data not shown here). In contrast, 53 percent of Latina/os overall are clustered in three states (California, Texas, and Florida). In fact, Latina/os are more than twice as likely as the country's overall population to be living in California (25.1% versus 11.9%) and Texas (18.4% versus 8.8%).

Similarly, the groups that comprise the Latina/o population were also concentrated in a few states in 2021 (data not shown here). The most extreme case is among Cubans with nearly two-thirds (64%) living in only one state (Florida). In addition, approximately three-fifths of Mexicans and Venezuelans reside in only two states (Mexicans: California and Texas; Venezuelans: Florida and Texas). Furthermore,

more than three-fifths of members of three other groups are clustered in three states: Dominicans (New York, New Jersey, and Florida), Ecuadorians (New York, New Jersey, and Florida), and Nicaraguans (New York, Florida, and New Jersey). Finally, close to three-fifths of Peruvians are located in four states (Florida, California, New Jersey, and New York).

We can also assess the degree to which the distribution of state residences of the different Latina/o groups compares to the distribution of the overall US population in 2021. To do this, we compute the index of dissimilarity (D) for each of the Latina/o groups (see Poston and Bouvier 2017). D ranges from 0 (the two groups being compared have identical distributions across geographic units, e.g. states) to 100 (the comparison groups do not share any common residence across the geographic units). The index represents the percentage of members of a given group being compared (say, Mexicans) to another group (say, the overall US population) that would have to move to another state in order for the two groups to have the same distributions across states. Compared to the overall US population, Dominicans (64.2) and Cuban (58.8) are the most dissimilar concerning their distribution across states (Figure 5.11). Four other groups (Ecuadorians, Venezuelans, Mexicans, and Nicaraguans) exhibit relatively high levels of variations from the overall national population on their states of residence with Ds between 46 and 53. On the other hand, Guatemalans (25.9) and Afro-Latina/os (26.0) exhibit the greatest degree of similarity to the US population with respect to their distribution of the population across states followed by All Other Latinos (27.3) and Spaniards (29.5).

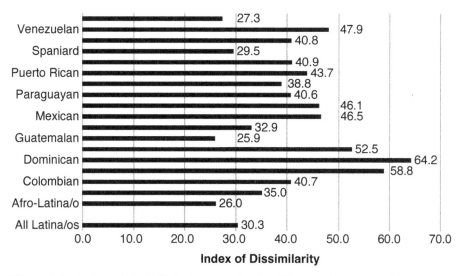

Figure 5.11 Indices of Dissimilarity Representing the Difference between Latina/o Groups and the US Population in States of Residence, 2021

Source: Data from 2021 American Community Survey 1-Year Estimates (Ruggles et al. 2024).

Nonetheless, over the last few decades, the Latina/o population has increasingly fanned out to areas beyond where they have been traditionally concentrated. The Mexican population epitomizes this movement to new areas where Latina/os have historically not inhabited in large numbers. We computed indices of dissimilarity based on data obtained from the 2021 ACS Public-Use Microdata Samples (PUMS) (Ruggles et al. 2024), the 2000 and 2010 Summary File 1 (US Census Bureau 2024), and the 1980 and 1990 5% Public-Use Microdata Samples (PUMS) (Ruggles et al. 2024). The index of dissimilarity comparing the state distributions of Mexicans and the US total population has declined significantly from 62.9 in 1980 to 61.4 in 1990 to 52.8 in 2000 to 47.5 in 2010 and to 46.5 in 2021. Similarly, the portion of Mexicans living in California and Texas has dropped from approximately three-fourth in 1980 (73.1%) and 1990 (74.3%) to two-thirds (65.5%) in 2000, and to three-fifths in 2010 (60.9%) and 2021 (60.3%). The movement into new areas among Mexicans and Latina/os, in general, illustrates how the Latina/o population is changing and having an impact on areas that have not traditionally had many members of this group. These areas have been referred to as Latina/o new-destination areas.

Latina/o New-Destination Areas

Latina/o new-destination states have experienced significant transformations of their populations characterized by a historical absence of Latina/os along with a rapid growth of this population over the course of the last several decades. In many of these places, the growth of the Latina/o population has been associated with transformations in the meat and poultry processing industry, beginning in the 1970s (Flippen and Farrell-Bryan 2021; Kandel and Parrado 2005; Marrow 2011; Ribas 2015). At that time, due to increasing global competition, meat and poultry packer executives sought to cut labor costs (Gouveia and Sáenz 2000). They did this through the movement of meat and poultry operations from urban areas to rural areas located largely in the Midwest and South (Zúñiga and Hernández-León 2006). These rural communities were hungry for economic growth, provided lucrative incentives to lure business, and were not friendly environments to labor unions (Ken and León 2022). As a result, the good-paying jobs in packing houses turned into low-wage jobs with limited benefits and even more dangerous work conditions, due to increasing speeds on the production line (Gouveia and Sáenz 2000). Accordingly, few workers in such localities were eager to take such jobs. Latina/o immigrants represented a sought-after labor pool. Recruitment of Latina/o immigrants took place in southwestern states, especially California and Texas, as well as in Mexico (Cohen 1998).

We use a procedure here to identify Latina/o new-destination states. In particular, we use the following criteria to classify new-destination states: (a) were not among the twenty states with the most Latina/os in 1980, (b) in 1980 Latina/os represented less than 3.2% of the state's overall population (i.e. half of the 6.4% value at the national level), and (c) had at least 245% growth in the Latina/o population between

1980 and 2020 (i.e. the same level of growth at the national level). Furthermore, the new-destination states that meet these criteria are further divided into two categories: (a) above average Latina/o percentage share of the state population in 2020 (9.4% or higher, which represents half of the Latina/o percentage share in the US in 2020) and (b) below average Latina/o percentage share of the state population in 2020 (below 9.4%, which represents half of the Latina/o percentage share in the US in 2020). This approach leads to the identification of 33 states as Latina/o new-destination states, one category including thirteen states, with the percentage share of Latina/os in the state being 9.4 percent or higher (Delaware, District of Columbia, Georgia, Kansas, Maryland, Massachusetts, Nebraska, North Carolina, Oklahoma, Oregon, Rhode Island, Virginia, and Washington) and the second category consisting of twenty states, where Latina/os account for less than 9.4 percent of the state's population (Alabama, Alaska, Arkansas, Indiana, Iowa, Kentucky, Maine, Minnesota, Mississippi, Missouri, Montana, New Hampshire, North Dakota, Ohio, Pennsylvania, South Carolina, South Dakota, Tennessee, Vermont, and Wisconsin). As shown in Figure 5.12, the thirteen states with above average Latina/o representation are located in the east coast, middle Great Plains, and the northwest, while those with below average Latina/o representation are largely located in the Midwest and South.

The Latina/o new-destination states share the commonalities that they had relatively few Latina/os in 1980 and have experienced dramatic increases in the Latina/o population since then. Georgia and North Carolina represent the quintessential Latina/o new-destination states. In 1980, Georgia was ranked 24th in respect to its

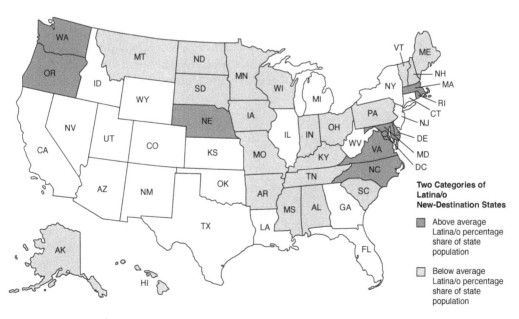

Figure 5.12 Two Categories of Latina/o New Destination States, 2020
Source: Hobbs and Stoops (2002) and US Census Bureau (2024).

size of the Latina/o population, with a population of 61,260, while North Carolina was 27th, with a population of 56,667, and Latina/os represented only 1 percent of the population of each state. By 2020, Georgia had the nation's ninth largest Latina/o population, with a population of 1,123,457, while North Carolina was ranked tenth, with a population of 1,118,596; thus, between 1980 and 2020, the Latina/o population grew approximately 18-fold in Georgia and 19-fold in North Carolina, with Latina/s representing just under 11 percent of the populations of the two states in 2020. Although less dramatic, the experience of the other 31 new-destination states shows similar trends.

Summary

The demographic journey of the Latina/o population over the last several decades has been profound. The population is expected to continue its domination of the nation's population growth in the coming decades, although Latina/os have experienced a slowdown in its growth rate relative to earlier decades, due to declines in fertility and immigration. A major question is whether Latina/o fertility and immigration will increase in the near future. Despite this slowdown, population projections indicate that Latina/os will continue to drive the nation's population growth over the next four decades.

An additional question to consider is whether the US will implement policies to ensure that Latina/o youth become key contributors to society. Demographic shifts driven by the growth of Latina/o youth translate to them becoming an increasing segment of the nation's workforce in the coming decades, as the US population increasingly ages, with the largest segment of older people being whites. Yet, as we will see in the chapter on education (Chapter 9), Latina/o youth continue to be underrepresented among persons with a bachelor's degree or higher.

We now shift our focus to gender and sexuality, topics that are of major importance today, as these dimensions of society have changed dramatically in the last few decades.

Discussion Questions

1. What is meant by the statement "Latina/os represent the engine of the US population change"?

2. What are factors that are associated with the faster growth of the Latino population compared to the white population?

3. What factors have been associated with the slowdown of the Latina/o population growth?

4. What does the term *natural change* mean?

5. How does the Latina/o distribution across US states compare to the US total population?

6. What does "Latina/o new destinations" mean? Provide a few examples of states considered new destinations for Latina/os.

7. Why did the Afro-Latina/o population decline between 2012 and 2022?

8. Which racial/ethnic group is projected to decline in the coming decades? Why?

6 Gender and Sexuality

> Obviously this chapter about my uncle's cockfighting ring and me being this
> really scared gay kid with machismo. Obviously this chapter about how you have
> a total inability to express your emotions has to do with the fact that that is a very
> machismo characteristic.   (Nylon 2022; see also Brammer 2022)

The above quote is taken from an interview with writer Edgar Gomez about his memoir, which tells his coming-of-age story through his experience as a Latino queer amid questions of Latinidad, machismo, and what it means to be queer, male, and Latino. He recalled moments in his early life when he found himself face-to-face with machismo in his uncle's Nicaraguan cockfighting ring, grappling with growing up in the literal face of machismo culture and even having his uncle pushing him to lose his virginity to a woman.

Understanding Latine/x[1] sexuality, gender, identity, and how these constructs intersect is integral to the Latine/x journey and experiences in the United States. Early Latina feminist scholars such as Cherríe Moraga and Gloria Anzaldúa (1981) are among the scholars who laid out the theoretical foundations for understanding the intersectionality of race/ethnicity, sex/gender, and class from a Latina perspective. Women of color are the founders of feminist and sexuality studies and intersectional approaches on how power relations of race/ethnicity, class, gender, and sexuality, for example, are not mutually exclusive but build on each other at both micro- and macro-levels (e.g. Collins 2022; Dow 2019; Fregoso 2003; hooks 1995; Mohanram 1999; Mohanty 1991; Moraga and Anzaldúa 1981; Romero 2017; Segura and Pesquera 1999). While the focus of our chapter is on Latina scholars' and organic intellectuals' work and on studies of Latine/x gender, sexuality, and how they intersect with other statuses, we want to pay homage to Black feminists who have advanced the scholarship and practices of intersectionality, such as Angela Davis, Marie Dawn Dow, Patricia Hill Collins, bell hooks, and Kimberlé Crenshaw, among others.

In reference to the study of intersectionality, prominent Latina scholars Maxine Baca Zinn and Ruth Enid Zambrana (2019: 678), asked, "Where are the Chicanas/Latinas in this burgeoning field of study and practice?" In *Chicanas/Latinas Advance Intersectional Thought and Practice,* Baca Zinn and Zambrana (2019) raised this

---

[1] For this chapter, we used gender neutral terms to be inclusive of all sexualities – Latine used in Latin America and Latine/x used in the English language.

question, not because Latina intersectionality scholarship does not exist but out of concerns about how the work of Latinas or Chicanas in this field is under-represented and under-valued. Chicana and Latina scholars of intersectionality do not get the citations they deserve, and Baca Zinn and Zambrana (2019) attributed this omission to "epistemic developments" where Black women have become the "normative standard for intersectional analysis" (p. 680) in part due to the long-standing Black–white race paradigm and the framework's genealogy and historical development.

For this reason and their theoretical insights, it is essential to highlight the contributions of Latinas in the US to the development and advancement of feminist, queer, and intersectional theory. Although the label of "intersectionality" is not always utilized, Latinas have examined how power relations by sex and gender, race/ethnicity, class, and others, are intertwined (Caballero et al. 2019; Carmona 2021; Ek, Cercer, and Rodríguez 2010; Facio and Lara 2014; Revilla 2004; Staudt and Coronado 2017). Other Latina scholars have engaged with the term "intersectionality" and have used this concept to expand on studies of citizenship, legality, and transnationalism (Alemán 2018; González-López 2005; Hernández and Upton, 2018; Hondagneu-Sotelo 1994, 1997; Morales and Bejerano 2009; Romero, 2002, 2008; Zavella 2011).

While all the chapters in this book provide a profile of the Latina/o sex disparities (both female and male) in the US, here we begin by acknowledging some of the theoretical contributions of Chicanas and Latinas in the US. In particular, we discuss theoretical paradigms that provided a foundation for intersectionality and/or those that provide a framework to have a more holistic understanding of the sexual diversities of Latine/xs in the US. We show how Latinas have expanded intersectionality literature by considering how sex and gender interlock with citizenship, legality, and transnationalism to capture the experiences of Latinas, queer Latine/xs, and Latina/o/e/x migrants in the US. Lastly, we focus on the experiences of LGBTQ+ Latine/xs and social constructions of sexual identities of Latine/x youth.

Early Chicana Feminist Scholars and Paths to Intersectionality

So, what is intersectionality? Patricia Hill Collins and Sirma Bilge (2020:2) accentuated how a core insight into intersectionality is ". . . that in a given society at a given time, power relations of race, class, and gender . . . are not discrete and mutually exclusive entities, but rather build on each other and work together; and that, while often invisible, these intersecting power relations affect all aspects of the social world." This is a good working definition, but it is also important to focus on what intersectionality does and not on what intersectionality is (Cho et al. 2013; Collins and Bilge 2020). In other words, what makes intersectionality scholarship is not using the term "intersectionality" nor drawing from a list of standard citations, but on what intersectionality does. This is particularly important to consider given that the scholarly work on Chicanas and Latinas experiences has not always used the "intersectionality" label but has nevertheless focused on how sex and gender are complicated by other membership categories, such as race and ethnicity, class, and citizenship, among others.

Although the term "intersectionality" was not yet popularized in academia or mainstream discussions about race during the time of her writing, in her essay "La Prieta" (1981), Gloria Anzaldúa wrote about the challenges of multiple identities and intersectionality. Specifically, Anzaldúa (1981) beautifully and critically wrote:

> You say my name is ambivalence? Think of me as Shiva, a many-armed and -legged body with one foot on brown soil, one on white, one in straight society, one in the gay world, the man's world, the women's, one limb in the literary world, another in the working class, the socialist, and the occult worlds. A sort of spider woman hanging by one thin strand of web. (228)

Anzaldúa's theoretical insights on identity and sexuality presented critical understandings that would later form part of queer theory. Indeed, her work is considered formative for developing queer theory (Barnad 1997). Again, in her essay "La Prieta," Anzaldúa (1981) described what it meant to be queer:

> We are the queer groups, the people that don't belong anywhere, not in the dominant world nor completely within our own respective cultures. Combined we cover so many oppressions. But the overwhelming oppression is the collective fact that we do not fit, and because we do not fit we are a threat. Not all of us have the same oppressions, but we empathize and identify with each other's oppressions. We do not have the same ideology, nor do we derive similar solutions. Some of us are leftists, some of us practitioners of magic. Some of us are both. But these different affinities are not opposed to each other. (233)

Elsewhere, Anzaldúa (2009) wrote more about identity, labels, and queerness in her essay "To(o) Queer the Writer – Loca, Escritora y Chicana." The challenge that Anzaldúa posed for us was in looking beyond heteronormative ways of thinking about gender, identity, and sexuality. To this day, Anzaldúa's writing is considered revolutionary as they transformed perspectives that are continually invoked across several academic disciplines today.

Another precursor to intersectionality that Maxine Baca Zinn and Ruth Enid Zambrana (2019) acknowledged is *This Bridge Called My Back: Radical Writings by Women of Color* (1981), edited by Cherríe Moraga and Gloria Anzaldúa and *Borderlands, La Frontera: The New Mestiza* (1987) by Gloria Anzaldúa (see Chapter 3). Cherríe Moraga is one of the most well-known Chicana writers and an activist, poet, playwright, and educator, who wrote about the multiple oppressions of being a lesbian and Chicana. In *Loving in the War Years: Lo Que Nunca Pasó Por Sus Labios* (1983), Moraga explores many topics, including sexuality, race, and culture. Predating the term intersectionality, Morga's critical analysis consisted of how multiple oppressions come together to shape the Chicana lesbian experience. For instance, Moraga (1983, p. 152) states, "In this country, lesbianism is a poverty – as is being brown, as is being a woman, as is being just plain poor."

Moraga's critical analyses provided the foundation to later bring forward the concept of "queer Aztlan" (Moraga 1993: 164), where she explained the struggle of finding a community that would accept her as a Chicana, a female Mexican American that embraces their Mexican and indigenous ancestry, and a Chicana lesbian. Aztlan refers to the Aztec homeland, geographically situated in the Southwest, and reclaimed by Chicanos during the Chicana/o Movement in the 1960s and 1970s (Herrera-Sobek 2006). Moraga (1993) argued that Chicana lesbians, while sharing in the struggle for justice, were often excluded within the Chicana/o Movement. In her poetics, Moraga (1993:173) drew parallels with the struggle she shared with Chicana/os and Indigenous people as one of self-autonomy or "the sovereign right to wholly inhabit oneself (*cuerpo y alma*) and one's territory (*pan y tierra*)." In her book, *The Last Generation: Prose and Poetry*, Moraga (1993:150) described the dilemma of Chicana sexuality as:

> Chicanos are an occupied nation within a nation, and women and women's sexuality are occupied within Chicano nation. If women's bodies and those of men and women who transgress their gender roles have been historically regarded as territories to be conquered, they are also territories to be liberated. Feminism has taught us this. The nationalism I seek is one that decolonizes the brown and female body as it decolonizes the brown and female earth. It is a new nationalism in which la Chicana Indígena stands at the center, and heterosexism and homophobia are no longer the cultural order of the day. (Moraga 1993, p. 150)

Moraga's response to the colonization of sexuality within the Chicana/o Movement and people called for the need to reimagine a more inclusive "Chicano nation," which she called "queer Aztlan." In particular, Moraga stated:

> Chicana lesbians and gay men do not merely seek inclusion in the Chicano nation; we seek a nation strong enough to embrace a full range of racial diversities, human sexualities, and expressions of gender. We seek a culture that can allow for the natural expression of our femaleness and maleness and our love without prejudice or punishment. In a "queer" Aztlán, there would be no freaks, no "others" to point one's finger at. (Moraga 1993, p. 164)

Moraga's scholarly poetics continue to be valued and have relevance today.

In 1987 Gloria Anzaldúa wrote *Borderlands/La Frontera: The New Meztiza* (1987), which transformed feminist literature and activism to this day. The University of Texas at San Antonio has an annual conference called *El Mundo Zuro* to celebrate the life and work of Gloria Anzaldúa (see Chapter 3). In *Borderlands/La Frontera* (1987), Anzaldúa expressed through her beautiful poetics that by not accepting her sexuality and seeking to make women subservient, she felt betrayed by her culture, which fueled a sense of rebellion. In addition, to the cultural estrangement, the patriarchal order established by colonization resonates. When colonizers established religious-cultural institutions, they embedded patriarchy in these institutions to control women's sexuality and attempt to desex Latinas. In culture and religion's quest to protect women from their own bodies and sexualities, it restrains women in rigidly defined gender roles.

In Anzaldúa's critical stance, not only is women's sexuality hidden, but those also who deviate from the sexual norm are ostracized. Anzaldúa (1987) writes "The queer are the mirror reflecting the heterosexual tribe's fear: being different, being other and therefore lesser, therefore sub-human, in-human, non-human" (p. 18). The "half and half's" (homosexuals) are not suffering from sexual identity confusion or gender confusion, rather they are suffering from a despot duality that says you must be one or the other. Within this dichotomy lies the fear of not being accepted by one's mother/culture/race. Elsewhere, Anzaldúa does not see sexual deviations from the norm as having less status; instead, these so-called sexual deviations are described as having supernatural powers by cultural-religious ideologies. Although there seems to be a contradiction about the status of those deviating from the sexual norm, both states describe being in an in-between ambivalent world.

Latine/x LGBTQ+ Scholarship

Similarly, research about queer male-identified Latine/xs in college is limited (Duran et al. 2020). Duran et al.'s (2020) qualitative research explores how male-identified Latine/x students enrolled at a four-year university experience heteronormativity and how those experiences influenced their notions of love. The authors employ a portraiture methodology that showcases the experiences of five gay male-identified Latine/xs. Duran et al. (2020) found that "Ultimately, these gay Latino men's portraits challenge professionals to view students as holistic beings who search for personal fulfillment while they explore their identities on campus" (p. 919).

In her 1993 essay "Tortillerismo: Work by Chicana Lesbians," Alicia Gaspar de Alba provided a review of three decades of early lesbian literature to ". . . bring Chicana lesbian writing out of the critical closet [and] . . . to historicize the exponential growth of Chicana/Latina lesbian literary production since 1991 (Gaspar de Alba 2013, p. 462). Gaspar de Alba believed that while Chicana feminists and lesbians Gloria Anzaldúa and Cherríe Moraga dominated the feminist, lesbian, and gender discourse in the 1980s in Chicana/o studies, the scholarship of other Chicana writers remained obscured. Gaspar de Alba (1993) described this omission as the colonization by people of color toward other people of color, as seen when Chicano/scholars excluded the work of their co-ethnics. Here, Gaspar de Alba highlighted the need for Chicana lesbian literature to be more inclusive about whose voices and scholarship get acknowledged.

Gaspar de Alba's goal to highlight the contributions of Chicana lesbians is seen in "Thirty Years of Chicana/Latina Lesbian Literary Production" (2013), where she delineated three distinct generations in this literature.

Generation A (1980 to 1990), also known as the ChicanA generation, challenged the patriarchal norms within the Chicano movement. Gaspar de Alba devised the ChicanA generation as the catalyst for examinations of the intersecting oppressions faced by Chicana lesbians, advocating for a feminism that considers the interlocking of sex and gender, alongside race and class. Toward the end of this era, we witnessed the emergence of pivotal texts such as *This Bridge Called My Back: Writings by Radical Women of Color* (1981), edited by Cherríe Moraga and Gloria Anzaldúa,

Third Woman: The Sexuality of Latinas (1990), edited by Norma Alarcón, Ana Castillo, and Cherríe Moraga, and *Chicana Lesbians: The Girls Our Mothers Warned Us About* (1991), edited by Carla Trujillo. Generation X (1990–2000) marked a surge in radical women of color texts, giving rise to a new era of Chicana lesbian visibility within academia. Notable works from this era include Jewelle Gómez's groundbreaking novel *The Gilda Stories* (1991), Achy Obejas's *We Came All the Way from Cuba So You Could Dress Like This?* (1994), and Chela Sandoval's influential *Methodology of the Oppressed* (2000).

Finally, Generation Q (2001 to 2011) signaled a pivotal shift toward a more nuanced exploration of gender and sexuality within Chicana/Latina lesbian literature that turned its focus inward, interrogating conventional notions of femininity, masculinity, queerness, and transgender identity. Here, Gaspar de Alba pointed us to the work of Lourdes Torres and Inmaculada Pertusa's *Tortilleras: Hispanic and US Latina Lesbian Expression* (2003), Carla Trujillo's *What Night Brings* (2003), and Laura G. Gutiérrez's *Performing Mexicanidad: Vendidas y Cabareteras on the Transnational Stage* (2010), among others. By outlining the evolution of Chicana/Latina feminist literary production into these three distinct generations, Gaspar de Alba provided a framework for tracing the contributions of Chicana lesbians in literature and expanding our understanding of the dynamic interplay between identity, activism, and creative expression.

Literature about the experiences of lesbian, gay, bisexual, transgender, and queer Latina/os has grown in the last decade. Different sociological, psychological, and medical perspectives have produced a variation of frameworks to study the different experiences of the Latine/x LGBTQ+ in the US. There are approximately more than 11.3 million LGBT adults living in the United States, approximately 40 percent are people of color, of which 20 percent identify as Latine/x (Wilson et al. 2021). Given the limitations of existing survey instruments, we believe these numbers are undercounted.

Latine/x Movements and Where We Are Now

Feeling connectedness to the broader LGBTQ+ community is essential for Latine/xs, including gay and bisexual men/womxn of color, in determining their likelihood of socio-political engagement (Harris et al. 2013). Latine/x contributions to the lesbian and gay movement for equal rights have persistently gone unnoticed. Unlocking the historical experiences of Latine/x LGBTQ+ individuals and understanding how race and ethnicity interplay with socio-political engagement is important because it challenges traditional understandings of civic engagement and what makes people interact with democratic processes.

Until the 1980s Latine/xs' contribution to the gay and lesbian movements was invisible in the media and in gay and lesbian organizations (Quesada et al. 2015). In *Queer Brown Voices*, Uriel Quesada, Leticia Gomez, and Salvador Vidal-Ortiz (2015) bring to the forefront the voices of Latine/xs and their often-marginalized activism and history within the more significant gay and lesbian movement in the 1970s through 1990s. The book covers over three decades of Latine/x activism across the US and Puerto Rico through the stories of fourteen activists. Each of these stories demonstrates the early organizing efforts of Latine/x people. As Vidal-Ortiz (2015) writes in the introduction to the book, "Brown queer people were visible in organizing and fighting for equal rights. Brown queer activists confronted these issues in their neighborhoods, in community-based organizations, in political movements, on college campuses, and in the government" (p. 2). In her essay titled "Dancing at the Crossroads: Mulata, Mestiza, Macha," Mujer, Luz Guerra (2015) discussed her challenges as an activist Latina lesbian mother. Guerra writes, "I was part of a generation of feminist lesbians who came of age at a time of great hope. We engaged in decolonization, liberation, and sovereignty struggles in communities in the United States and around the world that were still sexist, homophobic, and racist. We often found ourselves to be the only visible lesbians and the few women, indigenous individuals, or people of color in the room" (2015, p. 44). Guerra highlighted the contributions and intent of Queer Brown voices, including Puerto Rican, Black, Chicana, Filipina, Chinese, Lakota, and other people of color involved in the struggle for gay and human rights. In her oral history titled "An East L.A. Warrior Who Bridged the Latina/o and the Gay Worlds," Laura M. Esquivel's (2015) oral history "critically reflects on the contradictions and limitations of some of the LGBT organizations of the 1980s and 1990s and the success of the Latina/o LGBT movement" (Quesada et al. 2015, p. 78). A Mexican American, Esquivel (2015), discussed the difficulties in advocating for Latina/os and LGBT communities: "We were committed to both, but faced much resistance from both Latina/o and LGBT communities when raising the issues. At the time, gay issues were not perceived to affect Latinas/os, and the gay community was as resistant to addressing issues of race as the larger society was and is" (p. 93).

Intersectional scholarship and research highlighting the different life experiences of LGBTQ+ Latine/xs has grown in the last decades and continues to expand. Utilizing an intersectional and gendered analysis, Katie L. Acosta's (2013) research in *Amigas y Amantes: Sexually Nonconforming Latinas Negotiate Family* explores race, ethnicity, sexuality, gender, and family. In a society that still grapples with institutions and social norms dominated by white male ideals, Acosta's research illuminates the experiences of nonconforming Latinas in the New England area. In her introduction, Acosta (2013) acknowledged academia as a patriarchal institution that has yet to surpass the heteronormative ideas that continue in society today. For those reasons, research on Latine/x who identify as lesbians, bisexual, or queer continues to be underrepresented within academic work. Acosta (2013) based her analysis on detailed observations from forty-two interviews with sexually nonconforming Latinas and fourteen months of participant observations within various social groups (Acosta 2013). Acosta (2013) utilized Gloria Anzaldúa's theoretical concepts and framework to elucidate the experiences of nonconforming Latinas and "crystallize the strategies these women used to simultaneously negotiate families of both choice and origin" (p.11).

The incorporation of Anzaldúa's "nepantla" (1987, p. 135), as defined by Anzaldúa to mean a space of transition, motion, change and of being in between, is exemplified in the stories of these women who are, as Anzaldúa (1987, p. 135) describes, in *una lucha de fronteras*, "alma entre dos mundos, tres, cuatro" (1987, p. 77) which translates to soul in two worlds, three, or four. For instance, Acosta (2013, p. 3) wrote:

> *Amigas y Amantes* is an exploration of sexually nonconforming Latinas' acts of resistance. As women who have chosen to build their lives with other women, they are resisting societal and familial norms. *Amigas y Amantes* is about these mestizas' journeys to reconcile the contradictions in their lives as mothers, daughters, and lovers and to learn to live with their plural identities and to develop borderlands where they can become whole. Mostly, however, it is about how Latinas build families and the roles that their contradicting identities play in the process.

Acosta's body of work has also made an important contribution to understanding queer Latino families, and the need to utilize queer intersectional approaches to overcome traditional family social science approaches that often miss and misunderstand how race, gender, class, and sexuality shape Latine/x families and their real-life experiences.

Anzaldúa's concept of nepantla is the space in between, where you are neither this nor that and is constantly changing. In *Nepantla²: Transfender Mistiz@ Histories in Times of Global Shift*, Linda Heidenreich (2020) highlights the work of C. Riley Snorton and Kale Namtigue Fajardo, who are "mapping the trans-ness of space and time – drawing our attention to the multiple ways that gender, space, and time are indeed part of a great weave" (p. xvii). In her book *Nepantla*,[2] Heidenreich (2020) first explores the philosophical history of the concept of nepantla back to the Aztecs and describes, "Nepantla² mov[ing] beyond static historical excavation to engage trans as a fierce Chicanx tool, intersecting with our Chican@ histories, lives, politics, and migrations" (p. xxvi). Heidenreich (2020) illustrates this through the lives of two trans-Latine/x individuals, Jack Garland and Gwen Amber Rose Araujo. The story of Jack Garland reveals how late nineteenth-century capitalism and California's gender structures marginalized mestiz@s who lived between genders (Heidenreich 2020). The life of Gwen Amber Rose Araujo similarly addresses the economic contexts of the late twentieth century and highlights the disparity in media coverage between cisgender white gay males and transgender people of color, shedding light on the experiences of nepantler@s navigating race, sex, and gender inequalities within Western economies (Heidenreich 2020). Heidenreich's work not only contributes to LGBTQ+ scholarship but also deepens our understanding of the intersectionality between Latine/x trans-lives and the philosophical concept of nepantla. This intersection has enriched the field of queer studies, offering new perspectives on queerness and its complexities.

Theorizing for Latine/x empowerment Anita Tijerina Revilla and José Manuel Santillana (2014) developed characteristics of a *jotería* (Latine/x queerness) identity and consciousness in academia and activist realms. They list several tenets to *jotería* identity/consciousness, including it being rooted in fun and radical queer love, embedded in a Mexican, Latin American, Indigenous, and African diasporic past and present, and derived from reclaiming the terms *jota* (female-identified queer) and *joto* (male-identified queer) as an identity/consciousness of empowerment, among others. This process of identity and consciousness-making allows for self-empowerment and redefines what it means to be queer and brown.

Scholarship on Trans and Gay Latine/xs

The body of scholarship addressing the experiences of trans-Latine/xs is limited. Sharon Doetsch-Kidder (2011) published an interview with Latina trans activist Ruby Bracamonte. In the interview, Ruby provides an oral history that elucidates her experience as a Latina from El Salvador, an immigrant to the United States, and a transgender womxn. Much research on Latine/x transgender persons centers on health risks and sexual behaviors (e.g. Arrington-Sanders et al. 2022; Rhodes et al. 2020; Trujillo et al. 2022). While this line of research matters, it is essential to highlight lived experiences of transgender Latine/x persons outside the scope of medicine or health aspects to destigmatize and humanize their lived experiences, as testified by Ruby Bracamonte.

The literature addressing gay Latine/x life experiences is smaller in scope, but it is expanding. The racialization of male-identified gay Latine/xs makes coming out more detrimental for them than for male-identified gay whites (Villicana et al. 2016). In *Gay Latino Studies: A Critical Reader* (2011), edited by Michael Hames-García and Ernesto Javier Martínez, a collection of essays is brought together to elucidate a variation of the communal legacy of gay Latine/x people. The book is intended to "... highlight relationships among ongoing intellectual projects that take the lives of gay, bisexual, and queer Latino men as a starting point" (Hames-Garca and Martínez 2011, p. 4). The book takes an intersectional approach and includes authors such as María Lugones, Antonio Vega, Horacio N. Roque Ramírez, and Lionel Cantú.

Lionel Cantú was known for opening a new space for research at the intersection of sexuality and migration (UC Santa Cruz 2024). He was one of the first scholars to write about immigration and sexuality, challenging heterosexual assumptions within migration scholarship (Peña 2011). In his book published posthumously by Nancy A. Naples and Salvador Vidal-Ortiz, *The Sexuality of Migration: Border Crossings and Mexican Immigrant Men*, Cantú et al. (2009) examined how sexuality impacts the process of immigration and identity formation among Mexican gay immigrant men. Cantú filled an important gap in the migration literature, highlighting how sexuality had not been primarily or adequately studied.

Cantú's work in "De Ambiente: Queer Tourism and the Shifting Boundaries of Mexican Male Sexualities" (2002) was another of his research articles that brought forward the role of migration and sexuality. Here Cantú argues that dimensions of sexual colonization and liberation were at work in the relationship between gay and lesbian tourism and Mexican sexuality. In the article, Cantú (2002) lays out the capitalistic factors that influenced the development of queer tourism in Mexico, including "... the development and commodification of Mexican 'gay' culture and space and the rise of a Mexican gay and lesbian movement" (p. 144). Cantú's work examining the impact of transnationalism and globalization between the US and Mexico on identity and sexuality remains influential in migration and Latine/x LGBTQ+ scholarships.

In addition, Héctor Carrillo (2017) in *Pathways of Desire* examines the migration of gay Mexican men to the US and their sexual health Carrillo questions whether Mexican gay men migrate to the United States in pursuit of increased sexual autonomy and freedom. Carrillo negates this as Mexico is evolving to acceptance of diverse sexualities. Furthermore, the book delves into the dynamics of cross-cultural interactions resulting from sexual migration, highlighting how these intricacies may impact the sexual health and HIV risk among transnational immigrant populations.

It is essential to recognize that the relationship between migration and sexuality among lesbian, gay, and transgender Latine/xs is not a monolithic or singular experience. For example, a study by Marysol Asencio (2009b) provided a deeper understanding of Puerto Rican lesbians who migrated to New York City and their experiences negotiating their identities and sexuality while experiencing multiple oppressions and the effect of minority status. Asencio (2009) contends that research on Latina lesbians, especially Puerto Rican lesbians, is scant, but "[t]heir experiences, however, help us to understand the complex relationship between multiple minority statuses, points of oppressions, and lived experiences" (p. 1). By examining how socioeconomic status, gender conformity, migration, and geographic location interlock, we gain a better understanding of how Puerto Rican lesbians negotiate their identities (Asencio 2009b). In *Latina/o Sexualities: Probing Powers, Passions, Practices, and Policies*, Asencio's (2009a) collection of essays demonstrates various intersections, including sex work, religion, spirituality, popular culture, health, and others. Acencio's (2009a) contribution to LGBTQ+ scholarship challenges scholars to move beyond ethnocentric, pathological, and static models of the past and examine writing on a variety of intersections and diversity of Latine/x sexuality and gender.

A Note on Gender, Sexuality, Identity, Latina/o/e/xs, and Data

General population surveys, such as the US Census American Community Survey (ACS), today collect certain characteristics and geographic information about same-sex households in the United States. The 1990 Census introduced the category of "unmarried partner" in response to the relationship-to-householder question (Seem and Coombs 2017). Subsequent 2000 and 2010 censuses refined the relationship data to more accurately represent same-sex couples. However, instead of explicitly distinguishing between same-sex and opposite-sex spouses and partners, these censuses analyzed responses related to sex and relationships (Seem and Coombs 2017).

According to the 2022 American Community Survey estimates, there are over 1.2 million same-sex households in the United States. Of the total same-sex households, 17 percent are Hispanic or Latina/o origin of any race as married male–male households and 14 percent female–female married Latina households. The percentage is slightly higher for unmarried male–male households in which 19 percent include a

Latino. While these data provide estimates on same-sex households, not enough is known to capture the different Latine/x identities.

Summary

In this chapter, we have provided a brief overview of research and theory about Latine/x sexuality, gender, and identity. We traced the contributions of Chicanas and Latinas to intersectionality frameworks. Prior to the development of the concept of intersectionality, Latina and Chicana scholars explored how multiple statuses interlock. We also provided a review of the revolutionary contributions of early Chicana writers, whose work opened the space for evolving conversations about gender, sexuality, and queer studies. We ended with a discussion on Latine/x masculinity, migrant sexuality, and transnational experiences. The studies we highlighted here lay an important foundation for the future development of studies on intersectionality and the sexual diversity of the Latine/xs in the US.

Discussion Questions

1. What theoretical contributions did early Chicana writers contribute to the formation of the intersectional approach?

2. What did Cherríe Moraga observe about the Chicana lesbian experience in the US? What was her proposed solution?

3. What concepts and theories did Gloria Anzaldúa develop in relation to gender roles and gender identity?

4. How do the three generations of Chicana/Latina feminist literary outlined by Gaspar de Alba reflect the evolving socio-cultural landscape and the intersectional struggles faced by Chicana lesbians over the span of three decades?

5. How does the history of the Latino LGBTQ+ experience in relation to the broader LGBTQ+ movement inform future research about gender and sexuality?

6. What theoretical challenges have there been to traditional understandings of *machismo* or Latino masculinity?

7. What are some of the ways transnationalism intersects with sexuality to influence the experiences of Latine/x migrants?

7 Political Engagement

I often reflect on my campaign. I always knew I would run for something, but the path to running for state representative didn't become clear until the unexpected opportunity to fill a vacant seat became available. I felt ready. I knew that the district I was running for had not had a Latina represent it in over fifteen years. I had so many reasons to run for office. As a mother to two young children, I wanted to show them that we, as Latina/os, deserve to be represented. I wanted them to see that our voices and perspectives are important in this country. I wanted both of my young children to know and believe that we have so much to offer. I also wanted my children to learn that this is their community, and that they too have the power to change it when things aren't right or just. I grew up in poverty, and it was the sting of poverty that fueled my desire to figure out how to end it. If holding elected office was one way of changing policy, then that was what I would do. I expected it to be a difficult race because I did not have name recognition, coffers full of money, or the benefit of having been a politician at the local level. Regardless, I worked hard. Just like my parents taught me. I knocked on doors, introduced myself to people and hoped I would earn their support. In the end, this race did not get me a seat in the state legislature, but it gave me something great. The experience of running for office was an exercise in democracy that too few Latina/os have yet to undertake. I only hope that as we grow in numbers, so too in political representation, because we do matter, and this is our home too.

(Coda Rayo-Garza, Ph.D. candidate at the University of Texas at San Antonio and co-author of this book)

Coda Rayo-Garza, one of the co-authors of this book, shares her story of how she decided to run for political office and why she did so. Her story is inspiring and illustrates the importance of young people getting involved in the political process and run for office. As we will see below, Latina women have been at the forefront of political engagement, with a progressive political lens. Hopefully, some readers will be inspired by Coda's story and pick up the political banner to get politically engaged.

In this chapter, we seek to examine the location and exercise of power of Latina/os in the US. We question whether democracy, as a form of government for the people and by the people, is fully extended to Latina/os. The exclusion of Latina/os from the benefits of white privilege is legally embedded and determined by US courts. For example, historian George A. Martinez (1997) traced the legal construction of whiteness as it is applied to the Mexican-origin community. The question of whether Mexicans in the US are considered "white" and by extension granted citizenship has been historically contested in the Courts. On May 3, 1897, in *In Re Rodríguez*, Ricardo Rodríguez, a Mexican living in San Antonio, petitioned a federal district court to request approval of his US citizenship application, which by extension would grant him voting rights. Judge Thomas S. Maxey ruled in his favor, legally affirming the civil rights of Texas Mexicans to vote during a time when it was necessary to be "white" to naturalize. In 1930, Mexican Americans were considered "white" in *Independent School District v. Salvatierra*, a desegregation case in Del Rio, Texas. Here the courts ruled that Mexican American children cannot be separated from children of "other white races." Note that the court ruling still permitted for the segregation of Mexican Americans based on limited English proficiency. On March 4, 1942, in *Inland Steel Co. v. Barcena* an Indiana appellate court addressed whether Mexicans are white. The court noted that about one-fifth of Mexico's inhabitants are white, two-fifths are indigenous, and the remainder are mixed-blood Blacks, Japanese, and Chinese. Over twenty years later in *López Tijerina v. Henry* (1969), the court refused to allow Mexican Americans to define themselves as a group to seek a class action lawsuit to secure equality in local schools. These are just a few of the historical examples of racial projects to categorize Latina/os and that have served to uphold white supremacy (Gómez 2020).

A signal of the contemporary political disenfranchisement of Latina/os relates to alarmists' concerns about the "Browning of America" (Chavez 2013; Montejano 1999; Sáenz et al. 2007). In *The Latino Threat* (2013), for instance, Leo Chavez provided a picture of hegemonic truths that shape myths produced by the media, politicians, and individuals to dehumanize Latina/o immigrants.

Most of the marginalization of Latina/o immigrants is aligned with concerns about the growing Latina/o population and surface as efforts to minimize their political power. Sáenz (2012) elegantly stated:

> As the nation's demography has shifted dramatically over the last few decades with the disproportionate growth of non-whites, especially Latina/os, the political landscape has shifted . . . [A]nti-democracy forces have engineered political warfare against Latina/os and African Americans in an effort to minimize the political influence that, in a perfect world, would accompany their growing presence. And there has been no effort to try to mask this erosion of democracy. (5)

Sáenz (2012) notes several ways that democracy has been weakened in response to the disproportionate population growth of Latina/os and other people of color (see Chapter 5). First, the progress that Latina/os and Blacks made following civil rights legislation has been practically eliminated by the vilification of affirmative action, done under the pretense that this is reverse discrimination. Second, the establishment of oppressive drug and immigration policies over the last several decades exacerbated the incarceration of Latina/os and Blacks (particularly males) and their disenfranchisement (see Chapter 14). Third, the growth of non-white students in schools parallels the declining priority of education at the federal- and state levels. Fourth, states around the country, most notably Texas, have undertaken overt gerrymandering efforts with a variety of subterfuge to dilute the political potential of

Latina/os and Blacks, whose population growth has outpaced that of whites. Fifth, numerous states have passed legislation requiring photo identification for voting. Sáenz (2012) concluded by drawing historical continuity between measures preventing marginalized groups from fully participating in a democratic society – slavery, Jim Crow laws, poll taxes, and the presence of Ku Klux Klan and the Texas Rangers to – to what is happening today: "Contemporary efforts to shut out Latina/os and African Americans and, more widely, the poor, contribute only the latest acid eroding our nation's bedrock of democracy" (5).

More than a decade has passed since Sáenz (2012) noted the association between the growth of the Latina/o population and the erosion of democracy in this country. Unfortunately, the situation has deteriorated. Concerns initially centered on reversed discrimination have since evolved into broader issues encompassing eliminating diversity, equity, and inclusion, as well as introducing legislation against critical race theory in 23 states (see Table 7.4). The incarceration rates of Latina/os and Blacks, particularly males, have seen an alarming increase, a trend associated with capitalism as documented in the prison and immigration industrial complex framework (Alexander 2020). In June 2023, the Supreme Court struck down President Biden's proposal to forgive $20,000 in student loan debt, which is especially detrimental considering that 90 percent of the relief would have benefited those making under $75,000 (https://escobar.house.gov/news/email/). Since 2006, there has been a dramatic increase in school shootings within K-12 and higher education institutions. Economic and political threats loom over public education at the US Capitol. Moreover, the humanitarian migrant crisis at the southern border is being treated as an "invasion." A federal judge declared on September 13, 2023, that the Deferred Action for Childhood Arrivals (DACA) is illegal (see Chapter 9). These are just some of the political issues destabilizing the social standing of Laitna/os in the US today.

This chapter discusses not only the threats to Latina/o democracy but also the political participation of Latina/os. We begin with an overview of the Chicana/o Movement's contributions and its heroes. Following we turn to discussing the resiliency of Puerto Ricans. We then proceed to use data from Pew Hispanic Center's National Survey of Latinos (2018) based on registered voters to illustrate Latina/o political trends, political party affiliations, the degree of support for former President Trump, and the political engagement of new Americans. Next, we highlight Latina/o political leaders in the Supreme Court, US Congress, and at the local level. We end with a discussion of issues that can jeopardize the future of Latina/o political power – legislation against diversity, equity, and inclusion and critical race theory policy and the perilous status of DACA.

Chicana/o Movement

An integral component of the US civil rights struggles is the Chicana/o Movement (*El Movimiento*) of the 1960s and 1970s, centered in the Southwest (Montejano 1999). A catalyst for the movement was the farmworker strikes in California and Texas (1965–1966) that ignited broad civil rights mobilizations among all social classes of

Mexican Americans – street youth, high-school and college students, factory workers, businesspeople, and professionals (Montejano 1999). The farmworker movement originated with a focus on collective bargaining rights for Mexican Americans and Filipino agricultural workers in California. However, under the leadership of Cesar Chávez, it evolved to embrace nonviolent tactics and ethnic symbolism, resonating with Mexican Americans across the nation (Gutiérrez 2019a). Importantly, *El Movimiento* was not exclusive to Mexican Americans; the Puerto Rican Young Lords and the Filipino communities were also actively involved (Stavans 2017).

The evolution of the Chicana/o Movement is the subject of some debate. Rodolfo Acuña (2020), a noted Chicana/o scholar, contends that labelling the second half of the 1960s as the birth of the Chicana/o Movement is inaccurate. He argues that Mexicans have been responding to injustices since the US wars in Texas and the Southwest. While Chicana/o activism pre-dated this period, the radicalization of Chicana/os as part of the Chicana/o Movement occurred from 1965 to 1975 (Cuéllar 1970; Montejano 1999). The Chicana/o Movement played a crucial role in raising public and governmental awareness about the plight of Mexican Americans, even though there were disagreements among Mexican Americans about the militant style of the movement (Montejano 2010) and the marginalization of women within the movement (Blackwell 2011; Montoya 2023). Despite these internal struggles, the Chicana/o Movement gained several defining legal and political triumphs. In 1965, the California Agricultural Labor Relations Act extended labor rights to farm workers and brought some closure to the events that helped to ignite the movement (Montejano 1999). That same year, the Voting Rights Act extended protections to non-English dominant speakers (Montejano 1999). In 1971 a US District Court ruled in the landmark *Cisneros v. Independent School District* case that Mexican Americans were considered an identifiable minority group entitled to special federal protections. Other victories credited to the Chicana/o Movement included successful electoral victories in various rural counties and town governments in Texas, spearheaded by José Ángel Gutiérrez (1998). Additionally, there was a land reclamation movement in New Mexico led by Reies López Tijerina (Montejano 1999). Furthermore, the Chicana/o Movement played a pivotal role in the establishment of advocacy organizations – e.g. the Mexican American Legal Defense and Educational Fund (MALDEF), the Southwest Voter Registration and Education Project (SVREP), and the National Council of La Raza (NCLR), now UnidosUS.

Chicana/o Civil Rights Leaders

Before discussing the Four Horsemen of the Chicana/o Movement – César Chávez, Rodolfo "Corky" González, José Ángel Gutiérrez, and Reies López Tijerina –we want to start discussing the contributions of Dolores Huerta, whose siginificant role in *El Movimiento* often went unnoticed. Her labor and civil organizing during the United Farm Workers (UFW) and Chicana/o Movement firmly established her as a social movement icon. She was born in Dawson, New Mexico, on April 10, 1930. She met Cesar Chávez through their work as community organizers and they co-led marches, sit-ins, and boycotts together. As Stacey K. Sowards' ¡*Si, Ella Puede! The Rhetorical Legacy of Dolores Huerta and the United Farm Workers* (2019) illustrates, Huerta helped shift the male focus in the UFW and the Chicana/o Movement. Huerta strategically used motherhood and *familia* as rhetorical maneuvers to disrupt traditional speaking, negotiating, and bargaining styles (Sowards 2019). While Dolores Huerta's contribution to *El Movimiento* was overlooked compared to that of Cesar Chávez (Sowards 2019), she has been inducted into the National Women's Hall of Fame and President Bill Clinton gave her the Eleanor Roosevelt Award (Stavans 2018).

The farmworker strikes also gave the Chicana/o Movement a national leader – Huerta's colleague, César Chávez (1927–1993) (Montejano 1999). Chávez, born in Yuma, Arizona, had spent his childhood as a migrant farmworker and emerged as a central figure in the strike (Acuña 2020). Before the strike in 1962, César Chávez and Dolores Huerta established the United Farm Workers' (UFW) union, which played a central role in nationally publicizing the struggles of Mexican American farmworkers. Thanks to the UFWs' efforts, California passed the landmark Agriculture Labor Relations Act in 1975, giving farmworkers the right to unionize and negotiate for better wages. Cesar Chávez emerged as the prominent figurehead of the Chicana/o Movement. Drawing inspiration from Mahatma Gandhi's philosophy of nonviolence, he turned hunger strikes into political strategies (Stavans 2018). Chávez's leadership and political strategies led to alliances with important figures like Jessie Jackson and Robert F. Kennedy. His iconic organizing slogan, "sí se puede" remains influential and was even adopted by President Obama as "yes we can" during his presidential campaign.

Another icon of the Chicana/o Movement is Rodolfo "Corky" Gonzales, born in Denver, Colorado in 1928, who is known for his political organizing and protest poetry (see Chapter 8). He was a political activist who worked for the John F. Kennedy campaign (Stavans 2018) and founded the Crusade for Justice, an organization that promoted Latina/o empowerment (Vizcaíno-Alemán 2017). Gonzales is best known for his poem *Yo Soy Joaquín/ I am Joaquín*, published in El Gallo: La Voz de La Justicia in 1967, a newspaper he founded with the Crusade for Justice. *Yo Soy Joaquín/ I am Joaquín* (1967) captured the spirit of the resistance of the Chicana/o Movement and the struggles of Mexicans in the United States, who are forced to assimilate, yet when they do, they lose who they are (see Chapter 8 for a presentation of selected words from the poem). *Yo Soy Joaquín/ I am Joaquín* served as consciousness-raising during the Chicana/o Movement and today.

José Ángel Gutiérrez was another one of the four horsemen of the Chicana/o Movement. The lack of political representation for Mexican Americans drove him to start his organizing work at 18 years of age. He gave speeches, registered voters, and fundraised, so that poor Mexican Americans could pay the poll tax necessary to vote (Gutiérrez 1998; Medrano 2010b). Gutiérrez, along with Mario Compean, Juan Patlán, Ignacio Pérez, and Willie Velásquez, founded the Mexican American Youth Organization (MAYO) in 1967 in San Antonio (Medrano 2010b), which would shortly after become La Raza Unida Party (LRUP). LRUP was a Chicana/o third-party movement that supported candidates for office and became a national political and civic organization. In its third-party status, LRUP took votes away from the Democratic Party, which was seen as taking Chicana/os for granted and as not being any different from the Republican Party. Gutiérrez served in the US Army and then completed his education. In 1976, he completed his Ph.D. in Government and Jurisprudence and in 1988 finished his Law degree from the University of Houston Law Center. He was a professor who spent a large part of his career at the University of Texas at Arlington. He has authored twenty-eight books, including *The Making of a Chicano Militant: Lessons from Cristal* (1998), *Lucille Ball and Desi Arnaz: The FBI and HUAC Files* (2021), *Bashing Boricuas: The FBI's War* (2021), and *The American Eagle: Spying on Mexicans and Chicanos* (2022).

Another key figure of the Chicana/o Movement is Reies López Tijerina, born September 21, 1926, in Falls City, Texas. He was nicknamed "King Tiger" for his tenacious struggle for land recovery in New Mexico (Gutiérrez 2019). Tijerina formed the *Alianza Federal de Mercedes* to fight for the communal lands or *pueblos* for all the inhabitants and their descendants granted under the Treaty of Guadalupe Hidalgo. Alleging that they were communist and outsider agitators, District Attorney Alfonso Sanchez ordered the arrest of Tijerina and Alianza members. Tijerina escaped and orchestrated a rescue mission to free Alianzistas, and placed a citizen arrest of D.A. Sanchez at the Tierra Amarilla Courthouse on June 5, 1967 (Gutiérrez 2019). On June 10, 1967, the National Guard captured Tijerina but, a year later, he successfully defended himself in court (Stavans 2018).

Aside from the Four Horsemen of the Chicano Movement just overviewed, we highlight two additional important leaders. First, a notable figure in the Chicana/o Movement was Rubén Salazar (see Chapter 15), whose contributions to journalism were pivotal. Salazar, was born in Ciudad Juárez, Mexico on March 3, 1928 and raised in Texas, earned a BA from the University of Texas at El Paso before serving in the army (Stavans 2017). He played a crucial role in combatting misrepresentation of Latina/os and bringing to light the mistreatment faced by Mexican Americans and the Chicano Movement (Stavans 2017). Tragically, at the age of 42, Salazar was killed by a sheriff in August 1970 during a march organized by the National Chicano Moratorium Committee. In addition, Oscar "Zeta" Acosta, a lawyer, activist, and writer known for his work *The Autobiography of a Brown Buffalo* (1972) and *The Revolt of the Cockroach People* (1973) is another important figure of the Chicana/o Movement. Acosta gained recognition during *El Movimiento* for his rebellious personality and involvement in serval important legal cases in the latter half of the 1960s, including his work defending the Chicano 13 for their role in the East Los Angeles school walkouts in 1968. Acosta disappeared mysteriously in May 1974, while traveling in Mazatlán, Sinaloa, in Mexico.

Art and Culture in the Chicana/o Movement

The Chicana/o Movement extended beyond political activism aimed at sociopolitical equity; it also encompassed rich Latina/o artistic expressions that illuminated the cultural dynamics through which individuals interpret their social realities (Ontiveros 2014). Ontiveros (2014) eloquently emphasized the pivotal role of art by stating, "There can be no politics, no movement without art" (p. 30). Within the Chicana/o Movement, art served a dual purpose: first, as a tool for raising awareness and consciousness regarding Latina/o social inequality (Romo 1992), and second, as a means of establishing Mexican Americans as both producers and consumers of art (Ontiveros 2014). In Chapter 3, we highlighted the intellectual contributions of activist scholars emerging from the Chicana/o Movement, while Chapter 8 offers a broader exploration of the artistic and cultural contributions of Latina/os to the US. The discussion here aims to highlight some of the enduring impacts of the Chicana/o Movement.

The Chicana/o Movement fostered powerful artistic and cultural expressions. Through powerful murals, Chicana/o artists utilized public spaces to amplify messages of empowerment, such as "Si Se Puede" (Yes We Can) and UFW slogans such as "Ya Basta" (Enough) and "Venceremos" (We Will Overcome), all in support of the Chicana/o Movement. These murals transcended mere aesthetics, serving as symbols to awaken social consciousness during *El Movimiento* (Romo 1992). The played a pivotal role in shaping the evolution of contemporary murals, influencing projects seen along the US–Mexico border (Romo 1992). As the movement progressed, graffiti emerged as another potent form of cultural expression. Between the 1970s and the 1980s, particularly in the urban hubs like New York, Chicago, and Los Angeles, Latina/os including Mexican, Salvadoran, Honduran, and those of Caribbean descent used graffiti artwork to assert their cultural pride i.e. Aztec representations and depictions of the struggles faced by Latina/os in the US (Stavans 2017).

Poetry, literature, and theater also emerged as powerful tools of mobilization during the Chicana/o Movement. Renowned poets of the era and its aftermath include Alurista, Lorna Dee Cervantes, and Gary Soto, who left valuable marks on the cultural landscape (Stavans 2017). Alturista (see Chapter 8), for instance, wrote the influential *"El Plan Espiritual de Aztlán,"* delivered at the Chicano Youth Liberation Conference in 1969, which left an impact on the Movement (Ontiveros 2014). Meanwhile, in the 1970s in New York, the Nuyorican Poet Café (see Chapter 8) movement endeavored to make poetry of street life, featuring poets such as Miguel Piñero and Miguel Algarín (Stavans 2017). The movement's embrace of Latina/o culture, including the Spanish language, also spurred the establishment of publishing houses like Arte Público and Bilingual Press/Editorial Bilingüge (Stavans 2017). Theater, too, played a crucial role in mobilizing communities. *Teatro Campesino*, founded by the Chicana/o Movement leader Luis Valdez, utilized the arts as a means of gaining support (https://elteatrocampesino.com/). Valdez, who initially volunteered with César Chávez's UFW after college, used plays to entertain the strikers, while depicting the struggles of Mexican Americans and rallying support for *la huega*, the union strike.

Throughout the transformative years of the Chicana/o Movement, spanning from 1965 to 1975, arts and culture were deeply intertwined with the struggle for labor, social and political rights, and political empowerment of, at that time, mostly Mexican-origin and Puerto Rican communities but also Filipinos (see Stavans 2017). This era witnessed a profound convergence of artistic expression and socio-political activism, where murals, poetry, literature, theater, and other forms of cultural production became tools for advancing the goals of *El Movimiento*. Today, the cultural legacy of the Chicana/o Movement continues to resonate with artistic and cultural expressions in museums and galleries, corporate and independent publishing houses, and theater venues (Ontiveros 2014).

Puerto Rican Social Movements

Puerto Ricans have a long history of resistance against multiple crises, e.g. demanding the release of political prisoners, defending ecosystems, challenging economic inequality, and organizing against mining, militarization, and other economic and corporate interests (Soto 2023). Many of these social movements use the ideology of *just transformation* to emphasize the need to achieve decolonization, sovereignty, and self-determination (Soto 2023). Examples of coalitions and *just transformation* efforts can be seen in the collaborative publication *Pactos Ecosociales en Puerto Rico* (https://pactosecosocialespr.com).

A successful example of Boricua (term used to refer to people from Puerto Rico and their descendants) power and coalition building among Puerto Ricans is *Todo Puerto Rico con Vieques* (TPRCV) (1999–2004). TPRCV is a broad-based coalition to remove the US Navy from Vieques (Vélez-Vélez 2015). The success of TPRCV, however, was gradual. One must look back to the 1990s and mobilizations against electromagnetic radar in Vieques, the fight against privatization, and the status of referenda, and how these movements intersected and contributed to the preparation for TPRCV (Vélez-Vélez 2015).

More recently, Puerto Ricans have organized against capitalism and US economic oversight. In particular, there are the movements against La Junta and PROMESA (Puerto Rico Oversight, Management, and Economic Stability Act) and the privatization of public services (Soto 2023). The Puerto Rican economic crisis started in 2014 and extended to 2017, when the government filed for bankruptcy, with a governmental debt crisis exceeding $70 billion (Vázquez 2017). In response to this crisis, the US Congress approved the Puerto Rico Financial Oversight and Administration Board created under the Puerto Rico Oversight, Management and Economic Stability Act in 2016. Under this Act, Puerto Rico must share all economic and political decisions with this body, a challenge for a country that has experienced historical political polarization (Vázquez 2017). Grassroots efforts against PROMESA have arisen, including those with feminist ideologies, which have spearheaded solidarity economies that seek to transform dominant capitalist and state-dominated authoritarian systems and reduce dependence on external resources (Soto 2023). Puerto Rico recently, in 2022, exited bankruptcy (Coto 2022).

Trends on Latina/o Political Perceptions

In this section, we use data from the Pew Hispanic Center 2018 National Survey of Latina/os (NSL), collected between July 26 and September 9, 2018, to assess the political perceptions of Latina/os. The data consists of a national sample of 1,501

Table 7.1 Percentage Perceptions of Which Party is Most Concerned About Latina/os, 2018

	Democrats	Republicans	No Difference
Mexican	50.6	11.8	37.7
Puerto Rican	44.1	6.3	49.6
Cuban	47.3	29.1	23.6
Dominican	66.7	–	33.3
Central American	44.4	12.1	43.4
Spanish	32.6	19.6	47.8
South American	64.3	11.9	23.8
Other	47.9	11.9	23.8

Source: Data from Pew Research Center National Survey of Latinos, 2018.

adults (N= 742 US-born, including Puerto Ricans and N=759 foreign-born Latina/os). Interviews were conducted in English and Spanish. All the analyses in this section are weighted to represent a nationally representative profile of Latina/o adults in the US

Latina/o Political Party Identification, Voter Registration, and Group Position. So, which political party do Latina/os perceive as the most concerned about Latina/os? (Table 7.1). Overall, Latina/os perceive that the Democratic Party addresses more societal issues impacting Latin/os. Indeed, most Latina/o sub-groups have approximately 50 percent of members who perceive that Democrats care more about Latina/os. Above the trend, 66.7 percent of Dominicans feel that the Democrats are more concerned about their group interests. If these trends in Latina/o perceptions about which political party serves their best interest translate into voting behavior, it will represent a linked fates phenomenon where Latina/os vote as a bloc for prioritizing group interest.

What about their perceptions of Republicans concerning how much they care of Latina/o interests? Overall, around 12 percent of members of most Latina/o sub-groups feel that Republicans are the most concerned about their ethnic group (Table 7.1). Cubans (29.1%) and Spanish (19.6%) have the highest percentage of members who feel the Republicans prioritize their ethnic group's interests. It is worth noting that while Cubans believe Democrats (47.3%) have their best interest in mind, the Spanish tend to feel that political affiliation makes no difference (47.8%).

Surprisingly, a significant portion of Latina/os feel there is no difference between Democrats and Republicans when it comes to caring about their ethnic group issues. Over 40 percent of Puerto Ricans, Central Americans, and Spanish feel that there are no differences in which political party prioritizes Latina/os. Trailing close behind are 37.7 percent of Mexicans, 33.3 percent of Dominicans, and about a quarter of the other groups (Cubans, South American, and Other Latina/os) who feel that there is no difference between the two major political parties in the US on their degree of concern for Latina/os.

For decades, political commentators have referred to Latina/os as the "sleeping giant." Yet, Latina/o voting behavior did not live up to its potential. One of the

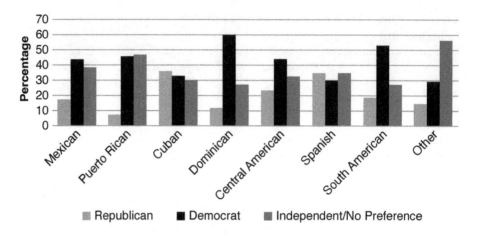

Figure 7.1 Percentage of Latina/o Registered Voters by Political Party
Source: Data from Pew Research Center National Survey of Latinos, 2018.

reasons for Latina/os' low voting rates is their youthfulness (see Chapter 5) (Sáenz 2012). Although the current young population among Latina/os limits the number of individuals eligible to vote at the present, this demographic pattern indicates a significant increase in voting potential in the near future. The Pew Hispanic Center also predicts a doubling in Latina/os who vote in presidential elections in 2023, due to not only to their youthful age, but also to increases in the rate of naturalization (Taylor et al. 2012a). On the other hand, disparities in Latina/o voter mobilization by political parties and candidates can influence their political subordination (Michelson 2005).

One other question is, what percentage of Latina/o citizens are registered voters? Figure 7.1 illustrates the percentages of Latina/os registered to vote (those who are sure they registered and those who are probably registered but their registration may have lapsed). We constructed a variable consisting of registered voters by the political party with whom they most identify, to more closely approximate Latina/o voting patterns (Figure 7.1) We found that among Latina/o citizens, Democrats are more likely to be registered to vote than those who identify with the Republican Party, or are Independent, or have no preference. This pattern held for all Latina/o subgroups, except Cubans and Spanish. Puerto Ricans' percentage of registered voters identifying as Democrat and Independent are nearly equal. Notably, the group with the highest percentage of registered Democratic voters is Dominican Americans, with 60 percent.

Although there are more registered Republicans among Cubans, the percentages across the three political party identifications are almost equal: Republicans 36.1 percent, Democrats 33.3 percent, and Independents 30.6 percent.

The high percentages of Latina/os who are registered voters and identify as Independents or have no preference is somewhat surprising. These percentages parallel registered Democrats in the case of Puerto Ricans, Cubans, and Spanish. Among

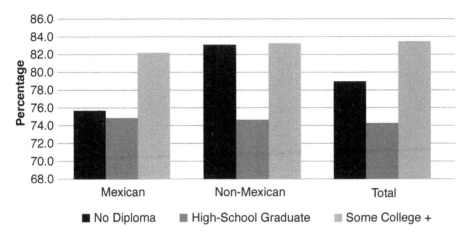

Figure 7.2 Percentage of Latina/o Registered Voters by Level of Education
Source: Data from Pew Research Center National Survey of Latinos, 2018.

Other Latina/o registered voters, the majority (56.1%) identify as Independent or have no preference (56.1%).

Next, we examine the influence of education on political party affiliation among Latina/o registered voters (Figure 7.2). Political scientists have long emphasized the role of socioeconomic resources, e.g. level of education, in shaping civic engagement (Verba et al. 1995; Jones-Correa et al. 2018). This is particularly concerning, as lower resources have been linked to reduced political participation among Latina/os (Bedolla 2009). Here data suggest a different narrative. In actuality, lower levels of education do not seem to hinder Latina/os from registering to vote. Among Mexican Americans, for instance, approximately three-fourths of those without a high-school diploma or with a high-school diploma are registered to vote, although more than four-fifths of those with some college education or more are registered to vote.

Due to small sample sizes, we had to merge the rest of the subgroups into a non-Mexican group. Among non-Mexican Latina/os, there is a u-shaped relationship with the highest level of registration at 83 percent among those with the highest and lowest level of schooling. Therefore, contrary to expectations, a lower level of education among Latina/os is not associated with lower levels of political participation.

Next, we examine the political party affiliation of registered voters by level of education (Figure 7.3). Among those with no diploma, nearly 55 percent are registered voters, identifying as Democrats. Registered voters identifying as Democrats represent about 40 percent of each educational category. Also, across all the educational categories, registered voters who identify as Independents, or have no political party preference, outnumber Republicans.

There are some interesting variations in party affiliation among Latina/o registered voters by sex (Figure 7.4). Previous research has found that Latino males and Latina females differ regarding political attitudes and behaviors (Bejarano 2014). Data from

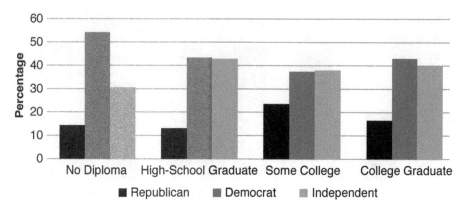

Figure 7.3 Percentage of Latina/o Registered Voters by Level of Education and Political Party

Source: Data from Pew Research Center National Survey of Latinos, 2018.

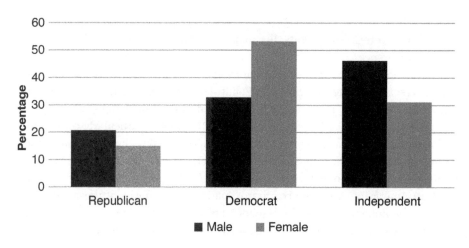

Figure 7.4 Percentage of Latina/o Registered Voters by Political Party and Sex

Source: Data from Pew Research Center National Survey of Latinos, 2018.

the 2018 National Survey of Latinos show that registered Latina females are much more likely to identify with the Democratic Party than Latino males – an absolute gap of 20 percentage points. Latino males are more likely to identify as Republicans (21%) and Independent/ No Preference (46%) compared to Latinas.

Now we examine the level of support of Latina/os for the Trump presidency (Figure 7.5). National data trends show that Latina/o citizens (US-born and naturalized citizens) had a low approval of the Trump presidency. While most subgroups show approval ratings for the Trump presidency ranging from the low to mid-20-percent range, there is a notable divergence among certain groups. Nearly 50 percent of Cubans and Spanish approve of the job that Donald Trump did as president, with South Americans trailing behind with a 30 percent approval rating. On the other

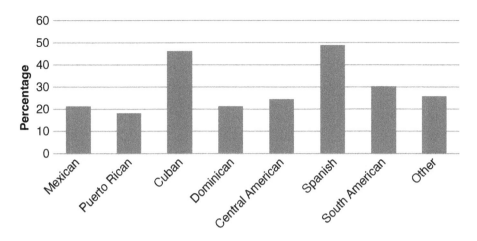

Figure 7.5 Percentage of Latina/os Who Approve of the 2017–2021 Trump presidency
Source: Data from Pew Research Center National Survey of Latinos, 2018.

hand, Puerto Ricans (18.5%) and Dominicans (20.0%) had the lowest approval of the Trump presidency. Overall, Latina/o citizens' relatively low approval of the Trump presidency is not surprising, given his criminalization of Latina/os. Indeed, the quote below became symbolic of President Donald Trump's anti-Latina/o stance and attitudes toward immigrants:

> When Mexico sends its people, they're not sending their best . . . They're sending people that have lots of problems, and they're bringing those problems with us. They're bringing drugs. They're bringing crime. They're rapists. And some, I assume, are good people. (see Phillips 2017)

Yet, the national trends do not capture local and regional support for Trump. Particularly surprising are the counties in South Texas, where, despite being over 80 percent Latina/o and having high levels of poverty, a disproportionately high share voted for Trump in 2020. While the national data showed that Mexicans tend to identify with the Democratic Party, there was support for Trump on the Texas–Mexico border. In the Biden–Trump presidential election, in the 14 border counties that Biden won, Trump gained a significant portion of the vote, ranging from nearly one-third in El Paso County to half in Culberson and Starr Counties (Sáenz 2021). What surprised many is that Trump won in six border counties in South Texas, including Zapata County, where just four years earlier, Hillary Clinton had beaten Trump by 30 percent points (Sáenz 2021). Therefore, while Latina/os mostly identify with the Democratic Party, there are ideological variations among Latinos across sub-groups and places (Jones-Correa et al. 2018).

Figure 7.6 Photograph of the Immigrant Rights March, 2006
Photograph by Maria Cristina Morales, April 10, 2006.

Political Participation of New Americans

What are some trends in the voting behavior of new American Latina/os? Jones-Correa et al. (2018) suggest that understanding the nuances of Latina/o political socialization and engagement is crucial. Foreign-born Latina/os in the US may exhibit distinct political participation patterns, as they have spent their formative years in another country and learned about American politics as adults. Historically, the Latina/o immigrant experience has been linked to uncertainties regarding American politics (Hajnal and Lee 2011). However, the immigrant mobilization of 2006 demonstrated that Latina/o immigrants are active participants in US social movements. Moreover, they display a notable desire to participate in the American voting process (Figure 7.6).

So, are naturalized Latina/o citizens more or less likely to be registered voters than US-born Latina/os (Figure 7.7)? There are no indications that naturalized citizens have less attachment to the American political system; on the contrary, among Mexican Americans, the percentage of registered voters is higher among naturalized citizens (83%) than US-born persons (80.5%). This trend is replicated among non-Mexican Latina/o Americans. Among naturalized non-Mexican Latina/os 82.6 percent are registered voters, as are 77 percent of non-Mexican US-born Latina/os.

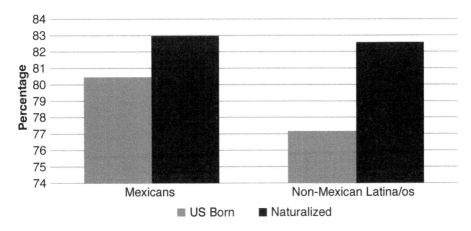

Figure 7.7 Percentage of Latina/o Registered Voters by US-Born and Naturalized Citizens
Source: Data from Pew Research Center National Survey of Latinos, 2018.

Latina/os Politicians

Despite the general political alienation of Latina/os in the US, Latina/o leaders are strong and exist at all levels of the government. We highlight next the legacy of some of the Latina/o politicians and political leaders, beginning with that of Sonia Sotomayor, who is the most powerful Latina/o in the field of law. We then discuss the Castro brothers together, given the strong influence that their mother's advocacy placed on them, and the different paths that they have taken in their political careers. Subsequently, we will overview the presence of Latina/os in different political offices at the federal, state, and local levels.

Among the most powerful Latina/os in politics is Supreme Court Justice Sonia Sotomayor. In her memoir, *My Beloved World* (2014), Sonia Sotomayor speaks candidly of her struggles, skills, and resiliency as she rose in political power from a Puerto Rican living in New York, to project to her position in the highest court as US Supreme Court Justice. Prior to her appointment to the US Supreme Court by President Obama, she was on the board of directors of the Puerto Rican Legal Defense and Education Fund and a judge on the US Court of Appeals for the Second Circuit (Stahl 2015).

In local, state, and federal politics, Julián and Joaquin Castro are two Latinos from Texas who have made their way through the political ranks. The twins from San Antonio, Texas, are no strangers to political advocacy, because it runs in their family. Their mother, Maria del Rosario "Rosie" Castro, began her career as a political and civil rights activist as a young woman. Her work runs back to the days when she attended Our Lady of the Lake College in San Antonio, where she created a campus chapter of Young Democrats and became president of the Bexar County Young Democrats (Voces Oral History Center 2015). She was greatly involved with the Mexican American Unity Council, was a co-founder of La Raza Unida (see above), and a San Antonio city council candidate of the Committee for Barrio Betterment (Voces Oral History Center 2015). Her sons, each with their distinct political direction, have continued in their mother's advocacy path. Joaquin Castro was elected to the Texas Legislature in 2005, where he represented House District 125 for five terms. In 2012 he was elected to the US House of Representatives for Texas's 20th District (Castro 2023a). His twin brother, Julián Castro, was first elected to the San Antonio City Council in 2001 and elected mayor of San Antonio in 2009, serving three terms (Biography 2020) until when President Barack Obama appointed him as US Secretary of Housing and Urban Development. Julián announced his candidacy for US president in 2019, in his hometown of San Antonio, Texas (Biography 2020).

Governors

Luis Muñoz Marín, the "Father of Modern Puerto Rico," was the first democratically elected Governor of Puerto Rico (Stahl 2015). He was reelected in 1952, 1956, and 1960 and, during his term, he expanded the Puerto Rican economy (Stahl 2015). Muñoz Marín, who had the reputation of being a political genius became the symbol of freedom for many poor Puerto Ricans *jíbaros* (country people) (Meier et al. 1997). He was awarded the Presidential Medal of Freedom in 1963.

Another impactful governor and Congress person is Mexican American William "Bill" Richardson (1947–2023). He served two terms as governor of New Mexico and fourteen years in Congress (Roberts 2023). Additionally, Richardson's public service includes being the US Ambassador to the United Nations (1997–1998) and the Secretary of Energy under President Clinton (1998–2000) (https://www.richardsondiplomacy.org/bill-richardson/). After his years in office, he continued to practice freelance diplomacy and became known as the champion of Americans held overseas (Roberts 2023). On behalf of about eighty families, he helped release American hostages from Iraq, Afghanistan, Cuba, and Colombia (Roberts 2023).

The US House of Representatives

The longest-serving Latina/o in Congress is Henry B. González (1916–2000) (The Office of the Historian and Office of the Clerk US House of Representatives 2013). Representative González, a Texas Democrat, served over 37 years from November 4, 1961, to January 3, 1999, in the US House of Representatives. Medrano (2010b) interviewed José Ángel Gutiérrez (see above), who recounted the impact of seeing and hearing Henry González for the first time. Prior to this encounter, Gutiérrez and the other youth had internalized societal messages suggesting that there were no Mexican American leaders. However, when Henry González visited Crystal City for his campaign, Gutiérrez remembered saying, "pues este Henry B. se avienta, man" (well, that Henry B. is awesome, man), though shortly later González would vigorously oppose the Chicana/o Movement (Gutiérrez 1998; Montejano 2010).

A rising politician of Afro-Latino background is Maxwell Alejandro Frost, representing Central Florida in the US House of Representatives (https://frost.house.gov/). He is the first member of Generation Z to be elected to Congress. Following the shooting at Sandy Hook Elementary, Representative Frost dedicated his community work to fighting gun violence and pushing for gun reform. As a member of Congress, Frost is especially driven to remedy the issues of housing affordability, health care, abortion rights, LGBTQ+ rights, voting rights, transportation, justice reform, and climate change, among others. Mr. Frost serves on the Oversight and Accountability and the Science, Space, and Technology Committees. Representing his ethno-racial identity, he is a member of both the Black and Hispanic Congressional Caucuses.

In 2018, at age 29, Alexandria Ocasio-Cortez (referred to as AOC) was the youngest woman and youngest Latina/o to be elected to the US Congress. Ocasio-Cortez ousted a ten-term New York Democrat in the primary, which earned her grassroots campaign great attention and recognition. Notably, Ocasio-Cortez also ran as a Democratic Socialist, on a platform for abolishing Immigration Customs Enforcement (ICE), criminal justice reform, and universal health care, among other political priorities (Biography 2023). Ocasio-Cortez was reelected for a second term, which began in 2021 (Ocasio-Cortez 2023).

Senators

Ted Cruz and Marco Rubio are Latino US Senators with similar ethnic backgrounds, political party representation, and career trajectories. Both Cruz and Rubio are Republicans and second-generation Cubans (Stahl 2015). They were both elected to the Senate in 2010 and were candidates in the 2016 Republican Party presidential primaries (Stahl 2015). Both Cruz and Rubio are still serving in the Senate. Ted Cruz has been a Texas Senator since 2013 and Marco Rubio has been a Senator for Florida since 2011. One difference, between the two, however, is that Rubio more visibly embraces his Latina/o heritage than Cruz.

Congress 2022 and Latina/o Representation

The 2022 Congress witnessed the highest representation of Latina/os to date, with members from both Democrat and Republican parties making significant strides across the US. Christian Paz (2022) wrote an article spotlighting the newly elected Latina/o lawmakers in Congress 2022. Among these new members of Congress, many are breaking through social barriers and/or making history as "the first" Latina/os elected to office in their respective states (Table 7.2).

Trends in Latina/o Political Representation at the City Level

As a proxy for Latina/o political power at the local level, we compiled data on the number of Latina/o politicians, i.e. mayors and city council members, among the top 25 cities with the largest Latina/o population. While research shows that Latina/os tend to prefer a co-ethnic mayor (Benjamin 2017), only El Paso, Miami, Hialeah, and Corpus Christi have a Latina/o mayor (16%). So, what makes these cities different from the rest? The Latina/o population average is 78.5 percent in cities with a Latina/o mayor. In contrast, cities without a Latina/o mayor average 44 percent of Latina/os in the population.

Table 7.2 Latina/o Lawmakers in Congress 2022 Making History

Name	Party	Representing	Ethnicity	First
Caraveo, Yadira	Democrat	Colorado House of Representatives 8th District	Second generation of Mexican descent	First Latina elected to Congress in Colorado
Chavez-DeRemer, Lori	Republican	Oregon House of Representatives 5th District	Mexican American	First Republican woman to represent Oregon in Congress
Ciscomani, Juan	Republican	Arizona House of Representatives 6th District	First generation Mexican (now naturalized)	First Republican Latino and the first immigrant Congress member
De La Cruz, Monica	Republican	Texas House of Representatives 15th District	Mexican American	First Republican woman to represent the 15th district
Garcia, Roberto	Democrat	California House of Representative 42nd Congressional District	First generation from Peru (now naturalized)	First LGBTQ+ Congress person
Gluesenkamp Pérez, Marie	Democrat	Washington House of Representatives 3rd District	Father immigrant from Mexico	First Democrat Latina to represent a seat that is nearly 90% white
Luna, Anna Paulina	Republican	Floria House of Representatives 13th District	Mexican American	First Mexican American woman elected in Florida Congress
Ramirez, Delia	Democrat	Illinois House of Representatives 4th District	Second generation from Guatemala	First Latina to be elected to Congress in the Midwest

Regarding the percentage of city council members that are Latina/o in the top 25 cities with a Latina/o population, there are four cities where 80 percent or more of the city council are Latina/os: Maimi, Santa Ana (California), Laredo (Texas) and Hialeah (Florida). Moreover, there are four cities that have between 50 and 60 percent of city council members being Latina/o: Las Vegas, Fresno, San Antonio, and El Paso. On the other hand, there are cities with a low percentage of Latina/os among the city council members. Particularly concerning are Houston and Philadelphia with 6 and 7 percent, respectively, of council members being Latina/o. The underrepresentation of Latina/s among the city council is especially apparent in Houston, which has the

Table 7.3 Cities with the Largest Latina/o Population and Local Political Representation, 2023

Rank by Latina/o Population	City	Mayor Latina/o	Pct. City Council Latina/o[a]	Pct. City Pop. Latina/o[b]	Pct. City CVAP Latina/o[b]	Ratio of Pct. City Council Latina/o to Pct. City CVAP Latina/o
1	New York, New York	No	35.3	28.9	25.2	1.40
2	Los Angeles, California	No	33.3	48.4	37.7	0.88
3	Houston, Texas	No	6.3	44.5	30.2	0.21
4	San Antonio, Texas	No	60.0	65.7	61.8	0.97
5	Chicago, Illinois	No	28.0	28.7	21.9	1.28
6	Phoenix, Arizona	No	25.0	42.7	31.9	0.78
7	El Paso, Texas	Yes	62.5	81.6	78.5	0.80
8	Dallas, Texas	No	28.6	42.0	27.2	1.05
9	San Diego, California	No	22.2	30.1	24.5	0.91
10	Fort Worth, Texas	No	20.0	35.3	24.2	0.83
11	Miami, Florida	Yes	80.0	72.3	66.3	1.21
12	San Jose, California	No	40.0	31.0	25.4	1.58
13	Austin, Texas	No	30.0	33.1	25.4	1.18
14	Albuquerque, New Mexico	No	22.2	49.8	45.7	0.49
15	Fresno, California	No	57.1	50.0	43.4	1.32
16	Philadelphia, Pennsylvania	No	6.7	15.4	11.8	0.57
17	Laredo, Texas	No	87.5	95.5	93.2	0.94
18	Santa Ana, California	No	83.3	76.7	65.2	1.28
19	Tucson, Arizona	No	33.3	44.6	39.0	0.85
20	Las Vegas, Nevada	No	50.0	34.1	24.1	2.07
21	Hialeah, Florida	Yes	100.0	95.8	95.3	1.05
1	Denver, Colorado	No	46.2	29.4	21.6	2.14
23	Bakersfield, California	No	14.3	52.0	44.4	0.32
24	Long Beach, California	No	22.2	43.9	35.0	0.64
25	Corpus Christi, Texas	Yes	37.5	64.2	61.3	0.61

[a] The term "City Council" is used for sake of convienence as it is the most common term but not all cities listed here use this term.

[b] CVAP denotes Citizens of Voting-Age Population, which represents US citizens 18 and older, the group that is ligible to vote.

Source: The authors compiled the data in this table from each of the cities' mayoral and city council webpage and identified Latina/os by bios in the webpage and other sources of information related to the elected officials. The information is current as of August 31 2023.

third largest Latina/o population, and where Latina/os account for 44 percent of the overall population, but they account for a mere 6 percent of city council members, a single Latina/o among a total of 16 city council members.

An important question is how the percentage of citizens of voting age population (CVAP) is associated with the percentage of Latina/o city council members. A ratio of percent Latina/o city council to percent Latina/os CVAP shows that Houston, again, is the city that has the lowest ratio (0.21). In Houston, despite Latinos representing 30.2 percent of the city's CVAP, they have no Latina/o mayor and only one of 16 city council members (6.3%). The cities with the best Latina/o representation in local politics are Las Vegas and Denver, with ratios of 2.07 and 2.14, respectively. In both cities, although their mayor is not Latina/o, the percentage of Latina/o council members is twice the percentage of Latina/o CVAP. About 40 percent of the cities with the largest Latina/o population have ratios above one, signifying that the percentage of council members that are Latina/os is representative of the Latina/o CVAP.

Issues Related to the Future of Latina/o Political Power

Having obtained an overview of Latina/o political behavior and attitudes, we now address some important political issues that affect the future of Latina/os. We will begin with the spread of anti-diversity, equity, and inclusion (DEI) and anti-critical race theory (CRT) state policies across the nation that can jeopardize the future standing of Latina/os and other groups of color (also see Chapter 9) The second issue we will discuss is the Deferred Action for Childhood Arrivals (DACA) implemented by President Obama, which of September 2023 is considered illegal.

State Laws Against Critical Race Theory and Diversity, Equity, and Inclusion (DEI)

W.E.B. Du Bois' famous quote in the impactful book *The Souls of Black Folk* (1903) stated "The problem of the twentieth century is the problem of the color-line" (Du Bois and Marable 2015, liii). Over a century later, American democracy continues to be tainted by racial equity and inclusion issues. Originating around the 1960s, diversity, equity, and inclusion evolved from emphasizing tolerance to multiculturalism to equity and inclusion (Zhao 2023). Diversity, equity, and inclusion (DEI) initiatives in education appeared to become mainstream. Indeed, in 2021 Taffye Benson Clayton of the American Council on Education stated that DEI is at the core of the mission of most institutions of higher education (Zhao 2023).

Yet, behind this appearance of DEI, the political landscape was changing rapidly. A growing polarization of race and sexuality has made its way into our schools and institutions of higher education (Zhao 2023). A political issue that will impact Latina/os and other groups of color into the foreseeable future is legislation against critical race theory and DEI. In the 2020 presidential campaign, Critical Race Theory (CRT) became a source of heated conversation in right-wing media, directly targeting K-12 and higher education (Cuevas 2022).

This political rhetoric became legislation in many states to dismantle CRT and DEI. As of 2023, 23 states have introduced legislation prohibiting DEI on several levels across the US (Table 7.4). Most anti-DEI legislation prohibits state funding for DEI offices and officers and requires the end of "political litmus tests" or diversity

Table 7.4 States with Anti-Diversity, Equity, and Inclusion Legislation Introduced, Approved, or Failed, June 2023

State	Policy	Snapshot of Provisions
Alabama	H.B. 7	Public institutions are prohibited from promoting, endorsing, or requiring affirmation of "divisive concepts," i.e. race, sex, or religion.
Arizona	S.B.1694	Public colleges are prohibited from requiring employees to engage in DEI, spending public funds on DEI, and establishing a DEI office.
Arkansas*	S.B. 71	Prohibited state and local governments from using affirmative action programs.
Florida	H.B.999, S.B. 266 (amended), H.B. 931, & S.B. 958	Prohibited funding of DEI programs, courses that teach "identify politics" or based on systemic racism, sexism, oppression, and privilege. State institutions are prohibited from giving preferential consideration for employment, admission, or promotion to individuals who support any ideology or movement that promotes the different treatment of a person or group based on race or ethnicity.
Georgia*	S.B. 261	Public institutions are prohibited from using "political litmus tests" in admissions and promotions.
Indiana	H.B. 1338	Prohibited public institutions from requiring students to engage in mandatory gender or sexual diversity training or counseling. Prohibits schools from presenting information on stereotyping based on race or sex.
Iowa	House File 616, successor to House Study Bill 218	If passed, prohibits colleges and universities governed by the Iowa State Board of Regents from funding DEI offices and officers.
Kansas	H.B. 2460	Post-secondary institutions are prohibited from providing admission or aid to students based on their support or opposition to political ideology. Ban schools to engage in DEI in hiring and spend state funds on requiring students, employees, or contractors to endorse DEI. (Note: Gov. Laura Kelly vetoed the parts of S.B. 155 based on higher education.)
Louisiana*	S.B. 128	Prohibited colleges and universities from providing preferential treatment through scholarships, grants, or financial aid to students based on race, sex, and national origin.
Missouri	S.B. 410, H.B. 75, S.B. 680, & H.B. 1196	If passed, it would prohibit higher education institutions from requiring students, instructors, or employees to answer questions about their ideology on DEI. Prohibits schools and higher education institutions from engaging in mandatory gender or sexual diversity training or counseling.
Montana	S.B. 283	Prohibited diversity training as a condition for employment and universities from compelling potential hires to believe in a list of inequalities, i.e. one class having privileges over another.

Table 7.4 (*cont.*)

State	Policy	Snapshot of Provisions
Nebraska	S.B. 283 (changed to a study)	Prohibited DEI offices and officers at public universities. The bill has been changed into a study.
North Carolina	H.B.607	Prohibited colleges and universities from asking students and employees about their political or social beliefs.
North Dakota	S.B. 2247	Students, professors, and other employees at higher education institutions cannot be asked about their political views.
Ohio	S.B. 83 (heading to Ohio House)	Prohibited DEI courses or training requirements for students, faculty, and staff. Would not be permitted to use the "political or ideology litmus tests" in hiring or promoting faculty.
Oklahoma	S.B. 870, S.B. 1008	Prohibited the funding of DEI offices and using "political tests" and diversity statements in hiring.
Oregon	H.B. 2430 & H.B.2475	Prohibited public educational institutions from requiring or compelling students to believe that any race, ethnicity, color, sex, gender, religion or national origin is inherently superior or inferior to another.
South Carolina	H.B. 4289 & H.B. 4290	Banned public institutions from establishing mandatory diversity training or statements and using diversity statements for hiring and admissions practices.
South Dakota	H.B. 1012	Targeted "divisive concepts" but does not restrict professors from teaching these subjects. Prohibited mandatory training or orientation about these concepts.
Tennessee	H.B.1376 & S.B. 102	Prohibited DEI training and education requirements on medical and health-related degrees and from using state funds to endorse or promote "divisive concepts." "Divisive concepts i.e. racism or sexism, are banned from teaching lessons. Students can report professors who teach "divisive concepts." Prohibited higher education institutions from firing faculty or employees who refuse to participate in implicit bias training.
Texas	H.B. 3164, S.B. 16, S.B. 17, & H.B. 1	DEI offices and officers, diversity training, and ideological oaths and statements are banned at public institutions. Critical race theory ban referred to the Higher Education Committee.
Utah	H.B. 451 & S.B. 283	Public institutions are prohibited from funding and promoting DEI offices and DEI statements from students, faculty, and staff for hiring or admission practices.
West Virginia*	H.B. 3503	Proposed eliminating mandatory diversity training i.e. discussions, workshops, and guest speakers on cultural appropriation, transphobia, homophobia, social justice, and inclusive language.

* Failed to pass.

Source: Data from Anti-DEI Tracker (Bryant and Appleby 2023).

statements for admission or employment. Several states also have language against promoting, endorsing, or requiring affirmation or training of what they call "divisive concepts," particularly race, sex, sexuality, religion, and national origin. By "divisive concepts," these laws imply that teaching about systemic oppression and inequality ensues in identity politics, pitting one group against another. Some states go even further and enact legislation against teachers and professors suspected of pushing critical race theory (CRT) onto "vulnerable" students. Indiana and Missouri even took this further by eliminating sexual diversity training and counseling. In this political context, there are concerns about how teachers and professors in the social sciences and humanities can teach, given that their fields are rooted in the understanding of culture, diversity, and inequality.

The elimination of CRT and DEI is detrimental to Latina/o students. For instance, Chicana/o, Mexican American, and Latina/o Studies courses and programs have helped to retain Latina/o students (Borom 2023). Ethnic study courses also improve academic success in terms of engagement, attendance, GPA, especially for at-risk students of color (Borom 2023).

There is a consensus that coursework on race benefits students' socio-emotional and cognitive development (de Novais and Spencer 2019); moreover, "divisive concepts" courses on Black and Latina/o Studies developed positive attitudes toward the group being studied and an understanding of systemic racism (de Novais and Spencer 2019).

Deferred Action for Childhood Arrivals (DACA)

For over twenty years, mobilizations have sought the legalization of youth who migrated as children, commonly called The Dreamers (also see Chapter 9). The name arose from proposed legislation titled the Development, Relief, and Education for Alien Minors Act, referred to as The Dream Act. For years, mostly Latina/o youth and their supporters have mobilized colleges, universities, and entire communities around this issue. Given that The Dreamers are largely Americanized, educated young adults who had no choice but to migrate because they were children when they were brought to the US, they gained some support during the Obama presidency. On June 15, 2012, there was a triumph for The Dreamers when the White House passed the Deferred Action for Childhood Arrivals (DACA). DACA legalized and authorized individuals for employment for two years if they came to the US as children and met other requirements. In the 10th-year anniversary of DACA, 800,000 individuals had registered, the majority of whom were born in Mexico.

In September 2017, the Trump administration announced it would rescind the DACA program (Mallet-García and García-Bedolla 2021). In June 2020, the US Supreme Court ruled that the Trump administration could not terminate DACA because it violated the Administrative Procedure Act (APA). However, it did provide an opening for eliminating DACA if they procedurally respect APA (Mallet-García and García-Bedolla 2021). The political turmoil behind DACA results in disenfranchisement and alienation of DACA recipients from American society for DACA recipients, even when they live in a welcoming state, e.g. California (Mallet-García and García-Bedolla 2021).

On September 13, 2023, a federal judge declared DACA illegal and made a declaration to immediately end the program and its protections. US District Judge Andrew Hanen sided with Texas and eight other states, suing to stop DACA. This decision is expected to be appealed to the US Supreme Court. The Court's rationale for terminating DACA is that the solution should lie with the legislature and not the executive or judicial branches. As such, the Executive Branch cannot bypass the power of Congress bestowed by the Constitution to make these decisions (Lozano 2023).

Summary

The story of Latina/os and US politics represents a mixture of efforts to disenfranchise them, but also shows political power and advocacy. This chapter has provided an overview of Latina/o political power and trends in voter registration, party affiliation, and group position. We also presented some highlights of the Chicana/o Movement and its leaders, i.e. César Chávez, Dolores Huerta, Reies López Tijerina, Rodolfo "Corky" Gonzales, and Jóse Ángel Gutiérrez. Since this civil rights movement, we have also witnessed the resiliency of Latina/os, as in the case of Puerto Ricans' victory at Vieques to remove the US Navy, and the current struggle to reclaim a say in the Puertan Rican economy.

The trends in Latina/o political participation are interesting. While Latina/os tend to identify more with the Democratic Party, there are growing numbers of Latina/os who identify as Independent, or who do not identify with a political party. This means that political parties still must work to win over Latina/o voters. Additionally, political parties should engage with new American Latina/os, as they are more likely to be registered voters than US-born Latina/os. Furthermore, there are also some interesting trends in terms of Latina/os support for President Trump in unlikely places such as South Texas. It will be interesting to see if the support for Trump in South Texas persists in the 2024 presidential election. Regarding Latina/o politicians there is a rich history of contribution to local, state, and federal governments. Building on this legacy, the US 2022 Congress has the highest number of Latina/os in history and there were several Congress people who broke records for being the first Latina/os elected in their states. While there is some point of optimism at the federal level, there are still more strides to be reached in local government. An analysis of the 25 most Latina/o populace cities, the ratio of the percentage of Latina/o council members to Latina/o citizens of voting age is above one in 40 percent of the cities, indicating proportional representation. Therefore, Latina/o voters are not being proportionately represented in city government in 60 percent of the 25 cities with the largest Latina/o populations. Particularly disturbing is the greatest Latina/o political underrepresentation in Houston, the third most populous city, where Latina/os account for 44 percent of the population and 30 percent of the CVAP but for only one of 16 city council members (6.3 percent).To make matters worse, Houston has never had a Latina/o mayor.

Discussion Questions

1. The Chicana/o Movement has mostly been associated with Mexican American rights in the Southwest. Do you believe that a pan-ethnic Latina/o movement is possible? Why, or why not?

2. Who are the "Four Horsemen" of the Chicana/o Movement?

3. There is a significant number of Latina/os who politically identify as Independent or who do not identify with Republicans or Democrats. What are the implications of this trend for future elections?

4. It had been speculated that Latina/os who are naturalized citizens may be less active in US politics. Here we show that they tend to be more engaged than the US-born when it comes to voter registration. How do you explain these results?

5. What are some concerns of Latina/o political representation in local government?

6. The banning of diversity, equity, and inclusion (DEI) across the US is spreading. What do you are the implications of these policies for Latina/os?

7. Why is DACA in legal limbo? What would it take to formalize DACA?

8 The Latina/o Arts

> In general, public art, art museums, and art galleries reflect settler colonialism and white supremacy because people of color are rarely decision makers in the art world. In essence, the wagons of settler colonialism have circled, creating a perimeter designed to keep people of color out. Anaya's struggle to find a publisher is the same experience that many Chicano artists endure in seeking venues to exhibit. Despite the obstacles and naysayers, we must believe in ourselves and in our work. The dominating white-controlled art community takes a toll on non-white artists due to the lack of access.   (Augustine "Gus" Romero 2021, p. 196)

Augustine "Gus" Romero's words are powerful. Romero, an artist and art curator living in Albuquerque, recently published these insightful observations concerning his experience of exclusion and marginalization. Many fellow artists, art curators, novelists, poets, and musicians would agree with Romero's thoughts. Countless numbers of Latina/o writers and artists have been shut out of the US mainstream publishing houses and museums because the "general public" would not understand or appreciate *that* work. As we discussed in Chapter 3, Octavio I. Romano and his collaborators started the Quinto Sol publishing house as well as *El Grito* to provide a place for Latina/o writers and scholars to publish their work and get it out to Latina/o readers – hungry to see themselves in these books, pages, and words. The exclusion of writers of color can be illustrated with the recent controversy (see Wheeler 2020) concerning the allegation of the appropriation of the immigrant experience by Jeanine Cummins, whose novel *American Dirt* drew bidding wars by the major publishing houses, with a lucrative advance never seen by the likes of well-established Latina/o writers, who write from insider lens. The struggle for acceptance into the mainstream continues, with many writers and artists of color themselves rejecting the rejectors by marketing their works in more friendly venues, which are less lucrative but reach audiences of color.

The Latina/o arts capture the heart and spirit of *la gente* or *la raza* (the people). Latina/o arts touches all aspects of the topics that we cover in this book. Latina/o novels, poetry, music, and paintings have long told the story of the Latina/o people in the areas of history, ties to the countries of origin, language, immigration, politics, education, work, resistance, crime and victimization, religion, gender and sexuality, among a multitude of other topics. One does not have to think for long to conjure powerful images or thoughts tied to our intimate lives and our cultures and histories from a variety of forms of art. The ubiquitous image of the Virgen de Guadalupe (in English, Virgin of Guadalupe) (see Chapter 12) regularly has been at the front and center in farmworker marches, demanding better wages and working conditions. Murals across the country, such as those found in Chicano Park in San Diego, depict the stories of the Latina/o people. There is a growing list of Latina/o novels, including early ones such as *Chicano: A Novel* by Richard Vasquez and *Down These Mean Streets* by Piri Thomas, which tell intimate accounts of the lives of Latina/os migrating to this country, or born here, and their life experiences and those of their families and loved ones. *Corridos*, folk ballads, written long ago and also recently, describe major events and personages, as well as the everyday and commonplace events and people. The image of Tejana singer Selena (Selena Quintanilla Pérez), who died tragically at such an early age in 1995, along with the rhythm and lyrics of her songs, is deeply etched in the minds and hearts of her many fans, who include a new generation that is being exposed to her iconicity and music in Netflix's *Selena: A Series* in 2020 and 2021. There is a wave of development of university courses on Selena, with Sonya Alemán, a professor of Mexican American Studies at the University of Texas at San Antonio, leading the way (Carrizales 2020; Garcia 2020).

In this chapter, we highlight two types of art: the written form (novels and poetry) and the musical form (music and songs). In doing so, we provide portraits emphasizing the historical roots and transformations that have occurred. In certain respects, the writers covered here represent the humanities' counterparts of scholars in the social sciences who have developed and shaped scholarship and social thought on Latina/os, as discussed in Chapter 3. The list of writers and musicians whom we introduce below is not meant to be exhaustive. Aside from the particular individuals whom we feature here, there are many others who have also made important contributions through their works.

Latina/o Literary Art

The Formative Period

There is a very rich tradition of literature in the US Latina/o community, beginning in the late 1950s. We highlight here two writers (Luis Leal and Américo Paredes) who were born in the early twentieth century and who made major contributions to the development of Latina/o letters. Luis Leal (1907–2010) was born in Linares, Nuevo Leon in Mexico, living through the Mexican Revolution during his formative years. Following the end of the Revolution, Leal immigrated to the US in pursuit of education and became a naturalized citizen. He received his undergraduate degree at Northwestern University in 1940 and continued his graduate education in Spanish at the University of Chicago, where he received his M.A. degree in 1941 and Ph.D. in 1950. He held faculty positions at the University of Mississippi, Emory University, the University of Illinois at Urbana-Champaign, and the University of California, Santa Barbara. Over a career expanding six decades, Leal was a prominent scholar of Mexican, Latin America, and Chicano literature (García 2000). While most of his works as a writer in the 1950s to 1970s focused on Mexican and Latin American literature, by the early 1980s he turned his attention to Chicana/o and Latina/o literature, a venture he had begun in the late 1960s. As he made this intellectual transition, Leal considered himself to be an "adopted Chicano" (García 2000, p. xiii). His prominence in the field is legendary, as he is called "the dean of Mexican American intellectuals in the United States" (García 2000, p. xi).

As a senior scholar, Leal played a prominent role in calling attention to and promoting the nascent Chicana/o literature. Leal's career working on Chicana/o literature spanned over three decades at the University of Illinois Urbana-Champaign and at the University of California, Santa Barbara. His publications include works overviewing the field and its historical roots, making linkages to the literature originating from Mexico, Latin America, and Spain (García 2000; Leal 1980, 1985a, 1985b; Leal and Barrón 1982; Leal et al. 1982), Chicana/o poetry (Leal 1984a, 1993), the concept of *Aztlan* (the mythical homeland of Aztecs) (Leal 1980, 1981, 1984a), writing on the works of Chicana/o writers, including Rolando Hinojosa (Leal 1984b), Miguel Méndez (Leal 1995), Alejandro Morales (Leal 1996), Américo Paredes (Leal 1987), and Tomás Rivera (Leal 1985c). Mario T. García's (2000) interview with Leal, who reflects back on his career and discussions on trends in Mexican, Latin American, and Chicana/o literature, is particularly enlightening. Leal died in 2010 at the age of 102. His legacy lives on through his writings, critiques, the writers he mentored, and through the Luis Leal Endowed Chair in the Department of Chicana and Chicano Studies at the University of California, Santa Barbara.

We now turn our attention to the second writer of the formative period. Earlier in the chapter on Latina/o social thought (Chapter 3), we introduced readers to him – Américo Paredes (1915–1999), a writer and folklorist originating from Brownsville, Texas, located along the Texas–Mexico border. Historian Ricardo Romo (2021) refers to Paredes as a "renaissance man" who was a journalist, poet, musician, and radio announcer before becoming a scholar. Paredes received his doctoral degree from the University of Texas at Austin in 1956, becoming the first Mexican American to receive a Ph.D. in English from this university. He turned his dissertation into a highly influential book titled *With His Pistol in His Hand* in 1958 (Paredes 1958). This work is based on the incident involving Gregorio Cortez (1875–1916), who was born in Mexico and lived in Karnes County, Texas (approximately 50 miles southeast of San Antonio), that took place there on June 14, 1901. The local sheriff W.T. (Brack) Morris was investigating a horse theft and was assisted by his deputy, Boone Choate, who spoke Spanish and served as interpreter when they visited the ranch where Gregorio and his brother, Romaldo, lived (Orozco 1995). The Mexican American man who reported the theft of his horse had already told the sheriff that he had swapped his horse for a mare that Gregorio owned. The sheriff and deputy's encounter with the Cortez brothers escalated quickly over the white lawmen, not knowing the distinction between the word *caballo* (horse or male horse) and *yegua* (mare or female horse). When Deputy Choate asked Gregorio if he had traded a *caballo* (horse), Gregorio explained that he had not traded a *caballo* but that he traded a *yegua* (mare). The deputy interpreted Gregorio's response as a denial and that he had something to hide (Orozco 1995). The sheriff informed the Cortez brothers that they were going to be arrested. When they questioned him, he took out his gun and fatally shot Romaldo, with Gregorio pulling out his gun and killing the sheriff. Using ingenious tactics and horsemanship skills, Gregorio Cortez was able to elude the Texas Rangers, who pursued him for thirteen days (Orozco 1995).

Gregorio Cortez became a hero of local Mexican Americans, who faced racism and treatment as second-class citizens at the hands of whites. Cortez was tried several times and eventually, in late April 1904, an all-white jury acquitted him of the murder of Sheriff Morris, due to self-defense, but convicted him on the murder of Gonzales County Sheriff Robert Glover, whom he had killed while evading his capture, and he was given a life sentence (Orozco 1995). Eight years later, Texas Governor O.B. Colquitt pardoned Cortez and set him free. Cortez died a few years later in 1916 at the age of 41 in Anson, Texas, approximately 200 miles east of Dallas (Orozco 1995). Paredes' book was translated into a movie titled *The Ballad of Gregorio Cortez*, with Edward James Olmos playing the role of Gregorio Cortez in 1982 (IMDb 1982).

In writing *With His Pistol in His Hand*, Paredes received hostility from the white establishment, including prominent historian Walter Prescott Webb, whose work glorified the Texas Rangers (Handelman 2002), for his critical but accurate assessment of the Texas Rangers, who for long tortured and killed Mexican Americans with impunity. Peña and Bauman (2000), in their obituary of Paredes published in *The Journal of American Folklore*, write that Paredes "forcefully argued, the biased views of such writers – in particular academics like Walter Prescott Webb – were intended not only to explain and rationalize Anglo dominance but to perpetuate it and to put a stamp of legitimacy on it" (p. 196). Moreover, in the Mexican American community, Paredes was lauded for presenting a more realistic portrait of Mexican Americans and demonstrating their agency in contrast to the stereotypical images that were consistently depicted by white scholars. Peña and Bauman (2000) provide us with a glimpse of Paredes' loathing of oppression in the following passage:

> . . . he [Paredes] abhorred hierarchy based on illegitimate power, particularly when such power was used to oppress entire groups of people, typically under the guise of some purportedly higher social imperative, such as saving America from the "yellow peril" or deporting thousands of Mexicans to protect the economic security of "real" Americans. He thus struggled, through his writings and his deeds, to expose the hidden motives – racism, classism, and even sexism – behind such undemocratic actions. In this process, Paredes became a defender of the disempowered, most often his own people, whom he saw as underdogs in a racially tinged struggle against Anglo-Americans for political control of the Southwest. (p. 196)

Paredes' work, coming on the heels of the Chicano Movement (see Chapter 7), was influential to the first wave of Chicana/o writers that would emerge during the next two decades. Like Luis Leal, Paredes had a long and distinguished career, for most of it serving on the faculty of the University of Texas at Austin. In 1997, the American Folklore Society's Section on Latina/o, Latin American, and Caribbean Folklore granted him an award as "the most important and influential American folklorist in the field of Mexican American and borderland folklore" (Peña and Bauman

2000, p. 197). In 1995, Texas singer-songwriter Tish Hinojosa, who was a student of Paredes, wrote a *corrido* (folk ballad) in honor of Paredes, titled "Con Su Pluma en Su Mano" ("With His Pen in His Hand"), substituting in the title Cortez's pistol for Paredes' pen.

The Chicana/o Movement Era

As the spark of the Chicana/o Movement gained strength in the 1960s and 1970s (see Chapter 7), we saw the blossoming of Chicana/o literature. Tomás Rivera (1935–1984) represents one of the most revered writers from this era. Rivera was born and raised in Crystal City, Texas, which was one of the most prominent sites of the development of the Chicana/o Movement. As a child, Rivera worked alongside his parents and siblings as a migrant farm worker, annually leaving Crystal City in April for the Midwest where they picked crops, and returning to South Texas in early fall. Rivera's (1971) book titled *Y No Se Lo Tragó la Tierra (And the Earth Did Not Devour Him)* is a classic in Chicana/o literature. The novel, consisting of more than a dozen short stories and vignettes, draws on his experiences as a migrant farm worker. Rivera paints a portrait of the vulnerable conditions of farmworker families and children, their expendability, and the racism that they experienced. Haunting stories illustrate this: a young Mexican American migrant farmworker child shot by a farmer for taking too many water breaks, two young Mexican American children burned to death in an accidental fire, as the farmer did not allow the parents to bring them to the fields, and a young Mexican student expelled by a school principal after he lashed out at his white classmate when he could no longer take their racism, with the principal justifying his decision by saying that Mexican children don't need education but are needed in the fields (Rivera 1971). An anthology of Rivera's work is available (see Olivares 1992).

In addition to being a highly celebrated writer, Rivera was a remarkably passionate and successful educator and administrator, holding faculty and administrative positions at Sam Houston State University, University of Texas at San Antonio, University of Texas at El Paso, and the University of California, Riverside, where he was the first Latina/o chancellor of a University of California institution and where he died at the tender age of 48.

Rolando Hinojosa-Smith (1929–2022), a very close and dear friend of Rivera, represents another major writer associated with the Chicana/o era. Hinojosa-Smith, son of a Mexican American father and white mother, was born and raised in Mercedes, Texas, the hometown of one of the co-authors of this book (Rogelio Sáenz). He had a long and distinguished career holding academic positions at Trinity University, Texas A&I University (now Texas A&M University-Kingsville), the University of Minnesota, and the University of Texas at Austin, where he spent the greatest part (35 years) of his career. Hinojosa-Smith wrote fifteen novels as part of his *Klail City Death Trip* (KCDT) series. Hinojosa-Smith is regularly compared to William Faulkner, who wrote about his fictional Yoknapatawpha County. For Hinojosa-Smith, the setting for novels that form the KCDT series is the fictitious Belken County, an amalgam of the four counties on the southernmost tip of Texas, an area known as "the Valley." Books that are part of the KCDT series include *Estampas del Valle y Otras Obras* (*Stamps from the Valley and Other Works*) (Hinojosa 1973), *Partners in Crime* (Hinojosa 1985), *Klail City* (Hinojosa 1987), *Becky and Her Friends* (Hinojosa 1990), *Ask a Policeman* (Hinojosa 1998), and *Dear Rafe/Mi Querido Rafa* (Hinojosa 2005).

Hinojosa-Smith aptly captured the major changes that have taken place in Belken County, extending back centuries to the present. Bruce-Novoa (1987), drawing on Hinojosa's work, notes that in the region "Anglos control[led] the centers of power, such as the banks, the government, and the legal system, they are the key players in events that directly affect the intimate lives of the Mexicano community" (p. 289). In Belken County, Hinojosa-Smith draws attention to the lives of Mexicanos in the region, their aspirations, their thoughts, their agency, which are commonly ignored in favor of stereotypical views of Mexicanos.

One of the profound insights that Hinojosa-Smith makes in his KCDT series is the deep connection that people who grew in the Valley region have to the region. Hinojosa (2011), in his short story titled "Es el Agua" ("It is the Water"), intimates:

> We have a saying here in the Rio Grande Valley: *es el agua*; it's the water, the Rio Grande water. It claims you, you understand? It's yours and you belong to it, too. No matter where we work, we always come back. To the border, to the Valley. (p. 125)

In an essay reflecting on Hinojosa-Smith's writings, Sáenz (2013b) observes:

> It is clear that while Rolando Hinojosa physically left the Valley, in a psychological and intellectual sense he never left Mercedes and its surrounding area. Indeed, the memories of his youth about the region and its people, language, and culture consistently emerge in his writings associated with the *Klail City Death Trap* series and beyond. He has a strong sense of place as he says and writes about the place and the people that he knows best.(p. 224)

Rolando Hinojosa-Smith passed away on April 19, 2022. His obituary appeared in the *New York Times* (Sandomir 2022). Nicolás Kanellos, founder and director of Arte Público, has noted that Hinojosa-Smith in the KCDT series was "a surveyor of the human scene, always keen to recognize the humor, irony and just plain outrageousness of people, especially as political animals" (Sandomir 2022). Sandomir, in the obituary observed that Hinojosa-Smith had said that his "hundreds of characters – fools, knaves, heroes and cowards among them – reside in a place called Belken County, of which I'm the sole owner and proprietor . . ." Hinojosa-Smith received numerous awards honoring his work, including the National Book Critics Circle's Ivan Landrof award for lifetime achievement in 2014, referring to him as the "dean of Chicano authors."

The Chicana/o Movement also produced many important poets. One of the most prominent poets of this era is Alberto Baltazar Urista Heredia, better known as Alurista (1947–) (see Chapter 7), which represents the combination of the shortened version of his first name along with his surname. Alurista was born in Mexico City and migrated with his family to San Diego when he was thirteen years of age. He received his bachelor's degree in psychology from San Diego State University and his M.A.

and Ph.D. in literature from the University of California, San Diego. His doctoral dissertation focused on the work of Oscar Zeta Acosta, a Chicano lawyer who defended Chicano organizations and activists in Los Angeles, including the Chicano 13 associated with the momentous East L.A. student walkouts in 1968 (López 2018) and author of *Autobiography of a Brown Buffalo* (Acosta 1972) and the *Revolt of the Cockroach People* (Acosta 1973) (see Stavans 1995) (see Chapter 7).

Alurista is commonly seen as the most influential poet of the Chicana/o Movement. Public accolades, highlighting his major influence, are plentiful: "the first postwar Chicano poet" (Dewey 2012, p. 44); "the poet laureate of Aztlán" (the mythical homeland of the Aztecs) . . . "poeta-maestro" (master poet) (González 2017, p. 27); the individual who "made the most significant contributions and innovations" to Chicano poetry (Bruce-Novoa 1981); and "our earliest activist and wordsmith" (González 2017, p. 20). Alurista gained notoriety when he, as a 21-year-old poet, took to the stage and delivered a captivating poem at the First National Youth Liberation conference organized by Rodolfo "Corky" González (see Chapter 7), one of the four major Chicano Movement leaders, in March 1969. Alurista's poem would become the preamble to *El Plan Espiritual de Aztlán* (*The Spiritual Plan of Aztlán*), a manifesto calling for Chicana/o nationalism and self-determination. Alurista's first section of what would become the manifesto's preamble reads:

> In the spirit of a new people that is conscious not only of its proud historical heritage, but also of the brutal "Gringo" invasion of our territories, we, the Chicano inhabitants and civilizers of the Northern land of Aztlán, from whence came our forefathers, reclaiming the land of their birth and consecrating the determination of our people of the sun, declare that the call of our blood is our power, our response and our inevitable destiny. (Burri 2010)

The preamble concludes:

> Before the world, before all of North America, before our brothers in the Bronze continent, We are a Nation of free pueblos, we are Aztlán. (Burri 2010)

Alurista's prominence in the Chicana/o Movement and in the world of Chicana/o letters soared over the next half century. He is commonly seen as a pioneer in Chicana/o poetry, with his work emphasizing the consciousness of a Chicana/o identity, the use of bilingualism in his poetry (codeswitching between Spanish and English), the incorporation of indigenous languages, emphasis on the spiritual indigenous roots of Chicana/os, and as one of the earliest writers to develop the meaning and significance of the concept of "Aztlán," the mythical homeland of the Aztecs (Dewey 2012; García 2000; González 2017; Lomelí 2005; López 2008). Alurista was highly critical of individualism and imperial capitalism, which symbolized the white conquerors. For him, the Chicana/o collectivity signified a key for gaining liberation from the oppression experienced by Chicana/os. As López (2008) notes, "Although Alurista shares the belief of many *Movimiento* activists that imperial capitalism is the foundation of Chicano/a oppression, he believes that liberation comes not simply from rectifying social inequities, but from each individual's recognition of themselves as connected, creative forces" (p. 98). Furthermore, López (2008), drawing on her interview with Jorge Ruffinelli, points out that to Alurista "liberation comes not from throwing off the shackles of capitalist oppression, but from realizing one's creative potential . . . [which] is not an individualistic quality, but a communal one" (p. 98).

Alurista is quite prolific, with his works spanning across five decades, beginning with such works as *Floricanto En Aztlan* (Alurista 1971), *The Chicano Cultural Revolution: Essays of Approach* (Alurista 1973), *Timespace Huracan: Poems, 1972–1975* (Alurista 1976) in the 1970s to *Zaz* published in 2020 (Alurista 2020). Sandwiched in between these books are other major works including *Spik in Glyph?* (Alurista 1981), *Et Tú . . . Raza?* (Alurista 1995a), *Z Eros* (Alurista 1995b), *Return: Poems Collected and New* (Alurista 1999), *As Our Barrio Turns: Who the Yoke B On?* (Alurista 2000), *Tunaluna* (Alurista 2010), and *Xicano Duende: A Select Anthology* (Alurista 2011).

Alurista has been a pioneer of Chicana/o – and, more broadly, Latina/o – poetry and has influenced countless poets through the last half century. Lomelí (2005) captures the significance of Alurista and his work when he writes "Of all the Chicano movement's leaders in the 1960s, Alurista demonstrated the greatest breadth and versatility by developing a social agenda, an artistic plan, a cultural design, and, most important, a new language." Moreover, López (2008) indicates that Alurista's "primary objective is to dismantle our notions of identity by troubling categories of language, nation, time, and history. Alurista seeks to disrupt hierarchies of imperialist capitalism, racist anthropological discourse, and defeatist essentialism" (p. 111). Moreover, Alurista never left behind his commitment to getting into, in the words of the Honorable John Lewis, "good trouble." He has been a lifetime activist, defending the rights of the Chicana/o community. Rigoberto González (2017) shows his frustration with academics who get too comfortable and so do not rock the boat, but highlights Alurista's commitment to the cause when he says "Thankfully, poets like Alurista have remained unafraid to mix the gunpowder into their ink" (p. 22). Alturista's writing, his passion, and his activism continue to date.

The organizer of the First National Youth Liberation conference, where Alurista gained national prominence, Rodolfo "Corky" Gonzales (1928–2005), was not only one of the four major leaders of the Chicano Movement (see Chapter 7), but he was also a boxer, political organizer, activist, and a writer. Gonzales, born in Denver, was one of the most influential leaders of the Chicano Movement. As a professional featherweight boxer, he compiled a record of 65 wins, nine losses, and one draw. Gonzales was ranked as the third highest featherweight in the world by the National Boxing Association and *Ring Magazine* (Denver Public Library 2022). Gonzales ran unsuccessfully for various political offices in Denver in 1955, 1964, and 1967. As a writer, Gonzales wrote throughout his life. However, his epic poem titled *Yo Soy Joaquin* became the spiritual anthem of the Chicana/o Movement. Gonzales first self-published the poem in 1965 and two years later it was published by Bantam Books (Gonzales 1967). In an interview by *La Cucaracha* (1977), which is part of the Colorado Historic Newspapers Collection, Gonzales disclosed the rapid manifestation in which the words came to him:

I wrote it in 1967. The Crusade was going to do a dramatic reading some little actos [acts] for a fund raiser. I sat down one night and asked "Who is Joaquin?" And then I told myself, "You are Joaquin." Then I asked "Who am I?" Then this historical story and the words just poured out . . . I wrote it in a narrative form. I started writing about 11 o'clock at night and I finished about 5 o'clock in the morning. (La Cucaracha 1977)

The poem captures the struggle that Chicanos face in the reality of colonialism, domination, and racism, with the route to success being assimilation and the foregoing of one's identity, culture, and history. The poem begins:

> Yo soy Joaquín,
> perdido en un mundo de confusión:
> I am Joaquín, lost in a world of confusion,
> caught up in the whirl of a gringo society,
> suppressed by manipulation, and destroyed by modern society.
> My fathers have lost the economic battle
> and won the struggle of cultural survival.
> And now! I must choose between the paradox of
> victory of the spirit, despite physical hunger,
> or to exist in the grasp of American social neurosis,
> sterilization of the soul and a full stomach.
>
> (Gonzales 1967, pp. 7 and 9).

The poem concludes:

> I am the masses of my people and
> I refuse to be absorbed.
> I am Joaquín.
> The odds are great
> But my spirit is strong,
> My faith unbreakable,
> My blood is pure.
> I am Aztec prince and Christian Christ.
> I SHALL ENDURE!
> I WILL ENDURE!
>
> (Gonzales 1967, p. 100)

Just as the Chicana/o Movement brought a surge of literary and artistic activity throughout the Southwest, the same was taking place on the other side of the country, as Puerto Ricans developed a literary and artistic movement.

The Nuyorican Movement

In the late 1960s to early 1970s, Puerto Rican writers, poets, artists, and musicians developed the Nuyorican Movement in New York City. The term Nuyorican was used to define Puerto Ricans who were from New York. Like the term Chicano, Nuyorican was previously used as a derogatory term. Like Chicano activists, Puerto Rican activists used it in a favorable fashion showing pride in being a Puerto Rican in New York. The Nuyorican Movement was very successful in galvanizing Puerto Ricans writers, poets, artists, and musicians, creating a space for significant artistic activity and collaboration along with the development of a variety of institutions, including art galleries, bookstores, theaters, cultural centers, and the iconic El Museo del Barrio and Nuyorican Poets Café. In some ways, the Nuyorican Movement is reminiscent of the Harlem Renaissance of the 1920s and 1930s. Gemma Solomons (2017) observes:

> One of the most iconic, important cultural and intellectual movements to come out of New York City, the Nuyorican Movement, produced some of the best works of poetry, literature, art, and music of the twentieth century. Miguel Algarín Jr., poet and founder of the historic cultural institution Nuyorican Poets Cafe on the Lower East Side, was one of the first to reclaim the title of Nuyorican. Some other notable artists from this movement include Esmeralda Santiago, Piri Thomas, Pedro Pietri, Miguel Piñero, Eddie Palmieri, and Tito Puente.

Now we highlight some prominent writers and poets from the Nuyorican Movement. Piri Thomas (1928–2011) was the son of a Puerto Rican mother and a Cuban father. Thomas (1967) gained great notoriety when he published his memoir, titled *Down These Mean Streets*, in 1967. The book is described as an "instant classic." Thomas lived a very tough life, being involved in gangs, drugs, and crimes. He served a seven-year prison sentence for armed robbery. The book came out of his decision while he was in prison to help turn the lives of youths like him, who could end up in the prison system or dead. In the book, Thomas writes about the struggles that he experienced as an Afro-Latino youth facing major racism, beginning in his own home with his father treating him worse than his siblings because of Piri's dark skin, and the racism extending to the streets. Thomas describes how he felt when he was writing the book: it "exploded out of my guts in an outpouring of long suppressed hurts and angers that had boiled over into an ice-cold rage" (see Berger 2011). The 30th anniversary edition of the book was published in 1997. Some of his other works include *Savior, Savior Hold My Hand* (1972), *Seven Long Years* (1974), and *Stories from el Barrio* (1979). Thomas died in 2011 from pneumonia at the age of 83 (for his obituary, see Berger 2011). He had a tremendous impact on influencing other writers of color. At the time of Thomas's death, Martin Espada, a Puerto Rican poet born in New York City, claimed that "Because he [Thomas] became a writer, many of us became writers . . . Before 'Down These Mean Streets,' we could not find a book by a Puerto Rican writer in the English language about the experience of that community, in that voice, with that tone and subject matter" (Berger 2011).

Nicholasa Mohr is a major Nuyorican Movement writer. She was born on November 5, 1938. At the time of the publication of *Down These Mean Streets: A Memoir* in 1967, Piri Thomas was the only Puerto Rican writer with a major book published by a mainstream press. Six years later, Mohr joined him in this coveted position with the publication of her book titled *Nilda* in 1973. Mohr became the first woman in the Nuyorican Movement to have a novel published by a major publishing house that year. Belén (2021) describes the semi-autobiographical *Nilda* as "the life of a Puerto Rican girl growing up in New York's El Barrio (Spanish Harlem) during the 1940s, as she discovers the complexities of a surrounding hostile environment, plagued with poverty and racial discrimination endured by many Puerto Ricans in US society." Other major works of Mohr include *El Bronx Remembered, Rituals of Survival: A Woman's Portfolio, The Song of El Cocquí and Other Tales of Puerto Rico.*

Tato Laviera (born Jesús Abraham Laviera) (1950–2013) is widely known as one of the major Nuyorican Movement poets. He was born in Santurce, Puerto Rico, and moved with his family to New York City when he was nine. Laviera took the name "Tato" (a nickname) after a teacher tried to get him to use his middle name "Abraham" instead of his given name Jesús. Laviera, who wrote in Spanish, English, and "Spanglish," was widely published. His books were regularly published by Arte Público Press. Laviera's major works include *La Carreta Made a U-Turn* (1979), *Enclave* (1981), *Mainstream Ethics-Ética Corriente* (1988), *AmeRícan* (1999), and *Mixturao and Other Poems* (2008–2009). In his poem titled "AmeRícan," which appears in the book with the same title, Laviera coins a new identity, which combines American and Rican and is drawn from the pride that he felt for being an American and a Puerto Rican. Laviera died in 2013 from diabetes at the age of 63 (for his obituary, see González 2013). Laviera embodied the spirit of the Nuyorican Movement. At the time of Laviera's death, Jesús Papoleto Meléndez, a fellow poet, observed that "The American thing is to forget who you are and become homogenized. The whole Nuyorican struggle was to maintain your roots because they are the groove that keeps it all together. Tato personified that struggle" (González 2013).

The works of writers and poets in the Chicana/o Movement and the Nuyorican Movement are very important in building an important foundation for Chicana/o and Puerto Rican and, more broadly, Latina/o literature. The work captured the spirit of the time filled with activism, calling out racism and injustices, and the hope of improving the lives of Latina/os. We can draw some patterns. For the most part, the publication outlets of Latina/o writers and poets of that era tended to be disproportionately limited to Latina/o publishing houses. Things were about to change, particularly with the increase in women authors.

The Next Generation

By the beginning of the 1980s, a new generation of Latina/o writers emerged. In certain respects, they shared a commonality with the writers of the formative period. Indeed, their work dealt with topics such as reflections of their youth and the places where they come from, issues of identity, racism, immigration, and politics. Yet, for the most part, similarities generally end there. Indeed, there were major changes that took place in this generation of Latina/o writers. First, the next generation was much more diverse in various ways. They were much more likely to be women, to come from outside the southwestern part of the US, to not be Chicana/os, and to be immigrants themselves or children of immigrants. Second, their range of topics was much broader, with gender, patriarchy, sexuality, domestic violence, citizenship, and transnationalism becoming much more prominent features of their work. Third, the new generation of Latina/o writers expanded their reach concerning its readership and publication outlets. While Latina/o writers of the formative period commonly encountered obstacles related to restrictive publishing outlets and readership, the new generation of Latina/o writers have been much more likely to publish their work with mainstream publishing houses Of course, the wider access has been due, in part, to the significant growth in the Latina/o population along with their greater distribution across the country. At the time of the earlier generation of Latina/o writers, the Latina/o population numbered nine to ten million, based on varying definitions in 1970 (Haub 2012), compared to nearly 63 million in 2021.

There are many prominent Latina/o writers who began their careers over the last couple of decades of the twentieth century. Undoubtedly, Sandra Cisneros is one of the most recognized Latina/o writers of this era. Cisneros was born in Chicago on December 20, 1954. She received her bachelor's degree from Loyola University and her M.F.A. from the University of Iowa Writer's Workshop. Cisneros broke into the writing mainstream with the publication of the prize-winning book titled *House on Mango Street*, first published by Arte Público Press in 1984 and by Vintage Contemporary in 1991. The prize-winning book, which has sold more than six million copies and been translated into twenty languages, was reviewed in the *New York Times Book Reviews* and listed in its best-sellers list. *House on Mango Street* is based on the life of Esperanza Cordero, a young Latina girl living in Chicago. In the book, Esperanza discovers her sexual awakening and the power that she has over boys and men in a bilingual–bicultural world with one side based on the Mexican life of her family and the other in which she makes her way in school and the larger city of Chicago. Cisneros has published numerous other notable books, which have received significant notoriety, including *Bad Boys*, her first book, published in 1980, *My Wicked, Wicked Ways* (1987), *Woman Hollering Creek and Other Stories* (1991), *Caramelo* (2002), *Have You Seen Marie?* (2012), *A House of My Own* (2015), *Puro Amor* (2018), and *Martita, I Remember You/Martita* (2021), and *Te Recuerdo* (2021).

Julia Alvarez is another prominent Latina/o writer. She was born in New York City on March 27, 1950, and lived the first ten years of her childhood in the Dominican Republic. Alvarez's novels focus on issues concerning identity, assimilation, acculturation, and immigration. Her first two novels *How the Garcia Girls Lost Their Accents* and *In the Time of the Butterflies*, both published in Algonquin Books in 1991 and 1994, respectively, achieved significant notoriety. *How the Garcia Girls Lost Their Accents* consists of fifteen short stories narrated by the Garcia sisters, beginning as adult women and tracing back to their upbringing in the Dominican Republic, until their father was forced to leave the island due to his opposition to Rafael Trujillo, the country's dictator (see Chapter 2). The book focuses on the alienation, acculturation, and assimilation that the four sisters experienced as they tried to find their way in New York City after being forced out of the Dominican Republic. *In the Time of the Butterflies*, Alvarez tells the story of the lives of the four Mirabal sisters living in the Dominican Republic during the Trujillo dictatorship and how they varied with respect to their support for the revolution set on overthrowing Trujillo. The book was adapted into a 2001 movie with the same title, featuring Selma Hayek and James

Edward Olmos. Other notable works of Alvarez featuring novels, poetry, essays, and nonfiction include *The Other Side: El Otro Lado* (published in 1995), *Homecoming: New and Selected Poems* (1996), *Yo!* (1997), *Something to Declare* (1998), *In the Name of Salomé* (2001), *The Woman I Kept to Myself* (2004), *Saving the World: A Novel* (2006), *Once Upon a Quinceañera: Coming of Age in the USA.* (2007), *A Wedding in Haiti: The Story of a Friendship* (2012), and *Afterlife: A Novel* (2020), and *The Cemetery of Untold Stories: A Novel* (2024). Alvarez has received numerous prestigious awards, including the National Medal of Arts, which she received from President Obama in 2013.

Ana Castillo is another acclaimed Latina/o writer who began her career in the 1980s. She was born on June 15, 1953, in Chicago. Her work deals with issues related to Chicana feminism and the concept of Xicanisma. Castillo, a highly prolific writer, has a wide range of writing genres. In many respects, the themes in her works extend back to the mid-1980s. Her writings have covered issues concerning intersectionality, Chicana feminism and the neglect of the major contributions of Chicanas to the Chicana/o Movement, border violence against women, and sexuality. Castillo's first novel, *The Mixquiahuala Letters*, takes an epistolary form, with Teresa, a writer of Mexican indigenous roots who grew up in Chicago, penning letters to Alicia, a white woman who grew up in New York. The forty letters cover events such as their meeting as exchange students in Mexico City, their relationships with men, Teresa's feelings regarding Alicia as a white woman, a deconstruction of their friendship, among a variety of other topics. Her novel *So Far From God*, published in 1993, gained a considerable amount of notoriety. The novel focuses on Sofi, a Latina mother, and her four daughters, Caridad (Charity), Esperanza (Hope), Fe (Faith), and La Loca (The Crazy One) living in a small town in New Mexico. The novel is influenced by the magical realism of such Latin American writers as Gabriel García Márquez, who wrote the classic novel *Cien Años de Solidad* (*One Hundred Years of Solitude*). La Loca dies when she is three years old but comes back to life after gaining healing powers, only to die a couple of decades later after contracting AIDS. The novel deals with issues concerning gender, spirituality, and rebellion.

There are many other prominent Latina/o authors who have emerged over the last few generations. Some of these include Erika Sánchez, a writer and poet, whose novel titled *I'm Not Your Perfect Mexican Daughter* (2017) received wide notoriety; Iliana Rocha, a poet, who recently published a book of poetry titled *The Many Deaths of Inocencio Rodriguez* (2022); Jaime Cortez, a writer, who recently published a book of short stories titled *Gordo* (2021); Ada Limón, the current national poet laureate who is the first Latina to hold this prestigious post, who recently wrote a book of poetry titled *Lucky Wreck* (2021); Myriam Gurba, a writer, whose recently wrote a book titled *Mean* (2017); Xochitl González, a writer, producer, and screenwriter, who recently published a novel titled *Olga Dies Dreaming* (2021); Cristina García, who recently published a novel titled *Vanishing Maps* (2023) in which she revisits the Del Pino family from her debut novel titled *Dreaming in Cuban* (1993), which she published thirty years earlier in 1993; Angie Cruz, who recently published a new novel titled *How Not to Drown in a Glass of Water: A Novel* (2022).

In sum, we have provided a deep overview extending through several generations of writers, beginning with the formative period, the Chicana/o Movement, and the newer generations, and concluding with a selection of recent books published by Latina/o writers. There has been much change in the publishing houses, where Latina/o writers publish their work with more recent authors publishing their work outside of traditional Latina/o outlets. We examine next another form of art that has undergone significant change – music.

Latina/o Music

Music plays a critical role in Latina/o culture, as it does for many other cultures. The Latina/o music we have encountered through the ages has been an expression of culture, time, history, and the lived experiences of diverse Latina/o groups. From emotive ballads and political *corridos* to the fast up-tempo reggaeton music and crossover Tejana/o music, Latina/o music is rich and has, naturally, evolved throughout time to reflect generational experiences.

Tejana/o music is a popular genre of music that combines musical elements from Mexican and Texan cultures. According to the Bob Bullock Texas State History (n.d.) Museum, the genre evolved primarily in South Texas during the nineteenth century. Throughout the nineteenth century, indigenous Mexican music began incorporating elements from French dance music, German polkas, and other influences. Lydia Mendoza, who began her music career as a young girl in the mid-1900s in the Lower Rio Grande Valley in Texas, is o ne of the most famous early Latina singers and one of the earliest women in Tejana/o music (National Endowment for the Arts 2022). Mendoza, who was known as the "queen," has been dubbed the "first lady of Tejano" (Burnett 2010). Other early Tejano artists included Ramón Ayala, Roberto Pulido, La Mafia, and Mazz. The twentieth century ushered in a new wave of Tejana/o musicians that would further popularize Tejana/o music, including Selena Quintanilla Pérez (commonly known as Selena), Emilio Navaira, and Bobby Pulido (son of early Tejano legend Roberto Pulido). While these three Tejana/o musicians experienced much success and fame, Selena's legendary stardom continues to influence the US cultural scene more than a quarter century after her fateful death. Two years after her tragic death, a movie about Selena's life was produced, with lead actress Jennifer Lopez becoming the first Latina to earn more than $1 million for a feature film (Franklin 2022). Tejana/o music continues to influence the music scene today, with artists like Veronique Medrano from Brownsville, Texas, and Chiquis Rivera (daughter of late banda Queen, Jenni Rivera).

In the genre of regional Mexican or *norteno* music, one of the most influential bands of all time is Los Tigres del Norte. Originally from the Mexican state of Sinaloa, the band formed in 1968 with the members beginning their careers playing in local restaurants, until they eventually brought their music to the US in the mid-1970s. Their music and *corridos* are famous for the message and the story they bring to Latina/o and Latin American music. They are famous for songs like their 1984 hit "La Jaula de Oro," which depicts the impact of migration on multiple generations within a family. The opening lyrics of the song set the stage, stating that even though "muchos años tengo ya" ("many years I have been here [in the United States]"), "sigo siendo un ilegal" ("I continue being illegal") (Los Tigres del Norte 1984).

The title of the song illustrates the way that the main character in the song feels. Even though he is here in this large nation with so many riches and owns a home, because he is undocumented, he is not free to get around for the fear of being deported. He laments that even though the cage (home or country) is made of gold, it continues to be a prison to him.

According to the Grammy's website, Los Tigres del Norte have been nominated for the award sixteen times and won a total of seven Grammys. The group's commitment to the preservation and education of Mexican music led them to founding the Los Tigres del Norte Foundation, which is headquartered at the University of California, Los Angeles (Gurza 2015). Other Mexican artists who have left their mark in regional Mexican music, especially in *cumbias*, include Los Angeles Azules, whose 37-year career reached a new peak when they performed at the American music festival of Coachella and gained massive attention when pop singer Justin Bieber was filmed dancing to their music during their performance (Roiz 2019). Young generations of Mexican Americans are continuing to preserve the cumbia and *corridos* of regional Mexican music, all the while evolving the genre based on their generational experiences. Contemporary bands like Fuerza Regida of California now produce urban corrido music that embrace "*pocho*," a slang and derogatory term used to identity persons of Mexican origin in the US who do not speak Spanish well or have lost their Mexican culture (Mier 2022). In Texas, a new generation of cumbia norteña music artists like Grupo Frontera have climbed to the top of the charts with hits like, "No Se Va" and their duet with Fuerza Regida in "Bebe Dame," which entered the top 50 of the Billboard Hot 100 charts in 2023. Grupo Frontera's musical styles reflect their life and experiences of growing up along the Texas–Mexico border and the unique culture of the borderlands.

Many Mexican and Mexican American musicians have left their mark on the US American music scene. Inarguably, one of the most iconic Mexican artists who brought a blend of genres to the music world was Juan Gabriel of Michoacán, Mexico. Juan Gabriel, who was born Alberto Aguilera Valadez, reportedly sold over 100 million albums during his 40-year career (Andrews 2017), with some of his greatest hits including "Querida" and "No Tengo Dinero," of which the latter was the first single of his debut album in 1971 (Gurza 2017). Gabriel's persona drew comparisons with artists like Prince, Michael Jackson, and David Bowie (Andrews 2017).

Marco Cervantes, a professor of Mexican American Studies at the University of Texas at San Antonio, has studied how the fusion of Mexican American and African American cultures has influenced music. Cervantes has talked about his work as "black and brown music solidarity." Cervantes says "I talk about a cultural afromestizaje [and] put on events that showcase some of the artists I feel fit that particular history. It's a way I think to look at Chicano music and really center Blackness and figure out ways to value and honor the Black roots of Mexican American, Tex-Mex, Chicano music" (Mendoza et al. 2022). The intersection of other cultures and ethnicities in Mexican music is also seen in the work of Lila Downs Sanchez (known musically as Lila Downs). Downs Sanchez, born in the Mexican state of Oaxaca to what she describes as a Mixtec Indian woman and a white man. Downs Sanchez grew up both in Minnesota and Oaxaca and her music reflects the many intersectionalities (e.g. race-class-gender and related intersectionalities) of her lived experience. According to her own website, Downs Sanchez combines "genres and rhythms as diverse as Mexican rancheras and *corridos*, boleros, jazz standards, hip-hop, cumbia and popular American music" (liladowns.com). Downs Sanchez has won six Grammy awards, marking the impact and significance of her music in the US music scene.

Latina/os from outside of Mexico have also made huge impacts on the American music scene across different genres. In the 1960s and 1970s, salsa music emerged as a vibrant emblem of cultural awakening within the barrios (Manuel 2007). Rooted in the visionary efforts of bandleader Johnny Pacheco and entrepreneur Jerry Masucci, Fania Records ignited a Latin music revolution (Manuel 2007). By infusing the New York Latin beat with unapologetic Latina/o pride and identity, Fania transformed it into the pulsating rhythm known as salsa (Manuel 2007). The rise of salsa harmonized with a period of heightened social consciousness among New York City's Latino communities, especially the Puerto Ricans, affectionately known as "Newyoricans" (Manuel 2007). Inspired by civil rights movements and fueled by a newfound ethnic pride, Latinos embraced their rich cultural heritage. Rejecting assimilationist pressures, they celebrated their distinct identity. Fania Records deftly capitalized on this cultural shift, positioning salsa as a vibrant reflection of barrio life, even as its stylistic roots traced back to Cuban dance music (Manuel 2007). Salsa became more than just music; it became a powerful expression of resilience and belonging. Co-founder Johnny Pacheco himself built an impressive musical career. Johnny Pacheco, born in the Dominican Republic, became known as the "Godfather of Salsa "and composed over 150 songs (EFE 2021). He famously shared the state with American jazz stars including Tony Bennett, Sammy Davis, Jr., and Stevie Wonder (EFE 2021). His company eventually acquired the Tico Imprint, and became home to Latin stars, including Pete Rodriguez, Joe Cuba, and Celia Cruz (Waring 2024). Cruz, undoubtedly, is one of the most legendary artists to have influenced the US music scene, and was known to many as the "Queen of Salsa." Cruz became the lead singer for the Afro-Cuban orchestra Sonora Matancera. According to the National Museum of African American History and Culture (2022), Cruz was "known for singing guarachas, a style of Cuban music with rapid tempo and comic or picaresque lyrics, earning the moniker 'La Guarachera de Cuba.'" In the mid-1900s, Cruz left Cuba for Mexico, eventually settling in the US, where her solo career took off in the New York music scene. Some of her most successful songs included, "Guantanamera," "Quimbara," and "La Vida es un Carnaval." Toward the end of her musical career, Cruz embraced the reggaeton genre, producing songs like "La Negra Tiene Tumba" (Cantor-Navas 2019). Three decades before the death of Celia Cruz, another young Cuban American woman began her musical career in 1975. Gloria Estefan and her husband, Emilio Estefan, married in 1978, and began their rise to global fame in 1985 with the Miami

Sound Machine, "creating a unique sound that blended Latin and pop rhythms" (Library of Congress 2022a). According to Horn (2022), Gloria Estefan's music career in the 1980s and 1990s "made Latin music part of mainstream pop culture and was essential in helping the next generation of Latin artists, such as Shakira and Jennifer Lopez, achieve massive crossover success."

In the twenty-first century, the reggaeton genre has dominated the US music industry. In 2020, Cobo (2020) reported that on *Billboard*'s overall Top 200 chart, Latin music was the third largest genre, behind rap/hip-hop and pop. In 2017, Puerto Rican-born singers Luis Fonsi and Daddy Yankee released their song, "Despacito," which later became the most streamed song in the United States, with 1.3 billion streams (Abad-Santos 2017; Cobo 2017). Since 2017, the number of Spanish language songs making it to Billboard's Hot 100 tracks has continued to grow. In 2017, only nineteen mostly Spanish songs made the Hot 100 list, but that number increased to 26 in 2021 (Cobo 2022). In the summer of 2022, Puerto Rican reggaeton superstar Bad Bunny's seventh album had nearly 357 million on-demand streams in the first week, making it the largest streaming week ever for a Latin music album. Reggaeton has been a phenomenon that has dominated social interests in the US, as evidenced by the prominence and demand for the music. For a more in-depth discussion of the social, cultural, and historical aspects of reggaeton, the sociologist Raquel Z. Rivera and her colleagues (2009) provide a comprehensive study of the genre in their book titled *Reggaeton*. Other contemporary Latina/o artists in the reggaeton genre currently influencing the music scene in the US include Pitbull, Nicky Jam, Karol G., and Becky G.

In the pop scene, Jennifer Lopez has continued to influence the US music scene. Lopez's most notable accomplishments include her headlining the Super Bowl half-time show, alongside Colombian singer Shakira. In January 2021, Lopez sang at the inauguration of President Joe Biden and Vice President Kamala Harris. During her performance, Lopez switched from English to Spanish and recited a portion of the pledge of allegiance, a move that resonated with Latina/os in the US. Other US-born Latina/os who have and continue to influence pop music include Marc Anthony, Camilla Cabello, and Jaime Luis Gomez of the Black Eyed Peas.

US-born Latina/os are also influencing and creating music outside of pop, regional music, and reggaeton. Carlos Santana is one of the most famous Latina/o guitarists to play a fusion of Latin rock, blues, and jazz. He rose to fame in the 1960s and 1970s with smash hits like "Black Magic Woman/Gypsy Queen" and "Oye Como Va." David Montgomery (2013a) of the *Washington Post* wrote that Santana redefined rock and roll with the inclusion of congas, timbales, and Afro-Latin guitar and organ rhythms. Santana's 1999 album, Supernatural, which included rock and pop superstars of the time like Dave Mathews and Lauren Hill, won nine Grammys that year. Santana was born in Autlan de Navarro, Mexico, where his father, who was a professional violin player, taught him how to play the instrument to Mexican folk tunes. Like many other Latina/o musicians of his era, Santana and his family immigrated to the United States in the 1960s, when he was a teenager (Montgomery 2013b). Santana has received a Kennedy Center Awards, Billboard Century Award, and has been inducted into the

Rock and Roll Hall of Fame. In 2021, he received the Legend Award at the 34th Annual Hispanic Heritage Awards (Hispanic Heritage 2021).

Latina/os in rock have also gone underrepresented for their contributions to the genre. Contemporary Latina/os include Mexican American bassist Robert Trujillo, who has played for some of the most revered metal bands, including Suicidal Tendencies and Ozzy Osbourne. He is currently playing with the band Metallica, one of the most famous metal bands of all time. Other Latina/os in US rock bands include Deftones lead singer Chino Moreno, Incubus drummer José Pasillas, and Rage Against the Machine lead singer Zack de la Rocha. In the neighboring genre of punk music, contemporary Latinas have also made their mark. Girl in A Coma, an all-Latina punk band originating from San Antonio, is one such band that earned worldwide success. They were the opening band for famous rock bands like Morrissey, the Smashing Pumpkins, Tegan and Sara, and Joan Jett (Vine 2022).

There are many more Latina/o artists who have influenced the American music scene and the evolution of genres and musical styles outside of those mentioned in this chapter. The music of other Latin American countries, such as merengue and bachata of the Dominican Republic, samba and bossa nova of Brazil, mambo and bolero of Cuba, and vallenato of Colombia, all beautiful and unique in their own way, have influenced much of the music we hear today in the US. Music can also serve as a conduit, connecting different cultures and enriching the growing diversity of the United States.

This section has provided an extensive overview of the Latina/o contributions to a wide variety of genres of music in the US scene. We began the discussion with some of the more traditional music stemming from the Texas–Mexico border and the great diversification and fusion found in the music of Latina/o musicians, reflecting the increasing diversity of the Latina/o population and expansion into all parts of the country, very different from what was the case back in the 1960s, when the Latina/o population was much smaller, more homogeneous, and concentrated in a few regions of the country.

Summary

This chapter has provided a wide swath of the development of literary works and music among Latina/o writers and musicians, respectively. We have provided some historical context to overview the changes that have taken place in Latina/o literary works and music. As we referred at the beginning of this chapter to the powerful words of Romero regarding the marginalization of artists and art curators in a white world and white space, which often marginalizes Latina/os and other people of color, this has been the case in many facets of the development of literature and music. But we have also seen that Latina/o writers and musicians, despite still encountering barriers, are also expanding their reach. The work covered in this chapter is intimately related to all of the chapters and topics covered in this book – from history to social thought, to immigration, to demography, to gender and sexuality, as well as to health and health care, crime and victimization, education, political engagement, religion, mass media, work and economic life, and family. For now, we turn our focus to education in the following chapter.

Discussion Questions

1. Who would you consider pioneers in the development of literary writings of Latina/os in the US? Why?

2. How do writers in the New Generation differ from their earlier counterparts in the Formative Period and the Chicana/o Movement era?

3. Which writer is associated with Belken County in his literary work? What does Belken County represent?

4. How have Latina/o musicians and genres, such as salsa, reggaeton, and Tejana/o, transformed and enriched the American music landscape?

5. What role have iconic Latina/o artists like Selena and Carlos Santana played, not only in popularizing their own music but also in breaking barriers and paving the way for future Latina/o musicians in the United States?

6. In what ways are the developments in literature and music among Latina/o artists related to the broader topics covered in the book?

7. What lasting impacts did Luis Leal and Américo Paredes have on the development of Latina/o literature, particularly in terms of challenging stereotypes and promoting agency within the community?

9 Education

Once, while at an airport, I started conversing with a woman who asked what I did for a living. At that time, my research focused on the Latina/o–white educational gap. As I discussed the data on how Latina/os lagged behind whites in education, she commented, "Ugh, some people are just not as smart as others!"

(Maria Cristina Morales)

The quote above represents the sentiments about biological perceptions of racial differences that have diminished in academia but are still prevalent in society. Following biological notions of race leads to erroneous conclusions that the Latina/o–white student education gap is attributed to intelligence rather than societal disparities. An examination of the racial disparities in educational achievement in the US among Latina/os shows the slow progress in closing the gap and that the gap persists for multiple generations (Telles and Ortiz 2008), or even downward assimilation in new destination regions (Marrow 2020a). Indeed, the racial gap in educational achievement has been virtually unchanged since the 1970s (Merolla and Jackson 2019). The US Department of Education's (2019) report, *Status and Trends in the Education of Racial and Ethnic Groups 2018*, highlighted troubling trends in reading and mathematical achievement between 1992 and 2017. Specifically, the Latina/o–white reading achievement gap from 1992 to 2017 is virtually unchanged for 4th graders. Among 8th graders, the Latina/o–white reading achievement gap narrowed from 26 points in 1992 to 19 points in 2017. Therefore, in 25 years, there has been little to no improvements in narrowing the Latina/o–white student achievement gap in reading and math in the US.

Moreover, there is evidence that Latina/o students value education and have higher educational aspirations than do their white peers (Goldsmith 2004). Given the continual Latina/o–white academic gap, this signals that the educational system needs to do more to develop such ambitions. Elsewhere, in a study of successful Latinas, education was a family goal, not just an individual one, and it took the sacrifices of the entire family to ensure the youths'/children's educational success. This means that theories of cultural deprivation or cultural deficit can fail to acknowledge the cultural wealth of Latina/o students and their families (Gonzales 2012).

There has been some progress regarding Latina/os' access to higher education. Latina/os disproportionately attend a two-year as opposed to a four-year institution of higher education (Ayala 2012). According to the American Association of Community Colleges (2022), 50% of Latina/o college students attend community college. Yet, socioeconomic disparities continue to present barriers to higher education. A barrier is socioeconomic status. Many Latina/o college students also have the added burden of helping their families economically. A study at a university in Southern California found that 40 percent of Latina/o students reported helping to meet the financial needs of their parents and siblings (Gandara and Orefield 2011). The labor of poor and working-class immigrant Latina/o youth is common and vital for their personal and families' economic stability and future mobility (Canizales and Hondagneu-Sotelo 2022). On the other hand, this financial help between parents and Latina/o college students is mutual. Latina/o parents also prioritize the financial needs of their children in college, even over their own needs, which is particularly difficult for undocumented parents to achieve (Cuevas 2019). Therefore, despite being economically strapped, Latina/o families attempt to offer economic help from both directions – students to parents and parents to students.

This chapter will illustrate the educational disparities among Latina/os in the US We begin with a theoretical discussion of perspectives used to examine Latina/o achievement and educational attainment from biological and culture deficiency perspectives to structural frameworks. We then highlight some pressing trends in Latina/o education, including the Deferred Action for Childhood Arrivals (DACA) and the impact of COVID-19 on virtual learning. Additionally, we present data from the 2019 American Community Survey (ACS) Public-Use Microdata Sample to examine Latina/o educational outcomes in school dropouts/pushouts, high-school graduates, and college graduations across Latina/o subgroups and two comparative groups (whites and Blacks). Lastly, we highlight the political climate that can hamper future academic success for Latina/os.

Theoretical Perspectives

Biological and Cultural Deficiency Theories

Today, various explanations are used to explain the Latina/o–white gaps in academic achievement, from biological and culture deficiencies theories to institutional and structural critiques (Ochoa 2013). Among the most problematic and erroneous are biological explanations that attribute the Latina/o educational lag to low IQs and thus say they are less capable of reaching the academic achievements of whites. The quote at the opening of this chapter, for instance, attributed the Latina/o–white gap in education to perceptions that Latina/o students are not as bright as their white peers. Therefore, in mainstream society, Latina/o students are subject to "blaming the victims" perspectives, rather than attributing any educational gap to structural inadequacies. While scholarly research based on biological perceptions of the Latina/o–white education gap has dwindled, this view remains relevant among the public and some K-12 academic institutions.

Biological deficiency perspectives have mostly been replaced by cultural deficiency theories that attribute the Latina/o–white education gap to "inadequacies" in

Latina/o culture. For instance, cultural deficiency or cultural deprivation perspectives have historically claimed that the social environment of disadvantaged children, i.e. Latina/os, slows their intellectual growth (see Hunt 1964). Both individual and cultural deficiency perspectives consequently blame Latina/os for their education lag, while downplaying institutional processes and structures (Ochoa 2013).

In the case of Latina/o students, a cultural feature that continues to be judged as a form of cultural deficiency is language. Educational research has illustrated that Spanish-speaking children have been evaluated from cultural and linguistic deficit views, rather than acknowledging failures in the educational system (Flores 2005). This is concerning, given that approximately two-thirds of Latina/o school-aged children have at least one immigrant parent, which indicates that Spanish is spoken at home (Gándara and Mordechay 2017). Moreover, 20 to 30 percent of low-income Latina/os reside in linguistically isolated households, where no adult speaks English (Wildsmith et al. 2016). Blaming Latina/o culture, i.e. Spanish speakers who lack English-language proficiency, fall under the umbrella of "blaming the victim," given that such views overly simplify Latina/o culture and disregard structural barriers responsible for educational disparities.

Arguably, some cultural deficiency perspectives in education are aligned with interpretations of the *culture of poverty* (e.g. Lewis 1966) paradigm and other similar theoretical perspectives, which are based on assumptions of white middle-class superiority and the devaluation of non-white cultures. According to such views, the low educational outcomes of Latina/os (and other groups of color) are attributed to the groups' culture that lacks ambition, supported by stereotypes of welfare dependency, low work ethic, and irresponsibility (Moynihan 1965). According to this view, the academic struggles of Latina/os are rooted in the low socioeconomic status, which creates a culture of disillusionment that presents barriers to succeeding in conventional ways, including educational attainment.

In disputing cultural deprivation perspectives, some scholars focus on the assets of Latina/o culture for educational attainment. Angela Valenzuela's (1999) *Subtractive Schooling: US–Mexican Youth and the Politics of Caring* accentuated how Latina/o youths' conceptualization of education is downplayed, and assimilationists' policies and practices minimize Latina/o culture in school in Houston. Latina/o high-school students feel the lack of authentic caring from teachers and administrators and see their education as rooted in subtractive assimilation or to dimmish their Spanish and disintegrated barrios (Latina/o neighborhoods). Latina/o students have a strong sense that the educational goal is to learn English, while not affirming their cultural worth as Mexicans. Therefore, the education of Latina/o students is focused on eliminating their cultural differences rather than embracing them. Consequently, Latina/o students are learning English at the cost of their Spanish skills, and this does not necessarily equate to gaining academic success. This subtractive education in the form of losing Spanish impedes healthy intergenerational interactions between immigrants and native-born. Moreover, Latina/o students perceive administrators' goals as providing the kind of subtractive education that will get them out of their barriers and prevent them from returning to their people again. Nearly twenty years later, cultural disparities that disproportionately impact Spanish-speaking Latina/os continue to be embedded in the American school system. There still is an urgent need for the K-12 school system to be aware of the cultural aspects of Spanish-speaking Black and Latina students and for educators to be culturally sensitive, provide culturally responsive pedagogy (Steketee et al. 2021; Contreras and Rodriguez 2021), and regularly assess the biases for positive academic (Steketee et al. 2021).

Other barriers for Latina/o students partly stem from a cultural mismatch between home and the educational setting. For example, even though parental involvement is important for the academic motivation of Latina/o children (e.g. Ayala 2012), some unfamiliarity with the educational system, being non-native English speakers, having low levels of education, residing in unsafe neighborhoods, and employment in secondary labor markets (see Chapter 10), all compromise their participation in the education of their children (e.g. Ayala 2012; Bean and Tienda 1987; Toldson and Lemmons 2013). Therefore, there is a mismatch between the culture at home and school. To alleviate this issue, schools need to engage parents from diverse cultural backgrounds, including those who speak a language other than English, and communicate about both positive and negative student achievements with parents (Toldson and Lemmons 2013).

This cultural mismatch between the students and their families and schools leads us to the notion of "cultural capital" developed by Bourdieu (1977). Accordingly, educational systems adapt to the attitudes and aptitudes of the dominant group. The elite, or the dominant social class, use knowledge, skills, and language to navigate educational institutions. By valuing the cultural capital of children from middle- and upper-class families, inequality is reinforced for the working-class and poor children in the school system. This, in turn, hampers the educational attainment of working-class Latina/o students. Consequently, academic institutions reinforce the inequality toward working-class and poor students, while contributing to the social reproduction of the dominant class.

By broadening the scope of the cultural capital of Latinas in the K-20 educational system, Gonzales (2012) questioned cultural deficit thinking. Aligned with the concept of familism (see Chapter 11), she found education to be a family goal, not just an individual one. The entire Latina/o family is working to ensure the children's academic success and college attendance (Gonzales 2012). In turn, rather than a cultural deficiency, the successful Latinas attributed their educational accomplishments to cultural values rooted in community, faith, and compassion (Gonzales 2012). Other scholars have also found that family and culture play a vital role in the success of Latina/os in higher education (Jabbar et al. 2019; Ramirez, Garcia, and Hudson 2020).

Social Reproduction and Social Transformation

Bourdieu's concept of social reproduction helps explain the cultural deficit lenses used to explain Latina/o academic achievement. Pierre Bourdieu and his associates (Wacquant and Bourdieu 1992; Bourdieu 1977; Bourdieu and Passeron 1977; Bourdieu 2018a) developed the theoretical perspective of *social reproduction* to contend that formal education perpetuates inequality by legitimizing the social hierarchy and transforming it into a hierarchy of merit, leading to the fact that educational systems are a social reproduction mechanism replicating existing social hierarchies outside the classroom.

Bourdieu's best-recognized concepts for explaining social reproduction are social and cultural capital. In social hierarchies, agents and institutions occupy dominant and subordinate positions. These positions are shaped by the resources or social capital (networks of people) and cultural capital (the social assets of a person) that explain unequal school achievement or the differential returns that children from different classes attain in the academic market (Bourdieu and Passeron 1977; Bourdieu 2018b). Education then plays a crucial role in legitimizing the hierarchy by naturalizing social divisions regarding cognitive classification and material privilege (Bourdieu and Wacquant 1992). As a result, social reproduction in education is a mechanism that preserves or enhances dominant interest and neglects how the distribution of different types of capital structures the social world (Bourdieu and Passeron 1977). A less prominent concept but integral to Bourdieu's social reproduction is *habitus* (Edgerton and Roberts 2014). Habitus refers to a set of learned preferences or cognitive schemas, structures of perception, conception, and action used to navigate the social world (Bourdieu 2004). Habitus is based on family socialization and conditions based on one's position in the social hierarchy. In examining Bourdieu's social reproduction theory, most theories use cultural capital and habitus to explain the intergenerational persistence of social inequality (Edgerton and Roberts 2014).

In Mitchell L. Stevens' (2007) *Creating a Class: College Admissions and the Education of Elites*, he outlines how formal schooling is part of social reproduction or the transfer of knowledge, culture, and social position from one generation to the next. Social reproduction occurs in the classroom, at home, and at other social gatherings to ensure that children have good lives. Forming schooling then provides the structure to organize and legitimize these processes. The organization of school, in turn, widely influences society, i.e. where people live, how children are raised, how money is spent, how to plan for the future, what achievements are valued in society, and even who they are in relation to others.

Yet, educational systems not only have social reproductive elements but are also transformative, where learning is geared to motivate and empower individuals to make informed decisions at the individual, community, and global levels (UNESCO 2023). Desjardins (2015, p. 239) argued that "Ideally, education would reproduce the 'good' and transform the 'bad', but 'good' and 'bad' are value-based and inherently political in nature." Stevens (2007) sees the contention between social reproduction and social transformation as based on contradictory national legacies. On the social transformation side, there is faith in education as a vehicle for upward mobility. Moreover, Americans have invested millions of tax dollars in education and programs to ensure college readiness. On the other hand, there is a long history of racial segregation and institutional exclusion. As a result, students of color remain outsiders to the higher education system built to serve Anglo-Europeans. Moreover, the context of heightened immigration enforcement and exclusionary policies has weakened the children of immigrants' opportunities for upward mobility (Marrow 2020b). On this topic, Stevens (2007: 142) argued: "The basic character of American higher education evolved over two full centuries before African American young people, let alone Latino and Asian American students, were welcomed to attend college with whites." The balance and tensions between social reproduction and social transformation are then based on governance and power relations, as reflected in the dominant socio-cultural and socio-political institutions (Desjardins 2015).

Structural Impediments to Latina/o Education

One of the most critical and documented structural factors affecting social reproduction in education is socioeconomic status (SES) (e.g. Bourdieu 1977). Social class has both a direct and indirect effect on educational attainment (Sullivan 2001). As a result, educational attainment is lower for those at the bottom of the socioeconomic hierarchy than for those at the top. Poverty is a significant impediment to educational success, which is especially concerning, given that approximately two-thirds of Latina/o children live in poverty (Gándara and Mordechay 2017). Within the educational system, poverty shapes students' access, their classmates, and who will teach them (Gándara and Mordechay 2017). Poverty influences nutrition, health care, and even time with their parents outside of school, which can impact educational outcomes (Gándara and Mordechay 2017). Furthermore, disparities in school funding result in middle-class children being primarily well-educated compared to children from working-class and poverty backgrounds, many of whom are disproportionately Latina/o, Black, and Native American.

Due to institutional barriers and a lack of socioeconomic resources, Latina/o parents, especially immigrants, have not had the tradition of US scholarship and schooling (see Bean and Tienda 1987). This pattern, in turn, becomes problematic when considering the strong relationship between the education of parents, an indicator of socioeconomic status, and that of their children. As a result of the low levels of educational attainment among Latina/o adults, these patterns place Latina/o youth in a vulnerable position for educational attainment, an indication of social reproduction. The persistent impact of social class is found among various educational indicators. In a study on the publishing rates of STEM students at a Hispanic-serving institution, undergraduate research programs designed to enhance diversity may close some gaps in line with social transformation perspectives but inadvertently reproduce class inequalities as predicted by social reproduction frameworks (Grineski et al. 2018).

Although the effects of SES on the academic success of Latina/os are widely acknowledged (Gándara and Contreras 2020), researchers disagree on the magnitude of this association. This is mainly due to how class intersects with race, which also positions people in the stratification system, shaping the type and number of resources people can access (e.g. Bonilla-Silva 2004; Feagin and Van Ausdale 2001; Omi and Winant 1994). Indeed, in a review of the literature on Latina/o educational attainment, Ayala (2012) argued that it is evident that the position of Latina/os in the racial hierarchy plays a significant role in lowering their educational achievement.

A useful theoretical lens that can be used to examine systemic racism in education is Bonilla-Silva's (1997, p. 469) concept of *racialized social systems*, which refers to "societies in which economic, political, social, and ideological levels are partially structured by the placement of actors in racial categories or races." Accordingly, the benefits of SES on academic achievement may be reduced in the case of Latina/os (and other groups of color) (Morales 2007). In such cases, Latina/os with higher SES may retain their cultural heritage and racial identifiers and still face discrimination from the larger society, dampening the positive effects of social class. Thus, not only is class structurally situated in society but race/ethnicity as well.

Applying structural racialization to unequal scholastic achievement is complex and entails analyzing how race impacts education and vice versa. For example, an examination of how race influences other elements, such as institutional processes and the racial hierarchy responsible for the substandard educational patterns, is warranted for the analysis of systemic racism in education. For instance, in a review of the literature on race and the achievement gap, Merolla and Jackson (2019) argue that a range of causes, including socioeconomic status, family cultural resources, school quality and racial composition, and bias and prejudice in schools, all link race to academics, culminating into structural racism or a system of social organization that privileges whites and disadvantages Americans of color.

Among the most impactful structural explanations for the Latina/o–white gap in education is unequal funding across public schools associated with living in racially and economically segregated neighborhoods or barrios. Some issues faced in underfunded public schools include quality of instruction, schools' curriculum, extracurricular activities (Aryaman et al. 2020), and crumbling school buildings needing repairs (Center for American Progress 2020). These inequalities are then magnified for students with mental health and learning disorders, whose needs are barely met, and who still need accommodations (Aryaman et al. 2020). Moreover, school budget cuts have narrowed opportunities for extra-curricular activities, mainly in the arts, which is problematic, considering the benefits of such programs for children's well-being in and out of the classroom (Knop and Siebens 2018). Also concerning are the disparities in extracurricular participation between low- and high-income families (Knop and Siebens 2018). These patterns of institutional disparities have ramifications for the upward mobility of present and future generations, given that children underserved by the educational system are more likely to become adults unable to provide for their families (Kozol 1991).

Many underfunded schools and racial disparities in public elementary and secondary schools are attributed to using property taxes as the main funding mechanism. Property-based school funding creates unequal funding when considering that neighborhoods occupied by low-income residents have lower property taxes, which translates to having schools with fewer resources for students. Dozens of lawsuits have been filed, based on the large gap in funding at high-income versus low-income schools (Aryaman et al. 2020). Moreover, the average differences in state per pupil funding range between $5,700 and $17,000 (Aryaman et al. 2020; Center for American Progress 2020). Due to the disparities in property tax-based school funding, some states are moving away from local property taxes to state property tax oversight (e.g. Illinois and Michigan). Still other states (i.e. California) are setting limits on local property tax growth (e.g. California) (https://www.ncsl.org/research/education/fun ding-approaches-the-property-tax-and-public-ed.aspx).

One way that Latina/o ethnicity structurally intersects with economic disparities is segregation. In the West, Latina/os students are the most racially segregated and isolated by poverty and language (Gándara and Mordechay 2017). Yet, Latina/os are not only segregated in the West. In a study of the education segregation of Latina/o children from 1998 to 2010, Fuller et al. (2019) found Latina/os have become more segregated in school. However, there are some variations in nativity status. The children of native-born Latinas benefit more from economic integration in school than those with immigrant mothers (Fuller et al. 2019). These patterns in ethnic and economic segregation are concerning, given that Ochoa (2004) found that schools in working-class Latina/o neighborhoods had less advanced placement classes and minimal representation in the school boards, compared to those in racially integrated middle-class neighborhoods.

Educational Trends among Latina/os

COVID-19 and the Digital Divide

Disparities in education became magnified due to issues with the digital divide within online and hybrid learning during the coronavirus (COVID-19) pandemic (Kim and Padilla 2020). One of the ways in which this happened is through the digital divide. Low-income Latina/o students are segregated in poor schools that have fewer resources for remote learning, in contrast to wealthier schools that distribute computers and internet (Lara 2021). According to Christina Quintanilla-Muñoz from the Intercultural Development Research Association (IDRA), the digital divide refers to a range of issues that impede access to digital technologies, such as access to broadband infrastructure, access to reliable, high-speed, affordable internet services, access to digital skills training, and access to technical support of digital technologies (personal interview on June 17, 2022). The digital divide in virtual learning did not impact all children equally. According to a national survey from Abriendo Puertas/ Opening Doors on June 12–19, 2020 about one-third of Latina/o families do not have regular internet access or access from cell phones, almost 60 percent of Latina/o parents feel that online schoolwork is difficult due to technical issues, about a half had higher internet or cell phone bills due to online school, and about a half do not have enough computers, laptops, or tablets for everyone in the household (https:// nationalsurvey.ap-od.org/#education). Similarly, a study in Silicon Valley found Latina/os faced inadequate access to technology in the home due to socioeconomic barriers (Kim and Padilla 2020). This is concerning, given the low SES among Latina/os (Chapter 11) and the importance of SES and cultural capital for social

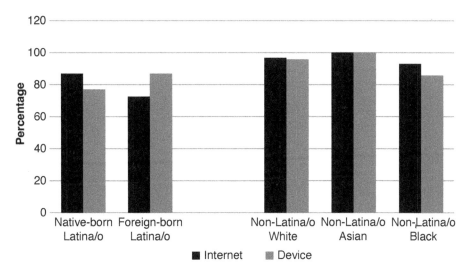

Figure 9.1 Percentage of Parents with Access to Internet and Computer Device by Race/Ethnic Group and Nativity, 2020

Source: Data from Pew Hispanic Center – January 25 to February 8, 2021, Core Trends Survey.

reproduction (Bourdieu 1977). The limited access to technology, and parents with the skills to utilize it, creates a social reproduction that places them further behind their middle- and upper-class peers. For a discussion on learning loss and COVID, see section below on "Issues of Concern for the Future of Latina/o Education."

To begin to determine racial disparities in the digital divide during the pandemic, we use data from the Pew Hispanic Center's Core Trends Survey conducted on January 25 to February 8, 2021. The analysis is restricted to individuals with children, to help gauge the implications of online learning for students. We found that most of the parental population had digital access, but there were some racial and nativity disparities. Regarding internet subscriptions at home, Latina/o immigrant parents are less likely to have internet in comparison to their native-born co-ethnics and the other native-born groups (non-Latina/o whites, non-Latina/o Asians, and non-Latina/o Blacks) (Figure 9.1). There are 25 percent fewer Latina/o immigrant parents with subscriptions to the internet in the household than non-Latina/o–whites and 16 percent less likely to have access than native-born Latina/os. Another indicator of the Latina/o digital divide that can hamper educational success is access to computers or tablets. Like trends on access to the internet, Latina/o immigrant parents are less likely to have a laptop or tablet at home than other ethnic-racial groups. Specifically, Latina/o immigrant parents have 20 percent less access to a computer or tablet at home than non-Latina/o–whites. In terms of disparities by nativity, there are 11 percent fewer Latina/o immigrant parents who have a computer or tablet than native-born Latina/os. While this measure does not directly measure Latina/o students' access to technology, we can see the differences in digital access at home. Regarding the racial digital divide, Latina/o immigrant parents are far worse off than any other group. This coincides with a study that found inadequate remote learning resources and training to be particularly detrimental for English learners (Sugarman and Lazarín 2020). Indeed, some of the school districts with the most significant numbers of English learners had less than half of the students logging into online instruction, due to limited access to digital devices and broadband, parents' limited capacity to support the student, inadequate remote learning resources and training for teachers, and family language barriers (Sugarman and Lazarín 2020).

Dropouts and Graduation Outcomes

Data from the 2022 American Community Survey (ACS) Public-Use Microdata Sample 1-Year Estimates Public-Use File (Ruggles et al. 2024) are used to examine the educational outcomes of Latina/o groups and two comparative groups (whites and Blacks) along three dimensions: dropping out, graduating from high school, and college graduates. The results will allow us to determine how well the various Latina/o groups are doing along various educational outcomes. The analyses are also carried out along the lines of national origin, nativity status (native-born versus foreign-born), and sex.

Dropouts/Pushed-outs

One of the more pressing issues that point to how the educational system is failing Latina/os relates to the high levels of high-school dropouts. Table 9.1 presents the percentage of Latina/os between the ages of sixteen and twenty-four who do not have a high-school diploma and are currently not enrolled in school – a proxy for being a high-school dropout – in 2022. The percentages are broken down by national origin, nativity, and sex. Overall, Latina/os (males, 9.6%; females, 6.1%) and Afro-Latina/os (males, 8.2%; females, 4.8%) have the highest dropout rates in comparison to white people (males, 4.9%; females, 3.7%) having the lowest dropout rates. In fact, Latina/os are nearly twice as likely to be dropouts compared to whites. The implications of such disparities are vast, given that Latina/os who do not complete high school with their peers tend to struggle to find and keep a job to support themselves and their families (Gándara and Mordechay 2017; Rumberger 2012).

Some interesting patterns emerge when we examine the prevalence of dropouts across all Latina/o subgroups. First, males are more likely than females to be dropouts. Among Other South Americans (males 3.4%; females 3.5%), the percentage of dropouts between males and females is almost equal. Second, foreign-born Latina/os are less likely to have a high-school diploma than their native-born counterparts. The largest Latina/o foreign-born-native-born gaps, favoring the native-born, are found among Guatemalans, Hondurans, Salvadorans, and Afro-Latina/o males. Third, the most elevated dropout rates among the Latina/o subgroups occur among foreign-born Guatemalans and Hondurans. Guatemalan immigrants are the most likely to be dropouts, with 46.2 percent of males and 37.2 percent of females being dropouts. Among Honduran immigrants, 36.8 percent of males and 34.4 percent of females

Table 9.1 Percentage of Persons 16 to 24 Years of Age who are Dropouts by Race/Ethnic Group, Sex, and Place of Birth, 2022

Race/Ethnic Group	Female			Male		
	Total	Native-Born	Foreign-Born	Total	Native-Born	Foreign-Born
Colombian	4.9	2.5	8.9	5.9	4.5	8.6
Cuban	5.1	3.8	8.3	7.9	5.6	13.6
Dominican	3.9	2.6	7.3	8.0	5.3	12.7
Guatemalan	18.4	2.3	37.2	28.6	7.4	46.2
Honduran	21.6	6.5	34.4	23.2	6.5	36.8
Mexican	5.3	4.4	12.9	8.9	7.2	22.0
Puerto Rican	5.7	5.8	15.2	7.0	7.0	12.9
Salvadoran	10.0	2.9	25.4	13.2	6.2	26.8
Spaniard	2.3	1.8	0.0	5.3	5.8	0.0
Other Central American	5.9	1.4	16.3	13.4	4.5	30.8
Other South American	3.5	1.2	7.6	3.4	1.2	7.0
Other Latina/o	6.6	5.9	16.1	9.0	8.0	19.6
Afro-Latina/o	4.8	5.0	2.7	8.2	6.9	28.6
Latina/o	6.1	4.3	16.4	9.6	6.8	23.4
Black	4.4			7.0		
White	3.7			4.9		

Source: Data from 2022 American Community Survey 1-Year Estimates Public-Use File (Ruggles et al. 2024).

are dropouts. Additionally, nearly one-third of foreign-born Afro-Latina/o are dropouts. Fourth, among females, native-born Colombians, Dominicans, Guatemalans, Salvadorans, Spaniards, Other Central Americans, and Other South Americans have dropout rates below whites. Fifth, among native-born Latina/os, the highest prevalence of not completing high school, above 7 percent, occurs among Guatemalan, Mexican, Puerto Rican, and Other Latina/o males. The number of dropouts or people without a high-school diploma is worse for Latina/o immigrants than native-born Latina/os. It is clear, then, that there is a significant variation in the prevalence of dropping out across the diverse Latina/o groups.

We need to point out, however, that the dropout measure we use here only partially applies to foreign-born individuals. Given that the measure is based on persons 16 to 24 years of age, it is likely that a particular portion of immigrants came to the United States at these ages and never attended school in this country. So, they did not "drop in" to US schools (for a discussion of methodological issues with the dropout rate, see Sáenz and Siordia 2012). Therefore, the dropout rates for foreign-born people need to be considered with some caution.

High-School and College Graduation

Now, we examine variations across groups regarding high-school and college gradu-ation among persons 25 and older. Table 9.2 provides the percentages of persons 25 and older high-school graduates, broken down by national origin, sex, and nativity. Again, Latina/os have the lowest high-school completion rates with only 74.8 percent of females and 71.7 percent of males holding a high-school diploma. Overall, Afro-Latina/os have higher high-school completion rates than Latina/os as a whole, but they lag significantly behind whites. In contrast, whites have the highest prevalence of high-school graduation (males, 93.6%; females, 94.8%). Such dispari-ties in high-school graduation are arguably the most crucial outcome measures for K-12 students, given that these achievements pave the way to future opportunities (Gándara and Mordechay 2017).

There are some commonalities between the dropout rate and high-school gradu-ation when we consider all subgroups of Latina/os. First, there are more female than male high-school graduates across all groups. Second, native-born Latina/os are more likely than their foreign-born peers to be high-school graduates, except for some subgroups among females (Colombian, Spaniard, and Other Central American) and comparable among Other South American females. Third, half or

Table 9.2 Percentage of Persons 25 Years of Age and Older who are High-School Graduates by Race/Ethnic Group, Sex, and Place of Birth, 2022

Race/Ethnic Group	Female			Male		
	Total	Native-Born	Foreign-Born	Total	Native-Born	Foreign-Born
Colombian	94.0	84.9	87.7	87.8	93.3	85.9
Cuban	92.9	79.6	75.7	83.3	91.6	79.2
Dominican	90.5	71.0	68.1	76.5	87.5	71.4
Guatemalan	85.8	47.3	45.5	48.8	77.4	41.6
Honduran	90.4	58.0	56.4	59.0	84.9	54.0
Mexican	86.7	51.3	48.4	67.6	84.9	47.7
Puerto Rican	84.6	72.2	69.1	82.8	83.2	68.9
Salvadoran	87.9	51.6	50.5	57.4	85.0	49.2
Spaniard	94.4	86.3	88.0	92.4	93.6	87.1
Other Central American	94.3	77.9	78.4	82.0	94.3	75.2
Other South American	93.3	87.6	87.2	87.6	92.6	86.3
Other Latina/o	85.8	66.8	68.0	78.1	82.5	63.4
Afro-Latina/o	86.4	91.5	72.0	83.5	87.9	71.2
Latina/o	74.8	87.1	61.3	71.7	85.2	57.2
Black	89.5			87.4		
White	94.8			93.6		

Source: Data from 2022 American Community Survey 1-Year Estimates Public-Use File (Ruggles et al. 2024).

Table 9.3 Percentage of Persons 25 Years of Age and Older with a Bachelor's Degree or Higher by Race/Ethnic Group, Sex, and Place of Birth, 2022

Race/Ethnic Group	Female			Male		
	Total	Native-Born	Foreign-Born	Total	Native-Born	Foreign-Born
Colombian	40.4	52.0	37.2	37.8	42.3	36.2
Cuban	33.0	47.3	26.5	30.0	39.5	25.2
Dominican	24.5	36.6	20.3	20.5	29.7	16.2
Guatemalan	13.4	32.0	7.9	10.5	22.4	7.5
Honduran	15.7	34.2	12.4	12.4	28.6	9.2
Mexican	17.6	23.6	10.2	14.1	19.2	8.3
Puerto Rican	26.1	26.3	19.7	21.9	22.0	17.4
Salvadoran	15.0	32.6	9.6	11.7	24.8	7.8
Spaniard	39.6	37.4	48.9	38.4	35.3	51.5
Other Central American	33.3	48.9	25.8	30.9	41.7	25.0
Other South American	40.7	51.1	38.0	38.5	43.9	37.0
Other Latina/o	25.7	27.1	21.0	21.4	22.6	17.3
Afro-Latina/o	30.8	32.9	24.9	24.2	25.0	22.3
Latina/o	22.4	27.2	17.0	18.5	22.5	14.3
Black	28.3			22.0		
White	40.3			38.8		

Source: Data from 2022 American Community Survey 1-Year Estimates Public-Use File (Ruggles et al. 2024).

less than half of foreign-born Guatemalans, Mexicans (males), and Salvadorans possess a high-school diploma, with foreign-born Guatemalan men (41.6%) having the lowest high-school graduation level. Fourth, no native-born female Latina subgroups surpass white females concerning high-school graduation rates. Other Central American males exceeded the white male graduation rate (94.3 v. 93.6%). Among males, native-born Colombians and Spaniards have high-school graduation rates comparable to white males. Finally, Guatemalan and Salvadoran males are less likely to have a high-school diploma. Again, there is great diversity concerning high-school graduation among Latina/os.

Table 9.3 shows the percentages of persons aged 25 and older who are college graduates, broken down by national origin, sex, and nativity status. Again, Latina/os have the lowest percentages of persons with a college diploma (males, 18.5%; females, 22.4%), with whites (males, 38.8%; females, 40.3%) being the most likely to be college graduates. White males are over twice as likely as Latino men to be college graduates, and white women are almost twice as likely as Latina women to have a college diploma. Again, Afro-Latina/os have higher rates of college completion than Latina/os as a whole as well as in comparison to Blacks, but they trail significantly behind whites.

Similar patterns observed above are revealed when we examine the prevalence of college graduates among Latina/o subgroups. For the most part, the patterns found earlier exist here as well, and so we will only highlight a few patterns of interest. Latina women are more likely to be college graduates than Latino men, except for foreign-born Spaniards. Indeed, the vanishing representation of Latina/o males from higher education continues but they do have cultural capital in the form of female family members who support their educational pursuits (Sáenz et al. 2020). Among females, native-born Colombians, Cubans, Other Central Americans, Other South Americans, and foreign-born Spaniards are more likely to be college graduates than whites. Among males, native-born Colombians, Cubans, Other Central Americans, Other South Americans, and foreign-born Spaniards are more likely than whites to have a bachelor's degree. Nearly or just over half of native-born females: Colombian (52.0%), Other Central American (48.9%), Other South American females (51.1%), and foreign-born Spaniard males (53.7%) and females (48.9%) have a college diploma. On the other hand, foreign-born Guatemalans and Hondurans (both males and females) and Honduran and Mexican males) have less than 10 percent of members with a college degree.

In sum, while Latina/os lag behind whites and Blacks in educational attainment, this is not true across the board. Instead, Cubans (native-born only), Colombians (all except foreign-born males), and Other South Americans (native-born only) stand out with the highest educational attainment levels, surpassing the educational standing of whites. On the other hand, foreign-born Guatemalans, Hondurans, Mexicans, and Salvadorans tend to trail behind other Latina/o groups, particularly among the foreign-born.

Issues of Concern for the Future of Latina/o Education

Latina/o educational disparities outlined not only have implications for the upward mobility of the Latina/o community but for the nation considering the growing presence of Latina/os in the US (Chapter 5). Indeed, Latina/o students represent most of the student body in many schools in the country – in the Southwest and beyond. So, the educational experiences of Latina/os should be a primary concern for the nation, given that they represent a significant share of the nation's labor force (Chapter 10). Educational disparities could dampen the integration of Latina/os in the labor force and their political and social integration. Below, we highlight a few examples of issues that concern the academic achievement of Latina/os.

Deferred Action for Childhood Arrivals (DACA)

In 2001, Senators Durbin (D-IL) and Hatch (R-UT) introduced the Development Relief and Education for Alien Minors (DREAM) Act. Still, they did not gain the 60 votes necessary to formalize it into law (Library of Congress 2020). The Illegal Immigration Reform and Immigrant Responsibility Act (IIRIRA) (1996) authorized states to allow aid for undocumented youth. The DREAM Act intended to offer undocumented youth who finished high school in the US and wanted to pursue higher education a pathway to citizenship. While this proposed immigration reform legislation had the most support, it failed. From 2007 to 2012, various Senators kept introducing iterations of the Dream Act, but it was unsuccessful (Library of Congress 2020). Indeed, it underwent twenty different iterations in the last twenty years (American Immigration Council 2021). The key aspect shared by all versions is a pathway to legal status for undocumented people who came to the US as children.

After the Dream Act failed congressional passage, President Obama issued an executive memorandum called the Deferred Action for Childhood Arrivals (DACA) on June 12, 2012. DACA provided legality for undocumented youth who migrated as children, work permits, and driver's licenses renewable for two years (Library of Congress 2020). The executive order gave "The Dreamers" (referring to the Dream Act that was not enacted) and undocumented veterans an opportunity to apply for a deferred action that will allow them a lawful presence in the US for two years. To qualify for DACA, undocumented immigrants must have arrived in the US when they were under the age of sixteen, be currently in school or have graduated from high school or attained a GED, or honorably discharged from the US Armed Forces, not be a risk to public safety or national security and be under age 30. DACA particularly benefited Latina/os (López and Krogstad 2017).

DACA presented a step toward immigrant integration and support for social transformation perspectives, given it granted legalization to undocumented individuals to remain in the US without fear of deportation (Gonzales 2016). Before DACA, undocumented students faced great financial hardships in pursuing higher education (Abrego and Gonzales 2010). Even undocumented people who graduated from top-tier universities had to resort to informal labor for economic survival (Huber et l. 2014). DACA provided some financial relief by giving the legal status necessary to apply for scholarships and internship opportunities, obtain work permits and driver's licenses, and obtain health insurance (Gonzales 2016; Huber et al. 2014). Obtaining work permits through DACA was especially important in providing incentives for higher education enrollment and graduation as they can now use their college degrees in the formal labor market (Gonzales 2016; Huber et al. 2014). Beyond opportunities for upward mobility, DACA recipients also found opportunities for civic engagement to give back to their community (Huber et al. 2014).

As vital as DACA was for the economic and social incorporation of undocumented individuals, it needed strengthening. For instance, DACA recipients do not qualify for federal financial aid (Huber et al. 2014) and lack the right to vote or travel freely (Gonzales 2016). The most significant concern is that DACA is temporary and offers no pathway to permanent legalization; therefore, enrollees can be deported in the future (Gonzales 2016). The temporality of DACA is problematic, given that recipients feel relieved upon receiving it, but then alienation returns, as it only temporarily mitigates the impact of being undocumented (Benuto et al. 2018). Another concern is that only an estimated 62 percent of those eligible for DACA applied (Gonzales 2016).

After the conclusion of the Obama presidency, the future of The Dreamers was in limbo, since it was not enacted into law. DACA came under heavy scrutiny during the presidency of Donald Trump, which led the US Citizenship and Immigration Services to pause new applicants (Canales 2022) temporarily. On December 4, 2020, in *Batalla Vidal et al. v. Mayorkas et al.*, the District Court for the Eastern District of New York ordered the government to accept first-time requests for DACA, renewal requests, and advance parole requests, based on the terms of the 2012 DACA program (National Immigration Law Center 2022).

During the presidency of Joe Biden, DACA remained in legal limbo. During its ten-year span, 800,000 Dreamers have received DACA (Biden 2023). On the 10th anniversary of DACA, President Biden issued a statement to express his commitment to providing Dreamers with the opportunities they needed to succeed, expand health care coverage for DACA recipients, and direct the Department of Homeland Security to "preserve and fortify" DACA (Biden 2023). Yet, the legality of the 2012 DACA policy has continued to be contested and revised in the courts. Months after President Biden supported DACA, a federal judge in the Southern District of Texas ruled DACA unlawful (https://www.nilc.org/issues/daca/). As a result, first-time DACA applications cannot be processed. Individuals who received DACA as of July 16, 2021, or whose DACA has lapsed for less than a year can apply for renewals (https://www.nilc.org/issues/daca/).

COVID-19 and Learning Loss

While the full effects of COVID-19 on learning loss are yet to be entirely determined, the current research signals a concerning trend in the decline in achievement for Latina/o students. Indeed, learning loss associated with the school shutdowns compounds the educational disparities between whites and Black and Latina/o students (Dorn et al. 2020). While the racial and ethnic educational gaps were narrowing in 2009, they had begun to widen before COVID-19 (Dorn et al. 2020). A study by Dorn et al. (2020) grouped high-school students into three groups. A group that experienced good-quality remote education continued progressing but at a slower pace. Students with lower-quality remote learning are staggering behind. Lastly, some students without remote instruction suffered the most significant learning loss, and even dropped out of school. This is a concern, as Black and Latina/o students received lower-quality instruction during COVID-19 (Lara 2021).

Erasure of Latina/o History, Culture, and Critical Race Theory in Academic Curricula

Some school districts and governments across the US are erasing Latina/o history and culture from educational curricula (Leyva 2002). Elements of Valenzuela's (1999) substrative schooling continue to resonate in the educational system. The educational experiences of Latina/os in the United States entail struggles to preserve their cultural roots against the endeavors of academic institutions to "Americanize" them by erasing the Spanish language and historical connections to Latin America (Garcia 2001). This leads Vélez (2008) to state that the historical context of Latina/o educational experiences in the US "can be summarized under relations of subjugation, colonization, and the specific institutional mechanisms used in different locations to segregate and track Latina/o students" (129).

An example of state-level initiatives rooted in viewing the Latina/o culture from the deficit model is the case of Arizona's SB 2211. In 2006, the famous Chicana activist Dolores Huerta told an assembly of Tucson high-school students that "Republicans hate Latina/os" (Lundholm 2011). As a response, the state's superintendent of public instruction began a mission to eliminate K-12 ethnic studies in Arizona because it promoted racism, hatred, and politically charged teaching (Lundholm 2011; Rodriguez 2012). In the spring of 2010, the Arizona legislature enacted SB 2211, and Governor Jan Brewer signed it into law in 2011, despite fierce protests (Lacey 2011). SB 2211 did more than discard Mexican American and Chicana/o Studies programs – it also removed curriculum decisions from local school boards (Lundholm 2011) and reduced funding from school districts that failed to comply with the law (Lacey 2011). Educational curricula presumed to promote the overthrow of the United States government are explicitly banned, which brings into question how US history will be taught (Lacey 2011). Such a ban erases the struggles and contributions that Latina/os and other racial and ethnic groups have made to the United States. This is an example of what historian Yolanda Levya (2002) refers to as an *erasure of memory* that deletes the cultural history of Latina/os from US history. Moreover, how can one understand US history without acknowledging the subjugation of minority groups and the 200-year-long struggles to overcome injustices (Rodriguez 2012)? Is a curriculum based only on the white majority perspective a form of ethnic studies? Such policy not only robs Latina/o students of their cultural gift but fails to educate all students about the struggles and accomplishments of all people of color in the US. This has led some to claim that ". . . Arizona banned ethnic studies to protect the reputation of the white majority" (Rodriguez 2012).

The rationale for enacting SB 2211 as ethnic studies creating racial hatred is ironic, given that this same legislature introduced SB 1070, which is controversial for legalizing the racial profiling of Latina/os (see Chapter 11). Aligned with S.B.1070, the ban was promoted to target all ethnic studies, mainly Latina/os and Latina/o ethnic studies. Indeed, the "Tucson Unified School District's Mexican American program has been declared illegal by the State of Arizona – even while similar programs for black, Asian and American Indian students have been left untouched" (Lacey 2011). Indeed, the superintendent who pushed the law, publicly scrutinized Chicana/o classics such as *The Pedagogy of the Oppressed* and *Occupied America* on the claim that they "inappropriately teach Latino youths that they are being mistreated" and that ethnic study instructors were sometimes unconventional by sprinkling their lessons with Spanish words (Lacey 2011).

Aligned are the issues above and the struggles for bilingual and dual-language education. Similar to the implementation of Arizona's SB 2211, there are nationwide efforts to erase the Spanish language. Spanish is often regarded as "the language of foreign immigrants, often undocumented, and blamed for poverty and low-level education of US Latina/os, Spanish is held in contempt in political and educational circles" (García 2009, p. 109). As a testament to the status of the Spanish language, there is evidence that whites' opposition to bilingual education is rooted in "racial threat," given that opposition is most vital in areas of substantial growth in already sizable Latina/o populations (Hempel et al. 2013). In Chapter 7, we highlighted some of the struggles in Latina/o civil rights in bilingual and bicultural education. Here, we only discuss some of the implications of the nationwide English-only movement in school districts.

While the value of learning English is recognized, what is scrutinized is the degree to which such endeavors focus on acculturation into white middle-class norms and the erasure of the Latina/o students' culture. The focus on educational curricula promoting students to be monolingual English speakers, writers, and readers is ironic, given the globalization forces in which students of all races and ethnicities would be well-served through foreign language instruction. Spanish is a global language (García 2009) and a valuable economic commodity in the US (García 2009). Indeed, Spanish–English speakers are an asset in the labor market, given that they perform work duties that matter to the public good (i.e. being bilingual) (Alarcón et al. 2014); as such, students speaking more than one language have an edge on job access. However, there is a double standard at play in taking Spanish-language classes. Accordingly, white students are often lauded for taking such courses, while Latina/os are discouraged or ridiculed for enrolling in Spanish-language classes.

Rather than policies aimed at criticizing Latina/o family values, their language and child-rearing, and household management practices, Valdes (1996) argued that programs designed to remedy educational disparities among Latina/os should be based on an understanding, appreciation, and respect for Latina/o students and their families. Administrators need to consider that disrupting the existing Latina/o culture will have profound costs to the culture and students' educational advancement (see Morales and Sáenz 2007). For instance, Morales and Sáenz (2007) found that having an English-only background is more influential in math than reading test scores. This indicates that language proficiency is needed and establishes a link between academic content and skills with the student's language and cultural identity. Thus, educational policies designed to improve the academic outcomes of Latina/o students need to work in unity with the Latina/o family and cultural practices. This is a trend that is not going away. As of January 2021, 42 states have introduced bills or taken other steps to restrict critical race theory in the classroom, or limit how teachers can discuss racism and sexism (Schwartz 2021).

These issues have currently intensified. Erroneous perceptions of Chicanx and Latina/o studies books teaching hate or promoting the overthrow of the government have fueled the legislative endorsement to eliminate critical race theory and diversity, equity, and inclusion (DEI). In Chapter 7, we discuss the growing polarization of race and sexuality that has made its way into our schools and institutions of higher education (Zhao 2023).

Summary

In this chapter, we highlighted the persistent Latina/o–white gap in educational attainment and some explanations for such disparity. While academia has stepped away from biological explanations of the Latina/o–white academic achievement gap, these perspectives continue to resonate with the public, as illustrated in the quote at the opening of this chapter. Most biological perspectives have given way to cultural deficiency explanations on Latina/o education that result in blaming the victim. In Angela Valenzuela's (1999) *Subtractive Education*, schools prioritize acculturation to white norms, mainly learning English, at the expense of losing their cultural gifts, i.e. Spanish fluency (also see Flores 2005; O. García 2009).

Academics have also accentuated structural explanations of the Latina/o–white education gap. Social conflict theory stresses the centralized role of socioeconomic status in educational disparities. For example, during the COVID-19 pandemic, socioeconomic inequality in schools created a situation where some schools struggled to provide the necessary tools for remote learning, i.e. computers and the internet, in contrast to others (Lara 2021). According to Bourdieusian theories of social reproduction (Wacquant and Bourdieu 1992; Bourdieu 1977; Bourdieu and Passeron 1977; Bourdieu 2018a), education perpetuates inequality by replicating the hierarchy in society and transforming it into a hierarchy of merit. As such, educational systems are social reproduction mechanisms replicating existing social hierarchies outside the classroom. In contrast to social reproduction frameworks, social transformation perspectives focus on the structural changes that reduce inequality. Under DACA, Dreamers received legalization for two years, which is crucial to alleviating some of the financial pressure to attend higher education. For example, with DACA, students qualify for scholarships and internships and access the formal labor market with better working conditions and higher wages. Social reproduction and social transformation can co-exist, and the balance between them is based on governance and power relations reflected in the dominant socio-cultural and socio-political institutions (Desjardins 2015).

We also used data from the 2022 American Community Survey (ACS) Public-Use Microdata Sample to illustrate the extent of the Latina/o–white and Latina/o–Black gaps in school dropouts, high-school completion, and higher-education graduation. The results show that Cubans, Colombians, and Other South Americans have high educational attainment rates, with native-born persons from these groups surpassing white people in educational attainment. In contrast, immigrant Mexicans and Central Americans have the lowest levels of education. Furthermore, native-born Latina/os, Mexicans, and Puerto Ricans lag significantly behind other groups and have lower educational attainment levels than immigrant Cubans, Colombians, and Other South Americans.

The findings discussed illustrate the need to narrow the Latina/o–white gap in educational achievement at K-12 and higher-education levels. Such policies should focus on macro-level solutions such as equalizing economic inequality among Latina/os (see Chapter 10), given that socioeconomic status significantly contributes to narrowing the ethnic gap in education (Morales and Sáenz 2007). Although not an easy feat, policies focused on equalizing wider societal inequalities will provide Latina/os with more equitable opportunities for educational advancement. This, in turn, will equip Latina/o parents with the necessary socioeconomic resources to help their children navigate the educational system.

Lastly, we raised some critical issues affecting the quality of education for Latina/os that need to be addressed to narrow the current and future Latina/o–white and Latina/o–Black education gaps. We highlighted some concerns: (1) the future of DACA, (2) learning loss associated with COVID-19, and (3) cultural deficiency paradigms that challenge bilingual education and spearhead the *erasure of memory* campaigns to eliminate ethnic studies. These are just some of the issues that are widening the Latina/o–white education gap.

Discussion Questions

1. What is the problem with cultural deficiency perspectives? What legislative changes are exacerbating the subtractive schooling of Latinas/os?

2. Is the future educational trajectory for Latina/os more aligned with social reproduction, social transformation, or both? Explain.

3. What are some of the variations in the educational patterns of Latina/os? How do these patterns vary by sex and nativity?

4. How does Afro-Latina/os' educational standing compare to other Latina/o groups?

5. How has the DACA program varied across Presidential administrations? What can be the implications for undocumented Dreamers if DACA is not extended?

6. How did COVID-19 affect the educational attainment of Latina/os? What do you predict will be the continuing impact of the pandemic on Latina/o education?

7. What are some of the ways that state efforts to restrict critical race theory are harmful to Latina/os?

10 Work and Economic Life

As a summary statistic for the economic performance of US Latinos, the 2021 US Latino GDP is revealing. The total economic output (or GDP) of Latinos living in the United States in 2021 was $3.2 trillion, up from $2.8 trillion in 2020, $2.1 trillion in 2015, and $1.7 trillion in 2010. If Latinos living in the United States were an independent country, the US Latino GDP would be the fifth largest GDP in the world, larger than the GDPs of India, the United Kingdom, or France.

(Hamilton et al. 2023)

In considering the work and economic life of Latina/os, there are two common stories. The first concerns a population that has experienced significant barriers in the workplace and in their financial resources despite overall elevated levels of work activities. The second relates to a population whose growing numbers are translating to a rapidly expanding gross domestic product (GDP), the fifth largest in the world if Latina/os were a country, as the opening quote (from the "US Latino GDP Report") attests. The two stories reflect the socioeconomic diversity within so many dimensions of life among Latina/os, including work and economic life. As we will show below, some Latina/os are doing very well while others continue to fall behind in the economy.

The low educational standing of Latina/os that we saw in the previous chapter is associated with the relatively low economic standing of the Latina/o population. Indeed, historically, certain racial/ethnic groups, including segments of the Latina/o population, have been positioned toward the lower rungs of the economic ladder. In particular, groups that were initially incorporated into the US as colonized or conquered groups – African Americans, Mexican Americans, Native Americans, and Puerto Ricans – continue to be disproportionately represented among persons with jobs that pay little, have limited benefits, and do not lift them out of poverty.

Scholars have increasingly pointed to the importance of place – or geographic location – in the socioeconomic outcomes of people, especially persons of color (Baker et al. 2022). For example, long-standing pockets of poverty have persisted along the Mexico–US border, where persons of Mexican origin disproportionately make their home, since the federal government began computing poverty rates (Betts 1994; Esparza and Donelson 2008; Fleuriet 2021; Sáenz 1997). Moreover, recent evidence has reconfirmed the importance of geographic location on the likelihood of Latina/o children born in the bottom quintile income category to low-income parents ascending to the top quintile based on individual income (Chetty et al. 2020; The

Opportunity Atlas 2024). For instance, Latina/o children in Pima County (Arizona) and in Travis County (Texas) have relatively low probabilities (0.0845) of making this income ascent, while those in three New York Counties (Queens, Westchester, and Nassau) have much higher probabilities (0.183) of doing so and are more than twice as likely to climb to the top one-fifth of income earners as those in Pima and Travis Counties.

Historically, Latina/os have lagged significantly behind whites on a wide variety of economic measures associated with wealth and income. According to data from the National Community Reinvestment Coalition, Latina/o households with a median wealth of $14,000 in 2019 had only 9 cents of every dollar in wealth of white households who have a median wealth of $160,200 (Asante-Muhammad et al. 2021). Moreover, according to data from the 2021 American Community Survey, Latina/o families had a median income that represented 68 cents for every dollar of white families and Latina/o families were 2.5 times more likely than white families to have incomes below the poverty level.

This chapter provides an overview of the economic standing of the Latina/o population. In particular, the chapter begins with a discussion of the various theoretical perspectives that have been put forth to understand the labor market and economic position of people. In addition, the chapter examines the labor market and economic characteristics of selected groups that comprise the Latina/o population and compares them to whites and Blacks. As will become evident, there is a significant amount of variation in the labor market and economic position of Latina/o subgroups, with certain groups faring relatively well, while others are not as fortunate. The chapter concludes with a discussion of major trends in the work and economic conditions of Latina/os and policies and programs that are needed to improve the overall socioeconomic standing of Latina/os.

Theoretical Perspectives

Theoretical perspectives have been developed to understand how individual and structural factors impact the labor market outcomes of individuals. In particular, we can think of labor market outcomes associated with three stages: securing employment, type of job, and reward for work. For the most part, individual and structural factors are related in a similar fashion to the three stages of labor market outcomes.

Individual Perspectives

The most basic perspectives developed to understand labor market outcomes are situated at the individual or personal level. As such, individual attributes, such as educational attainment, work experience, English language proficiency, cognitive skills, and "soft skills," are seen as factors that contribute to success in the labor market. The human capital perspective is the primary theory that has been used to explain variations in labor market outcomes. Gary Becker (1975), a Nobel laureate in economics, developed the human capital theory. The perspective argues that individuals invest in education, skills, and work experience to reap benefits in the labor market. Thus, for example, people pay tuition and related costs in the attainment of a college diploma or a postgraduate degree, which assists them in finding more favorable employment as well as greater monetary rewards in the labor market. Similarly, individuals seek out internship and apprenticeship opportunities to enhance their marketability on the job market. Much research has shown a strong positive association between levels of human capital attributes, such as educational attainment, and favorable labor market outcomes, including occupational prestige and wage and salary earnings.

Similarly, other personal characteristics are related to labor market outcomes. For example, work experience is generally associated with high wages and salaries. Thus, an extra year of experience is typically related to a bump in the pay of workers. However, as employers have cut labor costs, they have opted for younger workers, who earn significantly less than experienced older workers, thus making it difficult for older people to find employment, especially at pay levels that they commanded at an earlier time (Ghilarducci and Radpour 2019). Moreover, given that nearly one-third of Latina/os are foreign-born, English fluency is another factor that is important in obtaining a job as well as in labor market earnings. Persons who are fluent in English are more competitive in the attainment of jobs that require English language communication with co-workers, clients, or customers. Research has also shown that employers pay a premium for workers who are fluent in English (Hamilton et al. 2008; Mora and Davila 2006a, 2006b; Shin and Alba 2009).

In addition, researchers have increasingly turned their attention to the role that cognitive skills play in labor market outcomes, especially with respect to earnings. Research has demonstrated that people with higher cognitive skills attain higher earnings than those with more limited cognitive skills (Hall and Farkas 2011). Finally, employers often identify "soft skills" as attributes that they look for in employees. Soft skills, according to Moss and Tilly (1996) refer to "skills, abilities, and traits that pertain to personality, attitude, and behavior rather than formal or technical knowledge" (253). These are personal characteristics that translate to how well potential workers approximate the mainstream population, i.e. white middle-class standards. Yet, the preference for soft skills extends to jobs where few whites are found. For example, employers seeking to fill positions in low-wage jobs voice a strong preference for Latina/o immigrant workers over African American workers. They reason that Latina/os are diligent individuals with a strong work ethic. Of course, what is left unsaid is that because many Latina/o immigrants are undocumented they tend not to complain about the low wages that they receive and the treacherous work environments that they toil under. As Zamudio and Lichter (2008) observe, employers in the hotel industry in Los Angeles use terms such as "attitude," "motivation," and "work ethic" as code words for "tractability." Employers are drawn to the vulnerable status of Latina/o immigrants, which tends to keep the latter from complaining against low wages and arduous work conditions.

Individual-level perspectives place the focus directly on workers to understand their labor market outcomes. Thus, if a worker has difficulty finding employment, obtains a job that is not very prestigious, and obtains low wages for the work that he/she does, it is due to their personal characteristics, such as their level of education, work experience, cognitive skills, and soft skills. If they desire more favorable outcomes in the job market, individuals need to invest in attaining higher levels of education and related factors in order to reap more favorable labor market outcomes.

Social Relationships

The influence of factors affecting people's labor market outcomes stem beyond one's own personal attributes. One line of research focuses on the social ties and social networks that people have to others from whom they can draw valuable information and insights to gain entry into particular jobs (McDonald et al. 2009; Morales 2016). Due to the limited human capital resources of many Latina/os, especially immigrants, such social connections are important in obtaining information regarding the availability of jobs as well as in securing sponsorship from someone who can vouch for job applicants (Pfeffer and Parra 2009). We have seen earlier in the discussion of migration theories the significance of social networks in facilitating the immigration journey as well as in adjusting to life in the areas of destination (see Chapter 4). Hence, Latina/os who are well connected to social networks are likely to be in a better position to obtain employment (Morales 2016) as well as to receive more favorable earnings compared to their counterparts who lack such social connections (Pfeffer and Parra 2009).

Despite the value of social networks in labor markets, we need to pay attention to the particular forms of social networks. Indeed, one of the earliest observations on the value of such ties is the classic work of Granovetter (1973) highlighting the strength of weak ties. Intuitively, we would think that individuals benefit most favorably from their connections to people that constitute their strong ties (i.e. persons who are close to them and with whom they maintain regular interactions). However, given the principle of propinquity, we tend to be relatively similar in a variety of respects to persons with whom we share strong ties along the lines of socioeconomic status, race and ethnicity, and so forth. As such, we are likely to hold similar information that can help us navigate entry into jobs as those people who are close to us and with whom we come into contact most frequently. In contrast, people with whom we have weak ties are more different from us in a variety of dimensions, including socioeconomic status, residence, and race and ethnicity. Hence, people who are a friend of a friend, with whom we are not close and with whom we do not interact regularly, are likely to be different from us, interact in social settings that are different from the social circles we run in, and, as such, have information that is distinct from that which we possess. Information drawn from more varied sources is particularly valuable to people. Sáenz and Douglas (2009) suggest that Mexican women who were working as *domesticas* (maids) gain valuable information from their weak ties with employers, which they can relay to their husbands to pursue valuable work opportunities. In their analysis of 2000 Public Use Microdata Sample, they discover that Mexican men whose wives work as domesticas and who live in areas with a significant presence of co-ethnics have higher wages than their counterparts.

Structural Factors

The value of human capital characteristics and social networks in influencing labor market outcomes is pretty intuitive. However, we need to recognize that it is important to take into account the context in which such characteristics are employed in the labor market. For example, the value of a high-school diploma is likely to vary significantly across different demographic, industrial, geographical, and political settings. In the 1960s and 1970s, when manufacturing was a staple of the US economy, workers with a high-school diploma had high levels of employment and wage earnings in certain industries, such as the automobile industry. However, as the US shifted increasingly toward a service and technological industrial base, the economic situation worsened dramatically for workers with low levels of education.

The work of Peter Blau (1977) serves as a base for introducing structural influences to gain a fuller understanding of labor markets as well as intergroup relations. While Blau's macro-sociological perspective has found a significant amount of support in the study of intermarriage (Blau et al. 1982), sociologists have used the theory to understand labor market outcomes including the influence that structural factors have on earnings and English fluency among immigrants (Hwang and Xi 2008; Hwang et al. 2010; Morales 2015, 2016; Xi et al. 2010). We highlight below some of the primary dimensions of Blau's macro-sociological perspective that are related to labor market outcomes.

Group size is a primary structural factor that has a major influence on the experiences of racial and ethnic groups in the labor market. Hubert Blalock (1967) is one of the earliest sociologists to observe the relationship between the size of a given minority group, such as African Americans, and their socioeconomic standing. Minoritized groups that are larger in a given area represent a threat to the existing power structure dominated by whites. So, whites put in place practices and policies that make it difficult for minoritized group members to ascend the socioeconomic ladder. There is a significant amount of research that has demonstrated that Latina/os tend to fare worse socioeconomically when they live in areas with a larger presence of Latina/os. For example, Sáenz (1997) has shown that Chicanos (persons of Mexican origin) had higher poverty rates in places where Chicanos comprised a larger share of the overall population than in areas where they made up a smaller portion of the population.

There are other structural characteristics that influence the labor market outcomes of minority groups. For example, residential segregation – the extent to which members of a given minority group live apart from whites – is a crucial factor in structuring the lives of Latina/os and other minoritized group members. Massey and Denton (1993) in their influential book titled *American Apartheid: Segregation and the Making of the Underclass* show the historical processes that have created elevated levels of residential separation between whites and Blacks in many US cities. One of the important consequences of this geographic arrangement is that Blacks are isolated from the opportunity structure. Thus, in the case of Latina/os, people who are clustered in neighborhoods where the substantial majority of people living nearby are Latina/os tend to have limited access to high quality schools, health care, parks, museums, libraries, and other facilities that many people in better off areas take for granted. Latina/os who live in such areas also lack access to good jobs (Joassart-Marcelli 2009). Indeed, over the last six decades, whites are increasingly found in suburban areas with Latina/os and African Americans clustered in metropolitan centers. This racial living arrangement has created a spatial mismatch in jobs (Farley 2022; Massey and Denton 1993; Stacy and Meixell 2020; Wilson 1987). This mismatch involves the imbalance in the location of jobs (in suburban areas) and job seekers (in metropolitan centers). This mismatch becomes even more acute when public transportation routes are not available to get people from the central cities to suburban areas, a situation that is fairly common, as residents of suburban areas have tended to oppose measures to easily connect them to metropolitan centers for fear of attracting poor and minority populations. Dickerson vonLockette and Johnson (2010) in their study of the nation's largest 95 cities found that between 1980 and 2000 Latina/os tended to fare the worst in employment in cities where they were the most segregated from whites. These researchers also observed that Latina/os experienced worsening employment conditions in cities where Latina/os were becoming increasingly segregated.

Moreover, yet another structural attribute that is influential in labor market outcomes is the industrial diversity of a given area. Communities that have a diverse set of industrial pursuits offer their residents a wide variety of job opportunities and are better able to sustain the vicissitudes of the economy in which certain industries are affected disproportionately at a given period. In contrast, places that have more limited opportunities involving a narrow set of industrial options are vulnerable to economic shifts. Immigrants and minoritized group members with limited human capital resources are often routed into racial/ethnic or immigrant occupational niches, where they are disproportionately located in the labor market (Douglas and Sáenz 2008; Liu 2011, 2013; Morales 2008). Douglas and Sáenz (2008) identify 25 Mexican occupations comprising immigrant sex-specific occupational niches using 2000 census data. These occupations include jobs such as agriculture laborers; meat, poultry, and seafood processing; construction; waiters/waitresses; cooks; maids and housekeeping cleaners; and janitors and building cleaners (Douglas and Sáenz 2008). Slightly more than half of Mexican immigrants worked in the 25 occupations comprising the Mexican immigrant occupational niches. Ethnic and immigrant niche jobs tend to offer workers low wages (Liu 2011, 2013; Spindler-Ruiz 2021).

While human capital, particularly educational attainment, represents a primary ingredient for understanding how well people are likely to fare at the different stages of the labor market from the attainment of a job, the type of job, and the economic rewards for performing the job, it is important to realize that social networks and contextual factors are important features that need to be taken into account. For example, social networks may help people with limited human capital navigate the labor market in order to facilitate the attainment of a job. In addition, in the case of structural characteristics, the value of human capital resources may be diminished through residence in certain areas that are isolated from the opportunity structures including quality jobs.

Having provided an overview of the variety of theoretical perspectives used to gain an understanding of variations in labor market outcomes, we now turn to an examination of recent data to assess the labor market conditions of the groups that form the Latina/o population.

Labor Market Patterns of Latina/o Groups

Data from the 2022 American Community Survey (ACS) Public-Use Microdata Sample are used to examine the labor market outcomes of Latina/o groups and two comparative groups (whites and Blacks) along three dimensions: job attainment, job quality, and job pay. The results will allow us to determine how well the various Latina/o groups have fared in the various stages of the labor market. Because labor market outcomes vary by age, the analysis is conducted for only the "experienced labor force"; that is, persons 25 to 54 years of age who have the most stable labor market experiences. The analysis is also broken down by sex and, for the Latina/o groups, nativity status (native-born versus foreign-born). Note that among Puerto Ricans, those born on the island and mainland are part of the native-born population, while those born in a different country make up the foreign-born portion of this group. Note also that the Afro-Latina/o group is not mutually exclusive; rather, members of this group are also part of the Afro-Latina/o group and its statistics are also included in those of the Latina/o subgroup or nationality to which it belongs. Due to this unique feature of the Afro-Latino grouping, it is situated in the table apart from the other Latina/o subgroups.

Job Attainment

We begin our analysis with the first phase of labor market outcomes – simply whether people have a job. In this respect, we are not merely examining persons who are part of the labor force (i.e. they are working or unemployed and actively seeking a job), but all persons 25 to 54 years of age, to include discouraged workers who have left the labor force and typically are not captured in trends concerning employment. Overall, among men, Latinos have a high level of employment, with 86 percent working, just below the 87 percent rate of whites, with Blacks having a lower level of employment at 73 percent (Table 10.1). In contrast, among women, Latinas are the least likely to be employed (70%) compared to white (78%) and Black (77%) women. Nonetheless, there is a noticeable amount of variation in employment across Latina/o groups as well as on the basis of nativity status and gender. For example, among Latino males, foreign-born individuals are generally, with a few exceptions, more likely to be working compared to native-born persons, whereas among females the opposite is the case, that is, across all Latina subgroups, native-born Latinas are more likely to have a job than foreign-born women. High rates of employment exceeding 88 percent are posted by seven groups of foreign-born men (Salvadorans, 91.9%; Guatemalans, 91.1%; Mexicans, 90.6%; Hondurans, 89.1%; Colombians, 88.7%; Spaniards, 88.6%; and Other South Americans, 88.5%). Among the native-born, Colombians (men,

Table 10.1 Percentage of Persons 25 to 54 Years of Age Employed by Race/Ethnic Group, Place of Birth, and Sex, 2022

Race/Ethnic Group	Female			Male		
	Total	Native-Born	Foreign-Born	Total	Native-Born	Foreign-Born
Colombian	78.2	84.9	75.4	88.8	89.1	88.7
Cuban	74.9	78.0	72.5	86.2	86.4	86.0
Dominican	75.1	76.9	74.1	83.9	82.8	84.6
Guatemalan	64.1	75.6	59.9	90.4	87.9	91.1
Honduran	64.2	77.3	61.6	88.4	85.2	89.1
Mexican	68.2	74.9	58.7	86.6	83.5	90.6
Puerto Rican	73.0	73.1	70.8	79.4	79.3	83.1
Salvadoran	70.6	77.9	67.5	90.8	87.9	91.9
Spaniard	77.5	78.3	73.8	85.2	84.5	88.6
Other Central American	72.4	78.0	68.2	83.5	85.3	82.2
Other South American	74.1	81.0	71.5	88.7	89.2	88.5
Other Latina/o	69.2	71.4	61.5	71.9	71.5	73.2
Afro-Latina/o	75.0	77.0	67.7	76.7	76.1	79.2
Latina/o	69.9	75.1	63.4	85.6	82.5	89.3
Black	76.6			73.3		
White	78.2			86.9		

Source: Data from 2022 American Community Survey 1-Year Estimates Public-Use File (Ruggles et al. 2024).

89.1%; women, 84.9%) and Other South Americans (89.2%; 81.0%) fare the best in employment, with Cubans (men, 86.4%; women, 78.0%) and Salvadorans (87.9%; 77.9%) also having quite high rates of employment. Among the native-born, Spaniard women (78.3%) had the third highest rate of employment among females and Guatemalan men (87.9%) were tied for third place alongside Salvadoran men among males.

The lowest employment levels among men occur among Other Latinos (native-born, 71.5%; foreign-born, 73.2%), Afro-Latinos (76.1%; 79.2%), and native-born Puerto Ricans (79.3%) with these groups having less than four in five of their members working. For women, the lowest employment rates occur among six foreign-born groups including Mexicans (58.7%), Guatemalans (59.9%), Other Latinas (61.5%), Hondurans (61.6%), Salvadorans (67.5%), and Other Central Americans (68.2%), all with employment rates below 70 percent.

Job Quality

We now turn to the second phase of labor market outcomes, namely, the quality of the job that people hold. Keep in mind that this part of the analysis involves only people 25 to 54 years of age (experienced workers) who are employed and the characteristics of the particular job that they held at the time of the survey. We use here three indicators of job quality: the median Duncan Occupational Socioeconomic Index (SEI), Latina/o immigrant occupational niche, and the possession of health insurance through employment. The Duncan Occupational Socioeconomic Index, commonly referred to as the SEI measure, was developed by O.D. Duncan (1961) using data from the 1950 census. The SEI is a score ranging from 0 to 100 and is based on the educational attainment level and income level associated with each occupation, with occupations having low SEI scores representing less prestigious occupations, based on the educational and income level of people holding such occupations, and those with high SEI scores denoting more prestigious occupations.

The Latina/o immigrant occupational niche is a sex-specific measure that identifies the occupations where Latina/os are disproportionately concentrated on a relative and absolute basis. The approach used to identify these occupations is based on the work of Waldinger (1996; see also Douglas and Sáenz 2008; Model 1993). In particular, we first obtain two sex-specific percentages: (1) the percentage of workers in a given occupation who are Latina/o immigrants (p_i) and (2) the percentage of all workers (regardless of occupation) who are Latina/o immigrants (p_t). Subsequently, we obtain the sex-specific ratio of the percentage of workers in a given occupation who are Latina/o immigrants (p_i) to the percentage of all workers who are Latina/o immigrants (p_t) by the following formula:

Ratio = p_i / p_t

Finally, we use two criteria to identify sex-specific Latina/o immigrant jobs: (1) the ratio is 1.5 or higher and (2) there are a minimum number of workers in a given occupation (11,265 for males and 8,244 for females), with the minimum sex-specific number derived by dividing the total number of Latina/o sex-specific workers by the number of occupations (525) in which they work. The procedure identifies 38 occupations for men and 34 for women, in which Latina/o immigrants are disproportionately concentrated. A list of the occupations for men and women is found in Appendix A. Approximately 45 percent of all Latina/o immigrants in the country who hold a job are working in an occupation identified as a Latina/o immigrant job (females, 42.7%; males, 46.8%). The analysis below will examine the percentage of workers across Latina/o subgroups, broken down by nativity status, who are employed in the Latina/o immigrant occupational niche.

The third indicator of job quality is the percentage of workers who have health insurance attained through their employment.

Based on the three indicators of job quality, higher levels of job quality are associated with high levels on the SEI measure, low rates of participation in the Latina/o immigrant occupational niche, and high levels of health insurance coverage through one's job.

The results show clear distinctions between whites, on the one hand, and Latina/os and Blacks, on the other hand, on the basis of job quality. For example, white workers hold much more prestigious jobs than Latina/o and Black workers (Table 10.2). However, the examination of the aggregate Latina/o workers veils much internal

Table 10.2 Selected Characteristics Related to Job Quality by Race/Ethnic Group, Place of Birth, and Sex among Workers 25 to 54 Years of Age, 2022

Sex and Race/ Ethnic Group	Median Occupational Socioeconomic Index[a]			Pct. in Latina/o Immigrant Job[b]			Pct. with Employment Health Insurance		
	Total	Native-Born	Foreign-Born	Total	Native-Born	Foreign-Born	Total	Native-Born	Foreign-Born
Female									
Colombian	47	52	46	20.3	9.4	25.3	62.6	75.4	56.7
Cuban	47	63	44	17.4	7.6	25.6	58.6	76.4	43.7
Dominican	44	51	26	27.3	10.5	36.4	52.5	66.3	44.9
Guatemalan	26	51	16	45.7	11.5	61.4	43.4	66.3	32.8
Honduran	18	47	17	48.2	19.0	55.5	38.1	70.2	30.2
Mexican	44	46	19	24.9	13.1	46.0	60.0	68.1	45.5
Puerto Rican	47	47	44	14.8	14.4	29.4	64.6	64.6	61.6
Salvadoran	38	47	18	38.9	12.7	51.5	50.8	69.3	42.0
Spaniard	61	60	68	9.3	8.6	12.9	74.4	73.8	77.4
Other Central American	47	61	44	19.6	7.5	30.0	64.8	73.4	57.4
Other South American	48	61	46	21.0	8.8	26.1	59.1	74.9	52.5
Other Latina	47	49	44	16.9	12.8	33.2	65.5	69.4	50.3
Afro-Latina	46	48	44	15.1	11.6	29.7	63.7	65.9	55.1
Latina	44	46	19	24.2	12.7	41.4	59.5	67.0	50.0
Black	46			13.5			67.7		
White	61			7.6			78.6		
Male									
Colombian	47	56	44	20.3	9.6	25.5	61.7	74.9	55.3
Cuban	44	49	24	20.1	12.6	25.7	55.8	71.0	44.1
Dominican	31	44	19	23.7	14.8	29.4	57.3	64.9	52.4
Guatemalan	17	44	16	53.9	25.1	61.5	32.7	64.3	24.3
Honduran	19	47	18	52.7	19.6	59.3	31.6	60.6	25.8
Mexican	22	39	18	34.9	20.2	52.1	55.0	67.9	39.8
Puerto Rican	44	44	24	18.5	17.9	35.5	69.4	69.6	64.8
Salvadoran	19	44	18	42.6	20.8	50.6	46.8	67.8	39.1
Spaniard	52	50	65	11.3	11.8	8.9	75.0	74.8	75.9
Other Central American	44	48	27	23.4	11.4	32.4	63.6	76.3	54.2
Other South American	44	62	38	24.5	12.8	28.8	56.5	73.3	50.2
Other Latino	44	44	19	22.6	17.2	39.7	64.0	69.8	45.6
Afro-Latino	39	44	19	16.1	12.1	29.9	62.5	64.4	55.9
Latino	27	44	18	32.1	18.7	46.8	55.6	68.7	41.2
Black	38			16.3			68.8		
White	52			11.2			77.9		

Source: Data from 2022 American Community Survey 1-Year Estimates Public-Use File (Ruggles et al. 2024).

variation regarding the SEI standing of the jobs that Latina/os hold. In fact, foreign-born Spaniard (socioeconomic index of 68) and native-born Cuban (63) work in more prestigious jobs than white women (61), while foreign-born Spaniard (65) and native-born Other South American (62) and Colombian (56) men hold more eminent jobs than white men (52). These Latina/o workers have prominent levels of educational attainment and also tend to be lighter in skin complexion compared to other Latina/o groups. These Latina/o groups have tended to be well integrated socioeconomically in the US. In contrast, foreign-born Guatemalan, Honduran, Mexican, and Salvadoran men and women hold the least prestigious jobs. Indeed, as expected foreign-born Latina/os hold jobs that are located further down the socioeconomic ladder than do their native-born counterparts, the exception being Spaniard immigrant men and women, who are at the top of the occupation prestige hierarchy. Note that, overall, women work in jobs with higher socioeconomic standing compared to men. This is due to the gendered nature of occupations in which men are more likely to be employed in blue-collar jobs where educational levels are fairly low and women in administrative-support positions that tend to have moderate levels of education.

Overall, as expected, Latina/os are much more likely to be working in Latina/o immigrant jobs than Blacks and, particularly, whites (Table 10.2). Foreign-born Guatemalan, Honduran, Mexican, and Salvadoran men and women are the most likely to hold jobs in the Latina/o immigrant occupational niche. This is particularly the case among Guatemalan immigrant men and women with more than three-fifths employed in Latina/o immigrant jobs. Again, Cuban, Colombian, Spaniard, and Other South Americans, regardless of nativity, are the least likely to be in the Latina/o immigrant occupational niche. It is noteworthy that approximately one-fourth of native-born Guatemalan and one-fifth of native-born Honduran, Mexican, and Salvadoran men work in jobs where Latina/o immigrants are concentrated. US birth status does not offer native-born persons from low-ranking Latina/o groups a key to bypass the Latina/o occupational niche.

White workers fare much better than Latina/o and Black workers when it comes to receiving health insurance through their job, with more than three-fourths of white workers covered through their employer (Table 10.2). Latina/o workers fare the worst in the attainment of health insurance through their employment with only 56 percent of men and 60 percent of women enjoying this benefit. In examining the varying groups of Latina/os, native-born Cubans, Colombians, Spaniards, Other Central Americans, and Other South Americans as well as foreign-born Spaniards are the most likely to have health insurance through their employers. Guatemalan and Hondurans immigrants are the least likely to receive health insurance benefits with only one-fourth of men and nearly one-third of women enjoying this job benefit.

Thus, we have seen that Latina/o groups vary significantly on the basis of job quality. On the one hand, Cubans, Colombians, Spaniards, and Other South Americans have the better jobs, while Mexicans, Salvadorans, Guatemalans, Hondurans and Other Central Americans generally fare much worse especially the foreign-born members of these groups.

Job Pay

We now direct our attention to the third phase of labor market outcomes – job pay. In this part of the analysis, we examine the median job income among people 25 to 54 years of age.

The results of the analysis show that whites are situated at the higher socioeconomic levels while Latina/os and Blacks lag significantly behind (Table 10.3). Latino men earn 69 cents and Latina women 74 cents per dollar that white men and women earn, respectively. Nonetheless, across gender groups, foreign-born Spaniards and native-born Cubans, Colombians, Spaniards, Other South Americans, and Other Central Americans have the highest median job incomes among Latina/os. In fact, foreign-born Spaniards ($67,750) have a higher median job income than white men ($64,623) and foreign-born Spaniard women ($60,454) and native-born Colombian ($52,116), Other South American ($52,116), and Cuban ($51,438) women have a higher median job pay compared to white women ($48,989). In contrast, in general, across gender groups and nativity status, Guatemalans, Hondurans, Mexicans, and Salvadorans have the lowest job incomes along with foreign-born Dominican men and women and Afro-Latino men. However, foreign-born Guatemalan and Honduran workers have the lowest median job earnings, with men earning approximately $36,000 and women $25,000.

This analysis, based on three segments of labor market outcomes – job attainment, job quality, and economic rewards – has provided a valuable portrait of the socioeconomic standing of Latina/o groups. In general, although whites tend to do better than Latina/os and Blacks across the variety of dimensions examined, there are certain Latina/o groups that fare better, at times surpassing whites. These are consistently foreign-born Spaniards and native-born Cubans, Colombians, Spaniards, Other South Americans, and, in certain respects, Other Central Americans. By contrast, Guatemalans, Hondurans, Mexicans, and Salvadorans consistently tend to be worse off socioeconomically, especially in the case of immigrants. Overall, it is clear that the socioeconomic fortunes are not only driven by human capital variations but also by nativity status and gender. Moreover, as noted in Chapter 2, the mode of incorporation that the various groups have experienced also affects the ease or difficulty that they face in integrating socioeconomically in the US. For example, Cuban, Colombian, Spaniards, and Other South American immigrants have been drawn from the more prosperous and educationally advantaged sectors of their country of origin and have received, in general, more favorable treatment and acceptance in the US.

A shortcoming associated with this analysis is that it has been fairly descriptive. We have merely provided a ranking of the diverse groups that comprise the Latina/o population. Nonetheless, as the analysis suggests, the Latina/o groups vary substantially along the lines of human capital and other characteristics that are typically associated with labor market outcomes. We next seek to assess the level of wage and salary inequality after we consider factors that are associated with earnings.

Table 10.3 Median Job Income by Race/Ethnic Group, Place of Birth, and Sex among Workers 25 to 54 Years of Age, 2022

Sex and Race/Ethnic Group	Total	Native-Born	Foreign-Born
Female			
Colombian	$41,692	$52,116	$36,481
Cuban	$39,608	$51,438	$31,269
Dominican	$32,520	$43,777	$29,810
Guatemalan	$29,185	$38,149	$25,015
Honduran	$27,100	$39,608	$25,015
Mexican	$34,396	$38,566	$29,185
Puerto Rican	$40,650	$40,650	$34,396
Salvadoran	$31,269	$41,692	$29,185
Spaniard	$46,904	$44,819	$60,454
Other Central American	$41,692	$46,904	$36,481
Other South American	$39,087	$52,116	$34,396
Other Latina	$38,357	$40,650	$31,269
Afro-Latina	$40,650	$41,692	$31,269
Latina	$36,272	$40,650	$30,227
Black	$38,982		
White	$48,989		
Male			
Colombian	$52,116	$62,534	$46,904
Cuban	$50,031	$57,327	$43,777
Dominican	$46,904	$52,116	$42,735
Guatemalan	$36,481	$41,797	$35,439
Honduran	$37,002	$46,904	$36,481
Mexican	$43,777	$47,946	$41,692
Puerto Rican	$50,031	$50,030	$46,904
Salvadoran	$41,692	$44,819	$41,171
Spaniard	$62,539	$62,539	$67,750
Other Central American	$48,989	$57,327	$42,735
Other South American	$52,116	$58,369	$48,989
Other Latino	$47,946	$50,031	$43,777
Afro-Latino	$43,777	$44,507	$42,735
Latino	$44,819	$50,031	$41,692
Black	$43,777		
White	$64,623		

Source: Data from 2022 American Community Survey 1-Year Estimates Public-Use File (Ruggles et al. 2024).

An Assessment of Earnings Inequality

As we saw in Table 10.3, there are significant differences in the median wage and salary incomes of workers across race/ethnic groups, with some Latina/o groups being particularly at a disadvantage. Furthermore, we observed that some Latina/o groups actually had more favorable earnings than whites. Yet, because groups differ on a wide variety of factors related to earnings, such as on educational attainment, it is difficult to pinpoint how much of the earnings differences are due to labor market inequality, what some call the "cost of being a minority worker" (Darity and Myers 2001; Doodoo and Takyi 2002; Poston et al. 1976; Sáenz and Morales 2019; Verdugo 1992). Indeed, research indicates that some racial and ethnic groups pay a penalty in earnings due to their racial or ethnic group membership. In describing the research undertaken to get at this cost that persons of color pay, Sáenz and Morales (2019) point out:

> These studies typically do not obtain direct measures of labor market discrimination based on race and ethnicity. However, they commonly treat differences in earnings between minority and majority workers that remain after making appropriate statistical adjustments as proxies of such discrimination. (p. 193)

Following this approach, we use data from the 2022 American Community Survey Public-Use File (Ruggles et al. 2024) for persons 25 to 54 years of age who worked during the previous year. We use ordinary least square (OLS) multiple regression to conduct the analysis, with our two major variables of interest being the log of the wage and salary income of workers in 2010 (the dependent variable, or the factor that we seek to explain) and race/ethnic group membership (the independent variable, or the factor that we set forth as an explanation for earnings). In addition, we introduce in the model a series of control variables to account for the demographic and socio-economic differences across race/ethnic groups. In particular, we use eight control variables for the analysis, focusing on native-born workers: educational attainment; language spoken and English ability; self-employment status; weeks worked during the year; usual number of hours worked per week during the year; marital status; age; and region (Midwest, Northeast, South, and West) of residents. For foreign-born individuals, we use these eight control variables along with two additional control variables: years living in the US and US naturalized citizen status. The analysis seeks to determine the percentage difference in earnings that remains between each race/ethnic group and whites (the comparison group) after accounting for differences between these groups on the series of control variables. The analysis is conducted separately on the basis of nativity status and sex. Therefore, for native-born individuals, the comparison is between each native-born race/ethnic group and the native-born white group by sex; for foreign-born persons, the comparison is between each foreign-born race/ethnic group and the foreign-born white group by sex. Note that in the analysis conducted below, Afro-Latina/os will now be a mutually exclusive group in order to be in the analysis and determine their earnings relative to whites and all other Latina/o subgroups. For sake of analytical efficiency, we also aggregate

Other Central Americans, Other South Americans, and Other Latina/os into one category labeled as Other Latina/os.

The results examining the relationship between race/ethnic members and earnings are presented in Table 10.4 (for an examination of the results for the full model
containing the relationships between earnings and all of the control variables, see
Appendix B). Note that the values (coefficients) shown in Table 10.4 for males and
females across nativity groups are in proportion format (thus, they can be multiplied by 100 to obtain the percentage). Negative values indicate that the specific
race/ethnic group has wages that are lower than the respective white comparison
group, while positive values note that the specific race/ethnic group has wages that
are higher than the comparative white group. Note also that some coefficients have
asterisks. The asterisks denote statistical significance – i.e. the differences are large
enough that they could not have occurred by chance – at the 0.05 level and at the 0.01
level with the latter associated with a higher level of statistical significance.

Let us take a look first at the results for native-born women. We can see that among
Latina groups, after accounting for differences on the control variables used in the
analysis, US-born Colombian, Dominican, and Cuban women have wages that are
significantly higher than those of white women by 8.9 percent, 6.4 percent, and 5.9
percent, respectively (Table 10.4). On the other hand, Afro-Latina (–6.6%), Spaniard

Table 10.4 Disparities in Wage and Salary Income of Workers 25 to 54 Years of
Age Obtained from Multiple Regression Analysis for Selected Race/Ethnic Groups
Relative to Whites by Place of Birth and Sex, 2022

Race/Ethnic Group	Native-Born		Foreign-Born	
	Female	Male	Female	Male
Afro-Latina/o	−0.066**	−0.087**	−0.021	−0.055
Colombian	0.089**	0.141**	−0.007	−0.027
Cuban	0.059**	0.010	−0.111**	−0.224**
Dominican	0.064**	0.002	−0.198**	−0.244**
Guatemalan	−0.001	−0.018	−0.065*	−0.036
Honduran	0.011	−0.047	−0.031	0.002
Mexican	−0.045**	−0.089**	−0.213**	−0.254**
Puerto Rican	0.001	−0.097**	−0.061	−0.185**
Salvadoran	0.008	−0.003	0.004	0.006
Spaniard	−0.062**	−0.050*	0.064	0.033
Other Latina/o	−0.007	−0.071**	−0.141**	−0.221**
Black	−0.022**	−0.104**	0.110**	−0.060**

[a] The results from the full multiple regression models are available in Appendix B.

 * Statistically significant at the 0.05 level.

** Statistically significant at the 0.01 level.

Source: Data from 2022 American Community Survey 1-Year Estimates Public-Use File
(Ruggles et al. 2024).

(–6.2%), Mexican (–4.5%), and non-Hispanic Black women (–2.2%) pay a wage penalty for being a member of their racial/ethnic group relative to white women. You may wonder why Spaniard women actually have lower earnings than white women, when we have seen them fare so well economically above. The reason is likely to be that their earnings are high to begin with because of their elevated level of education. If they had the lower educational levels of white women, their wages would be even lower. The other five groups of Latina women (Guatemalan, Honduran, Puerto Rican, Salvadoran, and Other Latinas) have job earnings that do not differ significantly from those of white women, after adjusting for factors used in the analysis. One thing worth mentioning, as we proceed with the analysis for men, is that the differences in earnings of non-white women relative to white women are smaller than those among men, This is due to the smaller differences in earnings between white women and Black and Latina women due to all women, including white ones, facing gender costs in the labor market. Thus, gender discrimination across all groups of women narrows the earning gaps between white and non-white women.

We now examine the results for native-born men workers. After adjusting for differences in the factors used in our statistical model across all the groups, native-born Colombian men have earnings that are approximately 14 percent higher those of white men. The results provide support for the earlier findings regarding the high wages of Colombians. On the other hand, five groups of native-born Latino men as well as non-Hispanic Black men pay a wage cost for their race/ethnicity: relative to the earnings of white men, the wages of Black and Puerto Rican men are 10 percent lower, 9 percent lower for Afro-Latino and Mexican, 7 percent lower for Other Latino, and 5 percent lower for Spaniard men. Like native-born Spaniard women, Spaniard men also pay a wage cost in the workforce despite their high educational attainment level. Five groups (Cubans, Dominicans, Guatemalans, Hondurans, and Salvadorans) do not differ in their earnings from white men, after making statistical adjustments for their differences in demographic and socioeconomic traits.

Now we turn to the examination of the earnings of immigrants. Among foreign-born women, five groups of Latina women (Cuban, Dominican, Guatemalan, Mexican, and Other Latinas) have significantly lower wages than white women after adjusting for statistical differences in demographic and socioeconomic attributes. The greatest earnings disparities occur among Mexican, Dominican, and Other Latina women whose wages are 21 percent, 20 percent, and 14 percent, respectively, lower than those of white women. However, the wages of immigrant Black women are actually 11 percent higher than those of white women. Yet, there are no significant differences between the wages of white women and Afro-Latina, Colombian, Honduran, Puerto Rican, Salvadoran, and Spaniard women.

Among foreign-born men, the results are somewhat similar to those of foreign-born women. Five groups of Latino men and Black men have significantly lower wages than white immigrant men: Mexican (–25.4%), Dominican (–24.4%), Cuban (–22.4%), Other Latino (–22.1%), Puerto Rican (–18.5%), and Black (–6.0%) men. Note that Mexican and Dominican immigrants have wages approximately 25 percent lower than those of white immigrants. Finally, the wages of Afro-Latino, Colombian,

Guatemalan, Honduran, Salvadoran, and Spaniard immigrant men do not differ from those of white immigrant men.

One important observation is that the magnitude of differences in earnings between white and non-white immigrants are larger than is the case for native-born persons. Two reasons account for this. First, foreign-born whites tend to have higher socioeconomic levels compared to native-born whites. Second, Latino immigrants tend to have relatively low socioeconomic characteristics compared to their US-born counterparts. These two differences, then, magnify the earnings differences shown here.

These findings examining earnings inequality provide added substance to the earlier results presented in Tables 10.1, 10.2, and 10.3. They are also instructive in other ways. First, despite the favorable standing of Cubans, Colombians, and Spaniards observed earlier, only three subgroups of these national-origin groups (native-born Colombian men and women and native-born Cuban women) actually have more favorable earnings than their white counterparts, after making the appropriate statistical adjustments for socioeconomic and demographic characteristics. Second, Mexicans and Other Latinos tend to pay a wage cost most consistently across nativity and sex groups. Third, three native-born Central American groups – Guatemalans, Hondurans, and Salvadorans – largely have wages that do not differ significantly from their white counterparts. This suggests that a path toward economic integration exists for these groups and Other Central Americans.

Some Issues Related to the Future of Latina/o Work and Economic Life

We need to be aware of several important labor market and socioeconomic trends regarding the Latina/o population, for these are likely to play a vital role in the future. In this section, we will address three of these trends: (1) the increasing share of Latina/os in the US workforce, (2) the declining immigrant workforce among Latina/os, and (3) the recent decline of women in the Latina/o workforce. These trends have major implications and questions regarding the future course of Latina/os in the labor market and the economy in the coming years.

The Increasing Latina/o Workforce

As we have observed earlier in Chapter 5, Latina/os have been the engine of US population growth since 1980 and will continue to be in the future. The number of Latina/o workers grew more than five-fold from 5.5 million in 1980 to 28.6 million in 2021, compared to a 38 percent increase in non-Latina/o workers during this period. Moreover, the number of Latina/o workers more than doubled between 2000 and 2021, compared to a slow growth of 10 percent for non-Latina/o workers. As a consequence, the percentage share of Latina/o workers in the US workforce has soared over the last four decades, rising from 5.6 percent in 1980 to 18.1 percent in 2021 (Figure 10.1).

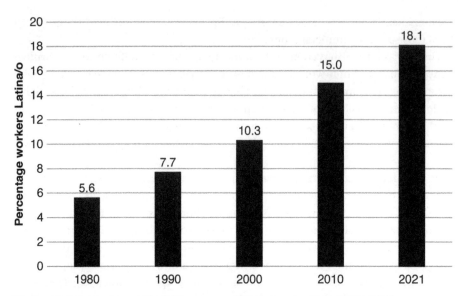

Figure 10.1 Percentage of Latina/os among US Workers by Year, 1980–2021
Source: Data from 1980, 1990, and 2000 Public Use Microdata Sample and 2010 and 2020 American Community Survey (ACS) Public Use Files (Ruggles et al. 2024).

The Bureau of Labor Statistics has developed projections of US workers for 2030. Between 2020 and 2030, the US workforce will become even more Latina/o, bolstered by new entrants into the workforce being Latina/o (Dubina 2021). It is projected that there will be 35.9 million Latina/o workers in 2030, an increase of 24 percent. Nearly four of five new workers between 2020 and 20230 are projected to be Latina/o. It is projected that Latina/os will make up 21.2 percent of the US workforce in 2030. The coming decades will continue to see more Latina/o workers and fewer white workers.

While US policy has grown increasingly color-blind over the last several decades, there are imperative public policy needs regarding the shifting demography of the US workforce. As the US population ages significantly, with Baby Boomers reaching age 65 and older from 2011 to 2029, there will be a major labor need to generate tax dollars to support a growing older population. Latina/os will disproportionately represent the new workers in the coming decades and, thus, will play a critical role in generating the tax dollars to support Baby Boomers and subsequent cohorts of older persons.

In order to meet this growing demand for supporting an older US population, policies must address the educational disparities of Latina/os. As we saw in Chapter 9, Latina/os continue to lag behind other racial/ethnic groups in educational attainment. To compete on a global scale in an increasingly technological world, there will need to be major investments to ensure that Latina/os increasingly go to college and earn bachelor's and more advanced degrees. The failure to make such investments will result in major opportunities being lost for this country.

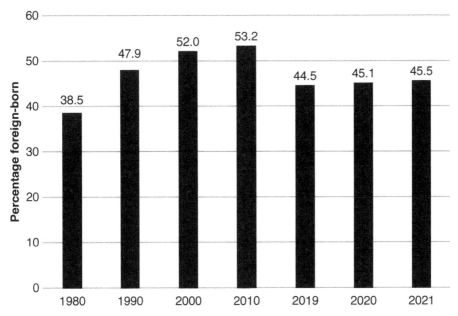

Figure 10.2 Percentage of Latina/o Workers Foreign-Born, 1980–2021

Source: Data from 1980, 1990, and 2000 Public Use Microdata Sample and 2010 and 2020 American Community Survey (ACS) Public Use Files (Ruggles et al. 2024).

The Recent Decline of Immigrants in the Latina/o Workforce

Over the last several decades, immigration has accounted for a sizable portion of the rapid growth of the Latina/o population and its workforce. This changed dramatically in more recent times, as we observed in Chapters 4 and 5. The volume of immigration from Mexico has plunged since the Great Recession (Sáenz 2019), resulting in a significant shift in the demography of the Latina/o workforce. In 2000 and 2010, immigrants made up more than half of all Latina/o workers, but in 2021 they accounted for 45.5 percent of Latina/o workers.

One of the most frequent questions is whether Mexican immigration will bounce back to levels seen at the close of the twentieth and opening of the twenty-first century. It is very unlikely that this will ever occur again. While Mexico had an excess of a youthful labor force for much of the twentieth century, that is no longer the case with the country becoming older and more so in the coming decades due to major drops in fertility (Sáenz 2015, 2019). In addition, most people coming to the US southern border are not Mexicans and are seeking to gain entrance as refugees and asylees. These individuals are largely not only from Latin American and Caribbean countries including Salvadorans, Hondurans, Cubans, Nicaraguans, Haitians, and Venezuelans, but from throughout the world, including Africa, Asia, and points beyond. Finally, despite growing anti-immigrant sentiments in the US, the aging of the US workforce and the waning levels of fertility in the nation will require the importation of new workers, many of whom are already at the US footsteps seeking asylum from the US government.

The Recent Decline of Women in the Latina/o Workforce

Latina women have historically had lower workforce participation compared to their counterparts from other racial/ethnic groups. Over the last several decades, Latinas have slowly increased their participation in the workforce with their percentage share of all Latina/o workers inching upwards from 39 percent in 1980 to 44 percent in 2019. Over the course of the pandemic, the percentage of Latina workers slipped to 43 percent of all Latina/o workers in 2021. Undoubtedly, this dip is due to the disproportionate pressure for women to deal with childcare needs and online schooling during the pandemic. What will the future hold?

On the one hand, there are a variety of factors that point to Latina women rebounding to an increasing share of all Latina/o workers. First, as we saw in Chapter 9, Latinas have experienced significant gains in educational attainment and they now surpass Latinos in the attainment of college degrees. As Latinas attain higher levels of education, they will increasingly be part of the workforce. Second, as we saw above, foreign-born Latinas continue to have relatively low levels of employment activity in the formal labor market. As more of these women enter the labor force with increasing time in the US, they will contribute to the increasing share of women among all Latina/o workers. Finally, as we will observe in the following chapter (Chapter 11), the share of families that are headed by Latina women has increased substantially over the last several decades. Under such circumstances, women will increasingly join the workforce in efforts to increase the economic resources of their families.

Yet, on the other hand, the US does not have family-friendly policies for its workforce. We have known for a long time that childcare is expensive, especially for families with limited resources. Furthermore, due to declining fertility and the high longevity of Latina/os, the Latina/o population will become older in the coming decades. One of the sidebars of the Latina/o paradox (see Chapter 13) is that Latina/os live longer lives than whites, but they do so with greater levels of disabilities and chronic and degenerative diseases. To complicate matters, older Latina/os have relatively high rates of dementia and Alzheimer's disease (Mather and Scommegna 2020). Thus, the care for an increasing number of older Latina/os in the coming years will place heavy demands on Latina/o families, with the responsibility for taking care of aging parents falling disproportionately on women – daughters, spouses, and granddaughters (see Cantu et al. 2023). Public policies will need to be enacted to ensure that family caretakers will be appropriately compensated for the care that they give to their loved ones and that they are not penalized for leaving the labor force.

Summary

This chapter has provided an overview of the work and economic patterns of the Latina/o population. We overviewed a variety of theoretical perspectives that sociologists and other social scientists have used to understand the various stages of labor market outcomes: job attainment, job quality, and economic rewards. The examination of contemporary data shows that there is a great degree of variability in the work and economic experiences of the diverse groups that comprise the Latina/o population. In particular, while some groups fare well socioeconomically (Cubans, Colombians, Spaniards, and Other South Americans), other groups are not as fortunate (Dominicans, Guatemalans, Hondurans, Mexicans, Puerto Ricans, Dominicans, and Salvadorans). In addition, analysis seeking to assess the extent to which Latina/o workers pay a penalty for their race/ethnic membership demonstrates that many subgroups of Latina/o face wage inequality, a pattern most consistent across place-of-birth and sex categories among Mexicans, Puerto Ricans, and Other Latinos. Finally, we highlighted three important trends in the Latina/o workforce involving their increasing share of the US workforce and downward trends in the share of immigrants and women among Latina/o workers.

We need to recognize the two stories of the work and economic life of Latina/os. Despite great challenges associated with racial/ethnic inequality and historical laws hurting Latina/o and non-white workers, the growing number of Latina/os cuts across all institutions, including the economy and workforce as Hamilton et al. (2023) illustrate at the outset of this chapter. We also see Latina/os playing a significant role in the enhancement of the national GDP, new businesses, workforce, and consumers. There is certainly a need to change the narrative that emphasizes the low socioeconomic standing of Latina/os as "takers" rather than "makers." Still, the challenges that confront so many Latina/os cannot be overlooked.

In conclusion, the work and economic activities of Latina/os are important for all phases of their lives, such as in the sphere of education, contributions to the larger society, and toward greater economic stability in the golden years. One area that is intimately related to the work and economic activities of Latina/os concerns their families. Indeed, family life affects one's work and economic conditions which subsequently are important for supporting and sustaining families. We now turn to an examination of the family life of Latina/os.

Discussion Questions

1. What are the two common stories regarding the work and economic standing of Latina/os?

2. What are the three theoretical perspectives concerning factors that impact labor market outcomes for workers? Is there a particular one that you find particularly useful? If so, why?

3. Overall, which Latina/o groups fare well and which fare worse on job attainment, job quality, and job pay?

4. Does the cost of being a minority worker equate to labor-market discrimination?

5. If US Latina/os were a country, how would they rank with respect to the GDP among all countries of the world?

6. Do you think that the recent decline of Latina/o immigrants and women in the US workforce will reverse? Why, or why not?

7. What are some of the jobs that are associated with the Latina/o immigrant occupational niche?

11 Families

Well, it (migration) has its advantages and its disadvantages. Having our paisanos (countrymen/women) there up North (US), um, it benefits the family. As I was saying, building a house with dignity and commodities, a floor, having a car, or even feeding our family. Still, as far as education or moral or paternal support, the children, in that sense, are left poor. An education in which the father leaves (migrates), and the mother, well, they (children) are not raised the same. In our society, that is how we're falling apart. We are developing materially, but as far as values, to have an education, the children of the paisanos (countrymen/women) who leave for many years or who come and go and only come to visit, well, the children do not feel a parent's warmth . . .

(Antonio, *transmigrant*, Otomí, The Sierra Nahñu, Hidalgo, Mexico [personal interview with Maria Cristina Morales and Leticia Saucedo])

The quote above is from an indigenous transnational Mexican migrant who described the struggle between being financial providers and the social and emotional costs of leaving children behind in their home country. This problem of having no option but to migrate to provide food and housing for the family at the sacrifice of parenting from miles away is painful, especially when feeling that the children are growing up without parental warmth, as Antonio stated (also see Abrego 2014 for an example on Salvadorans). The cultural changes that transnational families face are especially dreadful for indigenous communities, such as Antonio's, who also struggle against the erasure of their indigenous culture.

Ironically, even though being family-centric is perhaps the most established characteristic of Latina/os, early scholarship depicted Latina/o culture and families as dysfunctional. Arguably, such perceptions gained momentum after the work of anthropologist Oscar Lewis, who is best known for the "culture of poverty" framework. Recall that although the "culture of poverty" concept has been misapplied, it has come to be used to portray poor people of color as having a dysfunctional culture without ambition. Oscar Lewis published two books on Latina/o families and the culture of poverty – *Five Families: Mexican Case Studies in the Culture of Poverty* (1959) and *La Vida: A Puerto Rican Family in the Culture of Poverty – San Jose and New York* (1965), the latter which focused on a single Puerto Rican family in the "culture of poverty." Lewis's work unintentionally contributed to stereotypes of Mexican-origin and Puerto Rican families as culturally deficient and a social problem for American society (Zambrana 2011).

Perceptions of Latina/o family dysfunctionality can also occur through comparative analysis. Intentionally or unintentionally, studies contrasting whites and Latina/os at times assume that the former is the standard by which all other racial/ethnic groups are judged (Zambrana 2011). Particularly in the early 2000s, scholarship shifted from using dysfunctional frameworks to study Latina/o families to more closely examining the impact of social structure on Latina/o well-being. For instance, more structural racism perspectives began to be used to explain the unequal treatment of ethnic families based on a superior-versus-inferior binary (Bonilla-Silva 2021).

This chapter begins with an overview of the familismo or familism that signals the high importance Latina/os place on family. Then, we examine the cultural versus structural perspectives used to discuss Latina/o families. Afterward, we use data from the 2022 American Community Survey 1-Year Estimates Public-Use File to explore various trends related to family composition for various Latina/o subgroups by sex and place of birth. Lastly, we highlight some of the issues affecting the future of Latina/o families, historically impacting Mexican and Central American but now Venezuelan and Afro-Latina/o families separated at the US–Mexico border, mixed-status families and households, and struggles for inclusion for same-sex couples.

Familismo

Familisimo, or familism, is the concept that has received the most attention in the study of Latina/o families. Two of the most prevalent components associated with familismo are prioritizing the family over individual needs and conceptualizing family beyond the nuclear to the extended. First, the concept of familismo has been a central element describing Latina/os living in the US and in Latin America for over fifty years (Fussell and Palloni 2004; Hurtado 1995; Moore with Cuéllar 1970; Rodríguez, Pilcher, and Garcia-Tellez 2021). One of the earliest usages of familismo/familism is seen in Moore with Cuéllar (1970), who described it as the most significant part of life for Mexican Americans in South Texas, as it is a primary source of obligations and emotional and economic support. Familismo is also central to other Latina/o groups. Puerto Rican fathers, for instance, have child-rearing responsibilities that emphasize familismo/familism in addition to respect and solidarity (Mogro-Wilson, Rojas, and Haynes 2016). The second component of familismo emphasizes the importance of contributing to the well-being of the nuclear and the extended family (Smith-Morris et al. 2012).

Scholars have also identified various dimensions of familismo, including structural/demographic (e.g. family size, marriage, and family structure), attitudinal/normative (e.g. values placed on the family), and behavioral (e.g. activities that fulfill family roles and degree of interaction between families and kin networks) (Valenzuela and Dornbusch 1994). Below, we address each of these dimensions of familismo.

Demographic and Structural Familismo

Demographic and structural factors can influence various aspects of familismo, including family size and marriage patterns. Among Latina/o immigrants, regardless of social class, there exists a distinctive emphasis on family interdependence, which is a fundamental aspect of familism. This trait sets apart Latina/o immigrant families, as noted by Hooker et al. (2023). Research also indicates that lower income levels tend to correlate with higher levels of interdependence among European American and, to a lesser extent, US-born Latina/o families (Hooker et al. 2023).

It is also crucial to consider the significance of family structure, given its influence on several factors in the life course and family and child well-being (Zambrana 2011). Family structure is pivotal in shaping various life trajectories that contribute to family and child well-being. The family structure of Latina/o families has been distinguishable from non-Latina/o–white families over the last several decades. For example, Latina females are less likely to be married, more likely to be heads of household, and more likely to have children at younger ages outside of marriage than non-Latina-white females (Cauce and Domenech-Rodríguez 2002).

Attitudinal/Normative and Behavioral Familismo

Most of the literature on familismo has focused on attitudinal/normative values placed on the family and behavioral that allude to activities involving fulfilling family roles and interactions among family members. While both of these forms of familismo are distinct, they both have been applied to similar topics, including obligations to help the family economically and emotionally, consulting with family members for significant life decisions (Corona, Campos, and Chen 2017), spending time with family members (Ackert and Wikle 2022), familial support (Campos et al. 2014; Corona, Campos, and Chen 2017), and loyalty and reciprocity within the family (Steidel and Contreras 2003).

Comparative studies found that familism is associated with higher levels of social support among Latina/os, in contrast to other racial and ethnic groups in the United States (Campos, Yim, and Busse 2018; Corona, Campos, and Chen 2017). Indeed, Latina/o's valuing of family relationships, even over the self, is a feature that is less salient among whites (Campos et al. 2014). Moreover, when it comes to asking for help, proximity is the primary determinant among whites, whereas Latina/os prefer family support (Cauce and Domenech-Rodríguez 2002).

Another indicator of behavioral familismo is living in geographical proximity to family. Latina/os place higher value on geographical closeness to family and kin (Hurtado 1995). For instance, a distinguishable characteristic of Mexican Americans is that they tend to live in kin-based communities, unlike Anglos (Keefe 1984). Mexican Americans are less geographically mobile, even when controlling for socioeconomic status (Keefe 1984). In a comparative study in Los Angeles, Mexican immigrants were more likely to have kin in town, to be related to people in the household, and to have visited more households weekly than whites (Keefe 1984).

Such family cohesion also functions to embrace Latina/o values. Although they did not use the concept of familism, Villalobos Solís (2021) found that Puerto Ricans who visit Puerto Rico have a greater positive correlation with increased ethnic identity and a stronger embrace of Latina/o values, family obligations, and *respeto*/respect, all of which help the youth to confront challenging daily life situations. In the case of Latina/o immigrants, it is well established that proximity to kin has been a critical feature of ethnic enclaves (Wilson and Portes 1980).

Debates on Familismo

The impact of familism among Latina/os is mainly associated with positive outcomes on several societal factors, particularly education and health. Familism or Latina/o family support encourages educational attainment among youth (Stein et al. 2015) and helps the youth plan successful futures (Carey 2022). Scholarly attention is increasingly focused on the impact of familismo on physical and mental health. Familismo is generally beneficial for mental health, even under stress, self-esteem, and subjective health (Ayón, Marsiglia, and Bermudez-Parsai 2010; Campos, Yen, and Busse 2018; Corona, Campos, and Chen et al. 2017; Gallegos and Segrin 2022; Stein et al. 2015). Indeed, for Latina/os, in contrast to non-Latina/os, social support indirectly buffers cortisol responses, providing physiological evidence of the positive effects of familism (Campos, Yim, and Busse 2018). As such, perceived family support can buffer against the physiological consequences of stress and benefit physiological health processes. There is also an association between a higher affinity for familismo and healthy sexual behaviors (García 2022; Muñoz-Laboy 2008; Pérez, Santamaria, and Operario 2018).

Despite the broad support for the positive outcomes associated with familismo, there are several points of contestation. First, utilizing the anthropological lens, Smith-Morris et al. (2012) found through nostalgic recollections of Mexican migrants that community is equally or more important than family. Second, others disagree about whether families are restricted to Latina/o culture, given that unidimensional measures of familism are also found among other racial and ethnic groups (Christophe and Stein 2022). Finally, there is disagreement on the impact of familismo on social processes. For instance, in contrast to the positive depictions of familismo described above, this concept has also been connected to downward mobility for Mexican Americans (Harris 1980) and as a source of surveillance and pressure on reproductive decisions (Maternowska et al. 2010).

Culture versus Structural Perspectives on Latina/o Families

Central to the early frameworks in the sociology of the family are ethnocentric views of families focused on European cultural norms that have guided theorizing about racial/ethnic groups, including Latina/os, in the US. On this point, Zambrana (2011, p. 39) argued that it is essential to "interrogate the epistemological roots of the intellectual traditions (family theory and assimilation/acculturation theory) that have been used to capture the lived experiences of Latina/o subgroups in the

United States." Thus, debates about culture versus structure are fundamental to theoretical perspectives applied to Latina/o families. Below, we elaborate on the culture v. structure debate that surfaces in studies on Latina/o families.

Families, Sex Roles, and Latina/o Culture

Academic scholarship has mostly moved away from using cultural deficiency perspectives that blame Latina/o culture for social inequalities, although these perceptions still exist in popular culture. Two cultural perspectives rooted in the Latina/o family that can be controversial are *marianismo* and *machismo*. The concept of marianismo is based on the Catholic ideal of the Virgin Mary, used to highlight women's role as the self-sacrificing mother who suffers for her children (Ramirez 1990). In the early 2000s, there was a shift in perceptions of the role of Latina/o culture. According to traditional Latin American perspectives, mothers are expected to self-sacrifice for the sake of the family (Chant with Craske 2003), while fathers are associated with authority, protection, and guidance of the family through participation in public spheres (Arriagada 2002). However, numerous studies have questioned the applicability of marianismo to Latina mothers. For instance, motherhood is defined more broadly in Latin America: mothers are not expected to be confined to the private sphere but to be proactive in public spheres, such as employment outside of the home, political participation, and migration (Abrego 2009). Even in the US, a comparative study of Latina and white females in a public university found no differences in gender ideologies and behavior (Franco et al. 2004). Similarly, a study based on Mexican American students enrolled in a southwestern university found that attitudes toward the female role in the workplace and parental responsibility for childcare reflected more Euro-American orientations (Gowan and Treviño 1998). In a study on motherhood on both sides of the US–Mexico border, Bejarano and Morales (2024) developed the concept of *frontera madre(hood)* to describe how Brown mothers teach children how to navigate or challenge restrictive and regimented structures, images, and ideologies embedded in this region.

In contrast to marianismo, *machismo* emphasizes the role of head of household versus fatherhood (Cauce and Domenech-Rodríguez 2002). Early feminist perspectives describe *machismo* as "an exaggerated masculinity, physical prowess, and male chauvinism" (Baca Zinn 1994, p. 74). Lea Ybarra's (1983) research on the portrayal of Chicana/o families in the 1960s to 1970s emphasized the patriarchal structure of male domination, female submissiveness, and maternal self-sacrifice. *Machismo* has had a wide range of conceptualizations. The most controversial are those that depict Latino males as tyrannical or hyper-masculine. This is ironic given that nine out of an estimated 29 women elected presidents of their countries since the 1970s have been from Latin America and the Caribbean (Romero 2013). However, characterizations of *machismo* continue to broadly depict Latino men as dominant fathers and husbands (Cauce and Domenech-Rodríguez 2002).

Others have painted *machismo* more positively or have questioned the applicability of the concept by highlighting Latino men's roles as providers, protectors, and representatives of their families (Mirandé 1997) or have highlighted how it originates as a coping mechanism from discrimination (Hendy, Can, and Heep 2022; Mirandé 1997), or the structural economic factors that sustain and benefit from *machismo* (Saucedo and Morales 2010). Despite Latina/o male characterizations as "*machistas*" (male chauvinists), scholarship has documented the value of familismo (the importance of the family over the individual), which extends to fathers' household participation and childcare activities (see below). For example, compared to white fathers, Latino fathers are more parentally engaged with their children (Leavell et al. 2012). Moreover, in cases where Latino fathers are less engaged in caregiving than whites and African Americans, it is attributed to their low educational levels that relegate them to working more hours at low-paying jobs, which pulls them away from caregiving activities (Leavell et al. 2012). The scholarship on the household division of labor also raises questions about the applicability of *machismo* to Latino males.

Indeed, for nearly five decades, scholarship has documented that in Latina/o families, both genders roughly agree on perceptions that men should do housework, that it is all right for the wife to be the primary earner, and that women have the right to use and decide the methods of birth control (Hurtado et al. 1992). The term *caballerismo* has been used to highlight the more gentlemanly, respectful, and family-protective behaviors of Latino men (Arciniega et al. 2008; Miville et al. 2017; Saez et al. 2010). For example, a study about Puerto Rican fathers described their parenting roles as being there, maintaining open communication, building confidence, preparing for adulthood, teaching culture/values, and providing a role model for their children (Mogro-Wilson et al. 2019).

Structural Explanations of Latina/o Family Circumstances

One of the most critical advancements in family studies in about the 1990s and onward is the emphasizing of social-structural characteristics (McLoyd et al. 2000). While referring to immigrant families, Foner (1997) elegantly stated, "the family is seen as a place where there is a dynamic interplay between structure, culture, and agency – where creative culture-building takes place in the context of external social and economic forces as well as immigrants' pre-migration cultural frameworks" (p. 961). Some of the most important structural factors to consider are those associated with poverty that influences divorce, non-marital childbearing, and female-headed households (Landale and Oropesa 2007). Studies on Latina/o families must account for structural inequality at the neighborhood, community, and educational institutional levels and its influence on family processes, family relationships, and gender-role expectations (Zambrana 2011). Indeed, in a comparative study of Mexican, Puerto Rican, and white families, structure is more important than culture, given that higher social class is associated with living further away from family members and a reduction in the likelihood of living with family (Sarkisian et al. 2006). Consequently, family practices and culture should be differentiated to avoid attributing differences simply to culture (Sarkisian et al. 2006).

Structure affects not only family formation but also parenting styles. In Ayón and García's (2019) study they found that parents who are subjected to high levels of discrimination tend to practice harsher disciplinary styles and experience more hardship in their parenting practices. They conclude by highlighting how restrictive immigrant climates create a range of issues, such as discrimination, that impact families and entire communities.

Trends in Marriage, Family, and Households among Latina/os

Data from the 2022 American Community Survey (ACS) 1-Year Public-Use Estimates are used to examine trends in the family composition of Latina/o groups and two comparative groups (whites and Blacks) along five dimensions: (1) marriage and divorce, (2) intermarriages, (3) heterosexual and same-sex cohabitations, (4) female-headed households with no husband present, and (5) living with extended family members and residing alone. Because sex is such an important factor in family studies, all analyses are conducted separately for females and males. Furthermore, other central determinants that affect Latina/o family structure are included, in particular, Latina/o subgroup and place of birth. Note that the analysis presented below is based on individuals 25 to 44 years of age. This age band controls for age differences across racial and ethnic groups. For example, let us consider all individuals fifteen years or older. It is likely that some groups, such as Mexicans, would have very low rates of marriage, due principally to the youthfulness of the population.

Marriage and Divorce

We begin our analysis by examining the prevalence of marriage (Table 11.1). First, we will discuss the overall marriage patterns for Latina/os and Afro-Latina/os and compare them to the percentages for whites and Blacks. Afro-Latina/os and Latina/os have lower percentages of marriage than whites but more significant percentages than Blacks. The marriage patterns of female and male Afro-Latina/os are comparable to that of Blacks among the native-born. For instance, 29.7 percent of native-born Afro-Latina females are married compared to 28.3 percent of Black females. Similarly, among males, 32.6 percent of native-born Afro-Latinos are married compared to 31 percent of Black males. Latina females have 7 percent lower rates of marriage than their white counterparts (49% v. 56.6%), and Latino males have 6 percent lower rates of marriage than whites do (45.1% v. 51.4%). In contrast, when compared to Black females (28.3%), Latinas are 1.7 times more likely to be married (49%). Similarly, among males, Latinos are 1.5 times more likely to be married than Blacks. Second, foreign-born Latina/os are more likely to be married than native-born Latina/os among females and males. Third, among Latina/os, females are more likely than males to be married.

    Next, we use ACS (2022) data to examine variations in marriage across Latina/o groups. Among the foreign-born females, three-fifths or more of Other South Americans (61.0%), Mexicans (61.1%), and Colombians (61.3%) are married,

Table 11.1 Selected Marriage and Divorce Characteristics among Persons 25 to 44 Years of Age by Race/Ethnic Group, Sex, and Nativity, 2022

| Race/Ethnic Group | Pct. of Persons Currently Married | | | | | | Divorce Rate | | | | | |
| | Female | | | Male | | | Female | | | Male | | |
	Total	Native-Born	Foreign-Born	Total	Native-Born	Foreign-Born	Total	Native-Born	Foreign-Born	Total	Native-Born	Foreign-Born
Colombian	56.1	45.8	61.3	49.1	41.5	53.7	22.1	32.5	22.0	24.0	24.4	23.8
Cuban	47.0	47.6	46.5	44.1	42.2	46.0	16.1	10.9	19.7	16.4	14.4	18.1
Dominican	44.1	34.1	50.9	43.8	32.0	53.6	32.5	36.5	30.0	23.5	21.6	24.5
Guatemalan	51.2	42.0	55.1	45.7	36.7	48.6	13.4	32.0	5.9	15.0	36.3	9.8
Honduran	49.3	43.3	50.7	48.6	41.4	50.2	14.8	30.8	10.7	6.7	25.1	3.4
Mexican	50.3	44.5	61.1	46.1	39.2	57.3	17.4	19.9	12.3	15.0	17.1	12.6
Puerto Rican	39.1	39.0	43.9	39.3	38.9	50.2	18.8	19.3	40.6	24.4	25.3	0.0
Salvadoran	47.8	40.0	52.4	46.7	34.3	53.5	13.2	18.7	11.7	6.9	10.8	5.6
Spaniard	48.3	43.9	75.3	45.0	41.5	65.1	22.8	28.7	4.2	21.6	27.5	0.0
Other Central American	48.0	39.7	55.9	45.8	42.1	49.3	16.7	13.6	29.6	9.8	2.2	15.7
Other South American	56.2	45.9	61.0	50.3	37.1	56.3	17.9	12.2	17.4	18.8	28.0	16.0
Other Latina/o	44.8	41.6	56.9	35.6	33.6	42.7	18.7	15.0	11.4	27.7	26.7	30.4
Afro-Latina/o	31.3	29.7	38.3	34.3	32.6	41.4	43.2	50.9	15.5	20.4	22.6	13.3
Latina/o	49.0	43.2	58.2	45.1	38.7	54.7	18.0	19.9	15.7	16.5	19.5	13.3
Black	28.3			31.0			36.2			29.6		
White	57.5			51.4			19.6			17.1		

[a] Number of persons divorced in the past year per 1,000 married persons (including married and separated individuals as well as persons who were divorced or widowed in the past year).

Source: Data from 2022 American Community Survey 1-Year Estimates Public-Use File (Ruggles et al. 2024).

surpassing marriage percentages among whites (57.5%). The highest marriage prevalence is among foreign-born Spaniards (females, (75.3%; males, 65.1). In contrast, the lowest rates of marriage occur among native-born male Salvadorans, Other Latinos, and male and female Dominicans that have less than 35 percent of their group married.

We now examine the prevalence of divorce among the different racial and ethnic groups. We compute the divorce rate as the number of persons divorced in the past year per 1,000 married persons. Again, there are certain overall patterns. First, Latina/os, as a whole, have lower divorce rates than whites and blacks. Yet, half of native-born Afro-Latinas are divorced, which is more than twice as high as whites (male and females) and Latina/os (males and females). Second, in general, among Afro-Latina/os and Latina/os, females have a higher divorce rate than males. Third, native-born Latina/os have substantially higher divorce rates than foreign-born individuals, with some exceptions among females (e.g. Cuban, Puerto Rico, Other Central American, Other South American) and males (Cuban, Dominican, Other Central American, and Other Latino).

There is also wide variation in the prevalence of divorce across Latina/o groups. The lowest divorce rates (less than 6%) are found among foreign-born Guatemalan females, Spaniard females, Honduran males, and Salvadoran males. On the other hand, the highest divorce rates among Latina/o subgroups are found among foreign-born Puerto Rican females (40.6%), followed by native-born Dominican females (36.5%) and Guatemalan males (36.3%).

In-Marriages and Out-Marriages

Next, we examine another demographic family characteristic – the degree of racial and ethnic in-marriage (endogamy or marriage inside the race/ethnic group) and out-marriage (exogamy or marriage outside of one's group) (Table 11.2a). Historically, scholars interested in racial/ethnic boundaries have viewed exogamy marriages as the litmus test of the salience between racial/ethnic boundaries (Landale and Oropesa 2007). We illustrate trends in endogamy and exogamy across race/ethnic groups.

Regarding the general racial and ethnic trends, Latina/o immigrants have the highest percentage of in-group marriages (Table 11.2a and 11.2b), possibly reflecting ethnic cultural retention or lack of cultural assimilation. Specifically, over 85 percent of Latina/o immigrants marry within their ethnic group (husbands 89.3%; wives 85.3%). Foreign-born Afro-Latina/os also tend to have higher endogamy rates than their native-born counterparts, but foreign-born Afro-Latinas (65.4) are about three-fourths as likely to marry a Latina/o man compared to foreign-born Latinas as a whole (85.3%). In contrast, in-group marriages among the native-born Latina/os (wives 61.3%; husbands 62.8%) are about one-third lower than among foreign-born Latina/os (wives 85.3%; husbands 89.3%). The endogamy rates among native-born Afro-Latina/os (wives 35.3%; husbands 48.9%) are about half of their foreign-born counterparts (wives 65.4%; husbands 86.5%).

Table 11.2a Race/Ethnic Identity of Latina Wives Married in Last Ten Years by Place of Birth and Husband Race/Ethnic Identity, 2022

Wife Race/ Ethnic Identity	Wife Native-Born/Husband Race/Ethnic Identity					Wife Foreign-Born/Husband Race/Ethnic Identify				
	Ingroup[a]	Other Latino	NH Black[b]	NH White[b]	NH Other[b]	Ingroup[a]	Other Latino	NH Black[b]	NH White[b]	NH Other[b]
Colombian	15.9	26.9	5.6	45.2	6.4	43.0	28.1	1.6	23.6	3.7
Cuban	22.1	20.4	4.3	43.8	9.4	76.5	14.7	0.5	6.8	1.5
Dominican	38.9	27.5	10.9	17.5	5.2	70.8	17.1	4.1	6.8	1.2
Guatemalan	33.3	35.3	4.3	22.3	4.8	65.6	25.6	0.6	7.0	1.2
Honduran	28.6	45.6	2.9	20.9	2.0	55.8	33.3	0.8	9.3	0.8
Mexican	60.2	6.1	3.0	25.7	5.0	81.8	7.0	0.9	8.3	2.0
Puerto Rican	37.8	21.4	8.7	27.1	5.0	64.1	10.7	4.7	16.9	3.6
Salvadoran	24.1	42.6	5.0	22.2	6.1	60.4	29.3	1.9	6.1	2.3
Spaniard	13.1	16.6	3.0	57.2	10.1	30.7	18.0	5.3	34.5	11.5
Afro-Latina	18.4	16.9	40.1	16.6	8.1	44.5	20.9	27.0	7.6	0.0
Latina	61.3	—	4.1	29.1	5.6	85.3	—	1.3	11.2	2.2

[a] Ingroup marriages are those in which the husband and wife are members of the same specific race/ethnic group (e.g. Mexican, Puerto Rican, Cuban, etc.). For Latina/o subgroups, the broader ingroup marriage rate can be computed by summing the "ingroup" and "Other Latina/o" percentages to determine the percentage of Latina/o individuals from each subgroup married to another Latina/o person.

[b] NH refers to Non-Hispanic.

Source: Data from 2022 American Community Survey Public-Use File (Ruggles et al. 2024).

Table 11.2b Race/Ethnic Identity of Latino Husbands Married in Last Ten Years by Place of Birth and Wife Race/Ethnic Identity, 2022

Husband Race/ Ethnic Identity	Husband Native-Born/Wife Race/Ethnic Identity					Husband Foreign-Born/Wife Race/Ethnic Identity				
	Ingroup[a]	Other Latina	NH Black[b]	NH White[b]	NH Other[b]	Ingroup[a]	Other Latina	NH Black[b]	NH White[b]	NH Other[b]
Colombian	22.1	28.5	4.8	36.4	8.2	62.1	22.1	0.2	12.7	2.9
Cuban	20.8	29.7	3.4	37.7	8.4	69.2	20.1	0.8	6.7	3.2
Dominican	37.6	37.8	2.2	18.1	4.3	79.1	12.7	0.7	4.4	3.1
Guatemalan	20.9	49.1	2.0	23.0	5.0	60.5	32.3	0.3	5.6	1.3
Honduran	21.8	34.2	5.0	27.8	11.2	57.3	34.3	1.0	5.1	2.3
Mexican	61.2	6.2	1.0	25.0	6.6	82.9	8.1	0.2	6.8	2.0
Puerto Rican	38.3	22.1	3.6	27.8	8.2	35.0	20.6	5.5	21.3	17.6
Salvadoran	26.6	46.0	0.8	20.3	6.3	61.2	31.1	0.5	4.9	2.3
Spaniard	12.8	10.7	0.6	61.1	14.8	32.3	34.6	2.1	21.7	9.3
Afro-Latino	18.6	30.3	21.5	21.1	8.5	46.1	40.4	5.7	0.6	7.2
Latino	62.8	—	1.7	28.2	7.4	89.3	—	0.4	7.8	2.5

[a] Ingroup marriages are those in which the husband and wife are members of the same specific race/ethnic group (e.g. Mexican, Puerto Rican, Cuban, etc.). For Latina/o subgroups, the broader ingroup marriage rate can be computed by summing the "ingroup" and "Other Latina/o" percentages to determine the percentage of Latina/o individuals from each subgroup married to another Latina/o person.

[b] NH refers to Non-Hispanic.

Source: Data from 2022 American Community Survey Public-Use File (Ruggles et al. 2024).

To examine Latina/o subgroup variations in the percentages of those who marry within their racial/group we begin with wives. Mexican wives have the highest percentage of in-group marriages among native-born and foreign-born wives. Specifically, 60.2 percent of Mexican American and 81.8 percent of Mexican migrant wives married within their ethnic group. Foreign-born wives are more likely to marry within their group than native-born wives. The lowest percentages of in-group marriages; are among native-born Colombian (15.9%) and Spaniards (13.1%).

Wives who marry outside of their group, both native-born and foreign-born, across all the subgroups, tend to marry Other-Latina/os, except for native-born Cuban (43.8%) and Spaniard (57.2%) wives, who marry non-Hispanic-whites. This signals an integration into whiteness experienced by Cuban and Spaniard wives. Interestingly, 40 percent of native-born Afro-Latina wives are married to non-Hispanic-Blacks.

Among Latino husbands, foreign-born Latinos are much more likely to be wedded to a co-ethnic (89.3%) compared to their native-born counterparts (62.8%). Indeed, all subgroups of foreign-born Latino husbands are more likely to have a spouse from their ethnic group, except for Puerto Ricans (35%) and Spaniards (32.3%). Only Mexican Americans (61.2%) among native-born Latino husbands are mostly wedded within their ethnic group. The other remaining subgroups of native-born Latino husbands mostly have spouses of "Other Latina/o" background, except Cubans (37.7%) and Spaniards (61.1%), who tend to marry non-Hispanic whites.

Same-Sex Couple Rates

This section provides ACS (2022) data trends in same-sex married/cohabiting couples. Same-sex couple rates are calculated as the number of same-sex couples per 1,000 total (same-sex and opposite-sex) couples living in the same households for a given sex group. Overall, the rate of same-sex spouse/partners among female-identified Latinas (15.3) is slightly lower than whites (16.1) and about one-third lower than the rate for Blacks (22.9) (Table 11.3). The highest rates of same-sex spouses/partners considering both sex and nativity are foreign-born male-identified Spaniards (56.1) and native-born female-identified Afro-Latinas (43.9). So, in the case of native-born female-identified Afro-Latinas, for every 1,000 couples in which there is a native-born Afro-Latina, 43.9 are same-sex couples. This translates to 4.39% of all couples with native-born female-identified Afro-Latinas.

Nonetheless, across the Latina/o subgroups, there are some interesting trends. There are more same-sex partnerships among the native-born than the foreign-born among female-identified Latinas. Particularly interesting are female-identified native-born Afro-Latinas, who more than tripled the rate of same-sex partnerships of whites (57.5% v. 16.1%). Native-born female-identified Afro-Latina same-sex spouse/partnered households are almost twice as likely (57.5%) as the next highest groups, native-born Dominican (35.4%) and Columbian (32.4%). In contrast, nine foreign-born Latina subgroups, including Afro-Latinas, have same-sex couple rates below 10.

Table 11.3 Same-Sex Couple Rates by Race/Ethnic Group, Sex, and Nativity, 2022

| | Same-Sex Couple Rate[a] | | | | | |
| | Female | | | Male | | |
Race/Ethnic Group	Total	Native-Born	Foreign-Born	Total	Native-Born	Foreign-Born
Colombian	11.7	32.4	6.2	30.5	26.5	31.6
Cuban	18.4	32.2	10.5	28.7	32.8	26.8
Dominican	12.5	35.4	4.9	15.8	28.4	11.2
Guatemalan	10.6	27.1	6.2	12.5	29.3	9.1
Honduran	10.2	30.8	7.1	19.5	42.7	15.4
Mexican	14.4	20.9	7.1	13.7	19.7	8.1
Puerto Rican	24.8	25.0	17.1	19.3	19.6	10.4
Salvadoran	10.8	28.7	6.0	11.1	34.2	5.9
Spaniard	20.7	19.8	24.5	39.7	35.0	56.1
Other Central American	10.8	18.4	7.4	26.0	23.6	27.1
Other South American	12.6	29.1	8.3	21.7	27.7	20.4
Other Latina/o	21.5	23.0	16.5	18.7	19.0	17.4
Afro-Latina/o	43.9	57.5	6.0	24.2	26.6	18.3
Latina/o	15.3	22.9	7.6	16.7	21.4	12.5
Black	22.9			11.2		
White	16.1			13.9		

[a] For each specific sex and nativity group, the number of same-sex couples per 1,000 total (same- and opposite-sex) couples.

Source: Data from 2022 American Community Survey Public-Use File (Ruggles et al. 2024).

Among male-identified Latinos in same-sex partnerships the trends are more complex. Overall, among those who are male-identified, Afro-Latinos (24.2%) and Latinos (16.7) have the highest rates of same-sex spouses/partnerships followed by whites (13.9), and Blacks (11.2). When examining male-identified Latino subgroup variations, the highest percentages of same-sex spouses/partners are found among Spaniards (native-born 35.0, foreign-born 56.1) and Salvadorans (native-born 34.2). Interestingly, the lowest rates of same-sex spouses/partners among the male-identified are found among Salvadoran foreign-born (5.9%), Mexican foreign-born (8.1%) and Guatemalan foreign-born (9.1%).

One caveat is in order for the same-sex couple rates. The analysis is based only on couples who are living together. Same-sex couples who are in relationships but are not living together are not counted and, thus, are not part of the same-sex couple rates used here.

Table 11.4 Percentage of Children Living in Family Households with Female Householders No Husband Present by Race/Ethnic Group and Nativity, 2022

Race/Ethnic Group	Total	Native-Born	Foreign-Born
Colombian	20.2	20.6	18.0
Cuban	23.2	23.3	22.1
Dominican	40.1	40.4	38.1
Guatemalan	24.0	24.2	23.2
Honduran	32.9	32.2	34.5
Mexican	26.3	26.4	24.3
Puerto Rican	38.7	38.8	33.9
Salvadoran	28.5	27.8	33.2
Spaniard	19.9	19.5	9.5
Other Central American	24.6	23.8	32.1
Other South American	19.4	19.3	20.0
Other Latina/o	27.3	27.4	25.3
Afro-Latina/o	54.8	54.9	51.0
Latina/o	27.6	27.6	26.2
Black	53.9		
White	13.8		

Source: Data from 2022 American Community Survey Public-Use File (Ruggles et al. 2024).

Children Living in Family Households with Female Householders

Next, we examine the percentages of children living in family households with female householders and no husband present by race/ethnicity and nativity. Over 50 percent of Afro-Latina/o (54.8%) and Black (53.9%) children live in households headed by females without a husband present (Table 11.4). In contrast, slightly over a quarter of native-born Latina/o children (27.6%) and foreign-born Latina/o children (26.2), and less than one-seventh of white children (13.8%) live in this household type.

When considering Latina/o subgroup differences and place of birth, there are essential variations regarding the proportions of children living in female-headed households with no husbands present. Specifically, 40.4 percent of native-born Dominican children live in female-headed households with no husbands present. On the other hand, the lowest percentages of children living with a single-parent mother are among foreign-born Colombian (18.0%) and Spaniard (9.5%) children.

Households with Extended Families and Living Alone

The last feature of family structure we consider is adults living with extended family members and those living alone (Table 11.5). The results show that foreign-born Latina/os have higher percentages of adults living with extended family members

Table 11.5 Selected Household Arrangement Characteristics by Race/Ethnic Group, Sex, and Nativity, 2022

Race/Ethnic Group	Pct. of Adults Living as Extended Family Member						Pct. of Adults Living Alone					
	Female			Male			Female			Male		
	Total	Native-Born	Foreign-Born	Total	Native-Born	Foreign-Born	Total	Native-Born	Foreign-Born	Total	Native-Born	Foreign-Born
Colombian	10.4	7.4	11.4	7.5	5.5	8.4	9.5	6.3	10.6	10.3	12.6	9.3
Cuban	13.3	7.3	16.6	9.5	6.0	11.5	12.4	10.9	13.2	11.7	13.3	10.8
Dominican	11.7	7.2	13.7	10.3	7.4	11.9	10.4	9.9	10.5	8.7	8.6	8.8
Guatemalan	15.0	10.2	16.9	15.4	12.8	16.3	4.8	5.1	4.7	4.9	4.6	5.0
Honduran	11.9	9.7	12.4	15.5	13.7	15.9	5.1	9.7	3.9	4.4	6.2	3.9
Mexican	10.6	8.5	13.8	10.1	8.8	12.1	6.6	7.7	4.7	7.4	8.5	5.8
Puerto Rican	7.0	6.8	12.9	6.7	6.5	11.2	13.8	14.0	8.4	12.8	13.0	5.4
Salvadoran	15.1	9.6	17.4	13.6	8.7	15.6	4.2	4.3	4.2	4.7	6.0	4.2
Spaniard	4.1	3.9	5.2	4.5	4.3	5.6	15.4	15.2	16.5	13.8	13.9	13.3
Other Central American	11.9	7.3	14.5	12.6	6.7	16.3	10.0	9.9	10.0	10.4	12.9	8.9
Other South American	12.9	6.6	15.0	9.8	6.5	10.9	8.3	8.9	8.1	8.7	10.8	7.9
Other Latina/o	7.5	6.3	12.0	7.5	6.8	10.0	14.0	14.6	11.6	12.5	13.1	10.2
Afro-Latina/o	5.8	4.7	9.6	9.1	8.1	12.8	12.5	13.1	10.2	13.7	14.2	12.2
Latina/o	10.6	7.9	14.2	9.9	8.1	12.4	8.3	9.5	6.6	8.4	9.8	6.6
Black	7.7			8.1			20.5			18.4		
White	3.9			3.3			17.6			14.7		

Source: Data from 2022 American Community Survey Public-Use File (Ruggles et al. 2024).

than native-born individuals. Specifically, among the foreign-born, 14.2 percent of Latinas and 12.4 percent of Latino males are living in households with extended family arrangements (Table 11.5). Yet, native-born Latina/os (females 7.9%; males 8.1%) have comparable levels of living with extended family members to Blacks (females 7.7; males 8.1%). Interestingly, the percentage of white adults living with extended family members (females 3.9; male 3.3%) is about half that of Latina/os and Blacks.

While differences between males and females are not too pronounced, place of birth seems to be an essential characteristic in identifying patterns of Latina/o adults living in households with extended family members. The highest prevalence of this type of living arrangement – about 20 percent – is found among foreign-born Guatemalans and Salvadorans, as well as Cuban females and Other Central American males. This pattern affirms that immigrants are more likely to live in households with extended family given their newcomer status. On the other hand, nearly all native-born Latina/o subgroups (both males and females) have 10 percent or fewer adults living with extended family members. The exceptions include Guatemalan females (10.2%) and males (12.8%) and Honduran males (13.6%).

In contrast to living with family members are those who live alone. Overall, non-Latina/o adults are almost twice as likely as native-born Latina/os to live alone. In particular, the largest percentages of adults living alone are among white (17.6%) and Black (20.5%) females. Their male counterparts have slightly lower percentages with 14.7 percent among whites and 18.4 percent of Blacks. The lowest percentages of adults living alone are found among foreign-born Latina/os. Indeed, foreign-born Latinas and foreign-born Latinos each have about 7 percent of adults living alone. This is aligned with the concept of familism, that Latina/os, in particular immigrants, tend to reside with family members (Hooker et al. 2023).

Potential Future Trends in Latina/o Families

Immigration law not only has material outcomes for families but is instrumental to the family formation of contemporary Latina/o immigrant families (Delgado 2022). Indeed, immigration laws aid in the creation of Latina/o family typologies: citizen/lawful permanent resident families, transnational families, separated families, mixed-status families, and undocumented families (Delgado 2022). Below we discuss some of the family typologies and the detrimental impact of immigration policies and laws on Latina/o families. See Chapter 4 on the "Historical and Contemporary Latina/o Immigration" for a profile on the national-origin of contemporary migrant populations.

Family Separation and Immigration Enforcement

On March 6, 2007, Secretary of Homeland Security John Kelly told CNN that he was considering separating foreign-born children from the adults accompanying them seeking to enter the US, at the border, as a deterrent to illegal immigration (Cordero, Feldman, and Keitner 2019). This initiative was set in motion in April 2018 when the Trump Administration adopted a "zero-tolerance" policy to illegal border crossings, ending the "catch and release" border enforcement practice. Catch and release refers to the immigration enforcement practice of releasing the migrants to the community as they wait for their immigration hearing, as an alternative to detention. Under federal law it is a misdemeanor crime for anyone to enter the US without approval from an immigration agent, resulting in an offense that carries fines and up to six months in prison. Therefore, when "catch and release" ended, individuals crossing the border without inspection were sent to detention centers, with the consequence that more than 2,000 children were separated from parents, and caretakers from their children, the youngest being six months old (https://www.americanbar.org/advocacy/govern mental_legislative_work/priorities_policy/immigration/familyseparation/).

Slack and associates (2015) described a shift from using natural terrain as a deterrent for clandestine border crossings to an enforcement regime that separates families at the border. On February 2, 2021, President Biden formed an Interagency Task Force on the Reunification of Families. The task force identified 3,924 children who were separated between January 20, 2017 and January 20, 2021. As of February 1, 2023, 2,926 separated children have been reunified, either before the establishment of the Task Force or through the leadership of the Task Force. Families continued to come forward and identify themselves as separated under the previous administration's zero-tolerance policy. Records that would have allowed for the children to be reunited with their parents and caretakers were not implemented. The forced separation of families at the US–Mexico border has left families with significant levels of stress and trauma (Cervantes, Mejía, and Guerrero Mena 2010; Hampton et al. 2021) and lasting resentment of children toward their parents (Dreby 2015). On December 11, 2023, a federal judge approved a settlement prohibiting the separation of families at the border (Garsd 2023).

Deportations

In contrast to political rhetoric about the importance of family unity, federal administrative policies have separated families through other mechanisms such as deportations. Indeed, the Illegal Immigration Reform and Immigrant Responsibility Act (IIRIRA) of 1996 broadened the types of crimes in the US (including misdemeanors) for which a legal resident can be detained and deported.

Deportations not only impact the individual migrant but the entire family (Mathema 2017). Deportations produce a range of "unintended consequences" including "fracturing families and placing women in many harmful situations, specifically leaving mothers in emotional pain and severe danger of lasting physical and mental harm" (Gomes and Ross-Sheriff 2011, p. 122). In cases where one or both parents are deported, the children remain in the US in the care of other family members or friends. Attachment bonds are uniquely impacted by parent–child separation due to deportation as it causes immediate and long-term effects on children and parent(s) (Flores 2011; Dreby 2015). Unmitigated by sufficient coping skills, the intense stress caused by deportation leaves children at risk of feeling isolated, abandoned, hopeless, angry, and scared (Flores 2011). This would be an example of what Menjívar and Abrego (Menjívar and Abrego 2012; Abrego and Menjívar 2011), refer to as *legal violence* where laws and their implementation give rise to practices that result in physical, economic, psychological, and emotional harm. For instance, restrictive immigration policies, i.e. Illegal Immigration Reform and Immigrant Responsibility Act (1996), exposed immigrant mothers and entire families to legal violence by making it difficult for mothers to migrate together with their children, and post-migration keeping them from accessing state services and in fear of deportation and family separation (Abrego and Menjívar 2011). When one or more of the parents are undocumented, children also suffer the emotional burden of worrying about their parents' deportation (Dreby 2012; Enriquez 2015; Zayas et al. 2015). Even in everyday experiences, young children suffer a "de facto undocumented status" of their parents, who are trying to avoid deportation and thus restricting driving, traveling, and employment (Enriquez 2015). The direct and chronic socio-emotional exposure to immigration enforcement carries on into adulthood, creating negative consequences, particularly in the form of family adversity (Dreby, Silveira, and Lee 2022). Among the consequences are approximately 544,000 children of deported parents living with grandparents or "grandfamilies" (Delgado 2022).

Mixed-Status Families and Households

Another issue impacting Latina/o families is that of households with members of mixed citizenship statuses. As such, some family members may be US citizens, others could be documented (various types of visas), and still others may be unauthorized. This situation translates to inequality among household members. To date, most of the research on mixed-status households concerns the utilization of social services. Latina/o undocumented parent(s) may be apprehensive to seek services for their US-born children, given fears of deportation or detention. Yet, Latina/o families headed by undocumented parents access services for their children at equivalent rates to those of documented parents (Xu and Brabeck 2012). Fears of deportation are counteracted by undocumented parents' utilization of their social networks to help them navigate the system.

On the other hand, in cases of Latina/o children who are in the welfare system and in need of alternative housing, mixed-status households present a challenge. While the number of Latina/o children in need of alternative family placements has doubled in the last fifteen years, kinship placements are a challenge in mixed-status households (Ayón et al. 2013). Before being placed in a home, all the residents of the household must pass background checks, which create fears of deportation for undocumented members.

Moving beyond the impact of being in mixed-status families and having access to social benefits, Rodriguez (2019) examined how adult-age citizen children with undocumented parents manage their parents' illegality. She found that these young adults are shielded from parental deportation concerns through having less sustained contact with parents, and perceptions that their parents are cautious. Yet, financially, the adult-citizen children's access to the formal labor market gives them more breadwinning responsibilities. And so, young adult citizens with undocumented parents face challenges that differ from those of their documented peers and from those for children with lawfully present parents. The economic instability of immigrant families makes the labor of poor and working-class immigrant Latina/o youth vital for their personal and families' economic stability and future mobility (Canizales and Hondagneu-Sotelo 2022).

Latina/o Same-Sex Couples

Given that familismo/familism is a strong characteristic associated with Latina/o families, are same-sex Latina/o families still subjected to marginalization? While Latinx (gender neutral/nonbinary) same-sex couples do experience close ties to family members, homosexuality is not as frequently discussed, and they can still potentially face ostracism (Loughrin 2015). Latina/o/x same-sex couples are more vulnerable to the current political climate targeting same-sex persons. Anti-gay family policies have a stronger adversarial impact on Latina/o/x and Black same-sex couples than their white counterparts, given that they are more likely to be raising children, earn less, and are less likely to own their home (Cahill 2009).

Latinx LGBT adults also experience more economic insecurity, depression, report more disabilities and chronic health conditions. For instance, more Latina/o/x LGBT individuals experience economic insecurity, with nearly 40 percent living in a household with income below $24,000 a year and are more likely to experience food insecurity and unemployment than Latina/o/x non-LGBT persons (Wilson et al. 2021). In regard to mental health, Latina/o/x LGBT adults are twice as likely to be diagnosed with depression compared to Latina/o/x non-LGBT persons (Latina/o/x LGBT 30% v. non-LGBT 16%) (Wilson et al. 2021). Latina/o/x LGBT people are also more likely to report disabilities and other chronic health conditions than Latina/o/x non-LGBT, however, they are more likely to have health cover and to have Medicaid (Wilson 2021).

Summary

This chapter offers an examination of the trends of Latina/o family structure across various dimensions such as race, ethnicity, nativity and sexual orientation, along with theoretical frameworks that explain these patterns. We underscore how social, economic, and political forces are shaping the construction of Latina/o families (Baca Zinn and Pok 2001). Historically, depictions of Chicana/o (Mexican American) families emphasized concepts such as machismo, representing male dominance, and marianismo, portraying females as submissive and self-sacrificing mothers, while failing to provide empirical evidence of the heterogeneity of Latina/o families and the structural conditions that surround them (Romero et al. 1997; Segura and Pierce 1988; Ybarra 1983). Moreover, early representations of Latina/o culture, as seen in Oscar Lewis's works in *Five Families: Mexican Case Studies in the Culture of Poverty* (1959) and *La Vida: A Puerto Rican Family in the Culture of Poverty – San Jose and New York* (1965), inadvertently perpetuated stereotypes of Mexican-origin and Puerto Rican families as culturally deficient and socially problematic for American society (Zambrana 2011). This early scholarship on Latina/o families often portrayed them as culturally flawed and employed victim-blaming perspectives to justify their position at the bottom of the socioeconomic hierarchy.

Another significant critique of early scholarship on Latina/o families was its tendency to group Latina/o subgroups together, therefore obscuring important differences among them (Baca Zinn and Pok 2001; Romero et al. 1997). In this chapter, our focus is to present a demographic profile highlighting the diversity in family formation among Latina/o subgroups. While the demographic profile we offer remains descriptive, it is crucial to acknowledge the structural forces that shape Latina/o families, i.e. immigration policies and socioeconomic status (Baca Zinn 1994), as well as institutional racism and cultural survival strategies (Mirandé 1978). Drawing on data from the American Community Survey (2022), we outline the distinctions between Latina/os and Afro-Latina/os, whites, and Blacks, as well as differences between Latina/o subgroups, in terms of family structural patterns. A general pattern that we found is that Cubans, Colombians, South Americans, and Spaniards often exhibit family household patterns that resemble those in the white population. In contrast, the family structures of Afro-Latina/o more closely parallel those of Blacks rather than the broader Latina/o population.

What lies ahead for theorizing on Latina/o family formation and behaviors? Theoretical approaches must continue to evolve beyond solely individualistic and cultural-deficit perspectives. Relying solely on individual approaches often results in solutions that are simply individualistic, neglecting the broader structural context that reproduces social and economic inequalities among Latina/o families. Some of the structural dynamics influencing Latina/o families and their well-being, as discussed here, are closely linked with immigration and border enforcement policies and socioeconomic status. These factors currently affect the status of Latina/o families and are likely, without policy changes, to continue to impact them.

Discussion Questions

1. Is the family going to continue being among the most defining features of Latina/os given all the structural barriers (i.e immigration and border enforcement) aimed to separate families?

2. How do historical cultural depictions of Latina/o families, such as machismo and marianismo, contribute to cultural-deficit perspectives that attribute blame to Latina/os for the inequalities they face in US society?

3. Which characteristics of Latina/o families resemble those observed in whites? Which characteristics are the most distinct from those found in whites?

4. How do family patterns among Afro-Latina/os compare to those among Latina/os ? In what ways are they like the family trends observed among Blacks?

5. How will education and intermarriage impact current family structures? Why do stereotypes continue to persist? Are these trends a result of cultural factors, socioeconomic class distinctions, or both?

6. Intersectionality refers to the overlapping population characteristics (such as nativity, national-origin, sex, and sexuality) that deeply influences individuals' life opportunities and social standing in society. What indications of intersectionality do you observe within Latina/o families?

7. What are some policies contributing to the social construction of Latina/o families? How do these policies impact the well-being of these families?

12 Religion

Marcos Witt, a white man, is a rockstar in the world of the recruitment of Latina/os to Evangelical Protestantism, collaborating with megachurch pastor Joel Osteen, who runs Lakewood Church in the Houston area. He was raised in Durango, Mexico, by Anglo American Pentecostal parents and in 2002 began leading Spanish-language services at Osteen's megachurch. In Witt's ten years with Lakewood Church, the number of persons attending the church's Spanish-language soared, drawing congregations of 6,000 every Sunday (Valdez 2023).

With major demographic shifts associated with the aging of the white population, along with its congregants across the spectrum of religious denominations, there is a major void in the pews of these religions as the white population ages and dies off. The youthful and growing Latina/o population represents an ideal recruitment ground, drawing large numbers from Catholicism. We have seen over the last few decades, a considerable segment of Latina/os shifting their religious affiliation to Evangelical Protestantism and Pentecostal denominations. We will see below how theoretical perspectives, especially the religious marketplace, help us understand the religious life of Latina/os and the ongoing religious shifts or conversions that are underway. In addition, we draw on sociological literature, especially the work of López-Sanders (2012) to illustrate the ways in which white churches attempt to integrate Latina/os, especially those who are immigrants.

Despite the significant inroads of the Evangelical Protestant and Pentecostal religions into the long-dominant Catholic religion of Latina/os, Catholicism continues to be the most popular religious denomination among Latina/os. Today, more than two of every five Latina/os have an affiliation with the Catholic denomination (Krogstad et al. 2023). Catholicism has been part of the lives of Latina/os in the US over numerous generations and the Catholic roots of Latina/os extend deeply to their Latin American and Caribbean provenance and the colonial period in which the indigenous people and their *mestizo* offspring were transformed in so many ways including their religion (Badillo 2006; Matovina 2012; Palmer-Boyes 2010; Treviño 2006). As Mexicans and other Latin Americans have made their way to the US, they have brought with them their religion, which continues to be most commonly Catholic, although this has been shifting significantly. Yet, as we will see below, despite a certain segment of Latina/os who are strong and dedicated Catholics who attend mass regularly, significant portions of Latina/os who are Catholic differ in numerous respects from mainstream Catholics and have weaker or cultural ties to Catholicism, grounds for which undoubtedly contribute to the movement of Latina/os away from this religion and to Evangelical Protestant and Pentecostal denominations and even into the path of secularization.

This chapter provides an overview of the religious life of Latina/os. We begin with an examination of the deep historical roots of Catholicism, extending back to the colonial period and the unique form of the religion that emerged in Mexico involving the blending of traditional Catholic and indigenous influences. In addition, we will illustrate the uniqueness of Latina/o Catholics from mainstream Catholics and cultural connections that many have with the Catholic Church. Subsequently, we highlight the theoretical perspectives that are useful in understanding the role that religion plays in the lives of Latina/os. Moreover, we highlight data that illustrate the religious shifts taking place among Latina/os. Finally, we draw attention to major issues that are likely to have an impact on the religious life of Latina/os in the near future.

Historical Ties of Latina/os to Catholicism and Our Lady of Guadalupe

The roots of the Latina/o experience in the Americas extend back to the conquest of the indigenous population at the hands of Spanish colonizers. While indigenous people had been in the Americas for centuries, the Italian navigator, Christopher Columbus, exploring on behalf of the Spanish crown, made four round-trip voyages to the Americas between 1492 and 1503. The Catholic religion of Latina/os represents yet another strong legacy stemming from the Spanish conquest. The Spanish colonizers, armed with their superior weaponry including cannons, demolished indigenous religions. For example, Hernan Cortez reached the Aztec empire located in Tenochtitlan, situated in present-day Mexico City, in 1519 and in a matter of a couple of years had conquered the Aztec empire (León-Portilla 1962). The conquest included the razing of Aztec temples and pyramids. As these were leveled and buried, they were replaced by crosses and eventually Catholic churches. The Spanish conquerors saw part of their mission, aside from securing the riches of the conquered, being the saving of the souls of the indigenous which they saw as heathen savages (Rodriguez 1994). Indeed, the Spanish questioned whether the indigenous people even had a soul, thus doubting that they were human (Elizondo 1980; Rodriguez 1994). Nonetheless, the indigenous population did not easily accept Catholicism and the demolition of their religions and religious beliefs. Rodriguez (1994) outlines the bitterness that the Aztec people felt after the fall of the Aztec empire:

> The people . . . could not accept a religion that asked them to negate their entire metaphysics, the way they understood reality. They also could not comprehend the missionaries, who were admired and respected because of the simplicity of their lives, came from the same religion and spiritual origin as the abusive and brutal conquistadors. The Aztec insurgents of the day were fighting not merely against Spain but against Catholicism. It was evident to them that the two things were intimately connected. (p. 13)

Thus, Catholicism in Mexico, as is the case in other parts of Latin America, took on a different form. In particular, Catholicism in the Americas can best be characterized as religious syncretism which involves a blending of traditional Catholicism and indigenous influences.

The root of this melding of the two forms of religion in Mexico extends back to the apparition of the Virgin of Guadalupe to Juan Diego, an indigenous man who had recently converted to Catholicism, shortly after the fall of the Aztec empire. On December 9, 1531, Juan Diego encountered her on the hill of Tepeyac, located northwest of present-day Mexico City. Garibay (1967) describes the meeting:

> She [the Virgin] instructed him [Juan Diego] to have the Bishop Zumárraga build a church on the site. Three days later in a second appearance she told Juan Diego to pick flowers and take them to the bishop. When he presented them as instructed, roses fell out of his mantle and beneath them was the painted image of the Lady. (p. 821; see also Rodriguez 1994, p. 17)

The apparition of Our Lady of Guadalupe and the series of subsequent events is eloquently described by Elizondo (1980, pp. 75–79). Rodriguez (1994) stresses the significance of the apparition of the Virgin with her indigenous features to Juan Diego, an indigenous man, along two lines: "(1) it was the foundation of Mexican Christianity and (2) it provided a *connection* between the indigenous and Spanish cultures" (p. 45). Thus, the apparition marked the conversion of the indigenous people and the base of Mexican Christianity (Rodriguez 1994). Indeed, the apparition represented a watershed in the conversion of the indigenous, as Rodriguez (1994) points out. Madsen (1967) notes that this form of religion is aptly called "Guadalupinist Catholicism" (p. 378; see also Rodriguez 1994, p. 45). The impact of the apparition on the conversion of indigenous people is reflected in that nine million Aztec individuals were baptized into Christianity only six years following the apparition (Elizondo 1980; Madsen 1967; Rodriguez 1994).

The apparition also provides a link between indigenous and Spanish cultures; this link stems from the actual name of the Virgin. The apparition involved an episode in which the Virgin paid a visit to Juan Diego's uncle, who was seriously ill. The Spaniards asked the uncle if the Virgin told him her name. He responded by saying that she said her name was "Tlecuauhtlacupeuh," which in Nahuatl means "*La que viene volando de la luz como el águila de fuego*" ("she who comes flying from the region of light like an eagle of fire") (Echeagaray 1981, p. 21; Rodriguez 1994, p. 46). Rodriguez (1994) notes that "The region of light was the dwelling place of the Aztec gods, and the eagle was a sign from the gods" (p. 46). The Spaniards believed that they heard the name "Guadalupe," which they immediately associated with the Guadalupe of Estremadura in Spain (Rodriguez 1994). A significant share of Spanish conquerors originated from the Spanish province of Estremadura and devotion to Our Lady of Guadalupe de Estremadura was very high at the time that the Spanish started making their way to the Americas (Rodriguez 1994). Thus, the name of Guadalupe was quickly adopted by the Spanish. It has been observed that because the Nahuatl language does not contain the letters "d" and "g," the

Virgin's name could not have possibly been Guadalupe (Escalada 1965; Rodriguez 1994).

Nonetheless, the indigenous – through the name of Tlecuauhtlacupeuh – and the Spanish – through the name Guadalupe – were able to view the apparition in personal terms and as something that could be understood and embraced from their own perspectives (Rodriguez 1994). The linkage of the apparition to the culture of each group reflected the religious syncretism that was the outcome. This syncretism, involving the merging of mainstream Catholicism and indigenous religious beliefs and practices, was repeated throughout Latin America to incorporate Inca and Mayan patterns (Palmer-Boyes 2010; Stanzione 2003). One prominent event concerns the appearance of the Virgin de Caridad del Cobre (the word "cobre" refers to the local copper mines) in 1612 to three boys (two indigenous brothers named Rodrigo and Juan de Hoyos and an enslaved African boy named Juan Moreno), who had been sent to collect salt in the Bay of Nipe in Cuba's northern coast (Deleon 2023; see also Ferrer 1999, 2021). While they sought out on their canoe to gather salt in the bay, the trio spotted a mysterious object that turned out to be "an image of the Virgin Mother, cradling a child with one arm and clutching a gold cross in her other hand" (Deleon 2023, p. 3). Upon rescuing the object from the water, they "saw a wooden plaque fastened underneath her that said 'I am the Virgin of Charity' . . . even though La Virgin had been submerged in sea water, her cloth robes were completely dry" (Deleon 2023, p. 3). The Virgin de Caridad del Cobre would become a protectress for the people of Cuba, no matter their race or where they lived, including serving as a protective symbol of exiled Catholic Cubans in Miami in 1961 (Deleon 2023).

In sum, one of the most interesting features of the establishment of Catholicism and efforts to convert indigenous people in Mexico and beyond into the rest of the Americas, is the uniqueness of Catholicism and how indigenous people played a role in the development of that religion to fit their own lives and needs.

The Uniqueness of Latina/o Catholics and Cultural Ties to Catholicism in the US

The uniqueness of Catholicism in Mexico was brought to the US by immigrants who settled in this country. In the US, Latina/os continue to be distinct from mainstream Catholics in numerous manners (Palmer-Boyes 2010; Pew Hispanic Center 2007). For example, Palmer-Boyes (2010) observes that Latina/os are distinct from other Catholics in two ways: (1) based on cultural norms and (2) based on the immigrant status of congregants. In addition, Latina/o Catholics deviate from the more traditional and official practices that epitomize being Catholic – "Mass attendance, communion, and involvement in parish life" (Palmer-Boyes 2010). Latina/os are more likely to engage in broader practices and activities beyond the confines of the more traditional and official practices. As such, many Latina/os are seen not as "practicing Catholics" but as "cultural Catholics" who do not have a strong connection with the church nor attend mass regularly but who identify with common practices "more loosely related to institutional involvement, characterized instead by cultural rituals and devotions rooted in indigenous heritage and often fused with civic and social celebrations" (Palmer-Boyes 2010, p. 305). Such celebrations include baptisms, weddings, funerals, *las Posadas* (annual nine-day celebration reenacting Joseph and Mary's trek from Nazareth to Bethlehem), and the Feast of the Virgin of Guadalupe (Palmer-Boyes 2010). Moreover, Latina/o Catholics are significantly more likely than other Catholics to incorporate charismatic activities into their worship. Charismatic conventions include speaking in tongues, raising of hands, clapping, shouting, and jumping (Palmer-Boyes 2010). Latina/os are five times more likely than non-Latina/o Catholics to worship in a charismatic fashion (Pew Hispanic Center 2007). Furthermore, Latina/o parishes are more likely than non-Latina/o parishes to have social services and programs that cater to the needs of immigrants, providing such services as English-language courses, citizenship-training courses, job-training, and assistance with immigration-related matters (Martini 2012; Matovina 2012; Odem 2004; Palmer-Boyes 2010; Stevens-Arroyo 2010; Sullivan 2000). Finally, Latina/o Catholics are more likely than other Catholics to pray to saints and to Our Lady of Guadalupe rather than directly to God (Krause and Bastida 2011). It is felt that because of the purity of the saints and the belief that they inhabit heaven with God, they are in a much better position to intercede on their behalf than are people themselves (Krause and Bastida 2011; Oktavec 1995). Given the unique ways in which a certain segment of Latina/o Catholics practice their religion and the ways that they connect to God through charismatic means and speaking in tongues, it is not too surprising that some make the conversion to Evangelical Protestant and Pentecostal religions and, for that matter, that cultural Catholics who have weak ties to the Catholic Church can find a religious home in another denomination or forego religion completely (see below).

Indeed, over the last several decades, we have seen growing numbers of Catholics convert to Protestant and Evangelical religions (Ellison et al. 2005; Hunt 1999; Matovina 2012). Latina/os who leave the Catholic faith in favor of a different religion report that their reason for doing so was that they were searching for a smaller and more intimate group as well as more active engagement (Matovina 2012). Furthermore, these individuals tend to be drawn to a more "direct and personal experience of God" in the Protestant religion (Matovina 2012, p. 106). Nonetheless, as suggested by the religious marketplace perspective (see below), some Latina/os maintain attachments with multiple religions. Despite the growing numbers of Latina/os breaking away from the Catholic faith, however, Putnam and Campbell (2010) note that the defection of Latina/os from Catholicism is not an anomaly – rather, their defection rate is lower than that of whites. The proselytizing and recruitment of Latina/os on the part of non-Catholic denominations promises to be more intense as these face declines in their memberships due to an aging white population. Furthermore, due to the movement of Latina/os to new-destination areas (see Chapter 5), the influence of Latina/os on American religion extends to locations beyond the regions where Latina/os have historically been concentrated (López-Sanders 2012; Matovina 2012).

Having obtained a historical context for understanding the deep historical roots of Latina/os to Catholicism and to Our Lady of Guadalupe along with the uniqueness of Latina/os among US Catholics, we now turn to an overview of theoretical perspectives that are useful in understanding the contemporary religious life of Latina/os.

Theoretical Perspectives

Interest in the sociology of religion has grown significantly over the last several decades. Indeed, Sherkat and Ellison (1999) in their review of the sociology of religion literature observe that "The wealth of empirical findings about religious beliefs, commitments, and institutions and their consequences left the field open for new theoretical insights, and the trickle of theoretical developments that began in the late 1970s turned into a flood by the early 1990s" (p. 378). Interest in religious matters related to Latina/os has also increased tremendously.

Religion as Social Capital

Propelled by Robert Putnam's (2000) book titled *Bowling Alone: The Collapse and Revival of American Community*, social scientists have called significant attention to the concept of social capital over the last couple of decades. Putnam defines social capital as "connections among individuals – social networks and the norms of reciprocity and trustworthiness that arise from them" (p. 19; see also Wood and Bunn 2012). Religious associations represent the "producers and facilitators of social capital" (Hye-cheon et al. 2012, p. 332). Religion is at the center of many organizational and civic activities in the US. Putnam (2000) highlights the role of religion in the establishment of social capital. Accordingly, Putnam (2000) points out that "Faith communities in which people worship together are arguably the single most important repository of social capital in America" (p. 66). Bruhn (2011) adds that:

> Religion is an important source of social capital. People of like-minded faith come together to form social networks that create interest in each other's welfare and provide an ongoing resource for social support and trusting relationships. (p. 206).

It follows that people with a religious orientation draw a variety of benefits from their social connections with people with whom they join to participate in religious services and with whom they share deep religious convictions and fellowship. In particular, such people gain a "sense of community and group solidarity" from their religious social attachments (Bruhn 2011, p. 185).

Putnam (2000) distinguishes between two types of social capital based on whether people are linked within groups or across groups. Bonding social capital involves the strengthening of social ties among people who belong to the same group or organization, such as members of a given church. In such instances, people in the social network have very close and interpersonal relations and exhibit a great amount of care for the well-being of each other. On the other hand, bridging social capital involves the linkage of people to individuals from other groups or organizations, such as across denominational groups, racial and ethnic organizations, and non-religious organizations. Typically, religious organizations tend to facilitate bonding social capital to the neglect of bridging capital (Williams and Loret de Mola 2007).

Social capital derived from religious activities is associated with a variety of favorable outcomes. We highlight here the association between social capital and the deterrence of alcohol, drugs, and crime among teenagers and health outcomes.

Religion has long been observed to be a deterrent to crime and deviance. Sherkat and Ellison (1999) outline the reasons for the deterrence impact of religion on crime and deviance:

> (a) the internalization of religious norms and moral messages; (b) the fear of divine punishment (the so-called "hellfire" effect); (c) the threat of social sanctions for core-ligionists; (d) the desire for approval from reference groups within religious communities; and (e) the lack of exposure to (or time for) deviant pursuits due to involvement in religious activities and networks, among other possible effects. (pp. 375–376)

The context in which people participate in religious activities replete with shared norms and expectations, social sanctions for being out of line, the pursuit of social approval from one's network, and an immersion in church-related activities that reinforces in-group associations with like-minded individuals, serve to shelter individuals from crime and deviance.

Bartkowski and Xu (2007) use a social capital of religiosity framework to understand drug use among teenagers. Drawing on the work of Putnam (2000) and others (Baron et al. 2000), Bartkowski and Xu (2007) conceptualize social capital as comprised of three key components: norms, networks, and trust. In particular, Bartkowski and Xu (2007) characterize social capital as consisting of "exposure to and internalization of religious norms (gauged respectively by denominational affiliation and religious salience)"; "integration within religious networks (measured through worship service attendance as well as participation in faith-based youth groups and Scouts)"; and "expressions of religious trust (measured through trust in God)" (pp. S182–S183). In their study based on the 1996 wave of Monitoring the Future Study, a nationally representative study of high-school seniors, Bartkowski and Xu (2000) found that teenagers who were more integrated into their religious networks – measured by the frequency of church attendance – had lower levels of drug use compared to their peers who were less integrated into their religious networks. Thus, teenagers who regularly attend church services tend to associate with similar peers who do also, and they tend to be connected to adult church members who serve as role models related to pro-social behavior and values. As such, youngsters connected to church life are more likely than their peers without such ties to fall for peer pressure associated with drug use. As Bartkowski and Xu (2007) suggest the context involving regular church attendance "collectively [steer] youth toward positive development outcomes" (p. S192). Other indicators of social capital (denominational affiliation, religious salience, religious trust, and faith-based civic participation), however, were not significantly associated with teenage drug use.

While the Bartkowski and Xu (2007) study was based on a nationally representative sample of high-school seniors, it did not focus on the racial/ethnic group of respondents, aside from a variable that takes into account whether a person is Black or not. Unfortunately, this is a common trend as some researchers (Hodge et al. 2011) have noted the absence of much research examining the association between religion and substance abuse and related phenomena among Latina/o youth. Hodge et al. (2011) use the Bartkowski and Xu (2007) social capital of religiosity to examine substance use among Mexican-origin teenagers. Hodge et al. (2011) used data from a drug prevention study based on students in fifth grade in 39 elementary and middle schools located low-income and inner-city areas and collected data from students additionally at four points in time, resulting in five waves of data for students who were initially surveyed when they were in fifth grade. As was the case in the Bartkowski and Xu (2007) study, Hodge et al. (2011) also found that religious attendance – a measure of integration into religious networks – was the most important indicator of social capital deterring Mexican-origin students from substance use. Specifically, students who attended church more regularly at time 1 tended to have lower substance use at time 2 (30 days after the church attendance was measured as well as lifetime substance use at any time). Hodge et al. (2011) suggest that "Early integration into Latina/o religious networks may protect youths from later substance use as they make the journey through adolescence and acculturation" (p. 145). Thus, there is evidence that integration and participation in religious activities provide important social bonds that allow youngsters to refrain from substance use.

Similarly, research has observed the value of religion – particularly with respect to attendance in religious services – in health outcomes (Hye-cheon et al. 2012). Drawing on theoretical insights extending back to Durkheim on the integrative and regulatory functions of religion, Sherkat and Ellison (1999) argue that people who are integrated into religious groups gain a sense of community from which they benefit emotionally and socially from feeling "loved, valued, and cared for." Furthermore, individuals who are integrated into religious communities are subject to regulatory prohibitions against the use and abuse of tobacco, drugs, and alcohol, as well as against risky and deviant behaviors, with the result being more favorable health outcomes (Bruhn 2011; Sherkat and Ellison 1999). Older Latina/os who never attend religious services, those who are not affiliated with a religious denomination, and those who do not consider religion as important have higher rates of depression compared to their respective counterparts (Lerman et al. 2018). Religiosity, in the form of faith and spirituality, during the first six months of the COVID-19 pandemic was associated with lower levels of substance abuse among Latina/os and Blacks in New York City (Svob et al. 2023). In sum, Sherkat and Ellison (1999) argue that participation in religious activities is likely to govern personal behavior which in turn results in people having lower prospects of disease. In such a case, then, social capital serves as a mediator between religious attendance and health outcomes (Hye-cheon et al. 2012).

Hye-cheon et al.'s (2012) research, utilizing data from the 2006 Social Capital Community Benchmark Survey, supports the mediating role of social capital in the association between religiosity and health outcomes. In particular, Hye-cheon et al.

(2012) observe that people who are more involved in religious activities tend to have greater involvement in formal groups associated with giving and volunteering – a reflection of contribution to the public good (see Leonard et al. 2010) which results in more positive self-reported health. Furthermore, Strawbridge et al. (1997) found that adults in Alameda County in California, who had greater participation in their church or synagogue tended to have lower death rates compared to those with more limited religious participation. Bruhn (2011), reflecting on the findings of the Strawbridge et al. (1997) study, points out that people with more favorable risks of death tended to have better health practices, higher levels of social connections, and more stable marriages.

While these findings are based on general populations and do not focus exclusively on Latina/os, there are some studies that demonstrate the value of religiosity on the health conditions of Latina/os. For example, Berges et al. (2010), using data from the Hispanic Established Population for the Epidemiological Study of the Elderly (H-EPESE), discovered that Mexican American elderly who had a high frequency of religious attendance (nearly once a week or more than once a week) were significantly less likely to develop disabilities associated with activities of daily living (ADL) compared to their counterparts who did not have high rates of religious attendance. This finding held even after controlling for changes in health conditions and mobility over time.

Yet, Latina/os tend to deviate somewhat from other groups with respect to the recipient of prayers. Thus, rather than praying directly to God, Catholic Latina/os tend to be more likely than other groups to pray to saints and the Virgin of Guadalupe, who serve as intermediaries between the petitioner and God (see above) (Krause and Bastida 2011; Oktavec 1995; Rodriguez 1994). Based on a study of older Mexican American Catholics, Krause and Bastida (2011) found that people who attended church more frequently tended to be more likely to believe in the effectiveness of prayers to saints and the Virgin of Guadalupe. Saints play a central role for both immigrant and native-born Latina/os. In the case of Latina/o migrant journeys, Toribio Romo, known as the "holy smuggler," is a saint known to help migrants in the desert find their way to the US (Romo 2010). Jesús Malverde, a Robin-Hood-like figure, who is the patron saint of drug traffickers, has been appropriated by Mexican immigrants who call on him for assistance in making the trek to the US (Murphy 2008). Among older Mexican Americans, those who pray to religious entities are more likely to believe that God is helping them control important aspects of their lives (Krause and Bastida 2011). Finally, older Mexican Americans who believe that God is assisting them in this way are more likely to be optimistic, which, in turn, is associated with more favorable health. These studies provide some evidence of the importance of religion in the lives of Latina/os.

Immigration Integration

Extending back to the earliest immigrants to the US, religion has played an important role in providing adherents with an identity, support for co-religionists, and guidance in integrating into the host society. An interest in the religiosity of post-1965 immigrants has arisen since the early 1990s (Cadge and Ecklund 2007). Religious organizations have historically been helpful in the sustenance and integration of new immigrants into their new places where they settle. We highlight four ways in which churches assist immigrants in the incorporation process. In particular, we provide an overview below on the dimensions related to identity maintenance, boundary expansion, civic engagement, and political participation.

Upon arrival to the US, immigrants are drawn to others like themselves. For example, at varying points in time, Irish, Italian, and Mexican immigrants have settled in ethnic enclaves, geographic settings where people from their countries were concentrated. In ethnic enclaves, immigrants find others who are similar to them with respect to language, origin, culture, and socioeconomic status. Immigrants find people who can provide a variety of support adjusting to life in their new country, assistance in securing employment, and a setting where they can maintain their sense of ethnic community (Bruhn 2011; López-Sanders 2012; Warner and Wittner 1998). Religious organizations provide newcomers with a place where they can sustain their ethnic identity and culture in their new country (Cadge and Ecklund 2007).

López-Sanders (2012) conducted an ethnographic study of three churches located in the Greenville-Spartanburg-Anderson (GSA) region of South Carolina, to understand how they incorporated Colombian, Mexican, and Guatemalan immigrants. López-Sanders (2012) describes the central role that religion plays in the lives of Blacks, whites, and Latina/o newcomers in the region. The three churches differ not only in their structure and racial/ethnic composition of church members, but also in the activities that they pursue to assist Latina/os incorporating into the GSA region. Of the three churches in López-Sanders' (2012) study, the Catholic Church of the Resurrection best illustrates the incorporation dimension associated with identity maintenance. The congregants of Resurrection are exclusively Guatemalan and the leadership consists of a white bilingual priest, who presides over the sacrament, along with a dozen Guatemalan lay leaders, who are involved in the administrative affairs of the church. The roots of Resurrection stem to Los Angeles, the original settlement of this group of Guatemalan immigrants. The Guatemalan congregants are held together by language, the small size of the church membership, and the ethnic homogeneity of the worshippers (López-Sanders 2012). The Guatemalan immigrants are very much aware and conscious of their language and ethnic differences with other Latina/os in the GSA region. In particular, they are not comfortable speaking Spanish and their Mayan language and with their physical features along with their low levels of education, all set them apart from other Latina/os in the area. López-Sanders (2012) observes that the homogeneity of the group in the church allows Guatemalans to "reproduce the social cohesion characteristics of Mayan communities in their country of origin" (p. 142). Moreover, the Guatemalan congregants maintain strong ties to the communities from where they originate in Guatemala, as is evident in the number of remittances and community projects that they support in the sending community (e.g. renovation projects, funding the feasts of the patron saints of their home villages) (López-Sanders 2012). Thus, the Catholic Church of the Resurrection provides a haven for Guatemalan immigrants, where they maintain their ethnicity, speak their Mayan language, and sustain ties to their home communities, which help bridge their transnational existence.

A second element associated with the incorporation of immigrants concerns boundary expansion. Racial and ethnic groups exhibit social boundaries where they operate and interact with each other. Frederick Barth (1969) brought to the forefront the way in which racial and ethnic groups construct and negotiate boundaries (see Alba and Nee 2003; Frank et al. 2010).

In contrast to the experience of Guatemalans in the Catholic Church of the Resurrection, López-Sanders (2012) observes that whites and Mexicans made changes in their boundaries that brought Mexicans into Harvest Church, a white non-denominational Protestant church. Harvest Church is located in a suburban area close to trailer parks and other low-income housing where Latina/os live (López-Sanders 2012). The church membership ventured to attract Latina/o newcomers and to assist them to integrate into the community. The church members had some contact with the local Latina/o workers, as they either worked with them or were their employers. Some church members began to stop by the local Latina/o areas and encourage them to visit their church. Latina/os started coming to the church and now make up twenty of the 140 families that belong to the church. The church has developed a series of activities, including bible camps and hiring a community liaison, in efforts to help integrate Latina/os to the church, efforts that are somewhat difficult, given language barriers across groups (López-Sanders 2012).

Yet, for the most part, it is Latina/os who are being transformed rather than the white congregants themselves, as evident in their placement in the church, where Latinos sit at the back with a personal translation scripture from English to Spanish. Nonetheless, Latina/os largely have not ceded their Catholicism as well as their participation in religious oriented rites, such as baptisms, and traditions including the celebration of the Virgin of Guadalupe (López-Sanders 2012). This is in contrast to other more traditional Protestant churches in the area that do not allow Latina/os to join unless they renounce their Catholic religion. Moreover, Latina/os report that they gain benefits from their attendance and participation at church. For example, Mariana, a 45-year-old woman who attends the church, intimates that she learns how to think and behave like whites by paying attention to what her "hermanos Americanos [American brothers/sisters] at church do and say" (López-Sanders 2012, p. 137). Mariana also believes that her attendance and participation in church functions shows to her employer that "she is responsible" (López-Sanders 2012), which she credits for her advancement in her job.

Again, stratified relationships in which Latina/os are the beneficiaries of the so-called goodwill of whites are evident at Harvest. López-Sanders (2012) observes that Harvest openness to Latina/o cultural norms and the socioeconomic benefits that come with learning from Anglo-Saxon norms and developing social networks with whites comes at a price:

> This type of incorporation, however, has implications for the nature of Latina/o
> integration. In brokering this integration, the church reproduces the asymmetric

position that whites and Latina/os have in the social structure. For example, many white parishioners are the employers of Latina/o members in the church. Although the church has a participatory structure – decisions fall on members rather than on a board of directors – Latina/os participate very little, if at all, in the decision making process of the church. Latina/os depend on the "charity" of white parishioners, as they are the church's major economic contributors. As such, the well-intended efforts to integrate Latina/os into the community could be interpreted as patronizing or condescending . . . (p. 139).

Nonetheless, López-Sanders (2012) makes reference to two individuals – one white and one Latina/o – who see the relationship between whites and Latina/os in Harvest Church more favorably. Joseph, the white church pastor, points out:

We genuinely love the Hispanic community. We actually feel a connection with them. We feel that they give just as much to us as we give to them. They enrich our lives as much as we enrich theirs. So I think that they realize that we are not just there because of obligation. It is very rewarding for us to get to know them to learn about their culture, to learn about where they come from. (López-Sanders 2012, p. 139–140)

Eulalio, a Central American immigrant, adds that "Harvest is a mix of Americans and Hispanics, but we all get along, we have good friendships, and Joseph has a gift to make everyone feel welcome" (López-Sanders 2012, p. 140).

Thus, regardless of how we view the relationship between Latina/os and whites at Harvest Church, it is clear that both groups have expanded their social boundaries to relate to one another in the confines of the church and beyond.

A third manner in which religion serves to incorporate immigrants is through getting them civically engaged. Over the last couple of decades there has been growing interest in the association between religion and civic engagement (Cadge and Ecklund 2007). Cadge and Ecklund (2007) note that "Civil actions are generally voluntary, not aimed at reaping an economic profit, and are often concerned with improving some version of the common good" (p. 366). Churches and church leaders often can spur their members to become engaged in various forms of civic life to contribute to the overall common good. Latina/o parishes and congregations tend to be particularly active in the provision of social and community services (Martini 2012; Palmer-Boyes 2010). Such services include efforts to improve housing and schools and endeavors to reduce crime (Martini 2012). In San Antonio, Latina/o Catholics have a long history of civic engagement and efforts to better Latina/o neighborhoods through their work with San Antonio's Communities Organized for Public Service (COPS) (Matovina 2012). It has been observed that religious organizations are particularly important for Latina/os in the encouragement of civic engagement as whites are more likely to engage civically through a broader set of types of organizations (Jones-Correa and Leal 2001; Verba et al. 1995).

The fourth way by which religion promotes the incorporation of immigrants and people of color is through political mobilization. Religious leaders have a significant amount of influence over their congregants, especially when they share a variety of political interests (Brown 2011; Putnam and Campbell 2010). Certainly, in the African

American community religious leaders have played a prominent role in organizing and impelling their church members to vote as well as support civil rights causes (Brown 2011; Morris 1984; Williams 2003). In the Latina/o community, Chicano priests and nuns have been important in demanding that the Catholic Church pay more attention to issues affecting Latina/os as was the case through the development of Padres Asociades para los Derechos Religiosos, Educativos, y Sociales (PADRES; Priests Associated for Religious, Educational, and Social Rights) and Las Hermanas (the Sisters), an organization for Latina women, not only for nuns and not only for persons of Mexican origin (Chicanos and Chicanas). More recently, Latina/o parishes and congregants have been active in a variety of efforts related to the human rights of immigrants as well as in efforts to push for immigration reform (Hondagneu-Sotelo 2007; Hondagneu-Sotelo et al. 2004; Menjívar 2003).

In addition, religious leaders also stimulate their followers to support a range of conservative causes as well. These include issues involving pro-life, anti-homosexual, and related matters. Williams and Loret de Mola (2007) describe the fiery words of a Latina/o pastor in a Florida community:

> Pastor Rincón is politically conservative, and speaks openly in church of his fervent support for President Bush and his policies. He often employs an apocalyptic discourse and biblical literalism to denounce homosexuality and abortion, and to preach against drinking, smoking, and other pleasures "del mundo" [of the world]. (p. 244)

Research has also examined the degree to which Latina/os support the role of religion in politics. Martini (2012), analyzing 2006 survey data from the Pew Hispanic Center and Pew Forum on Religion and Public Life, discovered that Latina/os with greater church participation and deeper religious beliefs are more supportive of the role of religion in the political sphere. Martini (2012) also observed that Evangelical Protestants, in particular, had the greatest degree of support for the involvement of religious organizations in politics. Ellison et al. (2005), using data from the 1990 Latina/o National Political Survey, find that Latina/os who are Protestants with the strongest degree of religious commitment to conservative Evangelical, fundamentalist, and charismatic groups exhibit the greatest support for the most restrictive bans on abortion. In sum, Martini (2012) observes that the overall general findings related to how Latina/os view the association between religion and politics "add to the mounting evidence of the role that religion can play a . . . role for Latina/os in shaping public opinion" (p. 1,004). The growing popularity of Protestant Evangelical denominations among Latina/os has implications for a turn toward more conservative political views among the population (Ellison et al. 2005).

Religious Marketplace

While Latina/os have historically been Catholic, increasingly they are turning to other denominations (Greeley 1994; Hunt 1999). Given the demographic trends that we examined in Chapter 5, it is certain that religious denominations will increasingly try to recruit Latina/os into their folds. The religious marketplace theoretical perspective offers a context that allows us to understand the competition that takes place among religious organizations as they seek congregants (Finke and Stark 1992). The religious marketplace perspective derives from economics and more specifically the rational choice (RC) framework.

The religious marketplace perspective views religious denominations as suppliers of a religious product that is marketed to consumers in search of a religion that suits them. More specifically, Sherkat and Ellison (1999) describe the players in the religious marketplace across levels:

> Religious organizations are firms dedicated to the production of religious value. Congregations are franchises led by entrepreneurial salespeople (ministers), who create value for customers. Firms are limited in their range of product offerings, and only those lacking an organizational hierarchy (e.g. Baptists) or nourishing an institutional commitment to pluralism (e.g. Roman Catholics) can sustain much diversity. (p. 379)

Accordingly, we can think of the different religious denominations as firms such as McDonalds, Burger King, Wendy's, and so forth. The franchises (or congregations) of these firms (or religious denominations) are situated across neighborhoods, communities, and states.

Like any other product, the religious product is "produced, chosen, and consumed" (Sherkat and Ellison 1999, p. 378). Religious denominations offer a product that offers "promises of future rewards and supernatural explanations for life events and meaning" (Sherkat and Ellison 1999, p. 378). Consumers compare the varying religious products on how they deal with these big issues and they come to a determination on the selection of a particular religious product. Subsequently, people consume the selected religious product with respect to participating in the religious activities and following the religious prescriptions that adherents are expected to follow. However, in contrast to other types of products, as Sherkat and Ellison (1999) point out, the promises of the religious product cannot be truly assessed. Thus, religious products are risky. Consumers gain reassurance more indirectly – from their social relationships derived from other congregants and religious leaders (Sherkat and Ellison 1999). Nonetheless, the uncertainty associated with the religious product leads to potential for people to eschew the product in favor of another one (religious conversion), diversify their religious portfolio (by either holding on to a primary religious denomination and also connecting to other denominations or identifying with various denominations without a preference for any), or by exiting the religious marketplace (becoming agnostic or atheist) (Sherkat and Ellison 1999).

The religious marketplace perspective has received some criticism. It is difficult for some people to view religion as a product that is manufactured, marketed, and consumed. It is challenging for some to think about people comparing across religious denominations and assessing the costs and benefits associated with becoming a member of an array of faiths. Similar criticisms are made of the marriage market and the economic perspective of fertility. It is difficult to see love and babies as commodities, with consumers using reason to analyze costs and benefits associated with varying potential spouses and comparing whether or not to have a child, or how many, relative to other consumer products.

Despite these criticisms and others (see McKinnon 2011), the religious market-place framework is a useful metaphor to make sense of how Latina/os are involved in religious conversion – typically from Catholicism to other religions – and perhaps more importantly, how religious denominations seek to recruit Latina/os as con-gregants as they face membership losses due to aging white populations. With the disproportionate growth of the Latina/o population, we have seen how corporations and businesses market their products to Latina/o consumers and how political par-ties market their political candidates to the Latina/o electorate. We can also envision how religious denominations package their faiths to Latina/os, who are seen as potential congregants. Step in, Joel Osteen and his Lakewood megachurch, bringing into his organization Marcos Witt, to connect with, draw, and inspire Latina/os to join their church – and join they do, in soaring numbers.

Religious Patterns of Latina/os

We now turn to the examination of survey data from the Pew Hispanic Center on shifts in religious affiliation among Latina/os. We draw here on the report of Krogstad et al. (2023). Figure 12.1 illustrates the level of change in Latina/o affiliation across several religious groups. While Catholicism continues to be the most common religious affili-ation for Latina/os, the percentage of Latina/os who identify as Catholic has fallen significantly, dropping from 67 percent in 2010 to 43 percent in 2022. The percent-age of Latina/os identifying as Evangelical Protestant has ranged from 12 percent

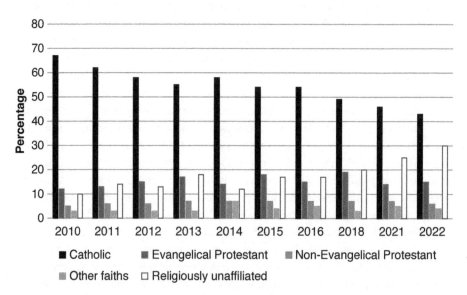

Figure 12.1 Percentage of Latina/os by Religious Affiliation, 2010 to 2022
Source: Data from Krogstad et al. (2023).

in 2010 to 19 percent in 2018 with 15 percent having an affiliation with Evangelical Protestantism in 2022. However, the greatest increase among Latina/os has been in the religiously unaffiliated group, with the percentage of people in this group ascending from 10 percent in 2010 to 30 percent in 2022. These trends suggest further shifts are likely to occur in the religious affiliations of Latina/os. Yet, recent research suggests Latina/os who report "no religion" or "no religious preference" tend to still be engaged religiously, with many also being former born-again individuals who are exploring different religions (Espinosa 2023). Espinosa (2023) used follow-up questions among Latina/os who report "no religion" or "no religious preference" and found that "60% of them reported believing in God or a higher power and/or being Christian, Catholic, or Protestant, religious, spiritual, or something other than no religion" (p. 1). He also observed that "17% of those who reported having 'no religion' also reported being born-again Christians" (p. 1). This is a significant finding that challenges conventional wisdom regarding the rise of unaffiliated or "no religion" Latina/os.

The Krogstad et al. (2023) report based on Pew Research Center survey data provides additional information on Latina/os and their religious patterns. First, for Latina/os 18 to 29 years of age, the lack of a religious affiliation is the most common religious selection, suggesting further declines in the future in the share of Latina/os identifying as Catholic and continual increases in the percentage who do not identify with any religion (Krogstad et al. 2023). Second, approximately one-third of Latinos have switched their religious affiliation from that of their childhood (Krogstad 2023). This religious switch is particularly likely among persons who leave the Catholic religion. One fourth of US Latina/os report that they were former Catholics. The Catholic religion is experiencing a major net outflow of Latina/o congregants. For every 23 Latinos that leave the Catholic religion, only one person converts to Catholicism from another religion. Finally, four in ten Latina/os consider religion to be an important part of their lives, Latina/os Protestants attend church more regularly than do Latina/o Catholics, and seven in ten Latina/o Evangelicals pray each day (Krogstad et al. 2023).

Another Pew Research Center report (Cooperman et al. 2014) allows us to assess variations among five Latina/o subgroups (Cubans, Dominicans, Mexicans, Puerto

Table 12.1 Percentage Distribution of Selected Latina/o Groups by Religious Affiliation, 2014

Latina/o Group	Catholic	Evangelical Protestant	Mainline Protestant	Unaffiliated	Other	Don't Know
Cuban	49	8	8	26	8	0
Dominican	59	16	6	16	3	1
Mexican	61	13	5	17	4	0
Puerto Rican	45	22	8	20	6	0
Salvadoran	42	32	5	15	5	1

Source: Data from Cooperman et al. (2014)

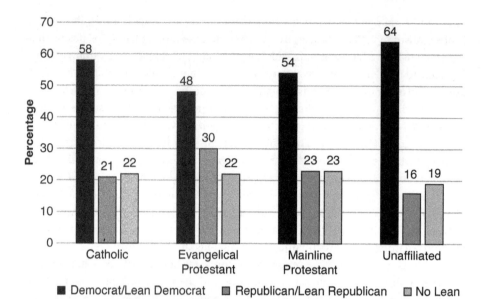

Figure 12.2 Latina/o Political Party Affiliation for Selected Religious Groups, 2014
Source: Data from Cooperman et al. (2014).

Ricans, and Salvadorans) in their religious affiliations. Catholicism is the most popular religious affiliation across the five Latina/o subgroups with three-fifths of Mexicans and Dominicans identifying as Catholic (Figure 12.2). Evangelical Protestantism is most common among Salvadorans and Puerto Ricans with one-third of Salvadorans and more than one-fifth of Puerto Ricans identifying with this religion. Finally, the religious unaffiliation category is the second most popular selection among Cubans and Mexicans, although the highest percentages of people reporting they have no religious affiliation occurs among Cubans (one-fourth) and Puerto Ricans (one-fifth).

The Cooperman et al. (2014) report allows us to examine the relationship between religious and political party affiliation. Figure 12.2 shows the variations in political preference among members of four religious groups (Catholic, Evangelical Protestant, Mainline Protestant, and Unaffiliated). The four religious groups identify most commonly with the Democrat Party with the unaffiliated (64%) and Catholics (58%) having the highest level of identification with the Democrat Party. Evangelical Protestants have the greatest level of support for the Republican Party with 30 percent identifying with this party. The religiously unaffiliated have the least level (16%) of identification with the Republican Party.

We now highlight some key questions related to religious patterns and trends that Latina/os will confront in the near future.

Issues Related to the Future of Latina/o Religious Life

There are a series of important trends that impact the religious life of Latina/os that we need to address and monitor. These revolve around the disproportionate growth of the Latina/o population and its role in the Catholic Church and as potential recruits for other religions, religious conversion, the secularization trend, and the impact of Pope Francis on Latina/os.

The Increasing Influence of Latina/os on the Catholic Church

As we saw in Chapter 5, the Latina/o population is shaping the demography of the US and its institutions. The impact of the Latina/o population will expand in the coming decades due to the relative youthfulness of this population (Huckle 2020). The Latina/o population is expected to have a particularly significant sway in religious life in the US. Over the final three decades of the twentieth century, the Latina/o Catholic population nearly tripled and accounted for close to 90 percent of the total population growth of Catholics in the US (Poyo 2010). Currently, Latina/os comprise approximately one-third of US Catholics (Matovina 2012; Pew Hispanic Center 2007). Matovina (2012) points out that in the absence of Latina/os, the US Catholic Church would be experiencing severe population declines, as is the case with mainline Protestant groups. The demographic influence of Latina/os in the Catholic Church will expand in the near future. Indeed, already Latina/os make up the majority of Catholics less than 25 years of age (Matovina 2012). Moreover, in Arizona, California, New Mexico, and Texas, Latina/os represent more than three-fourths of Catholics less than eighteen years of age. Furthermore, the demographic influence of Latina/os on the Catholic Church is also apparent in Latina/o new-destination areas. For example, Latina/os Catholics outnumber white Catholics in Georgia (Matovina 2012). Put simply, Putnam and Campbell (2010, p. 17; see also Matovina 2012, p. vii) claim that the US Catholic Church "is on its way to becoming a majority-Latina/o institution."

The influence of Latina/os on the US Catholic Church extends beyond numbers. There are two distinct aspects of Latina/o Catholics that are particularly noteworthy, for they stand to potentially alter the practice of Catholicism in this country. First, Latina/o Catholics are much more likely than other Catholics to engage in spirit-filled religious expression as part of their worship. As noted above, while only one-eighth of non-Latina/o Catholics view themselves as charismatic, more than half of Latina/os do (Pew Hispanic Center 2007). Moreover, Latina/os as a whole, regardless of religious faith, are more likely than non-Latina/os to believe that God is an active presence in their daily lives, to pray daily, to believe in religious miracles, and to possess religious objects in their homes (Pew Hispanic Center 2007). It is likely that with the growth of the Latina/o population, these beliefs and forms of worship will become a greater part of Catholicism in the US. Second, Latina/o Catholics tend to worship and attend churches with other Latina/os. For instance, two-thirds of Latina/o Catholics participate in churches that have Latina/o clergy, where masses are in Spanish, and where the majority of attendees are Latina/os, with three-fourths of foreign-born and half of native-born Latina/os attending such churches (Pew Hispanic Center 2007). Hence, the disproportionate growth of Latina/os in the US Catholic Church is likely to lead to more predominantly Latina/o churches. It will certainly be interesting to see how white Catholics will adjust to their declining numbers and potential for church closings in this changing environment.

This major demographic transformation involving the increasing influence of Latina/os in the Catholic Church represents another stage in the long history between Latina/os and the Catholic Church. For example, as the Mexican population grew in the early twentieth century due to people fleeing the Mexican Revolution, the Catholic Church largely neglected Mexicans, with its ideological model emphasizing Americanization, which stressed the abandoning of Spanish and Mexican culture in favor of English and mainstream white culture (Matovina 2012; Poyo 2010; Stevens-Arroyo 2010; Treviño 2006). There were important shifts in the relationship between Latina/os and the Catholic Church, beginning in the 1960s. In the midst of the Civil Rights Movement, the Second Vatican Council (1962–1965) of the Catholic Church made significant changes in bringing about greater democracy, diversity, transparency, and opened the door for concerns for social justice (Stevens-Arroyo 2010). Still, however, efforts to improve the conditions of Latina/os within the Catholic Church and, more generally, in the larger society did not originate from the mainstream Catholic structure. Rather, as the Chicano Movement emerged in the 1960s, Catholic priests, such as Ralph Ruiz, and nuns, such as Sisters Gregoria Ortega and Gloria Graciela Gallardo, played important roles in pushing for greater inclusion of Latina/os and on social justice concerns affecting Latina/os. Despite the more multicultural environment supporting the retention of the Spanish language and Latina/o cultures, Latina/os continue to be disproportionately underrepresented in the hierarchy of the Catholic Church (Poyo 2010; Treviño 2006). The major question that arises is whether the increasing numbers of Latina/os in the Catholic Church will translate into the actual positioning of Latina/os in the higher levels of the hierarchy of the Church. Moreover, Latina/os have historically been underrepresented as priests and nuns. Current trends suggest that Latina/o youth will forego careers as priests and nuns, which commonly has led to the importation of priests from abroad (Goodstein 2008a, 2008b; Heatherington 2023; Quintanilla 2023) or even outsourcing of prayer services to priests abroad (Rai 2004).

Finally, Huckle (2020) conducted an examination of the relationship between Latino population size and the presence of a Latino priest in the types of services that Catholic Churches in three cities provide to their Latina/o constituents. Huckle found that: (1) Latino population size was not related to the church's providing mass in Spanish nor other types of services and activities for Latina/os, (2) churches with a Latina/o priest were more likely to provide both types of services for Latina/os, (3) there was not a relationship between the Latino population size and the presence of a Latina/o priest, and (4) churches were more likely to provide masses in Spanish than other types of services to Latina/os. The findings suggest that these Catholic churches have much room for improving their services to the growing Latina/o population.

Huckle (2020) concludes with the urgency for Catholic churches to improve their services and direct activities toward Latina/os:

> ... we must consider the necessity of serving Latinos to the Church's institutional survival. The Church is dying, suffering from high attrition rates, church closures, and continued fallout from numerous sex scandals. Latinos, as the only source of membership and growth, represent a lifeline. As such, Church officials should be conducting as much welcoming, outreach, and service provision as possible in order to stave off closures, particularly since it is one of the primary responsibilities of leaders to maintain membership levels ... Incentives include not only offering mass in Spanish, but also the provision of other services and activities that directly appeal to Latinos. Indeed, many have theorized that it is precisely because of the Church's failure to provide these enticements that so many Latinos have left Catholicism ... The success or failure of the Catholic Church to accept – and take seriously – this reality should serve as a lesson to other institutions that will soon be reliant on the membership of a growing Latino population for their survival. (p. 190)

If the Catholic Church does not heed Huckle's (2020) words of advice, it is likely that Latina/os will seek other denominations to meet their spiritual and related needs.

Religious Conversion

As we have observed above, while Latina/os remain predominantly Catholic with 43 percent identifying with this religion, the share that converts to other religions has been rising the last few decades (Ellison et al. 2005; Hunt 1999; Krogstad et al. 2023; Matovina 2012). Given the fondness of Latina/os for spirit-filled forms of worship and belief that God is an active force in daily life, it is not surprising that Latina/os who leave the Catholic Church tend to gravitate to Evangelical and Pentecostal denominations (Pew Hispanic Center 2007). Moreover, these denominations also provide opportunities for Latina/os to assume leadership positions. The Latina/o clergy in these denominations tend to be working-class men without religious training, which make them particularly effective in connecting with and recruiting Latina/os of similar backgrounds (Walsh 2010). Mainline Protestant denominations, such as Methodists, Presbyterians, Congregationalists, and Baptists, will increasingly turn to Latina/os as potential congregants as their membership dwindles further, due to an aging white population. These denominations have increasingly created Latina/o ministries to attract Latina/os, with some degree of success in many cities, particularly in California, Florida, and Texas (Barton 2010).

One of the major implications of Latina/o converts is the degree to which they shift politically. There has been much discussion about the future political strength of the Latina/o population. While this scenario is largely associated with the assumption of a strong Democrat presence among Latina/os, given shifts toward Evangelical and Pentecostal denominations, it is likely that Latina/os making such changes will increasingly gravitate to the Republican Party, as we observed above, where Latina/o Evangelical Protestants were the most likely to identify with the Republican Party. Therefore, it can be argued that the rising conversion of Latina/os to Evangelical and

Pentecostal denominations may have played a role in the political swing that brought Trump increasing Latina/o support in Texas (see Sáenz 2021).

Finally, although religious conversion has primarily focused on Christian religions, there is a growing body of scholarship on Latina/o Muslims (Abeyta 2023; Bowen 2013; Cuartas 2020; Kaba 2008; Sierk 2016). This is a fascinating area of research with a need for more information on the experiences of Latina/o Muslims.

Secularization

As we observed above, one of the major religious trends among Latina/os is their increasing lack of identification with any religious denomination. Indeed, 30 percent of Latina/os were religiously unaffiliated in 2022, three times the rate of that in 2010 (Krogstad et al. 2023), particularly among younger adults. Earlier data showed that about 8 percent of Latina/os do not have a religion, or consider themselves to be secular. The percentage approximates the 11 percent in the general public that were secular in the mid-2000s (Goodstein 2007). However, one of the distinguishing attributes of secular Latina/os is that they are more likely than those in the general public to have belonged to a particular religion in the past – two-thirds of secular Latina/os, with the majority former Catholics (Goodstein 2007). The secularization of Latina/os has been dramatic. Indeed, data from the American Religious Identification Survey show that the percentage of Latina/os without a religion doubled from 6 percent in 1990 to 13 percent in 2001 (Goodstein 2007). Some have observed that the secularization trend is not limited to higher generation Latina/os, but also includes immigrants, who were devout church attendants in their home country but who have now abandoned church attendance and religion more generally (Goodstein 2007). To the extent that Latina/os achieve greater socioeconomic mobility in the future and move away from family influences, it is likely that secularization may be an increasing reality for Latina/os. However, given the recent findings of Espinosa (2023) concerning the continued religiosity of Latina/os who report "no religion" or "no religious preference," there is a word of caution in fully accepting the strong upward trend toward secularization. It is likely that the secularization is taking place, but perhaps not as dramatically.

The Pope Francis Factor

Despite Latin America having the largest share of Catholics in the world (Sáenz 2005), this region has largely been overlooked in selection of popes. This changed on March 13, 2013, when Jorge Mario Bergoglio, an Argentinian, was elected the 266th pope and the first originating from Latin America. Ordained as Pope Francis, he has been an extraordinarily popular and charismatic pope who shuns luxury and comfort and who has placed a high priority on addressing the conditions of the poor and social justice concerns. Undoubtedly, Latina/os feel a deep connection to Pope Francis, due to his Latin American roots and his enthusiastic attention to people on the margins. As a voice for social change in the Catholic Church, Pope Francis has the potential to bring back to the fold Catholics who have left the faith – many of these people who do not have a religion – due to dissonance between their views and those of the Catholic Church regarding a variety of issues such as contraceptive use, abortion, and the sexual abuse of children by priests that has rocked the Church. In addition, it is possible that Pope Francis will help stem the outflow of Catholics who have converted to Evangelical and Pentecostal denominations. Pope Francis has shone light on issues that are important to Latina/os such as immigration, human rights, poverty, and inequality. It will be interesting to see the impact he has on Latina/os, not only in keeping them within the religious fold, but also in how he can meet their spiritual needs.

The Issues of the Catholic Church

Major issues surrounding the many priests who have sexually assaulted children across so many decades have rocked the Catholic Church. Even more disturbing for many Catholics is that the church leadership knew about these abuses and turned a blind eye or simply reassigned abusive priests to other churches, where they put children in those places at risk of falling victim to the abusive priests. To make matters worse, the problem has not gone away, but we continue regularly to read about yet another priest who has abused children. Undoubtedly, this issue has driven some Latina/o Catholics away from the Church. If the situation persists, will there be more congregants who leave the Church?

Then there is the abortion issue. The Catholic Church continues to take a very hard stance against abortion, supporting the recent Supreme Court decision to overturn *Roe v. Wade*. The reproductive rights of US women, particularly of Latina women, who are disproportionately among women in their childbearing ages, have been severely cut. Many women with limited resources living in states where abortion is now outlawed have been trapped by a lack of funds to be able to travel to a state where abortion is legal. Like the majority of politicians who support the end of abortion, who are largely men, the Catholic Church power structure is made up exclusively of men. Will the Catholic Church's position on abortion drive progressive women out of Catholicism?

The Catholic Church's major issues related to priests sexually abusing children and its hardline position against abortion could possibly result in at least some people leaving the Church. There is undoubtedly a need for research to answer these questions.

Summary

This chapter has provided an overview of the religious patterns of the Latina/o population. We also examined the deep historical roots of Latina/os to Catholicism as well as the unique aspects related to worship among Latina/os and the strong presence of La Virgin de Guadalupe in their lives and La Virgen de la Caridad del Cobre in Cuba. In addition, we overviewed a variety of theoretical perspectives that sociologists and political scientists have used to understand various aspects of religion relating to Latina/os, including the role of religion as social capital, as a vehicle to integrate immigrants, and as a framework for viewing religion as a marketplace. The examination of recent data from the Pew Research Center shows that while Catholicism continues to be the most popular religion among Latina/os, a significant portion identify as Evangelical Protestant and an even larger portion are not affiliated to any religion. We saw at the outset of the chapter how Evangelical religions have developed strategies to tap into the rapidly growing Latino population. Finally, we highlighted five important issues and trends related to the religious life of Latina/os involving the increasing influence of Latina/os in the Catholic Church, religious conversion, secularization, the Pope Francis factor, and the issues of the Catholic Church.

Religion has sustained many Latina/os, providing a certain degree of security, predictability, and strength in dealing with all aspects of their lives, a topic that we have covered thus far. As we saw in this chapter, there is a significant association between religion and health and well-being. Indeed, individuals whose lives are intimately tied to religion tend to have more favorable health outcomes than others. We now turn to an examination of health and health care among Latina/os.

Discussion Questions

1. What is the significance of the apparition of the Virgin of Guadalupe to Juan Diego?

2. How are Latina/o Catholics unique among mainstream Catholics?

3. What is meant by "cultural Catholics"?

4. We examined three theoretical perspectives for understanding Latina/o religious life. Is there one that resonates with you the most? Any other? Is there one that you do not support?

5. Which is the group of Latina/os that has grown the most rapidly with respect to their religious affiliation or lack thereof?

6. Do you think that Latina/os will continue to leave the Catholic religion? If so, what can the Catholic Church do to halt this outflow?

7. Why do you think that Latina/os have increasingly converted to Evangelical denominations?

13 Health and Health Care

It is a real scary thing when you are little, you know, you don't know what is going on in the world . . . you know that your parent probably doesn't have a job. So, making sure that I was there was my priority, but their priority is also their education.

(Yajaira Rangel, school teacher, Austin, Texas)

As a Latino, a Mexican, we never stopped working. This affect us, maybe at the beginning, but right now is that everybody is looking for work. I work Monday to Friday, if I have work Saturday, Saturday too.

(Fernando Jiménez, construction worker, Phoenix, Arizona)

Just being there trying to get an iPad to make sure that their daughter or son or whatever family member was there for them. They were passing away and like and we didn't have that time to be like it is happening now.

(Natalia Useche, ICU nurse, Miami, Florida)

(Voces Oral History Project 2024)

The quotes above are part of the Voces Oral History Project at the University of Texas at Austin's Voces Oral History (2024) project, which consists of more than 400 oral interviews with Latina/os from all over the country telling their personal stories concerning the COVID-19 pandemic. This is an exceptional and rich source of data that provides the human voice and emotions to the devastation that the Latina/o community sustained as their members disproportionately died from the pandemic. We will provide below an overview of the devastation that Latina/os sustained in the midst of well-established mortality and life-expectancy advantages that they have long held eroding over the last several years.

Throughout the chapters we have covered thus far, we have seen that Latina/os as a whole are characterized by relatively low socioeconomic levels. Latina/os, particularly in the case of certain groups such as Mexicans, tend to have comparatively low levels of education, hold low-paying and physically demanding jobs with limited benefits, have high rates of poverty, and have high percentages of persons lacking health insurance. These conditions of Latina/os are consistent with the many challenges that they face in accessing quality health care and in having numerous negative health outcomes, as the theoretical perspectives that we present below illustrate. Yet, one of the major surprises that have baffled epidemiologists, public health specialists, and demographers is the finding that Latina/os actually have mortality rates that are lower and life expectancies that are more favorable than whites. This pattern, referred to as the "epidemiological paradox" or "Latina/o or Hispanic paradox" has been observed consistently for three decades (Hummer and Chinn 2011; Markides and Coreil 1986; Markides and Eschbach 2011). There has been much research that has attempted to unravel the paradox through the examination of various explanations that have been proposed (see below).

The unanticipated favorable mortality outcomes of Latina/os, however, hide other health and health care related patterns that are more disturbing. For example, Latina/os lack access to health care due to their low prevalence of health care insurance, particularly among undocumented immigrants (Chavez 2012). Latina/os without health care insurance resort to a variety of other ways to access health care, including depending on health care at the emergency room when ailments become severe (Chavez 2012), using alternative forms of health care, and traveling to Mexico to obtain health care (Bastida et al. 2008; Horton and Cole 2011). Moreover, Latina/os fare worse than whites on the prevalence of diabetes, obesity, and disability. It has, thus, been observed that Latina/os live longer than whites, but they do so with chronic and degenerative ailments. The COVID-19 pandemic sorrowfully revealed the fragility of the lives of Latina/os as they lost their lives disproportionately, bringing about the short-term disappearance of the Latina/o paradox for some age groups in the first year of the pandemic (Garcia and Sáenz 2023; Sáenz and Garcia 2021),

We begin with an overview of theoretical perspectives that have been used to understand the health and mortality outcome of individuals. Subsequently, we provide a discussion of the Latina/o paradox and examine the different explanations that have been proposed. In addition, we examine the other side of the paradox where Latina/os do not fare as well, including the COVID-19 era. Finally, we highlight major questions and issues that we need to recognize in order to better understand the future of Latina/os in the area of health and health care.

Stratification and Cumulative Advantages/Disadvantages

One of the most enduring sociological tenets is that one's position in the social class ladder is associated with one's position in the various domains of life (Domhoff 2013; Massey 2007). Thus, people born in the upper classes are endowed with a multitude of social, economic, political, and cultural resources that allow them to get into and graduate from the most prestigious universities, earn high incomes, accumulate vast amounts of wealth, live in prestigious neighborhoods, and have strong political connections that protect their wealth and societal position (Sáenz et al. 2007). In contrast, individuals born in the lower classes, bereft of social, economic, political, and cultural assets, are restricted to low-quality education, low levels of income, minuscule wealth, low-income neighborhoods, and do not have significant political connections (Sáenz et al. 2007). One's social class standing also affects health and mortality outcomes.

Our sociological understanding of the link between social class and mortality extends back to a very influential research project by Evelyn Kitagawa and Philip

Hauser, two sociologists and demographers at the University of Chicago, who examined the relationship between social class and mortality among some 500,000 people who died in the US in 1960. They published their findings in a landmark book titled *Differential Mortality in the US: A Study in Socioeconomic Epidemiology* (Kitagawa and Hauser 1973). Kitagawa and Hauser (1973) observed that white adults with the lowest education and income levels had the highest death rates and the probability of death declined with increasing educational and income levels. For example, they found that low-income women died at nearly twice the rate of high-income women.

The relationship between socioeconomic position and mortality persists today (Rogers et al. 2000). For example, among adults dying in the US in 2004, there is a strong and consistent negative association between educational level and death rate (Miniño et al. 2007). On average, US adults with less than twelve years of education had death rates that were more than three times higher than those of their counterparts with thirteen or more years of schooling in 2004 (Miniño et al. 2007). Furthermore, historical data show that whites have a longer life expectancy than Blacks (National Center for Health Statistics 2013). Despite the narrowing of the White–Black life expectancy gap since 1990, the life expectancy of white males was still about 7 percent higher than that of Black males in 2010, while white females had an advantage of 4 percent in their life expectancy compared to Black females (National Center for Health Statistics 2013).

Variations in mortality and health outcomes on the basis of socioeconomic status as well as race and ethnicity reflect the advantages and disadvantages that people have, due to their position in the stratification system. As people go through the life course extending from the utero stage to birth, infancy, childhood, teenage years, young adulthood, middle age, and elderly age, they have social and economic resources at their disposal to maintain their health (Geronimus et al. 2007; Ross and Wu 1996). Persons who are endowed with socioeconomic advantages – whites being disproportionately in this category – have greater access to health care, nutritious diets, living in safe and salubrious environments, and are also more likely to exercise compared to individuals with limited resources – people of color, especially African Americans, Latina/os, and Native Americans, being disproportionately in this category (Hummer 1996; Williams 1999; Williams and Jackson 2005). Over the life course, the advantages and disadvantages accumulate to produce greater disparities in health and mortality outcomes (Bowen 2009; Ross and Wu 1996). This is consistent with such adages as "success breeds further success," "failure breeds further failure," and "the rich get richer and the poor get poorer" (Ross and Wu 1996). Thus, people with greater access to quality health care have the ability to attain preventive care to minimize the risks of contracting serious health problems and can get medical care whenever illness arises. In contrast, people without health care insurance and those with limited access to quality health care may have to forego medical visits until health problems become unbearable, at which time health recovery is more difficult. Similarly, people working in physically demanding jobs, such as agricultural labor, machine operative work, meatpacking labor, construction, mining, and so forth, face the accumulation of stress on the body over time and, as such, become increasingly vulnerable to physical disabilities (Leigh and Fries 1992; Schlosser 2001) with immigrants particularly likely to work in risky and physically demanding jobs (Orrenius and Zavodny 2009).

Health disparities at old age, then, reflect the statuses that people had throughout the life course. People with more disadvantaged statuses, such as being poor, being a person of color, being an immigrant, and lacking US citizenship status, are particularly vulnerable in old age because of their cumulative disadvantages over the life course. Moreover, at the elderly stage of their lives they are likely to lack adequate socioeconomic resources to deal with the many health challenges that come at the later stages of life (Orrenius and Zavodny 2009; Schlosser 2001).

The Social Determinants of Health and Longevity Theoretical Perspectives

A variety of theoretical perspectives have been developed over the last several decades which provide an understanding of the complex and interrelated factors that result in varying health outcomes and longevity. These perspectives include the life course perspective, the social determinants of health, and the National Institute of Minority Health and Health Disparities (NIMHD) research framework. In general, these theoretical frameworks capture the multiple pillars or dimensions that impact how healthy or sickly we are throughout the course of our lives, from the time that we exist in our mother's womb to the time we make our entrance into the world to our childhood, teen years, young adulthood, middle adulthood, and into our older years. In many respects, our health circumstances are impacted by ancestors and where we are positioned on a variety of socioeconomic, racial and ethnic, gender, sexuality, ableism, and related hierarchies and systems of oppression or privilege.

We overview here the social determinants of health and the NIMHD research framework. There has been increasing attention to the role that social determinants play in health outcomes and the federal government has embraced the model (see Figure 13.1) as an inventory of factors that must be addressed to reduce health disparities. Healthy People 2030 (2024) defines the social determinants of health as "the environments where people are born, live, learn, work, play, worship, and age that affect a wide range of health, functioning, and quality-of-life outcomes and risks." The model reflects the increasing understanding that a significant portion of health outcomes happens outside of the health system. Hacker et al. (2022) delineate that "[w]hile health care is important, it is estimated that these conditions, ranging from structural racism to socioeconomic factors, drive as much as 50% of health outcomes" (p. 589). As Figure 13.1 shows, the five categories of social determinants of health include economic stability, educational access and quality, health care access and quality, neighborhood and built environment, and social and community context. Artiga and Hinton (2018) add a sixth social determinant, namely food, which involves hunger and access to healthy options. The social determinants of health represent pillars or dimensions of factors that contribute to health outcomes, which include mortality, morbidity (i.e. illness and disease), life expectancy, health care expenditures, health status, functional disabilities (Artiga and Hinton 2018).

Figure 13.1 The Social Determinants of Health
Source: Healthy People 2030 (2024).

Artiga and Hinton outline the indicators of the six social determinants of health: economic stability; neighborhood and physical environment; education; food; community and social context; and health care system. We can envision people having more favorable health outcomes if they had economic stability in their daily lives, lived in a safe neighborhood and in a physical environment that allowed them to get around and enjoy the amenities of the immediate and local surroundings, received a good-quality education, met their food necessities and had access to healthy food choices, were integrated into and felt supported and a part of their community, and had easy access to good-quality health care. In contrast, the opposite kinds of conditions would generate less favorable health outcomes.

The NIMHD research framework developed by the National Institute on Minority Health (2018) is similar with respect to the links between a variety of social determinants and health outcomes, but adds a biological component and has four sets of geographic levels, including the individual, interpersonal, community, and societal levels (Figure 13.2). In particular, the National Institute on Minority Health (2018), indicates that "[t]he framework serves as a vehicle for encouraging NIMHD- and NIH-supported research that addresses the complex and multi-faceted nature of minority health and health disparities, including research that spans different domains of influence (Biological, Behavioral, Physical/Built Environment, Socio-cultural Environment, Health Care System) as well as different levels of influence (Individual, Interpersonal, Community, Societal) within those domains." The NIMHD research framework and the Social Determinants of Health are used by the National Institute on Minority Health and the Healthy People 2030 to establish a research agenda and roadmap for researchers and federal agencies to reduce health disparities.

Domains of Influence (Over the Lifecourse)	Levels of Influence*			
	Individual	Interpersonal	Community	Societal
Biological	Biological Vulnerability and Mechanisms	Caregiver-Child Interaction Family Microbiome	Community Illness Exposure Herd Immunity	Sanitation Immunization Pathogen Exposure
Behavioral	Health Behaviors Coping Strategies	Family Functioning School/Work Functioning	Community Functioning	Policies and Laws
Physical/Built Environment	Personal Environment	Household Environment School/Work Environment	Community Environment Community Resources	Societal Structure
Sociocultural Environment	Sociodemographics Limited English Cultural Identity Response to Discrimination	Social Networks Family/Peer Norms Interpersonal Discrimination	Community Norms Local Structural Discrimination	Social Norms Societal Structural Discrimination
Health Care System	Insurance Coverage Health Literacy Treatment Preferences	Patient-Clinician Relationship Medical Decision-Making	Availability of Services Safety Net Services	Quality of Care Health Care Policies
Health Outcomes	Individual Health	Family/ Organizational Health	Community Health	Population Health

Figure 13.2 The National Institute on Minority Health and Health Disparities Research Framework

Source: National Institute on Minority Health (2018).

Now we introduce the Political Determinants of Health theoretical perspective, which pushes back on governmental interventions by emphasizing the role that federal and state governments, along with researchers and health specialists play in maintaining the system of inequality. We call attention here to Daniel E. Dawes' (2020) book titled *The Political Determinants of Health*. The book's opening chapter "The Allegory of the Orchard: The Political Determinants of Health Inequities" is a fascinating allegory that describes a farmer who sought to acquire land to establish an orchard. He located a plot of land that, though not ideal, would serve his purpose. The farmer discovers a massive, beautiful tree that was already bearing a significant amount of fruit. He did not want the tree there, for it would distract from the success-ful orchard that he will develop, and opted for relocating the tree to where it cannot be seen. The farmer subsequently acquires six seeds that he will plant to initiate the successful endeavor that he envisions. The plot has three sections: a section with rocky terrain, the second with poor soil, and the third with nutrient-rich soil. The farmer very quickly favors the two seeds that he planted in the latter sections, which features high quality soil and related endowments that are sure to produce trees that will thrive and abundantly bear fruit. He largely or completely ignores the seeds that he planted in the other two locations. The outcome is that at the end it is the two seeds in the section with the nutrient-rich soil that will eventually survive and thrive.

The author, then, lets us in on the moral and the lesson of the story. Dawes (2020) reveals that:

> The overarching moral of these stories warns us to take heed lest we follow the path of negligent farmers who were ultimately left with far less yield than they could have achieved had they taken proper care of their entire crops from beginning to end. The stories drive home the idea that improper planning, resources, care, and attention result in unfavorable outcomes, while proper care at the right time and in the right amount will encourage an endeavor to thrive.
>
> The preceding parable is an allegory for the history of health inequities in the United States. It underscores the impact that political forces have on an individual's and the larger society's health and well-being: the political determinants of health. It highlights how inequities, when left unchecked, can sap a nation's strength. The allegory also reminds us to be cautious about the judgments we make about people because their health status is often based on their limited choices and opportuni-ties. After all, regardless of our status, we all strive to improve our health and achieve health equity. (p. 18)

There are plenty of symbols in the allegory. The farmer represents the government:

> . . . which at every stage of our life, whether through policy or legal actions or inac-tions, through a complex web of political structures and processes that have been created at the international, federal, state, and local levels, impacts our health status. The government either exacerbates health inequities or advances health equity for individuals or communities across the country. Like the farmer who failed to recognize the value and potential of all of his seeds and who failed to acknowledge or understand how his actions resulted in the loss of his crop, the government has

oftentimes failed to take ownership for its actions or has been complicit with others, resulting in the outcomes we see today. (Dawes 2020, p. 19)

This section provides an overview of theoretical perspectives that have been used to address issues of health disparities, drawing on the social determinants of health care and introducing biological dimensions and the various levels at which social determinants impact health outcomes as well as the emphasis on the political determinants of health.

The Latina/o Paradox Before the Pandemic

It is now half a century since demographers first observed an unexpected pattern involving Latina/os exhibiting low levels of mortality despite their low socioeconomic status and related factors that would suggest that the group would have elevated levels of mortality. Teller and Clyburn (1974) were the first to observe this unexpected finding in their study of Latina/o infant mortality in Texas. A dozen years later Markides and Coreil (1986) observed the same phenomenon in their study of Latina/o infant mortality in the Southwest. These researchers referred to this unexpected pattern as an "epidemiological paradox." Markides and Coreil (1986; see also Hummer et al. 2007) elaborated on the paradox:

> Despite methodological limitations of much of the research, it can be concluded with some certainty that the health status of Hispanics in the Southwest is much more similar to the health status of other Whites than that of Blacks although socioeconomically, the status of Hispanics is closer to that of Blacks. This observation is supported by evidence of such key health indicators as infant mortality, life-expectancy, mortality from cardiovascular diseases, mortality from major types of cancer, and measures of functional health. On other health indicators, such as diabetes and infectious and parasitic diseases, Hispanics appear to be clearly disadvantaged relative to other Whites. (253)

The favorable mortality outcome of Latina/os is pretty well established over the last three decades in the areas of infant mortality, general mortality, and low birth weight (Crimmins et al 2007; Gorman et al. 2010; Hummer et al. 2007; Markides and Eschbach 2005, 2011; Palloni and Arias 2004; Turra and Elo 2008; Turra and Goldman 2007). The label of "epidemiological paradox" has been commonly used interchangeably with other terms such as "Hispanic paradox," "Latina/o paradox," and "Mexican immigrant paradox." Mexican immigrants, in particular, are associated with the paradoxical patterns involving unexpectedly favorable mortality among this group. Unfortunately, the data used to conduct the analysis below do not have specific mortality data for Latina/o subgroups.

The Latina/o paradox with respect to death rates is prevalent across both sexes and age groups. Table 13.1 shows the death rates of Latina/os, whites, and Blacks in 2021 broken down by sex and age. With the exception of the under-1 age category for males and the under-1 and 1–4 categories, Latina/os had the lowest death rates, while Blacks had the highest prevalence of death. The lowest death rates among

Table 13.1 Death Rates for Selected Race/Ethnic Groups by Age and Sex, 2022

| | Deaths Per 100,000 Population | | | | | |
| | Female | | | Male | | |
Age	Latina	Black	White	Latino	Black	White
Under 1	440.6	1,023.00	433.4	502.9	1,231.70	495.9
1–4	20.0	47.0	19.1	20.6	53.0	24.5
5–14	11.3	20.9	10.8	13.7	31.7	14.7
15–24	42.6	83.5	45.3	119.3	257.9	104.7
25–34	79.3	178.1	108.5	227.1	416.3	236.9
35–44	140.4	332.5	206.8	324.2	608.6	365.1
45–54	281.5	627.6	401.9	579.3	1,050.9	655.3
55–64	654.9	1,302.4	839.1	1,213.4	2,118.4	1,361.5
65–74	1475.0	2,459.4	1,697.7	2,374.1	3,935.6	2,587.2
75–84	3683.0	5,201.3	4,511.3	5,208.9	7,251.9	6,168.8
85 and over	11,396.2	13,780.5	15,883.6	12,927.3	15,908.6	18,352.7
Age-Adjusted Rate	582.7	917.2	751.4	884.9	1,374.0	1,055.6

Source: Centers for Disease Control and Prevention (2024a).

Latina/os at all but the young age groups represent the Latina/o paradox. Moreover, the age-adjusted death rates, which considers all the age groups and adjusts for age differences across all three groups, again show that, overall, Latina/os had the lowest death rates, followed by whites, with Blacks having the highest death rate. Indeed, comparison of the Latina/o and white age-adjusted death rates shows that Latinas died at a rate that was 22 percent lower than that of white females, while Latinos died at a rate that was 16 percent lower than that of white males. Note that the Latina/o mortality advantage over whites was weakened during the pandemic. In 2019, before the pandemic, Latinas died at a rate that was 31 percent lower compared to white females and Latinos 27 percent lower relative to white males.

Based on the favorable death rates of Latina/os compared to whites and Blacks, Latina/o babies born in 2021 were expected to outlive their white and Black counterparts. Latina baby girls born that year were expected to live an average of 81.1 years (1.6 years more than white baby girls and 6.1 years more than Black baby girls) (Figure 13.3). Latino baby boys born in 2021 were estimated to live an average of 74.6 years (0.6 years more than white baby boys and 7 years more than Black baby boys). Again, these patterns are consistent with the Latina/o paradox. However, during the COVID-19 pandemic, the Latina/o life-expectancy advantage narrowed significantly due to a major drop in Latina's life expectancy of 3.3 years (compared to a drop of 1.8 years for white females) and a decline of 4.5 years for Latino males (compared to a dip of 2.3 years for white males).

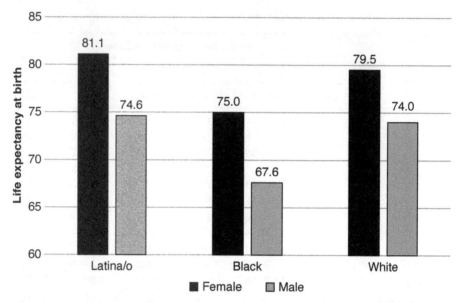

Figure 13.3 Life Expectancy at Birth for Selected Race/Ethnic Groups by Sex, 2021
Source: Data from Arias et al. (2023).

Paradox across Causes of Death?

We also can assess whether the Latina/o paradox is valid across some of the most common causes of death. We draw here on the work of Xu et al. (2021) concerning mortality, including causes of death in 2019. Table 13.2 shows the age-adjusted death rates for Latina/os, Blacks, and whites across the fifteen leading causes of death. For almost three-fourths (11) of the fifteen causes of death, whites had higher age-adjusted death rates than did Latina/os. In particular, whites had higher levels of death in the three most common causes of death (diseases of the heart, cerebrovascular diseases, and malignant neoplasms) – 75 percent of white deaths in 2019 were due to these three diseases compared to 67 percent of Latina/o deaths (Xu et al. 2021). In contrast, Latina/os had higher age-adjusted death rates than whites in four diseases (for both males and females: chronic liver disease and cirrhosis, diabetes mellitus, and essential hypertension and hypertensive renal disease; and for females: nephritis, nephrotic syndrome and nephrosis). Overall, Blacks had the highest age-adjusted death rates compared to Latina/os and whites for ten of the fifteen leading causes of death among males and nine of the fifteen among females. In general, there is some support for the generalizability of the Latina/o paradox for causes of death, especially with respect to the three leading causes of death.

Table 13.2 Age-Adjusted Death Rates for Fifteen Leading Causes of Death by Race/Ethnic Groups by Sex, 2019

| | Deaths Per 100,000 Population | | | | | |
| | Female | | | Male | | |
Cause of death	Latina	Black	White	Latino	Black	White
Diseases of heart	86.4	165.0	129.6	141.9	267.5	210.7
Malignant neoplasms	91.4	148.6	131.2	125.7	212.2	179.2
Accidents	18.0	29.4	36.4	52.6	78.8	74.3
Chronic lower respiratory diseases	13.4	24.2	41.8	19.8	37.2	46.3
Cerebrovascular diseases	30.3	48.8	35.2	35.3	58.1	35.7
Alzheimer disease	28.3	30.0	35.7	20.5	22.8	25.1
Diabetes mellitus	21.0	32.6	14.3	31.2	47.1	24.9
Nephritis, nephrotic syndrome and nephrosis	10.1	21.8	9.5	14.0	30.6	14.0
Influenza and pneumonia	8.3	11.9	11.0	12.1	17.0	14.4
Intentional self-harm	3.0	2.9	7.7	11.6	12.5	28.0
Chronic liver disease and cirrhosis	8.8	5.5	8.7	20.8	10.4	15.4
Septicemia	5.8	14.4	8.5	8.1	18.8	10.5
Essential hypertension and hypertensive renal disease	7.6	15.5	7.4	9.2	19.4	8.4
Parkinson disease	4.7	3.1	6.4	9.1	7.7	14.4
Pneumonitis due to solids and liquids	2.3	4.0	3.7	4.4	7.2	6.7

Source: Data from Xu et al. (2021).

Explanations for the Latina/o Paradox

What accounts for the Latina/o paradox? There have been several explanations proposed to resolve the paradox. First, it has been suggested that the paradox is due, at least in part, to the selectivity of immigrants. For long it has been established that immigrants are distinct in a variety of ways from others in the countries from which they originate, one of these being related to health. Immigrants who come to the US tend to be healthier than people who do not migrate from the country of origin (Jasso et al. 2004; Landale et al. 1999; Markides and Eschbach 2005; Palloni and Arias 2004; Palloni and Morenoff 2001). As such, given that Latina/o immigrants are a healthy lot, it is reasonable that they will have favorable health and mortality outcomes in the US. The migration selectivity explanation extends to Latina immigrant women who tend to have healthier infants than other women (Hummer et al. 2007; Montoya-Williams et al. 2021).

Second, it is proposed that the elements of the culture of Latina/o immigrants protect them in a variety of ways. Cultural dimensions that produce favorable outcomes include a high degree of importance for the family (familism), participation in supportive social networks, diets which are rich in vegetables, grains, and legumes, and relatively low levels of the use of alcohol, tobacco, and drugs (Abraído-Lanza et al. 2005; Bacio and Ray 2016; Liu et al. 2021; Pérez et al. 2001; Reichman et al. 2008;

Zambrana et al. 1997). The importance of culture in favorable health outcomes is evidenced by worsening health and mortality as Latina/o immigrants live longer in the US and acculturate (Bacong and Menjívar 2021; Horevitz and Organista 2013; Kaestner et al. 2009; Kimbro et al. 2012). The association between culture and health is also evident among Latina immigrant mothers (de la Rosa 2002; de la Torre and Rush 1987; Sussner et al. 2008). Furthermore, there is a growing body of literature showing that Latina/os who live in Latina/o areas with higher shares of immigrants tend to be healthier than those living in areas with fewer Latina/o immigrants (Aranda et al. 2011; Eschbach et al. 2005; McFarland and Smith 2011; Osypuk et al. 2010; Patel et al. 2003).

Third, it has also been posited that the Latina/o paradox represents a statistical artifact rather than reality, or at least is not as strong as it appears. The underlying problem, according to this argument, is that there is inconsistency between the numerator and denominator used to generate death rates, due to problems associated with age misreporting, inconsistencies in reporting of race and ethnicity, and return migration (Lariscy 2011; Liao et al. 1998). For example, it has been suggested that there tends to be the misreporting of age, with the result being more people in the older ages (the denominator in the computation of death rates), resulting in artificially lower death rates. In addition, death records may have inaccurate information regarding the race and ethnicity of deceased individuals, especially if persons other than family members fill out this information in death certificates (e.g. funeral directors, physicians, etc.), leading to the populations comprising the numerator and denominator in the calculation of death rates being different. This problem may have been especially acute during the early stages of the COVID-19 pandemic, when people were dying in hospitals without family members to provide details on their characteristics. Furthermore, return migration is problematic when immigrants living in the US become ill and return to their country of origin – if such persons die in the home country, their death is recorded there rather than in the US, resulting in an artificially lower death rate in the US. The phenomenon associated with the return of ill individuals to the home country to die is referred to as the "salmon bias," a term coined by Pablos-Mendez (1994). In general, there is a growing volume of research suggesting that the Mexican paradox is authentic rather than due to a statistical artifact (Elo et al. 2004; Hummer et al. 2007).

While the Latina/o paradox suggests that Latina/os tend to die at lower rates and live longer lives than whites and other groups, there is also a significant amount of information indicating that Latina/os suffer significantly from an array of health problems and from the lack of adequate health care.

The Other Side of the Latina/o Paradox

Evidence from the Latina/o paradox suggests that Latina/os are overachievers in the area of mortality. Latina/os tend to fare much better than expected with respect to avoiding death and actually living long lives. However, Latina/os are not as fortunate in other areas, such as elevated risks of dying from particular diseases, disability, risky behavior and lifestyles, and the lack of adequate health care. We will now examine each of these areas.

Prominent Causes of Death for Latina/os

As noted earlier, based on the fifteen leading causes of deaths, Latina/os fare better than whites on many of these causes of deaths including some diseases that take a heavy toll on people – heart disease, cancer, and cerebrovascular disease. There were only a handful of diseases in which Latina/os fare comparatively worse than whites. We now examine all specific causes of death drawing on data from Xu et al. (2021) for 2019. Again, as was the case with the fifteen leading causes of death, Latina/os have higher death rates than whites for a small number of causes of death drawn from all specific causes of death. Table 13.3 shows thirteen causes of deaths for which Latina/os have age-adjusted death rates of 1.0 or higher (to ensure that causes of deaths with very small number of deaths are not excluded from the analysis) and for which Latina/os have higher age-adjusted death rates than whites.

Of the thirteen causes of death, the six causes of deaths with the highest death rates among Latina/os include diabetes mellitus (25.6 deaths per 100,000 people); chronic liver disease and cirrhosis (14.6); nephritis, nephrotic syndrome and nephrosis (11.8); malignant neoplasms of liver and intrahepatic bile ducts (8.9);

Table 13.3 Causes of Death For Which Latina/os Have Higher Age-Adjusted Death Rates Compared to Whites, 2019[a]

Cause of Death	Latina/o	White	Ratio of Latina/o Death Rate to White Death Rate
Viral hepatitis	1.3	1.0	1.30
Human immunodeficiency virus (HIV) disease	1.4	0.6	2.33
Malignant neoplasm of stomach	4.6	2.1	2.19
Malignant neoplasms of liver and intrahepatic bile ducts	8.9	5.9	1.51
Malignant neoplasm of cervix uteri	1.2	1.0	1.20
Diabetes mellitus	25.6	19.1	1.34
Essential hypertension and hypertensive renal disease	8.3	8.0	1.04
Chronic liver disease and cirrhosis	14.6	11.9	1.23
Alcoholic liver disease	7.7	6.8	1.13
Nephritis, nephrotic syndrome and nephrosis	11.8	11.4	1.04
Certain conditions originating in the perinatal period	3.2	2.8	1.14
Assault (homicide)	5.0	2.7	1.85
Assault (homicide) by discharge of firearms	3.6	1.7	2.12

[a] The causes of death included here are those where the Latina/o adjusted death rate is 1.0 or higher and Latina/os have higher death rates than whites.

Source: Data from Xu et al. (2021).

essential hypertension and hypertensive renal disease (8.3); and alcoholic liver disease (7.7).

The seven causes of death with the greatest relative risk of dying for Latina/os compared to whites (measured by the ratio of the Latina/o-to-white death rates) are human immunodeficiency (HIV) disease (ratio of 2.33 based on the Latina/o death rate divided by the white death rate, indicating that Latina/os died at a rate that was 2.33 higher than that of whites); malignant neoplasms of stomach (2.19); assault (homicide) by discharge of firearms (2.12); assault (homicide) (1.85); malignant neoplasms of liver and intrahepatic bile ducts (1.51); diabetes mellitus (1.34); and viral hepatitis (1.30).

There are certain commonalities associated with the thirteen causes of death. The causes of death are largely associated with lifestyle and risky behavior. For example, two causes are directly related to liver problems, which are commonly associated with heavy alcohol use. Other causes of death are associated with smoking (stomach cancer), unprotected sex, multiple sexual partners (viral hepatitis, HIV diseases, and cervix cancer), and violence (both causes of death associated with homicide). Still other causes of death – primarily hypertension-related disease and type-2 diabetes) are associated with the lack of healthy diets featuring fruits and vegetables, obesity, and lack of exercise. So, it appears that a change in lifestyle behaviors and modifications in risky behavior could result in healthier Latina/os and even lower death rates.

Risky Behavior among Adolescents

Adolescents are at risk for engaging in an array of behaviors that are risky to their health and well-being. The degree to which they are exposed to such possibilities varies greatly and is influenced by many factors, including the schools they attend, the neighborhoods in which they live, the peers with whom they associate, as well as the level of guidance from their parents. The data used here are from the *Youth Risk Behavior Survey Explorer*, with the data pulled for the analysis below based on 2019 (Center for Disease Control and Prevention 2020).

Table 13.4 presents information on the percentage of students in grades 9 to 12 who engage in a series of health risk behaviors. Of the nine behaviors in the table, Latina/o youth are most likely to have engaged in sexual intercourse (females, 40.3%; males, 43.6%), had sex the last time without the use of a condom (females, 49.1; males, 37.7%), were in a physical fight (females, 17.8%; males, 27.7%), and rode in a vehicle with someone who has been drinking alcohol (females, 22.0%; males, 19.4%). In addition, 23 percent of Latina adolescent girls have seriously considered suicide in the past year, while 17 percent of Latino adolescent boys have carried a weapon in the last thirty days. Compared to white and Black youngsters, Latina/o females and males are the most likely to have ridden in a vehicle with a driver who had been drinking alcohol, while Latina adolescent girls are the most likely to have ever had sexual intercourse and to be physically forced to have sexual intercourse. Note in particular the gender differences among Latina/os. While Latino males are more likely than Latina females to have been in a fight and carried a weapon, Latina

Table 13.4 Percentage of Students in 9th to 12th Grade Engaging in Selected Health Risk Behaviors by Race/Ethnic Group and Sex, 2019

Selected Health Risk Behaviors	Female			Male		
	Latina	Black	White	Latino	Black	White
Seriously considered attempting suicide (last 12 months)	22.7	23.7	24.3	11.4	10.7	13.8
In a physical fight (last 30 days)	17.8	22.7	12.7	27.7	36.9	26.6
Carried a weapon (last 30 days)	6.6	5.3	7.1	17.1	13.0	22.8
Rarely or never wore a seatbelt	7.2	10.7	3.5	7.7	12.2	6.0
Rode with a driver who had been drinking alcohol (last 30 days)	22.0	13.8	16.0	19.4	17.4	14.1
Ever had sexual intercourse	40.3	34.0	39.2	43.6	50.1	36.7
Physically forced to have sexual intercourse	11.8	9.9	11.5	4.0	4.8	2.8
Did not use a condom during last sexual intercourse	49.1	55.5	48.4	37.7	48.2	39.1
Did not use any method to prevent pregnancy during last sexual intercourse	15.6	24.1	10.1	10.6	21.0	6.3

Source: Youth Risk Behavior Surveillance (YRBS) Explorer (Centers for Disease Control 2020).

females are more likely than Latino males to have been forced to have sexual intercourse and not to have used a condom or any method of contraception during the last sexual encounter. Obviously, the risky behaviors examined here are associated with a litany of serious consequences including injury, arrest, pregnancy, the contracting of a sexually transmitted disease, and death, all situations that can severely alter the life course of teenagers.

Obesity

Many of the health problems that Americans face are associated with the increasing prevalence of obesity (Monteverde et al. 2010). Obesity is associated with unhealthy diets lacking fruits and vegetables, lack of exercise, and sedentary lifestyles. The poor often have ready access to inexpensive processed unhealthy food and lack access to nutritious foods. The rise of obesity has been especially apparent among Latina/os, especially children. The National Hispanic Caucus of State Legislators (2010) has called the obesity of Latina/os (Hispanics) a "national crisis." The National Hispanic Caucus of State Legislators (2010) asserts that "For Latina/o communities, the obesity epidemic has reached crisis, with many states and communities reporting Latina/o obesity at staggering proportions, with Latina/o children becoming obese earlier in their lives" (p. 8). The National Hispanic Caucus of State Legislators goes on to warn

Table 13.5 Percentage of Children and Adolescents Who are Obese by Race/Ethnic Group and Sex, 2015–2018

	Female			Male		
Age Group	Latina	Black	White	Latino	Black	White
2 to 5 years	16.3	12.6	12.4	22.3	12.4	12.4
6 to 11 years	25.6	27.2	12.6	27.5	18.3	18.3
12 to 19 years	25.1	33.6	16.0	31.1	23.0	15.8

Source: National Center for Health Statistics (2021).

that "Increasing rates of obesity in Latina/o children suggest that, unless policymakers take action, the subsequent generation will be less healthy as it ages, affecting among other things, health care costs" (p. 9).

A significant share of the Latina/o population is considered obese as defined by a body mass index (BMI) of 30 or higher. The latest national data to examine child obesity are available from *Health, United States, 2019* (National Center for Health Statistics 2021). We examine these data to assess the prevalence of obesity among Latina/o, Black, and white children by age group and sex for the 2015–2018 period. Overall, Latino boys have the highest obesity levels compared to white and Black youngsters with more than one-fifth of Latino boys two to five years of age being obese, more than one-fourth at ages six to eleven, and nearly one-third at ages twelve to nineteen (Table 13.5). Latina girls have the highest levels of obesity at ages two to five – over Black and white girls – but Black girls are the most likely to be obese in the 6–11 and 12–19 age groups. White children are the least likely to be obese. These trends are disturbing for Latina/o and Black children and put at risk the mortality advantages of Latina/os that we observed above.

Disability

While Latina/os have an advantage over whites and Blacks in the area of mortality, the advantage is somewhat different in the area of disability. We present data here for Latina/os, whites, and Blacks of the percentage of persons across age and sex groups who have any disability. The list of possible disabilities includes cognitive difficulty, ambulatory difficulty, independent living difficulty, self-care difficulty, vision difficulty, and hearing difficulty. Overall, with very few exceptions, Blacks have the highest levels of disability throughout the age spectrum (Figure 13.4). There are noticeable differences between Latina/os and whites, however. In particular, Latinas have lower levels of disabilities than white females aged between 15 and 49 among females and Latino males have lower levels than white males between ages 15 and 59. Whites have lower disability rates than Latinos below age 15 and above age 49 for females, and above age 59 for males. Overall, then, there is a disability crossover between Latina/os and whites, with whites actually having the lower disability rates at the older ages compared with Latina/os.

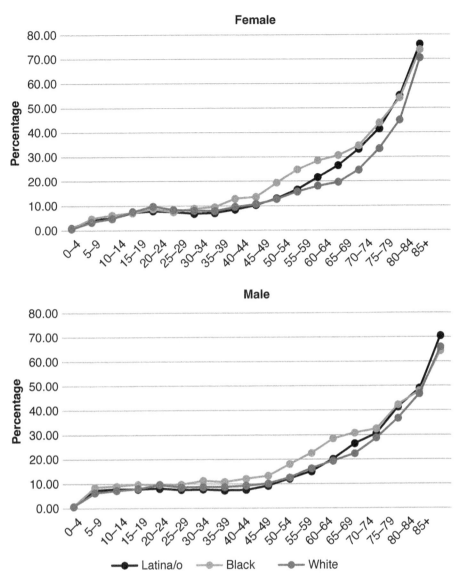

Figure 13.4 Percentage of Persons with a Disability for Selected Race/Ethnic Groups by Age and Sex, 2022

Source: Data from 2019 American Community Survey 1-Year Estimates Public-Use File (Ruggles et al. 2024).

The disability crossover is likely driven by the selectivity of Latina/o immigrants. As we learned earlier, Latina/o immigrants tend to be positively selected from the countries from where they originate, with people with disabilities being less likely to immigrate to the US. However, the situation is a bit more complicated because, in order to get the more complete panorama of the disability crossover, we need to examine whites, foreign-born Latina/os, and native-born Latina/os. For both males and females, we would hypothesize that the selectivity of Latina/o immigrants is clear, as they have lower disability rates compared to both whites and native-born Latina/os, but that eventually in the older ages, foreign-born Latina/os would have the highest levels of disability. Why would Latina/o immigrants suddenly have higher rates of disability as they reach the older ages? Latina/o immigrants are more likely than other groups to work in physically demanding jobs, which take a toll on the body. Thus, it is likely that by the time Latina/o immigrants reach the older ages, the wear-and-tear impact on the body becomes more debilitating. Because whites, in particular, tend to be employed in more prestigious occupations, their bodies are not subjected to physical demands on the job as much as Latina/os. The data in Figure 13.5 show that generally native-born Latina/os have the highest disability rates across much of the age spectrum. When we compare foreign-born Latina/os and whites, the hypothesis outlined above is supported. Among females, foreign-born Latinas have the lowest disability rates compared to native-born Latinas and white women, but at the 70–74 age category their rates of disability become higher than those of white women. However, it seems that Latino immigrant men are able to delay the point at which their disability rates become higher than those of whites. Foreign-born Latino men continue to have the lowest disability rates, spanning from ages 5 to 84. Thus, it seems that Latino immigrant men continue to fare better than white men, with their bodies holding up to the stress caused by the physically demanding jobs that they perform. At least in part, the lowest levels of disability among Latino immigrant men into their older ages is likely associated with their continued participation in the workforce into their older years. Indeed, they have the highest percentage of persons working among men 70–74, with 26 percent working, compared to 21 percent of whites and 17 percent of native-born Latino men. Starting at 75–79, white men have the highest work rates.

It is clear, then, that while Latina/os live longer than whites and Blacks, they do so with a greater prevalence of disability, especially relative to whites. Given the high incidence of diabetes among Latina/os (and Blacks as well), Latina/os are at risk of worsening health conditions, with the onset of a configuration of diabetes, obesity, and disability. People who are obese are at greater risk of diabetes and people who have diabetes are at risk of becoming physically disabled, with increasing probabilities of loss of sight and limbs. Due to the limited resources of Latina/os and the undocumented status of a noticeable share of the population, they tend to have health care challenges.

Health Care Needs

Latina/os have significant health care needs compared to other race/ethnic groups. For example, one-fourth of Latina/o adults do not have a usual source of health care, a rate that is 1.7 times as high as that of whites and about 1.4 times higher than that of Blacks (Table 13.6). Similarly, Latina/o and Black children are less likely than white children to have a usual source of health care. In fact, Latina/o and Black children are also more likely than white children to have gone the past year without a health care

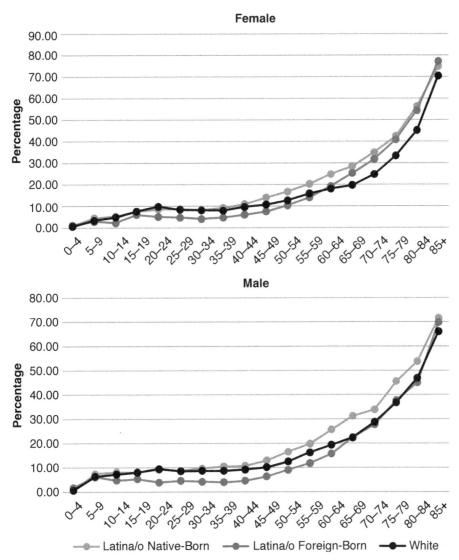

Figure 13.5 Percentage of Persons with a Disability among Native-Born Latina/os, Foreign-Born Latina/os, and Whites by Age and Sex, 2022

Source: Data from 2019 American Community Survey 1-Year Estimates Public-Use File (Ruggles et al. 2024).

visit. Latina/o children from six to seventeen years of age fare particularly poorly on these two health-dimensions.

The high prevalence of health care needs of Latina/os reflects the high rate of lack of health care insurance, the undocumented status of a considerable share of Latina/os, as well as the types of jobs that many Latina/os hold, which are low-paying and without significant benefits (see Chapter 10).

Table 13.6 Percentage of Persons by Health Care Needs by Race/Ethnic Group and Age, 2015–2016

Age Group	Percentage Without Usual Source of Health Care			Percentage Without a Health Care Visit in Past Year		
	Latina/o	Black	White	Latina/o	Black	White
Under 6 years	4.6	4.7	2.4	6.0	8.0	4.4
6 to 17 years	7.5	5.7	3.9	13.1	11.8	8.8
18 to 64 years	24.7	17.3	14.3	—	—	—

Source: National Center for Health Statistics (2017).

Lack of Health Care Insurance: A Major Impediment to Meeting Health Care Needs

Latina/os stand out among racial and ethnic groups with respect to the lack of health care insurance coverage (Sáenz 2010a), which makes their low mortality and high longevity particularly surprising. Overall, 17 percent of Latina/os lacked health insurance in 2022 compared to 5 percent of whites and 10 percent of Blacks. Across age groups, Latina/os are much more likely than whites and Blacks not to have insurance in 2022 (Figure 13.6). Approximately 1 in 12 Latina/o children (0 to 18 years of age), nearly one in four Latina/o adults 19 to 64 years of age, and one in 27 Latina/os 65

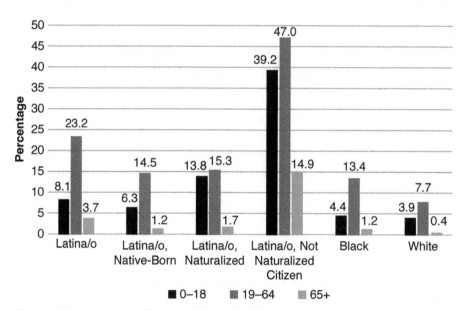

Figure 13.6 Percentage of Persons Without Health Insurance by Race/Ethnic Group, Age, and Place of Birth/Citizenship Status, 2022

Source: Data from 2019 American Community Survey 1-Year Estimates Public-Use File (Ruggles et al. 2024).

years and older lack insurance cover. Latina/o children are 2.1 times more likely than white children not to have insurance, with Latina/o adults aged nineteen to 64 being three times more likely than white adults of these ages to not have insurance. While health insurance coverage is pretty much universal for white and Black elderly, this not the case for Latina/o elderly, with 3.7 percent lacking insurance.

The absence of health care insurance coverage among Latina/os, however, varies by nativity and citizenship status. The lack of insurance is lowest among Latina/os born in the US, followed by Latina/o immigrants who are naturalized citizens with Latina/o immigrants who are not naturalized citizens being the most likely not to have insurance, with 44 percent not having this health security (Figure 13.6). Across the three age groups, a high percentage of Latina/os who are not US citizens do not have insurance cover: approximately two-fifths of children, nearly half of adults 19 to 64 years of age, and about one in seven persons 65 and older. Approximately 10 percent of Latina/s who are US citizens and 12 percent of those who are naturalized citizens do not have insurance cover.

As we have seen in earlier chapters, there are noticeable variations in the socio-economic standing of the different groups that constitute the overall Latina/o population. Overall, native-born Spaniards (5.7%), Colombians (5.9%), and Other South Americans (6.2%) are the least likely not to have insurance coverage. On the other hand, we call attention here (see Table 13.7) to the plight of foreign-born Guatemalans, Hondurans, Mexicans, and Salvadorans who have the highest percentages of persons going without health insurance. This is particularly the case among Hondurans (65% of children, 65% of persons 19–64, and 26% of persons 65 and older lack insurance) and Guatemalans (58% of children, 64% of persons 19–64, and 25% of persons 65 and older lack insurance). These individuals live in very precarious conditions, given what a serious health setback to a family member can mean for the entire family.

It has been suggested that the lack of health insurance and the prohibitive costs of health care in the US prompt Latina/o, especially Mexicans, to travel to Mexico for affordable health care, involving visits to doctors, dentists, as well as to obtain medicine (Bastida et al. 2008; Horton and Cole 2011). Research has shown that such

Table 13.7 Selected Foreign-Born Latina/o Groups with the Highest Percentages of Persons Lacking Health Insurance by Age, 2022

Selected Latina/o Group	Not US Citizen		
	0–18	19–64	65+
Guatemalan	58.0	63.5	25.1
Honduran	65.3	65.0	25.5
Mexican	37.8	49.2	14.7
Salvadoran	38.9	48.7	19.2

Source: Data from 2022 American Community Survey 1-Year Estimates Public-Use File (Ruggles et al. 2024).

travel is not restricted to people living along the US–Mexico border but also among those living further away from the border (Wallace et al. 2009). Moreover, it has been observed that even Latina/os with health insurance travel to Mexico for health care (Seid et al. 2003; Wallace et al. 2009), while still others even forego attaining insurance in the US in favor of the less expensive and more flexible health care system in Mexico (Brown 2008).

Given the broad segment of the Latina/o population that depends on travel to Mexico for health services, there are elements beyond costs and the lack of health insurance that motivate Latina/os to opt for the attainment of health care in Mexico. Horton and Cole (2011) observe a list of reasons that Latina/os give most often for their preference for travel to Mexico in search of health services. These include the low cost of health care, speed at which they are attended, the potency of medication in Mexico rather than the concern for extended diagnosis and referrals, costlier treatment, and impersonal form of health care delivery in the US (Horton and Cole 2011). Yet, it is important to understand that many Latina/os may find it costly to travel into Mexico and, of course, the surging violence, especially along the Mexican side of the border, makes it difficult for people to make the trip. Moreover, the militarization of the border serves to trap unauthorized immigrants in their home region and makes it practically impossible to cross into Mexico because of the realistic fear of not being able to reenter the US.

The Affordable Care Act, also known as Obamacare, promised to make affordable health care insurance available widely, although people who are undocumented are not eligible. While it is difficult to assess all aspects of the program to determine whether or not it has been successful, it did help in reducing the uninsured in the country (Williams and Schaffer 2021). We examine changes in the number of people lacking health insurance between 2011 and 2021 using data from the American Community Survey. Overall, in the US the percentage of persons without insurance coverage dropped from 15.1 percent in 2021 to 8.6 percent in 2021, a drop of 43 percent; for the Latina/o population, the percentage of persons lacking insurance coverage fell from 29.8 percent to 17.7 percent, a drop of 41 percent. Unfortunately, to date, ten states (Alabama, Florida, Georgia, Kansas, Mississippi, South Carolina, Tennessee, Texas, Wisconsin, and Wyoming) have not adopted Medicaid expansion, with another state (North Carolina) adopting it but not implementing it (Lopes et al. 2024). Texas, in particular, stands out given that Latina/os represent the largest racial/ethnic group in the state and the state annually has among the highest percentages of people without health insurance. Focusing only on Latina/os who are US citizens, Texas has the highest percentage of Latina/os not insured (21.2%), followed by Wyoming (20.5%), and Mississippi (19.5%). When we focus on Latinos who are US citizens and who are nineteen to 64 years of age, Texas has the second highest percentage of persons without insurance coverage at 28.9 percent, just behind Mississippi with 29.7 percent. The expansion of Medicaid would certainly increase the health-insurance coverage in the state without costing a penny; in fact, Texas taxpayers are paying their tax dollars to fund the insurance of residents of the forty states (including the District of Columbia) that have expanded Medicaid.

Issues Related to the Future of Latina/o Health and Health Care

There are several important trends regarding Latina/o health and health care that we need to recognize, due to their significance in shaping the future patterns of health well-being among Latina/os in the near future. We highlight here trends regarding the falling Mexican immigration and possible reduction in the Latina/o mortality advantage; the impact of the COVID-19 pandemic on Latina/o life expectancy; and obesity. These trends have important implications for how Latina/os will fare in terms of their health in the future.

Reduced Mexican Immigration and a Possible Decline in Latina/o Mortality Advantage?

As we have seen in this chapter, the favorable aspects of Latina/o health and health care are associated in one form or another with immigration. For example, favorable death rates, life expectancy, and disability levels reflect the selectivity of Latina/o immigrants on the basis of health status. Yet, immigration from Mexico to the US has plummeted over the last fifteen years or so. The volume of immigration from Mexico to the US fell 53 percent between the 2003–2007 period and the 2013–2017 period (Sáenz 2019) and the number of persons born in Mexico and living in the US fell by one million between 2010 and 2021, a drop of 9 percent (Rosenbloom and Batalova 2022). If the reduction of Mexican immigration persists over time, there will be fewer immigrants who come with their salubrious conditions, diets, and lifestyles. The reduced number of Mexican immigrants would represent a declining share of the overall Latina/o population, with the result being, perhaps, worsening death rates, longevity, and disability levels in the overall Latina/o population.

While the impact of declining immigration from Mexico may take a considerable amount of time before seeing adult mortality rise, preliminary data suggest that the declining immigration may be associated with Latina/o babies now having higher infant mortality rates (number of babies dying before reaching their first birthday per 1,000 live births) than white babies. Figure 13.7 shows the infant mortality rates of Latina/o and white infants between 1995 and 2021 and Figure 13.8 shows the percentage of Latina women giving birth in the past year, who are foreign-born, between 2000 and 2021 (these data were not available before 2000). First, while the infant mortality rates of Latina/o and white infants has been fairly close between 1995 and 2021, a major shift occurred. Over the period between 1995 and 2007, Latina/o babies had lower infant mortality rates than white babies in twelve of the thirteen years; between 2008 and 2021, white babies had lower infant mortality rates than Latina/o babies in twelve of the fourteen years. Second, the percentage of Latina women who have given birth in the past year who are foreign-born has declined significantly between 2000 and 2021. While foreign-born women accounted for more than half of Latina women giving birth in the past year between 2000 and 2009, they made up less than half of women giving birth between 2010 and 2021. In fact, the percentage share of immigrants among Latina women giving birth dropped from a peak of 57.4 percent

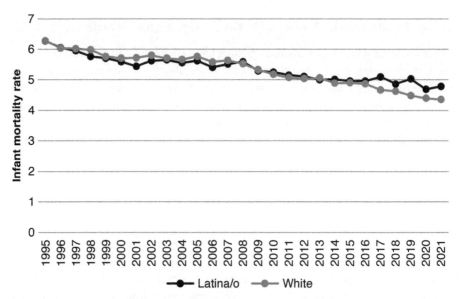

Figure 13.7 Infant Mortality Rates for Latina/os and Whites by Year
Source: Data from Centers for Disease Control and Prevention (2023d).

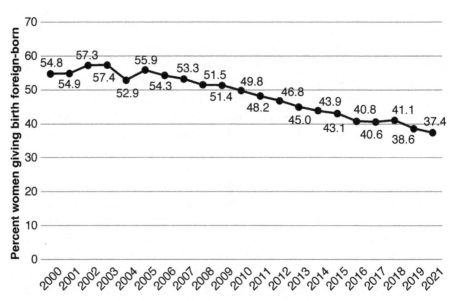

Figure 13.8 Percentage of Latina Women Giving Birth in Past Year Who Are Foreign-Born by Year
Source: Data from 2000–2021 American Community Survey 1-Year Estimates Public-Use File (Ruggles et al. 2024).

in 2003 to a low of 37.4 percent in 2021. Why is this trend important in explaining the significant drop in the Latina/o infant mortality rate? Recall that, consistent with the Latina/o paradox, Latina immigrant women have more favorable birth outcomes compared to native-born women (Hummer et al. 2007; Montoya-Williams et al. 2021). Over the course of time, when there are fewer immigrant women giving birth, the infant mortality rate has risen. Obviously, although we need more data and more sophisticated analysis to reach this conclusion, these data are suggestive. If this pattern is real, could we also see increasing death rates and longevity decline and the narrowing or possible disappearance of the Latina/o paradox across all age groups?

The Impact of COVID-19 on Latina/o Life Expectancy

The COVID-19 pandemic has inflicted so much pain and loss of life since it emerged in the beginning of 2020 in the US. People of color – American Indians and Alaska Natives, Blacks, and Latina/os – have died from COVID-19 at a higher rate than whites throughout the pandemic, but particularly in the initial stages of the pandemic. We draw here on data from the CDC Wonder (Centers for Disease Control and Prevention 2024a) to compare the COVID-19 death rates among racial/ethnic groups in the country. We focus below on Latina/os, Blacks, and whites by sex and examine the COVID-19 age-adjusted death rates (AADRs), which make statistical adjustments to take into account age differences between the race/ethnic and sex groups. The AADR signifies the number of deaths due to COVID-19 per 100,000 in the given population.

Latina/os and Blacks had much higher COVID-19 age-adjusted death rates than whites (Figure 13.9). In 2020, Black and Latina females died from the pandemic at twice the rate of white females, whereas Latino males died at a rate 2.6 times higher and Black males 2.3 times higher than white males. Blacks and Latina/os continued to die at higher rates than whites in 2021, although the gaps were narrower (ranging from rates 1.4 to 1.7 times higher than the rates of whites). Among males, Latinos had the highest COVID-19 death rates in both years; among females, Blacks sustained the highest death rates in both years. The COVID-19 death rates of Black and Latino males declined between 2020 and 2021, while they increased slightly among Black and Latina females. In contrast, the death rates of whites rose considerably between the two years, ascending by a 44 percent hike for males and a 34 percent ascent for females.

The pandemic has thus far resulted in more than 1.1 million deaths between January 1, 2020 and September 16, 2023 (Centers for Disease Control and Prevention 2024d). These deaths have impacted the life expectancy in the US with the disproportionate death of people of color resulting in greater decline in life expectancy for these groups. Now we examine the life expectancy of Latina/os, Blacks, and whites by sex for 2019 (before the pandemic, which we discussed above), 2020, and 2021.

Figure 13.10 clearly shows the disproportionate impact of COVID-19 on the reduction of life expectancy, particularly for Latina/os and Blacks. Between 2019 and 2021, the life expectancy of Latina/o males fell by 4.7 years and 4.6 years for

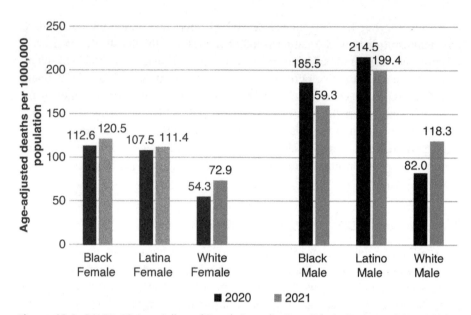

Figure 13.9 COVID-19 Age-Adjusted Death Rates by Race/Ethnic Group and Sex, 2020 and 2021

Source: Data from Centers for Disease Control and Prevention (2024a).

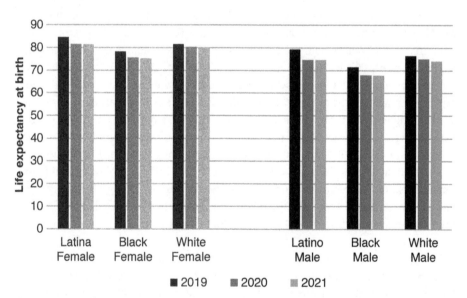

Figure 13.10 Life Expectancy at Birth by Race/Ethnic Group and Sex, 2019, 2020, and 2021

Sources: data from Arias and Xu (2022a, 2022b) and Arias et al. (2023).

Black males, while the reduction for Latina females was 3.4 years and 3.3 for Black females. The declines in life expectancy were much less pronounced for whites, with the reduction being about 37 percent lower for white females compared to Latina and Black females, and 44 percent lower for white males relative to Latino and Black males. These trends had an impact on the Latina/o paradox as well. For example, the Latina/o life-expectancy of Latina/os narrowed considerably between 2020 and 2022 – a drop from 3.1 to 1.8 years for Latina females and a fall of 2.8 to 0.7 years for Latino males. In fact, the Latina/o paradox disappeared in 2021 for Latino males when their life expectancy was 0.2 shorter than that of white males, but bounced back later (Garcia and Sáenz (2023).

The major question is whether these narrower gaps in the Latina/o paradox will remain or even disappear in the coming years, as we observe the long-term consequences of COVID-19 on people who contracted it. As we noted above, the major decline in immigration from Mexico may well contribute to the narrowing or, perhaps, even a disappearance of the Latina/o paradox. Only time will tell what will occur in the coming years concerning the long-lasting Latina/o life-expectancy and mortality advantage over whites.

Obesity

The escalating levels of obesity among Latina/os have the potential to have devastating impacts on the future health and economic well-being of Latina/os. Obesity is associated with a variety of chronic diseases, including diabetes, hypertension, heart disease, and particular types of cancer (Monteverde et al. 2010; World Health Organization 2000). Moreover, the onset of chronic diseases is also likely to limit the mobility of individuals, thus promoting a more sedentary life that does not include exercise. As we learned above, the causes of death that disproportionately affect Latina/os are related to obesity, lifestyle choices, and diet. Programs and policies need increasingly to promote healthy choices among Latina/os.

Nonetheless, we need to understand that the choices that people make involving diet, exercise, and other lifestyle choices do not occur in a vacuum. Rather they take place in a larger cultural, physical, and economic environment, which sets limitations. For example, many popular foods that Latina/os enjoy are unhealthy. These include such foods as *bañuelos, barbacoa, chile rellenos, chimichangas, empanadas, enchiladas,* flour tortillas, *gorditas, menudo, mofongo, nachos, pan dulce, quesadillas,* refried beans, and tamales. Often these foods can be modified with good ingredients to improve their nutritional value. Yet, there needs to be some modification of attitudes toward such alterations. In addition, poor Latina/os tend to be located in segregated areas, where they have few options for the acquisition of healthy foods, including fresh fruits and vegetables, and for engaging in exercise due to the lack of parks and sidewalks. For many Latina/os who live in "food deserts" in many US cities, stores at hand are disproportionately convenience stores, fast-food outlets, and liquor stores. Furthermore, a healthy diet tends to be more expensive than unhealthy food, which is cheap and convenient. Thus, the environments where Latina/os with limited resources live tend to promote unhealthy diets and lifestyle choices. Policymakers need to invest in bettering the availability of parks and recreational facilities in poor Latina/o communities and to develop incentives for the establishment of supermarkets and farmers' markets that provide a wider availability of fruits, vegetables, and other healthy foods in those communities.

These are certainly major challenges that policymakers and other community leaders must tackle in establishing policies and programs that provide healthier environments in order to allow people with limited resources to make healthier choices in their diets and lifestyles. In addition, there need to be options for unauthorized persons and others who cannot afford health insurance under Obamacare to ensure that they have access to preventive health care that can ward off medical catastrophes at early stages.

Summary

This chapter has provided an overview of the health and health care patterns of Latina/os. We provided an overview of the theoretical perspectives that for long have shown that people with limited socioeconomic resources tend to fare worse in mortality and health compared to individuals who are well off socioeconomically. Furthermore, we overviewed the Social Determinants of Health, the National Institute of Minority Health and Health Disparities (NIMHD) research framework, and the Political Determinants of Health, which help us understand how the determinants on which these models focus are linked to health outcomes. We presented data that demonstrated that Latina/os depart from this general pattern and represent an epidemiological paradox. Accordingly, despite their low socioeconomic profile, along with a variety of related factors, Latina/os actually have lower death rates and live longer than do whites. We provided an overview of several explanations that have been put forth to explain the Latina/o paradox. We also demonstrated the other side of the paradox, which reveals a variety of areas where Latina/os do not fare as well as whites and other groups. Finally, we highlighted several major trends that have major implications for the future course of Latina/o health and health care, including the significant decline of Mexican immigration, which could negatively impact the mortality and longevity of Latina/os, the disproportionate COVID-19 deaths among Latina/s and their significant decline in life expectancy, and the obesity epidemic.

We observed in this chapter that the other side of the paradox included disproportionate causes of death and practices related to violence and at-risk behavior. We now turn to an overview of crime and victimization among Latina/os.

Discussion Questions

1. How do cumulative advantages/disadvantages contribute to health outcomes among Latina/os?

2. What is the Latina/o paradox (also known as the epidemiological paradox and Hispanic paradox)? What are the explanations that have been proposed to account for it?

3. What are some causes of death from which Latina/os die at higher rates compared to whites?

4. Is there a possible relationship between the significant decline of Latina immigrant women among Latina women giving birth and Latina/o babies having higher infant mortality rates than white babies over the last fourteen years? If so, what is the logic behind the relationship? If not, why not?

5. What is the "salmon bias"?

6. Describe the Social Determinants of Health model.

7. How does the National Institute of Minority Health and Health Disparities (NIMHD) research framework differ from the Social Determinants of Health model?

14 Crime and Victimization

Riverside County Sheriff killed unarmed Ernie Serrano, a 33-year-old Chicano, on December 15, 2020. Mr. Serrano was at the market picking up snacks when the police received a call about a man wandering in and out of the store. When the sheriff arrived, they found Mr. Serrano grappling with a security guard. The sheriff's deputies began to beat Mr. Serrano with batons and used a Taser on him before wrestling him face down on the checkout counter, according to a bystander's video. The officers' body camera captured Mr. Serrano pleading for his life and saying, "I can't breathe." After several minutes, one officer noticed he was no longer breathing and tried to resuscitate him. The preliminary autopsy report lists the cause of death as methamphetamine, but an attorney for the family filed a wrongful death lawsuit and said he died of asphyxiation. (Foster-Frau 2021)

Police killings of Latinos (mostly male) are nearly double the rate of whites, but incidents such as the death of Chicano Ernie Serrano rarely receive national news coverage (Foster-Frau 2021). While the police killings of Black Americans out-number all ethno-racial groups, the Latina/o killings are extremely concerning but are left out of national media and debates on police reform. At the same time, it is difficult to ascertain the exact numbers of Latina/os killed by police, in part due to the lack of a standardized system for reporting policing killings (Foster-Frau 2021) and the racial ambiguity in identifying Latina/os in police reports (i.e. unknown race and Latina/o being an ethnicity rather than a racial category); an estimated 1,587 Latina/os have been killed by police since 2013–2020 (https://policeviolencereport.org/). In 2021, Latina/os represented 33 percent of those killed by police, who had been unarmed and who did not appear threatening (https://policeviolencereport.org/).

Latina/o disparities in the criminal justice system expand far beyond police kill-ings to numerous other injustices. The "criminal framework" is frequently used by the media and the criminal justice system to depict Mexican and Mexican American youth in gangs as violent and dangerous, while their gang membership is more of a strategy of belonging (Duran 2018). While examining whether racial disparities in the criminal justice system are institutionalized through legal case factors, Omori and Peterson (2020) found the most significant inequalities are between whites and Black Latina/os, increasing the probability for pretrial detention, conviction, and prison sentences. Elsewhere, studies found that Black and Latino male youths are sentenced more harshly than other groups (Lehmann 2018) and are less likely to be released on probation (Bales and Piquero 2012). Part of the Black and Latina/o disparities in the criminal justice system are also attributed to lacking financial resources to post bail, which results in a loss of bargaining power in sentencing (Leslie and Pope 2017).

According to nationwide data collected in 2019, Latina/o youth are 28 percent more likely to be detained or committed to juvenile facilities than their white peers (setencingproject.org). Yet, these disparities vary across states, with Maryland, Washington, Virginia, Texas, and Tennessee having at least 50 percent more Latina/o youth held in detention than whites (sentencingproject.org). Although criminal justice disparities for Latina/o youth are smaller than for Black and American Indian youth, Latina/os are 42 percent more likely than their white peers to be incarcerated (Rovner 2021). Yet, it is important to stress that injustices in the criminal justice system are not attributed to youth of color being more involved in criminal activities but due to their harsher enforcement and punishment (Rovner 2021). Indeed, violent crimes only account for about 6 percent of Latina/o arrests (Rovner 2021; Rios 2011).

When analyzing policing toward criminalized populations (i.e. Blacks and Latinos), the dispiriting ways of community policing are evident (Rios et al. 2020). Such racialized practices in policing result in the hyper-surveillance of Latina/os in schools and police harassment of those who are just hanging out with friends or playing at the park in their neighborhoods (Rios 2011). Police presence in Black and Latina/o communities (Menjivar and Bejarano 2004; Weitzer and Tuch 2005) is perceived as threatening rather than protective.

Additionally, the stop-and-frisk practice, where police officers, at their discretion, are legally able to question and inspect an individual regarding any suspicion of criminal activity, disproportionately targets Latina/os and Blacks who reside in neighborhoods denoted as high crime and poor (Levchak 2021; Rios et al. 2020). While officials claim that stop-and-frisk promotes crime deterrence and is thus beneficial for communities of color, in actuality, police officers instill fear and submission by this practice (Rios et al. 2020) and inflict a range of emotional and psychological harm (Bandes et al. 2019). There are also signs that racial- and citizenship-profiling in Latina/o-immigrant neighborhoods reduce cooperation with law enforcement (Morales and Curry 2021).

This chapter presents an overview of the criminalization and victimization of Latina/os in the US. While most of the literature on race and the criminal justice system, crime, and criminalization has focused on Black–White disparities, the scholarship on Latina/os is valuable and sizable. Below we begin by illustrating some of the historical and contemporary societal constructions of Latina/os as criminals. We then highlight some criminology theories used to explain Latina/o criminal activity. Next, we present some of the trends in the criminalization and victimization of Latina/os, utilizing data from the Pew Hispanic Center's National Survey of Latina/os (2018) and Pew Research Center's American Trends Panel Wave 68 (2020). We then focus on Latina/os involvement in the Black Lives Matter movement. Finally, we conclude by asking major questions about the future study of Latina/os and crime and victimization.

Criminalization of Latina/os in the Past and Today

The colonization of Latina/os has been ongoing since the annexation of the American Southwest as an internal colony (Acuña 1972). Since the inception of the US, Mexicans have been labeled as "bandidos" (Martinez 2018; Mirandé 1994). The criminalization of Chicana/os resulted not from being more criminal but from varying from mainstream society in terms of culture, worldviews, economic, political, and justice systems. Second, the Mexican–American War rendered Chicanos (Mexican Americans) landless and displaced them politically and economically, positioning them to become a vital source of cheap labor for developing the US capitalist system (Mirandé 1994; Martinez 2018). Chicana/os active resistance against white encroachment, being scapegoated for political corruption and crime, and not having the power to shape the images of criminality placed upon them, all led to the image of the Mexican *bandido* (Martinez 2018; Mirandé 1994; Montejano 2010) that continues to be prevalent in popular culture (Martinez 2015). Such images of criminality also legitimize the economic, political, and legal exploitation of Mexicans in the US (Mirande 1994) and violence against Mexicans in the US (Martinez 2018). Such history of Latina/o oppression is essential to understanding the contemporary US racial hierarchy and how Latina/os emerged as an intermediary category between Blacks and whites (Gómez 2020).

A notable example of the criminalization of Chicano young men and boys and the failing relationship with law enforcement in the twentieth century is the Zoot Suit riots. The tension between young Chicanos wearing a distinctive style of dress called a zoot suit and the service members and police officers in Los Angeles erupted between June 3 and June 10, 1943 (Escobar 1999). The riots began when service members attacked Zoot Suiters, beating them, tearing off their clothes, and leaving them bleeding and naked in the streets. The Los Angeles Police Department (LAPD) allowed this violence against the Chicano community to escalate to an attack on all Chicana/os, which highlights the violation of Mexican American rights. When LAPD finally got involved, they only arrested a handful of service members, but they incarcerated over 600 Chicanos for disturbing the peace. This incident of anti-Mexican racism in the criminal justice system has taken precedence in Chicana/o history.

Today's criminalization of Latina/os is exacerbated by laws to regulate immigration and border enforcement. In the case of entering without inspection, according to the American Immigration Council, a first offense of unlawful entry is a misdemeanor punishable by a fine, up to six months in prison, or both (8 USC § 1325) (https://www.americanimmigrationcouncil.org/sites/default/files/research/prosecuting_people_for_coming_to_the_united_states.pdf). Penalties for unlawful reentry or those found in the US after deportation, removal, or denied admission are more severe (8 USC § 1326). This crime is punishable as a felony with a maximum sentence of two years. However, higher penalties are applied if the person had been previously removed after a conviction of certain crimes. Prosecutions for entry-related offenses subsequently declined when the government began expelling migrants back into Mexico rather than prosecuting them.

The legal restrictions against undocumented Latina/o immigrants do not stop at the US–Mexico border. Criminalization of Latina/os also occurs through the local policing of immigration law. Some states initially developed immigration enforcement policies as a response to a perceived inability of the federal government to control migration flows from the southern border. State-level policies that aim to control immigration not only criminalize undocumented migrants but also their families and, consequently, the entire Latina/o community.

Among the most notable efforts by states to implement immigration law is Arizona's S.B.1070, signed in April 2010 (Sáenz et al. 2011) and amended as H.B. 2162, which legalized the *intensification* of surveillance efforts primarily targeted at Latina/os. Such legislative policing led to the criminalization of Latina/os in the form of increases in criminal arrests and detentions by state and local police (Heyman 2010). This law then extended the policing of immigration beyond the border and arguably legalized the racial profiling of Latina/os by giving local and state law enforcement the authority to arrest Latina/os on "reasonable suspicion" of being undocumented (Golash-Boza 2012).

On June 25, 2012, the US Supreme Court upheld most of the provisions of S.B.1070 in *Arizona v. the United States* (567 US 387). Some of the provisions of S.B.1070 that did *not* pass, mainly because they preempted federal laws, include not carrying proof of legal status that can result in a misdemeanor and making seeking work a crime. Additionally, state officers cannot arrest a removable immigrant without a warrant. While state officers may arrest a person who is removable/deportable, they could only do so when requested by a federal judge according to the revised provisions.

So, why are states getting involved with the enforcement of federal immigration laws? Sáenz et al. (2011) argued that Latina/os represent a racial threat where demographic changes are the impetus behind policies such as Arizona's S.B.1070. Specifically, from 1980 to 2008, Arizona experienced a growth in the immigration population from eighteen to 33 percent, with Latina/os growth driving this growth. Consequently, during this timeframe, the state's Latina/o population doubled, while White representation decreased. Therefore, while S.B.1070 targets all undocumented migrants, Latina/os are disproportionately targeted, given that they represent the majority of migrants in the state. Other states experiencing similar demographic shifts as Arizona for the first time, e.g. Alabama, Georgia, and Pennsylvania, have implemented similar policies.

The court battles over state rights to police federal immigration law continue. Even though the initial state-level policies to enforce immigration occurred in new migrant destination areas (Sáenz et al. 2021), Texas Governor Abbott signed S.B.4 on May 7, 2017. S.B.4 is designed for Texas to implement its own immigration law that will provide the legal mechanism for state police to arrest a person accused of crossing the border without inspection (https://capitol.texas.gov/tlodocs/85R/billtext/pdf/SB00 004F.pdf). While S.B.4 does not include penalties associated with the investigation of employers who allegedly hire an undocumented immigrant, it extends Arizona's S.B.1070. While S.B.1070 allowed for the local policing of federal immigration law, in S.B.4, Texas seeks to make unauthorized border crossings illegal at the state level, so that border and immigration enforcement would not solely be the jurisdiction of the federal government. On March 12, 2024, the US Supreme Court reviewed a lawsuit filed by the American Civil Liberties Union (ACLU) and the Texas Civil Rights Project (TCRP) on behalf of Las Americas Advocacy Center and El Paso County over concerns that the law would lead to racial profiling, separating families, and harm Black and Brown communities in Texas (https://www.aclu.org/press-releases/sup reme-court-extends-pause-on-anti-immigrant-texas-legislation-that-would-overst ep-federal-law#:~:text=The%20American%20Civil%20Liberties%20Union,is%20pree mpted%20by%20federal%20law).

Local and county policies also shape perceptions of Latina/o criminality and scapegoating. In Hazelton, Pennsylvania, for instance, the Illegal Immigration Relief Act (IIRA) was passed in 2006 after an allegation of a Latina/o-on-White homicide occurring against the background of demographic shifts and a deteriorating economy (Longazel 2013). For the passage of IIRA, officials heavily relied on a racialized rhetoric of the war on crime and socially constructed Latina/os as "illegal" and "unlawful." Such racialized rhetoric further marginalized immigrant communities and sustained the racial order of white hegemony (Longazel 2013).

In *Ortega Melendres v. Arpaio* (2009), the American Civil Liberties Union sued Maricopa County Sheriff Joe Arpaio for racially profiling groups of color, mainly Latina/os, during traffic patrols. Indeed, Sheriff Arpaio had been detaining individuals solely based on suspicion of being undocumented and disproportionately targeting Latina/os (Shahrasbi 2020). District Court Judge Murray Snow ordered the sheriff's office to discontinue this practice and ordered anti-bias training, a court-appointed monitor, and patrol cameras (among other things). When Sheriff Arpaio failed to follow the injunction, the court issued a civil contempt order, and eventually a criminal contempt of court, for failure to abide by previous injunctions (Shahrasbi 2020). A month later, Arpaio received a Presidential pardon from Donald Trump (Shahrasbi 2020), legitimizing the disparate treatment and criminalization of Latina/os.

Aligned with the increasing power given to local immigration policing is the Secure Communities initiative. Secure Communities is an administrative policy forming a partnership between US Immigration and Customs Enforcement (ICE) and local and state-level law enforcement aimed to remove criminal "aliens." It is based on a federal information-sharing partnership between ICE and the Federal Bureau of Investigation (FBI) that helps identify criminal aliens (http://www.ice.gov/secure_communities/). Under Secure Communities, the FBI automatically sends fingerprints to the Department of Homeland Security (DHS) to check against its immigration databases. Suppose these checks reveal that an individual is unlawfully present in the US. In that case, ICE takes enforcement action, prioritizing removing individuals who present the most significant threats to public safety, including those with repeated immigration law violations.

Nevertheless, accenting the racialization of deportation practices, it is Afro-Caribbean small-time drug peddlers and Latina/o undocumented workers that DHS has primarily targeted for removal rather than the "worst of the worst"

(Golash-Boza 2012). The convergence of criminal and immigration law and its implementation is what Stumpf (2006) referred to as "crimmigration" and Menjívar and Abrego (2012) devised as "legal violence." The local policing of federal immigration law has come to constitute a multilayer enforcement regime consisting of federal, state, and local laws and ordinances that act to enforce immigration (Menjívar 2014).

Adding to the policies described above are what some scholars call the *immigration–industrial complex* (Alexander 2020; Diaz 2012; Fernandez 2007; Douglas and Sáenz 2013; Golash-Boza 2012). Attempts to criminalize immigrants, in addition to creating parallels between migrants and terrorists in this post-9/11 era, have fueled policies that created the profit-making immigration–industrial complex focused on the detention and deportation of migrants (Fernandez 2007). According to Douglas and Sáenz (2013) the rise of the immigration–industrial complex is due to an association between the criminalization of immigrants and a corresponding growth in prison-like detention facilities. Detention centers are intended to house individuals and entire families, including children, who are waiting for hearings, deportation, or to be bonded out. According to data from the US DHS, the immigrant detainee population has expanded from 9,011 in 1996, 20,429 in 2001, 19,409 in 2006, to 33,330 in 2011 (Douglas and Sáenz 2013), and in FY 2019–2020, the detained population averaged 50,165 (US Immigration and Customs Enforcement 2021). These increases in individuals in detention are especially concerning, given that non-criminal immigrant detainees confront multiple forms of violence while in ICE custody, and the system of standards and audits is ineffectual (Hernández et al. 2018).

Central to the profit-making immigration–industrial complex is the privatization of detention centers. Corporations are becoming rich from detaining immigrants in prison-like conditions (Diaz 2012; Hallinan 2001). For instance, the Corrections Corporation of America (CCA) (now CoreCivic) increased its stock market value 9-fold after making significant political contributions of an estimated $3.1 million from 2003 to 2012 (Sáenz 2013a). As such, immigration policies are in the hands of powerful interest groups and corporations that lobby to prevent the passage of laws that would ameliorate the lives of undocumented migrants and their families (Golash-Boza 2012).

Donald Trump and Latina/os

In 2015, Donald Trump's presidential campaign marked a shift in the legitimacy of blatant racism against Latina/os when he stated:

> When Mexico sends its people, they are not sending their best. They're not sending you. They are not sending you. They're sending people that have lots of problems, and they're bringing those problems with us. They're bringing drugs. They're bringing crime. They're rapists. And some, I assume, are good people. But I speak to border guards and they tell us what we're getting. And it only makes common sense. It only makes common sense. They're sending us not the right people. It's coming from more than Mexico. It's coming from all over South and Latin America, and it's coming probably – probably – from the Middle East. (Phillips 2017)

Trump's racialization of Latina/os as "different" from his supporters and as "criminals" made it evident that Latina/os had to be eliminated to "Make America Great Again." Such sentiments not only negate the history of Latina/os in the American Southwest as the native inhabitants, along with the indigenous populations, but signaled a new racial order moving from covert to blatant racism against Latina/os during the Trump presidency (2017–2021). Donald Trump's white nativist anti-Latina/o politics continued throughout his "Make America Great Again" 2016 election cycle (González 2019). Trump's campaign proclaimed blatant lies about the so-called millions of "criminal aliens" living in the US, which stands in sharp contrast to the estimated 93 percent of the undocumented population without criminal records (Abrego et al. 2017).

Once elected, President Donald Trump's racial rhetoric transpired in actual administrative agendas that further strengthened punitive policies already in place during the Bush and Obama eras, which further criminalized immigrants and, by extension, Latina/os in the US. The criminalization of Latina/os during the Trump era essentially occurred through the lens that Latina/os are "criminal aliens," negating the historical presence of Latina/os in the US Trump's immigration-related executive orders (EO); e.g. "Border Security and Immigration Enforcement Improvements" from the onset stated "Aliens who illegally enter the United States without inspection or admission present a significant threat to national security and public safety" (Trump 2017: 2; see also Morales 2018). As a continuation of post-9/11 federal policies during the Bush and Obama eras (see Andreas and Nadelmann 2006; Bejarano et al. 2012; Dunn 2009; Macías-Rojas 2016; Payan 2016), the bureaucratization of border security under Trump conflated terrorists with undocumented migrants. These policy constructions, which make undocumented status synonymous with criminality, have been in place since the 1980s and enforced in 1996 through the Illegal Immigration Reform and Immigrant Responsibility Act and Antiterrorism (IIRIRA) and Effective Death Penalty Act (Abrego et al. 2017; Ewing, Martínez, and Rumbaut 2015). Moreover, this EO on border security also expanded immigration detention in line with the immigration prison industrial complex that subjected border crossers and the undocumented population in the US to prison-like conditions (see Abrego et al. 2017; Donato and Armenta 2011; Gonzales and Chavez 2012; Menjívar and Abrego 2012; Morales 2018).

Trump's border security EO also expanded the 287(g) program, allowing local law enforcement agents to enforce immigration law as indicated in the 1996 Illegal Immigration Reform and Immigration Responsibility Act (IIRIRA) (Abrego et al. 2017). In 2020, all the counties in Arizona, Massachusetts, Georgia, and Florida, and the counties with the most immigrants in the states of Texas, Oklahoma, Louisiana, Arkansas, Wisconsin, and South Carolina, had the jail model of 287(g) agreements that deputized local law enforcement as official to perform certain functions of federal immigration officials in jails. All the counties in the states of Montana, Wyoming, and Florida, and the counties with the most immigrants in Alaska, have 287(g) agreements, warrant service officer model where ICE trains, certifies, and authorizes selected state and local law enforcement officers to execute ICE administrative warrants and perform the arrest functions of an immigration officer within the law enforcement agency's jails and/or correctional facilities.

Migrant Crisis and Shifts in Border and Immigration Enforcement

The legal landscape in border and immigration enforcement changed drastically in response to the refugee crisis that began in the latter half of 2017. To contextualize the refugee crisis, CBP documented 949,450 encounters between 2014 and 2019 (Rosenblum, Gibson, and Leong 2022); this amount more than tripled, with 3,201,144 apprehensions in a single FY 2023 (https://www.cbp.gov/newsroom/stats/cbp-enforcement-statistics) (see Chapter 4). Texas Governor Gregg Abbott established *Operation Lone Star* (OLS) in March 2021 to respond to the refugee crisis. At its height, OLS has deployed more than 10,000 soldiers of the Texas National Guard (Martin 2023), plus officers from the Texas Department of Public Safety, to police border crossings in unauthorized locations. While the state did not have the jurisdiction to police federal immigration law, Governor Abbott invoked an invasion clause in the US and Texas Constitutions that authorized the state to take "unprecedented measures" to defend against the "invaders."

On the ground at the international southern border, tensions between state and federal agents ensued, i.e. state agents placed mires of concertina wire that prohibited CBP from patrolling the border. CBP cut the wire installed by state agents to access the border, resulting in a civil action no. 2:23-cv-00044, *The State of Texas v. US Department of Homeland Security*, on October 30, 2023, claiming that federal agents were committing conversion and trespassing. On January 22, 2024, the US Supreme Court ordered Texas to allow federal border-patrol agents the authority to access private land within 25 miles of the international border and to implement federal immigration law (The Supreme Court of the United States 2024).

Criminological Theoretical Frameworks

Criminologists have developed several theoretical perspectives to examine criminal patterns. One such perspective is the *labeling theory*, which stresses that society creates deviance by creating rules and laws, and violating these rules/laws constitutes deviance for individuals who do not have enough power to avoid such labels (Becker 1963). Even though deviant behavior cuts across social class and race, it is the undereducated, poor, and people of color who are disproportionately labeled as deviant in the criminal justice system and beyond. Therefore, labeling theory emphasizes the role of society in defining what is illegal and assigning a deviant status to specific individuals who break those rules. Eventually, people who are tagged with a deviant label can internalize it to the extent that it dominates their identities and behaviors.

Systematically imposed upon Latina/os and their communities are labels such as "bandido," "illegal," "foreigner," "criminal," and "violent" (Duran 2018; Mirandé 1994; Rios 2011). Such labeling is the basic premise behind racial profiling, where police stop Black and Latina/o drivers for routine traffic violations to search for evidence of criminal activity such as drugs or guns. The racialization of Latina/os as criminal and violent then interlocks with perceptions of unauthorized citizenship status, leading to citizenship profiling (Morales, Delgado, and Curry 2018) and the deportation regime (Duran 2018). Moreover, in describing the stigmatized labels imposed on young Latino and Black males, Rios (2011) called this process the "labeling hype," where agents of social control (i.e. schools, police, probation officers) systematically target these youths as criminal risks, thus creating a cycle of criminalization.

Latina/os are not only subjected to racial profiling but to *citizenship profiling*, where law enforcement determines whom to stop, question, and search, solely on determinations of Latina/o ethnicity and perception of lack of US citizenship (Morales, Delgado, and Curry 2018; Morales and Curry 2021). A study on citizenship profiling among Latina/os found that the second-generation are more likely to be stopped and questioned by law enforcement, and questioned about their citizenship status, than first- and third-and-later-generation Latina/os (Morales, Delgado and Curry 2018). Additionally, while residents in Latina/o–immigrant neighborhoods are more likely to cooperate with police, being profiled for citizenship compromises police legitimacy, raising concerns about the local policing of immigration on perceptions of procedural justice (Morales and Curry 2021).

Another criminological theoretical perspective is the *subculture of violence* thesis, which posits that violence becomes normalized and is an expected means for dispute resolution in structurally disadvantaged areas (i.e. poor neighborhoods) (Wolfgang and Ferracuti 1967). In the case of Latino male youth (Rios 2011), they display "tough front" subcultures that develop in the streets – not as a result of being cruel, hyper-masculine, and/or resistant, but as a resilience based on trying to succeed in a system that has systematically excluded them. Along the US–Mexico border, Duran (2018) explained how Disproportionate Minority Contact racializes Mexicans and Mexican American youth due to the label of gang memberships, which justifies additional resources in the juvenile justice system and endorses school policies and juvenile probation punishments. At the macro-level, however, there is less support for a subculture of violence perspective (Sampson 1985), suggesting that structure is more important than culture.

Attention has turned from cultural perspectives to examine the association between structural disadvantages and crime. Cloward and Ohlin's (1960) opportunity structure is an early framework studying the structural component, *built on* Robert Merton's (1949) theory of delinquency. According to this thesis, the opportunity structure represents access to societal institutions (e.g. employment and schooling) to support oneself and achieve goals. Merton argues that there is some consensus over central values and goals. However, when society does not provide equal access to legitimate means for achieving those goals, it will result in deviance/delinquency. According to this perspective, Latina/os residing in economically disadvantaged neighborhoods may be encouraged to turn to crime as a means of overcoming blocked opportunities (Martinez 2015).

Expanding upon the association between structural disadvantages and crime, Sampson and associates (Sampson and Bean 2006; Sampson and Wilson 1995) devised the *racial invariance thesis*. According to the racial invariance thesis, the role of concentrated disadvantage has two dimensions: (1) the convergence of an assortment of adverse economic and social conditions (e.g. joblessness, welfare dependency, poverty, family disruption, and residential instability), and (2) the concentration of these conditions in specific geographic areas (Martin et al. 2011). Consequently, due to structural racism, Latina/os and Blacks are relegated to neighborhoods with concentrated disadvantages and racial segregation, both of which are associated with crime rates, in particular, violent crime (Martin et al. 2011). This perspective has been applied to Black–white racial disparities in crime (Sampson and Bean 2006; Sampson and Wilson 1995) and Latina/os (Martinez 2008).

Another perspective to examine Latina/o crime is the *social disorganization* framework that posits that crime is spatially concentrated in specific neighborhoods, and structural conditions exert disparate influences on various types of crime across communities (Shaw and McKay 1942). A vital feature of the social disorganization perspective is that structural economic conditions do not directly influence crime but that crime results from the breakdown of informal social control associated with deteriorating structural conditions (Allen and Cancino 2012). According to the social disorganization thesis, in disorganized areas, community institutions cannot work together to protect the residents' values and control residents' behavior to conform to shared goals and values, thus creating a space for crime to prosper (Bursik 1988).

In the case of Latina/os, an assumption behind the *social disorganization* theory is that social change, such as demographic changes that come along with new settlements of Latina/os, is associated with the breakdown of social institutions, which weakens social control, allowing crime to flourish. However, the applicability of the social disorganization framework needs to be improved in the case of Latina/os, particularly Latina/o immigrants. While it has been argued that immigrants may undermine established institutions and hinder the establishment of shared values (Bankston 1998), current research does not support this.

The argument that immigration reduces crime or that there is no link between immigration and crime is substantially supported in the literature (Light and Miller 2018; Chalfin and Deza 2020; Chouhy and Madero-Hernandez 2019; Gunadi 2021; Lee and Martinez 2009; Sampson 2008; Allen and Cancino 2012). Indeed, in a nationwide study conducted by Light and Miller (2018) they found that undocumented migration does not increase violent crimes and that this association is not related to decreases in reporting or migrant selectivity.

The immigration–crime link has been examined under the *Latina/o immigration crime paradox*. Like the Latina/o epidemiological paradox examined in the health chapter, despite the structural disadvantages of Latina/o immigrants – high poverty, low levels of education, lack of adequate housing, and so forth – they have *lower* criminal patterns than Blacks, whites, and native-born Latina/os (Stowell and Gostjev 2018; Kubrin and Ishizawa 2012; Rumbaut, Dingeman, and Robles 2019; Durán 2018; Sampson 2008; Martinez 2015; Martinez et al. 2010). Furthermore, this relationship appears robust, emerging among immigrant groups from different national origins, including those from Central America and Mexico, and across different cities and periods (Martinez and Stowell 2012). Even for homicides, the rates for Latina/os are not as high as for other impoverished racial/ethnic groups (Martinez 2015). The lower-than-expected crime rates have also been found at the neighborhood level among Mexican Americans (Martinez Jr. and Sheppard 2019) and in larger geographical regions such as the US–Mexico border (Durán 2018; Allen and Cancino 2012). Duran (2018), for instance, referred to the border region as a "miracle" given its low levels of gang involvement and modest rates of violence in comparison to other urban areas.

While the research on the Latina/o immigrant crime paradox appears to be robust, there are still more research questions to be examined. Specifically, variations exist in the immigrant crime paradox across neighborhoods, cities, and other structural characteristics (Kubrin and Ishizawa 2012). At the school level, for instance, there is no association between immigration and a higher presence of immigrant students at the school level of crime (Peguero et al. 2023).

An alternative perspective used to explain the association between low crime rates and immigration, Martinez (2015) and Martinez and Valenzuela (2006) developed the *immigrant revitalization theory.* According to this perspective, immigration revitalizes impoverished urban neighborhoods with hard-working families and new businesses, therefore lowering crime. Indeed, Martinez (2002:6) claims that "the most plausible explanation for Latina/o homicide patterns being lower than expected is the strength of Latina/o immigrants and immigrant communities, which buffer Latina/os from criminal activity." This argument contrasts with the social disorganization perspective. Moreover, if there were an association between immigration and violent crime, Latina/os and Latina/o communities would have experienced the bulk of that crime, given the heavy representation of migrants from Latin America in the US (Martinez 2008).

Examining the extent to which social ties and collective efficacy (trust and informal social control) influence neighborhood crime, net of neighborhood characteristics, Burchfiekl and Silver (2012) found that collective efficacy mediates the association between concentrated disadvantage and robbery victimization. This effect was weaker in Latina/o versus non-Latina/o neighborhoods, suggesting that a Latina/o crime paradox may be present, given that crime rates in Latina/o neighborhoods have less to do with local levels of collective efficacy than in non-Latina/o neighborhoods (Burchfiekl and Silver 2012). While the reasons for this paradox are still being investigated, there are indications that the Mexican culture functions as a protective barrier (Zavala, Curry, and Morales 2020).

Latina/o Gangs

There is a long history of images of young Latina/os stereotypically associated with violent gang activity (Durán and Campos 2020; Thomas 2015). These images of Latina/o gangs are historically cemented in the Zoot Suit Riots that began on June 3, 1943, in Los Angeles, California, where violence between US naval personnel violently confronted the Zoot Suiters members of the Mexican-origin community (Turner and Surace 1956). In the aftermath, gang activity became interpreted through the Zoot Suiter lens (Turner and Surace 1956), even though only a small percentage of Zoot Suiters had gang involvement (Bogardus 1943).

Puerto Rican youth also confronted perceptions of criminal gang activity, this time from popular culture. Puerto Rican leaders in the 1950s worked on challenging images of Puerto Rican youth susceptible to gang membership (Thomas 2015). This became increasingly difficult when, in 1957, the popular Broadway show *West Side Story* helped to perpetuate societal images of young Puerto Ricans as delinquents and gang members (Thomas 2015; Sanchez 2018). Hysteria about Puerto Rican gang members intensified two years later, in 1959, with the high-profile murder of a young Puerto Rican gang member, "Capeman" (Thomas 2015).

The contemporary scholarship on barrio gangs began with the work of Joan Moore and James Diego Vigil (Dudley 2020). In Vigil's *Barrio Gangs* (1988), he contextualized the causes of Latina/o gang membership as rooted in marginality at all societal levels, i.e. macro-, meso-, and micro-levels. Moore's (1991) *Going Down to the Barrio* studied three generations of barrio gangs in East Los Angeles and compared the experiences of male and female gang members. She highlighted how gangs often became family-like, ensuing both loyalty and dependency. As the scholarship on Latina/o gangs developed rather than using solely a deviant lens, the focus has been placed on the structural context of Latina/o barrios with high levels of poverty, few occupational opportunities, and marginally minimal political inclusion (Moore and Pinderhughes 1993).

Stereotypes against Latina/o youth associated with violent gang activity have continued to this day. Durán and Campos (2020) documented the racial disparities in associations of gang membership. Data from police records found that Latina/os are four times more likely than whites to be labeled as gang members (Durán and Campos 2020). Not only is a small fraction of Latina/o youth involved in gang activities (Durán and Campos 2020), but most gang activities are non-violent (Durán 2013) or simply social recreational in nature (Vigil 1988; Durán and Campos 2020).

So, what are the conditions associated with Latina/o gang formation? Durán and Campos (2020) noted three conditions. First, Latina/o youth growing up in under-resourced communities had relied on gangs for self-protection. Second, despite the marginal structural conditions, most Latina/os do not join gangs. Third, while most Latina/o gang activities are formed to socialize with family and friends and reduce boredom, there are cases where group conflict results in harm that impacts Latina/o residents and brings about the interplay of being a victim or offender.

Latina/o gangs have also been examined from the subculture theoretical framework, where certain groups or subcultures in society have norms that are conducive to crime and violence. Tapia's (2019) study of Chicano gangs in San Antonio found that some gangs were established in the 1950s and are still active, spanning 50 to 60 years of continuity. Moreover, a common thread in the gangs in San Antonio is ethnic pride in shaping the identity of gang members but also intergenerational tensions between "gangsta" identity over Chicano pride (Tapia 2019).

Transnational Latina/o Gangs

Most of the public policy aimed to curb Latina/o gangs has focused on those with transnational members and activities that span national boundaries. Mara Salvatrucha, commonly known as MS-13, is perhaps the most notorious Latina/o transnational gang. While local and neighborhood gangs did exist in Central America prior to the evolvement of transnational gangs (Paarlberg 2022; Cruz 2010), this changed with civil wars and military conflict in Central America, the migration process that displaced the youth, and return migration both voluntary and in the form of deportations. In the early 1980s Central America was plagued by civil wars and military conflict (see Chapter 2), pushing many Central Americans, especially Salvadorans, to migrate to the US as refugees (Cruz 2010). As thousands of young Salvadoran immigrants found themselves culturally and economically excluded, they turned to gangs for identity and peer support. First they joined the 18th Street Gang (Barrio 18), a Mexican and Chicana/o gang but, as the population of Salvadorans grew, they formed MS-13 (Cruz 2010). When MS-13 originated it was not associated with the transnational criminal organization that it is today; it was mostly a stoner gang (Ward 2013). When the civil unrest in El Salvador slowed down in the 1990s, over 375,000 Salvadorans living in the US voluntarily returned and another 150,000 were deported. Many of the returnees were young males who barely spoke Spanish, had weak family ties in El Salvador, but they found a home with gang members who provided family-like ties (Ward 2013).This was the context where some argue that MS-13 was made in America and deported back to El Salvador (Dudley 2020).

While most of the disadvantaged Latina/o youth do not join gangs, macrosocial ills do play a role. The high-risk factors for gang involvement among Salvadorans, Guatemalans, and Hondureñas/os is growing up removed from both parents who migrated to the US, domestic violence, and school failure (Brenneman 2012; Ward 2013). However, even Salvadoran youth who migrated felt displaced in the US and found a sense of security in MS-13 (Ward 2013). Gangs became a sort of surrogate family in the streets for Latina/o youth, who came to rely on older gang members to protect them as though they were big brothers/sisters, who also taught them how to defend themselves from enemy gangs (Brenneman 2012).

MS-13 evolved into a social and criminal transnational gang, sustained by both individual, local, and transnational processes. While MS-13 reinforces its bond via individual and collective violence resulting from bad individual decisions (Dudley 2020), there were also social conditions that helped MS-13 evolve into a transnational criminal organization. At the local-level of marginalization and law enforcement strategies (Cruz 2010), national-level circumstances, i.e. flawed US and Central American policy and unequal economic systems (Dudley 2020), as well as transnational processes such as migration and the diffusion of Southern California gang norms and identities (Cruz 2010), all of these situations helped MS-13 evolve to what it is today.

While the Central American maras networks and identities are no longer dependent upon American dynamics, they have undergone a process of institutionalization enabling them to become organized protection rackets (Cruz 2010). (Paarlberg 2022) devised a framework of criminal remittances to describe the manner and conditions in which criminal activity and institutions, norms, and people cross borders. Specifically, instability in violence-receiving states transform them into migrant-sending states (Paarlberg 2022). Today, MS-13 is in nearly every state in the US and, in 2020, the first MS-13 leader was indicted on terrorism charges for his role as the leader of the gang's US East Coast Program (Bunker and Sullivan 2020).

Trends in Victimization

Latina/os as the Targets of Mass Shootings

A troubling trend in victimization is the domestic terrorist acts or mass shootings, some explicitly targeting Latina/os. On June 12, 2016, 49 people were killed and another 53 injured at the Pulse nightclub in Orlando, Florida, which catered to lesbian, gay, bisexual, and transgender people. This hate crime, however, targeted not only the LGBTQ+ community but Latinxs. The tragedy happened on the club's Latin night, and Latinxs comprised 90 percent of the victims. Koon (2017) argued that the social constructions of Latinx and LGBTQ+ intersect as systems of oppression, making the massacre at the Pulse nightclub inevitable, and showing that members of the LGBTQ+ Latinx community encounter hate violence from both their sexual and gender identities and their race and ethnicity. In 2018, the FBI recorded the highest levels of hate crimes in sixteen years, with a surge of attacks on Latina/os and transgender people (Levin 2019).

About three years after the mass shooting in Orlando, Florida, Latina/os became the target of a domestic terrorist act again in El Paso, Texas. The tragedy resulted in twenty-three dead and twenty-three wounded at the Cielo Vista Walmart in El Paso. Just before the mass shooting, the gunman posted a manifesto online called the Great Replacement, which subscribed to far-right white nationalist rhetoric and referenced a "Hispanic invasion." The El Paso community and its leaders, including Congresswoman Veronica Escobar and Beto O'Rourke, who served in the House of Representatives for Texas and as a Democratic Presidential candidate in 2020, both established a connection between Trump's racialization and criminalization of Latina/os and the gunman's manifesto.

Sadly, tragedy hit the Latina/o community once again on May 24, 2022, this time targeting children. Nineteen school-age children and two teachers, mostly of Mexican descent, were gunned down at Robb Elementary in Uvalde, Texas. Uvalde is a small city with a population of 15,217 according to the 2020 US census, of which 81.8 percent are Latina/o and with a percentage of people in poverty that nearly doubles that of the nation. The children were fatally shot, and their bodies decimated by a semi-automatic gun in the hands of an eighteen-year-old Latina/o gunman. The motive is currently unknown, although some preliminary connections have been made to the gunman's being a victim of bullying, mental health issues, and access to semi-automatic weapons. While this tragedy does not appear to be racially motivated, and mass shootings in educational institutions have occurred in regions of the US with a white population majority, such as Virginia Tech in 2007 and Sandy Hook Elementary School in 2012, the tragedy in Uvalde occurred against a backdrop of a history marked by structural racism. Enrique Figueroa (2022), who was born in Uvalde and resided there until age eleven, wrote a powerful op-ed that revealed some of the history of racism against Mexican Americans in Uvalde, a history that the media has failed to demonstrate. Figueroa (2022) described how, in the 1970s, there existed two Uvaldes – one Mexican and the other white. The city's public areas were deeply segregated. Additionally, in the 1970s, Mexican American-Chicana/o students walked out of Uvalde High School to protest the discriminatory treatment of Mexican Americans. These students were then confronted by armed law-enforcement agents in the Texas Rangers. Additionally, the retaliation against the students continued when the Uvalde Draft Board obtained a list of the protestors and reclassified them as 1A so they could be drafted (Figueroa 2022). This history matters because, five decades later, Uvalde is at the center of what many would say is the most tragic event in Latina/o history. Many questions have arisen about the local police response to the mass shooting, where the gunman terrorized the students and teachers for over an hour without any intervention. In the end, it was the US Border Patrol Tactical Unit (BORTAC) who entered the school and fatally shot the gunman.

Only a few days later, the National Rifle Association (NRA) held its annual convention in Houston, Texas. While some entertainers refrained from participating, out of respect for the families of the Uvalde massacre, Texas Governor Greg Abbott and Texas Senator Ted Cruz attended the NRA meeting. The support for the NRA and lack of motivation for gun control from the Texas governmental leadership raised questions about the worth of Latina/o children's lives in the state.

Some Trends in Latina/o Victimization and US Immigration and Border Enforcement

While US immigration and border enforcement policies are designed to control the undocumented population, they also affect native-born Latina/os and Latina/o communities more broadly. Below, we utilize the Pew Hispanic Center (2008, 2018) National Survey of Latinos to present data trends on how fearful Latina/os are about deportations of self, relatives, or friends and the changes in those trends from President Obama to Trump's administration. Table 14.1 presents the percentages of Latina/os who, regardless of their citizenship status, are concerned about their deportation or that of relatives or friends.

Based on the National Survey of Latinos for 2008 and 2018, it is evident that deportations of self, relatives, or friends are more concerning for immigrant Latina/os than native-born Latina/os, except for Salvadorans where the native-born expressed greater concern in 2018 (Table 14.1). In 2008, the Latina/o group most worried about deportations were Mexican immigrants, with 77 percent who are concerned about deportations, followed by 69.5 percent of Other Central American immigrants, 68.8 percent of Salvadoran immigrants, 66.5 percent of South American immigrants, and

Table 14.1 Percentages of Concern Regarding Deportations of Self, Relatives, or Friends, 2008–2018[a]

	2008		2018	
	Foreign-Born	Native-Born	Foreign-Born	Native-Born
Mexicans	77.0	39.2	65.7	43.1
Puerto Rican		36.2		40.8
Cuban	49.3	16.7	42.9	c
Salvadoran	68.8	62.5	57.1	63.6
Other Central American	69.5	31.0	73.5	
Other Caribbean Islander[b]	58.6	22.2	52.4	47.0
South American	66.5	26.3	52.5	42.8

[a] Categories of "a lot" and "some" concerned merged for this table.

[b] For 2018, the "other Caribbean Islander" category only includes Dominicans.

[c] Empty cells are attributed to low sample sizes.

Sources: National Survey of Latinos 2008, 2018.

58.6 percent of foreign-born Other Caribbean Islanders. In 2008, the groups that were the least concerned about deportations were native-born Cubans (16.7%) and native-born Other Caribbean Islanders (22.2%).

Ten years later, in 2018, there is a shift in the trends about which Latina/o subgroup feels the most threatened by deportation. The subgroup most concerned about deportations is that of Other Central American immigrants, with most of the group, 73.5 percent, being concerned about deportations, followed by Mexican immigrants, with about 9 percent less (65.7%) than Other Central American immigrants. The groups that are the least concerned about deportations in 2018 are native-born South Americans (42.8) and Cuban immigrants (42.9%). Interestingly, 40.8 percent of Puerto Ricans fear deportation, despite being American citizens, but this statistic also captures concerns about the deportations of friends.

Interestingly, Latina/o immigrants had more concerns about deportations in 2008 during the Obama presidency than in 2018 during Trump's. This is the case for all immigrant groups, i.e. Mexicans, Cubans, Salvadorans, Other Caribbean Islanders, and South Americans; the exception is Other Central American immigrants (Table 14.1). Even though Donald Trump pledged to expand the border wall and to deport as many as three million undocumented immigrants, mostly Latina/os, with criminal records living in the US, among other tough-on-immigration approaches, Latina/os had less fear of deportations.

Nevertheless, President Obama had the reputation of being the "Deporter in Chief" given the high numbers of removals/deportations of unauthorized immigrants during his presidency, in comparison to George W. Bush, who, despite being a Republican, had a much lower record of deportations (Chapter 4). Caution does need to be taken in interpreting Latina/os lower fears of deportation during the Trump Administration as a symbol of lower policing of immigration. When President Trump took office, ICE arrests initially increased but remained much lower than during most of Obama's tenure (Gramlich 2020). Trump's focus on policing the US–Mexico border resulted in ICE agents being reassigned to police the border, in contrast to the US interior. This reassignment decreased the federal policing of immigrants in the interior of the US. Furthermore, the lower Latina/o concerns about deportations are also symbolic of the growth of "sanctuary cities," where local officials refuse to honor ICE detainer's requirements to turn over undocumented immigrants for deportation. Given all these patterns – Obama's focus on immigrant detention, Trump's being overzealous with policing the US–Mexico border, and the growth of sanctuary cities – all contributed to lowering Latina/os victimization due to fears of deportation.

Latina/os and Racial Profiling in Policing

Next, we gauge perceptions of racial disparities in policing based on the Pew Research Center's American Trends Panel Wave 68, June 4 to June 10, 2020. Almost half of the non-Latina/o Blacks perceived that the police had unfairly stopped them. Following non-Latina/o Blacks, Puerto Ricans (27.1%) and Mexican Americans (24.3%) are more likely to feel that police have racially discriminated against them (Figure 14.1). Foreign-born Cubans are the least likely to perceive that they had been racially profiled by police, even less so than non-Latina/o whites (6.2% v. 7%). Unfortunately, data for the other Latina/o subgroups are not available.

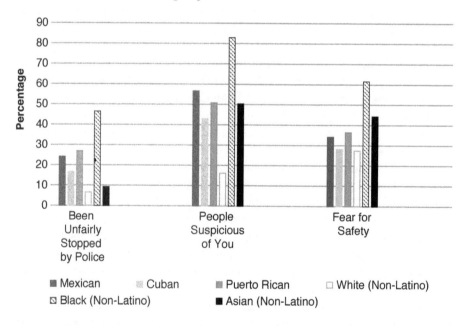

Figure 14.1 Percentage Perceptions of Racial and Ethnic Discrimination by Race/Ethnic Group, 2020

Source: Data from 2020 Pew Research Center's American Trends Panel Wave 68 June 4 to June 10, 2020.

There are also considerable gaps in perceptions of being unfairly stopped by the police because of their race between the native- and foreign-born Latina/os. Mexican immigrants are about 40 percent less likely to perceive racial discrimination in police stops than Mexican Americans. Similarly, among Cubans, foreign-born Cubans are about 65 percent less likely to feel racial discrimination in police stops than Cuban Americans.

Next, we examine perceptions of whether individuals think people are suspicious of them. More people of color feel that people are suspicious of them because of their race. Among Latina/os, like perceptions of racial biases in policing, 57 percent of Mexican Americans and 51 percent of Puerto Ricans feel that people are suspicious of them because of their race and ethnicity (Figure 14.1). However, the gap between native-born and their foreign-born co-ethnics is much closer. For instance, perceptions of people being suspicious of them because of their race and ethnicity are about 25 percent lower for Mexican immigrants than Mexican Americans and over 50 percent lower for Cuban immigrants than Cuban Americans. Therefore, more native-born Latina/os perceive that people are suspicious of them because of their race.

Next, we examine whether respondents feared for their safety because of race and ethnicity (Figure 14.1). In the case of Latina/os, similar to the trends above, Puerto Ricans and Mexican Americans reported higher perceptions of fearing for their safety with 36.8 percent and 34.7 percent, respectively. Among Latina/o immigrants, about 22 and 13 percent of Mexicans and Cubans, respectively, reported fearing for their safety because of their race. Among non-Latina/os, 62 percent of Blacks reported fearing for their safety, representing the highest percentages for all race and ethnic groupings. About 28 percent of whites reported fearing for their safety because of their race, which surprisingly is higher than the perceptions of both Mexican and Cuban immigrants. Therefore, in the case of differences by nativity, native-born Latina/os are more likely to fear for their safety than immigrants. This is probably attributed to the immigration crime paradox, where immigrant neighborhoods are safer than native-born neighborhoods.

Systemic Racism in Policing and Social Movements

So far, we have highlighted Latina/o criminalization and victimization, but it is also essential to acknowledge that Latina/os are not passive victims but active agents. There are numerous examples of Latina/o resiliency against criminalization and victimization. Among the most important social movements against racism in policing is the Black Lives Matter.

In July 2013, three women, Patrisse Cullors, Alicia Garza, and Opal Tometi, started #BlackLivesMatter (BLM) as a response to the acquittal of George Zimmerman in the murder of Trayvon Martin, a Black teenager. The movement had uneven support throughout the years, but this all changed in 2020 when the world witnessed the killing of an unarmed Black man, George Floyd, at the hands of a police officer.

Latina/os have been significantly involved in BLM. Indeed, Latina/os in college have had greater involvement in BLM than in political activism to protect the Deferred

Action for Childhood Arrivals (DACA) that legalizes those who are undocumented and migrated as children to the US (Hope, Keels, and Durke 2016) (Chapter 9). Pew Hispanic Center's American Trends Panel Wave 68 (June 4 to June 10, 2020) gauged the level of support for the Black Lives Matter (BLM) movement by ethnicity, race, and nativity. These national data sources confirm the broad support for BLM among Latina/os. Almost half of Mexican Americans (48.8%), Puerto Ricans (47.4%), and Mexican immigrants (46%) strongly support BLM. Latina/os are generally more supportive of BLM than non-Latina/o whites, with 37.4 percent of individuals strongly supporting BLM. About a quarter more US-born Blacks (75%) support BLM than Latina/os. However, non-Latina/o–white and Cuban immigrants have comparable percentages of individuals who strongly oppose BLM (18 and 19%, respectively).

When merging the results for "strongly support" and "somewhat support" BLM, most Latina/os support BLM on some level. In particular, Mexican immigrants are the most supportive, with 81.6 percent supporting BLM, followed by 79 percent of Mexican Americans, 78 percent of Cuban Americans, and 76 percent of Puerto Ricans. The group with the lowest percentage of support, but still over 50 percent, is Cuban immigrants (57%).

Nevertheless, Latina/o involvement in the Black Lives Matter movement is complex and plagued with identity politics. Some Latina/os are involved or supportive of the Black Lives Matter movement as a form of solidarity (Hatzipanagos 2020). Other Latina/os are cautious about what they see as the appropriation of the "Black Lives Matter" movement, even though Latina/os are also subjected to systemic racist practices in policing (Hatzipanaagos 2020). Still, others are critical of the "Latina/os for Black Lives Matter" slogan as it implies a denial of Blackness among Latina/os, given that Latina/os are mestizos and mulattos with a mixture of indigenous, African, and European ancestry (Hatzipanagos 2020).

Issues Related to the Future of Latina/o Crime and Victimization

In this section, we highlight some of the significant issues concerning Latina/o crime, criminalization, and victimization that are likely to affect their future stability in the US. We discuss structural violence that is associated with crime and victimization, laws and policies aimed to militarize the border, the hyper-criminalization, and victimization of Latina/o youth. These topics are relevant not only for future academic research but also for public policy.

Structural Violence

How should violence be conceptualized in the crime literature? For the most part, the criminal justice and criminology literature concentrates on interpersonal violence. In separate literature on social inequality, violence is conceptualized as interpersonal and structural. Galtung (1969) introduced the concept of structural violence to accentuate how violence shapes and reshapes our experiences beyond interpersonal liability-based models of agency and force. A basic premise of structural violence as a theoretical approach examines how violence is a consequence of a society's macro-level inequalities, which occur when a group of people suffers from avoidable conditions, while others do not (Morales and Bejarano 2009; Chasin 2004; Farmer 2004; Galtung 1969). To examine the root causes of Latina/o criminal behavior, such as criminalization and victimization, it is crucial to examine both interpersonal and structural approaches to violence. Thus far, structural violence approaches on Latina/o victimization have been used to conduct a historical analysis of anti-Latina/o and hate crimes (Pérez 2019), analysis of race and policing (Ihaza 2020), Latina/o families (Rodriguez et al. 2018), immigration enforcement and border crossings (Sabon 2018; Campos-Delgado 2021; Delgado 2020; Eidy, Alvarez, and Simone 2020), health (Mason-Jones and Nicholson 2018), immigration and sexual harassment (Rodríguez-Martínez and Cuenca-Piqueras 2019; Cheney et al. 2018), *crimmigration*, or the criminalization of immigration (Armenta and Vega 2017; Rumbaut, Dingeman, and Robles 2019).

Hyper-Surveillance of Latina/os

One of the most concerning issues facing Latina/os in the US is the criminalization and hyper-surveillance of Latina/o communities. Building upon Orlando Patterson's (1982) concept of "social death" or the systemic denial of humanity, Rios (2011) described the experiences of Latina/o youth as exposed to "social incapacities," or punitive social control measures used to marginalize and keep Latina/os from thriving. Moreover, such racialization practices in policing are linked to the national disparities in the incarceration of Black and American Indian youth that have remained practically unchanged for the last ten years, but the incarceration disparities for Latina/o youth did decrease 21 percent (Rovner 2021).

Summary

This chapter has provided an overview of the study and trends on Latina/o criminalization, criminal behavior, and victimization. We began by highlighting some historical and contemporary examples of how the law and the criminal justice system disproportionately criminalize Latina/os, from images of the Mexican "bandido" rooted in the aftermath of the Mexican-American War to the Zoot Suit riots of the 1940s, to the depiction of violent Latina/o youth, and today's immigration enforcement policies, which not only criminalize migrants but entire Latina/o communities. We then presented an overview of the criminological theoretical frameworks that are used to examine Latina/o criminalization (e.g. labeling theory), criminal behavior (e.g. subculture of violence, opportunity structure, racial invariance thesis, social disorganization, and collective efficacy), and racial and citizenship profiling. We also discussed the Latina/o immigrant crime paradox in which Latina/o immigrants exhibit lower levels of criminal behavior than whites, Blacks, and native-born Latina/os, despite the structural disadvantages they face (e.g. poverty, low levels of education, substandard housing, etc.). In addition, we provided an overview of patterns of criminal behavior and victimization among Latina/os based on data from the Pew Hispanic Center's National Survey of Latina/os (2008; 2018), and Pew Research Center's American Trends Panel Wave 68 (2020), to describe perceptions of racial biases in policing among Latina/o subgroups. Finally, we discussed issues that need to be considered in current and future discussions on Latina/o criminal behavior and victimization. We started with a plea to consider structural violence or structural-level perspectives in the analysis of Latina/o crime patterns and victimization.

Discussion Questions

1. What are some of the disparities that Latina/os face in the criminal justice system?

2. The US is witnessing an increase in hate crimes and mass shootings. How do societal racializations of Latina/os make them vulnerable to these types of crimes?

3. In a review of the literature on immigration and crime, Stowell and Gostjev (2018) argued that since 2010, research has focused on documenting how immigration is linked to crime rates. How are Latinas/os, both immigrant and native-born, subjected to "crimmigration" (Stumpf 2006)?

4. How did Latina/o gangs evolve from the neighborhood level to having transnational members and activities? What societal conditions in Central America and the US sustained the development of Latina/o transnational gangs?

5. How has the hyper-surveillance of Latina/os contributed to Patterson's (1982) concept of "social death"?

6. The responses to the refugee crisis have dramatically shifted approaches to border and immigration enforcement. What role has the state of Texas taken in border and immigration enforcement? How have communities and the federal government reacted to those enforcement efforts?

7. What is the difference between interpersonal violence and structural violence? Is one more damaging than the other?

15 Mass Media

The numbers in terms of representation are terrible in the media industry, and – whether it's Hollywood or hard news. For example, in entertainment, Latinos make up around three and four per cent of folks in front of and behind the camera. So we're woefully underrepresented both in front of and behind the camera, and that affects the stories that come out of Hollywood and how they're told, and oftentimes it's led to very negative portrayals and stereotypes of Latinos as drug dealers, as criminals, as the dregs of society, as illegals, and it affects how other Americans see our community and how our own children see themselves ... And in that dangerous mix, in its – in its worst form, you get what happened in El Paso, Texas, in August of 2019, where a madman drove ten hours and killed twenty-three people because he considered them quote-unquote Hispanic invaders to Texas. And so all of this represents, for me, a very dangerous void in narrative.

(Congressman Joaquin Castro in Taladrid 2021)

The mass media has historically played an important role in fostering and presenting a portrait of Latina/os locally, nationally, and internationally. As the Latina/o population has become more diverse along a variety of dimensions – generational status, national origin, language use, and socioeconomic status – this image is increasingly difficult to devise. Nonetheless, because many Americans know relatively little about Latina/os and the diversity that characterizes the group, many people rely on the mass media's depiction of Latina/os. Historically, Latina/os have been presented in stereotypical fashion, as Congressman Joaquin Castro discusses in the opening quote. Moreover, despite the major importance of Latina/os in the demographic patterns of the US, Latina/os continue to be disproportionately absent from the big screen, television, and other forms of mass media.

The absence of representation of Latina/os in the mass media results in the continuation of stereotypical images in the portrayal of Latina/os. Thus, the mainstream media tend to present Latina/os and frame issues involving them in a certain fashion. For example, they tend to stress immigration-related matters, resulting in the continuation of an image of Latina/os as immigrants. In contrast, the Spanish-language media also engage in the construction of counternarratives that give voice to people who have been marginalized in mainstream society. Yet, traditional forms of mass media including television and newspapers do not have a monopoly in the creation and dissemination of images and framing of matters related to Latina/os. This is particularly the case with the technological advancements – such as email, Facebook,

Twitter, blogs, and other forms of communication – which provide voice to a large swath of the population with mercurial speed in which images and stories can be dispersed. Such technology has made it possible to spread positive and negative images of Latina/os and the major issues that affect the community.

In this chapter, we begin with a discussion of theoretical perspectives that help us understand the framing of Latina/os in the mass media. Subsequently, we provide a discussion of the important role that the Spanish-language media has played in providing a more complete portrait of Latina/os compared to that of the mainstream media. Furthermore, we illustrate the distinct ways in which Latina/os are framed in the mainstream and Spanish-language mass media. Moreover, we assess the relative presence of Latina/os in a variety of dimensions of the mass media. Finally, we highlight some of the major issues involving Latina/os and the mass media in the near future.

Theoretical Overview

The mass media play an important role in shaping public opinion on particular issues as well as groups such as Latina/os (Markert 2010; McConnell 2011; Ordway 2020). In the case of groups of color, the mass media is particularly important in shaping opinions that members of the dominant group hold, given the lack of knowledge about and limited interaction with minority-group members. For example, Markert (2010) reports on a study that he undertook involving 136 white and Black college students concerning their interaction with and opinions about Latina/os. He found that both sets of students had a minimal number of friends and acquaintances that are Latina/o. Furthermore, Markert (2010) observed that students who had the greatest levels of animosity against Latina/os were more likely than other students to have been exposed to stories, shows, or news reports that presented Latina/os in a negative fashion compared to students who had lower levels of antagonism against Latina/os.

The mass media essentially package issues, individuals, and groups of people through frames that are presented to the general public. McConnell (2011) describes the role that framing plays in establishing an image about certain groups as well as attributes that are associated with them:

> Scholars invoking the framing perspective explore media professionals' use of media texts as organizing devices that structure information and help shape the social world . . . Through framing, members of the media create particular interpretations through the selection, emphasis and juxtaposition of material . . . Consequently, media organizations help produce discourses that do not simply reflect an objective reality. (p. 181)

As Hall (1997) argues, such discourses package what is significant, pertinent, and true for people of color (see also McConnell 2011). Without the nuances of the diversity that exists within groups of color, the group is packaged efficiently for the audience to consume and form opinions. The framing of groups of color – especially

Latina/os and African Americans – tends to provide images as the "other," people who are not like "us." Thus, Latina/os and African Americans tend to be portrayed as law breakers, criminals, hypersexual, aggressive, and so forth (McConnell 2011; Van Dijk 1991). Leo Chavez (2013) has documented in great detail the Latina/o Threat Narrative, which portrays Latina/os as criminals who are a threat to American ideals and institutions and who are not worthy of social services and education (see also Flores-Yeffal et al. 2011; Santa Ana 2002). This is a portrait that certainly does not engender empathy toward the plight of Latina/o unauthorized immigrants and, by extension, Latina/os in general.

There are three theoretical perspectives that we highlight here to help us understand how Latina/os are framed and the issues and attributes that are associated with them. These include the racial formation, powerthreat, and critical race theory perspectives.

Racial Formation Perspective

The racial formation perspective, developed by Michael Omi and Howard Winant (1994), describes how race is socially constructed through social, economic, and political forces and how it operates at the micro-level (personal interactions) and at the macro-level (institutions, laws, mass media, etc.). The racial formation perspective is especially useful in making sense of the role of the mass media in crafting frames and narratives to relay the storyline about groups of color and their societal standing (McConnell 2011). As McConnell (2011) asserts, "extensive research documents that members of the media actively construct ideologies and metaphors about racial and ethnic minorities in the US, select which information is relevant to readers, shape their depictions in texts and associated photographs and limit the variety of those depictions" (p. 181).

As noted above, Latina/os and African Americans tend to be depicted negatively as violent individuals who are prone to crime and who are outside of the mainstream. When the specter of Latina/os as criminals and as threats to the US ideals is raised, it is easy to see how people in the mainstream increase their level of hostility and distaste for "those" people (Chavez 2013; Santa Ana 2002). In addition, when Trayvon Martin was portrayed as a Black man up to no-good in a gated white community – the common frame that the mainstream "knows" – it was with ease that many in the mainstream no longer saw Martin as a scared teenager but as an aggressive man who did not belong where he was when he was murdered (Sáenz 2014). In contrast, when the mass media holds whites as the "norm," as a group without race, it supports white hegemony and white privilege, thus placing whites at the top of the racial hierarchy (Feagin 2013; Jensen 1998; McConnell 2011; Omi and Winant 1994). Accordingly, the mass media, as do other societal institutions, support and sustain the existing racial hierarchy.

Power Threat Perspective

The power threat perspective (or group size perspective), developed by Hubert Blalock (1967), overviewed in Chapter 10 provides some insights into understanding the role of the mass media in framing Latina/os, particularly with recent modifications to the original theory (Markert 2010; Weimann 2000). In its original formulation, Blalock (1967) argued that as a minority group increases in size, it becomes an economic and political threat to the dominant group, at which time – in order to protect its position of power – the dominant group establishes barriers in the form of policies and practices to limit the economic and political power of the minority group. Over the nearly sixty years since the development of the power threat perspective, a lot has changed. In particular, while the perspective focuses primarily on African Americans, Latina/os are now the largest minority groups. In addition, while the perspective placed emphasis on competition over economic resources and political power, due to the more limited influence of the mass media half a century earlier, the perspective did not take into account the role of the mass media in enhancing competition and in limiting opportunities for the minority group (Markert 2010).

Since the development of the power threat perspective, the mass media has played an increasingly powerful role in the development of frames, narratives, and images that can instantly define situations involving minority–majority relations and stir collective action to correct threats that the minority group poses to the dominant group (Markert 2010). Moreover, technological innovations, such as email, Facebook, and Twitter, can distribute mass media products instantaneously and widely. It has been suggested that the intensity of the competition rises when the minority group is quite distinct from the dominant group (Markert 2010). Markert (2010) asserts that, accordingly, Latina/os stand out from whites along the lines of their undocumented status and the perceived resistance toward learning English. Markert (2010) points out that over the last several decades there has been a shift from a greater predominance of news stories involving legal immigration over undocumented immigration to the opposite pattern. For example, Lee's (1998) research based on newspaper articles relating to immigration, published in the *New York Times* between 1965 and 1995, showed that reporting turned predominantly to undocumented immigration, beginning in 1975 with a 6:1 ratio in stories on undocumented immigration to legal immigration. Markert's (2010) replication revealed that the ratio had climbed to 30:1 during the 1996–2005 period, and the large majority of stories on undocumented immigration focused on Latina/os. In reality, as we observed back in Chapter 5, the majority of Latina/os – approximately seven out of ten – were born in the US and, thus, are not immigrants, much less undocumented immigrants.

Similarly, as the Latina/o population has grown there has been opposition to bilingual education programs as well as the increase of states around the country that have adopted English as the official language (Markert 2010). Opposition to bilingual education has been magnified further by the inaccurate belief among many opponents that bilingual education involves the instruction of students only in Spanish (Huddy and Sears 1990; Markert 2010). Rising attacks on bilingual education in California led to the passage of Proposition 227, which mandated that instruction in public schools be only in English (Markert 2010). Relatedly, 32 states in the country have made English their official language (Pro English 2023); this list includes six of the ten states with the most Latina/os: Arizona, California, Colorado, Florida, Georgia, and Illinois. Again, in actuality, 84 percent of Latina/os five years of age and older speak English, with 52 percent being bilingual (speaking Spanish at home and speaking English well or very well) and an additional 32 percent speaking English at home in 2022 (US Census Bureau 2024).

In sum, Markert (2010) seeks to extend Blalock's (1967) power threat perspective as a mediating variable that "affects the intensity of the public's hostility toward Hispanics, regardless of their population size, because media attention may make the group seem larger than it actually is, and thus more threatening" (p. 321). Inaccurate perceptions suggesting that the Latina/o population is larger than reality is fueled by news stories that tend to describe the growth to the Latina/o population in superlative terms often imbued with natural disaster prose, e.g. wave, surge, flood, etc. (Markert 2010; McConnell 2011).

Critical Race Theory

Critical race theory (CRT), developed by legal scholars such as Derrick Bell and Richard Delgado, originated as a critical response to critical legal studies and civil rights research in the 1970s, when gains from civil rights legislation waned (Delgado and Stefancic 2001; Milner and Howard 2013). In addition, CRT was critical of critical legal studies and civil rights scholarship for sidestepping the profound links between the legal system and racism. López (2006) points out that laws create racial categories and support the subordination of groups of color. One of the elements of CRT that is particularly relevant to our understanding of the role that the mass media plays in framing Latina/os is the counterstory or counternarrative that provides voice to marginalized people. As Waterman (2013) notes:

> Counterstory-telling is an important element of CRT ... Counterstories reveal the lived experiences of non-dominant groups that are typically not acknowledged by the dominant society. The popular notion that *the victor writes the history* is the common person's understanding ... that not all stories are told. CRT insists that those stories be told. (p. 340)

Thus, as the mainstream mass media present images, depictions, frames, narratives, and stories about groups of color, minority media sources provide counterimages, counterdepictions, counterframes, counternarratives, and counterstories that originate from the group and which serve to correct or provide greater nuance to tales put forth by the mainstream media.

Having provided an overview of three theoretical perspectives that allow us to gain an understanding of the framing of Latina/os, we now turn to a historical overview of the Spanish-language media and how it differs in many respects from the mainstream in its coverage of the Latina/o population. As we will see below, the Spanish-language mass media continues to be valuable in offering a counternarrative to the shallow and, oft, stereotypical narrative that the mainstream media constructs.

Historical Overview of Spanish-Language Mass Media

There is a common tendency to focus exclusively on the mainstream mass media in its treatment of Latina/os. Nonetheless, the Spanish-language media has a long history in the US. The first Spanish-language newspaper, New Orleans' *El Misisipí*, was published in 1808 (Gutiérrez 2013). In 1938, at the time that San Antonio's *La Prensa* celebrated its 25th anniversary, it published an inventory of 451 Spanish-language periodicals published in the US (Gutiérrez 2013).

The mainstream English-language and Spanish-language mass media differ significantly in their coverage of Latina/os. Gutiérrez (2013) notes the differences between the two. Gutiérrez (2013) provides an overview of the mainstream media method of appealing to an audience and in its views regarding people of color:

> They [mainstream media] seek to attract viewers, readers, and listeners by offering news, programs, or movies with broad appeal to people from different races, ages, sexes, income, and demographic categories. Although they reach multicultural, multiracial audiences, Anglo media have tended to view people of diverse cultures through eyes that see Anglo Americans as the norm and others as apart from the norm. This "us and others" media view has offered less accurate images, reporting, and coverage of people of color and the communities in which they live. This is especially apparent in the Anglo media's portrayal and coverage of Latinos. (p. 100)

Gutiérrez (2013) describes the contrasting way in which the Spanish-language and mainstream media view and portray Latina/os:

> Latino media are produced by, for, and about Latinos and their communities. Their success in drawing audiences and ultimately advertisers is built on having a close connection with the wide range of activities and issues of interest to Latinos in the US. They are more closely linked to their audiences and play important roles in explaining the US to their readers, listeners, and viewers, while also covering news in Latin America. (p. 100)

Further, David Hayes-Bautista illustrates the difference between the two media in its coverage of Latina/os:

> In the mainstream media, almost the only time you see a minority is a crime or welfare story, something negative. In the Spanish-language media, you also get the human interest, the arts and sport stories . . . Latinos are reduced to only one slice in the Anglo media, while in the Spanish media, a whole community is presented. (Gutiérrez 2013, p. 100; see also Garza 1997, p. 134)

The mainstream historically has had little knowledge of Latinos. For example, Gutiérrez (1977) conducted an analysis of magazine articles published between 1890 and 1970. Gutiérrez (1977) observed that relatively few stories reported on Latina/os and the few that were written tended to depict Latina/os as a problem or crisis. Gutiérrez (2013) notes that:

> When Latinos were covered in Anglo news media during much of the twentieth century, the editors, news directors, and reporters often used shorthand word symbols to trigger stereotypes of the Latinos seen as posing a threat, such as "Zoot Suiters" in the 1940s, "Wetbacks" [*sic*] in the 1950s, "Chicano Militants" in the 1960s, and "Illegal Aliens" in the 1970s and 1980s. (p. 102)

The lack of knowledge concerning Latina/os on the part of the mainstream media is illustrated in a 1967 magazine article in *The Atlantic* titled "A Minority Nobody Knows" (Rowan 1967; see also Gutiérrez 2013). Gutiérrez (2013) suggests that when the mass media did start paying attention to this minority nobody knows, "their stories sometimes revealed more of their own lack of knowledge or their Anglo preconceptions than the realities of the people they tried to cover" (p. 103). For example, the gulf separating white reporters and the Latina/o community is evident in a 1967 *Time* magazine article on East Los Angeles, a predominantly Mexican area in Los Angeles, which is described as "tawdry taco joints and rollicking cantinas . . . the reek of cheap wine . . . the fumes of frying tortillas . . . the machine gun patter of slang Spanish" (quoted in Gutiérrez 2013, p. 103; see also *Time* 1968). Rubén Salazar, a reporter for the *Los Angeles Times*, asserted at a conference held in San Antonio in 1969 that "It's as if the media, having finally discovered Mexican Americans, is not amused that under the serape and sombrero is a complex Chicano instead of a potential Gringo" (quoted in Gutiérrez 2013, p. 103; see also Salazar 1969). The following year Salazar was killed by a Los Angeles County sheriff's deputy during the National Chicano Moratorium.

Aside from providing the deeper more profound counternarrative to the shallow narrative of the mainstream media, the Spanish-language media serve a variety of other functions related to the Latina/o community. Luis Leal (1989), a scholar of Mexican, Chicano, and Latin American literature (see Chapter 8), lists these functions:

> . . . political and social activism; promotion of civic duties; the defense of the population against the abuse of the authorities and other organized groups; the sponsoring of national and religious holidays; the provision of an outlet for the public to express their ideas in the form of letters or to express their activity in the form of poems, short stories, essays, and an occasional serialized novel . . . Not less important has been the publication of community social news. (p. 159; see also Gutiérrez 2013, p. 105)

Gutiérrez (2013) summarizes the uniqueness of the Spanish-language press and its coverage of Latina/os in contrast to the mainstream media:

> One common theme across all Latino media is coverage of active, engaged, and ambitious people looking to make a better life for themselves and others in the US, first in print and later other media. Recognizing the fullness of Latino experiences in the US, these media show Latinos as participants, not bystanders, in events that shaped the nation and their communities. Such representation and documentation is important in countering prevailing images of Latinos as passive, unambitious, and uncultured additions to the nation. By documenting the literate tradition of Latinos and their use of new media technologies as they were developed, a more complete history of the nation and its communities can be told to a wider public. (p. 106)

The Spanish-language media, then, portray Latina/os as real people with agency who make important contributions to their communities and country. Latina/os are seen as people who have a long history in the US, who are vested in this country, and who belong here.

We can gain an understanding of the importance of the Spanish-language media in its role in calling attention to Latina/os and key issues that affect them. The spring of 2006 saw major waves of marches throughout the country bringing together undocumented immigrants along with family, friends, and supporters protesting the draconian HR 4437 – the Sensenbrenner Bill – which, among a variety of provisions, sought to enhance criminal penalties against undocumented immigrants and to make helping and abetting undocumented immigrants a felonious act. These marches, known as the Immigrant Rights Marches, also called for immigration reform with particular emphasis on the development of a path to US citizenship for undocumented immigrants. The marches caught the mainstream media off guard (Gutiérrez 2013). The mainstream media quickly placed the events within its handy, tried-and-true "sleeping giant" narrative. Accordingly, the marches represented the Latina/o sleeping giant being rousted from its somnolence (Gutiérrez 2013). The mainstream media, in fact, had been itself in a stupor while the planning of the massive marches were underway for some time earlier, illustrating its lack of connection to the Latina/o community and its grassroots organizations.

In fact, the Spanish-language media played a major role in the organizing of Latina/os. Indeed, radio personalities, most prominently Eduardo Sotelo (known as *El Piolín*), played an important part in "spreading advance word of the marches, where they would happen, and who should participate" (Gutiérrez 2013, p. 99). Yet, as Gutiérrez (2013) points out, other forms of Spanish-language mass media such as television networks (Univision and Telemundo) and newspapers played an important role as well. The morning of the 500,000-person march in Los Angeles started with the thunderous headline titled "*A Las Calles!*" ("To the Streets!") on the front page of *La Opinión*, one of the leading Spanish-language newspapers in the country housed in Los Angeles (Gutiérrez 2013).

In addition, as the traditional mass media sought answers to its query about whether the marches represented an awakening of Latina/os on the national political scene, it began to learn more about the history of Latina/o protest (Gutiérrez 2013). For example, on the *NewsHour with Jim Lehrer*, Félix Gutiérrez asserted that this was nothing new – *El Clamor Público* (The Public Clamor), a Los Angeles Spanish-language newspaper, back in 1855 was a forceful voice of protest calling attention to equal rights violations of Mexicans following the Treaty of Guadalupe Hidalgo (PBS NewsHour 2006). Gutiérrez also told of Pedro J. González, a radio personality, who opposed the repatriation of Mexicans during the Great Depression in the 1930s, *La Opinion's* critical coverage of Operation Wetback in the 1950s, among other important protests on the part of the Spanish-language mass media (PBS NewsHour 2006). In sum, the Spanish-language media provided a valuable counternarrative to the sleeping-giant narrative that the mainstream media erected.

We have presented an overview of the uniqueness of the Spanish-language media and its important role in presenting a counternarrative to the often superficial and stereotypical narrative that the mainstream promotes. We now turn to a discussion in which we draw attention to how the mainstream and Spanish-language media differ in their framing of Latina/os in the print media.

The Framing of Latina/os in the Print Media

The newspaper is an important mass media source that is quite effective in shaping opinions on political issues and on certain groups, such as groups of color and immigrants. The newspaper is a valuable source for researchers today as newspaper articles are digitalized which allow them to be compiled, culled, and sorted. Thus, scholars can analyze text and images to assess how issues or groups are framed and how the framing varies across media sources, such as mainstream versus ethnic media. We illustrate below how Latina/os are portrayed in a variety of contexts.

Framing Latina/o Population Growth in Georgia

As shown in Chapter 5, the Latina/o population has increased more rapidly than other racial and ethnic groups in the country. Newspapers around the country readily run headline stories about the growth of the Latina/o population following the release of population figures by the US Census Bureau. McConnell (2011) analyzed 70 newspaper articles appearing in the *Atlanta Journal-Constitution* between 2000 and 2003 to see how they reported the growth of different racial and ethnic groups in Gwinnett County, a suburban area that is part of the Atlanta Metropolitan Statistical Area (MSA), between 1990 and 2000.

McConnell's (2011) results indicate that while the four major racial and ethnic groups (whites, Blacks, Latina/os, and Asians) in Gwinnett County increased between 1990 and 2000, newspaper articles overwhelmingly focused on growth in the Asian and, especially, Latina/o populations. Only one-fifth of articles actually reported the growth across all four racial and ethnic groups. In contrast, 71 percent of the articles concentrated primarily on the increase of the Latina/o population, with 59 percent reporting principally on the growth of the Asian population. In fact, none of the articles focused exclusively on gains in the white or Black populations, although the absolute growth of each of these groups was larger than that of Latina/os and Asians.

Furthermore, even though whites make up the largest segment of the population of Gwinnett County and they accounted for the largest share of the county's growth between 1990 and 2000, their role in Gwinnett County's population change was minimized. Rather the focus was especially on Latina/o growth through the use of superlative words as illustrated by the following description:

> Gwinnett's population, with a whopping 657 per cent increase in Hispanics in the past decade, now claims the greatest number of Latinos in the Atlanta region. More are coming, too, furthering Gwinnett's explosive growth. (Chapman 2001; see also McConnell 2011, p. 187)

Again, minimizing the role of whites in Gwinnett County's population growth, another article focuses on the growth of gangs alongside the increase of non-white groups:

> Their names are colorful, sometimes menacing: La Gran Familia, Latin Lords, Asian Piru Bloods, Insane Blood Gangstas. There are many reasons gangs have flourished in Gwinnett, experts say, including an explosion of immigrants seeking better economic circumstances ... According to the 2000 Census, Gwinnett's Hispanic population grew from fewer than 9,000 in 1990 to 64,000 in 2000 – more than a sevenfold increase. More than 50 of the 175 gangs identified by Gwinnett police have Latino roots. The Asian community's numbers swelled even more spectacularly, from fewer than 1,000 residents from 1990 to 42,768 just a decade later. Police have identified 28 gangs with Asian ties. The Black population quadrupled from 1990 to 2000, rising to 78,224. Officials estimate 20 to 30 predominantly Black gangs in Gwinnett. Police have also identified a handful of white gangs and many white youths who are members of gangs with Asian, African-American or Latino roots. (Mungin and Davis 2003; see also McConnell 2011, p. 189)

The framing of non-white growth is simple – the massive growth of non-whites has brought an influx of gangs. This particular newspaper article illustrates the methodological caution that must be exercised in reporting percentage changes which McConnell (2011) points out, namely that an elevated percentage change is oft due to a very small population base at the earlier point in time in the comparison (e.g. 1990). Certainly, such reporting leads to the impression that the Latina/o population is larger than actuality (see above). In many Latina/o new-destination areas, such as Georgia, extraordinary high levels of growth were due largely to very small population sizes at the beginning of the comparative period.

The Framing of Latina/os in Virginia

Virginia represents another new-destination area for Latina/os. Stewart et al. (2011) conducted an analysis of the discourse of undocumented immigration in articles appearing in *The Virginian Pilot*, which serves the Hampton Roads region of Virginia – including Virginia Beach, the state's largest city, between 1994 and 2006. These researchers undertook two studies – the first based on articles, editorials, and letters to the editor appearing in the newspaper between 1994 and 2006 to examine the salience of the term "illegal immigrants" in these texts and the second based on an examination of two local events (an undocumented immigrant drunk driver who killed two teenage girls in a crash and undocumented workers employed for a Verizon contractor) associated with undocumented workers that occurred in 2007.

The findings of Stewart et al. (2011) suggest newspaper reports constructed "illegal immigrants" as a metonym – a word or phrase used as a substitute for something else – for Latina/o immigrants. Thus, just as "Washington" is used to represent the federal government, illegal immigrant is used to signify Latina/o immigrants. The analysis reveals discourse showing the threat that Latina/os represent: "Local policy let this illegal immigrant [Alfredo Ramos, the drunk driver] flout the law" (Stewart et al. 2011, p. 20); Ramos described in court as having a "zombie like demeanor" and unable to "muster any visible remorse" (Stewart et al. 2011, p. 21); "While we have heard repeated apologies from Hispanic leaders, most recently in announcing an alliance of sorts with MADD to combat drunk driving, I've yet to hear an apology from the people in the Hispanic community" (Stewart et al. 2011, p. 21).

Stewart et al. (2011) report a few incidences in which whites took action in response to their suspicions that some Latina/os were in the country illegally. In addition, Stewart et al.'s (2011) interviews with local Latina/os demonstrated that Latina/os feared a backlash. Stewart et al. (2011) describe the feelings of local Latina/os:

> These Latino community members clearly sensed that they were perceived as a threat by the majority and worked to counter stereotypes that were developing within the local news media. These out-group responses to this news discourse show how its rhetorical force is created through widespread public participation in the construction and definition of the illegal immigrant . . . This rhetorical force is strongly tied to the marker of race; despite being longtime residents and established business owners in the community they perceived that their identities as Latinos are still constrained by dominant media constructions of (illegal) immigrants. (p. 23)

This research project shows how the construction of the "illegal immigrant" term came to represent all Latina/os in the Hampton Roads region of Virginia. Latina/os clearly became marked as the "other," individuals who do not belong in the community.

Framing a Wise Latina

Thus far, we have examined how the mainstream media has framed, constructed, and represented Latina/os, as a group, in two new-destination areas. We now shift to how a particular individual Latina woman was framed differently by the mainstream media and the Spanish-language media. On May 26, 2009 President Barack Obama nominated Sonia Sotomayor to the Supreme Court. As the nomination process went into effect, pundits, journalists, legislators, and the general public began looking into her background, experience, politics, and legal decisions (Nielsen 2013). Nielsen (2013) conducted an analysis of 124 news articles related to Sotomayor that appeared in the *New York Times* (76 articles) and *El Diario-La Prensa* (48 articles) – a Spanish-language newspaper located in New York City – between the date of her nomination (May 26, 2009) and one week after she was sworn (August 15, 2009). Nielsen's (2013) analysis was based on the use of critical race theory and the intersectionality perspective, which takes into account the intersection between race, class, and gender.

The results of Nielsen's (2013) analysis clearly show that the two newspapers framed Sotomayor distinctly. In particular, the two outlets differed significantly in how they framed the issue of diversity. The *Times* articles focused primarily on the *burden of diversity* with the discourse primarily centered on concerns that Sotomayor has in-group biases and favoritism toward Latina/os. In contrast, *El Diario* articles emphasized the benefit of diversity, highlighting the favorable attributes that she brings to the job such as opening doors of opportunities for others.

The newspapers also diverged in the way that they defined the catchphrase "wise Latina" which was culled from a 3,932-word speech that Sotomayor had delivered at the University of California, Berkeley School of Law in 2002 (Nielsen 2013). In the speech she states, "I would hope that a wise Latina woman with the richness of her experiences would more often than not reach a better conclusion than a white male who hasn't lived that life" (Nielsen 2013, p. 127). The *Times* articles containing the catch phrase were either based on her opponents who found it to be racist or characterized as reverse racism or based on her supporters who offered apologies for Sotomayor (Nielsen 2013). In contrast, *El Diario* "reclaimed the phrase as an expression of pride" (Nielsen 2013, p. 127). *El Diario* saw the value in what a wise Latina brings to legal discourse. Nielsen (2013) points out that the reclamation of the catch phrase reached the marketplace: "The reclamation of 'wise Latina' created a marketing boom, with everything from mouse pads to baby bibs bearing phrases such as 'I love Wise Latinas' or 'Future Wise Latina'" (p. 127).

Moreover, the two newspapers varied also in yet another way, in the way that they covered and analyzed Sotomayor. Nielsen (2013) finds that the *Times* articles tend to highlight her ethnicity over other personal salient attributes. In contrast, *El Diario* articles presented a fuller panorama of Sotomayor, drawing on her ethnicity, class, and gender.

In sum, consistent with critical race theory, while the *Times* framed and developed a narrative on Sotomayor, *El Diario* represented the counternarrative. As Nielsen summarizes:

> *El Diario* provided a counternarrative to the *Times* in all aspects of this study from frames to news packages to exemplars, metaphors, and catchphrases ... by challenging mainstream media messages about racism, by including the stories of people who have experienced oppression, and by avoiding an Anglo-as-norm standpoint. (p. 129)

Having now provided some illustrations on how the print media frames and develops narratives on Latina/os and the role of the ethnic media in presenting counterframes and counternarratives, we now provide a discussion of how Latina/os are marketed.

Latina/o Spin: The Marketing of Latina/os

We have seen above how the mainstream mass media has defined and portrayed Latina/os. There is a long history of Latina/os portrayed on the big screen as well as the small screen as criminals, thugs, bandits, shiftless, people who are in this country illegally, and who do work that no one else wants to do (Rodríguez 2008). The phrase "illegal immigrant" has come to signify "Latino immigrant" and to a certain extent "Latino" (Stewart et al. 2011). Samuel Huntington (2004) two decades ago targeted Latina/os as a threat to national ideals, democracy, and institutions. Clearly, there are a lot of negative images in place that vilify Latina/os.

There are counterimages that have developed over the last couple of decades that attempt to counter these images. However, in contrast to the counternarrative from the critical race theory that calls attention to racism and the legal systems and institutions that create and support the subordination of people of color, these counterimages tend to be colorblind and attempt to make Latina/os palatable to mainstream society (Dávila 2008; Guillem and Briziarelli 2012; del Rio 2012). Arlene Dávila (2008) refers to these counterimages as the "Latino spin." We discuss here how the Latina/o spin packages Latina/os as a cultural product and as an economic product. Subsequently, we highlight two major projects that have sought to correct stereotypical images associated with Latina/os and how these can be classified as part of the Latina/o spin genre.

In response to portrayals of Latina/os in negative fashion associated with criminality, dishonesty, laziness, and other forms of moral turpitude, advocates of Latina/os have constructed descriptions of Latina/os that emphasize their hard-work ethic, strong family values, and conservative ideals (Dávila 2008). Dávila recalls interviewing Raul Yzaguirre, former president of the National Council for La Raza (now UnidosUS), in 2006 when he reflected about the biggest challenge being to correct the stereotypes that had been perpetuated against Latina/os. Yzaguirre states:

> We have to understand and internalize that Hispanics are the hardest working of Americans, the most patriotic of Americans, the most family oriented and entrepreneurial of Americans. Everything that is supposed to be uniquely American we embody. We originated these arguments a long time ago and I'm happy that they are being picked up but they are not picked up enough. The average American does not hear these arguments. When I make them to an Anglo audience they say, wow! They are surprised to learn that Hispanics have higher participation in the labor force, that they work more hours per week. These are surprising facts. (Dávila 2008, p. 33)

In addition, Jorge Ramos (2004; see also Dávila 2008), Univision anchor, argues that Latina/o conservative values, encompassed by opposition to abortion, homosexuality, and divorce, are the cherished values that Americans hold dearly. Ramos (2004; see also Dávila 2008) further asserts that through their strong moral and family values, Latina/os make important contributions to the American moral fabric. Moreover, Lionel Sosa, the highly successful advertising agent commonly contracted by Republican candidates, is fond of saying that the first time he met Ronald Reagan (prior to becoming president), he told him "Hispanics are Republicans, they just don't know it" (Dávila 2008, p. 59). These messages tend to draw Latina/os as a homogeneous group of people who are just like regular white Americans. Latina/os are not subverting and invading the US, they are strengthening its morals.

In contrast to the image of Latina/os as poor people dependent on public assistance, the Latina/o-spin counterimage emphasizes the hard-work ethic of Latina/os, upward mobility, entrepreneurial spirit and the expanding purchasing power of Latina/os. There is often pride in that American employers prefer to hire Latina/o immigrants over African American, native-born Latina/o, and even white workers, with the notion that Latina/o immigrants outperform other workers (see Wilson 1997). Of course, one of the reasons why US employers prefer Latina/o immigrants, especially those without documents, is that they can pay them lower wages and they are less likely to complain due to their lack of US citizenship. Furthermore, there is increasing attention to the growing Latina/o middle class and to the expanding Latina/o purchasing power. Indeed, according to the University of Georgia's Selig Center for Economic Growth (2012), the $1.2 trillion buying power of Latina/os in 2012 is larger than the market of all but thirteen countries around the world. While the Spanish-language Univision television station is a major promoter of the large and growing Latina/o market, it goes way beyond the Spanish-language media (Dávila 2008). For example, Dávila (2008) calls attention to an email that a Hispanic marketing agency owner sent to his clients: "Recognize that in just seven years, the 43 million plus Hispanics in the US today will have spending power equivalent to 60 percent of all 1.3 billion Chinese" (p. 71). The message is clear – Latina/os represent major dollars for the business community.

The cultural and economic packaging of Latina/os shows the importance of Latina/os for the US and its economy. The message is completely colorblind, as the issue of race is completely invisible from these narratives. There is no reference to the many Latina/o children who are poor, the many Latina/os who are working but still poor, and the many Latina/os who do not have health care insurance. There is no mention of the exploitation that many Latina/os encounter in their jobs. In fact, it has been suggested that there are some Latina/o political and economic leaders who make sure that statistics that make Latina/os look bad do not see the light of day. One analyst indicates that a report that he produced for the Puerto Rican Legal Defense Education Fund (PRLDEF) in 2004, which showed that Puerto Ricans were three times more likely to be poor than the national average, received much negative reaction from community leaders who wanted this fact buried because it would make Puerto Ricans look bad (Dávila 2008). Certainly, when the emphasis is on presenting an image of Latina/os as successful and content, the important concerns of people on the margins are hidden away.

We now turn to two major undertakings that sought to deal either with stereotypical or incomplete representations of Latina/os in a Latina/o-spin fashion. These two venues are the multimedia project *Americanos: Latino Life in the US/La Vida Latina en los Estados Unidos*, which started in 1999 (del Rio 2012; see also Olmos et al. 1999) and the CNN two-part documentary *Latino in America*, which aired in 2009 (Guillem and Briziarelli 2012; see also O'Brien 2009).

Esteban del Rio (2012) conducted a study analyzing the *Americanos* project. We highlight his work here. The project began in the late 1990s and involved collaboration between actor Edward James Olmos, sociologist Lea Ybarra, and photojournalist Manuel Monterrey, in partnership with the Smithsonian Institution and Time Warner (del Rio 2012). Olmos points out that the project had two aims: "(1) to present the diversity of *Latinidad* as a cultural signifier; and (2) . . . to build a coherent cultural unity for Latina/os" (del Rio 2012, p. 191; see also Sanches 1999). Del Rio (2012) offers a critique of the exhibit. He argues that the exhibit kept a white audience in mind. He points out that the work is couched within multicultural and universalistic frameworks, where despite our differences that we celebrate, in reality we are all the same, as shown by the daily rituals in which Latina/os engage. One photographer claims in the exhibit's brochure:

> By revealing our commonality through the daily rituals of home, family, and community, others can see that Latinos are a vital part of America and that we are more than the stereotypes portrayed in most of today's media. I hope that this exhibition can show America that we are all the same. (Goldson 1999; see also del Rio 2012, p. 186)

One segment of the exhibit hails the American Dream and what Latina/os can achieve through hard work. One part of this section features the story and photographs of US Representative from California Xavier Becerra's family. Becerra reflects on the life of his parents and what they have accomplished:

> Maria Teresa and Manuel married in Mexico and moved to California. Manuel helped build our nation from the ground up, laying pipe and concrete. While raising four children, Maria Teresa worked and attended night school to learn English . . . They were able to buy their first home. Now in retirement, Manuel and Maria Teresa own many homes. They are an American success story and they are my parents. (del Rio 2012, p. 194)

As del Rio (2012) points out, however, the exhibit is devoid of the discussion of political struggle as well as structural inequality, thus creating a sanitized colorblind portrait that makes mainstream America comfortable. Del Rio notes that few photographs feature the many activists who have struggled to bring justice to Latina/os over their long history in this country. Yet, the few photographs that show such individuals present them in a passive manner, e.g. a small group of union employees protesting against an unfair labor contract with the University of Southern California; a poet, artist, and activist sitting at his desk; and Luis Valdez, Teatro Campesino founder, shown sitting off to the side of a stage (del Rio 2012).

Obviously in exhibits such as this one that involve partnerships with governmental institutes (Smithsonian Institution) and corporations (Time Warner), the messaging is affected by what such sponsors require and the limitations that they impose. While *Americanos* confronted the many stereotypical images of Latina/os, it did so in a multicultural, universalistic, colorblind, and ahistorical fashion – a way which was palatable and not offensive to the mainstream (del Rio 2012).

The second work that we will examine is CNN's two-part documentary *Latino in America*, hosted by Soledad O'Brien, which was aired in 2009. We highlight here the research of Guillem and Briziarelli (2012) in which they analyzed *Latino in America*, along with Latina/o audience reaction. The producers of the documentary aimed to examine "how Latina/os are reshaping our communities and culture and forcing a nation of immigrants to rediscover what it means to be an American (CNN 2009; see also Guillem and Briziarelli 2012). Soledad O'Brien, then anchor of CNN and a person who is Latina and Irish, served as the host of the documentary.

Guillem and Briziarelli's (2012) findings offer a number of critiques of the documentary. Overall, these researchers suggest that the documentary reflects a two-way street involving assimilation – on the one hand, the show highlights the obstacles that Latina/os encounter when they retain their Latina/o ethnicity and, on the other hand, the fact that Latina/os are redefining the mainstream. Guillem and Briziarelli (2012) observe three paths that the documentary describes, in which Latina/os try to better their socioeconomic situation: (1) the loss of ethnic identity and the achievement of socioeconomic success; (2) the retention of Latina/o ethnicity and the barrier that it represents in attaining socioeconomic success; and (3) the maintenance of Latina/o ethnicity alongside socioeconomic success. Of the stories featured in the documentary that fit exclusively into one of these paths, four related to the first path, seven to the second, and eight to the third. Guillem and Briziarelli (2012) call attention to problems in the two most popular paths. First, the latter path, the one in which people reconcile their ethnicity and socioeconomic attainment, the individuals who are featured are not typical of the Latina/o cross-section, but are persons who are either celebrities or people in the entertainment industry, such as Eva Longoria and Chef Lorena Garcia (Guillem and Briziarelli 2012). Even in the case of Chef Lorena, who immigrated to the US, she is not the typical Latina immigrant, as initially she was going to attend law school and ended up pursuing a career as a chef (Guillem and Briziarelli 2012). Second, is the second path, the one in which people maintain their Latina/o ethnicity and encounter problems with socioeconomic achievement. A representative story is one about a Puerto Rican young man whose dream is to be a police officer, but his lack of English skills and thick accent prevent him from passing a requisite exam. He fails yet another attempt, but insists that he will keep trying. As Guillem and Briziarelli point out, the stories involving such failures end on an optimistic note, as O'Brien lauds their insistence that they will keep on trying and she does not critically examine the systemic inequities that keep people from achieving their dream.

Guillem and Briziarelli (2012) additionally analyze more than 500 commentaries from Latina/o viewers regarding the documentary. One of the main criticisms that the audience leveled against the documentary was that the primary emphasis was on failure rather than success. In particular, many audience commentators indicated that they viewed the path involving the maintenance of Latina/o ethnicity and the obstacle that it represented in attaining socioeconomic success as a failure, rather than as a success as depicted by O'Brien. In addition, viewers also were critical about the unrepresentativeness of celebrities as the people who have kept their ethnicity and achieved socioeconomic success. Viewers suggested that there are many successful Latina/os in the community from other walks of life who could have been featured.

In the end, while the documentary did feature the diversity that characterizes the Latina/o population, there were limitations in presenting an accurate representation of Latina/os as well as the structural inequities that block opportunities for Latina/os. Like *Americanos, Latino in America* comes across as a feel-good overview of Latina/os with the documentary not addressing underlying inequities that produce and maintain racial subordination.

Social Media, Misinformation, and Latina/os

As social media continues to become an important part of everyday lives, people are increasingly faced with many of the challenges that come from this form of media. The problematic side of social media in influencing real life was especially visible in the 2020 elections and the COVID-19 pandemic, where Latina/os were primary targets of campaigns promoting certain political angles to both of these events.

The spread of misinformation and disinformation through social media via advertisements was rampant during the 2020 presidential cycle. Facebook ads targeting Latina/o voters in Texas and Florida, describing Biden as a communist, were aimed at Spanish-speaking communities. In a study conducted by the Election Integrity Partnership, the group found that narratives and messages "took the form of religious commentary denouncing socialism and the left, which appeals to Latino audience members who come from religious, often Catholic, backgrounds and/or who fled a socialist regime in their birth country" (Center for an Informed Public 2021). Misinformation and disinformation are more likely to reach Latina/os, according to one source, because they spend more time on social media sites, including YouTube, Instagram, and WhatsApp (Seitz and Weissert 2021). According to a Pew Research Center survey, the percentage of adult Latina/os who use YouTube was 85 percent in 2021, compared to 79 percent of whites (Auxier and Anderson 2021). In Florida during the 2020 election, conspiracy theories referring to the "deep state" were found to be prominent (Rodriguez and Caputo 2020). The harm that misinformation and disinformation can cause to democracy is in the erosion of public trust, discouraging people from civic participation, and influencing elections that ultimately impact public policy. The movement of misinformation through social media sites targeted at Latina/os was also a huge problem after the onset of the COVID-19 pandemic that had a direct impact on Latina/o health and decision making.

Following the start of the COVID-19 pandemic, mortality rates began to rise, and many people began to hope for a vaccine. However, the spread of misinformation has largely been identified as part and parcel of the reason for what became known as the "vaccine gap," where Latina/os were less likely to get the COVID-19 vaccine, all the while having higher chances of becoming infected, primarily because many Latina/os have increased risk of exposure due to their occupation. One report published by First Draft (now the Information Futures Lab at Brown University) in 2021 examined vaccine misinformation and the Latina/o community and found that narratives promoting doubt about the vaccine targeted at Latina/os were the most widespread in social media (Longoria et al. 2021). These narratives included claims about the vaccine causing sterilization and death, which played into existing fears and distrust of the US health care system among many Latina/o communities (Longoria et al. 2021). Some other findings of the report highlight the need for platforms to combat Spanish-language misinformation, specifically, and to provide culturally informed moderation of Spanish-language content (Longoria et al. 2021).

In 2022, the Spanish Language Disinformation Coalition, which consists of civil rights, Latino leadership, and consumer advocacy organizations, called for stronger civic integrity policies from Meta, YouTube, Instagram, Twitter, TikTok, and Snap, urging that without stronger policies in place, Latinos would again be targets of disinformation and misinformation.

Social media, however, can also present a very real opportunity for marginalized voices to shake up political infrastructure, change narratives, and be heard. The Pew Research Center found in a recent study that social media platforms provide an important role in political activism, noting that almost half of all Black, Latina/o, and Asian users believe social media is very or somewhat important for finding other people who share their views about important issues (Bestvater et al. 2023). Social media platforms can serve to launch movements.

One example would be Puerto Rico's "RickyLeaks." In 2019, private messages between then-Governor Ricardo Rosselló and his aides by the Centro de Periodismo Investigativo (CPI), sparked widespread protests leading to Rosselló's resignation (Jin 2019). The leaked messages revealed attempts to manipulate media coverage, including discussions on influencing journalists and altering news content. The messages not only contained derogatory language toward women and victims of Hurricane María but also revealed instances of homophobia (Jin 2019). This incident highlighted concerns about the relationship between politicians and the press in Puerto Rico, where advertising revenue from the government plays a significant role in sustaining media outlets (Jin 2019). The hashtag #RickyRenuncia ignited a movement that called global attention to the issues being faced in Puerto Rico and "consequently, diaspora members used social media to call and celebrate demonstrations in Washington DC; Orlando, Florida; Denver, Colorado; Austin and Dallas, Texas; Seattle, Washington, and Saint Louis, Missouri" (Nieves-Pizarro and Mundel 2021).

In 2020, Army Specialist Vanessa Guillen was reported missing from Fort Hood in Texas and her remains were found later that year. This tragic case brought to light the history of sexual assault in the military. The hashtag #IAmVanessaGuillen became a social media movement bringing forward thousands of survivors to share their stories (Sicard 2020). The hashtag and the additional attention that it brought to the case sparked wider community support, the demand for answers, and social protests (J. Hernández 2022).

Mass Media Patterns Concerning Latina/os

As we have done in other chapters, we examine the current standing of Latina/os on the subject matter being covered in the particular chapter – in this case, mass media. In contrast to other chapters, there are limited sources of data available to undertake a systematic analysis of the state of Latina/os in the mass media. In this section we provide information on general patterns that we have observed in the literature and in related sources.

Latina/o Employment in the Media Industry

Noting the persistent lack of Latina/o representation in US media, in 2020 US congressman and then-chair of the Congressional Hispanic Caucus (CHC), Joaquin Castro of Texas, led a group of members of the CHC and the House Committee on Oversight and Reform, to request an official report on Latina/o employment in the media (including film, television, and publishing sectors) from the Government Accountability Office (GAO). Three years after the GAO released two separate reports with the findings of its investigation, the congressman wrote in response, "I wanted to know whether our nation's largest minority has a voice in America's narrative-creating and image-defining industry. The answer is a resounding no" (Castro 2023b).

In the first report released in 2021, the US Government Accounting Office (2021) report utilized American Community Survey data to estimate the number of Latina/o workers in the media workforce. Their study found that Latinas/os made up 12 percent of the media workforce in 2019, compared to 18 percent in the rest of the workforce. The report also found that Latina/o underrepresentation in the media industry has persisted. The GAO report shows that from 2014 to 2019, Latina/o representation in the media industry remained at an estimated 11 to 12 percent, while Latina/o representation in all other industries combined comprised 16 to 18 percent over the same time period (US Government Accounting Office 2021). In terms of print media, the report found that Latina/os make up 8 percent of the newspaper, periodical, book, and directory publishers' workforce. In television, the report found that Latina/os make up approximately 11 percent of news analysts, reporters and journalists. Unsurprisingly, the report also found that Latina/os have the largest percentage of service jobs within the sector and the lowest representation among management in media.

The second report released in 2022 included additional analysis of Latina/o representation in media, including representation disaggregated by gender. Further, the second report summarized the findings from efforts to identify the challenges that contribute to the lower representation of Latina/os in the media industry. Those challenges, according to the GAO report, include financial barriers, challenges obtaining education, limited access to professional networks, difficulty meeting requirements for union membership and lack of diversity among talent agents, media executives, and other decision makers (US Government Accounting Office 2022b). More data are needed to understand Latina/o representation in mass media employment, the role of the union membership in the media industry, and the roles of the Federal Communications Commission (FCC) and the Equal Employment Opportunity Commission (EEOC) in enforcing anti-discrimination laws in the industry.

The Representation of Latina/os in Movies and Television

Over the history of Hollywood movies there has been an increase of Latina/o actors, although they continue to be portrayed in stereotypical manners (Rodríguez 2008). Yet, despite these gains, Latina/os continue to be disproportionately underrepresented and to play supporting rather than leading roles (Rodríguez 2008). For example, a study by researchers at the University of Southern California's Annenberg School for Communication and Journalism analyzed 500 top-grossing movies and 20,000 speaking characters appearing between 2007 and 2012 (Keegan 2013). The study found that while Latina/os accounted for approximately 26 percent of all movie ticket sales, they only accounted for 4 percent of all speaking parts in the movies analyzed over the period (Keegan 2013). In contrast, while whites constituted 56 percent of all moviegoers, they comprised 76 percent of all speaking parts (Keegan 2013). Moreover, true to the stereotypical image of sexual objects, Latina women were the most likely racial/ethnic-gender group to be shown nude or donning sexy clothing (Keegan 2013). In addition, Latina/os did not appear or fare much better on television. For example, a study of prime-time television shows in March 2007 appearing on ABC, CBS, FOX, and NBC revealed that Latina/os only accounted for 5 percent of characters in these shows (Monk-Tanner et al. 2010) with an even smaller percentage (3%) a decade earlier (Mastro and Greenberg 2000).

Moreover, in many ways, Latina/os continue to be absent from movies and television in yet another way. In particular, Latina/os are noticeably removed from movies and television series that are based in particular locales where Latina/os are well represented. For example, Rodríguez (2008) observes that in the movie *Ghost* coming out in 1990, which took place in New York City, where Latina/os at the time comprised one-fourth of the city's population, Latina/os were completely absent, save for "the repellent villain and a confused spiritualist seeker" (p. 192). In addition, the hit series *Seinfeld*, which aired from 1989 to 1998, and which also took place in New York, featured almost exclusively white people. Latina/os were absent from this series, with a few exceptions, including the Puerto Rican parade episode, in which one of the regular characters, Kramer, accidentally set a Puerto Rican flag on fire and proceeded to stamp on it, which drew the rage of Puerto Rican bystanders; the episode received much complaint from the Latina/o community for showing the Puerto Rican flag being burned and stomped and the portrayal of Puerto Ricans as aggressive. Similarly, the HBO-aired series *Curb Your Enthusiasm*, which featured Larry David – the creator of *Seinfeld* – as the star, was based in Los Angeles but hardly included any Latina/o characters, except for an occasional maid. Rodríguez (2008) further notes that Latina/os are also virtually absent – aside from isolated parts as criminals or people performing cleaning jobs – in other major Hollywood movies including *Beverly Hills Cop*, *Beverly Hills Cop II*, *Down and Out in Beverly Hills*, *Forrest Gump*, *Pretty Woman*, *Terminator 2*, and *Rambo First Blood Part 2* (Rodríguez 2008).

The Representation of Latina/os on News Shows

While the Latina/o population is driving the US demography, is an increasingly important segment of the voting population, and is likely to account for the large majority of the nation's population growth over the coming decades, it is virtually invisible among political commentators discussing current political events and the future of the US. This represents yet another paradox, where the rising demographic and political strength of the Latina/o population does not translate to a representative voice in the mass media discussing important political issues. Jamie Reno (2012) in an article titled "Why Don't We Have More Hispanic Talking Heads?" commenting a few days after the November 2, 2012 election describes this situation:

> It's official: Latina/os are now the nation's most coveted 'new' voting bloc, and they'll have a record 31 members in Congress come January. But amid all the talk of Hispanics' new political clout, they're still barely visible as anchors or hosts on the national broadcast and cable news networks, even liberal channels such as MSNBC. And without these voices, several sources say, their power is weakened despite what happened on Tuesday.
>
> There's been a lot of talk on all the English-language television networks since the election about the increasing power of the Latina/o vote – but virtually all of the television pundits pontificating about this subject this past week have been non-Hispanic. On MSNBC's *Morning Joe* on Friday morning, for example, all four white males over 50 sat around and talked about the election, including the Latino vote.
>
> In fact, of the 23 MSNBC anchors and hosts listed on the network's website, apparently only one is Hispanic.
>
> And, while CNN has CNN en Español, on the main network only two of the 21 anchors and hosts are Hispanic: Soledad O'Brien and Zoraida Sambolin.

Furthermore, Otto Santa Ana (2013) in his book titled *Juan in a Hundred: The Representation of Latina/os on Network News* observes that less than 1 percent of all news covered on the evening news programs of ABC, CBS, CNN, and NBC focuses on Latina/os with the minuscule number of such stories slanted in a negative direction (see also Dominguez 2013). To date, there has been hardly any change (see Rendon 2024).

The Representation of Latina/os in Newspaper Articles

Latina/os do not fare much better in printed media. To examine the prevalence of articles in the *New York Times* we did a search of the keywords "Hispanic" or "Latino," using LexisNexis Academic, and selected the "On-High similarity" option in the Duplicate option. There are two caveats to be aware of with the analysis overviewed below. First, the identified articles merely contain the word "Latino" or "Hispanic" and, thus, the gist of the content may not be related specifically to Latina/os. Second, beginning in 2007 the *New York Times* started using blogs, which have become quite popular since 2011, and these are not considered in the analysis to be able to more effectively compare the number of articles across time periods, including when blogs were not used.

Over the period between 1980 and 2019, we found a total of 50,108 articles including the words "Hispanic" or "Latino," which appeared in the *New York Times*. Figure 15.1 presents the total number of these articles for four time periods: 1980–1989, 1990–1999, 2000–2009, and 2010–2019. There is a general increase in the number of articles related to Latina/os over the periods covered, rising from 9,062 in the 1980–1989 period to 16,003 in the 2010–2019 period, an increase of 77 percent between these periods. Despite the general upward trend in the number of articles in the *New York Times* containing the word Hispanic or Latino, it has not kept up with the quadrupling of the Latino population between 1980 and 2020 (see Chapter 5).

Moreover, supplementary analysis shows that the articles related to Latina/os are increasingly tied to immigration. We conducted this part of the analysis by computing the percentage of articles containing the word "Latino" or "Hispanic" that also contain the word "immigration" or "immigrant." Figure 15.2 shows the percentage of articles making reference to immigration over the four time periods. There is a rising share of articles related to Latina/os that are also connected to immigration, with the percentage rising steadily from roughly 14 percent in the 1980–1989 period to 37 percent in the 2010–2019 period.

The overall trends related to the relative absence of Latina/os in the mass media in general and in positions of political commentary on television are consistent with the assertion that Marco Portales (2000) makes that Latina/os are "crowded out" in the mass media and, by extension, in the public consciousness. As Portales (2000) suggests:

> African Americans have spokespeople . . . who continue to speak out against the distortions and misrepresentations. With two or possibly three not very widely known exceptions, Latinos have not had the benefit of being defended or promoted by known voices or champions. César Chávez spoke out for the California field migrant workers in the 1960s, but the leaders envisioned by enlightened intellectuals like Carey McWilliams and other less known Chicano activists in the late 1960s simply have not materialized during the last thirty years. (p. 57)

The absence of such individuals in the Latina/o community as was apparent during the Immigrant Rights marches of 2006 took place without a clearly recognized leader. In addition, when Paul Taylor and Mark Hugo Lopez (2010) at the Pew Hispanic Center queried a sample of Latina/os in 2010 about whom they consider to be the most important Latina/o leader in the nation, nearly two-thirds responded that they did not know, with an additional one-tenth indicating that there is no one who fits the bill. Supreme Court Justice Sonia Sotomayor was identified as the most recognized Latina/o leader in the country by only 7 percent of the sample, followed by Illinois Congressman Luis Gutierrez with 5 percent, then-mayor of Los Angeles Antonio Villaraigosa with 3 percent, Univision anchorman Jorge Ramos with 2 percent, and an open "other" category receiving 8 percent of the response. Taylor and Lopez (2010) jest that the job of national Latina/o leader is open.

The absence of a clearly recognized national Latina/o leader, in part, reflects the disproportionate absence of Latina/os in the mass media and stage of public discourse. In some ways, the absence of Latina/os in a variety of media sources and public dialogue reflects the view of Latina/os as newcomers – as a people who are immigrants – a view that ignores the fact that the majority of Latina/os were born in the US and a certain segment of the population has been here for many generations.

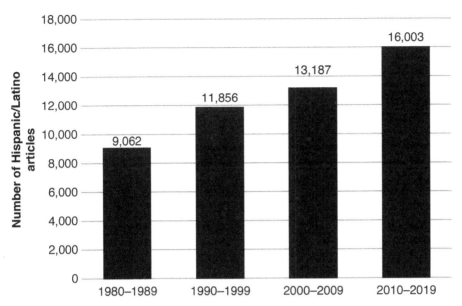

Figure 15.1 Number of Articles in the *New York Times* Containing "Hispanic" or "Latino" by Period

Source: Data from LexisNexis Academic search conducted on September 17, 2023.

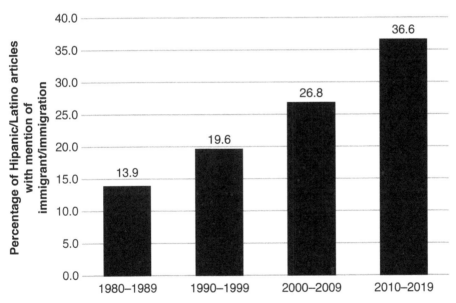

Figure 15.2 Percentage of Articles in the *New York Times* Containing "Hispanic" or "Latino" That Also Contain "Immigrant" or "Immigration" by Period

Source: Data from LexisNexis Academic search conducted on September 17, 2023.

Issues Related to the Future of Latina/os and the Mass Media

There are a number of questions on which we need to keep an eye in the coming decades, related to the imaging of Latina/os in the mass media in light of their disproportionate influence on the demography of the country. We examine two areas below – the framing of Latina/os in the context of expanding numbers and the future of the Spanish-language media.

The Framing of Latina/os in the Context of Expanding Numbers

As we saw in Chapter 5, the Latina/o population is projected to drive the demography of the US in the coming decades. The relative size of the Latina/o population is expected to rise and these shifts are no longer limited to a few regions of the country where Latina/os have been historically concentrated, as Latina/os have increasingly moved to new-destination areas. Earlier in this chapter, we examined Blalock's theoretical insights on how the growing presence of minority groups represents a threat to the dominant group, which then erects barriers and policies to limit the political and economic power of the minority group. In recent reformulations of Blalock's theory, the mass media has been introduced as an increasingly important resource that the dominant group uses to control the "threat" of the growing minority group through the framing of the group and salient political issues.

The growing numbers of Latina/os has certainly led to the mounting of efforts on the part of segments within the white community to portray Latina/o immigrants – and, by extension, Latina/os in general – as people who do not belong in the country, who are here illegally, and who negatively impact the communities where they live. This hostility directed against Latina/os existed before Donald Trump opened his presidential campaign, but Trump has escalated this attack against Latina/os. It remains to be seen whether the growing numbers of Latina/os and their increasing purchasing power will lead to more objective or sympathetic framing of Latina/os on the part of the traditional mass media. Undoubtedly, the mainstream mass media will need to enhance the recruitment of Latina/os as journalists, news analysts, correspondents, and commentators in order to gain a fuller understanding of Latina/os and to include them in the ongoing dialogue concerning issues that affect Latina/os. Currently, data from the 2021 American Community Survey public-use file suggests that Latina/os account for 9.5 percent of news analysts, reporters, and journalists in the country. Other sources provide earlier alternate statistics. For example, the American Society of News Editors reported that in 2012 Latina/os represented only 4.1 percent of journalists working in daily newspapers; the Radio Television Digital News Association announced that Latina/os made up 7.3 percent of local television news employees and 2.6 percent of radio news workers (Gutiérrez 2013). Moreover, as illustrated above, Latina/os are severely underrepresented among commentators – the talking heads – addressing critical issues affecting the country and world on popular news programs.

The Future of the Spanish-Language Media

The Spanish-language media is a strong presence in the lives of Latina/os and in closely reporting on Latina/os and the issues that affect them. As we have seen above, the Spanish-language media play an important role in providing a counternarrative to what the mainstream offers concerning Latina/os. The large-scale growth of the Latina/o population bodes well for the popularity of Spanish-language media in the future. For the first time ever, in June 2013 the Univision television network attracted more viewers among the coveted 18–34 and 18–49 age groupings than did English-language networks (ABC, CBS, FOX, and NBC) (Lopez 2013). The success of Univison has been concentrated in entertainment shows, such as *telenovelas* (Spanish-language soap operas) as well as local news shows, particularly in large cities (Lopez 2013).

However, there are some trends that do not bode as well for the future growth of Spanish-language media. First, there are significant signals over the last several years that point to the decline of immigration stemming from Latin America, especially from Mexico. For example, the level of immigration from Mexico has dropped significantly with a net outflow from the US to Mexico recently (Passel et al. 2012). In addition, due to rapidly falling fertility rates, Mexico will have fewer people in the age groups (e.g. 15–34) that have fueled the immigration of its workforce toward the US. Second, over the last several years there has been a tendency for Latina/os to get their news (from television, print, radio, and the internet) in English (Lopez and González-Barrera 2013). For instance, a growing percentage of Latina/os – 82 percent in 2012 compared to 78 percent in 2006 – report obtaining at least part of their news in English (Lopez and González-Barrera 2013). During the same period, there has been a fall in the share of Latina/os who get at least some of their news in Spanish or in both Spanish and English (Lopez and González-Barrera 2013). If the volume of immigrants coming to the US from Latin American continues to decline, a greater share of Latina/os will be born in the US, a group that is increasingly proficient in English. Thus, both of these trends – declining immigration alongside a rising share of Latina/os five and older who speak English at home (18.7 million persons or nearly one-third of all Latina/os) (US Census Bureau 2024) – have the potential to negatively impact the expansion of Spanish-language media. Nonetheless, Latina/os place a high premium on being bilingual and a large segment of native-born Latina/os have immigrant parents, who provide a link to the Spanish language (Lopez 2013).

In sum, overall, there are mixed patterns involving the future of Spanish-language media. We envision that these media will continue to grow, though the growth is likely to be somewhat tempered in the future, given current trends in immigration and English proficiency. Thus, we see the Spanish-language media continuing to play an important role in telling the story about Latina/os and engaging the community on salient political issues.

Summary

This chapter has provided an overview of the portrayal of Latina/os in the mass media. We introduced several theoretical perspectives that are useful in understanding the treatment of Latina/os in the media. In addition, we provided an overview of the long history of the Spanish-language media in more fully reporting on the Latina/o population and the variety of functions it plays in the lives of Latina/o communities compared to the mainstream media. Moreover, we illustrated the way that the mainstream and Spanish-language media differ in their portrayal of Latina/os. We also provided a discussion of how Latina/os are packaged through what is referred to as the Latino spin. The emergence of misinformation and disinformation and its impact on the Latina/o community was examined, with special attention to the influence of misinformation on the 2020 presidential election and the COVID-19 vaccine. Efforts to combat misinformation from the Latina/o community were also highlighted. Additionally, we assessed the representation of Latina/os in the mass media, which revealed the continued underrepresentation of Latina/os, particularly as political commentators contributing to debates on current and future policy issues. Finally, we spotlighted some important questions that have major implications for the future concerning the treatment of Latina/os in the mass media.

We now turn to the concluding chapter, in which we highlight some of the major patterns from all the chapters covered in the book. The chapter will address how Latina/os are changing our understanding of race relations in this country as well as discussing the impact that Latina/os will have on the various societal institutions.

Discussion Questions

1. What are some of the key differences in the portrayal of Latina/os in mainstream media compared to Spanish-language media, and how do these differences influence public perception?

2. What role does Spanish-language media serve in Latina/o communities, and how does it differ from mainstream media in its coverage and impact?

3. Given the impact of misinformation and disinformation on the Latina/o community during the COVID-19 pandemic and the 2020 presidential election, what other efforts need to be pursued to prevent the future spread of mis- and disinformation among Latina/o communities? How does the power threat perspective play a role?

4. What are some recent notable examples of the "Latina/o Spin" concept?

5. What is the significance of counterstories or counternarratives within the framework of critical race theory, and how do they provide a voice to marginalized groups, including Latina/os?

6. What other examples of Latina/o movements have been activated by social media platform and hashtag awareness?

7. What factors contribute to the persistent underrepresentation of Latina/os, particularly in managerial roles within the media sector?

16 Conclusions

Over the last fifteen chapters, we have provided a wide overview of the Latina/o population. The portrait that emerges is that of an increasingly diverse population that continues to represent the engine of the US population change. Latina/os continue to account for more than half of the US population growth, while the white population has declined over the last several years. As the population of Latina/os and other people of color has increased its share of the overall population, there have been numerous attempts to stem the potential political power that comes with rising numbers and to halt programs and laws that promote efforts that support diversity and equal opportunities. The growing diversity in the Latina/o population has also resulted in fewer commonalities related to generational status, national origin, socioeconomic status, language use, cultural attachment, religious denominations, gender and sexuality, political views and interests, and in other areas as well. Our analysis carried out above also demonstrates the significant stratification along socioeconomic lines that results in some Latina/o groups being at the top, others somewhere in the middle, and still others at the lower levels of the socioeconomic hierarchy. Finally, as we noted at the outset, despite Latina/os being the nation's largest population of color and its long history in this country, the US public continues to not know much about Latina/os. Latina/os continue to be underrepresented on the Hollywood screen and among political and business leaders assembled at the table to discuss important political and business issues of the day and of the future.

This chapter has several aims. First, we provide an overview and reflect on changes that we made in the book in this second edition. Second, we consider some of the challenges that Latina/os are making to the understanding of racial matters in the United States. Third, we provide a discussion of a theoretical framework that describes how the United States is changing with respect to how it sees race and how groups in the country are positioned along the hierarchy of the stratification system. Fourth, we address structural and systemic obstacles, including recent anti-race and anti-voting rights policies, which need to be confronted and challenged in order for Latina/os to gain social and economic upward mobility. Finally, we call attention to the many ways in which Latina/os will increasingly impact US institutions in the coming decades.

Changes from the First Edition

As we noted in Chapter 1, in this second edition of our book, we made several changes that serve to expand our understanding of the Latina/o experience in this country and to widen the reach of the audience beyond the traditional social sciences. We added three new chapters including Latina/o social thought, gender and sexuality, and the Latina/o arts. In addition, the focus of the Latina/o groups covered in the analysis was expanded to include Afro-Latina/os, Hondurans, and Spaniards.

The new chapter on Latina/o social thought incorporates early Latina/o social thought leaders, who advanced a more diverse and reflective understanding of the Latina/o experience in the US. The chapter highlights three eras of intellectual leader in the Latina/o community and the work that they carried out to call attention to issues impacting the Latina/o population and efforts to improve the lives of Latina/os. Particularly impressive was the institution building that took place between WWII and the 1960s, which resulted in the development of the major Latina/o civil rights organizations, as well as academic journals that supported and promoted scholarship on Latina/os. The group of Latina/o intellectual leaders featured in the chapter, along with many others not named, challenged a simplistic, myopic understanding of the Latina/o experience and paved the way for deeper research and theories that are more representative of the dynamics of the world in which Latina/os live today.

The new chapter on gender and sexuality provides an interplay of cultural identity, gender dynamics, and sexual orientation specific to the Latina/o community. It offers insight into the diverse, multifaceted, and historically excluded experiences of Latina/o individuals across the gender and sexuality spectrum. For example, this intersectionality allows us to better understand how the migratory experience of Latina/os varies along the lines of gender identity. By acknowledging the diversity of how Latina/os navigate gender and sexuality within the US, we are better able to understand how lived experiences vary, where vulnerabilities exist, and where it is imperative to push against harmful stereotypes and systems of patriarchy and heteronormativity. Further, the contextual additive of gender and sexuality and the Latina/o lived experiences ultimately provide a more comprehensive understanding of Latina/os in the US, fostering a more inclusive and informed perspective on our vibrant and diverse community.

The new chapter on the Latina/o arts provides a humanities perspective on the very rich Latina/o literature stemming from the early pioneer writers and novelists to contemporary writers and artists. As we note in the beginning of Chapter 8, the Latina/o arts capture the heart and spirit of *la gente* or *la raza* (the people). The Latina/o arts touch all aspects of the topics covered in this book. Indeed, Latina/o novels, poetry, music and songs, and paintings have long told the story of the Latina/o people in the areas of history, ties to the countries of origin, language, immigration, politics, education, work, resistance, crime and victimization, religion, gender and sexuality, among a multitude of other topics. We provide a relatively detailed overview of the development and shifts in Latina/o literature, with a primary focus on novels and poetry over three eras related to the formative period, the Chicana/o Movement, and the post-Chicana/o Movement periods. In addition, we highlight a variety of genres of Latina/o music. These music categories range from emotive ballads and political *corridos* (folk ballads) to the fast, up-tempo reggaeton music and crossover Tejana/o music. Latina/o music is quite diverse and rich and has, naturally, evolved throughout time to reflect generational experiences.

Finally, the addition of Afro-Latina/os, Hondurans, and Spaniards provides us the opportunity to further understand the diversity of the Latina/o population. The Afro-Latina/o population is one of the largest Latina/o groups in the country, although our knowledge of the group is relatively limited. To complicate matters, there was a significant change in the way that the US Census Bureau processed racial/ethnic data before and after the 2020 decennial census. The result is that there was a decline of over 373,000 Latina/os between 2019 and 2022, a 27 percent decline. This is incredible! No other Latina/o subgroup sustained a decline in their populations between 2019 and 2022. The ranking of Afro-Latina/os among the Latina/o population dropped from seventh in 2019 to ninth in 2022. Scholars such as Nancy López and her colleagues (see López and Hogan 2021) have been very concerned about the likelihood that shifts in the OMB racial and ethnic designations will lead to fewer Afro-Latina/os counting themselves as Latina/o if the one-race format is adopted by the OMB, and Afro-Latinos no longer have the choice of identifying ethnically as Latina/o and racially as Black.

Our analysis of the demographic and socioeconomic standing of the Afo-Latino population provides an interesting portrait that is somewhat varied. For example, the demographic attributes and socioeconomic standing of Afro-Latina/os in some ways reflects characteristics of non-Hispanic Blacks in matters related to marriage and household arrangements and on wage penalties that Blacks pay in the labor market. However, because they are quite young and high percentages are US-born, Afro-Latinos tend to fare a bit better than groups that are on the lower levels of the Latina/o socioeconomic hierarchy, which consists of Mexicans and Central Americans, whose socioeconomic standing is generally closer to that of Puerto Ricans and Dominicans. The Honduran population in many ways resembles other Central American groups – notably, Guatemalans and Salvadorans – as well as Mexican immigrants. The Spaniard group, in contrast, ranks very favorably in socioeconomic status alongside Cubans and Colombians. In sum, the addition of the three new groups in this second edition further illustrates the great diversity and nuances of the numerous groups that form the overall Latina/o population.

Overall, the four new elements to the second edition provide a broader and more inclusive portrait of the Latina/o population compared to the earlier edition of our book. In the process, we have expanded our reach to encompass the richness and nuances that make Latina/os who they are.

Challenges of Latina/os for US Racial Matters

Despite their growing significance to the future of the United States, Latina/os continue to be absent not only on Hollywood screens, but also in corporate boards and among people sitting at the proverbial table discussing current issues and policies and in planning for the future of the country. This, at least in part, reflects the challenges that Latina/os pose to a country that has had a relatively static framework for understanding race relations. Indeed, the United States continues to feature a Black–White framework, extending back to the institution of slavery, for making sense of racial matters in this country. The many groups that have immigrated to the United States have been forced into this dichotomy. In fact, many groups such as the Irish and Italians were initially seen as Black, while over time they came to be accepted as white. Today, because of the growing presence of Latina/os, the question about where Latina/os fit in the racial framework of this country is not trivial, as we discussed in Chapter 1. This is even the case of Afro-Latina/os, who are often not seen as "real" or "completely" Black or Latina/o within the African American and Latina/o community, respectively (Gosin 2017; Howard 2018). In addition, Spaniards do not easily fit into the Latina/o or Hispanic category. On the one hand, considerable segments of Latina/os do not see Spaniards as part of the Latina/o or Hispanic population, as they are seen as white or European, and as descendants of the colonizers who wreaked havoc throughout Latin America and the Caribbean, beginning in the late fifteenth century. Furthermore, as the newer focus of the concept of settler colonialism reminds us, minoritized people who themselves have been colonized, most prominently Chicana/os, have, in turn, colonized indigenous people (Pulido 2018). Finally, with increasing levels of intermarriage and Latina/o–white intermarriages being the most common, a considerable share of Latina/os are multiracial individuals, some of whom may elect not to associate with the group, while persons in the Latina/o community may also not consider them part of the group, depending on their physical appearance and other traits.

Latina/os also challenge sociological theories that have been used to understand the integration of racial and ethnic groups into the US. For long the assimilation perspective was used to understand the progress of white immigrant groups, with the general view that over approximately three generations white ethnic groups became integrated into the US mainstream. Yet, the two groups of Latina/os that have the longest presence in the US – Mexicans and Puerto Ricans – continue to lag significantly behind not only whites but numerous other Latina/o groups that have been in the United States for a much shorter period of time. Certainly, the assimilation perspective does not hold much weight for understanding the experiences of Mexicans, Puerto Ricans, and other non-white groups in the US.

The Shift from a Bi-Racial to a Tri-Racial Framework

Eduardo Bonilla-Silva (1997, 2001, 2004, 2021) has made major contributions in the development of theoretical frameworks in understanding the workings of white supremacy – how it was established, the means at its disposal that it uses to maintain its dominant position, and the adjustments that it makes to deal with challenges that allow it to persist. Just as we see how the capitalist system has been able to maintain its dominant position, Bonilla-Silva helps us to see how white supremacy has persisted through countless centuries. Throughout its existence, the bi-racial frame-work has been part of the system that has maintained white supremacy in the US. As whites established themselves as the dominant group in this country, the standing of racial and ethnic groups depended on whether they were seen as white or Black (the "other").

A number of significant demographic, social, and political changes in the US over the last several decades, however, is increasingly challenging the bi-racial framework that has been in place in this country for centuries. In particular, the US population is undergoing major shifts in its racial and ethnic composition. The share of the domi-nant white population is waning numerically and will continue to do so in the coming decades. In contrast, the portion of the population that is non-white is expanding and will continue to do so throughout the twenty-first century, driven largely by the growth of the Latina/o and Asian populations. Further, the passage of Civil Rights legislation brought about changes in racial discourse in the US, shifting from overt racial discrimination to a softer, covert, and colorblind form of racial discrimina-tion and the way people in the US think about race (Bonilla-Silva 1997, 2001, 2004, 2021). In essence, the storyline that has emerged in the US mainstream is that we are now beyond race, particularly in light of the nation electing its first Black president, now nearly two decades ago. Accordingly, people who continue talking about the continued existence of racism in the US are often accused of trying to inflame racial divisions. Finally, over the last several decades, there have been certain Asian and Latina/o groups that have been able to ascend the socioeconomic scale while others continue to lag behind, as we have seen above in the case of Latina/os.

In light of such changes and how the white supremacy system makes adjust-ments to maintain its dominance, Bonilla-Silva (2004) argues that the United States is moving from a bi-racial toward a tri-racial framework – one similar to that found in Latin America and the Caribbean (Bonilla-Silva 2004; Degler 1986; Wade 1997). Historically, Latin American and Caribbean societies have undertaken ways to whiten the population in light of the disproportionate increase of darker-skinned people in these countries (e.g. indigenous, Black, and mestizo populations). For example, light-skinned elites in these countries have sought to whiten the population through selective immigration from Europe and the redefinition of racial categories to allow certain non-whites to join the ranks of the white elite (Bonilla-Silva 2004; Helg 1990; Loveman and Muñiz 2007; Rodríguez 2000; Telles 2006). Bonilla-Silva suggests that the transformation toward a tri-racial framework in the US will occur through the inclusion of highly assimilated and light-skinned persons allowed to become white as well as the creation of "honorary whites," a group of people who will be almost white, receiving certain white privileges but still subject to some inequality – not being exclusive members of the select white group. In particular, Bonilla-Silva (2004) pro-poses that the tri-racial categories in the US will consist of: (1) *Whites*, consisting of "Whites, New Whites (Russians, Albanians, etc.), Assimilated white Latina/os, Some multiracials, Assimilated (urban) Native Americans, and a few Asian-origin people"; (2) *Honorary Whites*, composed of "Light-skinned Latina/os, Japanese Americans, Korean Americans, Asian Americans, Chinese Americans, Middle Eastern Americans,

Most multiracials, and Filipino Americans"; and (3) *Collective Black*, comprised of "Vietnamese Americans, Hmong Americans, Laotian Americans, Dark-skinned Latina/os, Blacks, New West Indian and African immigrants, and Reservation-bound Native Americans" (p. 933). The original White–Black racial framework exists at the poles of the tri-racial framework, with honorary whites serving as an intermediary group. The shifting of white boundaries to accommodate assimilated and honorary-white Latina/os and members of other groups will occur increasingly as the number of whites declines due to the aging of the white population alongside decreasing fertility rates and dwindling segments of white women capable of giving birth (ages of 15 to 44, the childbearing ages according to demographers). To compensate for their declining numbers, whites will increasingly expand racial boundaries to allow acceptable non-white people to enter the white group, some as full members and others as occasional and honorary members.

Thus, although there continues to be a lack of data to assess the skin color of Latina/os and the overall population in general (but see Telles 2014), following Bonilla-Silva's tri-racial framework, the diverse set of Latina/os in the United States will span the three categories that Bonilla-Silva outlines. First, completely assimilated light-skinned Latina/os are likely to be part of the white category. Second, light-skinned Latina/os who are well off economically are likely to be part of the honorary white group. Third, dark-skinned Latina/os are likely to be part of the collective Black category.

While this categorization is useful in understanding the role that skin color and socioeconomic standing plays in the positioning of Latina/o individuals across the emerging tri-racial framework in the US, it does not directly address the socioeconomic ranking and level of integration of Latina/o groups in the United States.

The Stratification of Latina/o Groups

In this book, we have provided an overview of the diverse histories of Latina/o groups and the varying ways in which they were initially incorporated into the US. We have also provided analyses showing variations across Latina/o groups on the basis of their social and economic characteristics. Overall, four groups – Cubans, Colombians, Spaniards, and Other South Americans – rank consistently high on the set of social and economic attributes that we examined. These groups tend to share certain commonalities – they tend to be of lighter-skin color, and members of these groups immigrated to the US with favorable socioeconomic resources. In a relatively short period of time, these groups have made impressive gains socially and economically in the US. In fact, in some instances, these groups surpass whites on certain social and economic indicators. Furthermore, foreign-born members of these groups consistently have more favorable social and economic standing compared to native-born members of other Latina/o groups that have been in this country for a long time, namely Mexicans and Puerto Ricans. Moreover, these four Latina/o high socioeconomic status groups, especially among native-born individuals, have high rates of intermarriage with whites. Thus, in many respects, Cubans, Columbians,

Spaniards, and Other South Americans are already or will soon be part of the white or honorary-white categories in Bonilla-Silva's tri-racial framework.

In contrast, certain other groups – especially Guatemalans, Hondurans, Mexicans, and Salvadorans, but also Dominicans, Puerto Ricans, and Afro-Latinos – fit into Bonilla-Silva's collective Black category. These groups tend to consistently fall at the lower levels of social and economic rankings among Latina/o groups. These groups tend to have certain commonalities, including a greater prevalence of people with darker skin as well as indigenous features, and immigrants tend to arrive in the US with limited socioeconomic resources. Particularly problematic is that Latina/o groups that were originally incorporated into the United States – ranging from approximately sixty years in the case of Dominicans, to more than 120 years in the case of Puerto Ricans, and to nearly 180 years in the case of Mexicans – continue to be positioned at the lowest tiers of the social and economic hierarchy among Latina/os. While some scholars (Perlman 2005) suggest that Mexicans today are following the path of Italians a century ago, our analysis suggests that Mexicans, as a whole, continue to lag behind socioeconomically compared to other Latina/o groups that have been in this country less time. Of course, the long history of African Americans and Indigenous Peoples in the United States and their continual positioning at the bottom of the US stratification system illustrates the structural aspects of this problem.

The Structural Aspects of Racial and Ethnic Stratification

The sociological roots of the study of race and ethnicity in the United States are in the tradition of the assimilation perspective developed by Robert Park (1950) and later modified by Milton Gordon (1964). This particular theoretical approach worked fairly well in explaining the experiences of white ethnic groups immigrating to the United States. For the most part, the process toward integration of these groups involved initial settlement in ethnic enclaves living alongside co-ethnics, experiences of hostility in the form of discrimination and prejudice against the group, followed by increasing levels of educational attainment, loss of the native language, and movement to suburban areas among subsequent generations. As mentioned above, in general, it took roughly three generations for white ethnic groups to fully integrate into US society. The commonality of these groups is that they were white, an attribute that was necessary to gain US citizenship over a long period of US history. Even though some of these groups, such as the Irish and Italians, were originally viewed as Black or non-white, eventually they attained white membership, alongside access to white privilege.

Ira Katznelson (2005) in his book titled *When Affirmative Action Was White: An Untold History of Racial Inequality in Twentieth-Century America* offers a historical overview of the privileges and advantages that whites have enjoyed due to their white race. The narrative associated with the assimilation perspective, in line with the country's Horatio Algier individual-oriented myth, is that success or failure is due simply to the individual person. Given the upward mobility that white ethnics experienced in the United States, the belief continues to be that if one works hard, plays by the rules, and becomes American through abandoning one's culture and language, then people eventually can get ahead and succeed. Accordingly, if people are unwilling to dedicate themselves in this way, they only have themselves to blame for their failure.

Such individualistic thinking blinds people from recognizing the structural factors that create and sustain racial stratification. Structural explanations of racial stratification argue that racism and racial inequality are systemic – etched in the foundations of the nation's institutions, laws, practices, policies, and general attitudes (Bonilla-Silva 1997, 2001, 2021; Feagin 2006, 2013). The contemporary low positioning of many Latina/os – especially Mexicans, Puerto Ricans, Dominicans, and Central Americans – reflects historical structural patterns that have defined Latina/os as not belonging in the United States – as the "other" – as people who could be easily deported and who had no interest in bettering themselves educationally. For much of the twentieth century Mexicans, in Texas and elsewhere in the Southwest, Mexicans were allowed to attend only segregated Mexican-only schools even after the *Brown v. Board of Education* (1954) ruling. Mexican schools were deplorably unequal compared to white schools. In these schools, Mexican students were commonly punished for speaking Spanish, experienced humiliation due to their culture, and were deloused. In such a setting, not surprisingly, few Mexican students made it to high school and even fewer graduated from high school.

In the mid-1950s the US Supreme Court outlawed "separate but equal" schools in its 1954 *Brown v. Board of Education* decision. From the outset white political officials protested the ruling and delayed complying with laws calling for the end of separate schools. When school desegregation was finally instituted, whites took steps to ensure that the desegregation ruling would be subverted. Whites used all means at their disposal alongside assistance from state and local officials and the court system to undermine school desegregation. In particular, whites sent their children to private schools and moved to white suburban areas (Clotfelter 2004). Moreover, the *Milliken v. Bradley* ruling of 1974, indicating that students could not be moved across school districts to achieve school desegregation, marked what Clotfelter (2004) refers to as "the beginning of a retreat from the proactive pursuit of racial balance as a judicial objective" (p. 31). In the opening decade of the twenty-first century, public schools were more segregated than they were toward the end of the 1960s (Orfield and Lee 2007). Orfield and Lee (2007) observe that:

> On a national scale, the segregation of Latina/o students has grown the most since the civil rights era. Since the early 1970s, the period in which the Supreme Court recognized Latina/os' right to desegregation there has been an uninterrupted national trend toward increased isolation. Latina/o students have become, by some measures, the most segregated group by both race and poverty and there are increasing patterns of triple segregation – ethnicity, poverty and linguistic isolation. (p. 31)

Furthermore, a recent report from the US Government Accountability Office (GAO) (2022a) noted that one-third of students in K-12 public schools go to schools where their own racial/ethnic group accounts for three-fourths or more of the student body.

In fact, whites are the most segregated, with 45 percent of white students going to schools that are 75 percent or more white, followed by Latina/o students with 31 percent and Black students with 23 percent attending schools that are 75 percent or more Latina/o or Black, respectively. In addition, a report from the Southern Education Foundation (2015) found that nationwide nearly half of Latina/o and Black students attend high-poverty public schools, while only one-tenth of white students do so. Moreover, a report by the Education Trust (2018) observed that public schools with the highest percentages of students of color (American Indian, Black, and Latina/o) received approximately $1,800 less in funding for each student, compared to those schools with the lowest percentage of students of color.

This backlash against Latina/os and other groups of color has become even more intense and wide, beginning with the Trump presidency and beyond, as far-right politicians compete with each other to develop harsher policies that muzzle critical thinking (i.e. critical race theory and diversity, equity, and inclusion programs and policies) on race, gender, and sexuality issues, with severe penalties for educators and others who stray from the rules, the banning of books in public school libraries and those for the general public, the criminalization of transsexual youth and their parents, and increasingly stringent policies to make it more difficult to vote. In essence, these efforts and many others alongside the attack of Trump supporters on the US Capitol on January 6, 2021, contribute toward the erosion of democracy. The political shift of the Supreme Court to the right has declawed voting rights legislation and has put a stop to the use of race as one of a number of factors used to make decisions on admissions to colleges and universities. These are all efforts to take the country back to the days when whites represented four out of every five persons in the US and people of color knew their place. The anti-race policies represent efforts to derail the demographic locomotive that has the potential to translate numbers into political power for Latina/o, Blacks, and other people of color. Nowhere are these efforts to turn back the demographic and political clock more intense than in Texas and Florida, the states with the second and third largest Latina/o populations in the US, respectively.

Thus, it will take strengthening of political power among Latina/os to overturn policies and programs that stem Latina/o political representation and upward mobility. At present, the demographic numbers of Latina/os do not translate to actual political power, particularly in states such as Texas, where the Latina/o population now outnumbers the white population. However, as we have seen, the Latina/o population is quite young, with 30 percent being less than 18 years of age in 2021 and thus ineligible to vote. One sign of optimism is the consistently large number of Latina/o children, beginning in 2021, who will be reaching eighteen years of age over the next eighteen years (2021 to 2039). The 18.9 million children in 2021 translates to a little more than one million Latina/os turning eighteen years of age every year during this period, and 95.5 percent are US citizens – a strong cadre of potential voters. Nonetheless, one-fourth of Latina/os 18 years of age or older are not US citizens and thus not eligible to vote. Furthermore, only 61.1 percent of Latina/os who are eligible to vote are actually registered to vote – this compares to a rate of 76.5 percent of whites and

69 percent of Blacks (US Census Bureau 2021). Finally, in the last presidential election the Latina/o eligible voter turnout was 53.7 percent – compared to 70.9 percent of whites and 62.6 percent of Blacks (US Census Bureau 2021). Obviously, there needs to be greater effort to register Latina/os and to make sure that they actually turn out to vote. The Southwest Voter Registration and Education Project (SVREP), founded by the late Willie Velasquez, is a major Latina/o organization with this function. SVREP has also organized the Latina/o Academy, which provides training to local Latina/o candidates and elected officials. As the last several presidential elections have shown, Latina/os are already becoming a major force in national politics. However, the significance of the Latina/o vote and its potential power will grow stronger in the coming years, as Latina/o youth turn eighteen years of age and, potentially, unauthorized Latina/os become US citizens, translating to a larger Latina/o populace. Ultimately, political power among Latina/os will allow for dealing with major structural obstacles that continue to block Latina/os from greater political participation and upward mobility.

Yet, the growing diversity of the Latina/o population stands to divide the political strength of the population. As we have seen, there is a certain segment of the Latina/o population – Cubans, Colombians, Spaniards, and Other South Americans – that has become integrated into the United States, and another segment that has not fared as well, particularly in the case of Mexicans, Puerto Ricans, and Dominicans, groups that have been in this country for a lengthy period of time. Certainly, there are rifts among Latina/o groups positioned at an elevated level and at a low level socioeconomically. In addition, even within Latina/o groups, people who are better off economically and those who are not doing well are likely to differ in the issues that they consider important, as well as the political party that they are most likely to support. While the Democratic Party has counted on the growing Latina/o population being Democrat, upward mobility and, as we observed earlier, association with Evangelical denominations are likely to move some Latina/os toward the Republican Party. The increasing Evangelical shift among Latina/os as well as Latina/os who work in the border patrol/Homeland Security industries along the US–Mexico border among the working-class point to political wedges among rank-and-file Latina/os.

In efforts to maximize political power to tackle structural impediments, Latina/o political leaders will need to forge alliances across racial and ethnic groups. For example, Bonilla-Silva (2004) suggests that in the emerging tri-racial society, the collective-Black and the honorary-White groups will need to recognize their common interests and forge ties. Similarly, Latina/os will need to develop stronger ties with Blacks, Asians, Native Americans, and progressive whites in order to maximize their political strengths. The US racial stratification system was built with the establishment of the country and has been fortified over the last five centuries. It will not crumble easily. Even in a country that is undergoing massive demographic shifts that will lead shortly to a population in which whites will be outnumbered by non-whites, whites will continue to be the dominant group, possessing economic, political, and social power. Corporate boardrooms, the halls of Congress, and the bench of the Supreme Court will still be filled disproportionately by whites. Nonetheless, the establishment of intergroup political linkages across groups of color will begin to make dents on the US racial-stratification house.

The Implications of the Growing Latina/o Population on Societal Institutions

We have asserted in this book that Latina/os are the engine of the US population. Indeed, the Latina/o population is driving the demography of the US. The future of the US will depend greatly on the fortunes of the Latina/o population. The last time that the US experienced such a dramatic impact on all of its societal institutions was the tremendous growth of its population that was born between 1946 and 1964, a group that was dubbed as 'baby boomers." The baby boom cohort has had a tremendous impact on all societal institutions as it has gone through its life course. For example, at infancy baby boomers had an impact on baby necessities and products; at the childhood stage they had an impact on the building of schools and the number of teachers that were needed; at the young adulthood phase they had an impact on the number of faculty positions to educate them in colleges and universities, they affected the number of jobs that were needed to accommodate them in the labor force, and they also impacted attitudes regarding war, sex, race, gender, environment, and music; at the middle age stage they have impacted the marketing of products, travel, and leisure; and now as they reach retirement age, baby boomers will impact the health care industry, the demand for assisted-care facilities, and so forth. Because of the youthfulness of the Latina/o population, and its significance in the changing demography of the United States over the coming decades, Latina/os will have an important impact on all US institutions.

Educational Institutions

Given the youthfulness of the Latina/o population, Latina/o youth will represent a growing share of our nation's students at the K-12 level and beyond. In fact, recent data show that Latina/os account for the largest segment of the growth among US undergraduate students between 2009 and 2017 (Sáenz 2020). While white undergraduate students declined by 1.7 million during this period, Latina/o undergraduates rose by 1.1 million. This shift will become even more dramatic in the coming years. The changing racial and ethnic profile of US schools can be illustrated by recent changes in the US child population. Between 2012 and 2022, the number of white children declined by 4.5 million, while the number of Latina/o children rose by 1.2 million.

These recent trends fuel further racial and ethnic changes in the country's child population that are on the horizon. Indeed, the latest population projections from the US Census Bureau (2023) show that while the white share of the nation's children less than eighteen years of age is expected to decline from 49 percent in 2022 to 36 percent in 2060, the percentage share of Latina/os is projected to rise from 26 percent to 32 percent, respectively. Overall, then, Latina/os accounted for one-third of the 3.5 million children who were added to the nation's population between 2012 and 2022 and their numbers will grow significantly in the coming decades. It is essential that policymakers make investments in providing Latina/o children with the educational skills that they will need to succeed educationally. Certainly, they are expected to become an even larger share of students on college campuses.

Economic Institutions

Latina/os will have an important impact on the economic institution. According to the US Bureau of Labor Statistics' (2023) population projections of the US civilian labor force between 2022 and 2032, Latina/os are projected to add 6.8 million persons to the nation's workforce, a 22 percent gain; in comparison, whites will add 926,000 workers, a 0.7 percent change. This is why it is so important that investments be made today to ensure that today's Latina/o youth succeed in the educational system in order to enhance their chances for economic success in the future. Some industries that will be largely affected by the aging of baby boomers, such as the health care and eldercare industries, will depend heavily on Latina/os to fill these new jobs. Moreover, the US consumer base will be increasingly Latina/o with the purchasing power of Latina/os expected to increase significantly alongside its projected population growth (Selig Center for Economic Growth 2012). According to the Latino Donors Collaborative (2023) report titled *LDC US Latino GDP Report*, the Latino Gross Domestic Product (GDP) stood at $3.2 trillion and the Latino Purchasing Power at $3.4 trillion, translating to Latina/os having the fifth largest economy in the world trailing only the US, China, Germany, and Japan. Businesses in the US will depend heavily on Latina/o consumers to buy their products. Furthermore, Latina/os stand to disproportionately represent the growth of entrepreneurs and self-employed workers in the coming decades. Latina/os are already experiencing significant growth in such business ventures (Valdez 2011). So, again, it is important that investments be made in the educational preparation of Latina/o youth today to ensure that they reach their maximum social and economic potential in the future.

Political Institutions

Over the last half century, Latina/os have shifted from a relatively small regional minority concentrated in certain parts of the country to the nation's largest minority group, which increasingly has the strength to sway national, state, and local elections. As suggested above, the Latina/o populace will grow significantly over the coming decades as Latina/o youth reach voting age alongside foreign-born individuals who become US naturalized citizens. Indeed, it is estimated that the Latina/o electorate will grow significantly (Taylor et al. 2012a). In addition, as Latina/os gain political strength, political slates will increasingly include Latina/o candidates.

On a national scale, the election of the presidency and related elections will shift dramatically if and when projected demographic changes turn Texas into a blue state. Texas currently has a major age split along the lines of race and ethnicity, which has major implications for changing the political landscape in the state. In particular, in 2022, whites outnumbered Latinos at age 50 and above, while Latinos outnumbered whites below the age of 50. Moreover, Latina/os already outnumber whites in the overall state population. The political influence of Latina/os will be prominent if and when Texas turns Democratic, which some observers believe is only a matter of time, although others are more skeptical

Health Institutions

We have seen that Latina/os pose a paradox in our understanding of mortality. Despite being a population that possesses a bundle of attributes – such as high poverty, low education, and low health insurance coverage – that suggest that Latina/os have high rates of mortality and truncated longevity, Latina/os actually have lower mortality rates and higher life expectancies compared to whites. Yet, as we saw in Chapter 13, there is another side of the paradox that is less favorable. In general, Latina/os are likely to live longer than whites, but they do so with a greater prevalence of disability, diabetes, and obesity. Moreover, Latina/os are much less likely than other racial and ethnic groups to have health insurance coverage and to receive adequate health care. Thus, particularly as Latina/os age, they will place an increasing stress on the health care system. It is therefore crucial that Latina/os have access to preventive health care that will allow for identifying health problems at an early stage where they can be treated, rather than at late stages when it is more difficult and costly to cure.

Moreover, as we suggested above, as baby boomers reach retirement age between 2011 and 2029, there will be greater demand for health care providers. Given the rising presence of Latina/os in the labor force, today's Latina/os will be part of the workforce that provides health care for an increasingly aging US population, largely made of whites but increasingly Latina/os. It is essential that Latina/os receive educational training opportunities to fill medical professional occupations.

Religious Institutions

The projected growth of the Latina/o population will impact the religious institution dramatically. As observed in Chapter 12, Latina/os are the driving force behind the changing demography of the US Catholic population. They accounted for 90 percent of the entire growth of the Catholic Church in the country between 1970 and 2000 (Poyo 2010). Latina/os a decade ago accounted for one-third of US Catholics (Matovina 2012; Pew Hispanic Center 2007), with their numbers expected to grow significantly in the coming decades. Putnam and Campbell (2010) point out that Latina/os will become the majority in the US Catholic Church in the near future. In fact, Latina/os already constitute the majority of Catholics less than 25 years of age (Matovina 2012). In addition, observers also suggest that Latina/os will transform the Church through their unique aspects of worship, such as engaging in spirit-filled religious expression and related practices (Pew Hispanic Center 2007).

Furthermore, as other religious denominations experience dwindling member-ships due to aging white populations, these will increasingly seek to recruit Latina/os into their fold. We have already seen over the last few decades a rising percentage of Latina/os who are converting to Evangelical and Pentecostal religions.

Military Institutions

Given the increasing Latina/o population throughout the twenty-first century, Latina/os will also have an impact on the military institution. Latina/os will increas-ingly be part of US forces protecting the country and participating in future wars. For many Latina/os throughout their presence in the United States, the military has rep-resented a career option. Latina/os have fought valiantly on the battlefield and have been decorated with medals of honor for these deeds (Buffalo Soldier 2014; Voces Oral History 2024).

Summary

This chapter has provided an overview of the highlights and implications that we have covered in the previous chapters. In particular, we called attention to how the grow-ing Latina/o population has challenged the long-standing US racial framework and sociological perspectives for understanding race relations in this country. We drew attention to the usefulness of Bonilla-Silva's (2004) theorizing, which argues that the United States is shifting from a bi-racial to a tri-racial framework and the role that Latina/os play in this shift. We also discussed the stratification that we have observed in our analysis presented earlier in the book, which shows that some groups, marked by lighter skin and socioeconomic advantages at the time of immigration, have fared well in the United States, while others have continued to lag significantly behind; this is particularly disturbing in the case of groups (Mexicans, Puerto Ricans, and Dominicans) that have been in this country for a long period of time. We also dis-cussed the structural and systemic elements of white supremacy, especially the many anti-race and anti-voting rights policies that have emerged recently; this needs to be confronted and challenged in order for Latina/os and other groups of color to make inroads into the social, economic, and political arenas. Finally, we called attention to the multitude of ways in which Latina/os will impact the nation's institutions in the coming decades.

The Latina/o population has a long history in this country, extending back to the original incorporation of Mexicans through the signing of the Treaty of Guadalupe Hidalgo at the conclusion of the US–Mexico War in 1848. This treaty created the Mexican American people. Over the span of the ensuing 180 years, the Latina/o population has been transformed in so many ways, including changes in the name of the group, the large numbers of groups that constitute the Latina/o population, the diverse histories that link them to the United States, which promoted immigration to this country, and the divergent paths toward integration that they have experienced in this nation. It is clear that Latina/os have had a significant mark on the history of the US. The aging of the white population alongside the youthfulness of the Latina/o population will result in a significant expansion of the Latina/o population throughout the twenty-first century. As such, Latina/os are the driving force behind the US population – its engine of population change. The growing Latina/o population will continue to make important contributions to the US throughout the century. Latina/os will play an increasingly important role in each of the country's institutions. Thus, it is essential that Americans gain a closer understanding and appreciation of the Latina/o population and that policies and programs be established to improve the lives of the Latina/o population, to ensure that they reach their full human potential and to shift from the margins of society to its core.

Discussion Questions

1. What do you consider the three or four most important findings of the book across all of the chapters?

2. Why does Eduardo Bonilla-Silva argue that the US is moving from a bi-racial to a tri-racial framework in the area of racial matters?

3. Based on the analysis in the book concerning the socioeconomic standing of the specific Latina/o subgroups analyzed, and on Bonilla-Silva's tri-racial categories, which Latina/o subgroups do you identify as being part of the white category, the honorary white category, and the collective Black category?

4. How many Latina/os will turn age eighteen every year, beginning in the year 2021?

5. Are there certain Latina/o groups that do not fit well into the Latina/o category? Which are these? Why do they not easily fit?

6. Pick three societal institutions and describe how Latina/os will impact these over the coming decades?

7. What are some of the major changes that the Latina/o population will undergo by 2040?

Appendices

A. List of Occupations Comprising "Latina/o Immigrant Jobs" by Sex

Code[a]	Occupation
Females	
2861	Interpreters and translators
3601	Home health aides
4010	First-line supervisors of food preparation and serving workers
4020	Cooks
4030	Food preparation workers
4110	Waiters and waitresses
4130	Dining room and cafeteria attendants and bartender helpers
4140	Dishwashers
4200	First-line supervisors of housekeeping and janitorial workers
4220	Janitors and building cleaners
4230	Maids and housekeeping cleaners
4252	Tree trimmers and pruners
4600	Childcare workers
4950	Door-to-door sales workers, news and street vendors, and related workers
5610	Shipping, receiving, and inventory clerks
6040	Graders and sorters, agricultural products
6050	Other agricultural workers
6260	Construction laborers
6410	Painters and paperhangers
7700	First-line supervisors of production and operating workers
7750	Other assemblers and fabricators
7800	Bakers
7810	Butchers and other meat, poultry, and fish processing workers
7855	Food processing workers, all other
8225	Other metal workers and plastic workers
8300	Laundry and dry-cleaning workers
8320	Sewing machine operators
8740	Inspectors, testers, sorters, samplers, and weighers
8800	Packaging and filling machine operators and tenders
8990	Miscellaneous production workers, including equipment operators and tenders
9142	Taxi drivers
9610	Cleaners of vehicles and equipment

Code[a]	Occupation
9620	Laborers and freight, stock, and material movers, hand
9640	Packers and packagers, hand

Males

4000	Chefs and head cooks
4020	Cooks
4030	Food preparation workers
4110	Waiters and waitresses
4130	Dining room and cafeteria attendants and bartender helpers
4140	Dishwashers
4200	First-line supervisors of housekeeping and janitorial workers
4210	First-line supervisors of landscaping, lawn service, and groundskeeping workers
4220	Janitors and building cleaners
4230	Maids and housekeeping cleaners
4251	Landscaping and groundskeeping workers
4252	Tree trimmers and pruners
4500	Barbers
6050	Other agricultural workers
6200	First-line supervisors of construction trades and extraction workers
6220	Brickmasons, blockmasons, stonemasons, and reinforcing iron and rebar workers
6230	Carpenters
6240	Carpet, floor, and tile installers and finishers
6250	Cement masons, concrete finishers, and terrazzo workers
6260	Construction laborers
6330	Drywall installers, ceiling tile installers, and tapers
6400	Insulation workers
6410	Painters and paperhangers
6460	Plasterers and stucco masons
6515	Roofers
6600	Helpers, construction trades
6765	Other construction and related workers
7150	Automotive body and related repairers
7640	Other installation, maintenance, and repair workers
7800	Bakers
7810	Butchers and other meat, poultry, and fish processing workers
8140	Welding, soldering, and brazing workers
8800	Packaging and filling machine operators and tenders
8810	Painting workers
9142	Taxi drivers
9600	Industrial truck and tractor operators
9610	Cleaners of vehicles and equipment
9640	Packers and packagers, hand

[a] American Community Survey occupational code.

Source: Data from 2022 American Community Survey 1-Year Estimates Public-Use File (Ruggles et al. 2024).

B. Results of Multiple Regression Analysis Examining the Relationships between Selected Predictors and the Logged Wage and Salary Income by Place of Birth and Sex, 2022

Race/Ethnic Group	Native-Born		Foreign-Born	
	Female	Male	Female	Male
Intercept	6.531**	7.005**	6.961**	7.628**
Afro-Latina/o	−0.066**	−0.087**	−0.021	−0.055
Colombian	0.089**	0.141**	−0.007	−0.027
Cuban	0.059**	0.010	−0.111**	−0.224**
Dominican	0.064**	0.002	−0.198**	−0.244**
Guatemalan	−0.001	−0.018	−0.065*	−0.036
Honduran	0.011	−0.047	−0.031	0.002
Mexican	−0.045**	−0.089**	−0.213**	−0.254**
Puerto Rican	0.001	−0.098**	−0.061	−0.185**
Salvadoran	0.008	−0.003	0.004	0.006
Spaniard	−0.062**	−0.050*	−0.198**	0.033
Other Latina/o	−0.007	−0.071**	−0.141**	−0.221**
Black	−0.022**	−0.104**	0.110**	−0.060**
Some high school	−0.032*	−0.035**	0.000	0.027*
High-school graduate	0.101**	0.117**	0.073**	0.086**
Some college	0.275**	0.285**	0.203**	0.199**
Bachelor's degree or higher	0.720**	0.717**	0.589**	0.650**
Bilingual	−0.025**	−0.028**	−0.073**	−0.139**
Limited or no English fluency	−0.110**	−0.114**	−0.181**	−0.280**
Age 35–44	0.143**	0.187**	0.085**	0.051**
Age 45–54	0.186**	0.279**	0.077*	0.088**
Married	0.096**	0.264**	0.041**	0.116**
Self-employed	−0.180**	−0.130**	−0.151**	−0.174**
Weeks worked per week	0.046**	0.046**	0.044**	0.041**
Usual hours worked per week	0.034**	0.025**	0.029**	0.021**
Midwest region	−0.145**	−0.135**	−0.126**	−0.117**
South region	−0.147**	−0.116**	−0.147**	−0.111**
West region	0.014**	0.008	−0.011	0.016
Naturalized citizen	—	—	0.052**	0.092**
Living in US 5 to 9 years	—	—	0.078**	0.088**
Living in US 10 to 14 years	—	—	0.105**	0.109**
Living in US 15 to 19 years	—	—	0.135**	0.121**
Living in US 20 to 24 years	—	—	0.157**	0.102**
Living in US 25 or more years'	—	—	0.207**	0.110**
Adjusted R^2	0.567	0.500	0.543	0.448
N	349,699	373,805	44,911	55,638

Source: Data from 2022 American Community Survey 1-Year Estimates Public-Use File (Ruggles et al. 2024).

Note: The comparison groups for the dummy variables are Whites; 0–8 years of education; persons who speak English at home; people who are not self-employed; persons who are not currently married; persons 25–34 years of age; persons living in the Northeast; and for foreign-born persons: persons who have lived in the US for less than five years and persons who are not naturalized citizens.

[a] The results are used to generate the coefficients appearing in Table 10.4.

* Statistically significant at the 0.05 level.

**Statistically significant at the 0.01 level.

References

Abad-Santos, Alex. 2017. "How 'Despacito' Became the Biggest Song of 2017." *Vox.* https://www.vox.com/culture/2017/8/18/16112710/despacito-biggest-song-of-2017-bieber-fonsi-daddy-yankee

Abeyta, Michael. 2023. "Why More Hispanics are Converting to Islam Faster Than Any Other Ethnic Group: 'I Feel Like I Just Found My Answer.'" *CBS News Colorado*, March 23. https://www.cbsnews.com/colorado/news/more-hispanics-converting-to-islam/

Abraído-Lanza, Ana F., Maria T. Chao, and Karen R. Flórez. 2005. "Do Healthy Behaviors Decline With Greater Acculturation?: Implications for the Latino Mortality Paradox." *Social Science & Medicine* 61: 1243–1255.

Abrego, Leisy. 2009. "Economic Well-Being in Salvadoran Transnational Families: How Gender Affects Remittance Practices." *Journal of Marriage and Family* 71 (4): 1070–1085.

Abrego, Leisy J. 2014. *Sacrificing Families: Navigating Laws, Labor, and Love Across Borders*. Stanford, CA: Stanford University Press.

Abrego, Leisy, Mat Coleman, Daniel E. Martínez, Cecilia Menjívar, and Jeremy Slack. 2017. "Making Immigrants into Criminals: Legal Processes of Criminalization in the Post-IIRIRA Era." *Journal on Migration and Human Security* 5 (3): 694–715.

Abrego, Leisy J. and Roberto G. Gonzales. 2010. "Blocked Paths, Uncertain Futures: The Postsecondary Education and Labor Market Prospects of Undocumented Latino Youth." *Journal of Education for Students Placed at Risk* 15 (1–2): 144–157.

Abrego, Leisy J. and Cecilia Menjívar. 2011. "Immigrant Latina Mothers as Targets of Legal Violence." *International Journal of Sociology of the Family* 37 (1): 9–26.

Ackert, Elizabeth and Jocelyn S. Wikle. 2022. "Familism among Latino/a Adolescents: Evidence from Time-Use Data." *Journal of Marriage and Family* 84 (3): 879–899.

Acosta, Katie. L. 2013. *Amigas y Amantes: Sexually Nonconforming Latinas Negotiate Family*. New Brunswick, NJ: Rutgers University Press.

Acosta, Oscar Zeta. 1972. *Autobiography of a Brown Buffalo*. San Francisco: Straight Arrow Press.

Acosta, Oscar Zeta. 1973. *Revolt of the Cockroach People*. San Francisco: Straight Arrow Press.

Acuña, Rodolfo. 1972. *Occupied America: The Chicano Struggle for Liberation*. 1st edn. New York: Harper and Row.

Acuña, Rodolfo F. 2020. *Occupied America: A History of Chicanos*. 9th edn. Pearson.

Aguilera, Michael Bernabè. 2004. "The Effect of Legalization on the Labor Markets of Latin American Immigrants: A Gendered Comparison." *Sociological Focus* 37 (4): 349–369.

Aguirre, B.E., Rogelio Sáenz, and Brian Sinclair. 1997. "Marielitos Ten Years Later: The Scarface Legacy." *Social Science Quarterly* 78 (2): 487–507.

Ahmed, Azam and Kirk Semple. 2019. "Photo of Drowned Migrants Captures Pathos of Those Who Risk It All." *New York Times*, June 25. https://www.nytimes.com/2019/06/25/us/father-daughter-border-drowning-picture-mexico.html

Alarcón, Amado, Josiah Heyman, and María Cristina Morales. 2014. "The Occupational Placement of Spanish-English Bilinguals in the New Information Economy: The Health and Criminal Justice Sectors in the U.S. Borderlands with Mexico," pp. 138–159 in R.M. Callahan and P.C. Gándara (eds.), *The Bilingual Advantage: Language, Literacy, and the Labor Market*. Clevedon, Bristol, UK: Multilingual Matters.

Alba, Richard and Victor Nee. 2003. *Remaking the American Mainstream: Assimilation and Contemporary Immigration*. Cambridge, MA: Harvard University Press.

Alemán, Sonya M. 2018. "Mapping Intersectionality and Latina/o and Chicana/o Students Along Educational Frameworks of Power." *Review of Research in Education* 42 (1): 177–202.

Alexander, Michelle. 2020. *The New Jim Crow: Mass Incarceration in the Age of Colorblindness.* Reprint Edition. New York: The New Press.

Allen, Jonathan and Jeffrey Cancino. 2012. "Social Disorganization, Latinos, and Juvenile Justice in the Texas Borderlands." *Journal of Criminal Justice* 40 (2): 152–163.

Allen, Walter, Edward Telles, and Margaret Hunter. "Skin Color, Income and Education: A Comparison of African Americans and Mexican Americans." *National Journal of Sociology* 12 (1): 129–180

Alurista. 1971. *Floricanto En Aztlan.* Los Angeles: Chicano Studies Center, University of California, Los Angeles.

Alurista. 1973. *The Chicano Cultural Revolution: Essays of Approach.* Unpublished manuscript.

Alurista. 1976. *Timespace Huracan: Poems, 1972–1975.* Los Alamos, NM: Pajarito Publications.

Alurista. 1981. *Spik in Glyph?* Houston: Arte Publico Press.

Alurista. 1995a. *Et Tú . . . Raza?* Tempe, AZ: Bilingual Review Press.

Alurista. 1995b. *Z Eros.* Tempe, AZ: Bilingual Review Press.

Alurista. 1999. *Return: Poems Collected and New.* Tempe, AZ: Bilingual Review Press.

Alurista. 2000. *As Our Barrio Turns: Who the Yoke B On?* San Diego: Calaca Press.

Alurista. 2010. *Tunaluna.* San Antonio: Aztlan Libre Press.

Alurista 2011. *Xicano Duende: A Select Anthology.* Tempe, AZ: Bilingual Review Press.

Alurista. 2020. *Zaz.* Berkeley, CA: Small Press Distribution.

Alvarez, Rodolfo. 1973. "The Psycho-Historical and Socioeconomic Development of the Chicano Community in the United States." *Social Science Quarterly* 53 (4): 920–942.

American Immigration Council. 2021. "Fact Sheet: The Dream Act: An Overview." https://www.amer icanimmigrationcouncil.org/research/dream-act-overview

Amuedo-Dorantes, Catalina and Cynthia Bansak. 2011. "The Impact of Amnesty on Labor Market Outcomes: A Panel Study Using the Legalized Population Survey." *Industrial Relations* 50 (3): 443–471.

Anderson, Thomas P. 1981. *The War of the Dispossessed: Honduras and El Salvador, 1969.* Lincoln, NE: University of Nebraska Press.

Andreas, Peter, and Ethan Nadelmann. 2006. *Policing the Globe: Criminalization and Crime Control in International Relations.* New York: Oxford University Press.

Andrews, Katherine. 2017. *The Life and Legacy of Juan Gabriel.* Panoramas. https://panoramas.secu re.pitt.edu/art-and-culture/life-and-legacy-juan-gabriel

Anzaldúa, Gloria. 1981. "La Prieta," pp. 220–233 in C. Moraga and G. Anzaldúa (eds.), *This Bridge Called My Back: Writings by Radical Women of Color.* Watertown, MA: Persephone Press.

Anzaldúa, Gloria. 1987. *Borderlands/ La Frontera: The New Mestiza.* San Francisco: Spinsters/Aunt Lute.

Anzaldúa, Gloria. 2009. "To(o) Queer the Writer – Loca, Escritora y Chicana," pp. 163–175 in A. Keating (ed.), *The Gloria Anzaldúa Reader.* Durham, NC: Duke University Press.

Aranda, Elizabeth M. 2007. *Emotional Bridges to Puerto Rico: Migration, Return Migration, and the Struggles of Incorporation.* Lanham, MD: Rowman & Littlefield.

Aranda, María, Laura A. Ray, Soham Al Snih, Kenneth J. Ottenbacher, and Kyriakos S. Markides. 2011. "The Protective Effect of Neighborhood Composition on Increasing Frailty among Older Mexican Americans: A Barrio Advantage?" *Journal of Aging and Health* 23 (7): 1189–1217.

Arciniega, G. Miguel, Thomas C. Anderson, Zoila G. Tovar-Blank, and Terence J.G. Tracey. 2008. "Toward a Fuller Conception of Machismo: Development of a Traditional Machismo and Caballerismo Scale." *Journal of Counseling Psychology* 55 (1): 19–33.

Argote-Freyre, Frank. 2006. *Fulgencio Batista: From Revolutionary to Strongman.* New Brunswick, NJ: Rutgers University Press.

Arias, Elizabeth and Jiaquan Xu. 2022a. "United States Life Tables, 2019." *National Vital Statistics Reports* 70 (19). https://stacks.cdc.gov/view/cdc/113096

Arias, Elizabeth and Jiaquan Xu. 2022b. "United States Life Tables, 2020." *National Vital Statistics Reports* 71 (1). https://stacks.cdc.gov/view/cdc/118055

Arias, Elizabeth, Jiaquan Xu, and Kenneth Kochanek. 2023. "United States Life Tables, 2021." *National Vital Statistics Reports* 72 (12). https://www.cdc.gov/nchs/data/nvsr/nvsr72/nvsr72-12.pdf

Armenta, Amada and Irene I. Vega. 2017 "Latinos and the Crimmigration System," pp. 221–236 in M. Deflem (ed.), *Race, Ethnicity and Law*. Vol. 22. Bingley, UK: Emerald Publishing Limited.

Arriagada, Irma. 2002. "Cambios y Desigualdad en las Familias Latinoamericanas." *Revista de CEPA* 77:143–161.

Arrington-Sanders, Renata, Aubrey Alvarenga, Noya Galai, Joyell Arscott, Andrea Wirtz, Rashida Carr, Alexander López, Chris Beyrer, Rebecca Nessen, and David Celentano. 2022. "Social Determinants of Transactional Sex in a Sample of Young Black and Latinx Sexual Minority Cisgender Men and Transgender Women." *Journal of Adolescent Health* 70 (2): 275–281.

Artiga, Samantha and Elizabeth Hinton. 2018. "Beyond Health Care: The Role of Social Determinants in Promoting Health and Health Equity." Kaiser Family Foundation, May 10. https://www.kff.org/racial-equity-and-health-policy/issue-brief/beyond-health-care-the-role-of-social-determinants-in-promoting-health-and-health-equity/

Aryaman, Archit, Shaira Jafar, Angie Mohamed, J.K. Rajjo Ronobir, Ryan Curran, Aarushi Kaushal, and Rehan Yazdani. 2020. "A Cause and Effect Analysis: Looking at the Effects of Lack of Funding for Schools on U.S. Students." *Finxerunt: Across the Spectrum of Socioeconomics* 41: 1–7.

Asante-Muhammad, Alexandra Perez, and Jamie Buell. 2021. "Racial Wealth Snapshot: Latino Americans." National Community Reinvestment Coalition. https://ncrc.org/racial-wealth-snapshot-latino-americans/

Asencio, Marysol. 2009a. *Latina/o Sexualities Probing Powers, Passions, Practices, and Policies*. New Brunswick, NJ: Rutgers University Press.

Asencio, Marysol. 2009b. "Migrant Puerto Rican Lesbians Negotiating Gender, Sexuality, and Ethnonationality." *NWSA Journal* 21 (3): 1–23.

Auxier, Brooke and Monica Anderson. 2021. "Social Media Use in 2021." Pew Research Center. https://www.pewresearch.org/internet/2021/04/07/social-media-use-in-2021/

Ayala, Maria I. 2012. "The State of Research in Latino Academic Attainment." *Sociological Forum* 27 (4): 1037–1045.

Ayón, Cecilia, Eugene Aisenberg, and Andrea Cimino. 2013. "Latino Families in the Nexus of Child Welfare, Welfare Reform, and Immigration Policies: Is Kinship Care a Lost Opportunity?" *Social Work* 58 (1): 91–94.

Ayón, Cecilia and San Juanita García. 2019. "Latino Immigrant Parents' Experiences with Discrimination: Implications for Parenting in a Hostile Immigration Policy Context." *Journal of Family Issues* 40 (6): 805–831.

Ayón, Cecilia, Flavio F. Marsiglia, and Monica Bermudez-Parsai. 2010. "Latino Family Mental Health: Exploring the Role of Discrimination and Familismo." *Journal of Community Psychology* 38 (6): 742–756.

Baca Zinn, Maxine. 1981. "Sociological Theory in Emergent Chicano Perspectives." *Pacific Sociological Review* 24 (2): 255–272.

Baca Zinn, Maxine. 1994. "Adaptation and Continuity in Mexican-Origin Families," pp. 64–94 in R. L. Taylor (ed.). *Minority Families in the United States: A Multicultural Perspective*. Englewood Cliffs, NJ: Prentice Hall.

Baca Zinn, Maxine and Angela Y.H. Pok. 2001. "Tradition and Transition in Mexican-Origin Families," pp. 79–100 in R. Taylor (ed.), *Minority Families in the United States: A Multicultural Perspective*. 3rd edn. Upper Saddle River, NJ: Prentice Hall.

Baca Zinn, Maxine and Ruth Enid Zambrana. 2019. "Chicanas/Latinas Advance Intersectional Thought and Practice." *Gender & Society* 33 (5): 677–701.

Bacio, Guadalupe A. and Lara A. Ray. 2016. "Patterns of Drinking Initiation Among Latino Youths: Cognitive and Contextual Explanations of the Immigrant Paradox." *Journal of Child & Adolescent Substance Abuse* 25 (6): 546–556.

Bacong, Adrian Matias and Cecilia Menjívar. 2021. "Recasting the Immigrant Health Paradox Through Intersections of Legal Status and Race." *Journal of Immigrant and Minority Health* 23 (5): 1092–1104.

Badillo, David A. 2006. *Latinos and the New Immigrant Church*. Baltimore, MD: Johns Hopkins University Press.

Baker, Regina S., David Brady, Zachary Parolin, Deadric T. Williams. 2022. "The Enduring Significance of Ethno-Racial Inequalities in Poverty in the U.S., 1993-2017." *Population Research and Policy Review* 41 (3): 1049-1083.

Balderrama, Francisco E. and Raymond Rodríguez. 2006. *Decade of Betrayal: Mexican Repatriation in the 1930s*. Revised edn. Albuquerque: University of New Mexico Press.

Bales, William D. and Alex R. Piquero. 2012. "Racial/Ethnic Differentials in Sentencing to Incarceration." *Justice Quarterly* 29 (5): 742-773.

Ballotpedia. 2024. "Presidential Election in Puerto Rico, 2024." https://ballotpedia.org/Presidential _election_in_Puerto_Rico,_2024

Bandes, Susan A., Marie Pryor, Erin M. Kerrison, and Phillip Atiba Goff. 2019 "The Mismeasure of Terry Stops: Assessing the Psychological and Emotional Harms of Stop and Frisk to Individuals and Communities." *Behavioral Sciences & the Law* 37 (2): 176-194.

Bankston, Carl L. III. 1998. "Youth Gangs and the New Second Generation: A Review Essay." *Aggression and Violent Behavior* 3: 35-45.

Barnard, Ian. 1997. "Gloria Anzaldua's Queer Mestisaje." *MELUS* 22 (1), 35+. https://link-gale-com. libweb.lib.utsa.edu/apps/doc/A19654386/BIC?u=txshracd2604&sid=summon&xid=7d5069e9

Baron, Stephen, John Field, and Tom Schuller (eds.). 2000. *Social Capital: Critical Perspectives*. New York: Oxford University Press.

Barrera, Mario. 1979. *Race and Class in the Southwest*. Notre Dame, IN: University of Notre Dame Press.

Barth, Frederik (ed.). 1969. *Ethnic Groups and Boundaries: The Social Organization of Culture Difference*. London: Allen and Unwin.

Bartkowski, John P. and Xiaohe Xu. 2007. "Religiosity and Teen Drug Use Reconsidered: A Social Capital Perspective." *American Journal of Preventive Medicine* 32 (6S): S182-S194.

Barton, Paul. 2010. "Latino American Religion: Mainline Protestants," pp. 1190-1195 in C.H. Lippy and P.W. Williams (eds.), *Encyclopedia of Religion in America*. Washington, DC: CQ Press.

Bastida, Elena, H. Shelton Brown, and José A. Pagán. 2008. "Persistent Disparities in the Use of Health Care along the U.S.-Mexico Border: An Ecological Perspective." *American Journal of Public Health* 98 (11): 1987-1995.

Batalova, Jeanne and Aaron Terrazas. 2010. "Frequently Requested Statistics on Immigrants and Immigration to the United States." *Migration Information Source*, December. http://www.mig rationinformation.org/USFocus/display.cfm?ID=818

Bean, Frank D. and Marta Tienda. 1987. *The Hispanic Population of the United States*. Newbury Park, CA: Russell Sage.

Becker, Gary S. 1975. *Human Capital: A Theoretical and Empirical Analysis, with Special Reference to Education*. 2nd edn. New York: Columbia University Press.

Becker, Howard. 1963. *Outsiders: Studies in the Sociology of Deviance*. New York: The Free Press of Glencoe.

Bedolla, Lisa García. 2009. *Introduction to Latino Politics in the US*. Vol. 4. Polity.

Bejarano, Christina E. 2014. "Latino Gender and Generation Gaps in Political Ideology." *Politics & Gender* 10 (1): 62-88.

Bejarano, Cynthia and Maria Cristina Morales. 2024. *Frontera Madre(hood): Brown Mothers Challenging Oppression and Transborder Violence at the US-Mexico Border*. Tucson, AZ: University of Arizona Press.

Bejarano, Cynthia, Maria Cristina Morales, and Said Saddiki. 2012. "A Comparative Analysis of the Mexico-U.S. and Moroccan-Spanish Regions: Understanding Conquest through a Border Lens," pp. 27-41 in J.M Loyd (ed.), *Beyond Walls & Cages*. Tucson, AZ: University of Arizona Press.

Belén, Edna Acosta. 2021. "Nicholasa Mohr." *Encyclopedia of Puerto Rico*. https://en.enciclopediapr. org/content/nicholasa-mohr/

Benavides, Lucía. 2020. "Why Labeling Antonio Banderas a 'Person of Color' Triggers Such a Backlash." *National Public Radio*, February 9. https://www.npr.org/2020/02/09/803809670/why-labeling-antonio-banderas-a-person-of-color-triggers-such-a-backlash

Benjamin, Andrea. 2017. *Racial Coalition Building in Local Elections: Elite Cues and Cross-Ethnic Voting.* Cambridge University Press.

Benuto, Lorraine T., Jena B. Casas, Caroline Cummings, and Rory Newlands. 2018. "Undocumented, to DACAmented, to DACAlimited: Narratives of Latino students with DACA status." *Hispanic Journal of Behavioral Sciences* 40 (3): 259–278.

Berger, Joseph. 2011. "Piri Thomas, Spanish Harlem Author Dies at 83." *New York Times*, October 19. https://www.nytimes.com/2011/10/20/books/piri-thomas-author-of-down-these-mean-streets-dies.html

Berges, Ivonne-Marie, Yong-Fang Kuo, M. Kristen Peek, and Kyriakos S. Markides. 2010. "Religious Involvement and Physical Functioning among Older Mexican Americans." *Journal of Aging* 12 (1): 1–10.

Betts, Dianne C. 1994. *Crisis on the Rio Grande: Poverty, Unemployment, and Economic Development on the Texas-Mexico Border.* New York: Routledge.

Bestvater, Sam, Risa Gelles-Watnick, Meltem Odabaş, Monica Anderson, and Aaron Smith. 2023. #BlackLivesMatter turns 10: Americans' views of and experiences with activism on social media. Pew Research Center. https://www.pewresearch.org/internet/2023/06/29/americans-views-of-and-experiences-with-activism-on-social-media/

Bialik, Kristen. 2017. "Key Facts about Race and Marriage, 50 Years after Loving v. Virginia." Pew Research Center, June 12.

Biden, Joe. 2023. Statement from President Joe Biden on the Anniversary of DACA. White House.

Biography. 2023. Alexandria Ocasio-Cortez. https://www.biography.com/political-figures/alexandria-ocasio-cortez

Biography. 2020. Julián Castro. https://www.biography.com/political-figures/julian-castro

Bizvibe. 2020. "World's Largest Bakery Companies – Leading Bakeries and Commercial Bread Companies." Bizvibe, August 19. https://blog.bizvibe.com/blog/largest-bakery-companies

Blackwell, Maylei. 2011.¡Chicana Power! Contested Histories of Feminism in the Chicano Movement. Austin: University of Texas Press.

Blalock, Hubert M. 1967. *Toward a Theory of Minority-Group Relations.* New York: John Wiley & Sons.

Blanton, Carlos. K. 2014. *George I. Sánchez: The Long Fight for Mexican American Integration.* New Haven, CT: Yale University Press.

Blau, Peter M. 1977. *Inequality and Heterogeneity.* New York: Free Press.

Blau, Peter M., Terry C. Blum, and Joseph E. Schwartz. 1982. "Heterogeneity and Intermarriage." *American Sociological Review* 47 (1): 45–62.

Blauner, Robert. 1972. *Racial Oppression in America.* New York: Harper and Row.

Bogardus, Emory S. 1943. "Gangs of Mexican-American Youth." *Sociology and Social Research* 28: 55–66.

Bonilla-Silva, Eduardo. 1997. "Rethinking Racism: Toward a Structural Interpretation." *American Sociological Review* 62: 465–480.

Bonilla-Silva, Eduardo. 2001. *White Supremacy and Racism in the Post-Civil Rights Era.* Boulder, CO: Lynne Rienner.

Bonilla-Silva, Eduardo. 2004. "From Bi-Racial to Tri-Racial: Towards a New System of Racial Stratification in the USA." *Ethnic and Racial Studies* 27 (6): 931–950.

Bonilla-Silva, Eduardo. 2019. "Feeling Race: Theorizing the Racial Economy of Emotions." *American Sociological Review* 84 (1): 1–25.

Bonilla-Silva, Eduardo. 2021. *Racism without Racists: Colorblind Racism and the Persistence of Racial Inequality in America.* 6th edn. Lanham, MD: Rowman & Littlefield.

Borom, Charles. 2023. *Another Chapter in the War on "Woke": Banning Ethnic Studies and the Anti-CRT Movement by the Unseasoned Elites.* Ph.D. dissertation, University of Minnesota.

Bourdieu, Pierre. 1977. "Cultural Reproduction and Social Reproduction," pp. 487–511 in J. Karabel and A.H. Halsey (eds.), *Power and Education Ideology.* New York: Oxford University Press.

Bourdieu, Pierre. 2004. "Structures and the Habitus." *Material Culture: Critical Concepts in the Social Sciences* 1 (part 1): 116–177.

Bourdieu, Pierre. 2018a. "Cultural Reproduction and Social Reproduction," pp. 71–112 in R. Brown (ed.), *Knowledge, Education, and Cultural Change*. Routledge.

Bourdieu, Pierre 2018b. "The Forms of Capital," pp. 78–92 in M. Granovetter (ed.), *The Sociology of Economic Life*. Routledge.

Bourdieu, Pierre, and Jean-Claude Passeron. 1977. *Reproduction in Education, Society and Culture*. Vol. 4. Thousand Oaks, CA: Sage.

Bourdieu, Pierre and Loïc Wacquant. 1992. *An Invitation to Reflexive Sociology*. Chicago: University of Chicago Press.

Bowen, Mary Elizabeth. 2009. "Childhood Socioeconomic Status and Racial Differences in Disability: Evidence from the Health and Retirement Study (1998–2006)." *Social Science & Medicine* 69 (3): 433–441.

Bowen, Patrick D. 2013. "U.S. Latina/o Muslims Since 1920: From 'Moors' to 'Latino Muslims'." *Journal of Religious History* 37 (2): 165–184.

Brammer, John Paul. 2022. "What Does It Mean to Be a 'High-Risk Homosexual'?" *New York Times*, January 14. https://www.nytimes.com/2022/01/14/books/review/high-risk-homosexual-edgar-gomez.html?unlocked_article_code=1.lk0.Gm2A.-R5gmPppTO2K&smid=em-share

Braswell, Mary. 2019. "Because of His Work, We're Ready for This Fight." UCLA Luskin School of Public Affairs. https://luskin.ucla.edu/symposium-honors-urban-planning-pioneer-leo-estrada

Brenneman, Robert. 2012. *Homies and Hermanos: God and Gangs in Central America*. New York: Oxford University Press.

Brown, Henry Shelton. 2008. "Do Mexican Immigrants Substitute Health Care in Mexico for Insurance in the United States? The Role of Distance." *Social Science & Medicine* 67: 2036–2042.

Brown, R. Khari. 2011. "Religion, Political Discourse, and Activism Among Varying Racial/Ethnic Groups in America." *Review of Religious Research* 53: 301–322.

Bruce-Novoa, Juan. 1981. *Chicano Poetry: A Response to Chaos*. Austin: University of Texas Press.

Bruce-Novola, Juan. 1987. "Who's Killing Whom in Belen County: Rolando Hinojosa's Narrative Production." *Monographic Review* 3 (1–2): 288–297.

Bruhn, J.G. 2011. *The Sociology of Community Connections*. New York: Springer.

Bryant, Jessica and Chole Appleby. 2023. "These States' Anti-DEI Legislation May Impact Higher Education." https://www.bestcolleges.com/news/anti-dei-legislation-tracker/

Buffalo Soldier. 2014. *Hispanic-American Medal of Honor Recipients*. http://www.buffalosoldier.net/Hispanic-AmericanMedalofHonorRecipients.htm

Bullock Texas State History Museum. (n.d.). Life and Death on the Border, 1910–1920. Musica Tejana. https://www.thestoryoftexas.com/visit/exhibits/life-and-death-on-the-border-1910-1920/musica-tejana

Bunker, Robert and John Sullivan (eds.). 2020. *Strategic Notes on Third Generation Gangs*. McLean, VA: Small Wars Foundation.

Burchfield, Keri B. and Eric Silver. 2012. "Collective Efficacy and Crime in Los Angeles Neighborhoods: Implications for the Latino Paradox." *Sociological Inquiry* 83 (1): 154–176.

Burnett, John. 2010. "Lydia Mendoza: The First Lady of Tejano." NPR, May 24. https://www.npr.org/2010/05/24/127033025/lydia-mendoza-the-first-lady-of-tejano

Burri, Breht. 2010. "Latina/opia Document – 1969 El Plan de Aztlán. *Latina/opia.com*. http://Latina/opia.com/Latina/o-history/plan-de-aztlan/

Bursik, Robert J. 1988. "Social Disorganization and Theories of Crime and Delinquency: Problems and Prospects." *Criminology* 26 (4): 519–552.

Bryant, Jessica and Chole Appleby. 2023. "These States' Anti-DEI Legislation May Impact Higher Education." https://www.bestcolleges.com/news/anti-dei-legislation-tracker/

Bustamante, Jorge. 1972. "The 'Wetback' as Deviant: An Application of Labeling Theory." *American Journal of Sociology* 77 (4): 706–718.

Caballero, Cecilia, Yvette Martínez-Vu, Judith Pérez-Torres, Michelle Téllez, Christine Vega, and Ana Castillo. 2019. *The Chicana Motherwork Anthology*. Tucson, AZ: University of Arizona Press.

Cadge, Wendy and Elaine Howard Ecklund. 2007. "Immigration and Religion." *Annual Review of Sociology* 33: 359–379.

Cahill, Sean. 2009. "The Disproportionate Impact of Antigay Family Policies on Black and Latino Same-Sex Couple Households." *Journal of African American Studies* 13 (3): 219–250.

Campos, Belinda, Jodie B. Ullman, Adrian Aguilera, and Christina Dunkel-Schetter. 2014. "Familism and Psychological Health: The Intervening Role of Closeness and Social Support." *Cultural Diversity and Ethnic Minority Psychology* 20 (2): 191–201.

Campos, Belinda, Ilona S. Yim, and David Busse. 2018. "Culture as a Pathway to Maximizing the Stress-Buffering Role of Social Support." *Hispanic Journal of Behavioral Sciences* 40 (3): 294–311.

Campos-Delgado, Amalia. 2021. "Emotional Geographies of Irregular Transmigrants' Journeys." *Migration Studies* 9 (2): 179–195.

Canales, Jesse. 2022. "DACA 10th Anniversary: Recipients Call for Immigration Reform." *Spectrum News*, Osceola County, Fl, June 6.

Candelario, Ginetta E.B. 2007. *Black Behind the Ears: Dominican Racial Identity from Museums to Beauty Shops*. Durham, NC: Duke University Press.

Canizales, Stephanie L. and Pierrette Hondagneu-Sotelo. 2022. "Working-Class Latina/o Youth Navigating Stratification and Inequality: A Review of Literature." *Sociology Compass* 16 (12): e13050.

Cantor-Navas, Judyú. 2019, "10 Eternal Celia Cruz Songs." *Billboard*, October 21. https://www.billboard.com/music/latin/ten-eternal-celia-cruz-songs-7865862/

Cantú, Lionel. 2002. "DE AMBIENTE: Queer Tourism and the Shifting Boundaries of Mexican Male Sexualities." *GLQ*, 8 (1–2): 139–166.

Cantú, Lionel, Nancy A. Naples, and Salvador Vidal-Ortiz. 2009. *The Sexuality of Migration: Border Crossings and Mexican Immigrant Men*. New York: New York University Press.

Cantu, Phillip, Joanna Chyu, Neil Mehta, and Kyriakos Markides. 2023. "Profiles of COVID-19 on Informal Caregivers of Older Mexican Americans." *Journal of Aging and Health* 35 (10): 819–825.

Card, David. 1990. "The Impact of the Mariel Boatlift on the Miami Labor Market." *Industrial and Labor Relations Review* 43 (2): 245–257.

Carey, Roderick L. 2022. "'Whatever You Become, Just Be Proud of It.' Uncovering the Ways Families Influence Black and Latino Adolescent Boys' Postsecondary Future Selves." *Journal of Adolescent Research* 37 (1): 59–97.

Carmona, Judith Flores. 2021. "'Dime Con Quién Andas y Te Diré Quién Eres': Theories and Methodologies that Center Latinx/a/o Epistemologies and Pedagogies," pp. 68–78 in N. Garcia, C. Salinas, and J. Cisneros (eds.) *Studying Latinx/a/o Students in Higher Education*. New York: Routledge.

Carrillo, Héctor. 2017. *Pathways of Desire: The Sexual Migration of Mexican Gay Men*. Chicago: University of Chicago Press.

Carrizales, Sylvia M. 2020. "Selena is the Subject of New UTSA Course This Fall." *Tejano Nation*, May 30. https://tejanonation.net/2020/05/30/selena-is-the-subject-of-new-utsa-course-this-fall/

Castro, Joaquin. 2023a. Official Website of Congressman Joaquin Castro. https://castro.house.gov/about

Castro, Joaquin. 2023b, "Texas Rep. Joaquin Castro Says Publishers Are Failing Latino Stories." *Publishers Weekly*, February 17. https://www.publishersweekly.com/pw/by-topic/columns-and-blogs/soapbox/article/91559-texas-rep-joaquin-castro-says-publishers-are-failing-latino-stories.html

Cauce, Ana Mari and Melanie Domenech-Rodríguez. 2002. "Latino Families: Myths and Realities," pp. 3–26 in J.M. Contreras, K.A. Kerns, and A.M. Neal-Barnett (eds.) *Latino Children and Families in the United States: Current Research and Future Directions*. Westport, CT: Praeger Publishers.

Cave, Damen. 2013. "In Mexican Villages, Few Are Left to Dream of U.S." *New York Times*, April 3. http://www.nytimes.com/2013/04/03/world/americas/new-wave-of-mexican-immigrants-seems-unlikely.html?hp

Cavendish, Richard. 1998. "The Sinking of the Maine." *History Today* 48 (2). http://www.historytoday.com/richard-cavendish/sinking-maine

Center for American Progress. 2020. "A Quality Approach to School Funding." Center for American Progress. https://www.americanprogress.org/article/fixing-chronic-disinvestment-k-12-schools/

Center for an Informed Public. 2021. *The Long Fuse: Misinformation and the 2020 Election*. Stanford, CA: Stanford Digital Repository, Election Integrity Partnership.

Center for Immigration Studies. 1995. "Three Decades of Mass Immigration: The Legacy of the 1965 Immigration Act." Washington, DC: Center for Immigration Studies.

Centers for Disease Control and Prevention. 2020. "Youth Risk Behavioral Surveillance Survey: 2019." https://npin.cdc.gov/publication/youth-risk-behavior-surveillance-survey-2019

Centers for Disease Control and Prevention. 2024a. "About Underlying Cause of Death, 2018–2021, Single Race." https://wonder.cdc.gov/ucd-icd10-expanded.html

Centers for Disease Control and Prevention. 2024b. "Life Tables." https://www.cdc.gov/nchs/produ cts/life_tables.htm

Centers for Disease Control and Prevention. 2024c. "Natality Information: Life Births." https://won der.cdc.gov/natality.html

Centers for Disease Control and Prevention. 2024d. "Linked Birth/Infant Death Records." https://wonder.cdc.gov/lbd.html

Cervantes, Joseph M., Olga L. Mejía, and Amalia Guerrero Mena. 2010. "Serial Migration and the Assessment of Extreme and Unusual Psychological Hardship with Undocumented Latina/o Families." *Hispanic Journal of Behavioral Sciences* 32 (2): 275–291.

Chalfin, Aaron and Monica Deza. 2020. "Immigration Enforcement, Crime, and Demography: Evidence from the Legal Arizona Workers Act." *Criminology & Public Policy* 19 (2): 515–562.

Chant, Sylvia with Nikki Craske. 2003. *Gender in Latin America*. New Brunswick, NJ: Rutgers University Press.

Chapman, Dan. 2001. "Gwinnett No. 1? Steady Growth May Put County in Top Spot by 2008." *Atlanta Journal-Constitution*, March 24: 1B.

Chasin, Barbara H. 2004. *Inequality and Violence in the United States: Casualties of Capitalism*. New York: Humanity Books.

Chavez, Leo R. 2012. "Undocumented Immigrants and Their Use of Medical Services in Orange County, California." Social Science & Medicine 74 (6): 887–893.

Chavez, Leo R. 2013. *The Latino Threat Narrative: Constructing Immigrants, Citizens, and the Nation*. 2nd edn. Stanford, CA: Stanford University Press.

Cheney, Ann M., Christine Newkirk, Katheryn Rodriguez, and Anselmo Montez. 2018. "Inequality and Health among Foreign-Born Latinos in Rural Borderland Communities." *Social Science & Medicine* 215: 115–122.

Chetty, Raj, John Friedman, Nathaniel Hendren, Maggie Jones, and Sonya Porter. 2020. "The Opportunity Atlas: Mapping the Childhood Roots of Social Mobility."

Cho, Sumi, Kimberlé Williams Crenshaw, and Leslie McCall. 2013. "Toward a Field of Intersectionality Studies: Theory, Applications, and Praxis." *Signs* 38 (4): 785–810.

Chouhy, Cecilia and Arelys Madero-Hernandez. 2019. "'Murderers, Rapists, and Bad Hombres': Deconstructing the Immigration-Crime Myths." *Victims & Offenders* 14 (8): 1010–1039.

Christophe, N. Keita and Gabriela L. Stein. 2022. "Facilitating the Study of Familism across Racial/Ethnic Groups: Creation of the Short Attitudinal Familism Scale." *Journal of Family Psychology* 36 (4): 534–544.

Cimini, Kate. 2020. "'Puro Cash': Latinos are Opening More Small Businesses than Anyone Else in the US." *USA Today*, May 23. https://www.usatoday.com/in-depth/news/nation/2020/02/24/latino-small-business-owners-becoming-economic-force-us/4748786002/

Clotfelter, Charles T. 2004. *After Brown: The Rise and Retreat of School Segregation*. Princeton, NJ: Princeton University Press.

Cloward, Richard A. and Lloyd E. Ohlin. 1960. *Delinquency and Opportunity: A Theory of Delinquent Gangs*. Glencoe, IL: Free Press.

CNN. 2019. "Latino in America."

Cobo, Leila. 2017. "How 'Despacito' Became the Biggest Song of the Year in Any Language." *Billboard*, July 21. https://www.billboard.com/articles/columns/latin/7873889/despacito-luis-fonsi-daddy-yankee-impact-changing-latin-music.

Cobo, Leila. 2020. "Latin Is the Third Largest Music Genre in the World, Plus More Key Facts." *Billboard*, October 20. https://www.billboard.com/music/latin/latin-third-largest-music-genre-facts-9468876/.

Cobo, Leila. 2022. "5 Ways 'Despacito' Changed Latin Music Forever." *Billboard*, June 1. https://www.billboard.com/music/latin/despacito-changed-latin-music-1235079900/

Cohen, Deborah. 2011. Braceros: Migrant Citizens and Transnational Subjects in the Postwar United States and Mexico. Chapel Hill, NC: University of North Carolina Press.

Cohen, Laurie. 1998. "Free Ride: With Help from INS, U.S. Meatpacker Taps Mexican Work Force." *Wall Street Journal*, October 15: A1.

Collins, Patricia Hill. 2022. *Black Feminists Thought*. 30th anniversary edn. New York: Routledge.

Collins, Patricia Hill and Sirma Bilge. 2020. *Intersectionality*. 2nd edn. Cambridge, UK: Polity.

Contreras, Frances and Jessica Rodriguez. 2021. "Investing in Educational Equity for Latinos: How Accountability, Access and Systemic Inequity Shape Opportunity," pp. 103–113 in E. Murillo, D. D. Bernal and S. Morales (eds.), *Handbook of Latinos and Education: Theory, Research, and Practice*. New York: Routledge.

Cooperman, Alan, Mark Hugo Lopez, Cary Funk, Jessica Hamar Martínez, and Katherine Ritchey. 2014. *The Shifting Religious Identity of Latinos in the United States: Nearly One-in-Four Latinos are Former Catholics*. Washington, DC: Pew Research Center.

Cordero, Carrie F., Heidi Li Feldman, and Chimène I Keitner. 2019. "The Law Against Family Separation." *Columbia Human Rights Law Review* 51(2): 432–508.

Corona, Karina, Belinda Campos, and Chuansheng Chen. 2017. "Familism is Associated with Psychological Well-Being and Physical Health: Main Effects and Stress-Buffering Effects." *Hispanic Journal of Behavioral Sciences* 39 (1): 46–65.

Correa, Jennifer G. and Joseph M. Simpson. 2022. "Building Walls, Destroying Borderlands: Repertoires of Militarization on the United States-Mexico Border." *Nature and Culture* 17 (1): 1–25.

Cortez, Jaime. 2022. *Gordo*. New York: Black Cat.

Coto, Dánica. 2022. "Puerto Rico Formally Exits Bankruptcy Following Largest Public Debt Restructuring." *USA Today*, March 16. https://www.usatoday.com/story/news/nation/2022/03/16/puerto-rico-exits-bankruptcy/7064653001/

Crandall, Russell. 2006. *Gunboat Democracy: U.S. Interventions in the Dominican Republic, Grenada, and Panama*. Lanham, MD: Rowman & Littlefield.

Crimmins, Eileen M., Jung Ki Kim, Dawn E. Alley, Arun Karlamangla, and Teresa Seeman. 2007. "Hispanic Paradox in Biological Risk Profiles." *American Journal of Public Health* 97: 1305–1310.

Cross Border Freight. 2019. "What are Maquiladoras and Where are They Located?" *Cross Border Freight*, August 15. https://mexicocrossborderfreight.com/what-are-maquiladoras-and-where-are-they-located/

Cruz, José Miguel. 2010. "Central American *Maras*: From Youth Street Gangs to Transnational Protection Rackets." *Global Crime* 11 (4): 379–398.

Cruz, Angie. 2022. *How Not to Drown in a Glass of Water: A Novel*. New York: Flatiron Books.

Cuartas, Victor Hugo. 2020. *Hispanic Muslims in the United States: Agency, Identity, and Religious Commitment*. Eugene, OR: Wipf and Stock Publishers.

Cuéllar, Alfredo. 1970. "Perspective on Politics, pp. 137–158 in J.W. Moore with A. Cuéllar, *Mexican Americans*. Englewood Cliffs, NJ: Prentice-Hall.

Cuevas, Joshua. 2022. "The Authoritarian Threat to Public Education: Attacks on Diversity, Equity, and Inclusion Undermine Teaching and Learning." *Journal of Language and Literacy Education* 18 (2): 1–6.

Cuevas, Stephany. 2019. "'Con Mucho Sacrificio, We Give Them Everything We Can': The Strategic Day-to-Day Sacrifices of Undocumented Latina/o Parents." *Harvard Educational Review* 89 (3): 473–518.

Danziger, Pamela A. 2023. "Cinco De Mayo Is Only One Day, Yet Latino Consumers Deserve Attention All Year." *Forbes*, May 1. https://www.forbes.com/sites/pamdanziger/2023/05/01/cinco-de-mayo-will-come-and-go-but-latino-consumers-will-be-here-long-after/?sh=3f85d1567217

Darity, William A., Jr. and Samuel L. Myers, Jr. 2001. "Why Did Black Relative Earnings Surge in the Early 1990s?" *Journal of Economic Issues* 35 (2): 533–542.

Dávila, Arlene. 2001. *Latino Inc.: The Marketing and Making of a People*. Berkeley, CA: University of California Press.

Dávila, Arlene. 2008. *Latino Spin: Public Image and the Whitewashing of Race.* New York: New York University Press.

Dawes, Daniel E. 2020. *The Political Determinants of Health.* Baltimore, MD: Johns Hopkins University Press.

de la Rosa, Ivan A. 2002. "Perinatal Outcomes among Mexican Americans: A Review of an Epidemiological Paradox." *Ethnicity & Disease* 12: 480–487.

de la Torre, Adela and Lynda Rush. 1987. "The Determinants of Breastfeeding for Mexican Migrant Women." *International Migration Review* 21 (3): 728–742.

de Novais, Janine and George Spencer. 2019. "Learning Race to Unlearn Racism: The Effects of Ethnic Studies Course-Taking." *Journal of Higher Education* 90 (6): 860–883.

de Ortego y Gasca, Felipe. 2008. "Why Chicano Studies?" *The Hispanic Outlook in Higher Education* 19 (1): 34–37.

del Rio, Esteban. 2012. "Accentuate the Positive: Americanos and the Articulation of Latina/o Life in the United States." *Journal of Communication Inquiry* 36 (3): 179–201.

Degler, Carl N. 1986. *Neither Black Nor White: Slavery and Race Relations in Brazil and the United States.* Madison, WI: University of Wisconsin Press.

Deleon, Lauren. 2023. "La Virgin de la Caridad del Cobre: The Protectress of Cuba." StMU Research Scholars, April 15. https://stmuscholars.org/la-virgin-de-la-caridad-del-cobre-the-protectress-of-cuba/

Delgado, Melvin. 2020. *State-Sanctioned Violence: Advancing a Social Work Social Justice Agenda.* New York: Oxford University Press.

Delgado, Richard and Jean Stefancic. 2001. *Critical Race Theory: An Introduction.* New York: New York University Press.

Delgado, Vanessa. 2022. "Family Formation Under the Law: How Immigration Laws Construct Contemporary Latino/a Immigrant Families in the US." *Sociology Compass* 16 (9): 1–13.

Denver Public Library. 2024. "Rodolfo 'Corky' Gonzales." https://history.denverlibrary.org/exhibit/rodolfo-corky-gonzales

Desjardins, Richard. 2015. "Education and Social Transformation." *European Journal of Education* 50 (3): 239–244.

DeVitt, Rachel. 2011. "Cheat Sheet: Latino Crossovers." *Rhapsody.com*, October 5. http://blog.rhapsody.com/2011/10/crossovers.html

Dewey, Joseph. 2012. "Alurista," pp. 42–44 in C. Tafolla and M.P. Cotera (eds.), *Great Lives from History: Latinos.* Vol. 1. Ipswich, MA: Salem Press.

Diaz, Jesse, Jr. 2012. "Prison and Immigration Industrial Complexes: The Ethnodistillation of People of Color and Immigrants as Economic, Political, and Demographic Threats to the US Hegemony." *International Journal of Criminology and Sociology* 1: 265–284.

Dickerson vonLockette, Niki T. and Jacqueline Johnson. 2010. "Latino Employment and Residential Segregation in Metropolitan Labor Markets." *Du Bois Review* 7 (1): 151–184.

Dinan, Stephen. 2012. "Obama Administration Sets Deportation Record." *Washington Post,* December 21. http://www.washingtontimes.com/news/2012/dec/21/obama-administration-sets-deportation-record/

Doetsch-Kidder, Sharon. 2011. "'My Story Is Really Not Mine': An Interview with Latina Trans Activist Ruby Bracamonte." *Feminist Studies* 37 (2): 441–467.

Domhoff, G. William. 2013. *Who Rules America?: The Triumph of the Corporate Rich.* 7th edn. New York: McGraw-Hill.

Dominguez, Jaime. 2013. "Latino Voices Missing in US Media: It's Time to Weigh In." *Al Jazeera,* April 2.

Donato, Katharine M., Chizuko Wakabayashi, Shirin Hakimzadeh, and Amada Armenta. 2008. "Shifts in the Employment Conditions of Mexican Migrant Men and Women: The Effect of U.S. Immigration Policy." *Work and Occupations* 35 (4): 462–495.

Donato, Katharine M. and Amada Armenta. 2011. "What We Know About Unauthorized Migration." *Annual Review of Sociology* 37: 529–543.

Donato, Katharine M. and Blake Sisk. 2012. "Shifts in the Employment Outcomes among Mexican Migrants to the United States, 1976–2009." *Research in Social Stratification and Mobility* 30 (1): 63–77.

Doodoo, Francis N.A. and Baffour K. Takyi. 2002. "Africans in the Diaspora: Black–White Earnings Differences among America's Africans." *Ethnic and Racial Studies* 25: 913–941.

Dorn, Emma, Bryan Hancock, Jimmy Sarakatsannis, and Ellen Viruleg. 2020. "COVID-19 and Student Learning in the United States: The Hurt Could Last a Lifetime." *McKinsey & Company* 1: 1–9.

Douglas, Karen Manges and Rogelio Sáenz. 2008. "No Phone, No Vehicle, No English, and No Citizenship: The Vulnerability of Mexican Immigrants in the United States," pp. 161–180 in A. Hattery, D.G. Embrick, and E. Smith (eds.), *Race, Human Rights and Inequality*. Lanham, MD: Rowman and Littlefield.

Douglas, Karen Manges and Rogelio Sáenz. 2013. "The Criminalization of Immigrants and the Immigration–Industrial Complex." *Daedalus, the Journal of the American Academy of Arts & Sciences* 142 (3): 199–227.

Dow, Mark. 2004. *American Gulag: Inside U.S. Immigration Prisons*. Berkeley, CA: University of California Press.

Dow, Dawn Marie. 2019. *Mothering While Black: Boundaries and Burdens of Middle-Class Parenthood*. Berkeley, CA: University of California Press.

Dreby, Joanna. 2012. "The Burden of Deportation on Children in Mexican Immigrant Families." *Journal of Marriage and Family* 74 (4): 829–845.

Dreby, Joanna. 2015. "US Immigration Policy and Family Separation: The Consequences for Children's Well-being." *Social Science & Medicine* 132: 245–251.

Dreby, Joanna, Florencia Silveira, and Eunju Lee. 2022. "The Anatomy of Immigration Enforcement: Long-Standing Socio-Emotional Impacts on Children as They Age into Adulthood." *Journal of Marriage and Family* 84 (3): 713–733.

Duany, Jorge. 2004. "Puerto Rico: Between the Nation and the Diaspora-Migration To and From Puerto Rico," pp. 177–195 in M.I. Torn-Morn and M. Alicea (eds.), *Migration and Immigration: A Global View*. Westport, CT: Greenwood Press.

Dubina, Kevin, Lindsey Ice, Janie-Lynn Kim, and Michael Rieley. 2021. "Projections Overview and Highlights, 2020–30." *Monthly Labor Review*, October.

Durán, Robert J. 2018. *The Gang Paradox: Inequalities and Miracles on the US-Mexico Border*. New York: Columbia University Press.

Du Bois, William, Edward Burghardt and Manning Marable. 2015. *The Souls of Black Folk*. New York: Routledge.

Dudley, Steven. 2020. *MS-13: The Making of America's Most Notorious Gang*. New York: Hanover Square Press.

Duncan, O.D. 1961. "A Socioeconomic Index for All Occupations," pp. 109–138 in A. Reiss, Jr., *Occupations and Social Status*. Glencoe, IL: Free Press.

Dunn, Timothy. 1996. *The Militarization of the U.S.–Mexico Border 1978–1992: Low-Intensity Conflict Doctrine Comes Home*. Austin, TX: Center for Mexican American Studies Books, University of Texas at Austin.

Dunn, Timothy. 2009. *Blockading the Border and Human: The El Paso Operation that Remade Immigration Enforcement*. Austin: University of Texas Press.

Duran, Antonio, Fernando Rodriguez, and Oscar E. Patrón. 2020. "Queer Love in the Lives of Gay Latino Men in College." *International Journal of Qualitative Studies in Education* 33 (9): 905–920.

Durán, Robert J. 2013. *Gang Life in Two Cities: An Insiders Journey*. New York: Columbia University Press.

Durán, Robert J. and Jason A. Campos. 2020. "Gangs, Gangsters, and the Impact of Settler Colonialism on the Latina/o Experience." *Sociology Compass* 14 (3): e12765.

Durand, Jorge and Douglas S. Massey. 2003. "The Costs of Contradiction: U.S. Border Policy 1986–2000." *Latino Studies* 1 (2): 233–252.

Dzidzienyo, Anani and Suzanne Oboler (eds.). 2005. *Neither Enemies Nor Friends: Latinos, Blacks, Afro-Latinos*. New York: Palgrave Macmillan.

Echeagaray, José Ignacio (ed.). 1981. *Album Conmemorativo del 450 Aniversario de la Apariciones de Nuestra Señora de Guadalupe*. Mexico City: Ediciones Buena Nueva.

Eckstein, Susan. 2009. *The Immigrant Divide: How Cuban Americans Changed the U.S. and Their Homeland*. New York: Routledge.

Edgerton, Jason D. and Lance W. Roberts. 2014. "Cultural Capital or Habitus? Bourdieu and Beyond in the Explanation of Enduring Educational Inequality." *Theory and Research in Education* 12 (2): 193–220.

Education Trust. 2018. *Funding Gaps: An Analysis of School Funding Equity Across the U.S. and Within Each State*. Washington, DC: Education Trust. https://edtrust.org/wp-content/uploads/20 14/09/FundingGapReport_2018_FINAL.pdf

EFE. 2021. "Johnny Pacheco, the 'Godfather of Salsa' and Soul of Fania Records, Dies at 85." *Los Angeles Times*, February 15. https://www.latimes.com/entertainment-arts/music/story/2021-02-15/johnny-pacheco-the-godfather-of-salsa-and-the-soul-of-fania-records-dies-at-85

Eidy, Nourel-Hoda, Ronnie Alvarez, and Madeline Simone. 2020. "State Sanctioned Violence across Latinx, Black, and Arab and Muslim Communities in a Post-9/11 America." *The Macksey Journal* 1 (1): Article 194.

Ek, Lucila D., Patricia D. Quijada Cerecer, Iliana Alanís, and Mariela A. Rodríguez. 2010. "'I Don't Belong Here': Chicanas/Latinas at a Hispanic Serving Institution Creating Community Through Muxerista Mentoring." *Equity & Excellence in Education* 43 (4): 539–553.

Elizondo, Virgilio P. 1980. *La Morenita: Evangelizer of the Americas*. San Antonio: Mexican American Cultural Center.

Ellison, Christopher G., Samuel Echevarria, and Brad Smith. 2005. "Religion and Abortion Attitudes among U.S. Hispanics: Findings from the 1990 Latino National Political Survey." *Social Science Quarterly* 86: 192–208.

Elo, Irma T., Cassio M. Turra, Bert Kestenbaum, and B. Reneé Ferguson. 2004. "Mortality among Elderly Hispanics in the United States: Past Evidence and New Results." *Demography* 41 (1): 109–128.

English, T.J. 2009. *Havana Nocturne: How the Mob Owned Cuba and Lost It To the Revolution*. New York: HarperCollins.

Enriquez, Laura E. 2015. "Multigenerational Punishment: Shared Experiences of Undocumented Immigration Status within Mixed-Status Families." *Journal of Marriage and Family* 77 (4): 939–953.

Escalada, Xavier. 1965. *Santa María Tequatlasupe: Pequeños Estudios en Torno al Gran Hecho Mexicano*. México City: Imprenta Murguía.

Eschbach, Karl, Jacqueline Hagan, Nestor Rodriguez, Rubén Hernández-León, and Stanley Bailey. 1999. "Death at the Border." *International Migration Review* 33 (2): 430–454.

Eschbach, Karl, Jonathan D. Mahnken, and James S. Goodwin. 2005. "Neighborhood Composition and Incidence of Cancer among Hispanics in the United States." *Cancer* 103 (5): 1036–1044.

Escobar, Edward J. 1999. *Race, Police, and the Making of a Political Identity: Mexican Americans and the Los Angeles Police Department, 1900–1945*. Berkeley, CA: University of California Press.

Esparza, Adrian X. and Angela J. Donelson. 2008. *Colonias in Arizona and New Mexico: Border Poverty and Community Development Solutions*. Tucson, AZ: University of Arizona Press.

Espino, Rodolfo and Michael M. Franz. 2002. "Latino Phenotypic Discrimination Revisited: The Impact of Skin Color on Occupational Status." *Social Science Quarterly* 83 (2): 612–623.

Espinosa, Gastón. 2023. "Nones, No Religious Preference, No Religion, and the Misclassification of Latino Religious Identity." *Religions* 14 (3): 420. https://doi.org/10.3390/rel14030420.

Esquivel, Laura M. 2021. "An East L.A. Warrior Who Bridged the Latina/o and the Gay Worlds," pp. 78–96 in U. Quesada, L. Gomez, and S. Vidal-Ortiz (eds.), *Queer Brown Voices: Personal Narratives of Latina/o LGBT Activism*. Austin: University of Texas Press.

Ewing, Walter A., Daniel Martinez, and Rubén G. Rumbaut. 2015. "The Criminalization of Immigration in the United States." American Immigration Council Special Report, July.

Facio, Elisa and Irene Lara. 2014. *Fleshing the Spirit: Spirituality and Activism in Chicana, Latina, and Indigenous Women's Lives*. Tucson, AZ: University of Arizona Press.

Farley, Reynolds. 2022. "Chocolate City, Vanilla Suburbs Revisited: The Racial Integration of Detroit's Suburbs." *Du Bois Review* 19 (1): 1–29.

Farmer, Paul. 2004. "An Anthropology of Structural Violence." *Current Anthropology* 45: 305–325.

Feagin, Joe R. 2006. *Systemic Racism: A Theory of Oppression*. New York Routledge.

Feagin Joe R. 2013. *The White Racial Frame: Centuries of Racial Framing and Counter-Framing*. 2nd edn. New York: Routledge.

Feagin, Joe. R. and Debra Van Ausdale, D. 2001. *The First R: How Children Learn Race and Racism*. Lanham, MD: Rowman & Littlefield Publishers.

Fernandez, Deepa. 2007. *Targeted: Homeland Security and the Business of Immigration*. New York: Seven Stories Press.

Ferrer, Ada. 1999. *Cuba: Race, Nation, and Revolution, 1868–1898*. Chapel Hill, NC: University of North Carolina Press.

Ferrer, Ada. 2021. *Cuba: An American History*. New York: Scribner.

Figueroa, Enrique. 2022. "Former Modesto Man Reflects on Racism in Uvalde, Texas." *The Modesto Bee: Issues and Ideas*, June 26.

Finke, Roger and Rodney Stark. 1992. *The Churching of America: Winners and Losers in Our Religious Economy*. New Brunswick, NJ: Rutgers University Press.

Fleuriet, K. Jill. 2021. *Rhetoric and Reality on the U.S.–Mexico Border: Place, Politics, Home*. Cham Switzerland: Springer Nature.

Flippen, Chenoa A. and Dylan Farrell-Bryan. 2021. "New Destinations and the Changing Geography of Immigrant Incorporation." *Annual Review of Sociology* 47: 479–500.

Flores, Barbara. 2005. "The Intellectual Presence of the Deficit View of Spanish-Speaking Children in the Educational Literature During the 20th Century," pp. 75–98 in P. Pedraza and M. Rivera (eds.), *Latino Education: An Agenda for Community Action Research*. New York: Routledge.

Flores, Erika Beckles. 2011. *Waiting for Your Return: A Phenomenological Study on Parental Deportation and the Impact of the Family and the Parent–Child Attachment Bond*. Ph.D. dissertation, Syracuse University.

Flores-Yeffal, Nadia Y. 2012. *Migration-Trust Networks: Social Cohesion in Mexican US-Bound Emigration*. College Station, TX: Texas A&M University Press.

Flores-Yeffal, Nadia Yamel, Guadalupe Vidales, and April Plemons. 2011. "The Latino Cyber-Moral Panic Process in the United States." *Information, Communication & Society* 14 (4): 568–589.

Foner, Nancy. 1997. "The Immigrant Family: Cultural Legacies and Cultural Changes." *International Migration Review* (31): 961–974.

Foster-Frau, Silvia. 2021. "Latinos, Disproportionately Killed by Police, are Often Left Out of Debate about Brutality, Advocates Say." *The Seattle Times*, June 2. https://www.seattletimes.com/nation-world/nation/latinos-disproportionately-killed-by-police-are-often-left-out-of-debate-about-brutality-advocates-say/

Franco, Jamie L., Laura Sabattini, and Faye J. Crosby. 2004. "Anticipating Work and Family: Exploring the Associations Among Gender-Related Ideologies, Values, and Behaviors in Latino and White Families in the United States." *Journal of Social Issues* 60 (4): 755–766.

Frank, Reanne, Ilana Redstone, and Bo Lu. 2010. "Latino Immigrants and the U.S. Racial Order." *American Sociological Review* 75 (3): 378–401.

Franklin, Jonathan. 2022. "'Selena' Movie Returns to Theaters." NPR, March 22. https://www.npr.org/2022/03/22/1088082740/selena-movie-returns-to-theaters

Fragomen, Austin T., Jr. 1997. "The Illegal Immigration Reform and Immigrant Responsibility Act of 1996: An Overview." International Migration Review 31 (2): 438–460.

Fregoso, Rosa Linda. 2003. *MeXicana Encounters: The Making of Social Identities on the Borderlands*. Berkeley, CA: University of California Press.

Fuller, Bruce, Yoonjeon Kim, Claudia Galindo, Shruti Bathia, Margaret Bridges, Greg J Duncan, and Isabel García Valdivia. 2019. "Worsening School Segregation for Latino Children?" *Educational Researcher* 48 (7): 407–420.

Furman, Nelly, David Goldberg, and Natalia Lusin. 2010. *Enrollments in Languages Other Than English in United States Institutions of Higher Education, Fall 2009*. New York: Modern Language Association.

Fussell Elizabeth and Palloni Alberto. 2004. "Persistent Marriage Regimes in Changing Times." *Journal of Marriage and Family* 66 (5): 1201–1213.

Galarza, Ernesto. 2011. *Barrio Boy*. 40th anniversary edn. Notre Dame, IN: University of Notre Dame Press.

Gallegos, Monica L. and Chris Segrin. 2022. "Family Connections and the Latino Health Paradox: Exploring the Mediating Role of Loneliness in the Relationships between the Latina/o Cultural Value of Familism and Health." *Health Communication* 37 (9): 1204–1214.

Galtung, Johan. 1969. "Violence, Peace, and Peace Research." *Journal of Peace Research* 6 (3): 167–191.

Gamboa, Erasmo. 2000. *Mexican Labor and World War II.* Seattle: University of Washington Press.

Gándara, Patricia and Frances Contreras. 2020. *The Latino Education Crisis: The Consequences of Failed Social Policies.* Cambridge, MA: Harvard University Press.

Gándara, Patricia and Kfir Mordechay. 2017. "Demographic Change and the New (and Not So New) Challenges for Latino Education." *The Educational Forum* 81 (2): 148–159.

Gandara, Patricia and Gary Orfield. 2011. "Squeezed from All Sides: The CSU Crisis and California's Future." Escholarship.org. https://escholarship.org/content/qt4cv8b8dx/qt4cv8b8dx.pdf

García, Cristina. 1993. *Dreaming in Cuban.* New York: Ballantine Books.

García, Cristina. 2023. *Vanishing Maps.* New York: Alfred A. Knopf.

Garcia, Eugene. 2001. *Hispanic Education in the United States.* Lanham, MD: Rowman and Littlefield.

Garcia, Jesse. 2020. "Episode 75: Dr. Sonya M. Aleman Brings Selena to Classroom." *The Jesse Garcia Show.* https://soundcloud.com/jessegarciashow/episode-75-dr-sonya-m-aleman-brings-selena -to-academia

Garcia, Marc A. and Rogelio Sáenz. 2023. "Latino Mortality Paradox Found (Again): COVID-19 Mortality A Tale of Two Years." *Journal of Aging and Health* 35 (10): 808–818.

García, Mario T. 2000. *Luis Leal: An Auto/Biography.* Austin: University of Texas Press.

Garcia, Moctezuma. 2022. "'You Are Not Alone': Family-Based HIV Risk and Protective Factors for Hispanic/Latino Men Who Have Sex with Men in San Juan, PR." *Plos one* 17 (6): e0268742.

García, Moctezuma, S. Raquel Ramos, Lisa Aponte-Soto, Tiarney D. Ritchwood, and Laurie A. Drabble. 2022. "'Family before Anyone Else': A Qualitative Study on Family, Marginalization, and HIV among Hispanic or Latina/o/a/x Mexican Sexual Minority Males." *International Journal of Environmental Research and Public Health* 19,8899.

García, Ofelia. 2009. "Racializing the Language Practices of U.S. Latinos: Impact in Their Education," pp. 101–115 in J.A. Cobas, J. Duany, and J.R. Feagin (eds.), *How the United States Racializes Latinos: White Hegemony and Its Consequences.* Boulder, CO: Paradigm Publishers.

Garibay, Angel. 1967. "Our Lady of Guadalupe," pp. 821–822 in Catholic University of America, *New Catholic Encyclopedia.* Vol. 8. New York: McGraw-Hill.

Garsd, Jasmine. 2023. "Federal Judge Prohibits Separating Migrant Families at the Border." NPR, December 8.

Gaspar de Alba, Alicia. 1993. "'*Tortillerismo*': Work by Chicana Lesbians. *Signs* 18 (4): 956–963.

Gaspar de Alba, Alicia. 2013. "Thirty Years of Chicana/Latina Lesbian Literary Production," pp. 462–475 in S. Bost and F. Aparicio (eds.), *The Routledge Companion to Latino/a Literature.* New York: Routledge.

Garza, Melita Marie. 1997. "Hola America! Newsstand 2000," pp. 129–136 in E.E. Dennis and E.C. Pease (eds.), *The Media in Black and White.* New Brunswick, NJ: Transaction Press.

Gearing, Jes. 2010. "The Most Popular Foreign Languages: Foreign Language Enrollment in U.S. Schools." *Beyond Words Language Blog,* April 5. http://www.altalang.com/beyond-words /2010/04/05/the-most-popular-foreign-languages-foreign-language-enrollment-in-u-s-schools/.

Geronimus, Arline, John Bound, Danya Keene, and Margaret Hicken. 2007. "Black–White Differences in Age Trajectories of Hypertension Prevalence among Adult Women and Men, 1999–2002." *Ethnicity and Disease* 17 (1): 40–48.

Ghilarducci, Teresa and Siavash Radpour. 2019. "Older Worker Exploitation: Magnitude, Causes, and Solutions." *Generations* 43 (3): 6–10.

Gibson, Ginger. 2023. "Trump Says Immigrants are 'Poisoning the Blood of Our Country.' Biden Campaign Likens Comments to Hitler." *NBC News,* December 17. https://www.nbcnews.com/poli tics/2024-election/trump-says-immigrants-are-poisoning-blood-country-biden-campaign-liken -rcna130141

Glazer, Nathan. 1987. "The Emergence of an American Pattern," pp. 11–23 in R. Takaki (ed.), *From Different Shores: Perspectives on Race and Ethnicity in America.* 2nd edn. New York: Oxford University Press.

Golash-Boza, Tanya. 2009. "A Confluence of Interests in Immigration Enforcement: How Politicians, the Media, and Corporations Profit from Immigration Policies Destined to Fail." *Sociology Compass* 3 (2): 283–294.

Golash-Boza, Tanya. 2012. *Immigration Nation: Raids, Detentions, and Deportations in Post-9/11 America.* Boulder, CO: Paradigm Publishers.

Goldsmith, Pat Antonio. 2004. "Schools' Racial Mix, Students' Optimism, and the Black–White and Latino–White Achievement Gaps." *Sociology of Education* 77: 121–147.

Goldson, E. 1999. *Americanos: Latino Life in the United States/La Vida de los Latinos en los Estados Unidos.* [Brochure.] Washington, DC: Smithsonian Institution.

Gomes, Maria and Fariyal Ross-Sheriff. 2011."The Impact of Unintended Consequences of the 1996 US Immigration Reform Act on Women." *Affilia: Journal of Women and Social Work* 26 (2): 117–124.

Gómez, Christina. 2000. "The Continual Significance of Skin Color: An Exploratory Study of Latinos in the Northeast." *Hispanic Journal of Behavioral Sciences* 22: 94–103.

Gómez, Laura. E. 2018. *Manifest Destinies: The Making of the Mexican American Race.* 2nd edn. New York: New York University Press.

Gómez, Laura E. 2020. *Inventing Latinos: A New Story of American Racism.* New York: The New Press.

Gonzales, Leslie D. 2012. "Stories of Success: Latinas Redefining Cultural Capital." *Journal of Latinos and Education* 11 (2): 124–138.

Gonzales, Roberto G. 2016. *Lives in Limbo: Undocumented and Coming of Age in America.* Berkeley, CA: University of California Press.

Gonzales, Roberto G. and Leo R. Chavez. 2012. "'Awakening to a Nightmare': Abjectivity and Illegality in the Lives of Undocumented 1.5-Generation Latino Immigrants in the United States." *Current Anthropology* 53 (3): 255–281.

Gonzales, Rodolfo. 1967. *I Am Joaquín/Yo Soy Joaquín: An Epic Poem.* New York: Bantam Books.

González, David. 2013. "Tato Laviera, 63, Poet of Nuyorican School." *New York Times,* November 5. https://www.nytimes.com/2013/11/06/arts/tato-laviera-nuyorican-poet-dies-at-63.html

González, Eduardo.2019."Stereotypical Depictions of Latino Criminality: U.S. Latinos in the Media During the MAGA Campaign." *Democratic Communiqué* 28 (1): 46–62.

González, Juan. 2000. *Harvest of Empire: The History of Latinos in America.* New York: Penguin Books.

González, Rigoberto. 2017. *Pivotal Voices, Era of Transition: Toward a 21st Century Poetics.* Ann Arbor, MI: University of Michigan Press.

González, Xochitl. 2021. *Olga Dies Dreaming.* New York: Flatiron Books.

González López, Gloria. 2005. *Erotic Journeys: Mexican Immigrants and Their Sex Lives.* Berkeley, CA: University of California Press.

Goodman, Adam. 2020. *The Deportation Machine: America's Long History of Expelling Immigrants.* Princeton, NJ: Princeton University Press.

Goodstein, Laurie. 2007. "For Some Hispanics, Coming to America Also Means Abandoning Religion." *New York Times,* April 15. http://www.nytimes.com/2007/04/15/us/15hispanic.html ?pagewanted=all

Goodstein, Laurie. 2008a. "In America for Job, a Kenyan Priest Finds a Home." *New York Times,* December 28.

Goodstein, Laurie. 2008b. "Serving U.S. Parishes, Fathers Without Borders." *New York Times,* December 28. http://www.nytimes.com/2008/12/28/us/28priest.html?pagewanted=all

Gordon, Milton M. 1964. *Assimilation in American Life: The Role of Race, Religion, and National Origins.* New York: Oxford University Press.

Gorman, Bridget K., Elaine Howard Ecklund, and Holly E. Heard. 2010. "Nativity Differences in Physical Health: The Roles of Emotional Support, Family, and Social Integration." *Sociological Spectrum* 30: 671–694.

Gorostiaga, Xabier and Peter Marchetti. 1988. "The Central American Economy: Conflict and Crisis," pp. 119–136 in N. Hamilton, J.A. Frieden, L. Fuller, and M. Pastor, Jr. (eds.), *Crisis in Central America: Regional Dynamics and US Policy in the 1980s.* Boulder, CO: Westview Press.

Gosin, Monika. 2017. "'A Bitter Diversion: Afro-Cuban Immigrants, Race, and Everyday-Life Resistance." *Latino Studies* 15 (1): 4–28.

Gouveia, Lourdes and Rogelio Sáenz. 2000. "Global Forces and Latino Population Growth in the Midwest: A Regional and Subregional Analysis." *Great Plains Research* 10: 305–328.

Gowan, Mary and Melanie Treviño. 1998. "An Examination of Gender Differences in Mexican-American Attitudes toward Family and Career Roles." *Sex Roles* 38 (11–12): 1079–1093.

Grasmuck, Sherri and Patricia R. Pessar. 1991. *Between Two Islands: Dominican International Migration*. Berkeley, CA: University of California Press.

Gramlich, John. 2020. "How Border Apprehensions, ICE Arrest and Deportations Have Changed Under Trump." Pew Hispanic Center. https://pewrsr.ch/3ap3x3l

Granovetter, Mark S. 1973. "The Strength of Weak Ties." *American Journal of Sociology* 78 (6): 1360–1380.

Grasmuck, Sherri and Ramón Grosfoguel. 1997. "Geopolitics, Economic Niches, and Gendered Social Capital among Recent Caribbean Immigrants in New York City." *Sociological Perspectives* 40 (3): 339–363.

Greeley, Andrew M. 1994. *The Sociology of Andrew M. Greeley*. Atlanta: Scholars Press.

Greenwood, Michael J. 1985. "Human Migration: Theory, Models, Empirical Studies." *Journal of Regional Science* 25 (4): 521–544.

Grineski, Sara, Heather Daniels, Timothy Collins, Danielle X Morales, Angela Frederick, and Marilyn Garcia. 2018. "The Conundrum of Social Class: Disparities in Publishing among STEM Students in Undergraduate Research Programs at a Hispanic Majority Institution." *Science Education* 102 (2): 283–303.

Grosfoguel, Ramon. 2016. "What is Racism?" *Journal of World-Systems Research* 22 (1): 9–15.

Guillem, Susana Martínez and Marco Briziarelli. 2012. "We Want Your Success! Hegemony, Materiality, and *Latino in America*." *Critical Studies in Media Communication* 29 (4): 292–312.

Gunadi, Christian. 2021. "On the Association between Undocumented Immigration and Crime in the United States." *Oxford Economic Papers* 73 (1): 200–224.

Gurba, Myriam. 2012. *Mean*. Minneapolis, MN: Coffee House Press.

Gurza, Agustin. 2015. "Artist Biography: Los Tigres del Norte. The Strachwitz Frontera Collection of Mexican and Mexican American Recordings.

Gurza, Agustin 2017. "Juan Gabriel: Una Apreciación. La Colección de Strachwitz Frontera de grabaciones mexicanas y méxico-americanas.

Gutiérrez, Félix F. 1977. "Chicanos and the Media," in M.C. Emery and T.C. Smythe (eds.), *Readings in Mass Communication: Concepts and Issues in the Mass Media*. 3rd edn. Dubuque, IA: Wm. C. Brown Co. Publishers.

Gutiérrez, Félix F. 2013. "More Than 200 Years of Latino Media in the United States." National Park System Advisory Board (ed.), *American Latinos and the Making of the United States: A Theme Study*. Washington, DC: National Park System.

Gutiérrez, José Angel. 1998. *The Making of a Chicano Militant: Lessons from Cristal*. Madison, WI: University of Wisconsin Press.

Gutiérrez, José Angel. 2019a. *The Eagle Has Eyes: The FBI Surveillance of César Estrada Chávez of the United Farm Workers Union of America, 1965–1975*. East Lansing, MI: Michigan State University Press.

Gutiérrez, José Angel. 2019b. *Tracking King Tiger: Reies López Tijerina and the FBI*. East Lansing, MI: Michigan University Press.

Gutiérrez, José Angel. 2021a. *Bashing Boricuas: The FBI's War*. Dallas: The Legal Center of José Angel Gutiérrez.

Gutiérrez, José Angel. 2021b. *Lucille Ball and Desi Arnaz: The FBI and HUAC Files*. Dallas: The Legal Center of José Angel Gutiérrez.

Gutiérrez, José Angel. 2022. *The American Eagle: Spying on Mexicans and Chicanos*. Dallas: The Legal Center of José Angel Gutiérrez.

Hacker, Karen, John Auerbach, Robin Ikeda, Celeste Philip, and Debra Houry. 2022. "Social Determinants of Health – An Approach Taken at CDC." *Journal of Public Health Management and Practice* 28 (6): 589–594.

Hajnal, Zoltan and Taeku Lee. 2011. *Race, Immigration and (Non) Partisanship in America*. Princeton, NJ: Princeton University Press.

Hall, Matthew and George Farkas. 2011. "Adolescent Cognitive Skills, Attitudinal/Behavioral Traits and Career Wages." *Social Forces* 89 (4): 1261–1285.

Hall, Stuart. 1997. "The Work of Representation," pp. 13–74 in S. Hall (ed.), *Representation: Cultural Representations and Signifying Practices*. London: Sage.

Hallinan, Joseph T. 2001. *Going Up the River: Travels in a Prison Nation*. New York: Random House.

Hames-García, Michael and Ernesto Javier Martínez. 2011. *Gay Latino Studies: A Critical Reader*. 1st edn. Durham: Duke University Press.

Hamilton, Dan, Matthew Fienup, David Hayes-Bautista, and Paul Hsu. 2023. *2023 U.S. Latino GDP Report*. https://blogs.callutheran.edu/cerf/files/2023/09/2023_USLatinoGDP_report.pdf

Hamilton, Darrick, Arthur H. Goldsmith, and William Darity. 2008. "Measuring the Wage Costs of Limited English: Issues with Using Interviewer Versus Self-Reports in Determining Latino Wages." *Hispanic Journal of Behavioral Sciences* 30 (3): 257–279.

Hampton, Kathryn, Elsa Raker, Hajar Habbach, Linda Camaj Deda, Michele Heisler, and Ranit Mishori. 2021."The Psychological Effects of Forced Family Separation on Asylum-Seeking Children and Parents at the US–Mexico Border: A Qualitative Analysis of Medico-Legal Documents." *Plos one* 16 (11): e0259576.

Handelman, Jonathan. 2002. "With His Pistol in His Hand: Touchstone for Border Study." *Interdisciplinary Literary Studies* 3 (2): 23–38.

Harris, Angelique, Juan Battle, Antonio (Jay) Pastrana, and Jessie Daniels. 2013. "The Sociopolitical Involvement of Black, Latino, and Asian/Pacific Islander Gay and Bisexual Men." *Journal of Men's Studies* 21 (3): 236–254.

Harris, Richard J. 1980. "An Examination of the Effects of Ethnicity, Socioeconomic Status and Generation on Familism and Sex Role Orientations." *Journal of Comparative Family Studies* 11: 173–193.

Hatzipanagos, Rachel. 2020. "Some Afro-Latinos Say the Phase 'Latinos for Black Lives Matter' Makes No Sense." *Washington Post*, August 28.

Haub, Carl. 2012. "Changing the Way U.S. Hispanics are Counted." Washington, DC: Population Reference Bureau. https://www.prb.org/resources/changing-the-way-u-s-hispanics-are-counted/

Haywood, Jasmine M. 2017. "Anti-Black Latino Racism in an Era of Trumpismo." *International Journal of Qualitative Studies in Education* 30 (10): 957–964.

Healthy People 2030. 2024. "Social Determinants of Health." U.S. Department of Health and Human Services, Office of Disease Prevention and Health Promotion. https://health.gov/healthypeople/objectives-and-data/social-determinants-health

Heatherington, Kimberley. 2023. "US Catholics' Priest Shortage Faces New 'Serious Crisis' Due to Immigration Law." *National Catholic Reporter*, December 15.

Heidenreich, Linda. 2020. *Nepantla Squared: Transgender Mestiz@ Histories in Times of Global Shift*. Lincoln, NE: University of Nebraska Press.

Helg, Aline. 1990. "Race in Argentina and Cuba, 1880–1930: Theory, Policies, and Popular Reaction," pp. 37–69 in R. Graham (ed.), *The Idea of Race in Latin America, 1870–1940*. Austin: University of Texas Press.

Hempel, Lynn M., Julie A. Dowling, Jason D. Boardman, and Christopher G. Ellison. 2013. "Racial Threat and White Opposition to Bilingual Education in Texas." *Hispanic Journal of Behavioral Sciences* 35 (1): 85–102.

Hendricks, Tyche. 2005. "Octavio I. Romano – Chicano Scholar." *SF Gate*, March 16. https://www.sfgate.com/bayarea/article/Octavio-I-Romano-Chicano-scholar-2722675.php

Hendy, Helen M., S. Hakan Can, and Hartmut Heep. 2022. "Machismo and Caballerismo Linked with Perceived Social Discrimination and Powerlessness in US Latina/o Men." *Journal of Cross-Cultural Psychology* 53 (1): 109–121.

Hernández, David, John M. Eason, Pat Rubio Goldsmith, Richard D. Abel, and Andrew McNeely. 2018. "With Mass Deportation Comes Mass Punishment: Punitive Capacity, Health, and Standards in U.S. Immigration Detention," pp. 260–269 in H.V. Miller and A. Peguero (eds.), *Routledge Handbook on Immigration and Crime*. New York: Routledge.

Hernández, Deluvina. 1970. "La Raza Satellite System." *Aztlan: A Journal of Chicano Studies* 1 (1): 13–36.

Hernández, Jeanette. 2022. "Three Takeaways from the 'I Am Vanessa Guillen' Documentary." *BELatina*, November 23. https://belatina.com/three-takeaways-i-am-vanessa-guillen-docu mentary/

Hernández, Kelly Lytle. 2006. "The Crimes and Consequences of Illegal Immigration: A Cross-Border Examination of Operation Wetback, 1943 to 1954." *Western Historical Quarterly* 37: 421–444.

Hernández, Leandra Hinojosa, and Sarah De Los Santos Upton. 2018. *Challenging Reproductive Control and Gendered Violence in the Américas: Intersectionality, Power, and Struggles for Rights.* Lanham, MD: Lexington Books.

Hernández, Ramona. 2002. *The Mobility of Workers Under Advanced á Capitalism: Dominican Migration to the United States.* New York: Columbia University Press.

Hernández, Tanya Katerí. 2022. *Racial Innocence: Unmasking Latino Anti-Black Bias and the Struggle for Equality.* New York: Beacon Press.

Hernández-León, Rubén and Víctor Zúñiga. 2000. "'Making Carpet by the Mile': The Emergence of a Mexican Immigrant Community in an Industrial Region of the U.S. Historic South." *Social Science Quarterly* 81 (1): 49–66.

Herrera-Sobek, Maria. 2006. "Gloria Anzaldúa: Place, Race, Language, and Sexuality in the Magic Valley." *PMLA* 121 (1), 266–271.

Heyman, Josiah. 2010. "Arizona's Immigration Law – S.B.1070." *News: A Publication for the Society of Applied Anthropology* 21 (3): 23–26.

Hickman, Christine B. 1997. "The Devil and the One Drop Rule: Racial Categories, African Americans, and the U.S. Census." *Michigan Law Review* 95 (5): 1161–1265.

Hines, Barbara. 2006. "An Overview of U.S. Immigration Law and Policy Since 9/11." *Texas Hispanic Journal of Law and Policy* 12 (9): 9–28.

Hinojosa, Rolando. 1973. *Estampas del Valle y Otras Obras.* Berkeley, CA: Quinto Sol.

Hinojosa, Rolando. 1985. *Partners in Crime.* Houston: Arte Público Press.

Hinojosa, Rolando. 1987. *Klail City.* Houston: Arte Público Press.

Hinojosa, Rolando. 1990. *Becky and Her Friends.* Houston: Arte Público Press.

Hinojosa, Rolando. 1998. *Ask a Policeman.* Houston: Arte Público Press.

Hinojosa, Rolando. 2005. *Dear Rafe/Mi Querido Rafa.* Houston: Arte Público Press.

Hinojosa, Rolando. 2011. *A Voice of My Own: Essays and Stories.* Houston: Arte Publico Press.

Hispanic Heritage Foundation. 2021. "Carlos Santana to Receive the 2021 Hispanic Heritage 'Legend' Award." Hispanic Heritage Foundation, June 30. https://hispanicheritage.org/carlos-santa na-to-receive-the-2021-hispanic-heritage-legend-award/

Hobbs, Frank and Nicole Stoops. 2002. *Demographic Trends in the 20th Century.* Census 2000 Special Reports, Series CENSR-4. Washington, DC: U.S. Government Printing Office. http://www.census .gov/prod/2002pubs/censr-4.pdf

Hodge, David R., Flavio F. Marsiglia, and Tanya Nieri. 2011. "Religion and Substance Use among Youths of Mexican Heritage: A Social Capital Perspective." *Social Work Research* 35 (3): 137–146.

Hoffman, Abraham. 1974. *Unwanted Mexican Americans in the Great Depression: Repatriation Pressures 1929–1939.* Tucson, AZ: University of Arizona Press.

Hondagneu-Sotelo, Pierrette. 1994. *Gendered Transitions: Mexican Experiences of Immigration.* Berkeley: University of California Press.

Hondagneu-Sotelo, Pierrette. 1997. "Working 'Without Papers' in the U.S.: Toward the Integrating of Legal Status in Frameworks of Race, Class, and Gender," pp. 101–125 in E. Higginbotham and M. Romero (eds.), *Women and Work: Race, Class, and Ethnicity.* Beverly Hills, CA: Sage Publications.

Hondagneu-Sotelo, Pierrette. 2001. *Doméstica: Immigrant Workers Cleaning and Caring in the Shadows of Affluence.* Berkeley: University of California Press.

Hondagneu-Sotelo, Pierrette (ed.). 2007. *Religion and Social Justice for Immigrants.* New Brunswick, NJ: Rutgers University Press.

Hondagneu-Sotelo, Pierrette. 2017. "Place, Nature and Masculinity in Immigrant Integration: Latino Immigrant Men in Inner-City Parks and Community Gardens." *International Journal for Masculinity Studies* 12 (2): 112–126.

Hondagneu-Sotelo, Pierrette. 2022. "Research." http://www.hondagneu-sotelo.org/

Hondagneu-Sotelo, Pierrette and Ernestine Avila. 1997. "'I'm Here, but I'm There': The Meanings of Latina Transnational Motherhood." *Gender and Society* 11 (5): 548–571.

Hondagneu-Sotelo, Pierrette, Genelle Gaudinez, Hector Lara, and Billie C. Ortiz. 2004. "There's a Spirit That Transcends the Border: Faith, Ritual, and Postnational Protest in the U.S.-Mexico Border." *Sociological Perspectives* 47:133–159.

Hooker, E.D., Corona, K., Guardino, C.M., Schetter, C.D., and Campos, B. 2023. "What Predicts Interdependence With Family? The Relative Contributions of Ethnicity/Race and Social Class." *Cultural Diversity and Ethnic Minority Psychology*. Advance online publication. https://dx.doi.org/10.1037/cdp0000593

hooks, bell. 1995. *Killing Rage: Ending Racism*. New York: Henry Holt & Company.

Hope, Elan C., Micere Keels, and Myles I. Durkee. 2016. "Participation in Black Lives Matter and Deferred Action for Childhood Arrivals: Modern Activism among Black and Latino College Students." *Journal of Diversity in Higher Education* 9 (3): 203–215.

Horevitz, Elizabeth and Kurt C. Organista. 2013. "The Mexican Health Paradox: Expanding the Explanatory Power of the Acculturation Construct." *Hispanic Journal of Behavioral Sciences* 35 (1): 3–34.

Horn, Xian. 2022. "Gloria Estefan: Music's Most Down-To-Earth Diva." *Forbes*, February 7. https://www.forbes.com/sites/xianhorn/2022/02/07/gloria-estefan-musics-most-down-to-earth-diva/?sh=527f522f38b5

Horton, Sarah and Stephanie Cole. 2011. "Medical Returns: Seeking Health Care in Mexico." *Social Science & Medicine* 72: 1846–1852.

Howard, Tiffany O. 2018. "Afro-Latinos and the Black–Hispanic Identity: Evaluating the Potential for Group Conflict and Cohesion." *National Political Science Review* 19 (1): 29–50.

Huber, Lindsay Pérez, Brenda Pulido Villanueva, Nancy Guarneros, Verónica N. Vélez, and Daniel G Solórzano. 2014. "DACAmented in California: The Impact of the Deferred Action for Childhood Arrivals Program on Latina/os." CSRC Research Report. No. 18." *UCLA Chicano Studies Research Center*.

Huckle, K.E. 2020. "Latinos and American Catholicism: Examining Service Provision Amidst Demographic Change." *Journal of Race, Ethnicity, and Politics* 5: 166–195.

Huddy, Leonie and David O. Sears. 1990. "Qualified Public Support for Bilingual Education: Some Policy Implications." *Annals of the American Academy of Political and Social Science* 508 (1): 119–125.

Humanities Texas. 2022. "Américo Paredes." https://www.humanitiestexas.org/programs/tx-originals/list/americo-paredes

Hummer, Robert A. 1996. "Black–White Differences in Health and Mortality: A Review and Conceptual Model." *Sociological Quarterly* 37 (1): 105–125.

Hummer, Robert A. and Juanita J. Chinn. 2011. "Race/Ethnicity and U.S. Adult Mortality: Progress, Prospects, and New Analyses." *Du Bois Review* 8 (1): 5–24.

Hummer, Robert A., Daniel A. Powers, Starling G. Pullum, Ginger L. Gossman, and W. Parker Frisbie. 2007. "Paradox Found (Again): Infant Mortality among the Mexican-Origin Population in the United States." *Demography* 44 (3): 441–457.

Hunt, John. 1964. "The Psychological Basis for Using Pre-School Environment as an Antidote for Cultural Deprivation." *Merrill-Palmer Quarterly* 10 (3): 209–248.

Hunt, Larry L. 1999. "Hispanic Protestantism in the United States: Trends by Decade and Generation." *Social Forces* 77: 1601–1623.

Huntington, Samuel P. 2004. *Who Are We? The Challenges to America's National Identity*. New York: Simon & Schuster.

Hurtado, Aida. 1995. "Creations, Combinations, and Evolutions: Latino Families in the United States," pp. 18–38 in R.E. Zambrana (ed.), *Understanding Latino Families, Scholarship, Policy, and Practice*. Thousand Oaks, CA: Sage.

Hurtado, Aida, David E. Hayes-Bautista, R. Burciaga Valdez, and Anthony C.R. Hernandez. 1992. *Redefining California: Latino Social Engagement in a Multicultural Society*. Los Angeles: UCLA Chicano Studies Research Center.

Hwang, Sean-Shong and Juan Xi. 2008. "Structural and Individual Covariates of English Language Proficiency." *Social Forces* 86: 1079–1104.

Hwang, Sean-Shong, Juan Xi, and Yue Cao. 2010. "The Conditional Relationship between English Language Proficiency and Earnings among U.S. Immigrants." *Social Forces* 33 (9): 1620–1647.

Hye-cheon, Karen, Kim Yeary, Songthip Ounpraseuth, Page Moore, Zoran Bursac, and Paul Greene. 2012. "Religion, Social Capital, and Health." *Review of Religious Research* 54: 331–347.

Ihaza, Itohen. 2020. "Police Brutality and State-Sanctioned Violence in 21st Century America." *Journal of Race, Gender, and Ethnicity* 9 (1): Article 10.

Ikas, Karin. 2012. "Interview with Gloria Anzaldúa," pp. 267–284 in G. Anzaldúa, *Borderlands: La Frontera: The New Mestiza*. 4th edn. San Francisco: Aunt Lute Books, San Francisco.

IMDb. 1982. "The Ballad of Gregorio Cortez." https://www.imdb.com/title/tt3551840/

Jabbar, Huriya, Carmen Serrata, Eliza Epstein, and Joanna Sánchez. 2019. "'Échale Ganas': Family Support of Latino/a Community College Students' Transfer to Four-Year Universities." *Journal of Latinos and Education* 18 (3): 258–276.

Jasso, Guillermina, Douglas S. Massey, Mark R. Rosenzweig, and James P. Smith. 2004. "Immigrant Health: Selectivity and Acculturation," pp. 227–266 in N.B. Anderson, R.A. Bulatao, and B. Cohen (eds.), *Critical Perspectives on Racial and Ethnic Differences in Health in Later Life*. Washington, DC: National Academies Press.

Jensen, Robert. 1998. "White Privilege Shapes the U.S." *Baltimore Sun*, July 19: 1C, 4C.

Jin, D. 2019. "Puerto Rican Journalism's 'New Awareness'." *Columbia Journalism Review*, December 19 https://www.cjr.org/analysis/puerto-rico-rickyleaks-media.php

Joassart-Marcelli, Pascale. 2009. "The Spatial Determinants of Wage Inequality: Evidence from Recent Latina Immigrants in Southern California." *Feminist Economics* 15 (April): 33–72.

Johnson, Lyndon B. 1965. "Remarks at the Signing of the Immigration Bill, Liberty Island, New York, October 3, 1965." Selected Speeches and Messages of LBJ. Austin, TX: LBJ Presidential Library. http://www.lbjlib.utexas.edu/johnson/archives.hom/speeches.hom/651003.asp

Jones, Nicholas, Rachel Marks, Roberto Ramirez, and Merarys Rios-Vargas. 2021. "2020 Census Illuminates Racial and Ethnic Composition of the Country."

Jones-Correa, Michael, Hajer Al-Faham, and David Cortez. 2018. "Political (Mis) behavior: Attention and Lacunae in the Study of Latino Politics." *Annual Review of Sociology* 44: 213–235.

Jones-Correa, Michael A. and David L. Leal. 2001. "Political Participation: Does Religion Matter?" *Political Research Quarterly* 54:751–770.

Julian Samora Research Institute. 2024. "Overview." https://jsri.msu.edu/about/overview

June, Sophia. 2022. "Inside Edgar Gomez's Buoyant, Queer Coming of Age Debut Memoir High Risk Homosexual." Nylon, January 12. https://www.nylon.com/life/edgar-gomez-high-risk-homosexual-interview

Kaba, Amadu Jacky. 2008. "Culture, Economic Progress and Immigration: The Hispanic/Latino Population in the U.S. and the North African/Muslim Population in European Countries." *Delaware Review of Latin American Studies* 9 (1): 1–11.

Kaestner, Robert, Jay A. Peterson, Danya Keene, and Arline T. Geronimus. 2009. "Stress, Allostatic Load, and Health of Mexican Immigrants." *Social Science Quarterly* 90 (5): 1089–1111.

Kandel, William and Emilio Parrado. 2005. "Restructuring of the U.S. Meat Processing Industry and New Hispanic Destinations." *Population and Development Review* 31 (3): 447–471.

Kang, Nancy and Silvio Torres-Saillant. 2010. "'Americaniards as Latinos: Spain in the United States Today." *Latino Studies* 8 (4): 556–568.

Katznelson, Ira. 2005. *When Affirmative Action Was White: An Untold History of Racial Inequality in Twentieth-Century America*. New York: W.W. Norton & Company.

Keating, AnaLouise. 2009. *The Gloria Anzaldúa Reader*. Durham, NC: Duke University Press.

Keefe, Susan E. 1984. "Real and Ideal Familism Among Mexican Americans and Anglo Americans: On the Meaning of 'Close' Family Ties." *Human Organization* 43 (1): 65–70.

Keegan, Rebecca. 2013. "USC Study: Minorities Still Under-Represented in Popular Films." *Los Angeles Times*, October 30. http://www.latimes.com/entertainment/movies/moviesnow/la-et-mn-race-and-movies-20131030,0,558698.story#axzz2jDAAhn4k

Ken, Ivy and Kenneth Sebastian León. 2022. "Regulatory Theater in the Pork Industry: How the Capitalist State Harms Workers, Farmers, and Unions." *Crime, Law and Social Change* 78: 599–619.

Khan, Sabith and Daisha M. Merritt. 2023. *Remittances and International Development: The Invisible Forces Shaping Community.* New York: Routledge.

Kim, Claire Ji Hee and Amado M. Padilla. 2020. "Technology for Educational Purposes among Low-Income Latino Children Living in a Mobile Park in Silicon Valley: A Case Study Before and During COVID-19." *Hispanic Journal of Behavioral Sciences* 42 (4): 497–514.

Kimbro, Rachel Tolbert, Bridget K. Gorman, and Ariela Schachter. 2012. "Acculturation and Self-Rated Health among Latino and Asian Immigrants to the United States." *Social Problems* 59 (3): 341–363.

Kitagawa Evelyn M. and Philip M. Hauser. 1973. *Differential Mortality in the United States: A Study in Socioeconomic Epidemiology.* Cambridge, MA: Harvard University Press.

Knop, Brian and Julie Siebens. 2018. "A Child's Day: Parental Interaction, School Engagement, and Extracurricular Activities: 2014, " United States Census Bureau (November 2018).

Koestler, Fred L. 2013. "Operation Wetback." *Handbook of Texas Online.* Denton, TX: Texas State Historical Association. http://www.tshaonline.org/handbook/online/articles/pqo01

Kolmar, Chris. 2023. "The 10 Largest Movie Theater Chains in the World." *Zippia.com,* April 24. https://www.zippia.com/advice/largest-movie-theater-chains/

Koons, Judith E. 2017. "Pulse: Finding Meaning in a Massacre through Gay Latinx Intersectional Justice." *19 Scholar* 19 (1): 1–55.

Kozol, Jonathan. 1991. *Savage Inequalities.* New York: Crown.

Krause, Neal and Elena Bastida. 2011. "Prayer to the Saints or the Virgin and Health Among Older Mexican Americans." *Hispanic Journal of Behavioral Sciences* 33: 71–87.

Krogstad, Jens Manuel, Joshua Alvarado, and Besheer Mohamed. 2023. *Among U.S. Latinos, Catholicism Continues to Decline but is Still the Largest Faith.* Washington, DC: Pew Research Center.

Kubrin, Charis and Hiromi Ishizawa. 2012. "Why Some Immigrant Neighborhoods Are Safer than Others: Divergent Findings from Los Angeles and Chicago." *Annals of the American Academy of Political and Social Science* 641 (1): 148–173.

La Cucaracha. 1977. "Interview with 'Corky' Gonzales." *La Cucaracha* 2 (No. 8, September 5). https://www.coloradohistoricnewspapers.org/

Lacey, Marc. 2011. "Rift in Arizona as Latino Class is Found Illegal." *New York Times,* January 7. http://www.nytimes.com/2011/01/08/us/08ethnic.html?pagewanted=all&_r=0

LaFeber, Walter. 1984. *Inevitable Revolutions: The United States in Central America.* New York: Norton.

Lakshmanan, Indira A.R. 2008. "U.S. Election Highlights Puerto Rico's 'Unequal' Status." *New York Times,* May 20. http://www.nytimes.com/2008/05/20/world/americas/20iht-letter.1.13044789.html

Landale, Nancy S. and R.S. Oropesa. 2007. "Hispanic Families: Stability and Change." *Annual Review of Sociology* 33: 381–405.

Landale, Nancy, R.S. Oropesa, and Bridget K. Gorman. 1999. "Immigration and Infant Health: Birth Outcomes of Immigrant and Native Women," pp. 244–286 in D.J. Hernandez (ed.), *Children of Immigrants: Health, Adjustment, and Public Assistance.* Washington, DC: National Academy Press.

Lara, Guadalupe Díaz, Lisa M. López, R. Gabriela Barajas-González, and Cynthia Garcia Coll. 2021. "COVID-19's Impact on Latinx Students." *The Learning Professional* 42 (6): 60–64.

Lariscy, Joseph T. 2011. "Differential Record Linkage by Hispanic Ethnicity and Age in Linked Mortality Studies: Implications for the Epidemiological Paradox." *Journal of Aging and Health* 23 (8): 1263–1284.

Latino Donors Collaborative. 2023. *2023 Official LDC U.S. Latino GDP Report.* https://www.latinodonorcollaborative.org/original-research/2023-ldc-u-s-latino-gdp-report

The Leadership Conference. 2014. "Voting Rights Act." http://www.civilrights.org/voting-rights/vra/

Leal, Luis. 1980. "Cuatro Siglos de Prosa Aztlanense." *La Palabra* 1: 2–12.

Leal, Luis. 1981. "In Search of Aztlán." *Denver Quarterly* 16 (3): 16–22.

Leal, Luis. 1984a. "El Concepto de Aztlán en la Poesía Chicana." *Imagine* 1 (1): 118–131.

Leal, Luis. 1984b. "History and Memory in *Estampas del Valle*." *Revista Chicano-Riqueña* 12 (3–4): 101–108.

Leal, Luis. 1985a. "Hispanic-Mexican Literature in the Southwest, 1521-1848," pp. 244–260 in J. A. Martínez and F. Lomelí (eds.), *Chicano Literature: A Reference Guide*. Westpoint, CT: Greenwood Press.

Leal, Luis. 1985b. "Mexican-American Literature, 1848–1942," pp. 280–299 in J. A. Martínez and F. Lomelí (eds.), *Chicano Literature: A Reference Guide*. Westpoint, CT: Greenwood Press.

Leal, Luis. 1985c. "Tomás Rivera: The Ritual of Remembering." *Revista Chicano-Riqueña* 13 (3–4): 30–38.

Leal, Luis. 1987. "Américo Paredes and Modern Mexican American Scholarship." *Ethnic Affairs* 1 (1): 1–11.

Leal, Luis. 1989. "The Spanish-Language Press Function and Use." *The Americas Review* 17 (3–4): 157–162.

Leal, Luis. 1993. "Truth Telling Tongues: Early Chicano Poetry," pp. 91–105 in R. Gutiérrez and G. Padilla (eds.), *Recovering the U.S. Hispanic Literary Heritage*. Houston: Arte Público Press.

Leal, Luis. 1995. "Mito y Realidad Social en *Peregrinos de Aztlán*," pp. 38–45 in G.D. Keller (ed.), *Miguel Méndez in Aztlán: Two Decades of Literary Production*." Tempe, AZ: Bilingual Review/Press.

Leal, Luis. 1996. "Historia y Ficción en la Narrativa de Alejandro Morales," pp. 31–42 in J.A. Gurpegui (ed.), *Alejandro Morales: Fiction Past, Present, Future Perfect*. Tempe, AZ: Bilingual Review Press.

Leal, Luis and Pepe Barrón. 1982. "Chicano Literature: An Overview," pp. 9–12 in H. Baker, Jr. (ed.), *Three American Literatures*. New York: The Modern Language Association of America.

Leal, Luis, Fernando de Necochea, Francisco, Lomeli, and Roberto G. Trujillo. 1982. *A Decade of Chicano Literature (1970-1979): Critical Essays and Bibliography*. Santa Barbara, CA: Editorial de la Causa.

Leavell, Ashley Smith, Catherine S. Tamis-LeMonda, Diane N. Ruble, Kristina M. Zosuls, and Natasha J. Cabrera. 2012. "African American, White and Latino Fathers' Activities with Their Sons and Daughters in Early Childhood." *Sex Roles* 66 (1–2): 53–65.

Lee, Everett S. 1966. "A Theory of Migration." *Demography* 3 (1): 47–57.

Lee, Kenneth K. 1998. *Huddled Masses, Muddled Laws*. Westport, CT: Praeger Publishers.

Lee, Matthew T. and Ramiro Martinez. 2009. "Immigration Reduces Crime: An Emerging Scholarly Consensus." *Immigration, Crime and Justice* 13: 3–16.

Lehmann, Peter S. 2018. "Sentencing Other People's Children: The Intersection of Race, Gender, and Juvenility in the Adult Criminal Court." *Journal of Crime and Justice* 41 (5): 553–572.

Leigh, J. Paul and James F. Fries. 1992. "Disability in Occupations in a National Sample." *American Journal of Public Health* 82 (11): 1517–1524.

León-Portilla, Miguel. 1962. *The Broken Spears: The Aztec Account of the Conquest of Mexico*. Boston: Beacon Press.

Leonard, Lubwa. 2023. "Top 10 Cement Producers in the US." *Constructionreview*, January 23. https://constructionreviewonline.com/top-companies/top-10-cement-producers-in-the-us/#google_vignette

Leonard, Tammy, Rachel T.A. Croson, and Angela C.M. de Oliveira. 2010. "Social Capital and Public Goods." *Journal of Socioeconomics* 39: 474–481.

Lerman, Shir, Molly Jung, Elva M. Arredondo, Janice M. Barnhart, Jianwen Cai, et al. 2018. "Religiosity Prevalence and its Association with Depression and Anxiety Symptoms among Hispanic/Latino Adults." *PLoS ONE* 13 (2): e0185661. https://doi.org/10.1371/journal. pone.0185661.

Leslie, Emily and Nolan G. Pope. 2017. "The Unintended Impact of Pretrial Detention on Case Outcomes: Evidence from New York City Arraignments." *Journal of Law and Economics* 60 (3): 529–557.

Levchak, Philip J. 2021. "Stop-and-Frisk in New York City: Estimating Racial Disparities in Post-top Outcomes." *Journal of Criminal Justice* 73: 101784. https://doi.org/10.1016/j.jcrimjus.2021.101784

Levin, Sam. 2019. "Violent Hate Crimes in US Reach Highest Levels in 16 Years, FBI reports." *The Guardian*, November 12. https://www.theguardian.com/society/2019/nov/12/hate-crimes-2018-latinos-transgender-fbi

Lewis, Oscar. 1959. *Five Families: Mexican Case Studies in the Culture of Poverty*. New York: Basic Books.

Lewis, Oscar. 1965. *La Vida: A Puerto Rican Family in the Culture of Poverty – San Jose and New York*. New York: Random House.

Lewis, Oscar. 1966. "The Culture of Poverty." *Scientific American* 215: 19–25.

Leyva, Yolanda Chávez. 2002. "The Revisioning of History Es Una Gran Limpia: Teaching and Historical Trauma in Chicana/o History." *La Voz de Esperanza*, September.

Liao, Youlian, Richard S. Cooper, Guichan Cao, Ramon Durazo-Arvizu, Jay S. Kaufman, Amy Luke, and Daniel L. McGee. 1998. "Mortality Patterns among Adult Hispanics." *American Journal of Public Health* 88: 227–232.

Library of Congress. 2020. "2002: Development Relief and Education for Alein Minors (DREAM) Act & 2012: Deferred Action for Childhood Arrivals (DACA)." *A Latinx Resource Guide: Civil Rights Cases and Events in the United States*.

Library of Congress. 2022a. "Emilio and Gloria Estefan." https://www.loc.gov/item/biographies/emilio-and-gloria-estefan/

Library of Congress. 2022b. "1911: Meeting of the Mexicanist Congress." A Latinx Resource Guide: Civil Rights Cases and Events in the United States. https://guides.loc.gov/latinx-civil-rights/mexicanist-congress

Light, Michael T. and Ty Miller. 2018. "Does Undocumented Immigration Increase Violent Crime?" *Criminology* 56 (2): 370–401.

Limón, Ada. 2021. *Lucky Wreck*. Pittsburg, PA: Autumn House Press.

Limón, José E., 1973. "Stereotyping and Chicano Resistance: An Historical Dimension." *Aztlan: A Journal of Chicano Studies* 4 (2): 257–270.

Limon, José E. 2012. *Américo Paredes: Culture and Critique*. 1st edn. Austin: University of Texas Press.

Liu, John M., Paul M. Ong, and Carolyn Rosenstein. 1991. "Dual Chain Migration: Post-1965 Filipino Immigration to the United States." *International Migration Review* 25 (3): 487–513.

Liu, Kathy Yang. 2011. "Employment Concentration and Job Quality for Low-Skilled Latino Immigrants." *Journal of Urban Affairs* 33 (2): 117–142.

Liu, Kathy Yang. 2013. "Latino Immigration and the Low-Skill Urban Labor Market: The Case of Atlanta." *Social Science Quarterly* 94 (1): 131–157.

Liu, P. Priscilla, Yuying Tsong, Savannah Pham, Banan Ramadan, et al. 2021. "Explaining the Alcohol Immigrant Paradox: Perspectives from Mexican American Adults." *Journal of Latinx Psychology* 9 (2): 109–124.

LoBreglio, Kiera. 2004. "The Border Security and Immigration Improvement Act: A Modern Solution to a Historic Problem?" *St. John's Law Review* 78 (3): 933–964.

Lomelí, Francisco A. 2005. "Alurista," pp. 68–71 in S. Oboler and D. J. González (eds.), *The Oxford Encyclopedia of Latina/os and Latinas in the United States*. New York: Oxford Press.

Longazel, Jamie G. 2013. "Moral Panic as Racial Degradation Ceremony: Racial Stratification and the Local-Level Backlash Against Latino/a Immigrants." *Punishment & Society* 15 (1): 96–119.

Longoria, Jaime, Daniel Acosta, Shaydanay Urbani, and Rory Smith. 2021. "A Limiting Lens: How Vaccine Misinformation Has Influenced Hispanic Conversations Online." First Draft. https://firstdraftnews.org/long-form-article/covid19–vaccine-misinformation-hispanic-latinx-social-media/

Looney, Dennis and Natalia Lusin. 2019. *Enrollments in Languages Other Than English in the United States Institutions of Higher Education, Summer 2016 and Fall 2016: Final Report*. New York: The Modern Language Association of America.

Lopes, Lunna, Grace Sparks, Marley Presiado, Jennifer Tolbert, Robin Rudowitz, Amaya Diana, and Ashley Kirzinger. 2024. "KFF Survey of Medicaid Unwinding." Kaiser Family Foundation, April 12. https://www.kff.org/medicaid/poll-finding/kff-survey-of-medicaid-unwinding/

López, Gustavo and Jens Manuel Krogstad. 2017. "Key Facts About Unauthorized Immigrants Enrolled in DACA." Pew Research Center. https://www.pewresearch.org/short-reads/2017/09/25/key-facts-about-unauthorized-immigrants-enrolled-in-daca/

López, Ian F. Haney. 2006. *White by Law: The Legal Construction of Race*. New York: New York University Press.

López, Marissa. 2008. "The Language of Resistance: Alurista's Global Poetics." *MELUS* 33 (1): 93–115.

Lopez, Mark Hugo. 2013. *What Univision's Milestone Says about U.S. Demographics*. Washington, DC: Pew Research Hispanic Trends Project.

Lopez, Mark Hugo, Ana González-Barrera, and Gustavo López. 2013. "A Growing Share of Latinos Get Their News in English." Pew Hispanic Center, July 23.

López, Nancy and Howard Hogan. 2021. "What's *Your* Street Race? The Urgency of Critical Race Theory and Intersectionality as Lenses for Revising the U.S. Office of Management and Budget Guidelines, Census and Administrative Data in Latinx Communities and Beyond." *Genealogy* 5: 75. https://doi.org/10.3390/genealogy5030075

López, Paul. 2010. "Samora, Julian (1920-1996)," pp. 492–494 in D.J. Leonard and C.R. Lugo-Lugo (eds.), *Latino History and Culture: An Encyclopedia*. 1st edn. New York: Routledge.

Lopez, Robert J. 2018. "The East L.A. Walkouts of 1968." *California State University, Los Angeles Magazine*, Winter. https://www.calstatelamagazine.com/university-news/cal-state-la-east-la-walkouts-1968

López-Sanders, Laura. 2012. "Bible Belt Immigrants: Latino Religion Incorporation in New Immigrant Destinations." *Latino Studies* 10 (1–2): 128–154.

Los Tigres del Norte. 1984. *La Jaula de Oro* [Album]. Hollywood, CA: Fonovisa Records.

Loughrin, Sandra Marie. 2015. "Queer Chicano Families: The Importance of Converging Literature on Queer Families, Chicano Families, and Chicano Queers." *Sociology Compass* 9 (3): 224–234.

Loveman, Mara and Jeronimo O. Muñiz. 2007. "How Puerto Rico Became White: Boundary Dynamics and Inter-Census Racial Reclassification." *American Sociological Review* 72 (6): 915–939.

Lowy, Richard F. and David V. Baker. 1988. "Transcendence, Critical Theory and Emancipation: Reconceptualizing the Framework for a Chicano Sociology." *Journal of Ethnic Studies* 15 (4): 57–67.

Lozano, Juan A. 2023. "Federal Judge Again Declares that DACA is Illegal with Issus Likely to be Decided by the Supreme Court." *Associated Press*, September 13.

Luibheid, Eithne. 1997. "The 1965 Immigration and Nationality Act: An 'End' to Exclusion." *Positions* 5 (2): 501–522.

Lundholm, Nicholas B. 2011. "Cutting Class: Why Arizona's Ethnic Studies Ban Won't Ban Ethnic Studies." *Arizona Law Review* 53 (3): 1041–1088.

Maccormack, John. 2012. "Immigrant Deaths Soar in South Texas." *San Antonio Express-News*, December 30. http://www.mysanantonio.com/news/local_news/article/Border-woes-no-longer-just-on-the-border-4155003.php

Macias-Rojas, Patrisia. 2016. *From Deportation to Prison: The Politics of Immigration Enforcement in Post-Civil Rights America*. New York: New York University Press.

Madsen, William. 1967. "Religious Syncretism," pp. 369–391 in M. Nash (ed.), *Handbook of Middle American Indians*. Vol. 6: Social Anthropology Austin: University of Texas at Austin.

Mallet-García, Marie L., and Lisa García-Bedolla. 2021."Immigration Policy and Belonging: Ramifications for DACA Recipients' Sense of Belonging." American Behavioral Scientist 65 (9): 1165–1179.

Manuel, Peter. 2007. "The Soul of the Barrio: 30 Years of Salsa." *NACLA*, September 25. https://nacla.org/article/soul-barrio-30-years-salsa

Maria, Caitriona. 2023. "10 Most-Learned Languages in Educational Institutions in the U.S." *TPR Teaching*, October 6. https://www.tprteaching.com/most-studied-languages-in-higher-education/

Markert, John. 2010. "The Changing Face of Racial Discrimination: Hispanics as the Dominant Minority in the USA – A New Application of Power-Threat Theory." *Critical Sociology* 36 (2): 307–327.

Markides, Kyriakos S. and Jeannine Coreil. 1986. "The Health of Hispanics in the Southwestern United States: An Epidemiological Paradox." *Public Health Reports* 101: 253–265.

Markides, Kyriakos S. and Karl Eschbach. 2005. "Aging, Migration, and Mortality: Current Status of Research on the Hispanic Paradox." *Journals of Gerontology, Series B: Psychological Sciences* 60B: 68–75.

Markides, Kyriakos S. and Karl Eschbach. 2011. "Hispanic Paradox in Adult Mortality in the United States," pp. 227–240 in R.G. Rogers and E.M. Crimmins (eds.), *International Handbook of Adult Mortality*. New York: Springer.

Marks, Rachel and Merarys Rios-Vargas. 2021. "Improvements to the 2020 Census Race and Hispanic Origin Question Designs, Data Processing, and Coding Procedures." https://www.census.gov/ne wsroom/blogs/random-samplings/2021/08/improvements-to-2020-census-race-hispanic-origin -question-designs.html

Marrow, Helen B. 2011. *New Destination Dreaming: Immigration, Race and Legal Status in the Rural American South*. Stanford, CA: Stanford University Press.

Marrow, Helen B. 2020a. "Hope Turned Sour: Second-Generation Incorporation and Mobility in U.S. New Immigrant Destinations." *Ethnic and Racial Studies* 43 (1): 99–118.

Marrow, Helen B. 2020b. "Hope Turned Sour: Second Generation Incorporation and Mobility in U.S. New Immigrant Destinations," in Portes, Alejandro, and Patricia Fernandez-Kelly, eds. *The End of Compassion: Children of Immigrants in the Age of Deportation*. Routledge.

Martin, Monica J., Bill McCarthy, Rand D. Conger, Frederick X. Gibbons, Ronald L. Simons, Carolyn E. Cutrona, and Gene H. Brody. 2011 "The Enduring Significance of Racism: Discrimination and Delinquency among Black American Youth." *Journal of Research on Adolescence* 21 (3): 662–676.

Martin, Will. 2023. "Southwest Border Mission Spurs 'Mixed Feelings' Among Guardsmen." *Reserve+ National Guard Magazine*, February 1.

Martinez, George A. 1997. "The Legal Construction of Race: Mexican-Americans and Whiteness." *Harvard Latino Law Review* 2: 321–347.

Martinez, Jaqueline M. 2014. "Culture, Communication, and Latina Feminist Philosophy: Toward a Critical Phenomenology of Culture." *Hypatia*, 29: 221–236.

Martínez, Mariana G., 2017. "The First 'Chicano' Journal: El Grito, A Journal of Contemporary Mexican-American Thought." *Diálogo* 20 (2): 47–53.

Martinez, Monica Muñoz. 2018. *The Injustice Never Leaves You: Anti-Mexican Violence in Texas*. Cambridge, MA: Harvard University Press.

Martinez, Ramiro, Jr. 2002. *Latino Homicide: Immigration, Violence, and Community*. 1st edn. New York: Routledge.

Martinez, Ramiro, Jr. 2008. "Latino Crime and Delinquency in the United States," pp. 114–126 in H. Rodríguez, R. Sáenz, and C. Menjívar (eds.), *Latinas/os in the United States: Changing the Face of América*. New York: Springer.

Martinez, Ramiro, Jr. 2015. *Latino Homicide: Immigration, Violence, and Community*. 2nd edn. New York: Routledge.

Martinez Jr, Ramiro and Keller Sheppard. 2019. "Were Mexican American Communities Safer than Others? Some Surprising Findings from San Antonio, 1960-1980." *UCLA Law Review*. 66: 1588-1615.

Martinez, Ramiro, Jr. and Jacob I Stowell. 2012. "Extending Immigration and Crime Studies: National Implications and Local Settings." *Annals of the American Academy of Political & Social Science* 641 (1): 174–191.

Martinez, Ramiro, Jr., Jacob I. Stowell, and Matthew T. Lee. 2010. "Immigration and Crime in an Era of Transformation: A Longitudinal Analysis of Homicides in San Diego Neighborhood, 1980-2000." *Criminology* 48 (3): 797–829.

Martinez, Ramiro, Jr. and Abel Valenzuela, Jr. (eds.) 2006. *Immigration and Crime: Race, Ethnicity, and Violence*. New York: New York University Press.

Martini, Nicholas F. 2012. "'La Iglesia' in Politics? Religion and Latino Public Opinion." *Social Science Quarterly* 93 (4): 988–1006.

Masarik, Elizabeth Garner. 2019. "Por la Raza, Para la Raza: Jovita Idar and Progressive-Era Mexicana Maternalism along the Texas–Mexico Border." *Southwestern Historical Quarterly* 122 (3): 278–299.

Mason-Jones, A.J. and Phoebe Nicholson. 2018. "Structural Violence and Marginalisation. The Sexual and Reproductive Health Experiences of Separated Young People on the Move. A Rapid Review with Relevance to the European Humanitarian Crisis." *Public Health* 158: 156–162.

Massey, Douglas S. 2007. *Categorically Unequal: The American Stratification System*. New York: Russell Sage Foundation.

Massey, Douglas S. 2020. "The Real Crisis at the Mexico-U.S. Border: A Humanitarian and Not an Immigration Emergency." *Sociological Forum* 35 (3): 787–805.

Massey, Douglas S., Joaquín Arango, Graeme Hugo, Ali Kouaouci, Adela Pellegrino, and J. Edward Taylor. 1993. "Theories of International Migration: A Review and Appraisal." *Population and Development Review* 19 (3): 431–466.

Massey, Douglas S., Joaquín Arango, Graeme Hugo, Ali Kouaouci, Adela Pellegrino, and J. Edward Taylor. 2005. *Worlds in Motion: Understanding World Migration at the End of the Millennium*. New York: Oxford University Press.

Massey, Douglas S. and Nancy Denton. 1993. *American Apartheid: Segregation and the Making of the Underclass*. Cambridge, MA: Harvard University Press.

Massey, Douglas S., Jorge Durand, and Nolan J. Malone. 2002. *Beyond Smoke and Mirrors: Mexican Immigration in an Era of Economic Integration*. New York: Russell Sage Foundation.

Massey, Douglas S. and Kristin E. Espinosa. 1997. "What's Driving Mexico–U.S. Migration? A Theoretical, Empirical, and Policy Analysis." *American Journal of Sociology* 102 (4): 939–999.

Massey, Douglas S. and Emilio Parrado. 1994. "Migradollars: The Remittances and Savings of Mexican Migrants to the USA." *Population Research and Policy Review* 13: 3–30.

Mastro, Dana E. and Bradley S. Greenberg. 2000. "The Portrayal of Racial Minorities on Prime Time Television." *Journal of Broadcasting and Electronic Media* 44: 690–703.

Maternowska, Catherine, Fátima Estrada, Lourdes Campero, Cristina Herrera, Claire D. Brindis, and Meredith Miller Vostrejs. 2010. "Gender, Culture and Reproductive Decision-Making among Recent Mexican Migrants in California." *Culture, Health & Sexuality* 12 (1): 29–43.

Mathema, Silva. 2017. "Keeping Families Together." Center for American Progress, March 16. https://www.americanprogress.org/issues/immigration/reports/2017/03/16/428335/families-together/

Mather, Mark and Paola Scommegna. 2020. "The Demography of Dementia and Dementia Caregiving." Population Reference Bureau, May 28. https://www.prb.org/resources/the-demography-of-dementia-and-dementia-caregiving/

Matovina, Timothy. 2012. *Latino Catholicism: Transformation in America's Largest Church*. Princeton, NJ: Princeton University Press.

McConnell, Eileen Diaz. 2011. "An 'Incredible Number of Latinos and Asians': Media Representations of Racial and Ethnic Population Change in Atlanta, Georgia." *Latino Studies* 9 (2/3): 177–197.

McDonald, Jill Anne and Leonard Joseph Paulozzi. 2019. "Parsing the Paradox: Hispanic Mortality in the US by Detailed Cause of Death." *Journal of Immigrant and Minority Health* 20 (2): 237–245.

McDonald, Steve, Nan Lin, and Dan Ao. 2009. "Networks of Opportunity: Gender, Race, and Job Leads." *Social Problems* 56 (3): 385–402.

McFarland, Michael and Cheryl A. Smith. 2011. "Segregation, Race, and Infant Well-Being." *Population Research and Policy Review* 30: 467–493.

McKinnon, Andrew M. 2011. "Ideology and the Market Metaphor in Rational Choice Theory of Religion: A Rhetorical Critique of 'Religious Economies.'" *Critical Sociology* 39 (4): 529–543.

McLoyd, Vonnie C., Ana Mari Cauce, David Takeuchi, and Leon Wilson. 2000. "Marital Processes and Parental Socialization in Families of Color: A Decade Review of Research." *Journal of Marriage and Family* 62: 1070–1093.

Medina, Jennifer. 2020. "Overlooked No More: Jovita Idár, Who Promoted Rights of Mexican-Americans and Women." *New York Times*, August 19. https://www.nytimes.com/2020/08/07/obituaries/jovita-idar-overlooked.html

Medrano, Manuel F. 2010a. *Americo Paredes: In His Own Words, an Authorized Biography*. Denton, TX: University of North Texas Press.

Medrano, Manuel. 2010b. "José Angel Gutierrez: An Oral History Conversation." *Journal of South Texas* 23 (1): 19–32.

Meier, Matt S. with Conchita Franco Serri and Richard A. Garcia. 1997. "Luis Muñoz Marín (1898–1980) Puerto Rican Patriot, Statesman, Politician, Poet, Editor." *Notable Latino Americans: A Biographical Dictionary*. Greenwood Press: Westport, CT.

Mendoza, Sylvia, Gloria Vásquez Gonzáles, and N. Geremy Landin. 2022. "West Side Sound: How Black Musicians Influenced Chicano Soul." *San Antonio Report*, July 29. https://sanantonioreport.org/west-side-sound-how-black-musicians-influenced-chicano-soul/

Menjívar, Cecilia. 2000. *Fragmented Ties: Salvadoran Immigrant Networks in America*. Berkeley: University of California Press.

Menjívar, Cecilia. 2003. "Religion and Immigration in Comparative Perspective: Catholic and Evangelical Salvadorans in San Francisco, Washington DC and Phoenix." *Sociology of Religion* 64 (1): 21–45.

Menjívar, Cecilia. 2014. "The 'Poli-Migra': Multi-Layered Legislation, Enforcement Practices, and What We Can Learn About and From Today's Approaches." American Behavioral Scientist 58 (13): 1805–1819.

Menjivar, Cecilia and Cynthia Bejarano. 2004. "Latino Immigrants' Perceptions of Crime and Police Authorities in the United States: A Case Study from the Phoenix Metropolitan Area." *Ethnic and Racial Studies* 27 (1): 120–148.

Menjívar, Cecilia and Leisy Abrego. 2012. "Legal Violence: Immigration Law and the Lives of Central American Immigrants." *American Journal of Sociology* 117 (5): 1380–1421.

Merolla, David M. and Omari Jackson. 2019."Structural Racism as the Fundamental Cause of the Academic Achievement Gap." *Sociology Compass* 13 (6): 1–13.

Merton, Robert. 1949. *Social Theory and Social Structure*. New York: Free Press.

Michelson, Melissa R. 2005. "Meeting the Challenge of Latino Voter Mobilization." *Annals of the American Academy of Political and Social Science* 601 (1): 85–101.

Mier, Tomás. 2022. "Mexican-American Band Fuerza Régida is Making Music 'For the People.'" Rolling Stone, December 30. https://www.rollingstone.com/music/music-latin/fuerza-regida-interview-pa-que-hablen-1234654239/

Mills, Claire Kramer, Jessica Battisto, Scott Liberman, Marlene Orozco, Iliana Perez, and Nancy S. Lee. 2018. *Latino-Owned Businesses: Shining a Light on National Trends*. Palo Alto, CA: Stanford Business Graduate School of Business. https://www.gsb.stanford.edu/sites/gsb/files/publication-pdf/slei-report-2018-latino-owned-businesses-shinging-light-national-trends.pdf

Milner, J. Richard and Tyrone C. Howard. 2013. "Counter-Narrative as Method: Race, Policy and Research for Teacher Education." *Race Ethnicity and Education* 16 (4): 536–561.

Miniño, Arialdi M., Melonie P. Heron, Sherry L. Murphy, and Kenneth D. Kochanek. 2007. *Deaths: Final Data for 2004*. National Vital Statistics Reports 55 (19). Hyattsville, MD: National Center for Health Statistics.

Mirandé, Alfredo, 1978. "Chicano Sociology: A New Paradigm for Social Science." *Pacific Sociological Review* 21 (3): 293–312.

Mirandé, Alfredo, 1982. "Chicano Sociology: A Critique and Evaluation of Prevailing Theoretical Perspectives." *Humboldt Journal of Social Relations* 10 (1): 204–223.

Mirandé, Alfredo. 1994. *Gringo Justice*. 2nd ed. Notre Dame, IN: University of Notre Dame Pess.

Mirandé, Alfredo. 1997. *Hombres y Machos: Masculinity and Latino Culture*. Boulder, CO: Westview Press.

Miville Marie L., Narolyn Mendez, and Mark Louie. 2017. "Latina/o Gender Roles: A Content Analysis of Empirical Research from 1982 to 2013." *Journal of Latinx Psychology* 5 (3): 173–194.

Model, Suzanne. 1993. "The Ethnic Niche and the Structure of Opportunity: Immigrants and Minorities in New York City," pp. 161–193 in M. Katz (ed.), *The "Underclass" Debate: Views from History*. Princeton, NJ: Princeton University Press.

Mogro-Wilson, Cristina, Alysse Melville Loomis, Crystal Hayes, and Reinaldo Rojas. 2019. "Emerging Bicultural Views of Fatherhood: Perspectives of Puerto Rican Fathers." *Advances in Social Work* 19 (2): 311–328.

Mogro-Wilson, Cristina, Reinaldo Rojas, and Jasmin Haynes. 2016."A Cultural Understanding of the Parenting Practices of Puerto Rican Fathers." *Social Work Research* 40 (4): 1–11.

Mohanram, Radhika. 1999. *Black Body: Women, Colonialism and Space*. Minneapolis, MN: University of Minnesota Press.

Mohanty, Chandra Talpade. 1991. "Under Western Eyes: Feminist Scholarship and Colonial Discourse," pp. 51–80 in C.T. Mohanty, A. Russo, and L. Torres (eds.), *Third-World Women and the Politics of Feminism*. Bloomington, IN: Indiana University Press.

Montoya-Williams, Diana, Victoria Guazzelli Williamson, Michelle Cardel, Elena Fuentes-Afflick, Mildred Maldonado-Molina, and Lindsay Thompson. 2021. "The Hispanic/Latinx Perinatal Paradox in the United States: A Scoping Review and Recommendations to Guide Future Research." *Journal of Immigrant and Minority Health* 23 (5): 1078–1091.

Monk-Tanner, Elizabeth, Mary Heiserman, Crystle Johnson, Vanity Cotton, and Manny Jackson. 2010. "The Portrayal of Racial Minorities on Prime Time Television: A Replication of the Masto and Greenberg Study a Decade Later." *Studies in Popular Culture* 32 (2): 101–114.

Montejano, David. 1987. *Anglos and Mexicans in the Making of Texas, 1836–1986.* Austin: University of Texas Press.

Montejano, David. 1999. "On the Question of Inclusion," pp.xi–xxvi in D. Montejano (ed.), *Chicano Politics and Society in the Late Twentieth Century.* Austin, TX: University of Texas Press.

Montejano, David. 2010. *Quixote's Soldiers: A Local History of the Chicano Movement, 1966–1981.* Austin: University of Texas Press.

Montes, Segundo. 1987. *El Compadrazgo: Una Estructura de Poder en los Estados Unidos.* San Salvador, El Salvador: UCA Editores.

Monteverde, Malena, Kenya Noronha, Alberto Palloni, and Beatriz Novak. 2010. "Obesity and Excess Mortality among the Elderly in the United States and Mexico." *Demography* 47 (1): 79–96.

Montgomery, David. 2013. "Carlos Santana Finds Kennedy Center Honors After a Lifelong Search for the 'Universal Tone.'" *Washington Post*, December 6. https://www.washingtonpost.com/entertainment/music/carlos-santana-finds-kennedy-center-honors-after-a-lifelong-search-for-the-universal-tone/2013/12/05/7f4c6e98-4bcf-11e3-ac54-aa84301ced81_story.html

Montgomery, Tommie Sue. 1982. *Revolution in El Salvador: Origins and Evolution.* Boulder, CO: Westview Press.

Montoya, Celeste. 2023. "Studying Latina Mobilization Intersectionally, Studying Latinas Mobilizing Intersectionality." *Journal of Women, Politics & Policy* 44 (4): 405–421.

Montoya, Margaret E. 1994 "Mascaras, Trenzas, y Greñas: Un/masking the Self While Un/Braiding Latina Stories and Legal Discourse." *Chicana/o Latina/o Law Review* 15:185–220.

Montoya-Galvez, Camilo. 2022. "At Least 853 Migrants Died Crossing the U.S.-Mexico Border in the Past 12 Months – A Record High." *CBS News*, October 28. https://www.cbsnews.com/news/migrant-deaths-crossing-us-mexico-border-2022-record-high/

Moore, Joan. 1991. *Going Down to the Barrio: Homeboys and Homegirls in Change.* Philadelphia: Temple University Press.

Moore, Joan W. with Alfredo B. Cuéllar. 1970. *Mexican Americans.* Englewood Cliffs, NJ: Prentice-Hall.

Moore, Joan and Raquel Pinderhughes (eds.). 1993. *In the Barrios: Latinos and the Underclass Debate.* New York: Russell Sage Foundation.

Mora, G. Cristina, Reuben Perez, and Nicholas Vargas. 2021. "About 25 Percent of US-Born Identify with 'Latinx" Term Regularly." Berkeley IGS Poll. Release #2021-07. https://escholarship.org/uc/item/07v7b7d1

Mora, G. Cristina, Reuben Perez, and Nicholas Vargas. 2022. "Who Identifies as 'Latinx'? The Generational Politics of Ethnoracial Labels." *Social Forces* 100 (3): 1170–1194.

Mora, Marie T. and Alberto Davila. 2006a. "Hispanic Ethnicity, Gender, and the Change in the LEP-Earnings Penalty in the United States During the 1990s." *Social Science Quarterly* 87 (supp. 1): 1295–1318.

Mora, Marie T. and Alberto Davila. 2006b. "A Note on the Changes in the Relative Wages of LEP Hispanic Men Between 1980 and 2000." *Industrial Relations* 45 (2): 169–172.

Moraga, Cherríe. 1983. *Loving in the War Years: Lo Que Nunca Pasó Por Sus Labios.* Boston: South End Press.

Moraga, Cherríe. 1993. *The Last Generation: Prose and Poetry.* Boston: South End Press.

Moraga, Cherríe and Gloria Anzaldúa (eds.). 1981. *This Bridge Called My Back: Writings by Radical Women of Color.* 1st edn. Watertown, MA: Persephone Press.

Moraga, Cherríe and Gloria Anzaldúa (eds.) 2015. *This Bridge Called My Back: Writings by Radical Women of Color.* 4th edn. Albany, NY: State University of New York Press.

Morales, Maria Cristina. 2008. "The Ethnic Niche as an Economic Pathway for the Dark Skinned: Labor Market Incorporation of Latina/o Workers." *Hispanic Journal of Behavioral Sciences* 30 (3): 280–298.

Morales, Maria Cristina. 2016. "From Social Capital to Inequality: Migrant Networks in Different Stages of Labor Incorporation." *Sociological Forum* 31 (3): 509–530.

Morales, Maria Cristina. 2018. "The Manufacturing of the U.S.-Mexico Border Crisis." pp 145–161 in C. Menjívar, M. Ruiz, and I. Ness (eds.), *The Oxford Handbook of Migration Crises*. New York: Oxford University Press.

Morales, Maria Cristina and Cynthia Bejarano. 2009 "Transnational Sexual and Gendered Violence: An Application of Border Sexual Conquest at a Mexico-US border." *Global Networks* 9 (3): 420–439.

Morales, Maria Cristina, Denise Delgado, and Theodore Curry. 2018. "Variations in Citizenship Profiling by Generational Status: Individual and Neighborhood Characteristics of Latina/os Questioned by Law Enforcement About Their Legal Status." *Race and Social Problems* 10 (4): 293–305.

Morales, Maria Cristina and Theodore R. Curry. 2021. "Citizenship Profiling and Diminishing Procedural Justice: Local Immigration Enforcement and the Reduction of Police Legitimacy among Individuals and in Latina/o Neighbourhoods." *Ethnic and Racial Studies* 44 (1): 134–153.

Morales, M. Cristina and Rogelio Sáenz. 2007. "Correlates of Mexican American Students Standardized Test Scores: An Integrated Model Approach." *Hispanic Journal of Behavior Sciences* 29 (3): 349–365.

Moreno, J. Edward. 2023. "How a Mexican Lager Quitely Rose to Become America's Best-Selling Beer." *New York Times*, July 23. https://www.nytimes.com/2023/07/23/business/modelo-bud-light.html

Morín, José R. 2006. *The Legacy of Américo Paredes*. College Station, TX: Texas A&M University Press.

Morris, Aldon D. 1984. *The Origins of the Civil Rights Movement: Black Communities Organizing for Change*. New York: Free Press.

Moss, Philip and Chris Tilly. 1996. "'Soft' Skills and Race: An Investigation of Black Men's Employment Problems." *Work and Occupations* 23: 252–276.

Moynihan, Daniel Patrick. 1965. *The Negro Family: The Case for National Action*. Washington, DC: Office of Policy Planning and Research, U.S. Department of Labor. http://www.dol.gov/asp/programs/history/webid-meynihan.htm

Mungin, Lateef and Mark Davis. 2003. "Gangs Put Their Mark on Gwinnett." *Atlanta Journal-Constitution*, April 13: 1A.

Muñoz-Laboy, Miguel A. 2008. "Familism and Sexual Regulation Among Bisexual Latina/o Men." *Archives of Sexual Behavior* 37 (5): 773–782.

Murguia, Edward and Edward E. Telles. 1996. "Phenotype and Schooling Among Mexican Americans." *Sociology of Education* 69: 276–289.

Murphy, Kate. 2008. "Mexican Robin Hood Figures Gains a Kind of Notoriety in U.S." *New York Times*, November 8. http://www.nytimes.com/2008/02/08/us/08narcosaint.html?_r=0

Myrdal, Gunnar. 1957. *Rich Lands and Poor*. New York: Harper and Row.

Natarajan, Anusha and Carolyne Im. 2022. "Key Facts about Hispanic Eligible Voters in 2022." Pew Research Center, October 12. https://www.pewresearch.org/short-reads/2022/10/12/key-facts-about-hispanic-eligible-voters-in-2022/

National Archives. 2024. "The Treaty of Guadalupe Hidalgo." https://www.archives.gov/education/lessons/guadalupe-hidalgo#background

National Center for Health Statistics. 2013. *Health, United States, 2012: With Special Feature on Emergency Care*. Hyattsville, MD: National Center for Health Statistics.

National Center for Health Statistics. 2017. *Health, United States, 2017: With Special Features on Mortality*. Hyattsville, MD: National Center for Health Statistics. file:///C:/Users/Owner/Downloads/cdc_59199_DS1.pdf

National Center for Health Statistics. 2021. *Health, United States, 2019*. Hyattsville, MD: National Center for Health Statistics. https://www.cdc.gov/nchs/data/hus/hus19-508.pdf

National Endowment for the Arts. 2022. "Lydia Mendoza Mexican American Singer." https://www.arts.gov/honors/heritage/lydia-mendoza

National Hispanic Caucus of State Legislators. 2010. *Hispanic Obesity: A National Crisis.* Washington, DC: National Hispanic Caucus of State Legislators.

National Immigration Law Center. 2022. "DACA." https://www.nilc.org/issues/daca/

National Institute on Minority Health. 2018. "The National Institute on Minority Health and Health Disparities Research Framework." https://www.nimhd.nih.gov/about/overview/research-frame work/

National Museum of African American History and Culture. 2022. "Celia Cruz." https://nmaahc.si.edu /latinx/celia-cruz

Nerudo, Pablo. 1991. *Canto General.* Berkeley: University of California Press.

Newman, Andrew Adam. 2012. "Rolling Stones Pages Aimed at Latinos, Even the Ads." *New York Times,* November 6. http://www.nytimes.com/2012/11/07/business/media/rolling-stone-section -is-aimed-at-latinos-even-the-ads.html?_r=0

Ngai, Mae. 2004. *Impossible Subjects: Illegal Aliens and the Making of Modern America.* Princeton, NJ: Princeton University Press.

Nielsen, Carolyn. 2013. "Wise Latina: Framing Sonia Sotomayor in the General-Market and Latina/o-Oriented Prestige Press." *The Howard Journal of Communications* 24: 117–133.

Nieves-Pizarro, Yadira and Juan Mundel. 2021. "#RickyRenuncia: The Hashtag That Took Collective Outrage from Social Media to the Streets," pp. 159–187 in V. Bravo and M. De Moya (eds.), *Latin American Diasporas in Public Diplomacy.* Cham, Switzerland: Palgrave Macmillan.

Niu, Sunny Xinchun, Teresa Sullivan, and Marta Tienda. 2008. "Minority Talent Loss and the Texas Top 10 Percent Law." *Social Science Quarterly* 89 (4): 831–845.

Noe-Bustamante, Luis, Lauren Mora, and Mark Hugo Lopez. 2020. "Views on Latinx as a Pan-Ethnic Term for U.S. Latinos." Pew Research Center, August 11. https://www.pewresearch.org/his panic/2020/08/11/views-on-latinx-as-a-pan-ethnic-term-for-u-s-hispanics/

O'Brien, Soledad. 2009. *Latino in America.* Atlanta: CNN. http://www.cnn.com/SPECIALS/2009/ latino.in.america/

O'Neil, Shannon K. 2013. *Two Nations Indivisible: Mexico, the United States, and the Road Ahead.* New York: Oxford University Press.

O'Neill, Molly. 1992. "New Mainstream: Hot Dogs, Apple Pie and Salsa." *New York Times,* March 11. http://www.nytimes.com/1992/03/11/garden/new-mainstream-hot-dogs-apple-pie-and-sal sa.html

Obolenskaya, Christina. 2021. "Hispanic Buying Power Rising in US, Bolstering Consumer Sectors." *EMARKETER,* December 21.

Ocasio-Cortez, Alexandria. 2023. Official Website of Congresswoman Alexandria Ocasio-Cortez. https://ocasio-cortez.house.gov/about

Ochoa, Gilda. 2004. *Becoming Neighbors in a Mexican American Community: Power, Conflict, and Solidarity.* Austin: University of Texas Press.

Ochoa, Gilda L. 2013. *Academic Profiling: Latinos, Asian Americans, and the Achievement Gap.* Minneapolis: University of Minnesota Press.

Odem, Mary E. 2004. "Our Lady of Guadalupe in the New South: Latino Immigrants and the Politics of Integration in the Catholic Church." *Journal of American Ethnic History* 24: 26–57.

Office of the Historian and Office of the Clerk US House of Representatives. 2013. "Hispanics in Congress 1822–2012." US Government Printing Office.

Oktavec, Eileen. 1995. *Answered Prayers: Miracles and Milagros Along the Border.* Tucson: University of Arizona Press.

Olivares, Julián. 1992. *Tomás Rivera: The Complete Works.* Houston: Arte Público Press.

Olmos, Edward J., Lea Ybarra, and Manuel Monterrey (eds.) 1999. *Americanos.* Boston: Little, Brown.

Omi, Michael and Howard Winant. 1994. *Racial Formation in the United States: From the 1960s to the 1980s.* New York: Routledge and Kegan Paul.

Omori, Marisa, and Nick Petersen. 2020. "Institutionalizing Inequality in the Courts: Decomposing Racial and Ethnic Disparities in Detention, Conviction, and Sentencing." *Criminology* 58 (4): 678–713.

Ontiveros, Randy J. 2014. *In the Spirit of a New People: The Cultural Politics of the Chicano Movement.* Vol. 6. New York: New York University Press.

The Opportunity Atlas. 2024. "The Opportunity Atlas." https://opportunityatlas.org/

Ordway, D. 2020. "Media, Race and Gender: How the News Media Portray Latinos in Stories and Images: 5 Studies to Know." *Journalist's Resource.* https://journalistsresource.org/race-and-gen der/news-media-portray-latinos/

Orfield, Gary and Chungmei Lee. 2007. *Historic Reversals, Accelerating Resegregation, and the Need for New Integration Strategies.* Los Angeles: The Civil Rights Project, Proyecto Derechos Civilies.

Orozco, Cynthia E. 1995. "Cortez Lira, Gregorio (1875–1916)." *Texas State Historical Association.* https://www.tshaonline.org/handbook/entries/cortez-lira-gregorio

Orrenius, Pia M. and Madeline Zavodny. 2009. "Do Immigrants Work in Riskier Jobs?" *Demography* 46 (3): 535–551.

Osterman, Michelle J.K., Brady E. Hamilton, Joyce A. Martin, Anne K. Driscoll, and Claudia P. Valenzuela. 2023. "Births: Final Data for 2021." *National Vital Statistics Reports* 70 (17). Hyattsville, MD: National Center for Health Statistics.

Osypuk, Theresa L., Lisa M. Bates, and Dolores Acevedo-Garcia. 2010. "Another Mexican Birthweight Paradox? The Role of Residential Enclaves and Neighborhood Poverty in the Birthweight of Mexican-Origin Infants." *Social Science & Medicine* 70: 550–560.

Paarlberg, Michael Ahn. 2022. "Transnational Gangs and Criminal Remittances: A Conceptual Framework." *Comparative Migration Studies* 10: 24.

Pablos-Mendez, Ariel. 1994. "Mortality among Hispanics." *Journal of the American Medical Association* 271 (16): 1237–1238.

Palloni, Alberto and Elizabeth Arias. 2004. "Paradox Lost: Explaining the Hispanic Adult Mortality Advantage." *Demography* 41 (3): 385–415.

Palloni, Alberto and Jeffrey D. Morenoff. 2001. "Interpreting the Paradoxical in the Hispanic Paradox." *Annals of the New York Academy of Science* 954: 140–174.

Palmer-Boyes, Ashley. 2010. "The Latino Catholic Parish as a Specialist Organization: Distinguishing Characteristics." *Review of Religious Research* 51 (3): 302–323.

Paredes, Américo. 1958. *With His Pistol in His Hand.* Austin: University of Texas Press.

Paredes, Americo. 1995. *Folklore and Culture on the Texas–Mexican Border.* Austin: University of Texas Press.

Park, Robert E. 1950. *Race and Culture.* Glencoe, IL: The Free Press.

Passel, Jeffrey S., D'Vera Cohn, and Ana González-Barrera. 2012. *Net Migration from Mexico Falls to Zero – And Perhaps Less.* Washington, DC: Pew Hispanic Center.

Patel, Kushang V., Karl Eschbach, Laura L. Rudkin, M. Kristen Peek, and Kyriakos S. Markides. 2003. "Neighborhood Context and Self-Rated Health in Older Mexican Americans." *Annals of Epidemiology* 13 (9): 620–628.

Patterson, Orlando. 1982. *Slavery and Social Death: A Comparative Study.* Cambridge, MA: Harvard University Press.

Payan, Tony. 2016. *The Three US–Mexico Border Wars: Drugs, Immigration, and Homeland Security.* Bloomsbury Publishing USA.

Paz, Christian. 2022. "The Next Congress Will Be the Most Representative of Latino Identity Ever." *Vox,* December 3.

PBS NewsHour. 2006. "The Spanish Media Organize their Listeners to React to the Immigration Bill." *PBS NewsHour,* April 11. http://www.pbs.org/newshour/bb/latin_america-jan-june06-immigr ation_4-11/

Peguero, Anthony A., Yasmiyn Irizarry, Janice Iwama, Sanna King, Jessica L. Dunning-Lozano, Jun Sung Hong, and Jennifer M. Bondy. 2023. "Is There an Immigration and School-Level Crime Link?" *Crime & Delinquency* 69 (8): 1339–1368.

Peña, Manuel and Richard Bauman. 2000. "Obituaries: Américo Paredes (1915–99)." *Journal of American Folklore* 113 (no. 448): 195–198.

Peña, Susana. 2011. "The Sexuality of Migration: Border Crossings and Mexican Immigrant Men." *Latino Studies* 9 (1), 155–157.

Pérez, Ashley, E. Karina Santamaria, and Don Operario. 2018. "A Systematic Review of Behavioral Interventions to Reduce Condomless Sex and Increase HIV Testing for Latina/o MSM." *Journal of Immigrant Minority Health* 20: 1261–1276.

Pérez, Eliseo J., Amelie Ramirez, Roberto Villarreal, Gregory A. Talavara, Edward Trapido, Lucina Suarez, José Marti, and Alfred McAlister. 2001. "Cigarette Smoking Behavior among US Latino Men and Women in Different Counties of Origin." *American Journal of Public Health* 91 (9): 1424–1430.

Pérez, Maritza. 2019. "A History of Anti-Latino State-Sanctioned Violence: Executions, Lynchings, and Hate Crimes," pp. 25–43, in A. Mirandé (ed.), *Gringo Injustice: Insider Perspectives on Police, Gangs, and Law.* New York: Routledge.

Perlman, Joel. 2005. *Italians Then, Mexicans Now: Immigrant Origins and Second-Generation Progress, 1890–2000.* New York: Russell Sage Foundation.

Pew Hispanic Center. 2007. *Changing Faiths: Latinos and the Transformation of American Religion.* Washington, DC: Pew Hispanic Center.

Pew Hispanic Center. 2020. American Trends Panel Wave 68, June 4–June 10, 2020. https://www.pew research.org/datasets/.

Pew Research Center. 2008 National Survey of Latinos.

Pew Research Center. 2018. National Survey of Latinos. https://www.pewresearch.org/datasets/.

Pew Research Center. 2024. *How Americans View the Situation at the U.S.–Mexico Border, Its Causes and Consequences.* Washington, DC: Pew Research Center.

Pfeffer, Max J. and Pilar A. Parra. 2009. "Strong Ties, Weak Ties, and Human Capital: Latino Employment Outside the Enclave." *Rural Sociology* 74 (2): 241–269.

Phillips, Amber. 2017. "'They're Rapists.' President Trump's Campaign Launch Speech Two Years Later, Annotated." *Washington Post*, June 16. https://www.washingtonpost.com/news/the-fix/wp/2017/06/16/theyre-rapists-presidents-trump-campaign-launch-speech-two-years-later-ann otated/

Phillips, Julie A. and Douglas S. Massey. 1999. "The New Labor Market: Immigrants and Wages after IRCA." *Demography* 36 (2): 233–246.

Piore, Michael J. 1979. *Birds of Passage: Migrant Labor in Industrial Societies.* Cambridge, UK: Cambridge University Press.

Ponce, Richard C. 2022. "Letters to the Editor: American Cowboys Owe Their Lifestyle to Mexican Vaqueros." *Los Angeles Times*, December 8. https://www.latimes.com/opinion/letters-to-the-edit or/story/2022-12-08/american-cowboys-mexican-vaqueros

Population Reference Bureau. 2020. *2020 World Population Data Sheet.* Washington, DC: Population Reference Bureau.

Population Reference Bureau. 2022. *2022 World Population Data Sheet.* Washington, DC: Population Reference Bureau.

Portales, Marco. 2000. *Crowding Out Latinos: Mexican Americans in the Public Consciousness.* Philadelphia: Temple University Press.

Portes, Alejandro and Robert L. Bach. 1985. *Latin Journey: Cuban and Mexican Immigrants in the United States.* Berkeley: University of California Press.

Poston, Dudley L., Jr., David Alvirez, and Marta Tienda. 1976. "Earnings Differences Between Anglo and Mexican American Male Workers in 1960 and 1970: Changes in the 'Cost' of Being Mexican American." *Social Science Quarterly* 57: 618–631.

Poston, Dudley L., Jr. and Leon F. Bouvier. 2017. *Population and Society: An Introduction to Demography.* 2nd edn. New York: Cambridge University Press.

Powell, John. 2005. *Encyclopedia of North American Immigration.* New York: Facts on File, Inc.

Poyo, Gerald E. 2010. "Latino American Religion: Catholics, Twentieth Century," pp. 1185–1189 in C.H. Lippy and P.W. Williams (eds.), *Encyclopedia of Religion in America.* Washington, DC: CQ Press.

Pro English. 2024. "Official English Map." https://proenglish.org/official-english-map-2/

Puerto Rico Report. 2022. "Puerto Rico Plebiscites." Puerto Rico Report, December 21. https://www .puertoricoreport.com/puerto-ricos-plebiscites/

Pulido, Laura. 2018. "Geographies of Race and Ethnicity III: Settler Colonialism and Nonnative People of Color." *Progress in Human Geography* 42 (2): 309–318.

Putnam, Robert D. 2000. *Bowling Alone: The Collapse and Revival of American Community.* New York: Simon and Schuster.

Putnam, Robert D. and David E. Campbell. 2010. *American Grace: How Religion Divides and Unites Us.* New York: Simon and Schuster.

Quesada, Uriel, Letitia Gomez, and Salvador Vidal-Ortiz (eds.). 2015. *Queer Brown Voices: Personal Narratives of Latina/o LGBT Activism.* Austin: University of Texas Press.

Quinnell, Kenneth. 2020. *National Hispanic Heritage Month Profiles: Ernesto Galarza.* AFL-CIO.

Quintanilla, Esther. 2023. "A Shortage of Catholic Priests is Why the Largest Congregation in the U.S. is So Big." *National Public Radio*, February 20.

Rai, Saritha. 2004. "Short on Priests U.S. Catholics Outsource Prayers to Indian Clergy." *New York Times*, June 13.

Ramirez, Jenesis J., Gina A. Garcia, and Lisanne T. Hudson. 2020. "Mothers' Influences on Latino Collegians: Understanding Latinx Mother-Son Pedagogies." *International Journal of Qualitative Studies in Education* 33 (10): 1022-1041.

Ramirez, Oscar. 1990. "Mexican American Children and Adolescents," pp. 224-250 in J.T. Gibbs and L.N. Huang (eds.), *Children of Color: Psychological Interventions with Minority Youth.* San Francisco: Jossey-Bass.

Ramos, Jorge. 2004. *The Latino Wave: How Hispanics Will Elect the Next American President.* New York: Rayo.

Ratha, Dilip, Eung Ju Kim, Sonia Plaza, Elliott J. Riordan, Vandana Chandra, and William Shaw. 2022. *Remittances Brave Global Headwinds.* Migration and Development Brief 37. Special Focus: Climate Migration. https://www.knomad.org/sites/default/files/publication-doc/migration_and_develop ment_brief_37_nov_2022.pdf

Reichman, Nancy E., Erin R. Hamilton, Robert A. Hummer, and Yolanda C. Padilla. 2008. "Racial and Ethnic Disparities in Low Birthweight among Urban Unmarried Mothers." *Maternal and Child Health Journal* 12: 204-215.

Reimers, David M. 1983. "An Unintended Reform: The 1965 Immigration Act and Third World Immigration to the United States." *Journal of American Ethnic History* 3 (1): 9-28.

Rendon, Hector. 2024. "News Media Representations: Audience Perceptions of News Frames About Latinxs and Hispanics." *Journalism & Mass Communication Quarterly* 101 (1): 20-44.

Reno, Jamie. 2012. "Why Don't We Have More Hispanic Talking Heads?" *The Daily Beast*, November 11. http://www.thedailybeast.com/articles/2012/11/10/why-don-t-we-have-more-hispanic-talki ng-heads.html

Revilla, Anita Tijerina. 2004. *Raza Womyn Re-constructing Revolution: Exploring the Intersections of Race, Class, Gender and Sexuality in the Lives of Chicana/Latina Student Activists.* Ph.D. dissertation, University of California, Los Angeles.

Revilla, Anita Tijerina and José Manuel Santillana. 2014. "Jotería Identity and Consciousness." *Aztlán* 39 (1): 167-180.

Rhodes, Scott D., Lilli Mann-Jackson, Jorge Alonzo, Jonathan C. Bell, Amanda E. Tanner, Omar Martínez, Florence M. Simán. 2020. "The Health and Well-Being of Latinx Sexual and Gender Minorities in the USA: A Call to Action," pp. 217-236 in A.D. Martínez and S.D. Rhodes (eds.), *New and Emerging Issues in Latinx Health.* Cham, Switzerland: Springer Nature.

Ribas, Vanesa. 2015. *On the Line: Slaughterhouse Lives and the Making of the New South.* Berkeley: University of California Press.

Rios, Victor, Jr. 2008. "Samora, Julian (1920-1996)," pp. 1191-1193 in R.T. Schaefer (ed.), *Encyclopedia of Race, Ethnicity, and Society.* Vol. 4. Thousand Oaks, CA: Sage Publications.

Rios, Victor M. 2011. *Punished: Policing the Lives of Black and Latino Boys.* New York: New York University Press.

Rios, Victor M., Greg Prieto, and Jonathan M. Ibarra. 2020. "Mano Suave–Mano Dura: Legitimacy Policing and Latino Stop-and-Frisk." *American Sociological Review* 85 (1): 58-75.

Riosmena, Fernando. 2010. "Policy Shocks: On the Legal Auspices of Latin American Migration to the United States." *Annals of the American Academy of Political and Social Research* 630: 270-293.

Rivera, Raquel Z., Wayne Marshall, and Deborah Pacini Hernandez (eds.) 2009. Reggaeton. Durham, NC: Duke University Press.

Rivera, Tomás. 1971. *Y No Se Lo Tragó la Tierra (And the Earth Did Not Devour Him)*. Berkeley, CA: Quinto Sol.

Roberts, Sam. 2023. "Bill Richardson, Champion of Americans Held Overseas, Dies at 75." *New York Times*, September 2, updated September 5.

Rocha, Iliana. 2022. *The Many Deaths of Inocencio Rodriguez*. North Adams, MA: Tupelo Press.

Rodriguez, Cassaundra. 2019. "Latina/o/a Citizen Children of Undocumented Parents Negotiating Illegality." *Journal of Marriage and Family* 81 (3): 713–728.

Rodríguez, Clara E. 2000. *Changing Race: Latinos, the Census, and the History of Ethnicity in the United States*. New York: New York University Press.

Rodríguez, Clara E. 2008. *Heroes, Lovers, and Others: The Story of Latinos in Hollywood*. New York: Oxford University Press.

Rodriguez, Gregory. 2012. "Why Arizona Banned Ethnic Studies." *Los Angeles Times*, February 20. http://articles.latimes.com/2012/feb/20/opinion/la-oe-rodriguez-ethnic-studies-20120220

Rodriguez, Jeanette. 1994. *Our Lady of Guadalupe: Faith and Empowerment among Mexican-American Women*. Austin: University of Texas Press.

Rodriguez, Rebecca, R. Lillianne Macias, Reyna Perez-Garcia, Griselda Landeros, and Aida Martinez. 2018. "Action Research at the Intersection of Structural and Family Violence in an Immigrant Latino Community: A Youth-Led Study." *Journal of Family Violence* 33 (8): 587–596.

Rodriguez, Sabrina and Marc Caputo. 2020. "Disinformation Plagues Florida Latinos." https://www.politico.com/news/2020/09/14/florida-latinos-disinformation-413923

Rodriguez, Sarah, Amy Pilcher, and Norma Garcia-Tellez. 2021. "The Influence of Familismo on Latina Student STEM Identity Development." *Journal of Latinos and Education* 20 (2): 177–189.

Rodríguez-Martínez, Pilar and Cristina Cuenca-Piqueras. 2019. "Interactions between Direct and Structural Violence in Sexual Harassment against Spanish and Unauthorized Migrant Women." *Archives of Sexual Behavior* 48 (2): 577–588.

Rogers, Richard G., Robert A. Hummer, and Charles B. Nam. 2000. *Living and Dying in the USA: Behavioral, Health, and Social Differentials of Adult Mortality*. San Diego: Academic Press.

Roiz, Jessica. 2019. "How Los Angeles Azules Got Their Groove Back, Landing Their First No. 1 Hit in 19 Years With 'Nunca Es Suficiente.'" *Billboard*, March 6. https://www.billboard.com/music/latin/los-angeles-azules-no-es-suficiente-interview-cumbia-8501379/

Romano, Octavio I., 1967. "Minorities, History, and The Cultural Mystique." *El Grito: A Journal of Contemporary Mexican-American Thought* 1 (1): 5–11.

Romero, Augustine "Gus." 2021. "The Ghetto Curator and the Curandera." *Aztlan: A Journal of Chicano Studies* 46 (1): 195–207.

Romero, Mary. 2002. *Maid in the USA*. 10th anniversary edn. New York: Routledge.

Romero, Mary. 2008. "The Inclusion of Citizenship Status in Intersectionality: What Immigration Raids Tells Us About Mixed-Status Families, the State and Assimilation." *International Journal of Sociology of the Family* 34: 131–152.

Romero, Mary. 2017. *Introducing Intersectionality*. Hoboken, NJ: John Wiley & Sons.

Romero, Mary, Pierrette Hondagneu-Sotelo, and Vilma Ortiz (eds.) 1997. *Challenging Fronteras: Structuring Latina and Latino Lives in the U.S.* New York: Routledge.

Romero, Simon. 2013. "On Election Day, Latin America Willingly Trades Machismo for Female Clout." *New York Times*, December 15. http://nytimes.com/2013/12/15/world/americas/on-oelection-day-latin-america-willingly-trades-machismo-for-female-clout.html?_r=0&pageewanted=print

Romo, David. 2010. "My Tío, the Saint." *Texas Monthly*, November. http://www.texasmonthly.com/story/my-t%C3%ADo-saint

Romo, Ricardo. 1992. "Borderland Murals: Chicano Artifacts in Transition." *Aztlan: A Journal of Chicano Studies* 21 (1–2): 125–154.

Romo, Ricardo. 2021. "Americo Paredes: Scholar, Poet, Musician, Teacher, and Mentor." *La Prensa Texas*, September 10. https://laprensatexas.com/americo-paredes-scholar-poet-musician-teacher-and-mentor/

Rosenbloom, Raquel and Jeanne Batalova. 2022. "Mexican Immigrants in the United States." Migration Policy Institute Migration Information Source, October 13.

Rosenblum, Marc R., Irene Gibson, and Sean Leong. 2022. *Fiscal Year 2021 Southwest Border Enforcement Report*, Washington, DC: Office of Immigration Statistics, US Department of Homeland Security.

Rosenfeld, Michael J. and Byung-Soo Kim. 2005. "The Independence of Young Adults and the Rise of Interracial and Same-Sex Unions." *American Sociological Review* 70 (4): 541–562.

Ross, Catherine E. and Chia-Ling Wu. 1996. "Education, Age, and the Cumulative Advantage in Health." *Journal of Health and Social Behavior* 37 (March): 104–120.

Rovner, Josh. 2021. "Racial Disparities in Youth Incarceration Rates Persist." The Sentencing Project, February 3. https://www.sentencingproject.org/publications/racial-disparities-in-youth-incarceration-persist/

Rowan, Helen. 1967. "A Minority Nobody Knows." *The Atlantic* 219, June: 47–52.

Ruggles, Steven, Sarah Flood, Matthew Sobek, Daniel Backman, Annie Chen, Grace Cooper, Stephanie Richards, Renae Rodgers, and Megan Schouweiler. 2024. IPUMS USA: Version 15.0 [dataset]. Minneapolis, MN: IPUMS. https://doi.org/10.18128/D010.V15.0

Rumbaut, Rubén G., Katie Dingeman, and Anthony Robles. 2019. "Immigration and Crime and the Criminalization of Immigration," pp. 472–482 in S.J. Gold and S.J. Nawyn (eds.), *Routledge International Handbook of Migration Studies*. New York: Routledge.

Rumberger, Russell W. 2012. *Dropping Out: Why Students Drop out of High School and What Can be Done About It*. Cambridge, MA: Harvard University Press.

Sabon, Lauren Copley. 2018. "Force, Fraud, and Coercion – What Do They Mean? A Study of Victimization Experiences in a New Destination Latino Sex Trafficking Network." *Feminist Criminology* 13 (5): 456–476.

Sáenz, Rogelio. 1997. "Ethnic Concentration and Chicano Poverty: A Comparative Approach." *Social Science Research* 26: 205–28.

Sáenz, Rogelio. 2005. "The Changing Demographics of Roman Catholics." *Population Reference Bureau*, August 1. http://www.prb.org/Publications/Articles/2005/TheChangingDemographicsof RomanCatholics.aspx

Sáenz, Rogelio. 2012. "Changing Demography, Eroding Democracy." *La Voz de Esperanza* 25 (7): 5.

Sáenz, Rogelio. 2013a. "The Rise of the Immigration Industrial Complex." *La Voz De Esperanza* 26 (1): 5–6.

Sáenz, Rogelio. 2013b. "Rolando Hinojosa's Klail City: Sociological and Demographic Reflections of a Hometown," pp. 198–229 in S. Miller and J.P. Villalobos (eds.), *Rolando Hinojosa's "Klail City Death Trap Series": A Retrospective, New Directions*. Houston: Arte Publico Press.

Sáenz, Rogelio. 2014. "Fifty Years of the Deferment of the Dream for Racial Justice: From Hattie Carroll to Trayvon Martin," pp. 119–124 in K.J. Fasching-Varner, A. Dixon, R. Reynolds, and K. Albert (eds.), *Trayvon Martin, Race, and American Justice: Writing Wrong*. Rotterdam, The Netherlands: SensePublishers.

Sáenz, Rogelio. 2015. "The Demography of the Elderly in the Americas: The Case of the United States and Mexico," pp. 197–223 in W.A. Vega, K.S. Markides, J.L. Angel, and F.M. Torres-Gil (eds.), *Challenges of Latino Aging in the Americas*. Cham, Switzerland: Springer.

Sáenz, Rogelio. 2019. "Far Fewer Mexican Migrants are Coming to the US and Those Who Do are More Educated." *The Conversation*, September 9. https://theconversation.com/far-fewer-mexican -immigrants-are-coming-to-the-us-and-those-who-do-are-more-educated-122524

Sáenz, Rogelio. 2020. "Latino Continual Demographic Growth: Implications for Educational Practices and Policy." *Journal of Hispanic Higher Education* 19 (2): 134–148.

Sáenz, Rogelio. 2021. "A Reflection on the Latino Vote in Texas." *Mexican American Civil Rights Institute Brown Paper*s 1 (1): 29–44. https://drive.google.com/file/d/1E-vgDEPxM6VajAJtR_X7N cPd2LwfNO8p/

Sáenz, Rogelio and Aurelia Lorena Murga. 2011. *Latino Issues: A Reference Handbook*. Santa Barbara, CA: ABC-CLIO.

Sáenz, Rogelio and Carlos Siordia. 2012. "The Inter-Cohort Reproduction of Mexican American Dropouts." *Race and Social Problems* 4 (1): 68–81.

Sáenz, Rogelio and Karen Manges Douglas. 2009. "The Economic Benefits of Domestica Employment: The Case of Mexicans." *Journal of Latino/Latin American Studies* 3 (4): 98–114.

Sáenz, Rogelio and Karen Manges Douglas. 2015. "A Call for the Racialization of Immigration Studies: On the Transition of Ethnic Immigrants to Racialized Immigrants." *Sociology of Race and Ethnicity* 1 (1): 166–180.

Sáenz, Rogelio and Marc A. Garcia. 2021. "The Disproportionate Impact of Covid-19 on Older Latino Mortality: The Rapidly Diminishing Latino Paradox." *Journals of Gerontology Series B Psychological Sciences and Social Sciences* 76 (3): e81–e87.

Sáenz, Rogelio and M. Cristina Morales. 2019. "Demography of Race and Ethnicity," pp. 163–207 in D.L. Poston, Jr. (ed.), *The Handbook of Population*. 2nd edn. Cham, Switzerland: Springer Nature.

Sáenz, Rogelio and Trinidad Morales. 2012. "The Latino Paradox," pp. 47–73 in R.R Verdugo (ed.), *The Demography of the Hispanic Population: Selected Essays*. Charlotte, NC: Information Age Publishing.

Saenz, Rogelio, Cecilia Menjivar, and San Juanita Edilia Garcia. 2011. "Arizona's SB 1070: Setting Conditions for Violations of Human Rights Here and Beyond," pp. 155–178 in J. Blau and M. Frezzo (eds.), *Sociology and Human Rights: A Bill of Rights in the Twenty-First Century*. Newbury Park, CA: Pine Forge Press.

Sáenz, Rogelio, Janie Filoteo, and Aurelia Lorena Murga. 2007. "Are Mexicans in the United States a Threat to the American Way of Life?" *Du Bois Review: Social Science and Research on Race* 4: 375–393.

Sáenz, Rogelio, Karen Manges Douglas, David Geronimo Embrick, and Gideon Sjoberg. 2007. "Pathways to Downward Mobility: The Impact of Schools, Welfare, and Prisons on People of Color," pp. 373–409 in H. Vera and J.R. Feagin (eds.), *Handbook of the Study of Racial and Ethnic Relations*. New York: Springer.

Sáenz, Victor B., Claudia García-Louis, Carmen De Las Mercédez, and Sarah L Rodriguez. 2020. "Mujeres Supporting: How Female Family Members Influence the Educational Success of Latino Males in Postsecondary Education." *Journal of Hispanic Higher Education* 19 (2): 169–194.

Saez, Pedro A., Adonaid Casado, and Jay C. Wade. 2010. "Factors Influencing Masculinity Ideology among Latino Men." *Journal of Men's Studies* 17 (2): 116–128.

Salazar, Rubén. 1969. "The Mexican-American Newsbeat – Past Practices and New Concepts," pp. 33–38 in US Department of Justice, Community Relations Service (ed.), *Southwest Texas Conference on Mass Media and Mexican-Americans*. San Antonio: St. Mary's University.

Sampson, Robert J. 1985. "Race and Criminal Violence: A Demographically Disaggregated Analysis of Urban Homicide. *Crime and Delinquency* 31 (1): 47–82.

Sampson, Robert J. 2008. "Rethinking Crime and Immigration." *Contexts* 7 (1): 28–33.

Sampson, Robert J. and Lydia Bean. 2006. "Cultural Mechanisms and Killing Fields: A Revised Theory of Community-Level Racial Inequality," pp. 8–38 in R.D. Peterson, L.J. Krivo, and J. Hagan (eds.), *The Many Colors of Crime: Inequalities of Race Ethnicity and Crime in America*. New York: New York University Press.

Sampson, Robert J. and William Julius Wilson. 1995. "Toward a Theory of Race, Crime, and Urban Inequality," pp. 37–54 in J. Hagan and R.D. Peterson (eds.), *Crime and Inequality*. Stanford, CA: Stanford University Press.

Sanches, L. 1999. "Olmos Touts Latinos' Contributions." *San Diego Union Tribune*, April 17: B1.

Sanchez, Alberto Sandoval. 2018. "West Side Story: A Puerto Rican Reading of 'America,'" pp. 164–179 in C.E. Rodríguez (ed.), *Latin Looks: Images of Latinas and Latinos in the US Media*. New York: Routledge.

Sánchez, Erika. 2017. *I'm Not Your Perfect Mexican Daughter*. New York: Alfred A. Knopf.

Sandomir, Ricard. 2022. "Rolando Hinojosa-Smith, Award-Winning Hispanic Novelist, Dies at 93." *New York Times*, April 27. https://www.nytimes.com/2022/04/27/books/rolando-hinojosa-smith -dead.html

Santa Ana, Otto. 2002. *Brown Tide Rising: Metaphors of Latinos in Contemporary American Public Discourse*. Austin: University of Texas Press.

Santa Ana, Otto. 2013. *Juan in a Hundred: The Representation of Latinos on Network News*. Austin: University of Texas Press.

Santana, Emilce. 2018. "Situating Perceived Discrimination: How Do Skin Color and Acculturation Shape Perceptions of Discrimination Among Latinos?" *Sociological Quarterly* 59 (4): 655–677.

Santos, Fernanda and Rebekah Zemansky. 2013. "Arizona Desert Swallows Migrants on Riskier Paths." *New York Times*, May 20. http://www.nytimes.com/2013/05/21/us/immigrant-death-rate -rises-on-illegal-crossings.html

Sarkisian, Natalia, Mariana Gerena, and Naomi Gerstel. 2006. "Extended Family Ties Among Mexicans, Puerto Ricans, and Whites: Superintegration or Disintegration?" *Family Relations* 55: 331–44.

Saucedo, Leticia and Maria Cristina Morales. 2010."Masculinities Narratives and Latino Immigrant Workers: A Case Study of the Las Vegas Residential Construction Trades." *Harvard Journal of Law and Gender* 33: 625–659.

Schlosser, Eric. 2001. "The Most Dangerous Jobs in America." *Mother Jones*, July/August. http://www .motherjones.com/politics/2001/07/dangerous-meatpacking-jobs-eric-schlosser

Schmalzbauer, Leah. 2005. *Striving and Surviving: A Daily Life Analysis of Honduran Transnational Families*. New York: Routledge.

Schwartz, Sarah. 2021. "Map. Where Critical Race Theory is Under Attack." Education Week, June 15. https://www.edweek.org/policy-politics/map-where-critical-race-theory-is-under-atta ck/2021/06?s_kwcid=AL!6416!3!602270476281!!!g!!&utm_source=goog&utm_medium=cpc&utm_ campaign=ew+dynamic+recent&ccid=dynamic+ads+recent+articles&ccag=recent+articles+dyna mic&cckw=&cccv=dynamic+ad&gclid=Cj0KCQjwl92XBhC7ARIsAHLl9amiQbRukcLoX5sdlSRpds v9ea3xQ-lyu5nGbdwENr9YJkGgO212xvEaAspUEALw_wcB

Seem, E. and J. Coombs. 2017. 2020 Research and Testing: 2015 National Content Test Relationship Question Experiment Analysis Report (Version 2.1). US Census Bureau website.

Segura, Denise A. and Beatríz M. Pesquera. 1999. "Chicana Political Consciousness: Re-Negotiating Culture, Class, and Gender with Oppositional Practices." *Aztlán* 24: 1–32.

Segura, Denise A. and Jennifer L. Pierce. 1993. "Chicana/o Family Structure and Gender Personality: Chodorow, Familism, and Psychoanalytic Sociology Revisited." *Signs* 19 (1): 62–91.

Seid, Michael, Donna Castañeda, Ronald Mize, Mirjana Zivkovic, and James W. Varni. 2003. "Crossing the Border for Health Care: Access and Primary Care Characteristics for Young Children of Latino Farm Workers along the U.S.-Mexico Border." *Ambulatory Pediatrics* 3 (3): 121–130.

Seitz, Amanda and Will Weissert. 2021. "Latinos, Misinformation, and the 2020 Election." *Associated Press*, December 1. https://apnews.com/article/latinos-misinformation-election-334d779a4ec4 1aa0eef9ea80636f9595

Selig Center for Economic Growth. 2012. *Hispanic Consumer Market in the U.S. is Larger than the Entire Economies of All but 13 Countries in the World, According to Annual UGA Selig Center Multicultural Economy Study*. Athens, GA: University of Georgia, Selig Center for Economic Growth.

Shahrasbi, Sanya. 2020. "Can a Presidential Pardon Trump an Article III Court's Criminal Contempt Conviction? A Separation of Powers Analysis of President: Trump's Pardon of Sheriff Joe Arpaio." *Georgetown Journal of Law & Public Policy* 18: 207–226.

Shaw, Clifford R. and Henry D. McKay. 1942. *Juvenile Delinquency and Urban Areas*. Chicago: University of Chicago Press.

Sherkat, Darren E. and Christopher G. Ellison. 1999. "Recent Developments and Current Controversies in the Sociology of Religion." *Annual Review of Sociology* 25: 363–394.

Shin, Hyoung-jin and Richard Alba. 2009. "The Economic Value of Bilingualism for Asians and Hispanics." *Sociological Forum* 24 (2): 254–275.

Sicard, Sarah. 2020. "Hundreds Come Forward as #IAmVanessaGuillen Movement Surges Online." *Military Times*, July 13. https://www.militarytimes.com/off-duty/military-culture/2020/07/13/hu ndreds-come-forward-as-iamvanessaguillen-movement-surges-online/

Sierk, Jessica. 2016. "Religious Literacy in the New Latino Diaspora: Combatting the 'Othering' of Muslim Refugee Students in Nebraska." *Journal of Inquiry and Action in Education* 7 (1): 1–17.

Sierra, Jerry A. 2014. "Fulgencio Batista."

Siskin, Alison. 2007. *Immigration-Related Detention: Current Legislative Issues*. Congressional Research Service Report for Congress. Order Code RL32369. Washington, DC: Congressional Research Service. http://www.ilw.com/immigdaily/news/2007,0406–crs.pdf

Siskin, Alison. 2012. *Immigration-Related Detention: Current Legislative Issues.* Congressional Research Service Report for Congress. Order Code RL 32369. Washington, DC: Congressional Research Service. http://www.fas.org/irp/crs/RL32369.pdf

Slack, Jeremy, Daniel E. Martínez, Scott Whiteford, and Emily Peiffer. 2015. "In Harm's Way: Family Separation, Immigration Enforcement Programs and Security on the US-Mexico Border." *Journal on Migration and Human Security* 3 (2): 109–128.

Smith-Morris, Carolyn, Daisy Morales-Campos, Edith Alejandra Castaneda Alvarez, and Matthew Turner. 2012. "An Anthropology of Familismo: On Narratives and Description of Mexican/ Immigrants." *Hispanic Journal of Behavioral Science* 35 (1): 35–60.

Solís, Myriam Villalobos. 2021."Puerto Rican Adolescents' Visits to the Island, Familial Ethnic Socialization, and Cultural Orientation." *Journal of Social Issues* 77 (4): 1213–1233.

Solomons, Gemma. 2017. "Beyond 'Nuyorican': The History of Puerto Rican Migration to NYC." National Trust for Historic Preservation. https://savingplaces.org/stories/becoming-nuyorican -history-puerto-rican-migration-nyc

Soto, Andrew C. 2020. "Chicano/a Philosophy: Rupturing Gringo Anti-Chicano/a Paradigms and Philosophies." *The American Philosophical Association Newsletter: Hispanic/Latino Issues in Philosophy*, 19 (2): 8–17.

Soto, Jovanna Garcia. 2023. "The Discipline of Hope: Reflections on Walking with Social Movements in Puerto Rico." Grassroots International: Funding Global Movements for Social Change.

Soto-Márquez, José G. 2019. "'I'm Not Spanish, I'm from Spain': Spaniards' Bifurcated Ethnicity and the Boundaries of Whiteness and Hispanic Panethnic Identity." *Sociology of Race and Ethnicity* 5 (1): 85–99.

Sotomayor, Sonia. 2014. *My Beloved World.* Vintage. New York.

Southern Education Foundation. 2015. *A New Majority: Low Income Students Now a Majority in the Nation's Public Schools.* Atlanta: Southern Education Foundation. https://southerneducation.org /wp-content/uploads/documents/new-majority-update-bulletin.pdf

Sowards, Stacey K. 2019. *¡Sí, Ella Puede! The Rhetorical Legacy of Dolores Huerta and the United Farm Workers.* Austin: University of Texas Press.

Spindler-Ruiz, Pedro. 2021. "Mexican Niches in the US Construction Industry: 2009-2015." *Journal of International Migration and Integration* 22 (2): 405–427.

Stacy, Christina and Brady Meixell. 2020. "The Changing Geography of Spatial Mismatch." *Cityscape* 22 (3): 373–378.

Stahl, Jonathan. 2015. "10 Influential Hispanic Americans in U.S. Politics." National Constitutional Center Blog, October 14. https://constitutioncenter.org/blog/10-influential-hispanic-americans- in-u-s-politics

Stanzione, Vincent. 2003. *Rituals of Sacrifice: Walking the Face of the Earth on the Sacred Path of the Sun.* Albuquerque: University of New Mexico Press.

Staudt, Kathleen and Irasema Coronado. 2017."Gendering Border Studies: Biopolitics in the Elusive US Wars on Drugs and Immigrants." *Eurasia Border Review* 8 (1): 59–72.

Stavans, Ilan. 1995. *Bandido: Oscar "Zeta" Acosta and the Chicano Experience.* New York: Routledge.

Stavans, Ilan. 2018. *Latinos in the United States: What Everyone Needs to Know.* Oxford University Press.

Steidel, Angel G. Lugo and Josefina M. Contreras. 2003."A New Familism Scale for Use With Latino Populations." *Hispanic Journal of Behavioral Sciences* 25 (3): 312–330.

Stein, Gabriela L., Laura M. González, Alexandra M. Cupito, Lisa Kiang, and Andrew J. Supple. 2015. "The Protective Role of Familism in the Lives of Latina/o Adolescents." *Journal of Family Issues* 36 (10): 1255–1273.

Steketee, Anne, Monnica T. Williams, Beatriz T.Valencia, Destiny Printz, and Lisa M. Hooper. 2021. "Racial and Language Microaggressions in the School Ecology." *Perspectives on Psychological Science* 16 (5): 1075–1098.

Stevens, Mitchell L. 2007. *Creating a Class.* Cambridge, MA: Harvard University Press.

Stevens-Arroyo, Anthony M. 2010. "Latino American Religion: Struggles for Justice," in C.H. Lippy and P.W. Williams (eds.), *Encyclopedia of Religion in America.* Washington, DC: CQ Press.

Stewart, Craig O., Margaret J. Pitts, and Helena Osborne. 2011. "Mediated Intergroup Conflict: The Discursive Construction of 'Illegal Immigrants' in a Regional U.S. Newspaper." *Journal of Language and Social Psychology* 30 (1): 8–27.

Stowell, Jacob I. and Feodor A. Gostjev. 2018."Immigration and Crime Rates: Lasting Trends and New Understandings," pp. 81–92 in H.V. Miller and A. Peguero (eds.), *Routledge Handbook on Immigration and Crime*. New York: Routledge.

Strawbridge, William A., Richard D. Cohen, Sarah J. Shema, and George A. Kaplan. 1997. "Frequent Attendance at Religious Services and Mortality Over 28 Years." *American Journal of Public Health* 87 (6): 957–961.

Stumpf, Juliet. 2006. "The Crimmigration Crisis: Immigrants, Crime, and Sovereign Power." *American University Law Review* 56 (2): 368–419.

Sugarman, Julie and Melissa Lazarín. 2020. "Educating English Learners during the COVID-19 Pandemic." Migration Policy Institute, September.

Sullivan, Alice. 2001. "Cultural Capital and Educational Attainment." *Sociology* 35 (4): 893–912.

Sullivan, Kathleen. 2000. "St. Catherine's Catholic Church: One Church, Parallel Congregations," pp. 255–289 in H. Ebaugh and J. Chafetz (eds.), *Religion and the New Immigrants*. Walnut Creek, CA: AltaMira Press.

Supreme Court of the United States. 2024. Department of Homeland Security v. State of Texas, Application to Vacate the Injunction in Pending Appeals for the Fifth Circuit.

Sussner, Katarina M., Ana C. Lindsay, and Karen E. Peterson. 2007. "The Influence of Acculturation on Breast-Feeding Initiation and Duration in Low-Income Women in the US." *Journal of Biosocial Science* 40: 673–696.

Svob, Connie, Susan X. Lin, Keely Cheslack-Postava, Michaeline Bresnahan, Renee D. Goodwin, et al. 2023. "Religiosity, Mental Health and Substance Use among Black and Hispanic Adults during the First Six Months of the COVID-19 Pandemic in New York City." *International Journal of Environmental Research and Public Health* 20 (9): 5632. https://doi.org/10.3390/ijerph20095632.

Taladrid, Stephania. 2021. "The Exclusion of Latinos from American Media and History Books." *The New Yorker*, September 21. https://www.newyorker.com/news/q-and-a/the-exclusion-of-la tinos-from-american-media-and-history-books

Tapia, Bertha Alicia Bermúdez. 2022. "'I Want to Get on the Next Bus and Leave This City Now': A Study of Violence and Deportation on the Texas-Tamaulipas Border." *Qualitative Sociology* 45: 483–509.

Tapia, Mike. 2019. "Modern Chicano Street Gangs: Ethnic Pride Versus 'Gangsta' Subculture." *Hispanic Journal of Behavioral Sciences* 41 (3): 312–330.

Taylor, J. Edward, Philip L. Martin, and Michael Fix. 1997. *Poverty Amid Prosperity: Immigration and the Changing Face of Rural California*. Washington, DC: Urban Institute.

Taylor, Paul, Ana González-Barrera, Jeffrey Passel, and Mark Hugo Lopez. 2012a. *An Awakened Giant: The Hispanic Electorate is Likely to Double by 2030*. Washington, DC: Pew Hispanic Center.

Taylor, Paul and Mark Hugo Lopez. 2010. *National Latino Leader? The Job is Open*. Washington, DC: Pew Research Hispanic Trends Program.

Taylor, Paul, Mark Hugo Lopez, Jessica Hamar Martinez, and Gabriel Velasco. 2012b. *When Labels Don't Fit: Hispanics and Their Views of Identity*. Washington, DC: Pew Hispanic Center.

Telemundo. 2023. "Biden Extiende 18 Meses el TPS Que Protege a 340,000 Inmigrantes de El Salvador, Honduras, Nicaragua y Nepal." *Noticias Telemundo*, June 13. https://www.telemundo .com/noticias/noticias-telemundo/inmigracion/tps-el-salvador-honduras-nicaragua-biden-rcna 89057

Teller, Charles H. and Steve Clyburn. 1974. "Trends in Infant Mortality." *Texas Business Review* 48: 240–246.

Telles, Edward E. 2006. *Race in Another America: The Significance of Skin Color in Brazil*. Princeton, NJ: Princeton University Press.

Telles, Edward E. 2014. *Pigmentocracies: Ethnicity, Race, and Color in Latin America*. Chapel Hill, NC: University of North Carolina Press.

Telles, Edward E. and Edward Murguia. 1990. "Phenotypic Discrimination and Income Differences among Mexican Americans." *Social Science Quarterly* 71 (4): 682–696.

Telles, Edward E. and Vilma Ortiz. 2008. *Generations of Exclusion: Mexican Americans, Assimilation, and Race.* New York: Russell Sage Foundation.

Thomas, Lorrin. 2015. "Puerto Ricans in the United States," in *Oxford Research Encyclopedia of American History.*

Thomas, Piri. 1967. *Down These Streets: A Memoir.* New York: Alfred A. Knopf.

Time. 1967. "Minorities: Pocho's Progress." *Time* 89, April 28: 24–25.

Toldson, Ivory A. and Brianna P. Lemmons. 2013. "Social Demographics, The School Environment, and Parenting Practices Associated With Parents' Participation in Schools and Academic Success Among Black, Hispanic, and White Students." *Journal of Human Behavior in the Social Environment* 23 (2): 237–255.

Torres-Saillant, Silvio. 2000. "The Tribulations of Blackness: Stages in Dominican Racial Identity." *Callaloo* 23 (3): 1086–1111.

Treviño, Robert R. 2006. *The Church in the Barrio: Mexican American Ethno-Catholicism in Houston.* Chapel Hill: University of North Carolina Press.

Trujillo, Dillon, Sean Arayasirikul, Hui Xie, Sofia Sicro, Joaquin Meza, Mackie Bella, Emperatriz Daza, Francisco Torres, Willi McFarland, and Erin C. Wilson. 2022. "Disparities in Sexually Transmitted Infection Testing and the Need to Strengthen Comprehensive Sexual Health Services for Trans Women." *Transgender Health* 7 (3): 230–236.

Trump, Donald J. 2017. Executive Order: Border Security and Immigration Enforcement Improvements. The White House, Office of the Press Secretary. January 25, 2017.

Tse, Don. 2023. "Modelo Extends Its Lead Over Bud Light and Budweiser in the U.S."

Turner, Elizabeth Hayes, Stephanie Cole, and Rebecca Sharpless. 2015. *Texas Women: Their Histories, Their Lives.* First edn. University of Georgia Press.

Turner, Ralph H. and Samuel J. Surace. 1956. "Zoot-Suiters and Mexicans: Symbols in Crowd Behavior." *American Journal of Sociology* 62 (1): 14–20.

Turra, Cassio M. and Irma T. Elo. 2008. "The Impact of Salmon Bias on the Hispanic Mortality Advantage: New Evidence from Social Security Data." *Population Research and Policy Review* 27 (5): 515–530.

Turra, Cassio M. and Noreen Goldman. 2007. "Socioeconomic Differences in Mortality among U.S. Adults: Insights Into the Hispanic Paradox." *Journals of Gerontology Series B Psychological Sciences and Social Sciences* 62 (3): S184–S192.

UC Santa Cruz. 2024. "Lionel Cantú Queer Center. Center's Namesake." https://queer.ucsc.edu/about-us/centers-namesake.html

UNESCO. 2023. "Five Questions on Transformative Education." https://www.unesco.org/en/articles/five-questions-transformative-education

United Nations. 1993. *Report of the UN Truth Commission on El Salvador.* New York: United Nations, Security Council. http://www.derechos.org/nizkor/salvador/informes/truth.html

University of Massachusetts Boston. 2024. "About Us. Gastón Institute." https://www.umb.edu/gaston-institute/about/

University of Notre Dame. 2024. "Julian Samora," in Latino Studies at Notre Dame. https://latinostudies.nd.edu/about/history/julian-samora/

US Bureau of Labor Statistics. 2023. "Employment Projections: Civilian Labor Force, by Age, Sex, Race, and Ethnicity." https://www.bls.gov/emp/tables/civilian-labor-force-summary.htm

US Census Bureau. 2021. *Voting and Registration in the Election of November 2020.* https://www.census.gov/data/tables/time-series/demo/voting-and-registration/p20-585.html

US Census Bureau. 2023. *2023 Population Projections for the Nation by Age, Sex, Race, Hispanic Origin and Nativity.* https://www.census.gov/newsroom/press-kits/2023/population-projections.html

US Census Bureau. 2024. Explore Census Data. https://data.census.gov/

US Department of Education. 2019. *Status and Trends in the Education of Racial and Ethnic Groups 2018.* Washington, DC: US Department of Education.

US Department of Homeland Security. 2023. *2022 Yearbook of Immigration Statistics.* Washington, DC: US Department of Homeland Security, Office of Homeland Security Statistics.

US Government Accountability Office. 2006. *Border-Crossing Deaths Have Doubled Since 1995; Border Patrol's Efforts to Prevent Deaths Have Not Been Fully Evaluated.* Washington, DC: US Government Accountability Office. http://www.gao.gov/new.items/d06770.pdf

US Government Accountability Office. 2021. *Workforce Diversity: Analysis of Federal Data Shows Hispanics Are Underrepresented in the Media Industry.* www.gao.gov/assets/gao-21-105322.pdf

US Government Accountability Office. 2022a. *K-12 Education: Student Population Has Significantly Diversified, But Many Schools Remain Divided Along Racial, Ethnic, and Economic Lines.* Report to the Chairman, Committee on Education and Labor, House of Representatives. https://www.gao.gov/assets/gao-22-104737.pdf

US Government Accountability Office. 2022b. *Workforce Diversity: Hispanic Workers Are Underrepresented in the Media, and More Data Are Needed for Federal Enforcement Efforts.* www.gao.gov/assets/gao-22-104669.pdf

US Immigration and Customs Enforcement. 2021. EROFY 2019 Achievements. Department of Homeland Security.

US Immigration and Naturalization Service. 1948. *Annual Report of the Immigration and Naturalization Service for the Fiscal Year Ending 1948.* Washington, DC: Immigration and Naturalization Service.

Vaca, Nick. 1967. "Editorial." *El Grito: Journal of Contemporary Mexican–American Thought* 1 (1): 4.

Valdés, Dionicio. 2005. "Galarza, Ernesto," pp. 159–160 in S. Oboler and D.J. González (eds.), *The Oxford Encyclopedia of Latinos and Latinas in the United States.* New York: Oxford University Press.

Valdes, Guadalupe. 1996. *Con Respeto: Bridging the Distances between Culturally Diverse Families and Schools.* New York: Teaching College Press.

Valdes, Marcela. 2023. "The Christian Pop Star Bringing Latino Evangelicals to the Pews." *New York Times Magazine,* June 28. https://www.nytimes.com/2023/06/28/magazine/marcos-witts.html

Valdez, Zulema. 2011. *The New Entrepreneurs: How Race, Class, and Gender Shape American Enterprise.* Stanford, CA: University of Stanford Press.

Valenzuela, Angela. 1999. *Subtractive Schooling US –Mexican Youth and the Politics of Caring.* State Albany, NY: University of New York Press.

Valenzuela, Angela and Sanford M. Dornbusch. 1994. "Familism and Social Capital in the Academic Achievement of Mexican Origin and Anglo Adolescents." *Social Science Quarterly* 75: 18–36.

Van Dijk, Teun A. 1991. *Racism in the Press.* London: Routledge.

Vasquez, Jessica M. 2014. "The Whitening Hypothesis Challenged: Biculturalism in Latino and Non-Hispanic White Marriage." *Sociological Forum* 29 (2): 386–407.

Vázquez, Victor. 2017. "Anthropological Analysis on the Development Model, and the Social, Political and Economic Inequality of Puerto Rico." Revista Decumanus. Ciudad Juarez, México: Universidad Autónoma de Ciudad Juárez.

Vélez, William. 2008. "The Educational Experiences of Latinos in the United States," pp. 129–148, in H. Rodríguez, R. Sáenz, C. Menjívar (eds.), *Latina/os in the United States: Changing the Face of America.* New York: Springer.

Vélez-Vélez, Roberto. 2015. "All Puerto Rico with Vieques: Mobilizing Support through Social Skills and Field Dynamics." *Social Movement Studies* 14 (5): 539–556.

Verba, Sidney, Kay Lehman Schlozman, and Henry E. Brady. 1995. *Voice and Equality: Civic Voluntarism in American Politics.* Cambridge, MA: Harvard University Press.

Verdeja, Ernesto. 2002. "Law, Terrorism, and the Plenary Power Doctrine: Limiting Alien Rights." *Constellations* 9 (1): 89–97.

Verdugo, Richard R. 1992. "Earnings Differentials between Black, Mexican American, and Non-Hispanic White Male Workers: On the Cost of Being a Minority Worker, 1972-1987." *Social Science Quarterly* 73 (3): 663–673.

Vidal-Ortiz, Salvador. 2015. "Introduction. Brown Writing Queer: A Composite of Latina/o LGBT Activism," pp. 1–27 in U. Quesada, L. Gomez, and S. Vidal-Ortiz (eds.), *Queer Brown Voices: Personal Narratives of Latina/o LGBT Activism.* Austin: University of Texas Press.

Videla, Nancy Plankey. 2008. "Maquiladoras," pp. 591–594 in W.A. Darity, Jr. (ed.), *International Encyclopedia of the Social Sciences.* Vol. 4, 2nd edn. Detroit: Macmillan Reference USA.

Vigil, James Diego. 1988. *Barrio Gangs: Street life and Identity in Southern California.* Austin: University of Texas Press.

Villicana, Adrian J., Kevin Delucio, and Monica Biernat. 2016. "'Coming Out' Among Gay Latino and Gay White Men: Implications of Verbal Disclosure for Well-Being." *Self and Identity* 15 (4): 468–487.

Vine, Katy. 2022. "Nina Diaz Almost Lost It All. Now She Wants to Guide SanAntonio's Next Rock Star." *Texas Monthly*, March 8. https://www.texasmonthly.com/arts-entertainment/nina-diaz-san-antonio-rock-heroine/

Visser, M. Anne. 2019. "The Color Gradient of Economic Opportunity: Implications of Skin Tone Labor Market Segmentation for Puerto Ricans in the United States." *Centro Journal* 31 (3): 47–71.

Vizcaíno-Alemán, Melina V. 2017. "Chicano Poetry, Chicana Art: Rodolfo 'Corky' Gonzales and Carlota d.Z. EspinoZa," pp. 99–122 in Vizcaíno-Alemán, Melina (ed.) *Gender and Place in Chicana/o Literature: Critical Regionalism and the Mexican American Southwest.* Cham, Switzerland: Palgrave Macmillian.

Voces Oral History Center. 2015. "Maria del Rosario Castro." Interview.

Voces Oral History. 2024. *Voces Oral History.* http://www.lib.utexas.edu/voces/.

Voces Oral History Center. 2024. *Voces of a Pandemic.* https://www.youtube.com/playlist?list=PLWhomroDwfXu942xEdE80f0WpwHZ3bP1M

Wade, Peter. 1997. *Race and Ethnicity in Latin America.* London: Pluto Press.

Waldinger, Roger. 1996. *Still the Promised City? African-Americans and New Immigrants in Postindustrial New York.* Cambridge, MA: Harvard University Press.

Wallace, Steven P., Carolyn Mendez-Luck, and Xóchitl Castañeda. 2009. "Heading South: Why Mexican Immigrants in California Seek Health Services in Mexico." *Medical Care* 47 (6): 662–669.

Wallerstein, Immanuel. 1974. *The Modern World System, Capitalist Agriculture and the Origins of the European World Economy in the Sixteenth Century.* New York: Academic Press.

Walsh, Arlene M. Sánchez. 2010. "Latino American Religion: Pentecostals," pp. 1196–1200 in C.H. Lippy and P.W. Williams (eds.), *Encyclopedia of Religion in America.* Washington, DC: CQ Press.

Ward, Thomas W. 2013. *Gangsters without Borders: An Ethnography of a Salvadoran Street Gang.* New York: Oxford University Press.

Waring, Charles. 2024. "Fania Records: How A New York Label Took Salsa To The World." *uDiscoverMusic*, January 13. https://www.udiscovermusic.com/stories/fania-records-story/

Warner, R. Stephen and Judith G. Wittner. 1998. *Gatherings in Diaspora: Religious Communities and the New Immigration.* Philadelphia: Temple University Press.

Waterman, Stephanie J. 2013. "Using Theory To Tell It Like It Is." *Urban Review* 45: 335–354.

Weimann, Gabriel. 2000. *Communicating Unreality: Modern Media and the Reconstruction of Reality.* Thousand Oaks, CA: Sage Publications.

Weitzer, Ronald and Steven A. Tuch. 2005 "Determinants of Public Satisfaction with the Police." *Police Quarterly* 8 (3): 279–297.

Wheeler, André. 2020. "American Dirt: Why Critics are Calling Oprah's Book Club Pick Exploitative and Divisive." *Guardian*, January 22. https://www.theguardian.com/books/2020/jan/21/american-dirt-controversy-trauma-jeanine-cummins

White, Christopher M. 2009. *The History of El Salvador.* Westport, CT: Greenwood Press.

Wikipedia. 2024. *List of English Words of Spanish Origin.* http://en.wikipedia.org/wiki/List_of_English_words_of_Spanish_origin

Wildsmith, Elizabeth, Marta Alvira-Hammond, and Lina Guzman. 2016. *A National Portrait of Hispanic Children in Need.* National Research Center on Hispanic Children and Families.

Williams, Caroline. 2020. "Most Popular Ethnic Cuisines in America According to Google." *Chef's Pencil,* February 26. https://www.chefspencil.com/most-popular-ethnic-cuisines-in-america/

Williams, David R. 1999. "Race, Socioeconomic Status, and Health: The Added Effects of Racism and Discrimination." *Annals of the New York Academy of Sciences* 896 (1): 173–188.

Williams, David R. and Pamela Braboy Jackson. 2005. "Social Sources of Racial Disparities in Health." *Health Affairs* 24 (2): 325–334.

Williams, Jennifer L. and Virginia O. Schaffer. 2021. "The Affordable Care Act: A Success?" *The American Journal of Surgery* 222 (2): 254–255.

Williams, Johnny E. 2003. *African-American Religion and the Civil Rights Movement in Arkansas*. Jackson, MS: University of Mississippi Press.

Williams, Philip J. and Patricia Fortuny Loret de Mola. 2007. "Religion and Social Capital Among Mexican Immigrants in Southwest Florida." *Latino Studies* 5: 233–253.

Wilson, Bianca D. M., Christy Mallory, Lauren Bouton, and Soon Kyu Choi. 2021. "Latinx LGBT Adults in the US: LGBT Well-Being at the Intersection of Race." School of Law Williams Institute, UCLA. http://efaidnbmnnnibpcajpcglclefindmkaj/https://williamsinstitute.law.ucla.edu/wp-content/up loads/LGBT-Latinx-SES-Sep-2021.pdf

Wilson, Kenneth L. and Alejandro Portes. 1980. "Immigrant Enclaves: An Analysis of the Labor Market Experiences of Cubans in Miami." *American Journal of Sociology* 86 (2): 295–319.

Wilson, William Julius. 1987. *The Truly Disadvantaged: The Inner City, the Underclass, and Public Policy*. Chicago: University of Chicago Press.

Wilson, William Julius. 1997. *When Work Disappears: The World of the New Urban Poor*. New York: Vintage.

Wolfgang, Marvin E. and Franco Ferracuti. 1967. *The Subculture of Violence: Towards an Integrated Theory in Criminology*. New York: Tavistock.

Wood, Matthew and Christopher Bunn. 2009. "Strategy in a Religious Network: A Bourdieuian Critique of the Sociology of Spirituality." *Sociology* 43 (2): 286–303.

World Health Organization. 2000. *Obesity: Preventing and Managing the Global Epidemic*. Technical Report Series 894. Geneva: World Health Organization.

Xi, Juan, Sean-Shong Hwang, and Yue Cao. 2010. "Ecological Context and Immigrants' Earnings: English Ability as a Mediator." *Social Science Research* 39: 652–661.

Xu, Jiaquan, Sherry L. Murphy, Kenneth D. Kochanek, and Elizabeth Arias. 2021. "Deaths: Final Data for 2019." *National Vital Statistics Records* 70 (8).

Xu, Jiaquan, Sherry L. Murphy, Kenneth D. Kochanek, and Elizabeth Arias. 2022. "Mortality in the United States, 2021." NCHS Data Brief No. 446. file:///C:/Users/Owner/Downloads/cdc_122516 _DS1.pdf

Xu, Qingwen and Kalina Brabeck. 2012. "Service Utilization for Latino Children in Mixed-Status Families." *Social Work Research* 36 (3): 209–221.

Ybarra, Lea. 1983. "Empirical and Theoretical Developments in the Study of Chicano Families," pp. 93–110 in A. Valdez, A. Camarillo, and T. Almaguer (eds.), *The State of Chicano Research in Family, Labor and Migration Studies: Proceedings of the First Stanford Symposium on Chicano Research and Public Policy*. Stanford, CA: Stanford University Press.

Zambrana, Ruth Enid. 2011. *Latinos in American Society: Families and Communities in Transition*. Ithaca, NY: Cornell University Press.

Zambrana, Ruth E., C.M. Scrimshaw, Nancy L. Collins, and Christine Dunkel-Schetter. 1997. "Prenatal Health Behaviors and Psychosocial Risk Factors in Pregnant Women of Mexican Origin: The Role of Acculturation." *American Journal of Public Health* 87 (6): 1022–1026.

Zamudio, Margaret M. and Michael I. Lichter. 2008. "Bad Attitudes and Good Soldiers: Soft Skills as a Code for Tractability: Immigrant Latina/os Over Native Blacks in the Hotel Industry." *Social Problems* 55 (4): 573–589.

Zavala, Egbert, Theodore R. Curry, and Maria Cristina Morales. 2020. "Explaining the Cultural Retention–Delinquency Relationship Using Differential Support and Coercion Theory: A Study of Native-Born and Immigrant Latino Youth." *Social Science Quarterly* 101 (2): 623–640.

Zayas, Luis H., Sergio Aguilar-Gaxiola, Hyunwoo Yoon, and Guillermina Natera Rey. 2015. "The Distress of Citizen-Children with Detained and Deported Parents." *Journal of Child and Family Studies* 24: 3213–3223.

Zhao, Guoping. 2023. "DEI and the Crisis of Liberal Democracy." *Philosophy* 79 (1): 36–70.

Zúñiga, Víctor and Rubén Hernández-León (eds.) 2006. *New Destinations: Mexican Immigration in the United States*. New York: Russell Sage Foundation.

Index

abortion 137, 240, 249, 313
academic achievement gap 9, 165–166, 173, 178–183
academia 35–36, 38, 40, 43, 49–51
    see also intellectuals; Latino spin; Latino threat narrative
Affordable Care Act 272
    see also Obamacare
age divide 93
age-sex 93
age-sex pyramid 94
agribusinesses 65
Alurista 127, 151–153
Alvarez, Julia 151
American Civil Liberties Union (ACLU) 284
Americanos: Latino Life in the US/La Vida Latina en los Estados Unidos (Americanos) 314
Anti-Terrorism and Effective Death Penalty Act (AEDPA) 73
Anzaldúa, Gloria 47–48, 112–114
    also see music
assimilation 45, 125, 154, 157, 161, 165, 167, 210, 215, 316, 331–334
Aztlán 11, 148, 151–152

baby boomers 338–339, 341
Baca Zinn, Maxine 41, 45–46,110–112
Bad Bunny 162
Baltazar Urista Heredia, Alberto (Alurista) 151–153
bandido (bandit) 2, 282, 287, 299, 312
Becerra, Xavier 314
Bejarano, Cynthia L. 211
bilingual education 71, 75–76, 84, 97, 99, 167–168, 181–182
    see also bicultural education
biological deficiency 165–168
bi-racial framework 51, 331–332, 341
    see also tri-racial framework
Black Lives Matter (BLM) 297–298
Blalock, Hubert 189, 304
blaming the victim 166–167, 183, 226

Bonilla-Silva, Eduardo 170–171, 208, 331–333, 341
Border Industrialization Program 5, 19
border enforcement 222, 226, 285–287
    see also border patrol; Department of Homeland Security; detention; US Customs and Border Patrol; US–Mexico border security
Bracero Program 19, 63–66
Brown v Board of Education 335

caballerismo 212
Cantú, Lionel 118
Castillo, Ana 115, 158
Castro, Fidel 4, 4, 20, 32
Castro, Joaquin 135–136, 301, 319
Castro, Julián 136
Castro, Maria del Rosario "Rosie", 135
Catholicism 228–231, 242– 245, 247
Chávez, César 124–125
Chicano artists 146
Chicano literature 147
Chicano Movement 123–128, 150–154
Cisneros, Sandra 157
citizenship, US 8–10, 12–13, 19, 37–38, 69–70, 73-74, 76–77, 82–84, 87, 116–118, 138, 160, 173–174, 178, 206, 221, 223–225
    see also rights claiming
collective black 51, 333–334
college graduation rates 177–178
colonization 11–12, 16, 181, 282
    also see colonization of sexuality; colonized group; colonized minority; decolonization; settler colonization
colonization of sexuality 113
    see also colonization; colonized group; colonized minority; decolonization; settler colonization
colonized group 19, 21
    see also colonization; colonized minority; colonization of sexuality; decolonization; settler colonization

colonized minority
  see also colonization; colonized group;
    colonization of sexuality; decolonization;
    settler colonization
colorblind 5, 202, 313–315, 332
CoreCivic formally Corrections Corporation of
    America (CCA) 285
corridos 147
Cortez, Gregorio 148–149
counterimage 305, 313
  see also counternarrative; counterstory
counternarrative 301, 305–309, 312–313, 325
  see also counterimage; counterstory
counterstory 200–201, 305
  see also counterimage; counternarrative
COVID-19 13, 53, 74, 99–100, 166, 172–173, 180,
    235, 251–252, 258–259, 263, 265, 275–276,
    317, 326
criminalization of immigrants 73–74
  see also criminalization of Latina/os;
    crimmigration
criminalization of Latina/os 133, 282–287
  see also criminalization of immigrants;
    crimmigration
crimmigration 53, 285, 299
critical race theory (CRT) 13, 140–143, 180, 182,
    303, 305, 311–313, 336
  see also diversity, equity, and inclusion
Cruz, Celia 4, 161–162
cultural capital 167–168, 172, 178
cultural Catholic 231–232
cultural deficiency 165–168, 180–181, 184
culture of poverty 167, 207, 226
cumulative advantages/disadvantages
    252–254
cumulative causation 61–62
  see also social capital; social networks

Daddy Yankee 4, 162
  see also reggaeton
Davila, Arlene 313–314
decolonization 45, 50, 116, 128
Deferred Action for Childhood Arrivals (DACA)
    84, 87, 143–144; 178–180, 182, 184, 297
  see also Dreamers; Dream Act
denominational affiliation 234
deportation 82, 179, 223–225, 285, 288, 292,
    294–296
Department of Homeland Security 19, 21–22, 40,
    42, 44–45, 84, 136, 182
  see also border enforcement; detention
    centers; US-Mexico border national
    security; US border patrol
detention centers 53, 74, 82, 223, 285

diabetes 48, 98, 156, 252, 258, 260–264, 268, 270,
    340
Diego, Juan 230
digital divide 172–174
disability 252, 263, 266–269, 273
discouraged workers 191
diversity, equity, and inclusion, anti 140–143
  see also critical race theory
DREAM (Development Relief and Education for
    Alien Minors) Act 143, 178–179
  see also Deferred Action for Childhood
    Arrivals (DACA); Dreamers
Dreamers 143, 179–180
dropout rates 174–175, 182
Downs, Lila 160–161
dual labor market theory 57–58
Duncan Occupational Socioeconomic Index
    (SEI) 193

English as official language 304–305
English-only 182
epidemiological paradox 98, 252–254, 258,
    262–263, 273–274, 278, 289
  see also Latina/o paradox; other side of the
    paradox
erasure of memory 181–182
Estefan, Gloria 161
Estrada, Leobardo 89
ethnic v. racial group 7, 10, 12
  also see social construction of race
ethnic enclave 21, 156, 210, 237, 334
ethnic studies 180–182
Evangelical Protestantism 228–229, 247–248
expulsions and deportations 82–84

Fania Records 161
Feagin, Joe 303
familism 168, 208–210, 208, 225, 261
  see also familismo
familismo 123–125; 208–210, 212, 225
  see also familism
family separation 222–224
fertility 96–97
food desert 277
Floyd, George 13, 297
framing of Latinos 302, 304–305, 309–310
frontera madre(hood) 258

Galarza, Ernesto 39, 41–42, 49
Gaspar de Alba, Alicia 114–115
Gastón, Mauricio Miguel 44
GEO group 74
golden exiles 4, 21
González, Rodolfo "Corky" 124–125, 153–154

Government Accountability Office 72, 319, 335

Grosfoguel, Ramón 49–51

group size perspective 189, 304
    see also power threat perspective

Gutiérrez, José Ángel 124–125, 136, 144

Guillen, Vanessa 318

habitus 169

health insurance 98, 179, 193, 195, 251, 270–272, 278, 340

Hernandez, Deluvina 39, 41, 43–44

high-school graduation rates 176–177, 182

Hinojosa-Smith, Rolando 150–151

history, Colombia 30–33

history, Cuba 20–21

history, Dominican Republic 23–25

history, El Salvador 25–30

history, Guatemala 30–32

history, Mexico 18–20

history, Puerto Rico 21–23

Hondagneu-Sotelo, Pierrette 49–50, 111, 166, 225, 240

honorary whites 332–333, 337

HR 4437 (Border Protection Anti-Terrorism and Illegal Immigration Control Act of 2005, Sensenbrenner Bill) 308
    see also criminalization of immigrants; criminalization of Latinos; crimmigration

Huerta, Dolores 124–125, 181

human capital 86, 189, 190, 195, 204

Huntington, Samuel 313

hyper-surveillance of Latina/os 281, 299

Idár, Jovita 35–38

identity, politics 143, 153, 160, 298
    see also López Tijerina v. Henry

identity, race, and ethnicity 5, 8, 11, 38, 42, 44, 47–48, 50, 119, 112, 114–115, 117–120, 156, 161, 210, 216–217, 237, 291, 316

identity, sex, and gender 119

Illegal Immigration Reform and Immigrant Responsibility Act (IIRIRA) 73–74, 178, 223, 286

income inequality 198–200

immigrant jobs 61, 193, 195, 343–344
    see also immigrant niche

immigrant niche 58, 190, 193, 195
    see also immigrant jobs

immigrant revitalization theory 290

immigrant rights movement 308, 322

immigrant students 165–166, 172–177

Immigration and Nationality Act of 1965 (Hart-Celler Act) 68–70, 75

immigration–industrial complex 74, 285
    see also prison industrial complex 285–286

immigration reform 308

Immigration Reform and Control Act of 1986 (IRCA, Simpson-Mazzoli Act of 1986) 30, 70–71, 87

indigenous 6–8, 11–12, 16, 20, 26–27, 41, 47, 71, 86, 113, 116–118, 122, 152, 158–159, 207, 228–232, 286, 331, 334

intersectionality 44, 47–50, 110–112

institutional theory 60–61

intermarriage 3, 189, 213, 331

intellectuals 38–45, 48–49

January 6, 2021 13

Jones Act 22

jotería 117

La Matanza (The Massacre) 27

La Violencia (The Violence) 32–33

labeling hype 288

labeling theory 287

labor unions 16–17, 20–21, 65, 70, 74, 82, 124, 210

Latina/o businesses 3, 21

Latina/o immigrant crime paradox 289–290, 297, 299

Latina/o gangs 155, 280 288, 290–291
    see also transnational gangs; zoot suit

Latina/o literature 148–159

Latina/o music 159–163

Latina/o spin 207–209, 217, 312– 314

Latino threat narrative 198

Latina/o economic contributions 86, 205, 248

Latina/o purchasing power 313–314, 324, 339

Latina/o-white comparison, 9, 165–166, 173, 178–183

Latino in America 314–316

Laviera, Tato 156

League of United Latin American Citizens (LULAC) 75

Leal, Luis 147–148

legal permanent resident 74–79

LGBTQ+ 111, 114–120

life expectancy 98–99, 252–254, 259, 273–277

linked fated 129

López, Ian 306

López Tijerina, Reies 124

López Tijerina v. Henry 122

Los Tigres del Norte 159–160

machismo 211–212, 225

manifest destiny 17 18

maquiladora 67–68

Mara Salvatrucha (MS-13) 292–293
marianismo 211–212
marriage 209, 213–218
Marielitos 21
Marin, Luis Muñoz 22, 136
Martin, Trayvon 297, 303
mass media 313, 318, 321–322, 324–325
mass shootings 293–294
Mayan 30–31; 231; 237–238
Mendoza, Lydia 159
mestizo 286, 298, 332
Mexican-American War 1, 19, 36, 38, 86, 282
Mexican American Legal Defense and
   Education Fund (MALDEF) 40–41, 49, 89,
   124
militarization of the US–Mexico border 53,
   72–73, 193–195, 225
  also see Department of Homeland Security;
   US border patrol; US–Mexico border
   security
Mirandé, Alfredo 41, 45–46, 212, 226, 282, 287
misinformation 317–318, 326
mixed-status families (households) 208, 222, 224
Moraga, Cherríe 112–113
mortality 98–99
multiracial 12
  see also social construction of race
murals 147

National Council for La Raza (NCLR), now
   UnidosUS 39, 49, 75, 82, 137
  see also rights claiming
narco violence 10
National Association of Latino Elected Officials
   89
National Rifle Association (NRA) 29
nativity 174–177
natural increase (decrease) 99–10
neoclassical economics perspective 55
neoliberalism 18, 71–72
  see also North American Free Trade
   Agreement; United States-Mexico-Canada
   Agreement
Nepantla 48, 116–117
network theory 59–60
new-destination areas (states) 106–108
new economics of migration perspective 56–57
New York Times, 35, 151, 157, 304, 311, 321, 323,
   329
North American Free Trade Agreement
   (NAFTA) 19, 59, 71–72
  see also the United States-Mexico-Canada
   Agreement
Nuyorican Movement 154–156

Obamacare 272, 278
  see also Affordable Care Act
obesity 265–266, 277–278
occupational prestige 186, 194–195
Operation Bootstrap 59
Operation Lone Star (OLS) 287
Operation Wetback 66–68
opportunity structure 189, 288, 299
Ortega Melendres v. Arpaio 283
other side of the paradox 252, 278, 340
  see also epidemiological paradox
Our Lady of Guadalupe 230–231, 245–246,
   247
  see also Virgin of Guadalupe

Pacheco, Johnny 161
pan-ethnic 6
Paredes, Américo 148–149
passport 15, 30
  see also political asylum; political refugees
people of color 70, 88, 90, 97, 121, 127, 138,
   148, 159–160, 180–181, 184, 195, 197–198,
   200–201, 204, 207, 227–228, 231
Piñero, Miguel 127, 155
police killings 280
  see also policing 283–285, 288, 295–297,
   299–300
political asylum 10, 19
  see also political refugees
political determinants of health 257
political participation 134
  see also voting behavior
political party affiliation 71–71, 77, 153, 224
political party 128–134
political refugees 11, 19, 21, 38
politicians 135–138
political representation 139–140
Pope Francis 248–249
population change 4, 91, 309, 328, 342
population growth, Latina/os 100–103
population, immigrants 79–85, 96
population projections 1, 90, 101–102, 108,
   338–339 4
Portes, Alejandro 21, 44–45, 49, 210
poverty 169–171
power threat perspective 304–305
  see also group size perspective
prison industrial complex 285–286
  see also immigrant industrial complex
Puerto Rican Legal Defense Education Fund
   (PRLDEF) 209
  see also rights claiming
Puerto Rican Oversight, Management, and
   Economic Stability Act (PROMESA) 128

Puerto Rican, movements 128
    see also social movements
Pulse nightclub shooting 293

queer Aztlán 112

race, biological perceptions 6
    see also social construction
racial formation perspective 303
racial census identification 6
racial identity 7–10
racial profiling 83, 97, 180, 183, 185–186, 288,
    296–297
racial invariance thesis 289
racial mixture 7
    also see mestizo
racialized racial system 224
racism 36, 39, 50–52, 63, 141–143, 149–150,
    154–156, 171
Ramos, Jorge 313, 322
reggaeton 161–162
    see also Bad Bunny, Daddy Yankee
religion as social capital, 233–235
religious affiliation 242–244
religious conversion 241–242, 245, 247–248
religious marketplace 241
remittances 56–57, 61, 237, 293
Repatriation Program 63
residential segregation 103–104
RickyLeaks 318
rights, civil rights 36–38, 70–71, 73, 76, 82–85,
    96–97, 149, 182–183, 200, 219, 222–223
    see also Chicana/o Movement
rights, human rights 30, 70, 74, 149, 156, 184,
    194–195, 225
rights, immigrant rights 41, 69–70, 73, 81–85,
    149, 224–225
rights, labor 20, 70, 75, 225
rights claiming: 70, 73–74, 203, 215, 224
    see also League of United Latin American
        Citizens (LULAC); Mexican American Legal
        Defense and Education Fund (MALDEF);
        National Council of La Raza (NCLR);
        Puerto Rican Legal Defense Education
        Fund (PRLDEF)
Rivera, Tomás 40, 148, 150
Robb Elementary 293
Roe v. Wade 249
    see also abortion
Romano, Octavio I. 39–41, 146
Romero, Augustine "Gus" 146–147

Salazar, Rubén 126
Salmon bias 262, 278

same-sex couples (cohabitation) 213, 218–219,
    225
    see also same-sex households
same-sex households 119–120
Samora, Julian 39–41, 43, 49
Sanchez, George I. 39, 41
sanctuary cities 296
Santana, Carlos 162
S.B.4 283–284
S.B.1070 181, 283
school segregation 171–172
secularization 229, 245, 248
Secure Communities 284
Selena Quintanilla Pérez 147, 159–160
settler colonization 11
sex ratio 103–104
skin color 113–114
social construction of race 5,7, 121–123
social capital 56, 59, 61, 67, 169, 233–236
    see also social networks
social determinants 254–255, 258, 278
social disorganization theory 289–290
social media 317–318
social movements 115–118
    see also Chicana/o movement; political
        participation; Puerto Rican movement
social networks 56, 59–60, 103, 188–190, 224,
    233, 238, 261
    see also cumulative causation; social capital
socioeconomic 166–167, 170–172, 184–186, 189,
    193, 195–196, 198, 201, 253–254, 271, 316
soft skills 186–188
Sotomayor, Sonia 311–312, 322
Spanish–American War 11–12
Spanish language 2, 3, 77
stop-and-frisk 281
stratification of Latina/o groups 333–335, 337
structural violence 298–300
    see also Frontera Madre(hood)
subculture of violence 288
subtractive education 167, 187

Tejano music 159–160
Telemundo 308
Teller Act 10
temporary protected status (TPS) 30
Texas Rangers 35, 40, 123, 149, 294
theories of criminology 287–290
theories of education 166–172
theories of mass media 302–306
theories of migration 55–62
theories of sex and sexuality 110–118
theories of social determinants of health and
    longevity 254–258

theories of religion 233–242

theories of work and economic life 186–191

Thomas, Piri 155

   see also Nuyorican Movement

Tienda, Marta x, 44–45, 49

Tijerina, Reis López 122, 124, 126, 144

Title 42 53, 82, 84

trans-Latine/x 118–119

   see also same-sex households; transgender

transgender 115, 117–119, 293

transnational/transnationalism 38, 42, 47–50,
   111, 115, 118–120, 156, 207, 222, 238,
   292–293

   see also transnational families, transnational
   gangs

transnational families 207, 222

   see also transnational/transnationalism

transnational gangs 292–293

Treaty of Guadalupe Hidalgo 1, 19, 86, 126, 308,
   341

Treaty of Paris 20–21

tri-racial framework 51, 331–334, 337, 341

   see also bi-racial framework

Trump, Donald 13 53, 285–287, 293–296, 324,
   336

undocumented (unauthorized) 19, 21, 30–35,
   38–42, 46, 70. 73, 81–82, 87, 97, 102, 106,
   118, 137–138, 158, 172–174, 177–179,
   182–185, 198–200, 203, 205, 223–225

unequal funding of education 170–172, 181,
   336

United Fruit Company (UFCO) 30

Univision 325

United States–Mexico–Canada Agreement 59,
   68, 71

   see also North American Free Trade
   Agreement

US–Mexico border operations 22, 53, 66, 67,
   72–73, 287, 308

   see also Department of Homeland Security;
   militarization of US–Mexico border;

Operation Bootstrap; Operation Lone Star;
   Operation Wetback; US–Mexico border
   security

US Border Patrol 62–63, 65–66, 72, 294, 337

   see also border enforcement; Department of
   Homeland Security; US–Mexico border
   security

US–Mexico border security (national security)
   19, 179, 222, 226, 285–287, 290. 296, 337

   see also Department of Homeland Security;
   militarization of US–Mexico border;
   Secure Communities, US–Mexico border
   operations

USA PATRIOT Act of 2001 73

Uvalde 293–294

Vaca, Nick 41

Valdez, Luis 127, 315

Virgin of Guadalupe 146–147

   see also Our Lady of Guadalupe

Voces Oral History Project 251

voting behavior 2, 13, 22–24, 122–126, 129–135,
   139, 144, 240, 317, 321, 336–337

   see also political participation

Voting Rights Act (VRA) 124

white hegemony 284, 303

   see also white privilege; white supremacy

white privilege 121, 303, 332, 334

   see also white hegemony; white supremacy

white supremacy 6, 51, 122, 146, 331–332,
   341

   see also white hegemony; white privilege

workforce 191–192, 194, 195, 202, 204

world system theory 16, 58–59

Yo soy Joaquín/ I am Joaquín 154

Youth Risk Behavior Survey (YRBS) 264–265

Zambrana, Ruth E. 208, 213, 225–226

zoot suit 282, 290–291, 299, 307

   see also Latina/o gangs